The New York Times

1·0·0·0
GARDENING
QUESTIONS
& ANSWERS

BASED ON *THE NEW YORK TIMES*
COLUMN "GARDEN Q. & A."

WITH ADDITIONAL MATERIAL BY LESLIE LAND

BOTANICAL ILLUSTRATIONS BY BOBBI ANGELL

HOW-TO ILLUSTRATIONS BY ELAYNE SEARS

WORKMAN PUBLISHING · NEW YORK

A High Tides Press book

Cover design by Paul Hanson
Design by Elizabeth Johnsboen with Noah Levine and Patrick Borelli
Cover photograph by Sandra Johnson
Botanical illustrations by Bobbi Angell
How-to illustrations by Elayne Sears

Typesetting by NK Graphics and Barbara Peragine

Library of Congress Cataloging-in-Publication Data
The New York Times 1000 gardening questions & answers : based on
the column "Gardeners Q. & A." / by the garden editors of the New York
Times ; with additional material by Leslie Land.
       p. cm
   ISBN 0-7611-2886-7—ISBN 0-7611-1997-3 (pbk. : alk. paper)
   1. Gardening—Miscellanea. I. Title: New York times one thousand
gardening questions and answers. II. Land, Leslie. III. New York times.
SB453.N468 2003
635—dc21   2002034206

WORKMAN PUBLISHING COMPANY, INC.
708 Broadway
New York, NY 10003-9555
www.workman.com

Printed in the U.S.A.
First printing March 2003
10 9 8 7 6 5 4 3 2 1

Acknowledgments

This book first sprouted in the fertile mind of *The New York Times*'s Mike Levitas, who looked at the archives of "Garden Q. & A." and saw the seeds of something more than a simple collection of columns. That vision grew into a manuscript under the guidance of Lisa MacDonald at High Tide Press, who tirelessly weeded, pruned, and transplanted until the huge pile of published pieces became a coherent whole. Suzanne Rafer and Mary Wilkinson, the project's editors at Workman, continued the work of cultivation, trimming, shaping, and refining, while Beth Doty helped us all keeep track of each other, and Marta Jaremko kept track of the process itself. Meanwhile, Elizabeth Johnsboen created a beautiful design, smoothly incorporating the work of Bobbi Angell, Q.&A.'s botanical illustrator, who contributed a wealth of drawings that both energize the text and make it far lovelier than it would otherwise be, and of Elayne Sears, who produced illustrations that have made it far more helpful.

Of course, there would be no book without the columns themselves, and for them thanks are due to many at the paper: Barbara Graustark and Michael Cannell, the editors who have made the column a part of the *Times*'s Home section; Martha Wilson, whose skill and dedication to garden coverage is unparalleled; and the patient crew at the copy desk, who have helped us speak the clear *Times* language without losing our own voices.

But the greatest gratitude must be reserved for the scores of university botanists, USDA researchers, county extension agents, professional growers, and other specialists who have so generously answered whenever *Times* writers called. Their wisdom informs the column over and over, and though their names don't appear in the text, I know I speak for my fellow writers when I say that we couldn't do it without them. Finally (or perhaps first), thanks go to the *Times* readers, whose endlessly interesting questions keep us thinking about the garden at all seasons, in all ways.

Contents

Got Questions? Get Answers.

Why won't my wisteria bloom? Will heirloom tomatoes grow in a container on a fourteenth-floor balcony? What's the best way to prune an overgrown yew . . . and by the way, could you suggest some fragrant flowers that don't attract bees?

The questions come from beginners and old hands, from apartment dwellers with only one (moderately) sunny windowsill, suburbanites with large yards, and readers with country gardens of all sizes and descriptions. While the majority are from the Northeast and Mid-Atlantic states, there are also plenty from the South, Midwest, and West. Every once in a while we get one that appears to come from outer space.

No matter where it originates, if the question is about some aspect of gardening that has general interest, *The New York Times* answers. Or, more specifically, I do. And before me there was Dora Galitzki, and before her,

Linda Yang, the "Garden Q.& A." columnists whose voices speak through this book.

Of course, we are but the latest in a long line of garden advisers that stretches back, approximately, to Adam, who we can be sure was frequently asked about the niceties of apple culture. But alas for Adam, he had to work without the resources available to the *Times*. He couldn't consult the hundreds of university professors, USDA researchers, commercial growers, and other specialists whose expertise is the ultimate source of our ostensible omniscience.

On the other hand, Adam didn't have the *Times*'s copy editors (who probably would have made me change the preceding sentence). And he didn't have deadlines or space limitations, either. These are the constraints that shape newspaper writing, and to the extent that they are positive, the editors in charge of this book have worked to retain them. Brevity, for instance, is always wise, and so is jargon-free prose that's clear to all readers.

But it would be no service to simply reproduce the columns. In the years since the first of them saw print, there have been substantial changes not only in the world of gardening, but also in the interests of readers, and in the willingness of the *Times* to permit a more colloquial, conversational style.

Why not? Gardening is, in many ways, a series of conversations: between the gardener and the site, the site and the weather, the weather and the plants, to say nothing of that famous duo, the gardener and the budget. Our readers may occasionally hire help, but they do most of the gardening themselves, and their questions frequently reflect that reality.

They also reflect a growing adventurousness about plants and designs, along with an increasing insistence on nontoxic solutions to insect, disease, and weed problems. These days, gardeners are environmentalists; they want to be water-wise, to be assured that a spiffy new plant will not become Darth Invader.

And often they want, quite reasonably, to know the correct botanical name of a plant. No problem—as a general rule. But there are exceptions. In the dozen years since "Q.&A." emerged in its present form, hundreds of plants have been reclassified: moved from one genus into another, demoted from being species to being merely subspecies or varieties. Unfortunately, the botanists who make these decisions do not always agree with one another, and respected sources occasionally conflict. When it comes to naming names, the editors have tried to steer a middle course, updating in cases where taxonomists agree, retaining older usages when those will be more useful to the general reader.

For the sake of that same reader, the book is divided into five broad sections that do not rely on climate or geography. First comes **The Flower Garden,** which deals with annuals, perennials, roses and bulbs, plants that bloom in spring, summer, and/or fall, then fade back in the cold(er) season. This is followed by **The Landscape Garden,** where you'll find answers to questions about the bigger picture, including ground covers and lawns, shrubs, trees, and vines, as well as a chapter called "Special Situations," about things like pathway materials and period garden design. Next comes **The Kitchen Garden,** wherein grows the information about vegetables, fruits, and herbs. After that **The Potted Garden,** containing the myriad questions we get about container gardening, both indoors and out. Finally, in **Garden Keeping,** the nitty gritty: soil, fertility, compost, and mulch, as well as disease control and pest abatement.

All those subcategories—and the good old alphabet—will probably lead you to what you want within the sections, but there is also a large index to help make sure you don't miss anything.

Onward, then, into the garden. But first, a small confession: this book is somewhat misleadingly named. There are indeed a thousand questions. But many of them are about multiple plants or multiple problems. Those that pose one problem sometimes have multiple solutions, and there are also dozens of sidebars packed with additional pointers. Result? Six, seven, eight, perhaps as many as 10,000 answers.

Have fun. Stay curious. And keep those cards and letters coming. We love to hear from you.

—LESLIE LAND

PART ONE

The Flower Garden

CHAPTER ONE

Annuals and Biennials

Annuals in General

Easy Growers

Q **What are the easiest annuals to grow from seed?**

A The easiest annuals to grow from seed are those that sow themselves. Alyssum, calendula, cosmos, larkspur, nicotiana, nigella, and poppies will all come back the following year as long you as leave some seed heads and the seeds fall on receptive ground. With this group, you only have to plant once.

The next easiest are those whose seed is large: marigolds, nasturtiums, sunflowers, and zinnias. Annual phlox is also a reliable choice, as is portulaca (moss rose).

Bear in mind that larkspur, nigella, and poppies are cool-weather germinators, so if you're starting from scratch, be sure to sow their seeds as soon as the ground can be worked. 🌰

Calendula officinalis

RECEPTIVE GROUND

As it relates to self-sown seed, receptive ground is nothing more complicated than reasonably loose soil that has room at the surface for something new to take hold. It need not be weed-free, or as soft and smooth as soil that has been thoroughly cultivated and raked. All that is necessary is an occasional bare place; the seeds will take it from there.

Quick Season

Q **I'm in northern Vermont and if possible would like to grow some annuals from seed despite my short growing season. What quick grower can you recommend that is also reliable? I don't have a lot of time, so I am not interested in starting seed indoors.**

Black-eyed Susan
(*Rudbeckia hirta*)

A No matter how quickly they grow, annuals need a couple of months to make it to blooming size, so if you want them to flower in summer you'll need to choose things that get growing in early spring, well before the last frost. The list is short but there are a few, including annual poppies, annual phlox, larkspur, nigella, silene, and bupleurum, a little-known but valuable bouquet filler that looks a bit like chartreuse eucalyptus. For best results, plant the seeds in fall the way the flowers themselves do. They will sprout in spring when conditions are right.

If you don't mind waiting until late summer for your flowers to bloom, the list can be expanded to include calendula, rudbeckia (black-eyed Susans), and asters. These need a bit more warmth to germinate, or in the case of the asters, a longer growing time, so they don't start flowering as soon as those listed above; but they don't mind light frosts and can (usually) be relied on for color in September and October. 🌰

The Wrong Seeds

Q **I've never grown annual phlox before, but this year I was seduced by a pastel star-shaped variety called 'Twinkle.' The plants grew quickly and looked healthy, but when they bloomed all the flowers were round and magenta colored. What did I do wrong?**

A Nothing—unless you want to count failing to complain to the seed company. Your problem is a packing error, at the seed house or with their suppliers. Characteristics like color and shape are genetically determined; if you'd gotten 'Twinkle' seeds, you would have gotten 'Twinkle' flowers.

The source of the error is especially clear because these were your first attempt. If you had planted annual phlox in the same spot before, the self-sown progeny of those plants might have crowded out the newcomers. Self-sown plants could easily be reversions to the species, and *Phlox drummondii* is by nature a sort of dull rose-purple.

In this case, though, the culprit is clear and it is neither you nor any former phlox. Fortunately, mistakes of this kind are uncommon. Most seed companies guarantee their products to be true to name and will cheerfully refund your money if you let them know you had trouble. You are entitled to see this as pretty minor compensation, but it's better than nothing. 🌱

AWAKENING A SEED

S eeds are amazing. These small packages contain everything needed to make a whole plant, and many also contain tiny sensors to tell them if the time is ripe for germination. Among those sensors is phytochrome, a pigment that is sensitive to certain wavelengths of red light.

Who cares? You will if you sow these seeds and cover them with soil. Seeds that need light, and often they are smaller seeds, will not germinate if they are buried too deeply. When a seed is struck by sunlight (or light from a regular incandescent bulb), the phytochrome changes. If the seed has warmth, moisture, and oxygen, the change in the phytochrome breaks the seed's dormancy and allows germination. If the environment is not to the seed's liking, the phytochrome slowly changes back and the seed waits for another blast of light when conditions are better.

Among seeds that need light to germinate are ageratum, California poppy, gaillardia, coleus, columbine, love-in-a-mist, snapdragon, Shasta daisy, strawflower, sweet alyssum, and sweet rocket. You can't tell by looking, so following seed-package instructions is always a good idea.

HARDY, HALF-HARDY, AND NOT HARDY AT ALL

In England, annuals are often classified **hardy, half-hardy,** and **tender** based on the cold resistance of newly planted seeds. This can lead to some confusion because most garden writers in the United States use the same names to rate the cold resistance of the plants themselves. When in doubt, assume the term applies both to plants and to their planted seeds. (Dry seeds that you want to keep can be packed airtight and frozen for storage, even if they are tender types that could not stand being frozen in the ground.)

Hardy annual seeds don't mind being frozen while in the ground, so they can be planted in late fall or very early spring. Hardy annual plants will not be killed until temperatures dip well below freezing, though how far below will depend in good part on how quickly it gets cold. Plants that have slowly toughened up can come through colder nights than those for which it is a sudden shock.

Half-hardy seeds are fence sitters, somewhat resistant to cold but not as tough as the truly hardy. They shouldn't be planted before the last frost-free date, but they don't mind extended periods at 35° to 45°F. Plants rated half-hardy are more delicate than hardy ones, though they can usually survive at least a few nights where it drops to 30° or so. Just as with plants that are hardy, their vulnerability depends somewhat on the speed with which frost arrives.

Last on the list are *tender* annuals and the many tropical perennials that are grown as annuals in the North. Though dry seeds can be kept in the freezer, they won't survive in frozen ground, and the slightest frost will kill these plants. Even mild cold should be avoided, since neither seeds nor plants will thrive until the air and soil are above 55°.

Unusual Annuals for Summer Color

Q **I would like to have color in my garden all season, but want something more unusual than marigolds and petunias. Can you suggest some?**

A For those willing to take the time to look, there is no dearth of flowers that bloom all summer. The Mexican tulip poppy, or golden cup (*Hunnemannia fumariifolia*), has finely cut blue-green leaves on nearly 2-foot stems, and yellow poppylike flowers. Love-in-a-mist (*Nigella damascena*) grows 18 to 24 inches tall and has fluffy blue, white, or bicolored blooms nestled in finely cut leaves.

Painted tongue (*Salpiglossis sinuata*), a bit over 2 feet tall, has trumpet-shaped purple, blue, yellow, or red summer flowers streaked with veins. Heat can blast it out of bloom, but it is ideal for regions where the summers are cool. The stately spider flower (*Cleome hassleriana*) tops out around 4 feet, with spidery-looking white, pink, or purple summer blooms.

Try also million bells (*Calibracoa*) and verbena, two good long-blooming trailers.

Tall Annuals

Q I have a sunny space at the back of my garden that I would like to fill with tall annuals. What do you suggest?

A Given good sun, rich soil, and plenty of water, many species of annuals—or plants that can be treated as annuals—grow quickly, reaching at least 3 feet in height.

Included in this group are spider flowers (*Cleome hassleriana*), flowering tobaccos (*Nicotiana alata* and the even taller *N. sylvestris*), four-o'clocks (*Mirabilis jalapa*), ornamental amaranths, including love-lies-bleeding and Joseph's coat, annual hollyhocks, scabiosas, sunflowers, and zinnias. Be sure you get tall varieties; many plants also come in dwarf versions that will not give you the height you want.

ANNUALS FOR SMALL SPACES

Sunny Spaces Window boxes, curbside planters, and the small areas of open soil next to mailboxes and light poles are often in direct sunshine for six or more hours a day, but they don't have room for exuberant growers like cosmos and four-o'clocks. Small annuals that should thrive in these situations include ornamental peppers, alyssum, dwarf dahlias, heliotrope, lantana, love-in-a-mist, ageratum, verbena, creeping zinnia, signet and other small marigolds, petunias, cockscomb, and geranium.

Shady Places Small planting areas that get only three hours or so of direct sunlight are often ideal for houseplants enjoying a summer outdoors, as well as nursery staples such as begonias, impatiens, lobelias, and torenia. Browallia, caladium, coleus, cigar plant, shrimp plant, purple passion vine, rabbit's-foot fern, and maidenhair fern are also choices to consider.

Daytime Fragrance—and Color, Too

Q Can you suggest some fragrant annuals besides boring old alyssum? We'd like to plant them below our living room window in a spot that gets sun for most of the day. We don't mind white but would like strong colors, too, if possible.

A Don't be so quick to dismiss sweet alyssum (*Lobularia maritima*); some clichés are there for a reason. It blooms all summer, it smells terrific, it doesn't crowd out other plants, and it's drought tolerant.

Among whites, the old-fashioned, small-flowered 'Carpet of Snow' is more fragrant than the larger-flowered 'Snow Crystals.' The colored forms vary: take a good sniff before making your choice.

In addition to its other virtues, alyssum is day-perfumed. Most of the best fragrant annuals—consider nicotiana, moonflowers, and four-o'clocks—are night bloomers.

In fact, the easiest way to be showy and smell good at the same time is to interplant night-blooming stock (*Matthiola bicornis* or *M. longipetala*) with whatever gaudy items catch your fancy. Just scatter a few pinches of seed here and there, and remember where they are so you don't weed them out. The inconspicuous little plants look a lot like weeds, and the flowers stay rolled up during the day. Then at dusk, they open and heaven pours out. Shear them back periodically, and they'll bloom all summer. 🌿

ANNUALS FOR CUTTING

Because it is the nature of annuals to keep making flowers until they are able to make seeds, it would seem that most of them would make good cutting material. In fact, cutting is as much about stems as it is about flowers, and many of the best plants for garden color aren't worth much in the vase because the flower stems are too short.

That said, choices still run into the hundreds. This is only a partial list of annuals that make good cut flowers. Be sure when choosing varieties to notice how tall the plants grow. When it comes to cutting, taller is better; "dwarf" is to be avoided at all costs, and beware of anything that's touted as "bushy" or "covered with flowers." No matter how tall the plant itself is, these are code words for short flower stems.

Ball Shapes Quilled aster, bachelor's button, globe amaranth, love-in-a-mist, marigold, scabiosa, double zinnia

Daisy Shapes Single aster, calendula, chrysanthemum, coreopsis, cosmos, gaillardia, rudbeckia, strawflower, sunflower, single zinnia

Spikes Bells of Ireland, annual foxglove, larkspur, lupine, pink poker, salvia, snapdragon, wheat celosia, stock

Other Flowers California poppy, Chinese lantern (*Physalis alkekengi*), corn cockle (*Agrostemma*), Iceland poppy, prairie gentian (*Lisianthius*), love-lies-bleeding, nasturtium, nicotiana, salpiglossis, statice, sweet pea

Foliage and Filler Amaranth, baby's breath, bearded wheat, blue lace flower (*Trachymene coerulea*), bupleurum, castor bean, cerinthe, coleus, euphorbia, quaking grass, bronze fennel, white dill (aka false Queen-Anne's lace; *Ammi majus*)

A Cutting Garden

Q I'd like to plant a cutting section in my vegetable garden. We rototill every year and plant cover crops, so only annuals need apply. How do I make sure I have a good selection?

A Serious self-control will be needed when you confront the thousand or so choices available, so start by figuring out how many plants you have room for. Allow 2 feet between rows and allot 1 foot of row per plant. This is admittedly arbitrary. Many cutting flowers can be planted as little as 8 inches apart. But since many others need 18 inches or more, it tends to even out.

Take a sheet of paper and divide it into five columns. Label them for the flower shapes: Ball, Daisy, Spike, Other, and Foliage and Filler.

Put the flowers you know you want in the appropriate columns. Perhaps you're a snapdragon lover. Goes in the Spike column. Maybe you fancy bachelor's buttons (Ball). Sweet peas? They're Other. Gotta have cosmos (Daisy). Is baby's breath your favorite filler, or do you prefer false Queen-Anne's lace?

Whatever your pleasure, write it in. Observe the gaps. Impulse shop accordingly, aiming for at least two choices in each column. If your space is small, stick to things that respond to cutting by producing more flowers, such as cosmos and zinnias. If you have more room, you can plant some of the beauties that produce only one flush of bloom, like China asters, and summer bulbs such as gladiolus. ✿

Flowers with Good-Looking Foliage

Q I'd like to grow some annuals from seed for cutting, but want to be sure the foliage is as good to look at as the flowers. Seed catalogs aren't much help—they scarcely show a single leaf! Do you have any suggestions?

A Most annual flowers grown for cutting are no great shakes in the pretty leaf department, but many gardeners think highly of *Cosmos bipinnatus,* the common cosmos. Its foliage is a bright light green, so deeply cut it's often called feathery, and the plants make lots of it so they're attractive even when not in flower.

The same is true of annual chrysanthemums, *Chrysanthemum carinatum,* with dark green leaves that are almost lacy, and of some of the tall African marigolds, *Tagetes erecta.* The marigold leaves are beautifully fernlike, though they do have a strong odor that not everyone finds pleasant.

While we're on the subject of old favorites, don't forget nasturtiums. The cutting stems are on the short side if you take individual flowers; but if you plant a long-vining type and pinch the seedlings to encourage branching, you'll soon have enough of the graceful stems to cut lengths of a foot or more, adorned not only with buds and blossoms but also with lovely round leaves. ✿

HOLDING PATTERNS

The loose look can be very attractive, but there are times when you want the flowers in an arrangement to stay just where you put them. The two most common aids for doing this are old-fashioned flower frogs (metal plates topped with rings or spikes) and florist's foam, usually referred to as Oasis, the name of the best-known brand.

They are both easy to find, and easy to use—you just insert the stem ends—but neither is much help to the arranger who must deal with a clear vase.

For that, there are two solutions: florist's tape and twigs. The tape is green and very sticky on one side. You can use it to anchor a single stem or tie a small group of stems together, but it really comes into its own as grid-making material. Stretch it across the top of the vase in a checkerboard pattern, leaving small holes between the strips. Insert flower stems into the holes. (Make sure there are enough leaves and filler to conceal the tape when the arrangement's done.)

For a more natural alternative, use long twigs. Willow works well, as do forsythia trimmings and the water sprouts that rise from neglected fruit trees. If necessary, clip off all the side branches, so you have simple sticks.

Put enough sticks in the vase to use about a third of the available space, then add flowers, using the sticks to help them stay more or less where you want them.

Florist's foam and tape are available at craft stores and through obliging florists. Frogs are available at garden and craft stores, flea markets, and antique shops (they're collectible). Twigs can be reused several times if you wash and dry them before storage.

Sparkling Vases

Q **I love cut flowers but find it impossible to get my glass vases clean. Any suggestions?**

A Are you scrubbing them out well between uses? If the usual dish liquid fails, try a vinegar rinse, which sometimes dislodges scum that soap can't get. If there are spots a bottle brush can't reach, try impaling a bit of an abrasive dish pad on the handle end of a wooden spoon.

You can also put about a tablespoon of coarse sand, clay kitty litter, or crushed eggshells in the vase, fill it with hot water, and shake vigorously.

And don't forget the fizzy denture cleaner, which not only helps keep vases clear but disinfects as well. After you've gotten them as clean as possible, fill the vases with very warm water and add one to three tablets of cleaner, depending on the size of the container. Allow it to sit for at least two hours, then rinse well with warm water.

If none of these things deliver sparkle, it's likely that the glass has become permanently clouded. Some of the minerals in hard water will bond to glass if they are in contact with it long enough, and antique glass pieces are occasionally marred by unknown chemicals. But clouded glass is usually not objectionable when it has water in it. 🌢

A TEMPORARY HEDGE

At first, "annual hedge" sounds like an oxymoron; a hedge's first name is usually something permanent, like "boxwood" or "hemlock." But it doesn't have to be that way. Short annual hedges offer an orderly neatness similar to that of clipped boxwood; tall ones can give (almost) as much privacy as evergreens.

And either is an excellent way to try out the idea of a hedge at minimal expense. Leaf shapes will be different; flowers will further complicate the issue, but so what? A trial run based on annuals will show you a wall of plants where you're thinking about building one, and it will show it to you *before* you undertake major construction.

For short hedges, kochia (*Kochia scoparia,* aka *Bassia scoparia*) is the best as well as the best-known choice. Until it turns red in the fall, it looks like a bright little cypress. But you can also get a hedgelike effect with tall marigolds, short (not dwarf) dahlias, or dark green ruffled kale.

For tall hedges, consider castor bean, sunflowers, curly mallow (*Malva crispa,* also sold as *M. verticillata* 'Crispa'), sorghum, corn, or tall amaranth.

No matter what you choose, set the plants slightly closer together than is recommended on the packet. You want them to knit into each other and intertwine their leaves, even though the shade thus created will reduce flowering. But don't overdo it; if the plants are really packed in tight, they'll just get spindly, and if the year is wet, they'll be targets for disease.

Annuals for Drying

Q **What are the best annuals to plant for dried flowers?**

A Old favorites include strawflowers (*Helichrysum bracteatum*), which come in a wide range of yellows, oranges, and reds; daisylike Swan River everlastings (*Rhodanthe manglesii*), available in white, rose, and deep pink; *Gomphrena globosa,* the pompon plant, in pink, purple, white, or a very strong red (cultivar 'Strawberry Fields'); and German statice (*Limonium sinuatum,* aka *L. tataricum*), offering brushlike panicles of blue, purple, yellow, salmon, pink, and white.

Statice also comes in the Russian variety (formerly *L. suworowii,* now *Psylliostachys suworowii*), commonly called pink poker. Instead of the well-known fans-on-sticks produced by the German sort, it makes foot-long, hot pink spires. Bells of Ireland (*Moluccella laevis*) offers cup-shaped green bracts all up and down the stem, while the fantastical cockscombs (*Celosia argentea,* Cristata group) look much like neon-velvet coral.

All these will keep their colors when simply bound into small bunches and hung upside down in a dark, warm, airy place. If you want to venture into using commercial desiccants, almost everything that blooms is fair game. 🌷

Drying Flowers the Easy Way

Q **I would like to start drying flowers now for winter arrangements. What is the easiest way to do this?**

A Early in the morning on a clear, dry day after the dew evaporates, snip several stems of flowers that are just approaching their peak of bloom. Shake them lightly to knock off any insects, wrap the stems with a rubber band, and hang them upside down in a well-ventilated spot away from the sun. Some gardeners strip the leaves off the stems before drying, but you can also wait to see if the dried foliage looks attractive.

Drying time can vary from two days to two weeks, depending on species, humidity, and temperature. Be patient, and don't set the dried flowers upright too soon or they will droop. 🌷

Traditional Annuals

Q **I have a reproduction eighteenth-century house in southern New Jersey, and would like to plan a traditional flower garden. What annuals would be appropriate?**

A The small, dark houses of most ordinary eighteenth-century folks don't get reproduced much, so it seems safe to assume your place would have been pretty grand in its time. That means its ornamental gardens would likely have been planted following the formal, highly symmetrical models popular in Europe the century before. (The natural look was all the rage in England by the eighteenth century, but it took a while to get here.) Order was paramount, and flower beds were used to further a geometry that echoed that of the house. Think of a teeny, tiny Versailles.

Color came largely from perennials and shrubs. The big infusion of flowering annuals didn't start until the turn of the nineteenth century. But some annuals were planted earlier, and not all of them were hidden in the utilitarian gardens placed out of view of the house.

Like other flowers, annuals for viewing were usually confined in beds defined by hedges or low walls. Bearing that in mind, you could use China asters, blue or red pimpernel (*Anagallis*), calendula, coreopsis, four-o'clocks, larkspur, opium poppy, safflower (*Carthamus tinctorius*), strawflower, sweet pea, and wallflower.

As always when hoping to create a genuine period feeling, try to find antique or heritage cultivars; even old-fashioned plants now come mostly in "improved" versions. That means their colors are stronger, flowers increased, singles turned to doubles, and in many cases, tall and graceful plants made shorter and bushier. These may be very pretty, but they don't look like they grew in the eighteenth century—because they didn't. 🌿

Safflower
(*Carthamus tinctorius*)

Growing a Patchwork Quilt

Q We recently bought a cottage with four raised beds in a very visible side yard that gets bright sun all day. I would like to plant each bed with a different annual to make a sort of patchwork quilt. My aim is to have the annuals grow low like a ground cover but be full of color all season, and to plant things that will not require a lot of maintenance. What do you recommend?

A Yours is one of the situations for which the plants called bedding annuals were created. These include *Salvia splendens,* traditionally bright red but now available in a wide color range including purple, white, salmon, and pink; French marigold (*Tagetes patula*), in shades of yellow, orange, and bronze; New Guinea impatiens; and dwarf forms of snapdragon, dahlia, and zinnia. All these will bloom stalwartly, even if not deadheaded or sheared back.

Garden centers offer a wide range of possibilities, depending on just how much maintenance is "not a lot," but be sure to think carefully about the effect before choosing. You have a cottage, not a gas station, and everyone who sees your yard—including, in the long run, you—will take more pleasure in your patchwork if it is well designed.

For instance, consider planting all the beds with just one kind of plant: marigolds, salvias, whatever. Choose two or more sympathetic colors and repeat them in each of the beds (take your analogy seriously and look at a quilt book for ideas about patterns).

Alternatively, think formal parterre instead of quilt. Stick with plants of the same type but vary the height, setting a short border around a mass of tall plants, or setting tall plants in the corners of beds otherwise smoothly short.

You can also go for less common subjects: silvery dusty miller, for instance, or the dark-leaved basil 'Purple Ruffles.' 🌿

For a Beautiful Backdrop

Q **What tall annual or biennial—other than hollyhocks or foxgloves— would look good massed together in front of a weathered red barn? We will be working on the siding soon, so I don't want to plant perennials.**

Scotch thistle
(*Onopordum* spp.)

A Well, sunflowers, of course, especially the shrublike, multi-branched *Helianthus cucumerifolius* (sometimes listed as *H. debilis* ssp. *cucumerifolius*) 'Italian White,' with small, dark centered flowers in shades of very pale cream. The bold foliage of castor beans should look good against the barn siding, and so would the long pnk-and-cream-striped green leaves of *Zea mays* var. *japonica,* an ornamental corn.

If you're willing to control them, consider the biennial Scotch thistle (*Onopordum* spp.), statuesque silver plants (up to 10 feet in the second year) with long, intricately sculptured leaves and pink to purple flowers. Onopordums can be very invasive, so if you plant them where that's a danger (zones 6 to 9), you should remove the flowers before they can set seed. That means work if you've got a lot of them, and hazardous work as well. Onopordum leaves sport wicked thorns wherever there's a point. Gorgeous, though. 🌱

A Single Color

Q The seeds for many of my favorite annuals—bachelor's buttons, cosmos, love-in-a-mist, and snapdragons—come as mixtures of different colors. Having an assortment is fine, but I'd like to arrange the colors in patterns instead of having them come up randomly. Is there any way to tell what color the flowers will be before the plants start blooming?

A Seedlings of bachelor's buttons and love-in-a-mist give no outward clues, but young cosmos and snapdragon plants do show a little of what's to come in their stems. The darker these are at seedling stage, the darker the flowers will be.

This works best as a predictor of darkness; stems of cosmos that will bear deep magenta flowers have a lot of strong color themselves, and the stems and leaves of dark-red-flowered snapdragons have a black-green cast.

Once you get into anything paler, though, guesswork takes over. Cosmos with stems that show no pink at all are usually white, but not always, and light-colored snapdragons can be anything from pink to pale yellow.

The best way to grow colors-to-order is to start with the seeds. Flower seeds segregated by color are seldom sold on racks in garden centers, but they are reasonably common in mail-order catalogs. 🌱

WHAT SMELLS SO GOOD?

Annuals offer some of the sweetest perfumes in the flower kingdom, so if you are a fan of good scents, be sure your strolling and cutting gardens include as many of these as possible: sweet alyssum, hesperis, the annual lupine called 'Sunrise' (*Lupinus hartwegii* ssp. *cruickshankii*), nicotiana (*Nicotiana alata* and *N. sylvestris,* but not *N. langsdorffii*), stock (*Matthiola incana*), night-scented stock (*M. longipetala*), mignonette, and sweet peas.

Petunias should be on the list, too, but be sure to read seed catalogs carefully or smell plants before buying. Some, like the old-fashioned trailing singles, are powerfully fragrant, while others, including many large-flowered hybrids, are very faint in the perfume department.

A White Annual Garden

Q I would like to add some unusual annuals to my all-white garden. Nurseries around here sell things like alyssum, nicotiana, and petunias—and last year I saw some white mini-zinnias—but I'm sure there's more to it than that.

A There is, indeed. You can have a wide array of white annuals as long as you're willing to get mail-order seeds and then grow your own.

To start with, there are white selections of common nursery annuals such as snapdragons, asters, bachelor's buttons, cosmos, nigella, and bedding dahlias. Demand isn't strong enough for most nurseries to bother growing them, but seed is available so you can do it yourself.

There are also lots of white sweet peas and an outstanding black-centered white venidium 'Star of the Veldt.' The sunflower 'White Italian' just squeaks in; it's closer to cream. But the plant world is rich with different hues of white, and displaying a good array of them is part of a white garden's charm. ❧

A Fifties Garden

Q I want to plant a "fifties garden," where all the flowers are black, pink, and turquoise, but so far I'm not having much luck finding plants. The idea is to start out with annuals so I don't end up wasting a lot of money if this doesn't work out, but there don't seem to be many black choices and I can't find any turquoise annuals at all. Any ideas?

A Finding turquoise flowers is going to be quite a trick no matter what category they're in. As a general rule, the only time you see them is in print, in catalogs and magazines where they're trying, unsuccessfully, to show something that's supposed to be blue. If you're determined to stick with annuals, your best bet in the turquoise department is probably Chinese forget-me-not, though the foliage of (purple-flowered) cerinthe just might pass muster as well.

Black is equally hard to get. With annuals as with everything else, most cultivars that have "black" in their names are actually dark maroon. Among them are 'Black Leaf' amaranth, a scabiosa called 'Ace of Spades,' and a white-edged nemophila called 'Pennie Black.' If you're willing to extend yourself to biennials, there's a terrific black pansy (actually a viola) called 'Black Prince,' and a sweet William called 'Sooty.' ☙

Foliage Annuals

Q **I would like to plant a small garden this summer, but I'm at a rented house and don't want to invest in perennials. What annuals would you recommend that have interesting foliage? I am hoping for something simple, just three or four different shapes and colors that could be planted in large groups.**

A There are a number of good foliage plants that are either annual or sold as such. Coleus, for instance, is enjoying a great revival and now comes in a wide range of leaf shapes and colors: large and small, plain and frilly, grass green, dark green, chartreuse, near yellow, dull pink, purple, and burgundy. For silver accents there's dusty miller. And don't overlook the ornamental effect of leafy vegetables. Scotch kale, to name one, is gorgeous—deep blue-green and heavily frilled—and it's most delicious after a frost. With any luck, it will be just ready to harvest when it's time to pack up and go.

For height, try a tall amaranth such as 'Opopeo' or 'Black Leaf.' Striped corn, usually sold as *Zea mays* var. *japonica,* is also an eye-catching choice. The leaves must get full sun to really shine, but at their best they are graceful ribbons of bright green, deeply edged with pink, magenta, and cream. ☙

Filling in the Gap

Q **My perennial border always looks kind of tired by mid summer. I know annuals are supposed to fill in the gaps, but I don't have any gaps. The border is full—it's just that it's full of foliage, and I'd like to have summer flowers. Can you help?**

A Fortunately, mid summer is a good time to lift and divide bearded iris, and as long as you have enough water to keep them from being stressed, you can also attend to other spring-blooming perennials, including early varieties of day lilies, cranesbill (true geraniums), perennial salvias, and tradescantia, all plants that *need* to be divided every three to five years if they are to remain healthy and floriferous.

If you divide each plant in half and give one half away, there should be plenty of room for annuals next to the slimmed-down dividees. And next time you decide to build a border, think about including some small clumps of spring bulbs as spacers between the perennials.

You do have to leave the bulb foliage to nourish the bulbs for next year, and it will for a time be less than lovely as it ripens. But the leaves of the perennials will partially screen out the wilted foliage, and before long it will have shrunk enough so that you can (carefully!) plant your annuals above the sleeping bulbs. 🌱

A Bed or a Border

Q **What's the difference, if any, between a flower border and a flower bed? My friend claims a flower bed is all annuals while a border contains perennials as well. Is she right?**

A Technically, a garden border is just like any other border; it marks the boundary between a garden and something else: a walk, a wall, or a lawn. A bed, on the other hand, is a discrete collection of plants located inside a garden area. There is no rule about which plants can be used in either situation. You could have a very effective border of tall amaranth, cosmos, and kochia. And beds of roses are so widely used, they've entered the language in their own right.

But many gardeners still define their terms as though they were in late-Victorian England. For this group, borders were forever defined by garden designer Gertrude Jekyll, who became famous for filling them with shrubs and perennials (and some annuals), thereby creating long, rhythmic sweeps of color and texture that were a breakthrough in their time.

For much of that same period, the word "bed" was short-hand for "carpet bedding," a style that uses brightly colored annuals to create patterns. It was all the rage for a while, and it is still sometimes used, especially in public gardens.

The patterns might be anything from simple stripes to intricate swirls mimicking Persian carpets, and they can occasionally be very decorative. But if you've ever seen a company logo spelled out in orange marigolds on a field of mixed alyssum, you know why borders became chic and carpet bedding fell from grace. ❧

Picking Plants

Q When I buy annuals at the nursery, most are in bloom. Should I pinch them back after I have planted them in the garden?

A Nurseries offer annuals in bloom because color is what loosens wallets, but you are right to guess that they should be encouraged to bush out while they are still small. Pinching back blooming plants will help, but it's better, where possible, to pinch seedlings that haven't started flowering yet.

During the heaviest period of demand (May and June in the North, earlier and earlier the farther south you go), most large nurseries will have at least one or two generations of young stock coming along to replace the bloomers as they get sold. Try to find this junior class and buy from it if you can.

Whether they are in flower or not, choose stocky, deep green plants that have thick, healthy main stems and several branches. Pinch off the branch tips, right above a pair of leaves that show strong buds in the nodes next to the stem. This will delay flowering for a while, but when the plants do start blooming they will be larger and stronger.

Note: Asters are an exception. They won't branch any more strongly when pinched, and may indeed be stunted. Rosette-forming plants such as arctotis and gazania are also best left alone. ❧

Deadhead We Must

Q I want my garden to have a natural look—and I don't have much time. Is deadheading really all that important if I don't care how tidy things look?

A Deadheading is not simply a matter of keeping things neat. When you remove spent flowers promptly after they bloom, you direct the energy of the plant away from seed making. Most annuals (asters are an exception) will, when deadheaded, use that energy to bloom and bloom, since making seeds is their whole mission in life. The more you thwart them, the harder they try. And don't wait until the blossoms look tired. As a general rule, annual flowers signal "mission accomplished" shortly after they're pollinated, so you get the longest season of bloom if you cut lots of bouquets.

It does pay to let a few seeds form; many annuals will self-sow for next year, among them nigella, alyssum, nicotiana, calendula, cleome, larkspur, and poppies. ✿

THE KEYS TO LONGER BLOOM: DEADHEADING AND CUTTING BACK

Annuals will keep making new flowers as long as they are deadheaded—but after a while they tend to get leggy, and the new flowers tend to get smaller as the stems elongate. In order to have the best blossoms on the handsomest plants, it becomes necessary to cut the plants back after they have been in bloom for six weeks or so.

Cutting back is a bit of an art. You want to remove stems that have already done most of their flowering, but you also want to leave as large and shapely a plant as possible. Annuals that have large, distinct bearing stems, such as salpiglossis, cosmos, and zinnias, can be cut back on a stem-by-stem basis. Work from the top down and the outside in, cutting right above strong side buds that will make new flowering branches.

This one-at-a-time method doesn't suit bushy or lanky-stemmed plants such as lobelia and alyssum; if you had time to do *them* stem by stem you'd have too much time on your hands. Instead, wait until the bloom season is about half over, then shear as though you were pruning a hedge, reducing the plants to about two-thirds of their former girth. They will look naked and injured for a few days, but fresh growth will soon cover their wounds, and they'll send out a whole new flush of bloom that should keep coming until fall.

Welcoming Seeds

Q **For two springs now, I have tried scattering the seeds of poppies, bachelor's buttons, and coreopsis over a part of the yard that used to have a children's pool on it. I've read that these flowers can be relied on to sow themselves, so I assumed just scratching the ground and then sprinkling them on top—as though they had fallen from the plants—would be a good way to plant them. Not so. All I ever get is more and more dandelions. What gives?**

A Even things that sow themselves must fall on receptive ground. Your soil has been compacted by its years under the pool, and the annuals, which are comparatively weak plants, are having a hard time getting through it. Dandelions, on the other hand, are strong perennial weeds with long-lived seeds and deep taproots. Not only were they just lying in wait for pool removal, but now they're well established and highly competitive.

To get the annuals going, start with the soil. Scratching the surface was the right idea; you just didn't go deep enough. Starting in late fall or in early spring, remove the weeds and loosen the soil to a depth of at least 8 inches. While you're at it, dig in some compost or composted manure to encourage soil-improving worms.

Scatter the seeds, then use a rake to scratch them gently into the soil. If you're working in fall, most will lie dormant, waiting for the warmth of spring, though a few may make tiny plants that will overwinter.

In the spring, your annuals will sprout in 8 to 21 days. Weeds will sprout, too. Pull as many as you can so they don't smother the flower seedlings.

It is true that many annuals will self-sow and come back year after year, but don't forget that the weeds are just as dedicated. You can have a whole bed of self-sown flowers that never needs replanting, but that doesn't mean you can have one that doesn't need any care. 🌰

Feeding Annuals

Q I'm confused about how much to fertilize the annuals I plan to plant. Do the ones for cutting need more or less than the ones in flower beds? Should I use the same kind of fertilizer for everything, and if so, how much?

A You can get fairly good results by feeding everything once a month with a bloom-boosting fertilizer. Bloom boosters are high in phosphorus, which supports the formation of flowers and seeds.

But you will have stronger plants and more flowers if you do just a bit of fine-tuning. Plants that are cut back repeatedly are being asked to put out more growth than those that simply sit and bloom, and they need more food to do it. This is especially true of cutting flowers, which lose substantial amounts of stem and leaf as well as blossoms. The more you take, the more important it will be to give the plant something to eat.

Usually. Like all rules, this one has exceptions: nasturtiums, nigella, morning glories, and poppies, among others, will flower most abundantly if they are given no extra fertilizer at all. Just plant them in good, well-drained garden soil.

At the other extreme, hybrid petunias, million bells, and the new sunflowers bred for cutting are heavy feeders. They need rich soil and biweekly doses of bloom booster if they are to live up to their full potential as flowering machines. 🌶

Where Are the Flowers?

Q **I have just planted my first garden. I've included a number of annuals because I would like a lot of blooms and color. So far I've had lots of leaf and a disappointing number of flowers. What's going wrong?**

A The likeliest answer is that you have been feeding your plants with a high-nitrogen plant food. Nitrogen is important for photosynthesis. Plants need it to make stems and leaves that contain sufficient life-sustaining chlorophyll. Nitrogen promotes rapid growth, too. But the growth it promotes is vegetative, not developmental, and if you add too much it will retard the formation of flowers.

On the other hand, you may just need to wait a little while. Many common annuals take at least three months to flower from seed, and some take a great deal longer. Even the speediest need about nine weeks before they start blossoming. 🌶

Seeking Pest-Free Annuals

Q **I have an organic garden and am committed to planting annuals that will be pest free. What do you suggest?**

A When it comes to pests, the goal for organic gardeners is to have pest levels low enough so they do no significant damage. The aim is for minimization rather than eradication. A garden that is totally pest free would only be possible through the use of toxic chemicals that would also "free" it of a wide assortment of beneficials.

That said, there *are* some annuals more resistant to pests than others. Strong-smelling flowers like marigolds, calendulas, and annual chrysanthemums (*Chrysanthemum carinatum*), for example, are seldom bothered by bugs, and the same is—sometimes—true of plants that contain strong toxins, such as castor beans, larkspurs, and the annual foxglove 'Foxy.' 🌿

Too Many Plants

Q **I like planting annuals from seed, but I hate thinning. I try to space seeds far enough apart to keep this from being a problem but it doesn't help—there are always way too many plants.**

A There are a couple of ways to cut overplanting to a minimum. One is to mix small seeds with sand, so when you dribble them along the row you're planting far fewer seeds. The other is to plant in pinches.

Say you want an eventual spacing of 8 inches. Use a dibble or your thumb to make shallow planting holes at 4-inch intervals. Drop a *small* pinch, three or four seeds, into each hole and cover if appropriate. When the seeds come up, let them develop a set of true leaves, then use a thin-bladed scissors to snip off all but the healthiest seedling. (Pulling up the extras would disturb the roots of the plant left behind.)

In theory, this plan will still leave you with twice as many plants as you need, but in practice not everything comes up, and there are slugs and cutworms waiting for the things that do. With this and with that, half-interval pinch spacing generally produces very few extras, and if you hate waste as much as you hate thinning, the well-spaced seedlings are easy to transplant or give away. 🌿

Pelleted Seed Explained

Q **Some catalogs state that they sell pelleted seed. Can you explain what this means?**

A There are some popular plants, like petunias, coleus, and snapdragons, that have very fine seeds and are therefore difficult to sow evenly. To make them easier to work with, such seeds are sometimes given a coating that increases their size. In addition to making them easier to plant, the coating helps protect them from disease. Some coatings also provide plant food—if they do, it should say so on the packet (or in the catalog).

Pelleted seeds should not be covered heavily with soil. Just press them lightly into the soil's surface. 🌱

Getting Seeds to Grow

Q **Flower packets sometimes reccommend "scarifying" the seeds. While I get the gist of this, can you add more details?**

Scarifying seeds

A Seeds vary in the texture and thickness of their seed coat, which affects how fast water can penetrate. The presence of water in turn allows germination.

Some plants, among them flowers like morning glory, lupine, and moonflower, have rather thick seed coats. To get them going, suppliers often recommend that they be scarified—nicked, scraped, or chipped—to create tiny breaks in the seed coat. With these cracks, moisture can penetrate easily and the plant will spring to life more quickly.

What happens if there's no human around to do this job? Nature has methods, but they take longer. Thick seed coats are eventually worn away by soil fungi, bacteria, the elements, or a trip through the digestive system of a bird or other animal. 🌱

Warming Seeds

Q **In a few weeks I expect to start sowing flower and vegetable seeds on my kitchen windowsill. Shouldn't I control the temperature there? How can I do this?**

A You're right to suspect that good seed germination depends on more than adequate light and moisture. It's also affected by soil temperature.

Different plants have different needs in the temperature department, but almost all of them will do okay at 70° to 75°F.

Because cold tap water can lower the temperature considerably, use tepid. And don't forget that temperatures warm enough to keep the soil in the 70s will probably make the air above the soil too warm for the seedlings when they *do* come up. The solution? Either supply bottom heat only, using a gardener's heat mat or heating cable, or put the flats on top of the fridge until about half of the seeds have sprouted and then move them to the windowsill. 🌱

SEED STORAGE

Unless you have a very large garden or many deserving friends, chances are good you will have leftover seeds when you're done planting annuals. Not all of them are worth saving; asters and larkspurs, for instance, have very short storage lives. But most will be perfectly usable next year *if* they are stored dry, cool, and dark.

Date each packet and reseal it with tape. Put the packets in a glass jar with a screw cap, or in a thick-plastic freezer-storage bag. Put the jar or bag in a cool place or in the freezer (away from the coils if it is a self-defrosting model). When you're ready to use the frozen seeds, remove the packets from the jar or bag and spread them out flat before letting them thaw, so they don't get wet from condensation.

A few seeds will die, no matter how carefully they are stored, so plant saved seed a little more thickly to allow for the reduced germination rate.

Gathering Seed Heads

Q As a result of a hectic fall, I have not yet gone out to clean up my garden. All the annual flowers are thoroughly dead, but it looks like there are many seed heads still attached to the zinnia, marigold, and cosmos plants. Can I save these seeds for next year, or is it too late to gather them?

A When you look more closely (especially at the cosmos) you may find that although the seed heads are there, the seeds themselves have already been gathered by the birds.

If not, they can be gathered by you, though whether the exercise will be worthwhile will depend on the nature of the plants and the quality of the seeds.

If your plants were hybrids, there's not much point in saving the seeds, which cannot be counted on to "come true."

Annuals in General

You'll get some kind of zinnias (or cosmos, as the case may be), but very few if any of them will resemble this year's plants.

Assuming the plants are not hybrids, the seeds will work fine next year as long as they are sound. The best guarantee of this is seed heads that are well filled and evenly dry and brown. Don't bother to harvest any that show signs of mold or other soft decay. The seeds inside might be okay, but there's also a good chance they won't be. 🥕

Rotating Annuals

Q **I rotate my vegetable crops, but is it also necessary to rotate the annuals I put in my annual bed?**

A Rotating annual plants is always a good idea—if nothing else, it confuses the bugs. But it can also help avoid trace-nutrient depletion, and even more important, prevent the buildup of soil-borne diseases that take a particular toll on asters, marigolds, snapdragons, and zinnias.

That said, most annual flowers do fine when planted in the same place year after year, as long as the soil in that place is regularly amended with compost and fed appropriately (pansies, for example, want more fertilizer than nasturtiums do). If you have a planting pattern that has worked well, there's no reason to change it unless you see definite signs that something is amiss. These symptoms include wilting or yellowing leaves, blasted buds, diminished flowering, and a tendency on the part of the gardener to yawn when viewing the same-old, same-old one more time. 🥕

Mysterious Deaths

Q **My annual bed, which flourished last year, died off plant by plant this season. Admittedly, it was a hot summer and I probably didn't water quite enough. But I'm suspicious at the way they seemed to die one by one. It's a raised bed. Do I need to change the soil? I'd rather not, but will if I must.**

A It sounds as though your plants were fine right up until they were dead, and if that's the case, they were almost surely cut off at the base. If it happened while they were still young and tender, the culprit is probably cutworms, the soil-dwelling larvae of a number of different moths. If the plants were already good sized before they bit the dust, blame mice or voles.

Cutworm damage, top; cutworm, inset; cutworm collar, bottom

There's not much point in changing the soil. Though that might get rid of the cutworms, it would only do so for one season. As soon as a new generation of moths laid their eggs, you'd be back where you started. And rodents don't care what they scamper over on their way to a tasty stem.

If you live in zones 3 to 6, the easiest way to deal with cutworms is to delay planting until the weather is settled and warm: mid May in zone 6 to late June in zone 3. By then most of the larvae will have pupated and left the soil. If you are in zone 7 or warmer (where each year presents multiple cutworm generations), or if you need to plant earlier, protect each stem with a cutworm collar when you set out the plants.

There is no easy cure for rodents, but traps, poison baits, and cats are all effective if correctly deployed.

It's also distantly possible that you had an attack of fusarium wilt, which can fell healthy plants overnight, but this virulent scourge usually causes mass slaughter, rather than killing serially. 🌱

ANNUALS THAT BEAT THE HEAT

Most flowering annuals are happiest when night temperatures stay below 80°F, but not everything gets cooked when the weather is baking hot. The following plants are extreme-summer stalwarts, providing color when lesser plants fade (as long as you keep them well watered):

Gaillardia, globe amaranth, four-o'clocks, lantana, Madagascar periwinkle, ornamental peppers, portulaca, salvia, sunflower, torenia, narrow-leaf zinnia (*Z. haageana*).

Warning: Most plants, like most people, can take heat more easily if humidity is low. Even when temperatures are moderate, long runs of muggy weather are usually synonymous with fungus invasions.

Annuals in Particular

The Two Amaranths

Q I've seen amaranth listed in my seed catalogs as both a vegetable and a flower. Are these the same plants? Do they have the same needs in terms of soil and climate?

A The various garden amaranths are from the same botanical genus and have very similar needs. They like warm weather, and fertile soil with a lot of organic matter in it. The flowering sorts, such as love-lies-bleeding and elephant head, can get by with somewhat less nitrogen than those grown for their leaves, such as 'Tampala' and 'Red Stripe.'

All amaranth leaves, including those of the common weeds often referred to as pigweed, are edible. So are all of the seeds, though only those amaranths sold as grain plants produce enough seeds to make harvesting worthwhile. 🍂

China Aster Problems

Q I love the shapes and colors of China asters—singles, doubles, and especially the wonderful quilled ones—and I set aside a special bed for growing them all. It was spectacular the first year and pretty good the second, but this year (the third) almost all the plants seem to have some kind of disease. Some of the flowers rot at the neck and are deformed. Leaves are turning yellow and most of the plants are stunted. What's happening and how can I stop it? I'd rather not use chemical fungicides, but at this point I'd do anything to save these plants.

A The first and best line of defense is to stop planting asters in that spot. It sounds as though your plants have contracted two very common afflictions: aster yellows, which stunts and deforms them, and aster wilt, a deadly rot that attacks both roots and stems.

There is no fungicide, natural or chemical, that can fully vanquish these diseases, and they persist in the soil for years. But all is not lost if you follow these three rules:

1. Remove all infected plants and burn or send them to the landfill. Don't bury them or put them in the compost.

China aster
(*Callistephus chinensis*)

2. Plant asters in a different place each year.

3. Work on getting rid of the leafhoppers that spread the contagions from one plant (or garden) to another. Although leafhoppers are very small, fast moving, and difficult to target, you can usually hit them in the cool of early morning. Spray with a mixture of 1 tablespoon isopropyl alcohol to 1 pint insecticidal soap, aiming particularly for the underside of the leaves.

It will take at least two or three applications to reduce a large population of leafhoppers to a tolerably small one. Spray at three-day intervals, and if extended treatment is necessary, give the plants a 10-day rest after every three sprayings. 🌿

Wedding Bells

Q **I am planning a homemade wedding and will be growing the flowers for my bouquet. My groom and I are both Irish, and the cousin who is helping us thought it would be fun to have bells of Ireland as a floral motif. Although I grew up in Ireland, I never heard of them. Are they difficult to grow?**

A The stately, old-fashioned annual bells of Ireland (*Moluccella laevis*), also sometimes called shell flower, has long been a mainstay of English cottage gardens although it is actually native to western Asia. The 2- to 3-foot-tall stems, which are often gracefully bent or twisted, are strung up and down with very small, fragrant white flowers. The flowers are encased in large, round green calyxes, like open bells, which give the plant its name. The leaves are sparse and interfere with the symmetry of the calyx rows, so they are usually removed before the stems are used in arrangements.

Nurseries seldom offer seedlings, but the plants can be grown from seed, which is widely available. Use peat pots or other plantable pots—moluccella makes sensitive taproots that resent transplanting. Start seed indoors six weeks before the last frost, and don't cover the very fine seed; it needs light to germinate. 🌿

Domesticated Texas Bluebells

Q I've loved lisianthius in florists' arrangements, so I bought a potted one. But now I realize that I know nothing about the plant. It seems to need a lot of water because it wilts readily. I assume it's an annual. Can it be planted outside? Does it bloom constantly?

A *Lisianthius russellianus* is another name for *Eustoma grandiflorum*, the prairie gentian, or Texas bluebell, originally a wildflower of the western plains.

Of course you can plant it outside. You can plant anything outside, at least temporarily. Choose a spot in full but not broiling sun, where the soil is neutral to slightly alkaline, well drained, and not too rich. Be careful when transplanting; the delicate taproot resents disturbance.

Feed sparingly, and water only when the soil is dry an inch down. Unless it has outgrown its pot, there's a good chance your plant is wilting because it's too wet rather than the reverse. Lisianthius is vulnerable to a wide range of fungi and bacteria, all of which thrive in damp conditions.

Prairie gentian is a slow-growing annual (or biennial grown as an annual) that will flower for two months or more, depending on the variety. Frost will kill it, but by then it will probably be all bloomed out. ✿

Calendula Weather

Q When I lived in New Hampshire, I grew calendulas in my herb garden that were to die for. Now we've moved near Washington, D.C., and they just aren't performing well. I'm baffled and need your help, please, as these are among my favorite easy-to-grow annuals.

A Welcome to summer heat. Calendula, also called pot marigold, takes little effort to grow other than remembering to put it in full sun. But while it loves cool climates, in warmer areas it quits blooming in mid summer.

If yours have grown long and rangy, mid summer is a perfect time to cut them back by a third to half. As cool weather returns, they'll rebloom. When they start again, continue your religious devotion to deadheading so they keep flowering cheerfully right until a hard frost finally takes them.

Calendula selections range from under a foot tall to over two. The flowers are usually bright orange or shades of yellow, and are often fully double. Knockout cultivars include 'Pink Surprise,' with soft peach-melba petals and a well-behaved habit, and 'Touch of Red,' whose many petals are edged in a mahogany blush. 🌸

Castor-Bean Plants

Q **I have long been intrigued by castor-bean plants and would like to grow one. What do they need, and where can I find seeds?**

A A native of Africa and member of the spurge family, the castor bean (*Ricinus communis*) is a fast-growing shrub that is treated as a summer annual in frosty climes.

The shiny, star-shaped leaves, which often grow up to 3 feet wide, make a strong architectural statement whether they are the more common green or tinged with red, as in the variety 'Carmencita.'

Castor-bean flowers range in color from cream through pink to bright red, and are followed by spiny red fruits that contain the (poisonous) seeds that are the source of castor oil.

Castor-bean plants are easily grown in full sun or light shade; they do best in fertile, well-drained soil. The seeds may be either started indoors in mid April, or sown directly into the garden in May once the ground is no longer cold and soggy.

Seeds are widely available from mail-order houses that specialize in flowers. 🌸

Tender Is the Plant

Q **I just noticed that my cerinthe has resprouted! I'm thrilled to see it come back, since I thought it was an annual, but what do I do now that winter is coming? Can I protect the plants where they are (in my backyard, in Brooklyn) or must I bring them inside?**

A Cerinthes are indeed thrilling plants: handsome in both garden and vase, seldom bothered by pests or diseases, and drought tolerant to boot.

Give them plenty of sun and well-drained soil, and they will produce multitudes of gracefully arching stems, clothed in spoon-shaped green or gray leaves and tipped with colorful bracts that last far longer than the flowers.

If you have plain *Cerinthe major,* also known as honeywort, with sage-gray bracts around yellow flowers, you were right the first time. It is an annual. The sprouts are self-sown seedlings, and unless you're fond of scrawny, bug-infested houseplants, you should bid them goodbye.

If you have the subspecies *C. major purpurescens* (turquoise to deep blue bracts and purple flowers), it has greater staying power. It can last for a year or more where winter temperatures are mild, so some sources call it a short-lived tender perennial.

Tender is the word, however. *C. major* is a Mediterranean native, only hardy down to about 25°F. The purple form is fond of cool weather and might resprout quite late in the fall. But it won't survive outdoors in Brooklyn, even with protection, unless the winter is record-breakingly balmy and then some.

You could bring it in. With tender care—and lots of insecticidal soap—it would probably come through. But it probably wouldn't last for long after you brought it out again; and cerinthes grow so quickly from seed, you might as well just skip the hassle and start over next spring. 🌰

Cerinthe major purpurescens

Cleomes from Seed

Q Recently, I bought cut flowers identified as cleomes. I would like to plant the seeds from the pods. Can this be done, and if so, when and what are the proper conditions?

A You certainly can grow them from seed, and with very little trouble. But keep in mind that cleomes (also known as spider flowers) cross freely, so the children may not be the same color as their parents.

About two months before the end of winter, start cleome seeds indoors on a sunny windowsill. Seeds can also be sown outdoors anytime in early spring; established plants will often self-sow. 🌰

Naming Cornflowers

Q **Why are bachelor's buttons called cornflowers? The plants don't look like corn plants, and the flowers certainly don't look like anything that grows on cornstalks.**

A Neither do corn cockles, *Agrostemma githago,* or corn poppies, *Papaver rhoeas.* But all three plants first came to notice as weeds of European grainfields. In England, grain was called "corn"—hence the name of these old-fashioned flowers. The stuff that grows on cobs came to Europe as "maize," and still often goes by that name on the other side of the Pond. ✿

Cosmos Count the Hours

Q **My cosmos 'Sensation Mix' has lovely ferny foliage, but not a single bloom, no hint of a bud for that matter. They have been fertilized and get plenty of sun. What is the problem? I have never had trouble with these easy-care plants before.**

*Cosmos
bipinnatus*

A The cosmos timetable is nearly as strict as a Swiss train schedule. *Cosmos bipinnatus,* whose tall, lithe stalks hold magenta, pink, or white flowers, are short-day plants. They initiate flower production only when the photoperiod, or day length, is shorter than a certain number of hours. For cosmos, the critical number is 14.

If your plants did not start the process of making flower buds in the spring, perhaps because they were stressed by the heat or were too young, they will patiently wait until long enough after the summer solstice that the daylight is once again less than 14 hours. In the meantime, they will continue to keep an eye on the clock and just grow taller. When they do flower, you'll be practically eye-to-eye with them.

But if a few of them never flower, blame genetics, not the calendar. *C. bipinnatus* 'Sensation Mix' is not a highly controlled hybrid, where the performance of every plant is uniform. Its genetic diversity means that among the variations in a population there may be a few blind plants, those that never flower. Enjoy the foliage. ✿

Cosmos Clinic

Q **I have been very conscientious about deadheading my cosmos plants, but they are nevertheless producing fewer and smaller flowers. Is mid August the end, or is there a way to make them look lush again?**

A The mid-summer beauty treatment for tired cosmos has three parts: surgery, nutrition, and hydration. The stems that have been bearing flowers should be cut back and the plants pepped up with a little food and a lot of water.

Cutting back is a bit of an art, since you want to remove about half of the plant while leaving it as large and shapely as possible. Work from the top down and the outside in, cutting spent stems right above strong, young green growth that will make new flowering branches.

Water deeply before fertilizing, then apply balanced liquid fertilizer, diluted to half-strength. Keep the soil moist from now on, and feed again, at half-strength, in 10 days. The cosmos should get their second wind in early September and continue to bloom well until they are killed by frost. ✿

Bringing Up Cape Daisy

Q **Late last spring I purchased two small Cape daisies. The labels said only *Osteospermum*. Over the summer they became huge. I cut them back late in the season, and when the first frost turned the foliage to slime, I cut them back again. Was this a mistake? Should I have mulched them for winter? The greengrocer I bought them from knew only that "it will come back again next year," so I assume osteospermum is a perennial. I would appreciate any tips on growing them.**

A Most osteospermums are indeed perennial, but only in their native South Africa and similarly frost-free climates. Everywhere else, they are treated as annuals.

Osteospermums, sometimes labeled *Dimorphotheca*, or star of the Veldt, come in a wide range of colors from bright oranges and rich purple-reds to yellow, pink, and cream. Though a few are golden-centered, most have dark hearts, and this is especially striking in the lavender-tinged whites.

Cape daisies are sun lovers that close at night and on dark cloudy days. They don't mind heat, and once established, will tolerate some drought. Seeds need warm soil to germinate, but grow so easily and quickly that they can be sown in the garden in spring for summer bloom about nine weeks later. They'll flower all season if you keep them deadheaded; and should the plants start looking used up, you can cut them back to strong buds and they will put out vigorous new flowering shoots. 🌶

Evolvulus

Q **My daughter gave me a blue flowering plant called evolvulus, which no one seems to have heard of. It's been outdoors all summer. Now what do I do with it?**

A Your gift plant is very likely one of the newer introductions to the market, *Evolvulus glomeratus* 'Blue Daze.' This is a delightful and very easily grown plant. It is one of several dozen species within the genus, and a member of the morning glory family, Convolvulaceae. Evolvulus differs from its morning glory cousins in that it does not twine; hence its name, which comes from the Latin verb for "unroll."

Native to Brazil, this plant is a tender herbaceous perennial. You could just let it die and start over again next spring, but because it can be hard to find, you might prefer to carry it over as a houseplant. Place it on a sunny sill in a cool room and feed it regularly with a diluted high-phosphorus fertilizer to keep it blooming. 🌶

4 O'Clock and All's Abloom

Q **Can you tell me how the four-o'clock plant knows it's 4 o'clock, and time to open?**

A Flowering plants are pretty clever, but how they decide exactly when to open their flowers is about as complicated as building a watch.

Nobody seems to have actually studied four-o'clocks, but according to Dr. Thomas Whitlow, an associate professor of horticultural physiology at Cornell, what most likely happens suggests some Rube Goldberg machine in minia-ture. If you didn't have a lot of respect for the ingenuity of plants before, you will if you read on.

It all begins when the sun gets low enough. The atmos-phere is a huge sphere, and sunlight has to travel through more of it in late afternoon to reach the earth because the rays are traveling at an angle, not straight down as at noon. Water in the air absorbs more blue light than red, which is why sunsets are often red.

Phytochrome, a protein in the flower buds, is sensitive to the balance between red and blue light. Extra red makes it turn the space just outside the cell walls slightly acidic. The wall membranes then begin letting potassium ions pass through from the liquid surrounding the cells. Once the potassium balance is off-kilter, osmotic pressure forces extra water into the cells in an effort to restore the balance of the inner and outer potassium.

Still with me?

All that extra water makes the cells expand like a balloon. As the cells in the flower buds expand, they press on the bud scales, the outer petals. The flower scales respond to the pres-sure by opening, and the flower blooms.

Why doesn't this happen at 4 a.m., as the sun rises? In some plants it does. Four-o'clocks prefer afternoon, and no one really knows why. Perhaps they're just not morning plants. 🍂

Fragrance and Four-O'Clocks

Q **I grew four-o'clocks from seed last year. They had no fragrance. Has this been caused by "improvement" in seed?**

A Modern flowers are infamous for having lost fragrance on the way to greater gaudiness, but that's probably not the case with four-o'clocks. Though catalogs and garden guides describe the common four-o'clock (*Mirabilis jalapa*) as very fragrant, individual strains are highly variable in this regard.

Breeders and seed savers have done some selecting for color, but no one seems to have done much about stabilizing the perfume, even though four-o'clocks have been around a long time. They were introduced to European gardens from

South America in the sixteenth century—hence their common name marvel-of-Peru. The marvel is the way the brightly colored, trumpet-shaped blooms open and put out fragrance as evening falls.

Marvel-of-Peru is also a name for the sweet four-o'clock, *M. longiflora,* a fragrant cousin of the common kind. The common one is famous for its riotous colors: magenta, orange-yellow, and candy pink, sometimes with multi-colored stripes, spots, and blotches. The sweet one comes in a more limited palette, heaviest on whites and pale pastels. Perhaps as compensation, the flowers of sweet four-o'clocks are larger, and they are reliably fragrant.

If you want the bright colors of *M. jalapa* and some perfume as well, it's best to try named cultivars; 'Don Pedro' is one that gets good marks.

Four-o'clocks make tubers that, like dahlia tubers, can be dug up and stored frost-free over the winter for spring planting. So if you grow some that have good perfume, consider saving them that way. 🌱

Mirabilis jalapa, left;
M. longiflora, right

HEIRLOOMS FROM THE FLOWER AND HERB EXCHANGE

The Flower and Herb Exchange is an offshoot of the Seed Savers Exchange, granddaddy of seed-preservation groups, and it is similarly dedicated to saving heirloom varieties. But SSE's focus is on vegetables and grains, whereas FHE, as its name makes clear, is about flowers and herbs.

The pages of the FHE catalog are filled with old-fashioned beauties, the pass-along plants that flourished in our grandmothers' gardens. Though some of these are familiar, many are obscure or rare. They are not available commercially, and owe their continued life to the network of seed savers who treasure them.

Because this is a seed listing, most of the plants are annuals, but perennials also have a place and there are a few oddball items that defy categorization.

FHE is a garden-to-garden network. Join as a non-listed member and buy the more common stuff; or by offering seeds yourself, become a listed member and gain access to the rarities. Contact them at 3076 North Winn Road, Decorah, IA 52101; (563) 382-5990; *www.seedsavers.org.*

'Foxy' Foxglove

Q **Does the annual foxglove really bloom in one season?**

A Yes, the variety called 'Foxy' will travel from seed to flower in about five months. Assuming, that is, that the season is a long, cool one, and that the plants are growing in well-drained, nearly neutral soil (ideally, in partial shade).

The plants won't do well if they are still small when spring turns into summer, so plan to get them going early: sow seed outdoors in late February if you're in zone 7 or 8, indoors about 8 to 10 weeks before the last expected frost if you live in zones 3 to 6. 🌶

No Need for Improvement

Q **I used to buy gazania seedlings and get the most beautiful flowers. They were mostly shades of orange, yellow, red, and brown, with elaborate patterns on the petals and a glowing eye at the base. But for several years now, all the ones I've bought have much plainer flowers. What happened?**

A What happened was the usual: a perfectly nice flower was seen by marketers as being in need of improvement. In the case of gazanias, there are two perceived problems (perceived by the breeders, that is). One is that gazanias close at night; the other is that it takes them a long time to bloom from seed, a grave disadvantage to the nursery trade, where bloom-by-sales-season is the *sine qua non* of attractiveness in annuals.

You might have better luck if you start your own from seed. The hybrids called 'Harlequin' sometimes come through with zippy combos, and some growers have had luck with 'Sundance.' If you do find a strain that produces the flowers you like, buy several packets and freeze them (see page 26). Almost all the gazanias in commerce are hybrids, so it won't do you much good to save seeds. 🌶

New York's Flying Geraniums

Q Every time I visit New York, I marvel at the huge pots of flowers hanging on lampposts all around the city. The geraniums look as if they were flying. I bought what I thought had the same characteristics: leaves and flowers on long curly stems. Not the same thing at all. What variety are the city geraniums, and why are they so prolific?

A The geraniums you admire are the same kind of container-planted ivy geraniums (*Pelargonium peltatum*) that also make Americans traveling in Europe so envious. Members of the Balcon series (ask for them by name or you'll get something else), they have a wild, trailing growth habit and are covered in flowers. As a bonus, they practically clean themselves, as the petals quickly drop off once the flower fades.

If you like to pinch back, these geraniums could take it every hour on the hour. Or you can just pinch them back when they get too far out of shape for your taste. Either way, full sun and weekly fertilizing will reward you amply.

The four members of the series are 'Balcon Royale' (scarlet), 'Princess Balcon' (light orchid), 'King of Balcon' (light coral pink), and 'Balcon Pink Star' (pink with a white eye).

Garden centers with the healthy attitude that convent neatness and manicured shapes aren't everything may carry them; otherwise, ask to have them ordered. 🌶

Geranium Spots

Q My ivy geraniums have tiny brown pimples on the underside of their leaves. Is this some weird disease?

A No. It is a common, environmentally caused condition called edema, which occurs when the soil is warm and damp and the air is cool and damp. This situation causes a rapid upward movement of the water within the plant's system, but a slow transpiration through the leaves. As a result, some of the cells on the leaves' undersides burst. When they callous over, they develop corky brown spots. Although the damaged leaves won't recover, new leaf growth should be fine if you improve ventilation and reduce watering. 🌶

The Geranium in Winter

Q I purchased 15 to 20 geraniums this year and had a tapestry of color—lavender, pink, burgundy, white, hot pink. It was a beautiful mass effect. I would like to keep them in the basement this winter for next year. Should I pot them up and water them occasionally, or just hang them upside down? I have no sunny space to keep them in.

A The perfect solution would be a cool, damp basement, where you could just hang them upside down. Shake the excess dirt from the roots, but leave all that clings. Loosely tie a string around the neck area, where the stem meets the roots, and use this to hang them from a rafter or beam. They should get good air circulation; be sure they don't touch each other, or anything else.

A dry basement—as long as it is cool (35° to 45°F)—is a distant second choice. In that case, you will need to pot them up and they will need a place that's light. They should be watered thoroughly about once a month, but let them go dry in between—they're hardly growing.

No matter which way you store them, remove buds and flowers, where the disease botrytis hides, and any leaves that turn yellow. Cut the plants back to 6 inches after planting them outside next year.

Even though your geraniums appear healthy, they could have picked up at least one of the many diseases that affect geraniums during the summer. When they are ready to go back outside, the geraniums will be stressed from their winter treatment, but any disease organisms will be just fine so the plants may not be as healthy as you expect. Keep a little extra in the gardening budget for replacements. 🌰

Zonal geranium
(*Pelargonium* ×
hortorum)

Quaking Grass or Bearded Wheat

Q My husband and I saw a beautiful dried flower wreath that had big fat wheat seed heads dangling from it. Or at least I think they were wheat. He says they weren't because they didn't have "beards." If they weren't wheat, what were they?

A Bearded wheat, *Triticum turgidum,* is often used in dried arrangements because the long, beardlike wisps (called awns) that sweep from each grain are so airy and graceful. But the majority of wheats do not sport these extra ornaments, so beardlessness doesn't rule out wheat.

The fact that the seed heads were dangling, however, suggests that they were something else (wheat can droop, but it's too stiff to really dangle). If the seed heads you saw were attached to their stems by a fine thread, they were probably big quaking grass, *Briza maxima,* also known as puffed wheat plant.

Bearded wheat and quaking grass are both annuals that are easy to grow in average garden soil in full sun. Harvest for drying when the seed heads are fully formed but before they start to dry. Tie in loose bundles and hang upside down in a warm, dry place where there is good air circulation. ✿

Saving Impatiens

Q **Each year in late summer, I collect impatiens seeds from hardy plants. I grow them indoors over the winter in flats placed in windows facing southeast. I get many good plants by spring and plant them outside in May, but they never blossom as profusely as nursery plants. Any explanations or suggestions?**

A The problem may be cultural. Although *Impatiens walleriana* is famous for blooming in the shade, the plants flower most exuberantly with a couple of hours of early-morning or late-afternoon sun. If yours are someplace truly gloomy, that might be the problem.

It's also possible that you may be carefully perpetuating your own special strain of shy-blooming plants—like parents, like offspring.

On the other hand, if the original group of plants came from a nursery, you could be disappointed even if you did make efforts at selective breeding. A lot of commercially grown heavy bloomers are first-generation hybrids, crosses between parent strains that are quite different from each other as well as from their progeny. The crosses themselves have "hybrid vigor" and bloom their little heads off, but saving their seeds seldom works out—only a few replicate their parents. Unless you know you've got a seed-saver's (non-hybrid) strain, when it comes to impatiens you're probably better off buying fresh seeds (or plants) each year. 🍂

Saving Gray Larkspur

Q **Last year I planted a larkspur called 'Major Grey.' It was a beautiful gray-mauve, almost the color of smoke, and I was very excited when seedlings showed up this year. Unfortunately, almost none of this year's plants have the same color. My blue larkspurs were on the other side of the garden, so I'm sure these plants are the children of the gray ones. What happened?**

A No doubt they *are* the children of the gray ones. But thanks to the bees, they are probably also the children of the blue flowers on the other side of the garden.

The gray color is a special selection, and the genes that produce it are fairly weak, easily dominated by the aboriginal purple-blue. If you want to perpetuate the gray strain, you'll have to grow only that color—unless you want to grow it in a bee-thwarting gauze cage and pollinate it by hand. 🍂

Starting Lavateras

Q **For several years I have had the pleasure of growing pink and white lavateras ('Silver Cup' and 'Mont Blanc') because I had a great source of seedlings: a woman two towns away who had a small greenhouse. Now she has gone out of business and I'm on my own. Are these plants difficult to start on a windowsill?**

A The annual mallow *Lavatera trimestris* is quite easy to start inside—the trick is transplanting it, since the roots resent disturbance. Although you don't say so, your former supplier probably grew them in larger than usual plastic cells, or else in individual peat pots.

Now that you're on your own, you have two options. One is to simply plant the seeds where they are to grow. Sow them in mid spring, about a week before the frost-free date. They will start blooming about 10 weeks later.

For earlier bloom, start the seeds indoors six weeks before the last expected frost. Use plastic cells or peat pots that are about 1½ to 2 inches wide across the top. Fill them to ⅓ inch of the rim with moistened commercial seed-starting mix. Put three or four seeds in each pot and sprinkle dry mix over them until the pots are almost full.

Set the pots in a pan of water and let them wick up moisture until the tops are wet. Remove from the water, place on a tray, and loosely cover with plastic wrap.

Put the tray on top of the refrigerator or somewhere else warm (70° to 85°F) until the seeds start sprouting, anywhere from three to eight days, then uncover and move them to a bright, cool windowsill.

Water (by the wick-up method) only when the soil surface is dry, and keep turning the pots so the plants grow evenly. As soon as they have two true leaves, clip off all but the strongest seedling in each pot.

Start hardening off the seedlings as soon as the danger of frost is past, and plant them where they are to grow as soon as possible. 🍎

HOW HARD DOES HARDENING OFF HAVE TO BE?

Plants that have been raised indoors have thin skins—their stems and leaves are easily damaged by sun and wind—so it is always recommended that seedlings be "hardened off," i.e., gradually made tougher, before they are planted outside.

The standard advice suggests leaving plants outdoors for gradually increasing amounts of time each day. You start with an hour or so in the shade, then move, over the course of a week or 10 days, to full days in the sun. Every day you take them out. Every day, you take them back in.

It works, but it isn't what you'd call convenient, and it isn't necessary if you give the plants a week or so in a transitional space, perhaps on a covered porch or against the east side of a building. If you are using an east- or north-facing porch, for example, you can probably get by with nothing more than a windbreak, rigged up at the end from which the wind usually blows.

If the plants are against the side of the house, they'll need a bit more protection. Set up a support of sawhorses in front of the plants (or boards leaning against the house), and put window sashes or spun-bonded row cover like Reemay against them for the first couple of days. Be sure there's plenty of air circulation at the top so the seedlings don't get cooked.

That's it, assuming you stay alert and use common sense. Bring the plants in if frost or a heavy rainstorm threatens, and shade them if it decides to be unseasonably hot. (Yes, you can use a picnic umbrella; just be sure the sun's hot rays don't get a chance to sneak in underneath.)

Malope, Not Musk Mallow

Q On a trip to Arkansas, we ate at a restaurant where the table bouquets were made from wildflowers. Included were some unusual flowers with alternate large and small petals of bright pink and bright green. Our waitress said they were musk mallows, but I was sure they weren't. After I got home, I looked them up. Sure enough, they were not musk mallows, but now I'm stumped. Do you have any idea what they could have been?

A Had you turned backward, from *Malva* to *Malope*, you would have found your quarry. The two plants are both Malvaceae, and bear a close family resemblance.

Musk mallow, *Malva moschata,* is large and long blooming, and could be classed either as a perennial or as a nuisance, depending on how well it's doing. Malope, *Malope trifida,* is an annual. It can grow as large as musk mallow, but although it will sometimes self-sow, it's not usually aggressive enough to qualify for wildflower status. The ones you saw were probably garden grown.

It must have been quite dark in the restaurant. If the place had been well lit, you would have seen that the bright green petals were nothing of the kind. The pink petals of the true flower are fan shaped, widely separated at the base where only their points touch. The brilliant green is the calyx, shining through the gaps. 🌱

Slouchy Marigolds

Q The 'Sophia' marigolds I grew this summer made very tidy little bushes, but the 'Crackerjack' and 'Vanilla Delight' I purchased (because they were sold as "good for cutting") got so tall and floppy I had to tie them up. Do all cutting varieties present this problem?

A Short, bushy marigolds like 'Sophia' are the French type, *Tagetes patula;* cutting varieties are usually African marigolds, *T. erecta.* In this case the Latin name is not entirely accurate; *erecta* can sometimes be quite *sloucha,* especially if it is growing in well-watered, fertile soil.

To encourage the tall growers to stand up straight, try pinching out the tips of the seedlings while they are still

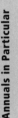

French marigold
(*Tagetes patula*)

small. This will delay flowering for a while, but it will also force denser branching and sturdier plants.

Don't stint on water, but don't keep them soggy; and don't fertilize more than twice. Tall marigolds grown for cutting do benefit from one dose of bloom booster at planting time, and another about halfway through the season, but feeding them much more than that is likely to produce soft growth that cannot hold itself up.

Finally, you can try some of the large-flowered *T. erecta* hybrids that have been bred for more compact habit, such as 'Inca' and 'Discovery.' They do stand up quite politely, but nothing is free; the plants are on the short side and so are the cutting stems. 🖋

Habits of Nicotiana

Q **I love the scent of nicotiana and try to have it bloom as long as possible. I start *Nicotiana alata* and *N. sylvestris* seed indoors in April to set out in late May, and these transplanted seedlings always do well. So does the self-sown *N. alata,* though it doesn't bloom until late summer. But the self-sown *N. sylvestris* doesn't make as many plants and the ones it does make seldom flower. Why do these closely related species behave so differently?**

A Why does the country mouse prefer to go to bed at 10 o'clock while the city mouse club-hops all night? Why does chicken taste so much better than turkey? The species are indeed closely related, but that doesn't mean they behave the same way. *N. alata* is, to put it bluntly, a weedier plant, hardier and more aggressive than its cousin *N. sylvestris*.

All nicotianas need warmth to germinate, but *N. alata* doesn't need quite as much as *N. sylvestris*. In your area, which sounds like zone 5, self-sown seedlings of *N. alata* usually appear in late May or early June, whereas *N. sylvestris* bides its time until mid June or early July. The seedlings look exactly alike, so it's easy to assume that you're seeing both kinds when you aren't.

This late start creates two problems for the self-sown *N. sylvestris:* personal space issues and time constraints.

Nicotiana alata, left;
N. sylvestris, right

N. alata will produce *something* even when competition is quite severe. *N. sylvestris* is less crowd-tolerant, and since its seedlings show up later, they usually have more to compete with.

And *N. sylvestris* takes longer to grow all the way from seed to flower. In years when summer's warmth hangs on, there's a chance these late starters can manage to be late bloomers as well; but most of the time, shortening days and cooling nights are telling the young *N. sylvestris* plants there's no point in bothering. ❧

Perking Up Pansies

Q **Every spring I buy all kinds of pretty-colored pansies and plant them at the edge of the garden. There is partial shade there and the plants do well until the beginning of July. Then they kind of peter out, not really dying but not doing well, either, even though I keep them well watered and fertilized. Sometimes they perk up in the fall, but usually they don't. Is there a trick to getting these plants to be more consistent?**

A Pansies are cool-weather plants, and nothing will keep them happy in mid summer except being planted so far north that temperatures never rise above 70°F for more than a few days.

Breeders keep working on creating more heat-tolerant types, but there are also some tricks that will help with any and all of them. You are already planting your pansies where they have some protection from full sun, which is very important, and as long as the regular fertilization is not heavy, that too is appropriate. Pansies need more food than most other annuals, but it should come in the form of a light foliar spray, delivered once a month or so. (Heavy feeding can lead to soft, leggy growth, and vulnerability to disease.)

Deadheading is another key to a long bloom season; pansies will put out larger flowers, and more of them, if they are prevented from setting seed. It will also help to shear them back when they start to flag. As soon as that happens, remove about half of the plant: stems, leaves, flowers, everything, cutting each stem all the way back to healthy branch buds. This will uglify them briefly, but not for long. By the time the weather cools down, they will again be full and strong and ready to bloom through fall.

Finally (or firstly), start with stocky, well-branched young plants that have not yet begun to bloom or that have, at most, one or two open flowers and a few buds. Plants that are already covered with flowers are also already stressed by cramped quarters. They will have a harder time getting settled in the garden, and will tend to stop blooming sooner than plants that are just starting when you set them out. 🌿

ENCOURAGING LATE BLOOMERS

There are three ways to make sure you have annuals blooming all through fall, right up until the hard frost.

1. Be faithful about deadheading and shearing back. If you stay on top of it, this potentially boring but effective tidying up will greatly extend the blooming time of most annual flowers.

2. Start a few hardy bloomers from seed in early June. They won't do much until the end of the season, but that's the idea. Choices include asters, calendula, coreopsis, larkspur, *Nicotiana alata,* nigella, phlox, seven-week stock.

This is the calendar for zones 5 and 6. If you are in zone 3 or 4, plant everything on the list as soon as the weather warms. If you're in zone 7 or 8, push the planting times back to mid May and mid June, then plant a last batch of alyssum, candytuft, Drummond phlox, larkspur, and nigella in mid August (keep the seedbed well watered and, if possible, lightly shaded for the first couple of weeks).

3. Be sure you have lots of plants that don't mind a little frost. After the nasturtiums and dahlias have been reduced to sad brown heaps, these flowers will still be smiling: alyssum, anagallis, asters, calendula, cerinthe, Chinese forget-me-not, annual chrysanthemum (*Chyrsanthemum carinatum*), larkspur, annual lupine (*Lupinus densiflorus, L. hartwegii*), malope, nigella, scabiosa, and snapdragon.

Peter's Purse? It's Pocketbook

Q In England, I fell in love with a flower called Peter's purse. They look like miniature pita breads—little pouches—and I remember them in startlingly bright colors. No one seems to recognize the name, but I wonder if Peter's purse is just British for a plant that is available here. If it is, will it thrive in zone 5 in upstate New York?

A Most likely Peter's neon-yellow, orange, or red purse is the common pocketbook plant, *Calceolaria herbeohybrida,* a hybrid of several tender species that is treated as an annual.

Pocketbook plants in full riotous bloom are widely sold throughout the spring and early summer at many florists and most well-stocked garden centers. Before you buy, bear in mind that they only bloom for about six weeks, and that they are somewhat fussy about growing conditions.

They need ample moisture but are also vulnerable to rot, so good drainage is essential. They must be kept cool; 60° to 65°F is best. They burn easily in strong sunlight and if stressed invite white flies, aphids, and spider mites.

For best results, choose plants that are starting to bloom but still have unopened buds. Check lower leaves for mold or insects. If the soil seems compacted or muddy, make sure the roots are not starting to rot. 🍎

Starting Petunias

Q I'm attracted to the many gorgeous colors and shapes of petunias I see in seed catalogs. There are so many more choices than at nurseries! Unfortunately, I don't seem to have much luck starting them. Any pointers?

A Petunias are easy to grow from seed, though you do have to start well in advance: 10 to 12 weeks before the frost-free date.

The tiny seeds need light to germinate, so just sprinkle them—sparingly—on top of some sterile seed-starting medium and press them in gently. Water from below until the medium is damp, then cover loosely with plastic wrap, and put in a warm place (70° to 75°F) until they sprout, usually in about 10 days.

Move the babies to a bright spot, preferably under grow lights, and grow them on until they have two sets of true leaves. As soon as they do, transplant to market packs or plug flats filled with a loose, light growing medium such as Pro-Mix.

From this point on, they should do fine. Keep them moist but not wet and make sure they get plenty of air circulation (petunias are highly vulnerable to damp-off, a fungus disease promoted by wet soil and/or stale, humid air).

When the plants have six to eight true leaves, pinch out the growing tips to encourage branching. Pinch the branches after they have formed four leaves of their own.

Spray with an all-purposed houseplant fertilizer, diluted to half-strength, when the seedlings are about six weeks old. Repeat when they reach the eight-week mark, but don't feed them any more than that until after they're in the garden.

As soon as the danger of frost is past, harden off the seedlings and plant them out as usual, being sure to include some that are on the small, weak side. With most annual flowers, you want only the biggest, strongest seedlings, but the prettiest petunias are often rather puny as children. ☙

TO PINCH OR NOT TO PINCH

Pinching out the growing tips of annual seedlings forces them to make multiple branches, so you get stockier, bushier plants and—eventually— more flowers. But pinching does delay flowering, and many gardeners find it hard to bring themselves to do it.

Try to be strong; it really does make a difference. If you are growing from seed, pinch at the six- to eight-leaf stage. If you are buying seedlings, pinch them as soon as you get them home. It hurts to remove flowers and buds, but the pinched-back plants will suffer much less stress at transplanting and will pull ahead of unpinched ones in about two weeks.

Most of the time. As with all general rules, this one has a few exceptions. Plants that don't benefit from being pinched include asters, poppies, stocks, and rosette-formers like venidium and gazania.

Not Quite Petunia

Q Last summer I saw a flowering plant that looked like—but wasn't— a petunia, with unusual veined blossoms. Do you know this plant and where I can get it?

A The flower you saw is probably the delightful summer-blooming annual from Chile called painted tongue (*Salpiglossis sinuata*). This free-flowering petunia relative deserves to be more widely grown. Its handsome, velvety, funnel-shaped blooms come in red, yellow, orange, brown, and purple; most have handsome contrasting veins. The blooms average between 2 and 3 inches in both length and width. Hybrids are a bit bushier than the species, which tends to be somewhat lank.

Painted tongue grows to between 2 and 3 feet tall, with the flowers clustered at the ends of the branches. It does best in rich, well-drained soil, full sun, and cool weather. Although the seed is very small, it's not difficult to start. Germination takes about two and a half weeks. 🌰

Wild Petunias

Q **When I was a child, my mother had small pink petunias that made a colorful, floppy display. I think they were wild plants, since the seeds spread easily and they returned each year. But I cannot find them.**

A It sounds as though your mother's plants were *Petunia violacea,* a rose-red or violet native of Argentina.

There are at least a dozen species of petunias, annuals and tender perennials from Mexico and South America. The smaller-flowered, more sprawling types are difficult to find now; they have been replaced by larger, tidier, more colorful hybrids. Unfortunately, these plants lack the original powerful aroma and are often sterile.

Check heirloom seed catalogs for old-fashioned varieties of species petunias, and remember these plants prefer full sun and well-drained soil that is not overly rich or moist. 🌰

Longing for Pale Poppies

Q **Two years ago I planted some annual poppies called 'Angel Wings,' which were supposed to have soft colors of lilac, very pale blue-gray, peach, and pink. Mostly they did, but there were also some bright red flowers, which kind of spoiled the effect. So this year I tried 'Mother of Pearl,' but there were even more red ones. Is there any soft-colored variety that really *is* all soft colors, or should I just give up?**

A 'Angel Wings' and 'Mother of Pearl' are both selections of good old *Papaver rhoeas,* a highly variable species that is, in the original wild form, almost always bright red with a black blotch at its heart.

The genes for those lavenders, grays, and pinks are rare, and tend to be recessive, so if you keep selecting for them over several generations, you can breed out most of the ones that say "I wanna be red."

But a few of them do remain, which means these mixtures often include a small proportion of red flowers, as you saw in your 'Angel Wings.'

Don't think bad thoughts about 'Mother of Pearl,' which may well have been innocent in the scarlet department. This year's larger contingent of red flowers probably came from self-sown seeds, deposited last year by those first red flowers (and by the pale flowers that were pollinated by them).

The only way to have an all-pastel poppy patch is to pull up every red-flowered plant as soon as the first blossom opens. It's difficult at first; the red-flowered plants are usually the largest and healthiest-looking, but if you think of them as weeds you'll get used to it soon enough. 🌿

Poppy Secrets

Q **What is the secret to growing lovely Iceland and Flanders and California poppies? I've had no luck with them in my area, on the New York–New Jersey border.**

A Iceland and Flanders are true poppies, *Papaver nudicaule* and *P. rhoeas*. California poppies are in the poppy family but are a different genus and species: *Eschscholzia californica.*

All three have tissue-paper-thin petals, bright colors, and a preference for cool, dry weather, bright sunshine, and very well drained soil.

But after that, the differences start to kick in. Iceland poppies are biennials or short-lived perennials. Although they will flower in one season if started early enough, you get the biggest, healthiest plants if you sow them in late summer for bloom the following year. Flanders poppies are annuals that should be sown in late fall or very early spring. Both species are erect growers, with long, fuzzy leaves with deeply cut edges.

California poppies are sprawlers, with smooth leaves cut so fine that they're feathery. The plants are classed as annuals, though they may overwinter in mild climates. They too are best sown in late fall or early spring, but unlike either of their *Papaver* cousins, they have a very long bloom season. And they last longer as cut flowers.

The key to success with these poppies is planting at the right time, ideally in sandy soil that gets lots of sun. If the soil is poor, it should be enriched with compost before planting, but don't add fertilizer or fertilize the plants once they are up. 🌰

THE POPPIES THAT AREN'T

Not all "poppies" are members of the genus *Papaver*. Other delicate-flowered sun lovers that are grown as annuals and belong to the poppy family (Papaveraceae) include:

Tulip poppy, aka golden cup (*Hunnemannia fumariifolia*), has bright yellow flowers. The variety 'Sunlight' starts flowering earlier than the species.

California poppy (*Eschscholzia californica*) comes in a wide range of strong colors—clear reds, yellows, and oranges, as well as peach and white. The very finely cut foliage has a bluish cast. Plants are low and spreading and bloom for a long season. Flowers may be single or double, the petals plain or frilled; and they make better cut flowers than true poppies because they last longer in the vase.

Prickly poppy (*Argemone grandiflora*) has sharp thorns, so don't plant it right next to paths where people might brush against it, but do choose a spot where the large, almost translucent white flowers will be easy to see. Where conditions are right, prickly poppies will form bushy plants 3 to 5 feet tall.

Chances are you won't find any of these plants at your local nursery, but seeds are widely available. They don't transplant well, so unless your season is very short, sow them where they are to grow, ideally in a soil that is not too rich, and very well drained.

Tulip poppy

A Mat of Portulaca

Q The 'Calypso' portulaca I grew last year made wonderful thick mats, covered with bright colored flowers, about 4 inches tall. Could I use this plant as a ground cover under my roses?

A You could try it, but the results are unlikely to be all that thrilling. It will be quite shady underneath the roses, and portulaca needs lots of sun. It won't make many flowers unless it gets bright light for most of the day, and it won't open the ones it does make unless they too get sun (you may be forgetting that they closed on cloudy days).

Food and drink are additional problems. Roses want lots of water and quite a bit to eat, while portulaca, a succulent designed to do well in drought, prefers dryer conditions and will go all to leaf if overfertilized.

But both do thrive in well-drained soil, it *is* wise to mulch under the roses, and portulaca seed is inexpensive so it won't cost much to give it a go. Choose a rose that tapers toward the base, and portulaca seeds from the Sundial series. They have been bred to open even when the weather is gray. ✿

Moss rose
(*Portulaca grandiflora*)

A More Relaxed Salvia

Q I love the color of the bright red annual salvias, but I don't like the way the plants look—they're so stiff and uniform they look out of place in my informal garden. Is there any way to grow them into a looser shape?

A Plant breeders have spent a lot of time and energy getting *Salvia splendens,* commonly called bedding salvia, to make stiff, short, uniform plants topped with stiff, short spires of fat flowers. Undoing their efforts would be difficult.

Also unnecessary. The way to get an even more brilliant red on a slightly taller, much looser plant, is to plant *S. coccinea* 'Lady in Red.' Like *S. splendens,* it's actually a tender perennial, and also like *S. splendens,* it will bloom from seed in its first summer even in the North, as long as you start it indoors six to eight weeks before setting out.

The individual flowers are more delicate than those of bedding salvia, and they are less tightly packed on the stem, but there are still more than enough of them to make 'Lady in Red' a plant that must be used judiciously. Especially in an informal garden, scattered groups of threes and fives will look better than a long row or a mass planting. ⚘

Snapdragons from Seed

Q I'd like to try some of the beautiful snapdragons I see in seed catalogs, but I've heard they're hard to grow. Are they?

A Growing from seed allows you to enjoy all sorts of unusual snapdragons, including the Brighton Rock strain, which resembles the parti-colored varieties popular in the nineteenth century, and the dark-foliaged, velvety red-flowered 'Black Prince,' neither of which is commonly sold in seedling form.

Read the catalog carefully; snapdragons range in size from 8-inch dwarfs to 3-foot giants. Flowers may be the classic lipped tube or a more open, ruffled shape called azalea- or butterfly-flowered.

Snapdragons take a long time to flower and must be started early to give a long season of bloom. Gardeners in zones 7 through 9 can sow seeds in late summer or early fall and let the young plants winter outdoors. From zone 6 north the seeds should be started indoors, about 12 weeks before the last-frost date.

Press the very tiny seeds into a well-prepared seedbed (or flat of seed-starting mix) and water, but don't cover with soil—snapdragons need light to germinate. Keep the surface moist but not soggy until they sprout, which may take several weeks.

Snapdragon
(*Antirrhinum majus*)

When the seedlings have two to four true leaves, transplant them to stand as far apart as the packet recommends (outdoors) or 2 inches apart (inside). When they are about 4 inches tall, pinch out the growing tips to encourage branching.

Overwintered babies will start blooming sometime between May and July, depending on age and variety. Indoor-started seedlings will bloom six to eight weeks after setting out. ⚘

Annuals in Particular

Snow-on-the-Mountain

Q **Last autumn I bought some branches that had white-striped leaves and tiny green flowers. I was told it was snow-on-the-mountain. I'd like to grow it myself. How?**

A The native American *Euphorbia marginata,* also called ghost weed, grows wild from Texas to Minnesota. Start seeds indoors six weeks before the last frost, or plant directly outside in well-drained soil after all danger of frost is past. Full sun is best, although it will tolerate light shade.

The milky sap from these beautiful succulents can cause skin rashes, so be careful when you handle the plants or cut stems for bouquets. 🌿

Shoofly!

Q **One of my coworkers who is interested in folk ways heard in a discussion group that tomatillo plants repel mosquitoes. Can this be true? How does it work?**

Shoofly plant
(*Nicandra physaloides*)

A The sharp-sweet fruits of the tomatillo (*Physalis ixocarpa*) are indispensable in Mexican cuisine, but that's about the extent of the plant's utility. It seems likely your coworker's informant was thinking of the shoofly plant, *Nicandra physaloides,* which is supposed to have a repellent effect on flies.

Some say the flies in question are houseflies; others contend that whiteflies are the ones that will be kept at bay. They might as well say butterflies for all the truth that's in it. Though nicandra, a member of the nightshade family, does contain toxic alkaloids, there's no evidence that the plants do anything to earn their keep except look handsome.

The fruits do resemble tomatillos; they're round berries inside lantern-shaped husks. But the flowers are much larger and prettier, pale purple bells about 1½ inches wide, and the plants are prettier, too. Tomatillos are so sprawly they make tomatoes look well behaved, but nicandra has trunklike main stems 3 to 5 feet tall and the lanterns hang from stiff, arched branches that are good material for the vase.

On the other hand, nicandra fruits are inedible, and if you don't tidy them out of the garden you'll have shoofly all over the place. 🍎

Spindly Strawflowers

Q **The instructions on the packet said strawflowers were easy to grow, but although mine were tall, they were spindly and they did not make many blossoms. I kept them weeded, watered faithfully, and fed them every six weeks. What more could I do?**

A The feeding may have been a bit too enthusiastic—annuals that are overfed often make leaves, lots of leaves, at the expense of flowers. But such plants are usually bushy as well as bloomless, so it seems more likely that your plants simply didn't get enough sun.

Strawflowers need at least six hours of sun a day, and except in the Deep South, are happier if they are exposed to those rays from dawn to dusk. 🍎

Summer Cypress

Q **Last year on a garden tour in Pennsylvania, I saw an herb garden where the beds were all edged with low bushes that had very spiky, light green leaves. They looked like some kind of evergreen, but they didn't feel like one. The leaves were very soft. The owner said the plants were called kochia. I've never seen seedlings for sale here in upstate New York. Is it hard to grow? How long does it take to make bushes?**

A The annual *Kochia scoparia* (or *Bassia scoparia*), commonly known as summer cypress, is easy to grow as long as it gets full sun and the soil is well drained. Depending on the cultivar, it will take about three months to go from seed to its full-grown size of 2 or 3 feet tall and as much as 2 feet wide.

Start six to eight weeks before the last expected frost. Sparingly sprinkle the seeds over the surface of a pot of moistened starting medium. Press in firmly but don't cover; the seeds need light to germinate.

Keep the pot at room temperature, about 70°F, and water from below as necessary to keep the medium moist but not wet. Seedlings should appear in about two weeks. Thin or transplant so they're 1½ inches apart, then grow on in bright light until all danger of frost is past. Plant them out 1½ to 2 feet apart.

Kochia plants can be left to grow informally into rounded bushes, or they can be shorn into formal hedges as though they were evergreens. Unlike evergreens, they will turn bright red in autumn and die at hard frost. 🍂

Thwarting Birds

Q **What is the best way to keep the birds from eating the sunflower seeds I've just planted?**

A It depends on your definition of "best." The fastest and easiest protection is a row cover of light, spun-bonded polyester such as Reemay. But anchoring a cover loose enough to allow for the sunflowers' fast growth can be tricky, and the polyester is very unattractive.

A tent of small-mesh chicken wire, on the other hand, is almost invisible once it is in place, and though it takes a small amount of work to make, it will be reusable for years.

Use the type of chicken wire that's 4 feet wide. Wearing gloves, cut it to a length equal to that of your planting, plus 2 feet—1 extra foot for each end. Pieces that measure 6 feet or less are easiest to work with, so if you have long rows, make several and overlap them.

Fold the wire in half and crease it, so it stands up in a triangle. Fold up a 6-inch-wide flap on each long side, and crease that fold as well. Bend the folded flaps back down so they stick out at right angles, like feet, and place them flat on the ground, centering the top of the tent over the planted area. Anchor the flaps with bricks, rocks, or dirt. That's it; just don't forget to remove the tent before it bends the young plants. (Although the ends of the tunnel are open, birds seldom walk in to get at the goodies; they tend to avoid places where aerial takeoff isn't instant.)

A chicken-wire cage will protect baby sunflowers.

Alternatively, you can try to scare away the birds. Numerous commercial scare devices exist, everything from plastic enemies such as snakes and owls to mylar ribbons that suggest danger by fluttering in the wind. Homemade flutterers, cut from aluminum pie plates or white rags, work just as well. Or just as badly. Putting the fear to the birds seldom works in the long term. Crows in particular are quick learners, and scare tactics seldom keep them away longer than a week or two. 🍂

Mexican Sunflowers

Q **I've always admired the large stature and velvety leaves of Mexican sunflower, but found the garish orange flowers a little hard to take. Now I notice that there's a golden variety. Are the plants the same shape and height? Are the flowers any better for cutting? I've tried using the orange ones in bouquets, but they always wilt very quickly no matter what stage the buds are in when I cut them.**

A Mexican sunflower (*Tithonia rotundifolia*) can easily top 6 feet if the plants get plenty of sun, and they are very bushy, which makes them a good choice for a temporary privacy hedge. The standard variety, 'Torch,' is indeed a very strong orange, though many would argue that the color's clarity saves it from being vulgar.

If the golden was 'Goldfinger,' be warned that the color is closer to copper than anything typically measured in carats. 'Yellow Torch' is genuinely yellow, though it too can have brassy notes. The seed seems to be somewhat variable; if possible, grow a few more plants than you need and get rid of the off-color ones as soon as they start flowering.

'Goldfinger' plants are comparatively compact, only half the size of 'Torch.' 'Yellow Torch' is supposedly the same size as its sibling, but it's often a bit smaller.

When it comes to cutting Mexican sunflowers, the only thing that really matters is sealing the stems. Either sear the bases over a flame or dip them in boiling water, just as you would poppies. Although tithonias are not notably long-lived in the vase, they will last three or four days if properly sealed. 🍂

Sunflower Toxins

Q Please explain how to manage sunflowers in a garden or bed with other plants, both while they are growing and in subsequent years. What can be done to prevent and counteract any toxins they may produce?

A Studies conducted by the United States Department of Agriculture have proven that sunflowers do secrete substances that can suppress the germination and growth of other plants. Fortunately, the ones that proved most strongly suppressive are semi-wild perennial types that are seldom grown in gardens.

The annual sunflowers most commonly grown for seed and/or ornament don't produce enough toxin to cause problems. In the experiments, plants as close as a foot away showed no signs of failing to thrive.

And no matter how strong it is, the allelopathic (growth-inhibiting) effect does not persist in the soil after the plant material is gone. So if you want to be on the super-safe side, remove sunflower plants—roots and all—after they are finished each year, and don't put them on the compost. 🌿

Wrong Sunflower

Q We have a large terrace and each year we plant sunflower seeds. We always manage to get lovely blooms, but the centers are yellow rather than the black pictured on the packet, which is somewhat disappointing. Do you know the reason for this? Is it the soil?

Sunflower
(*Helianthus annuus*)

A If they grow at all, the soil's not to blame. Unlike hydrangeas, which can be sweet-talked into changing from pink to blue and back again by alternating the soil pH, sunflowers are stubborn—their colors are genetically determined.

Dr. Jerry Miller, a geneticist and one of the country's foremost sunflower experts at the Agriculture Department's Northeast Crop Science Laboratory in Fargo, North Dakota, said that dark centers, or disk flowers, are controlled by a gene that produces dark pigments. Because this is a dominant gene, any sunflower that has it will have a dark center no matter how you grow it.

Since you don't mention growing a particular sunflower, you may have ended up with a package of seeds that simply had a generic photograph of a sunflower on it, but a different seed inside.

Next season, don't grow just any old sunflower—choose one (or a dozen) that will really turn heads. There are a wide range of interesting cultivars available, including 'Sonia' and 'Holiday,' both of which have dark centers. ✿

Love Among the Wildflowers

Q This summer I planted a packet of wildflower seeds. One of the plants that emerged grew almost 5 feet tall and produced bunches of long, furry-looking, dangling crimson flowers. Can you tell me about this plant?

A Your surprise plant is love-lies-bleeding or tassel flower (*Amaranthus caudatus*), said Elvin McDonald, who oversees the Brooklyn Botanic Garden's Signature Seed Program, which supplies members of the garden with seeds of unusual plants. In tropical parts of the world, amaranthus cousins are used to make flour, and the leaves of *A. tricolor* are cooked or used in salads. The genus is also related to the cockscomb (*Celosia*).

Love-lies-bleeding grows easily from seed when the warm weather arrives, and does best in full sun with well-drained soil.

The plant is an annual, so if you want to be sure of having it again next year, you will have to replant it. In addition to the crimson flowers you had this summer, you might consider such cultivars as 'Pigmy Torch,' which has upright, dark maroon flower spikes; 'Illumination,' which has scarlet, orange, yellow, and green flowers; or 'Green Thumb,' which has dark green flower spikes. ✿

Longer Than Ten-Week Stock

Q What is the best way to get good bloom from plants of ten-week stock? I start the seedlings indoors in late April and set them out in late May, but they seem to sulk for a long time and the flowers are scanty when they do finally show up.

A You don't say where you are gardening, but if it is anywhere warmer than zone 4, the problem is probably that you are starting too late. Ten-week stock, an annual selection from the biennial *Matthiola incana,* is slightly misnamed. It often takes 11 or 12 weeks to go from seed to bloom, and it prefers to make most of that growth in cool weather.

Plants should be started indoors quite early, about eight weeks before the last expected frost date. You want them to be all hardened off and ready for setting out as soon as the danger of hard frost is past. (Assuming they have been toughened up, a few 30° nights won't bother them at all.)

Stocks also thrive best in moist, fertile soil that contains generous amounts of organic matter. If your garden is on the dry and sandy side, work in some composted manure before planting, and give the stock bed a thin mulch of compost after you set the plants out.

Finally, stocks are happiest in soil that is neutral to slightly alkaline. They can tolerate a bit of acid but not much, so if you are in doubt, have the soil tested, and if necessary add enough limestone to raise the pH to 6.5 or above. 🌶

Old-Fashioned Zinnias

Q **I have had trouble getting the old-fashioned, tall, large-flowered zinnias to grow well in my cutting garden in northwestern Connecticut, although the soil here is good and other flowers do fine. I start the seedlings indoors in early March, and set the plants out in early May when they are about a foot tall. They usually have the first flower at that point, and it goes ahead and blooms, but then the plants just sort of sit there. They make only a few side branches and always look kind of weak.**

A It sounds as though you may be giving them too much of a head start—at both ends. Old-fashioned largeflowered zinnias are fast-growing heat and light lovers that do not take well to long sojourns on the windowsill, and they will sulk if transplanted out before the soil is warm.

Plants started too far in advance tend to become leggy from stretching toward the sun, and unless the seedling pots are larger than average, they may become rootbound as well.

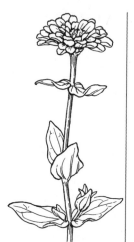

Common zinnia
(*Zinnia elegans*)

So it's important to get them out into the garden quickly, but it's also important that the garden is toasty enough to welcome them. Temperatures in the 50s and 60s won't kill zinnias, but they won't encourage them, either.

Next year, start the seeds indoors one month before the last expected frost, and don't plant them out until two weeks after that date has passed. In your zone (5), that should make the little plants six weeks old at the end of May, which should be just about right.

As long as they are healthy, these zinnias will branch well even if they are not pinched, but for maximum bushiness, pinch out the growing tips when the seedlings have six or eight true leaves. 🌿

NURSERY SCHOOL

Though annuals are famous for being able to bloom all summer, they are equally famous for getting rather tired looking in August. (You'd look tired, too, if you'd been blooming nonstop for six weeks.) In many cases, shearing them back will provoke a new round of bloom three or four weeks later, but then you're looking at sheared-back plants when you'd like to be looking at flowers.

The solution is to grow a second generation that can be just coming into bloom as the first group goes on vacation. All you need is a nursery bed, a small patch of good soil devoted to the purpose.

The best site for a nursery bed is in a large vegetable garden, out by the compost, or in some other open space where utility is beauty. But what do you do if there is no such place in your gardenscape?

Just think "spot," rather than bed. Start the seedlings in pots outdoors, ideally on the patio where you will remember to water them. When they are ready to transplant, move them to whatever crumbs of open space are available. Distributed in ones and twos and threes, they will not be noticeable.

Possible parking spots include the ground near spring-blooming perennials that have just been cut back, and the edge of the mulch skirts around the shrubs. Sometimes there's room near the service area where things like garbage cans and natural gas tanks are stored. (Seedlings placed where there is a lot of foot traffic do need protection; you might put an old dish drainer over them so they don't get stomped by accident.)

As holes open up in the annual beds, move the seedlings right on in.

Biennials in General

Biennial Confusion

Q **I am confused about the life span of biennials. Can you clarify?**

A A biennial is a plant that requires most of two growing seasons to complete its life cycle; that is, to develop to the point of producing flowers and seeds, and then die. During the first year, the plant builds (below ground) the food reserves needed to nourish the following year's flowers.

Biennials grown for their food reserves include onions, carrots, parsnips, and beets. These are usually sown in early spring and harvested that same year, as soon as they have reached optimum size.

Biennials grown for their flowers, on the other hand, are typically sown in mid to late summer, in the ground or in a cold frame. Planting dates vary, but in all cases the goal is to let the plants develop only partially. They should be large and strong, yet not so close to maturity that they try to flower in autumn. This group includes Canterbury bells, hollyhocks, foxglove, honesty (money plant), and pansies.

Confusion arises because some biennials seem perennial; they either self-sow or multiply by offshoots and reappear. Many short-lived perennials are, for convenience, also treated as biennials. To add to everyone's confusion, some biennials can be brought to bloom in a single year if the seed is sown early in a greenhouse.

Waiting for Biennials to Fill In

Q **I'd like to have biennials like hollyhocks, foxgloves, and wallflowers reseed themselves in my garden, but I don't quite see how to do it without having ugly bare spots. It seems like you'd get big holes in mid summer, when the plants that flowered have died and the young ones haven't sprouted yet.**

A Once you've established your biennials, you have them at three different stages each year: big plants that bloom and then die; robust first-year plants from last year's seeds; and toward the end of the season, tiny seedlings from seeds of the current year. By the time the bloomers die, the year-old plants are big enough to keep the garden from looking patchy.

For the first couple of years, though, you do get big holes—and that's why God made annuals. Either start some from seed in a nursery bed, or purchase them in spring and keep them in reserve in pots until the big biennials die back.

If you go for potted annuals, remember to move them into larger containers as soon as they start to outgrow the ones they came in. They need room to expand if they are to be big and bushy when called on for fill-in duty, and they need this freedom early; they never will amount to much if you let them get rootbound. 🍎

Biennials in Particular

Cup-and-Saucer Plants

Q **Is it possible to grow cup-and-saucer plants in zone 4? We had them when I was a child in New Jersey and I'd love to have them again, but I'm afraid they wouldn't make it through the winter here in Minnesota.**

A Regrettably, your fears are well founded. Cup-and-saucer is a variety of Canterbury bells, *Campanula medium* 'Calycanthema,' rated hardy only to zone 5. And the truth is they're marginal in the colder parts of that.

On the other hand, zones are only approximations and not every winter is as cold as the worst-case scenario. If you give your plants the neutral to slightly alkaline soil they prefer, a sheltered planting spot, and a winter blanket of dry straw mulch, you may well be able to revisit your youth.

Start the seeds in late spring, so the plants are medium-large at frost. (For some reason, biennials that make their full prebloom size before frost are more prone to winterkill than those that still have some growing to do.) Wait until the ground freezes hard before applying the mulch, and be sure to remove it as soon as the spring rains begin; wet roots are likely to rot.

Alternatively, you can start the seeds extra early indoors, and probably get bloom the same year. You'll need to plant seeds in February for flowers the following July or August, and because they will be indoors for so long, you'll need a greenhouse or grow lights to produce seedlings that will be worth bothering with. 🌿

Foxglove Safety

Q How poisonous is foxglove? I know it is the source of digitalis, a very strong drug. Is it safe to plant it in the border around my vegetable garden? Can I add it to my compost heap? I use the compost for my vegetable garden.

A The leaves of foxgloves—and to a lesser extent, the flowers, stems, and roots—could in extreme cases be deadly, but only if you ate them. The digitalin they contain will not migrate into the soil while they are alive, or out of the compost after they are dead. 🌿

Missing Hollyhocks

Q I planted year-old hollyhocks last year. They weren't spectacular, but they did flower. I was hoping to start a colony, but it looks like they didn't reseed. My early perennials are well on their way and there's no hint of a hollyhock plant. What happened?

Hollyhock (*Alcea rosea*)

A There are lots of things that might account for the absence of hollyhock progeny. One is that the flowers withered before they could make seeds. Another is that the seeds weren't pollinated, and were therefore infertile. Yet another is that they *were* fertile, and something happened to them.

The seeds might have rotted on the plant, which happens quite often in wet years. Or they may have fallen into nests of dead leaves and been removed by fall cleanup.

It could also be that you got as far as baby plants but they bit the mud before you noticed them. Hollyhocks sometimes germinate early, then rot out in prolonged cold, damp weather. If this spring was dank, you might have lost your small plants then. But take heart—and don't start weeding yet. If the problem is drought, the seeds may just be biding their time; they need moisture to germinate. ❧

Hollyhock Spot

Q **My hollyhocks start out healthy but then get brown spots on the leaves that eventually damage the growth and keep them from flowering. Can I solve the problem organically?**

A Unfortunately, hollyhocks (*Alcea rosea*) are subject to many fungal diseases, including anthracnose, leaf spot, and rust, which cause various kinds of leaf disfigurement. Since some fungi can winter over, garden sanitation is important: in autumn, remove and destroy infected leaves from around the plants. During the growing period it is also useful to remove some of the growth that shows early signs of disease.

A traditional organic fungus control is a spray or dusting of Bordeaux mix, a combination of lime and copper sulfate that has been used in French vineyards since the nineteenth century. If you want to use it, apply every two to three weeks starting in early spring; its power is preventative, not curative. ❧

Managing Mulleins

Q **I'd like to try planting some of the unusual mulleins offered in seed catalogs, but I'm afraid they might become invasive. We already have a weed problem with the wild ones, even though we try to pull them up whenever we see them. Are the fancy ones safe to plant or is there a danger they will take off and create more weed problems?**

A It depends on which fancy ones have caught your fancy; there are dozens of mulleins available, and while most of them will self-sow, some do it much more aggressively than others. The delicate, short-lived perennial *Verbascum chaixii,* for instance, which has matte green leaves and pink or white flowers, is quite well behaved, spreading, but not agressively. The bold biennial *V. bombyciferum,* on the other hand, is a much more vigorous character. Plant it for its silvery leaves and tall spires of golden flowers and watch it become just as weedy as common mullein, *V. thapsus,* also known as flannel leaf, Aaron's rod, and a royal pain in the neck.

Catalog pictures show all mulleins to their best advantage, so it pays to look carefully at the words. Avoid anything described as "robust," especially if you are in the middle of its zone range.

Of course, nothing can self-sow if you don't let it go to seed, so as long as you're willing to deadhead conscientiously, you can plant whatever you want. Alternatively, stick to 'Copper Rose,' an F_1 (first-generation) hybrid that comes in a range of pinks, creams, apricots, and tans, and is advertised as completely sterile. ❦

Poppies All Season Long

Q **On a garden tour, I saw a poppy that blooms later in the season than the poppy I'm familiar with. I would love to include it in my garden. What can you tell me about it?**

A How late was it? And which poppy are you pals with already? There are about a dozen species that are quite widely grown, and if you planted all of them, you could have poppies almost all season. In order of bloom, the first are usually the perennial types—small, delicate *Papaver alpinum* and *P. burseri,* as well as the old-fashioned, large-flowered *P. orientale,* a big plant with distinctly hairy leaves. The classic version is bright orange, but it also comes in reds, pinks, and whites.

The annuals bloom next: delicate, tissue-paper-petaled corn poppies, *P. rhoeas,* and the hunkier opium poppy, *P. somniferum,* also called lettuce leaf poppy because of its broad leaves. Opium poppies are usually pink or mauve, though they can also be red or white. The original *P. rhoeas* is scarlet (it's the poppy of Flanders fields), but most seed mixtures offer softer pinks, whites, and picotees as well.

Shortly after the annuals open, on come the biennial Iceland poppies, *P. nudicaule* (aka *P. croceum*), similar to corn poppies but a bit more substantial, better for cutting,

Iceland poppy
(*Papaver nudicaule*)

and more likely to be yellow or orange than pink (there are no reds). These can bloom quite late in the season, and so can the *P. alpinum,* which will keep putting out flowers all summer if the weather is cool and you are hot on deadheading. 🥕

Queen-Anne's Lace

Q Could you tell me about growing the wildflower Queen-Anne's lace? Can I start it from gathered seeds?

A The beautiful, dainty-leaved Queen-Anne's lace (*Daucus carota*) strongly resembles its edible cousin, the carrot. And indeed, wild carrot is still the British name for the plant that Americans, depending on their locale, call either Queen-Anne's lace, cow parsley, fool's parsley, or bird's-nest plant.

Queen-Anne's lace is a biennial that typically grows from 1 to 3 feet tall. It prefers full sun and well-drained to dry soil, though it will tolerate almost any ground that isn't constantly wet. It can be found blooming abundantly from June through August along roadsides and in open meadows. Once established in an area, it sows itself easily, or the seeds can be harvested when the heads have turned dark. The plant's white flowers are superb for fresh bouquets if you don't mind the pollen shed, and they are also good for drying (be sure to pick them before the seeds ripen.) 🥕

What Is It? Rose Campion

Q When I was out walking in Portsmouth, New Hampshire, last summer, I saw a flower I'd love to grow, in the front yard of a house I passed. There was no one at home to tell me what it was, so I'm hoping you can help. It had a rosette of silvery green leaves at the base, then tall, many-branched stems with round, flat flowers at the tips of all the branches. The flowers were a beautiful deep rose-red. Can you tell me what it was?

A It's hard to say for sure, of course, but you seem to be describing old-fashioned rose campion, *Lychnis coronaria,* which has been a staple of dooryard gardens for centuries in spite of its straggly habits and neon magenta flowers.

Lychnis does have a few merits. It thrives in tough conditions, unbothered by poor soil and drought, and it blooms for a long time. Though the flowers are small and widely separated, rose campion keeps putting out new ones (albeit fewer and fewer of them) for six to eight weeks after the initial burst of blossom in early July.

On the other hand, it may be that the plant persists simply because each flower makes roughly a zillion seeds, all of which germinate, so before long your garden is full of the silvery little rosettes of the first-year leaves. But don't worry. As long as you keep your place well fertilized and amply watered, most of them will rot.

L. coronaria is classed as both biennial and perennial. It flowers in its second year and usually, but not always, dies after flowering. To keep a clump going in the same spot, just thin out all but two or three of the babies that sprout near the parent plant. The only difficult part of growing these almost-weeds is having the discipline to cut them down when they start looking tatty, even though they're still covered with buds.

The easiest way to get campion plants is to beg a few babies from someone who has them. Otherwise, rose campion plants and seeds are available from perennial and seed catalogs.

Rose
campion
(*Lychnis
coronaria*)
second year, left;
first year, right

Profits from Silver Dollars

Q **I have been looking for silver dollar plants for years, and in September a friend gave me a small handful of seeds. Now that they've sprouted, I need advice. Should I grow them on the terrace, where it is very windy and gets only morning sun, or should they be on a sunny windowsill inside? I live on the nineteenth floor of an apartment building, so these are my only options.**

A Exercising either of your options is unlikely to yield much profit.

Silver dollars, also called money plant, moonwort, and honesty (for the way the seeds show through the translucent pods), is a biennial. It is usually started in late spring, grows best in a lightly shaded garden, and takes two grow-ing seasons to provide a payoff.

Your seedlings, started in pots in the fall, are thus both out of season and out of their element. But full winter dor-mancy is not essential, so if you're game for an experiment, transplant them to 4-inch pots and grow them indoors in a cool, bright place like the sill of an east window or under grow lights in a back room. Start feeding them in early February, and move them up to 8- or 10-inch pots shortly afterward.

As soon as day temperatures rise above 50°F, rig up a windbreak on the terrace and start hardening them off. Move them out as soon as nights stay above 45°.

With luck, the plants will grow large enough to make their small purple or white flowers. With more luck, they will do it early enough to also make the seedpods, called silicles.

The silicles come in a thin green envelope. Remove them after they dry to reveal the silvery disks that give *Lunaria annua* its first name. What suggested the sec-ond is a mystery, and many sources do refer to the plant as *L. biennis.*

CHAPTER TWO

Perennials

Perennials in General

A Long-Blooming Garden

Q Are there perennials that bloom for longer than three or four weeks a year? I know I can have flowers all summer by planning a sequence of bloom from lots of different plants, but is there a way to have something similar without going through all that?

A One of the pleasures you get from "all that" is constantly unfolding novelty, and a sense of the garden as a place moving through time. Having the same assortment all summer will not offer satisfactions similar to that one.

But there are many perennials that do have long blooming seasons, and if you mix them with a few of the best-loved short-term thrills—peonies, poppies, and Japanese anemones, for instance—you should have a perennial bed that delivers all summer without becoming monotonous.

Choices include bee balms (*Monarda didyma*); the bright-colored yarrows (*Achillea millefolium*); coreopsis (both *C. grandiflora* and *C. verticillata*); hollyhock mallow (*Malva alcea*); many day lilies, including 'Stella d'Oro,' 'Happy Returns,' and 'Pardon Me'; and sedums and *Hylotelephium* species, most famously 'Autumn Joy.'

Garden phlox, perennial scabiosa, *Aster × frikartii, Salvia nemorosa,* and hybrid veronicas all offer several cultivars that can be very long lasting, especially if the first flowers are cut off as soon as they fade. Exactly which ones will perform well for you will depend on climate, exposure, soil, and care (or the lack thereof).

If you are determined to get maximal performance for minimal effort, take the trouble to keep notes for the first couple of years. Notice what works best, both in your garden and in those nearby, then ruthlessly remove anything that doesn't measure up and replace it with something that does. ✿

Sedum 'Autumn Joy' (*Hylotelephium spectabile*)

Damp and Woodsy

Q I have a country house in Connecticut, with a moist area at the edge of a woodland that I would like to landscape. What flowers and foliage plants can I use here?

A Moist ground at the edge of the woods is an ideal environment for many plants that do not flourish in the bright heat of a conventional flower garden. Among them are low growers such as sweet woodruff (*Galium odoratum*), foamflower (*Tiarella cordifolia*), Virginia bluebells (*Mertensia virginica*), marsh marigold (*Caltha palustris*), bunchberry (*Cornus canadensis*), lily-of-the-valley (*Convallaria majalis*), Canada mayflower (*Maianthemum canadense*), and Jack-in-the-pulpit (*Arisaema triphyllum*). Taller choices include blue lobelia (*Lobelia siphilitica*), astilbe, turtlehead (*Chelone glabra*), and black snakeroot (*Cimicifuga racemosa*). You can also go to town with hostas, which should be very happy in the conditions you describe. ✿

Shady Bloomers

Q I would like to use flowering perennials, but much of my garden is very shady, so I'm afraid that won't be possible. Are there any I can grow?

A That depends on what you mean by "very." Even plants described as shade lovers need some light to grow, and plants that must produce flowers need more light than those that don't.

If conditions are truly gloomy, you'll be better off concentrating on things like ferns and mosses, exploiting the interplay of feathery frond and velvet drape. But if the area does get at least some filtered light, and is reasonably moist, you can try toad lilies (*Tricyrtis* spp.), whose orchidlike flowers are white, yellow, or mauve; *Kirengeshoma palmata,* which has yellow flowers; fringed bleeding heart (*Dicentra eximia*), which has pink or white flowers; and *Corydalis lutea,* with its delicate yellow blooms.

Bold Flowers for Shade

Q I would like to grow some flowers in the shady backyard of my summer rental and am hoping you can suggest something bolder than impatiens. Though I don't expect to be back next year, I don't mind planting perennials as long as they are relatively inexpensive.

A Not many annuals flower well in shade, and most of the ones that do—like torenia and monkey flower—are no bolder than impatiens.

The shade "annuals" with the greatest presence are begonias and fuchsias, both of which are actually tender perennials. Fortunately, there are several hardy perennials that would suit your purpose, including astilbe, which has long-blooming plumes of flowers in strong reds and creamy yellows, as well as white and many shades of pastel pink and coral. You might also go for ligularia, which has very shapely leaves in addition to spikes of bright yellow flowers.

And of course, there are hostas. Though best known for their beautiful foliage, most hostas also produce handsome flowers: white, pink, or lavender bells (fragrant, in some varieties), hung on tall stems that rise well above the leaves.

Blooming-size plants of hardy perennials will be not be too easy to find—look only in large, well-stocked nurseries—and they will cost quite a bit more than inexpensive annuals like impatiens. But they'll be comparable in price to expensive "annuals" like large begonias and fuchsias, and a rare bargain if you compare them to cut flowers. 🌱

Grace in the Shade

Q **I live in a wooded, partly shaded area and would like to have at least a few flowers among the ferns. I don't mean annuals like impatiens, but something perennial, and with a bit more grace. Any suggestions?**

Solomon's seal
(*Polygonatum* spp.)

A There are quite a few graceful perennials that will produce flowers and also do well in shade. Low growers that can be used as ground covers include sweet woodruff, ajuga, creeping blue phlox, moneywort, bunchberry, and epimedium. Showier, larger, and in most cases more graceful plants include bleeding heart, columbine, hellebore, hosta, celandine poppy (*Stylophorum diphyllum*), Solomon's seal, turtlehead, foamflower (*Tiarella cordifolia*), hardy begonia, and astilbe. 🌱

PERENNIALS FOR MOIST LOCATIONS

Dampness can be challenging, even without the shade that so often accompanies it. But there are plants that revel in having a root zone that stays on the wet side. Choices include:

Althaea officinalis (marsh mallow); *Aruncus dioicus* (goatsbeard); *Astilbe* spp; *Caltha palustris* (marsh marigold); *Filipendula ulmaria* (queen-of-the-meadow); *Iris ensata* and *I. pseudacorus* (Japanese iris and water iris); *Ligularia* spp.; *Lobelia siphilitica* and *L. cardinalis* (great blue lobelia and cardinal flower); *Rodgersia podophylla* (bronze-leaf rodgersia); *Thalictrum* spp. (meadow rue); *Trollius* spp. (globeflower).

PERENNIALS FOR DRY LOCATIONS

Note that many plants that tolerate drought have leaves that are narrow, hairy, or silvery (or all three)—strategies to keep evaporation to a minimum. Or they may have the alternative: very thick, succulent leaves that act as water-storage devices. Choices include:

Achillea spp. (yarrow); *Armeria* spp. (thrift, sea pink); *Artemisia* spp.; *Aurinia saxatilis* (basket-of-gold); *Catanache caerulea* (Cupid's dart); *Centaurea* spp. (perennial cornflower); *Cerastium tomentosum* (snow-in-summer); *Coreopsis* spp. (tickseed); *Echinops* spp.; *Eryngium maritimum* (blue sea holly); *Gaillardia* spp. (blanketflower); *Nepeta* spp. (catmints); *Papaver orientale; Portulaca* spp.; *Santolina chamaecyparissus* (lavender cotton); *Sedum* spp.; *Stachys byzantina* (lamb's ears); *Yucca* spp.

Indian blanket
(*Gaillardia pulchella*)

Summer Bloomers

Q **I recently moved into a home on the Connecticut shore that has beautiful gardens. One garden, which gets southeastern exposure, also gets a fair amount of shade. I would like to add a few perennials that will bloom in July and August. What do you suggest?**

A Since you say the gardens are lovely already and don't mention major trees, let's assume that your soil is relatively free of roots and in good health, and that by southeastern exposure you mean the garden gets sunlight for most of the morning. If these assumptions are correct, your only problem will be leaving room for later bloomers after you fill up the joint with spring delights such as columbines, violas, bleeding hearts, trout lilies, primroses, and bluebells.

Most partial-shade gardeners fall heavily for coralbells (*Heuchera sanguinea*) because they are such hard workers. Though they start putting out airy stalks of little red, pink, or white bells in late spring, heucheras often repeat right through the season and, if deadheaded, can usually be counted on to rebloom at summer's end. The leaves are equally lovely, basically round, but sometimes also scalloped and cut. Several varieties, including 'Palace Purple' and 'Pewter Moon,' are grown primarily for their deep maroon or maroon-and-silver foliage. These darklings are prettiest when backed by something bright, like the chartreuse blades of golden sedge, which also does well in partial shade.

Many hostas have lovely mid-summer flowers. Don't forget the puffy spires of astilbes or the taller, more delicate meadow rue (*Thalictrum* spp.), which comes in yellow as well as pink and white. There's great blue lobelia (*Lobelia siphilitica*), and all the wonderful, intense purples of monkshood (*Aconitum* spp.). For architectural drama, consider black snakeroot (*Cimicifuga racemosa*) or, as fall comes on, the exquisite blossoms of Japanese anemones. 🌿

Designing Tall

Q **I would like to add some color and height to the back areas of my garden, but don't want to plant shrubs. What flowers do you suggest?**

A There are many tall flowers that can anchor the back of a border. Which ones you choose will depend on the space available (some of them are as wide as they are tall) and on your growing conditions.

Foxgloves, for instance, will grow to 6 feet if they're in moist, nearly neutral soil in semi-shade, but they might top out a bit below 4 feet if they're in average soil in the sun. The same goes for black snakeroot (*Cimicifuga racemosa*), which might stretch to 7 feet or more if happy and dwindle utterly if not.

Foxgloves are usefully columnar, their tall flower spikes rising almost leafless from a broad rosette at the bottom. Snakeroot is rangier; sending out beautifully cut-edged leaves almost all the way up the stem. Meadow rue (*Thalictrum* spp.) also sends out leaves all the way up, but they, like the flowers, are lacy and delicate, so the overall effect is light. *T. rochebrunianum,* which has purple blooms, and *T. speciosissimum,* (aka *T. flavum* ssp. *glaucum*), which has pale yellow flowers and bluish leaves, are both 4 to 6 feet tall. White-flowered *T. polygamum* can grow to 8 feet.

Black snakeroot
(*Cimicifuga racemosa*)

Other tall flowers include delphinium, Carolina lupine (*Thermopsis caroliniana*), plume poppy (*Macleaya cordata*), *Ligularia* spp., Japanese meadowsweet (*Filipendula purpurea*), foxtail lily (*Eremurus stenophyllus*), Joe Pye weed (*Eupatorium purpureum*), and globe thistle (*Echinops bannaticus*). Read cultural descriptions carefully before you buy; many of these plants have very specific needs and some—especially plume poppy and Joe Pye weed—are very aggressive spreaders. 🌰

Easy Wildflowers

Q **I have a country house in Pennsylvania, but don't have a lot of time to garden there. Can you suggest some perennials that are still close to being wildflowers, and would be easy for a beginner?**

A The sundry wildflowers that accompany the seasonal cycles vary considerably in their habitats, from unobstructed sun in meadows to dappled shade in woodlands. Before choosing, take time to observe light and soil conditions where you intend to plant.

For a sunny spot, you might consider rose mallow (*Hibiscus moscheutos*), which bears large, late-summer white or pink flowers on stately 5½-foot stems; bluets or Quaker ladies (*Houstonia caerulea*), which have delicate, late-spring lilac-blue flowers on 8-inch stems; Carolina lupine (*Thermopsis caroliniana*), a 3-footer whose long spikes of yellow flowers appear in early summer; and wild pinks (*Silene caroliniana*), whose graceful, early-summer flowers rise above rosettes of blue-green leaves.

For light shade, there is white snakeroot (*Eupatorium rugosum,* or *Ageratina altissima*), which can reach 6 feet tall. It bears fluffy white blooms in late summer on very long stems. Wild bleeding heart (*Dicentra eximia*) has pink flowers that bloom almost all summer long on 10-inch stems set among ferny-looking blue-green leaves. If the soil is moist, you can grow the great blue lobelia (*Lobelia siphilitica*), whose 2-foot-tall purple-blue flower spikes brighten the late summer. 🌰

HELPING THE CONSERVATION OF WILDFLOWERS

New England Wild Flower Society (Name notwithstanding, they are actually involved with the entire northeastern quadrant of the U.S.)
    180 Hemenway Road
    Framingham, MA 01701
    (508) 877-7630
    www.newfs.org

North American Native Plant Society (Formerly the Canadian Wildflower Society, but they, too, have expanded their franchise and have a lot to say about, for instance, the Upper Midwest.)
    P.O. Box 84, Station D
    Etobicoke, ON M9A 4X1, Canada
    (416) 631-4438
    www.nanps.org

Lady Bird Johnson Wildflower Center (Emphasis on the West and South, of course, but with the center's help, enthusiasts can find wildflower societies from Oregon to Florida and most places in between.)
    4801 La Crosse Avenue
    Austin, TX 78739
    (512) 292-4200
    www.wildflower.org

Perennials for Cutting

Q **I love flowers like delphiniums and peonies, but when you cut them, their blooms are sorely missed in the garden. What perennials could I plant that would provide flowers for the house and yet not look denuded?**

A The best way to keep perennials from looking denuded when their flowers are cut is to plant enough of them. A thick hedge of mature peonies will yield armloads for the house without appearing to have surrendered a single blossom. Multiple clumps of big delphiniums, each with many flowering spires, will still be impressive when the grand total has been reduced by several vases' worth. Even lilies can be cut if there are dozens in a comparatively confined space.

Easier said than done, unfortuately, if you have a small garden and a big appetite for variety, so the next best thing is to choose plants with a great many flowering stems. Their individual flowers are smaller than the show stoppers you mention, but they make up for it by producing lots and lots of them.

Examples include blanketflower (*Gaillardia* × *grandiflora*); coreopsis; painted daisies and Shasta daisies; echinaceas; foxgloves (if you live in a cool climate); globe thistles; Joe Pye weed; mountain bluet (*Centaurea montana*) and the other perennial centaureas; phlox; Russian sage (*Perovskia atriplicifolia*); and yarrow. 🌿

A Garden for Fall

Q **I know most perennials bloom in spring, but I'm always traveling then and not around to enjoy them. Is it possible to plan a perennial garden that is at the height of bloom in fall?**

A It's easy, as long as your plans can include someone to take care of the place until you get home to enjoy it. Most of the stalwart bloomers of autumn need attention earlier in the season to be at their best when showtime comes.

Typical examples include New England asters (*Aster novae-angliae*) and Michaelmas daisies (*A. novi-belgii*), chrysanthemums, and Montauk daisies. All will get floppy and naked-stemmed if not pruned to encourage branching when they're about a foot tall, and they are even prettier if pruned again at the 18-inch mark.

Gardeners who are there to cut things back as soon as they finish blooming can also enjoy autumn color from a second round of early to midsummer flowers like peach-leaved bellflowers, delphiniums, and globe thistles.

That said, there are still a few late-flowering perennials that can be left to their own devices all season. If you have the partial shade it prefers, you could go in heavily for the stately—and fragrant—*Cimicifuga racemosa*. Japanese anenomes should do fine, and you should have no trouble with late-blooming day lilies like 'Happy Returns' and 'Stella

New England aster
(*Aster novae-angliae*)

d'Oro.' Interplant them with late-blooming sedums to get a handsome contrast in leaf forms.

There are also many wonderful fall-flowering bulbs, including Oriental lilies, colchicums, and autumn crocus. Repeat-blooming roses should be included too; you'll miss the spring and summer flowers, but roses often keep at it until very hard frost (in fact, if you have Japanese beetles, the fall show may be the only one worth looking at). You won't be there to care for them, so ask your local extension service to recommend the toughest varieties for your area.

No matter what you plant, don't forget to put down a layer of porous weed barrier (landscape fabric, covered with an organic mulch), or you won't be able to find your blossoms in the sea of weeds come fall. ❧

Taming a Garden

Q We recently bought a house and I am busy trying to get the perennial garden back in shape. It's not big, about 8 by 25 feet, but it has been neglected for some time and is now almost completely taken over by mint (the purple-blooming kind), some form of artemisia, and a couple of other unknown plants. Should I get weeding, or must I just abandon this good spot and start from scratch somewhere else?

A Never mind the unknowns—the mint and artemisia are reason enough to take drastic action. Both of these invasive characters spread by runners that can travel long distances, especially in the loose soil of gardens, and each runner has multiple growth nodes, any one of which can start a new plant.

The runners are tenaciously rooted and tend to break when tugged, so hand weeding is better at spreading them than it is at eradication. But if you don't want to start somewhere else, you can renovate the bed.

Begin by digging up the plants you want to keep and storing them in pots. (If the unknowns are not runner-makers, pot up a few of them, too; they might turn out to be something nifty.)

Next, use a digging fork to turn all the soil, sifting each forkful through the tines to remove the unwanted plants, their runners, and any stray weeds. Throw all this debris into the underbrush, bury or burn it, but don't put it on the compost pile, where it can easily take root and form new colonies.

Always stand on unworked ground so you don't compact the fluffy soil you are creating by your efforts.

When the whole bed has been cleaned out, replant the saved material and mulch with a 2- or 3-inch layer of compost. Expect to start hand-weeding almost at once—all that stirring of the soil will turn up lots of buried weed seeds, including those of mint and artemisia. 🌿

Building Up a Bed

Q I plan to build up a perennial bed with an extra 2 to 3 inches of soil and compost. Now that bulbs are blooming and new shoots have started to grow, is it necessary to dig up and replant everything, or will my bulbs and perennials adapt to being buried deeper?

A There are a few perennials that are fussy about being buried no matter what the season. Peonies, for instance, will fail to bloom if the shoot-forming buds are more than about 2 inches below the ground. And the lumpy rhizomes of bearded iris are prone to rot if their tops don't get light and air.

Special exceptions like these aside, the rest depends on how much of your mixture is compost and how much is soil.

Compost is organic matter that's partly decomposed. It's lighter and fluffier than soil, so it doesn't (usually) promote rot, and vigorous shoots can push right through it. Over the season, compost will break down, adding nutrients, improving structure, and encouraging beneficial organisms. Two or 3 inches of pure compost won't hurt your plants, but it will disappear—by fall the bed won't be any taller than it was before.

Soil is a different story. The kinds vary greatly, but all of them are heavier than compost, and because they contain mostly sand and clay rather than organic matter, they don't keep breaking down the way compost does. A 3-inch layer of soil would permanently raise the height of your beds, but if you applied it now it would be likely to rot any foliage it's pressed against, and it would damage (or kill) most new shoots if you heaped it right on them.

So if by "build up" you mean "improve," you can add compost right now. But if your goal is the altitude provided by a thick layer of soil, it's better to lift the plants—or even better, wait until next winter.

As long as they're still underground, most bulbs won't mind being buried a bit deeper, and established perennials should have no trouble pushing new growth up 2 or 3 inches farther to reach the light. 🌸

Picking a Winner

Q **How do I pick out a good perennial at the nursery? Should I avoid what's in bloom, or what's past?**

A You're buying the plant for its potential, not its current performance, so a strong youngster is better than something mature enough to be flowering.

Start by checking for good health: no bugs, no mottled or curled leaves, no denuded stems. Then look for signs that the kid is on the verge of a growth spurt: the crown should be robust, with two or more stems, and the stems should be well spaced so you won't have to remove anything to end up with a shapely plant.

Small plants surrounded by lots of fresh soil are unlikely to be good buys; chances are they were just moved up from a smaller, less-expensive-size pot. To get the most for your money, look for plants with large crowns. But not too large—if the top of the plant seems to fill the pot, its roots are probably overcrowded and running around in circles, which is every bit as unhealthy as it sounds. Check by tipping the plant from the pot and taking a look.

Ideally, the plant has not even started to think about blooming. Making buds and opening flowers takes energy the confined root system can ill afford to spare; and plants that have already bloomed are even less desirable. (Not only did they have to make flowers, they may well have tried to make seeds before someone at the nursery got around to deadheading them.)

In the real world, however, many perennials bloom in spring. Your shopping window would be pretty tight if you rigidly followed the no-flowers rule. So as long as you look for healthy young plants that have not overgrown their pots, it won't be the end of the world if they have a few blossoms.

And on the positive side, those blooms will be insurance that you're getting what you are supposed to get. The pointers about avoiding bloom assume that the plant is correctly labeled, an assumption that isn't always warranted. ☙

Planting Peat Pots

Q **Several perennials I bought this year came in peat pots, and the nurseryman told me to just plant the entire thing. Is this a good idea?**

A Lately it seems that more perennials, small woody species, and even some vegetables and herbs are being sold in rather thick peat pots. Theoretically, the roots will grow through these pots and the peat will disintegrate completely with time. But the roots are often unable to penetrate the peat, and the plant becomes potbound.

Therefore, it is rarely a good idea to plant the pot. Unless the roots have infiltrated the sides, treat a plant grown in a peat pot as you would any plant in a container, slipping it out before planting. Then snip the pot into small pieces and either incorporate it into the soil or add it to your compost pile. ☙

MORE ON PLANTABLE POTS

It's traditional (and appropriate) to start seeds in small, thin peat pots when growing things like poppies and cucumbers, which do not transplant well. Planting the babies "pot and all" helps ensure that delicate roots can safely survive the transition.

But large plants are a different story. The heavy-duty pots in which they are sold do not break down easily, no matter what the label says, and the plants in them will do much better if they are removed from the pots before being set in the soil.

The one exception is when plants sold in peat pots have bonded with their containers. In that case, it's better to plant pot and all than risk damaging roots.

For best results when planting peat pots of any size, first soak them in water until thoroughly saturated. Once the larger ones are soft and soggy, cut several slits in the sides with a sharp knife (don't slit the little guys).

Cut off the upper rim of the pot, so the top is even with the soil inside. Bury the pot in the planting hole, making sure none of it sticks above the surface (exposed peat wicks water away). Pack the soil around the plant firmly, and water it in well.

Moving Plants

Q We are moving to a new home and brought along a fair number of perennials that we dug up and potted from our old garden. It's almost fall and our new house still isn't ready. What is the latest date we can safely put them in the ground? The plants we have include hostas, cranesbill, corn-flowers, rudbeckia, campanula, and coreopsis. Should we divide them if they become potbound?

A The garden stalwarts on your list should survive nicely as long as they have six weeks or so for the roots to settle in before the ground freezes for the winter.

If your house is not ready at the six-weeks mark (and we are after all talking about house construction), you can winter the plants over in the pots they're in now. Leave them outdoors and let them go dormant, then stash them in a place where they will stay dormant but not frozen (32° to 45°F, and the less light the better).

Don't divide the plants until spring. Even if by some miracle your house is actually ready soon, the plants should be heading toward dormancy and not be forced to grow lots of new roots. Division is healthy in the long run, but it does temporarily weaken plants and is best done when they'll have plenty of time to recover. ☙

Grumpy When Moved

Q I have a garden on eastern Long Island, New York. It gets sun three-fourths of the day and the soil, which has been improved over the years, drains well. I have a *Baptisia australis* that did not bloom last year (it was divided the previous year). Can you tell me what the problem is, and what can be done to make it bloom?

A Descriptions of blue false indigo (*Baptisia australis*) may vary in how they rave over the blue flowers or pealike blue-green leaves, but the one phrase you'll always encounter is "slow to get established." That's horticulture-speak for grumpy, stubborn, or resentful plants, those that don't appreciate being transplanted, divided, or having their roots disturbed. These plants show their resentment by refusing to bloom for a year or two. Or three.

Impatient gardeners wish everything worked on the same timetable as annuals. Although an annual is always in a hurry, perennials take their time settling in and getting to know the neighborhood before they commit to something as energy-sapping as a flower. Assuming your baptisia has decided that this is home, you should see flowers this summer or next.

Anytime you divide, plant, or transplant something whose description includes phrases like "a challenge to transplant" or "slow to take hold," do a little research so you can move it at the proper time. Take a big ball of soil with the plants, to disturb the roots as little as possible, and prepare to wait it out.

Among the challenges are balloon flower (*Platycodon*), hellebore (*Helleborus*), gas plant (*Dictamnus*), monkshood (*Aconitum*), and butterfly weed (*Asclepias*). ✿

Dividing and Multiplying

Q **My first perennial garden is now almost five years old, and I think several of the plants need dividing. Can you give me any general guidelines?**

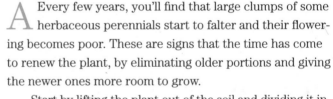

A Every few years, you'll find that large clumps of some herbaceous perennials start to falter and their flowering becomes poor. These are signs that the time has come to renew the plant, by eliminating older portions and giving the newer ones more room to grow.

Start by lifting the plant out of the soil and dividing it in half. Sometimes the halves part easily; sometimes the clump is so dense, it's necessary to place two digging forks back to back in the mass and then pull them apart; and sometimes, the roots are so firmly tangled that the only thing you can do is slice through the mass with a very sharp spade and finish the job with a knife or pruner.

After dividing the clump, cut away and discard any of the center portion that shows signs of disease, decay, or old age. Add some compost to renew the soil, then replant. If you have had to cut away substantial amounts of material, all the remaining healthy looking clusters of fibrous roots (the ones with lots of new leaf shoots or growth buds) may fit back into the same hole. But the replanted division

If you wait until fall, you can cut back the leaves, which makes division easier.

should have plenty of room to grow, so if most of the original plant was sound, find a new space—or a new home—for the other half.

Early-flowering or spring bloomers are best divided immediately after they bloom. Most others can be divided in either early spring or fall.

Note: A few perennials do not form clumps but grow from a single taproot, a single crown, or a woody stem. These plants cannot be divided. 🌱

Cleanup Caution

Q Does it matter if I cut my perennials down in fall or spring? I never seem to have the time in the fall, but I'm wondering if it's healthier for the plants if I make an extra effort to make time.

A In the madness of fall cleanup, that rush to make the garden neat, pruning sometimes seems as sensible as raking. But early cleanup means missing the wonderful bronzy red to golden yellow leaves, the bobbing seed heads, and the last hurrah for plants that are glad the summer heat is gone. Besides, many perennials, including perovskia (Russian sage), santolina, buddleia (butterfly bush), sage, lavender, caryopteris, and Montauk daisy should be left alone until well into spring, when new growth is visibly swelling. Pruning too early can pave the way for dieback. 🌱

Dormant Perennials

Q Some of my perennials—like Virginia bluebells and bleeding heart—go dormant in late summer and vanish. Should I continue watering the area where they're planted?

A Most perennials do need some moisture even while they're dormant, but whether you have to supply it by watering will depend on the quality of your soil and the regularity of the rain.

Sandy soils dry out more quickly than clay; soils rich in organic matter hold water better than poor ones. All soils dry out faster when it's warm and windy than when it's cool and still. So before hauling out the hose, dig down a bit and check. Although moist is good and dry is not, dormant plants don't need as much water as plants that have leaves, and if they get too much of it they'll rot. 🌶

Preserving by Drying

Q **Is it possible to preserve fern fronds, small branches, or similar live materials without ending up with the ghastly artificial colors that I've seen?**

A The revolting colors are a result of certain plants' reactions to being dried in a glycerine solution or an antifreeze liquid. You can avoid these unnatural hues if you use sand, borax, or silica gel as your drying material. Most herbalists consider silica gel the best, although it is also the most expensive.

Despite its name, silica gel is really a sandlike crystal that varies in texture from very rough to fine. It is sold at some hardware stores, pharmacies, and craft shops. (The packets you may find in pill bottles to absorb moisture are silica gel.)

To dry flowers, leaves, or twigs, you'll need a box or other container, preferably airtight, that is large enough to hold them comfortably. Pour the silica gel to a depth of several inches, and position the plant material so that it lies in its most natural form. Work the crystals around it, adding more as needed, so that every part is covered and no petals or leaves touch. Depending on the species, drying can take two to five days.

Drying flowers with silica gel

Among the flowering plants that respond well to drying in silica gel are bird of paradise (*Strelitzia reginae*), Christmas rose (*Helleborus niger*), daffodils, tulips, dahlias, dogwood, peonies, Queen Anne's lace, and rhododendron. 🌶

Patents and Trademarks

Q **Some plants at my local nursery are patented and others are trademarked. Would you explain the difference? Does being patented or trademarked mean they are better in some way than the other plants?**

A Plant patents, given to the breeder of a new plant, prevent anyone else from selling that plant or using it as one of the parents in a breeding program without permission—and without paying royalty fees, which are promptly passed on to those who buy the plants. Patents aren't a guarantee that a plant is better, just that it is different.

The benefit to gardeners is that breeding new plants is a very long, expensive process, filled with many more failures than successes. Without patent protection, and royalties, fewer companies would take the risks.

Trademarks are names or symbols used to identify a product. The raised letters ™ mean that the designation is claimed as a trademark, and ® means it has been registered with the United States Patent and Trademark Office.

A trademark is simply a marketing tool, used to create an identification between the plant and the company. The company hopes that your previous good experience with one of its plants will convince you to buy from it again.

Theoretically, companies put their reputations on the line and have a vested interest in providing you with a high-quality, well-grown plant. They hope that if gardeners have an easier time making choices, they may find it worth the additional cost.

Paying more for trademarked and patented plants may mean a future of fewer small nurseries with a wide range of plants, and more large-chain garden centers with rows of the same plants. But remember, a lot of things can happen between the grower and your yard. How a local nursery or mail-order supplier handles a plant before you buy it makes everything else moot. Good plants come from people who care about them. 🍎

Organic Wildflowers?

Q **A friend has just bought a house with a good parcel of land. She wants to garden organically and has organic wildflower seeds on her wish list. Do these actually exist? It's hard to believe they spray chemicals on wildflower meadows.**

A True wildflower meadows are not sprayed, and neither are organic seeds. But that doesn't mean the former are the source of the latter. When you buy "mixed wildflower seeds," you are buying a mixture created by the packager, not Mother Nature.

No matter how wild their ancestors were, the seeds in these blends come from flowers that were farmed, just as tomatoes and corn are farmed. And as with vegetables, so with seeds: only those from farms with government-approved certification can be labeled organic.

For most flower growers, the cost of organic certification outweighs any advantage it might confer, but now that "organic " is so useful as a marketing tool, there are a few who have found it worthwhile. That said, it does pay to keep in mind that the most important key to success with wildflower mixtures is careful blending of regionally appropriate seeds. Before you go to a national company with a big advertising budget, consider finding a supplier who specializes in seeds for your area, and asking them about their sources; you might be pleasantly surprised. ☙

A mixture of wildflowers

THE RELUCTANT SEED

The seeds of many perennials (and temperate-zone shrubs and trees) have built-in inhibitors that keep them from sprouting as soon as they hit moist soil. This protects them from getting started in the fall and then having the baby seedlings frozen when winter comes.

Although there are various delaying mechanisms, and various ways to defuse them, the most common retardant is the need for a cold, moist period—a winter in the ground—and the most common way to overcome that is to provide a shortened version, called **stratification.**

To stratify seeds, moisten some freely draining, sterile medium (either vermiculite, sand, or a mixture of sand and peat) until it is damp but not wet. Place a generous layer in a plastic bag, then put the seeds on top. Cover the seeds with another thick layer of the damp medium; close up the bag, and put it where the temperature will stay at about 40°F. The refrigerator (not the freezer) is a popular spot.

Leave the bag for the length of time specified by the seed packet. If the packet recommends stratification without giving any time frame, stratify more seeds than you need, to allow for experimentation, then start looking for signs of germination after six weeks. Look again at the two-month mark, and at regular intervals thereafter; three or even four months may be required.

Inconveniently, some seeds need a warm period after the cold one before they sprout, and if you don't know how long to stratify, you may not have this information either. So starting at the two-month mark, remove a few seeds every couple of weeks and plant them in the usual way, in pots of seed-starting soil. When the potted seeds sprout, you'll know the others are ready to get started as well.

Bringing Home Wildflower Seeds

Q On a late summer vacation in the Adirondacks, I collected the seeds of wild columbine (*Aquilegia canadensis*), and some fruits of bunchberry (*Cornus canadensis*) and clintonia (*Clintonia borealis*). All are—I hope!—to be planted in my garden in northern New Jersey. But how can I tell when the berries are ripe? Do the seeds need a cool period?

A The seeds of all three of those wildflowers have similar requirements to germinate: three months of moist cold at about 40°F, followed by 70° temperatures. Planting them directly outside is best because they seem to like the variations in climate that a real winter brings, but your refrigerator (not freezer) will do. The seeds can be potted up or just mixed with moist vermiculite and placed in a sealed plastic bag.

Bunchberries are bright red; clintonia turns blue when ripe. Both have germination-inhibiting chemicals in their pulp. The seeds have to be really clean before planting, or they won't germinate until all the pulp rots away. In the wild, the cleaning as well as the planting is neatly done by passing through an animal, complete with fertilizer. For humans, it is better to soak the pulpy seeds in water for a week, dry them, and rub against a screen or between fingers until the seeds come free of the pulp.

For the plants to survive, each needs the kind of environment it is used to. Bunchberry and clintonia need cool, moist soil in dappled shade, with summer nights in the 50s or low 60s. Wild columbine needs abundant moisture in the spring, but dry summers. If your property offers the right conditions, wildflower seeds make a great vacation souvenir. Otherwise, you're better off with a sweatshirt or a coffee mug. 🌶

Perennials in Particular

A Flower for Fall

Q **I just bought a Japanese anemone that my garden center insists will flower all fall. What conditions does it require?**

A With 70 or so species in the genus, there seems to be an anemone for every season, and the Japanese anemone (*Anemone hupehensis* var. *japonica*) is certainly one no autumn garden should be without.

The many hybrids sold under this name bear their graceful flowers from late summer until well into fall, in shades that vary from the clear white of the cultivar 'Alba' to the rosy pink of 'September Charm.' Depending on the hybrid, the wiry branching stems can reach from 2 to nearly 5 feet tall.

This hardy perennial, which is rarely plagued by insects or disease, grows easily in fertile, well-drained soil but does need some shade from the hot afternoon sun.

Most Japanese anemonies grow well as far south as zone 8 and are hardy at least to zone 5. In colder areas, protect new plants over their first winter by adding mulch after they've gone dormant and the ground is frozen. ☙

Bamboo Invasion

Q **A bamboo I planted a few years ago has appeared at the other end of my yard. Can you explain how it got there?**

A Bamboos spread by underground stems called rhizomes, which grow out and away from the plant and enable new territory to be colonized. What the plant looks like depends on its rhizomes, which are divided into two growth types.

One, the pachymorph rhizome, is short and thick and curves upward. The new above-ground stems (properly called culms or canes) emerge close to each other and to the parent plant, resulting in a tight clump that expands only a short distance each year. This pattern is typical of the tropical bamboos, including the popular genus *Bambusa*.

The other, the leptomorph rhizome, is thin and grows horizontally, often spreading out over great distances before sending up new culms. This pattern is typical of bamboos from temperate regions and is seen in the genus *Phyllostachys*. As you have seen in your garden, it is this type that often produces surprises.

Striped Bamboo

Q **Recently I saw a small green-and-yellow-striped bamboo growing in shade that I wish to try. Can you tell me what it might be?**

A It's hard to know exactly which of the many handsome striped bamboos you saw. If the plant was young, it might have been *Sasa palmata*, but given the size, it's more likely to have been *S. ramosa* (also called *Sasaella ramosa*).

Several members of the genus *Sasa* (and their close relatives in the genus *Sasaella*) have striped leaves, and both genera are widely planted because they are so adaptable. They prefer some shade and moist, well-drained soil, but will also grow in sun as long as they get plenty of water.

Tenderness varies quite a bit. The tall and vigorous *Sasa palmata*, which has bright green leaves with yellow midribs, is hardy as far north as zone 5. The shorter but also yellow-striped *Sasa ramosa* (aka *Sasaella ramosa*) grows only in zones 8 to 10, while the lovely white- or cream-striped *Sasaella masumuneana albostriata* thrives in zones 7 to 9.

If you have a protected spot, you can often get away with granting yourself an extra zone, but do keep in mind that all of these are "running" bamboos. It is prudent to grow them where they can be controlled, such as between a paved walk and a building, or in a container.

A list of mail-order sources for bamboos is published each spring by the American Bamboo Society, P.O. Box 640, Springville, CA 93265.

Make Room for a Grower

Q **I have an old-fashioned white bleeding heart (*Dicentra spectabilis* 'Alba'), too large for my small garden. How do I divide it, and when?**

A The old-fashioned bleeding heart does not like to be moved or disturbed, and if you really must divide it, be careful, because its thick, fleshy roots are brittle and break off easily. Mark the plant's site before it goes dormant in mid summer; otherwise you will not find it when the foliage has died and disappeared and the surrounding plants have sprawled into the bare area.

Dig it up in late August or early September, and divide the crown with a sharp spade or knife into sections at least 4 inches across, each with a few large roots 6 to 8 inches long plus a couple of eyes (small buds at the base of the crown). If a root breaks, trim the end to a clean cut. Plant one section at the same depth as before. Remaining pieces can be shared with friends.

Common bleeding heart (*Dicentra spectabilis*)

Why not clear out a few plants around your bleeding heart, rather than punish a wonderful plant for growing 3 feet tall and 3 feet wide as it is supposed to? Its graceful, arching sprays of locket-shaped flowers make it a welcome addition to every garden, but it should never have to compete for space. 🌰

Never Bluebells Enough

Q I have a patch of Virginia bluebells that is lovely but doesn't seem to be expanding on its own. When is the proper time to divide them and increase my supply?

A To have *Mertensia virginica* at all is to want to have more, even though—or perhaps because—the smooth gray-green leaves, pink buds, and nodding blue flowers of this native wildflower are such a fleeting pleasure.

Virginia bluebells tend to self-sow into large patches where conditions are right, so it is possible that yours have run out of the soil they prefer: fertile, moist, and neutral to slightly acid. They will not spread into boggy areas, or into territory that is dry all year.

Alternatively, it may be that they are not getting enough sunshine. Since they go dormant by early summer, the shade of deciduous trees doesn't bother them—that's why they often grow in woodlands—but they need light while they are growing.

Assuming you have the right environment, the most reliable way to fill it with bluebells is by planting lots of seeds. Gather the seeds after the pods have browned and sow them in early fall, about half an inch deep. Not all of them will germinate, but a fair number should sprout the next spring and give you flowers a year later.

Some gardeners have success with division, but there is a good chance that splitting the clumps will reduce your supply instead of increasing it. Once established, the plants resent disturbance and tend to express their displeasure by dwindling. If you want to try it anyway, divide them in early summer, just as the foliage starts to yellow. 🌰

Virginia bluebells
(*Mertensia virginica*)

Heroic Cephalaria

Q **Does scabiosa come in a giant form? I saw something on a garden tour that sure looked like one. The plants were weird, well over 6 feet tall, with yellow flowers on long stems, far above most of the foliage. They looked just like the pincushion flowers I've been growing for years, but there's no sign of anything like them in my seed catalogs.**

A The plants you saw were almost certainly *Cephalaria gigantea,* sometimes (incorrectly but understandably) known as *Scabiosa gigantea*. It tends to be sprawly, as well as tall, and can look a bit overheroic in the average perennial border.

Cephalaria is at its best when planted where the flowers are set off by a simple background, either a dark hedge or a clear sky, and where there is lots of other substantial material—shrubby perennials like *Thermopsis* species, and/or clumps of tall grasses like *Miscanthus* species—to balance its big, coarse leaves and towering flower stems.

The plants come readily from seed but are seldom offered that way. In fact, they're seldom offered by nurseries,

Cephalaria gigantea

either, which is a bit of a mystery. Given plenty of sun and well-drained, moderately fertile soil, cephalarias are a gardener's delight: long-lasting, long-blooming, and seldom troubled by bugs or diseases. 🌰

Better Redder

Q When I recently purchased a maroon-leaved form of *Cimicifuga*, the nurseryman told me it needed a lot of sun. I have other, green-leaved cimicifugas that I know are shade plants. Where will the maroon-leaved one do best?

A Exactly why some plants have purple-red foliage is not completely understood, but their appeal is clear, and plant breeders have been offering more of them.

The compounds in the leaves that cause the red color are anthocyanins, which are composed of, among other things, sugars. The more light the plant receives, the more sugars it makes, and more sugars mean more anthocyanins. So everything else being equal, the purple colors will be more vivid when the plant gets more light, and duller, with more green, when grown in shade.

Remember that when there is more sun, the soil dries out faster, so the maroon-leaved cimicifuga will use water faster than its green relatives in the shade. 🌰

Getting Rarer

Q When I was growing up, we could find trailing pine (fan-shaped branches on a runner) and princess pine (which resembles 3-inch evergreen seedlings) in the woods each winter. I haven't seen either of these in the woods for years. If I did find some, could they be introduced into my property?

A Princess pine (*Lycopodium obscurum*) and trailing pine (*L. digitatum*) are among the few remaining species of club mosses, plants that have been around for about 300 million years. Unfortunately, we may yet see them disappear altogether because they are so appealing in Christmas wreaths and garlands.

It isn't surprising that you haven't seen them in the woods recently. Harvesting from the wild has seriously diminished many populations, and in some states, including New York, they are listed as "exploitably threatened," which means they are in danger of becoming endangered if people keep picking them.

They are both difficult to cultivate, and slow growing. Trailing pine, like most other *Lycopodium* species, forms a complex relationship with a fungus that lives among its roots and contributes to its nutrition. It is almost impossible to transplant trailing pine without destroying the relationship, so it can't be grown commercially. Princess pine doesn't have this relationship, but it is also very fussy about its growing conditions, so you are unlikely to have success introducing it even if you do find a nursery that propagates it for sale.

Every garland or wreath you see made of these two ancient survivors represents about 25 years' growth of plants taken from the wild. They have survived dinosaurs, ice ages, and upheavals of all sorts. It seems a shame to use them in Christmas decorations that are thrown out after a week or two. 🍂

Trailing pine (*Lycopodium digitatum*), left; princess pine (*L. obscurm*), right

Columbine Collector

Q The seed heads on my white columbines have browned, and before they open and scatter, I would like to gather them. Since the seeds are ready to go, it seems as if August is the right time to plant, but I wonder if they can be held until spring?

A Saving columbine seeds to start new plants is a good idea because the plants tend to be short-lived, dying out after three or four years. When the slender seed heads split open, the small, shiny black seeds are ready. But you needn't stand around waiting for them because the seed heads are held upright so the seeds don't all fall out when the head opens. Instead, the seeds scatter a few at a time whenever the wind blows. By tipping the heads into an envelope, you'll capture nearly all of their seeds.

As to when to plant, your options are limited. Robert Bartholomei, director of outdoor gardens at the New York Botanical Garden in the Bronx, said that columbine

(*Aquilegia* spp.) requires stratification, which breaks down inhibitors to germination. While many seeds that need stratification can be kept slightly damp in a refrigerator for a month or two, columbine seems to need a changing environment with alternate cooling and warming.

Nature is the best stratifier. Plant seeds now or later in the fall; either way, they won't germinate until next spring. Lightly scratch up the soil, scatter the seeds, and just barely cover them. Have a drink to their health and wait for spring.

Columbines are easy to transplant when they have two to three sets of leaves, but not when they are mature plants. So if you want to move them around in the garden or give a few away, do it while they're young.

Will you get those beautiful white columbines back? Most likely. Normally, they are notorious for cross-pollinating with any other neighborhood columbines in bloom, and the offspring is unpredictable. But white columbines are almost guaranteed to be a cultivar of *Aquilegia flabellata,* which blooms earlier than other columbines. Pollination without competition is the ideal way to ensure that seedlings will look like their parents. 🌸

Tunneling Terrors

Q The leaves on my columbine (*Aquilegia* 'Music Mix') have tracks resembling those seen in tree bark created by bark beetles. What is killing my once happy and blooming plant?

A Your columbine may look bad, but those squiggly white markings probably won't kill it.

Even if you're very observant, it's unlikely that you'd have noticed the nondescript $\frac{1}{16}$-inch grayish flies occasionally hovering around your plant. The females were busy making small pinholes in the leaves, through which they took a bit of nourishing sap and left an egg behind. The maggot that hatches is appropriately called a columbine leaf miner.

In less than two weeks it chews a tunnel between the leaf surfaces, exits through a small slit it makes, and falls to the ground, where it pupates for about two more weeks and then emerges as an adult. The life cycle is fast enough that there are several generations each year, with the last pupa overwintering in the soil, dreaming about more delicious columbine next spring.

You can limit damage if you happen to notice the pin-holes when first made, or spot the tunnels when they are still short. Just remove and destroy the affected leaves. But longer tunnels mean the leaf miner has likely packed her pickax and left; and once she's gone, there is no reason to remove the evidence of her residence. Leaves with long tunnels may look bad, but they are still useful to the plant since there is plenty of chlorophyll left.

Faced with a serious infestation, some gardeners cut columbines to the ground, destroy the leaves, and enjoy the fresh foliage that regrows (knowing they won't get flowers).

If you are willing to exchange the wide color range possible with hybrids for the yellow-rimmed reddish flowers of the elegant *Aquilegia canadensis*, you'll find that they are much less susceptible to leaf miners while being every bit as beautiful. 🍎

Moving Wild Canada Columbine

Q Each day on the way to work, I drive past a hillside that has many clumps of beautiful bright red-and-yellow flowers growing among the rocks. They look like little rocket ships on tall stems. What are they? Will they survive transplanting?

Wild Canada columbine
(*Aquilegia canadensis*)

A The wildflowers brightening your commute are Canada columbines, *Aquilegia canadensis*. This delicate-looking but tough species, ancestor of many garden hybrids, grows in open woodlands and along road-sides from eastern Canada through northern Florida and westward into New Mexico.

For the moment, at least, they are not endangered; but that doesn't mean it's all right to start kidnapping them. Removal of wild plants is not only a threat to the parent colony, but also a bad idea from the point of view of pure survival. Digging them up often causes root damage, and even when roots are preserved intact, the transition to different soils and light levels puts a lot of strain on the plants. Container-grown (or adapted) plants are expressly created to deal with moving and usually do better at it.

Canada columbine's flowers bloom only in spring and the fernlike blue-green foliage is too delicate to attract the casual browser's eye, so this plant is seldom sold in garden centers, but it is widely available by mail order.

Canada columbines prefer light shade but will tolerate full sun if it isn't baking hot, and they are adaptable to a wide range of soils as long as those soils are well drained. 🌿

Morning Glory Cousins

Q **In a book on Sissinghurst (an English National Trust house), I came across a lovely trailing plant with pink blossoms called *Convolvulus elegantissimus*. Can you tell me about it? Will it grow in zone 4, by any chance?**

A The plant you saw is a member of the morning glory family, Convolvulaceae. This group includes many trailing or twining herbaceous plants, some of which, like bindweed (*Convolvulus arvensis*) are pernicious weeds.

The plant you have fallen for is an attractive perennial that is more often known by one of its synonyms, among them *Convolvulus althaeoides tenuissimus*. This sun lover has lacy silvery foliage, and pink flowers 1 to 2 inches in diameter, on trailing stems. It typically inhabits dry soils in southern Europe and apparently has become naturalized in parts of California.

Unfortunately, this particular species is only hardy in zone 8 and warmer. You can grow it as an annual in zone 4, but it won't winter over. 🌿

The Lovely Corydalis

Q **During a visit to England last summer, I saw a lovely yellow flower called corydalis in wall cracks and on rustic paths. Will it grow here in the U.S.?**

A It certainly will. Growers in zones 5 to 8 can enjoy the blooms of the yellow corydalis, *Corydalis lutea*, nearly nonstop from late spring to autumn. Its graceful, tube-shaped blossoms sit on top of neat, low-growing mounds of ferny-looking blue-green leaves.

One of several hundred species in the genus, this hardy perennial, a European native, grows in sun or light shade. Both its foliage and tiny flowers somewhat resemble its cousin, the fringed bleeding heart, and like its cousin, corydalis does best with humus-rich, well-drained, slightly moist soil. If garden conditions are to its liking, it may surprise you by sowing itself where you least expect.

Corydalis lutea is sometimes labeled yellow fumitory, and is sold by many well-stocked nurseries. You might also find room in your garden for a blue variety, but it's not as tolerant of the summer heat as the yellow. Its heaviest flowering occurs in spring, and a second good flush appears in fall, but there are only sporadic flowers through summer. A creamy white or ivory form is also available, flowering nearly as well as the yellow. 🌰

Caring for Day Lilies

Q Last spring I planted my first day lilies. They were bought as container plants and bloomed nicely through summer. What care do they need for winter, and when should I divide them?

A Day lilies are undemanding members of the lily family whose genus name, *Hemerocallis*, is Greek for "beauty for a day." The only attention these hardy perennials need in winter is a blanket of mulch. After the first hard frost, cover the ground with a loose, 3- to 5-inch layer of evergreen boughs, bark chips, straw, or leaves. By holding cold in the ground, you help prevent the alternate thawing and freezing that can heave roots from the earth. Many gardeners skip the mulch after clumps are well established, but it's a good idea when the plants are young and not yet well anchored.

You don't have to worry about dividing them yet. Division is needed only in established clumps that have become too large, or those whose flowers have become sparse or small. This may be several years away. 🌰

Day lily
(*Hemerocallis* spp.)

The Fruiting Body

Q **I've been told that in deadheading day lilies, it's necessary to take off the fruiting body. What's that?**

A Technically, a fruiting body is the spore-making part of plants that don't flower, like mosses, or of nonplants, like mushrooms. But the term is also often used to mean the fleshy green seedpods (technically, the fruit) of plants not known for fruit making. Snap them off carefully where they meet the stem, so you don't hurt developing buds on the same scape (the leafless flower-bearing stem that rises from ground level). 🌶

Constant Bloomers?

Q **I read that 'Stella d'Oro' day lilies will bloom all summer if you deadhead them. So I went out every day and scrupulously pulled off all the spent flowers. About two weeks later, however, I started seeing what seem to be big green seedpods developing. What am I doing wrong? Do I need to literally cut off the spent blooms with a little bit of stem? And when a stem seems finished, should it be cut back too?**

A This may not be the place to say "Don't believe everything you read," but these day lilies, like most perennials that are supposed to be constant bloomers, are more accurately described as frequent re-bloomers. They will indeed make flowers over a long season, but usually in waves, called flushes, rather than all the time.

Deadheading does help encourage more flowers by preventing the development of seeds, but only if you also consistently remove the baby fruits (seedpods) while they are still small. Look for them right below the flowers, at the top of the small stems that join the flowers to the larger stalks.

The plant will look better if you cut spent stalks to the ground after they have finished blooming, but as long as the incipient seedpods have already been removed, there's no "should" involved. 🌶

Day Lily Jungle

Q Is it safe to dig up and transplant day lilies in the middle of the summer? I am tempted to throw them out, as they have turned the path to my door into a jungle, but I'm told disposing of them is a sin. Maybe I'll put them by the side of the road with a sign reading "Free to a Good Home."

A Day lilies are justly famous for their ability to survive anything, including being divided in the middle of summer. They will do better if you wait until the weather cools a bit, but as long as they have finished flowering, they should be all right.

Of course, if you just want to get rid of them, who cares? You can even leave stalks of unopened flowers as an incentive for adoption. That will stress the plants considerably, but it probably won't kill them.

If you set the plants out, cover their roots with a thick layer of damp newspaper and be sure they will be in the shade. Leave a few plastic bags next to them, so the new parents have something to put their babies in for the trip home. 🌿

Delphinium Blues

Q A year ago I bought five yellow delphinium seedlings at a plant sale. They didn't grow large or bloom, but they seemed healthy, and I thought they would flower this year. Instead, they all died. Delphiniums usually do well here in western Connecticut (my others are fine). Do you have any idea what happened? Is the problem likely to spread?

Delphinium semibarbatum

A Winter is what happened. It's likely that your other delphiniums are hardy garden stalwarts such as tall Pacific hybrids, mid-size Connecticut Yankees, and short grandiflorum types. No matter what colors they are, light or dark blue, purple, pink, or white, all of them can survive temperatures that dip well below zero.

Unfortunately, the yellow one, *Delphinium semibarbatum,* also known as *D. zalil,* is a more tender creature. Temperatures below 10°F will do it in. If it's any consolation, the yellowness doesn't stay constant from plant to plant. Some flowers are a wan cream color; others have an orange cast.

If you want to try again, and don't mind that you will be growing an annual, give the seedlings a longer head start. Plant fresh seeds indoors in December. Give the seedlings bright sun, moderate temperatures (55° to 65°F), and monthly doses of half-strength fertilizer. Make sure they have plenty of root room.

Established plants set out in early May should send up spikes of loosely packed flowers in summer. 🍂

Delphinium Blahs

Q **My delphiniums were gorgeous for the last three years, but when they came up this spring they looked spindly and weak. I see no signs of bugs or disease, and I'm providing the same care and fertilizer I always have. What happened?**

A Nothing. Or at least nothing wrong. Delphiniums belong to that class of plants called short-lived perennials, which means that they tend to peter out over time. It's not inevitable, but it is likely, no matter how carefully you provide the good drainage, correct soil (they like lime), and rot-discouraging air circulation that are essential to healthy delphiniums.

For best results, experiment with different species to find out what's most durable in your garden. For instance, *Delphinium grandiflorum* (also known as *D. chinense*) 'Blue Mirror,' a lacy 3-footer with flowers of the most beguiling gentian blue, is supposedly very short lived, but where the soil is well drained and the summers are cool, it sometimes hangs on for a long time. The statuesque Pacific Giant hybrids usually do best— no surprise—in the Pacific Northwest, but some New Englanders have found them even tougher than 'Connecticut Yankee,' which is generally among the most durable of the lot.

It's also wise to hedge your bets. Experienced growers keep a supply of new plants coming, starting them from seeds, cuttings, or divisions, and growing them in nursery beds or the vegetable garden for their first year. 🍂

Delphinium
'Connecticut Yankee'

Tough Maidenhair

Q **I think of maidenhair fern as a tropical plant to be grown indoors, but I saw a picture of maidenhairs in a Quebec garden. What does that gardener know that I don't?**

A That gardener knows that of the 300 species of *Adiantum*, maidenhair fern, a few are quite hardy.

One of the loveliest and most readily available is *A. pedatum*, the Northern maidenhair fern, which grows a foot or two tall. Its pinkish crosiers unfurl into elegant fan-shape fronds on wiry black stalks. All it needs is moist, rich, loose soil, well amended with compost, and light to medium shade, especially from the hot afternoon sun. *A. pedatum* may look delicate, but it is hardy to zone 2, or –50°F. If you live anyplace colder than that, you probably aren't gardening.

Maidenhair fern
(*Adiantum pedatum*)

Fern Foliage

Q **I would like to landscape a damp area that has bright dappled sun, and I thought of using ferns. Which would you suggest for good foliage combinations?**

A Ferns predate the dinosaurs but are often overlooked by gardeners despite the enormous variety of shape, texture, and tone of their leaves, which are referred to as fronds.

The Japanese painted fern (*Athyrium nipponicum* 'Pictum') has silvery serrated fronds on wine-red stems, and grows about 18 inches high. The Christmas fern (*Polystichum acrostichoides*) has leathery, dark green fronds growing to about 30 inches, and stubbornly endures through the snow.

The Northern maidenhair fern (*Adiantum pedatum*) has dark wiry stems with dainty fronds set in a flat, fanlike pattern, and grows to about 18 inches. The ostrich fern (*Matteuccia struthiopteris*) grows fast, to about 4 feet, with graceful feathery fronds.

Choice Ferns for Beginners

Q **I'd like to start some ferns in a shady part of my yard, but I've never grown them before. Any suggestions?**

A Many ferns thrive in partial shade, in well-drained but moist soil that contains plenty of humus. For starters, consider the cinnamon fern, *Osmunda cinnamonea*, which grows 2½ to 5 feet tall and has cinnamon-colored fertile fronds; the interrupted fern, *O. claytonia*, a majestic plant that can reach a height of 8 feet in the damp-to-wet soils it prefers; the crested shield fern, *Dryopteris cristata*, with wide, leathery foliage that grows 1 to 3 feet tall; and the Japanese painted fern, *Athyrium nipponicum* 'Pictum,' whose burgundy stems and striking gray-, white-, and green-patterned fronds can grow to about a foot and a half. 🌰

Withering Ferns

Q **Early this summer I planted a group of beautiful maidenhair ferns, but now they look withered and ratty. What happened?**

A Your problem may have been a result of drought. Maidenhair ferns (*Adiantum* spp.) need a rich, loose, well-drained soil, and must be kept evenly moist. If the soil is allowed to dry completely, even for a day, the plants' leaves will wither and die.

Snip off the dead leaves at the point where the stems emerge from the ground, then begin watering regularly. If there is still life in the roots, the fern will send up new shoots.

Be sure to remove only those stems that are truly dead. Fronds that still have life in them should be left to help nourish the roots. Once there is plenty of new growth, you can remove the unsightly older foliage. 🌰

Fiddleheads for the Table

Q **A bowl of steamed fiddleheads is my idea of the perfect spring celebration. I have only a few ostrich ferns, and it takes a lot of fiddleheads to make the meal worthwhile. If I harvest them all, will it kill the ferns?**

A Fiddleheads, or crosiers, are a spring delicacy that makes it worthwhile getting mud on your shoes. Before the new fronds of the ostrich fern (*Matteuccia struthiopteris*) unfurl, they form a tightly curled spiral that really does resemble the head of a violin or a bishop's staff.

They are tender and delicious, but don't celebrate to excess. Dr. John Mickel, senior curator of ferns at the New York Botanical Garden in the Bronx, said not to cut more than three or four from a fern crown, which typically produces about a dozen fiddleheads. If you harvest them all, the plant will send out new fronds, but perhaps at a price. Producing the second set reduces the supply of nutrients stored in the fern's rhizome, weakening the plant. A droughty summer or a hard winter and the fern, especially an older one, may not make it. Since ostrich ferns spread rapidly by underground runners, have patience. In a few years, you'll be able to move from clump to clump, harvesting all the fiddleheads you want without endangering the plants.

But right from the start, it's important to be sure you really have ostrich ferns. (Their fiddleheads should have only a few tan scales, which should rub off easily.) Several other common ferns, including royal and bracken, are carcinogenic. And don't forget to cook your fiddleheads thoroughly; even ostrich ferns can cause stomach upset if they are eaten while they're still crunchy. 🌰

Ostrich fern
(*Matteuccia
struthiopteris*),
at the fiddlehead stage

The Geranium Conundrum

Q I've always heard that geraniums aren't hardy, but I saw some plants at a B & B in New Hampshire that were labeled "hardy geraniums," and they had clearly been growing in the garden for years (other stuff was all mixed in with them). Are they a new development?

A Not at all. Hardy geraniums are distant cousins of the tender plants known as geraniums. The irony is that the hardy plants have technical rights to the name (they belong to the genus *Geranium*), but it is the tender ones that most people think of when they hear "geranium."

Technically, the familiar houseplants are not geraniums. They belong to the genus *Pelargonium*. But the confusion is natural. Both the hardy and tender versions belong to the Geraniaceae family, and they both used to be in the genus *Geranium*. Then the tender ones got split off into *Pelargonium*, but people kept right on calling them geraniums.

Pelargoniums were brought to Europe from South Africa early in the seventeenth century. They found immediate favor, but it was their scented leaves and not their flowers that caused the sensation. By the time they came to the U.S., more than a century later, Pelargoniums' large clusters of bright red, orange, or hot pink flowers had taken center stage, a position they still hold; scented-leaved geranium fans are passionate, but a minority.

Meanwhile, back in the temperate British and American countrysides, numerous species of native *Geranium*, known to the populace as cranesbills, were finding their way into gardens. The cranesbills do double duty, offering beautiful, long-lasting leaves as well as loose umbels of flowers in a wide range of pinks, blues, and purples.

You can usually tell these plants apart by general appearance: the leaves of *Pelargonium* are thicker than than those of true *Geranium*, their flower stems are stiffer, and though individual flowers are smaller, they tend to be clustered more densely. And if you look closely at the individual flowers, you can usually see a tiny spur on the pelargonium flower stalk (geranium flowers don't have them).

Color helps too: although both kinds might be white, plants in the genus *Geranium* come in purples, blues, and blue-tinged reds and pinks; those in *Pelargonium* may be true red, orange-red, pink, or orange, but they do not sing the blues. ✿

Hardy geranium
(*Geranium
macrorrhizum*)

Wild Geraniums

Q **I've heard that the wild geranium is recommended for naturalizing. Is this true?**

A It is true. Wild geranium (*Geranium maculatum*) is a hardy perennial excellent for naturalizing, or filling in, under bushes and trees or wherever there is dappled shade or part sun. Also known as cranesbill, *Geranium maculatum* is a very distant cousin of the tender geraniums known botanically as *Pelargonium*.

This American native wildflower, with its flat, delicate-looking pink-lavender flowers and deeply notched foliage, is very easy to grow, ultimately reaching between 12 and 18 inches. 🌱

A Tough Perennial

Q **I have a partially shaded spot and was advised to plant something called goatsbeard. What is it, and do you recommend it?**

A This plant is indeed superb for partial shade, especially areas where the soil tends to remain moist. Goatsbeard (*Aruncus dioicus*) is a shrublike herbaceous perennial and a tough one at that, surviving winter temperatures well below freezing. A native of North America and a member of the rose family, the plant has ferny-looking foliage that may grow from 5 to 7 feet tall. In June and July this handsome plant comes into its glory with the appearance of 4- to 5-foot-tall, frothy white-plumed flowers that rustle in the wind. The sexes are on separate plants and male flowers tend to be more ornamental.

Goatsbeard is easy to care for, seemingly impervious to insects or disease. If your space is limited, look for the dwarf varieties, including *A. d.* var. *astilboides,* which grows about 2 feet tall, and *A. aethusifolius,* which reaches only about 10 inches. 🌱

Seeking Well-Behaved Grasses

Q **I'd like to add some ornamental grasses to my garden, but I've had so much trouble with weeds, I confess I'm a little scared. Is there any way to tell which grasses are likely to be invasive before I plunge in?**

A Anything with runners—ribbon grass (*Phalaris arundinacea*), blue lyme grass (*Leymus arenarius*), and switch grass (*Panicum virgatum*) are the classic examples—is likely to be a problem, so if you're taken with something that doesn't come with a description, tip it out of

Switch grass
(*Panicum virgatum*)
tends to invade.

the pot and look for signs of runners (underground shoots with upward-pointing tips) before you take it home.

And almost anything with seeds will self-sow, that being what the seeds are for, though some, such as the fountain grasses (*Pennisetum* spp.), do it far more agressively than others. Be careful of plants described as self-sowing "manageably"; someone has got to do the managing, and that someone will be you.

Fortunately for grass lovers, invasiveness is always situational. Pampas grass (*Cortaderia selloana*) is a real pest where winters are warm, but it's not going to cause any problems in the Frost Belt. A moisture lover like dwarf cat tail (*Typha minima*), though inadmissibly pushy in marshy areas, will probably be a safe bet in a pond in a dry garden, as long as there are no vulnerable wetlands in the immediate area.

Nurseries are increasingly conscientious about labeling possible invaders, but it's still best to check with your local extension service before you purchase and plant. 🌿

Blue Lyme Grass

Q At the Central Park Zoo recently, I saw some spectacular bluegrass. Is it blue lyme grass? Is it invasive?

A Through the years, various grasses have been used in the spectacular perennial borders at the Central Park Zoo, which were designed by Lynden B. Miller in 1988. The grass that caught your eye is indeed blue lyme grass.

Also known as sea lyme grass (*Leymus arenarius* or *Elymus arenarius*), it is a hardy perennial native to Europe and Asia, with handsome, shiny blue-green foliage. At 2 to 5 feet tall, it is one of the largest of the ornamental grasses. It does best in full sun, is easily cared for, and tolerates a range of soils from dry to wet.

The color persists well into the fall, and many gardeners leave it standing for winter interest, but it should be cut down in early spring, long before new growth starts.

And oh, yes, blue lyme grass can be invasive. If a noninvasive bluegrass is what you need, you might take note of blue wild rye (*Elymus glaucus*). Its bright blue-green foliage is not so broad as lyme grass's, but it develops in clumps and does not spread aggressively. 🌱

Ornamental Grasses for Part Sun

Q **To improve the foliage texture in a partly shaded area, I would like to add some ornamental grasses. Are there any that will manage with about four hours of sun?**

A It is true that the majority of ornamental grasses do best in full sun, but a number will also tolerate shade, as long as it is not too heavy and their other cultural needs are met.

Among these useful grasses or grasslike plants are tufted hair grass (*Deschampsia caespitosa*), millet grass (*Milium effusum*), *Hakonechloa macra* 'Albo-aurea,' variegated lily turf (*Liriope muscari* 'Variegata'), and ribbon grass (*Phalaris arundinacea* var. *picta*). These vary from about 1 to 3 feet tall. Somewhat shorter are Virginia wild rye (*Elymus virginicus*), Alpine hair grass (*Deschampsia alpina*), and blue fescue (*Festuca ovina glauca*). And quite a bit taller are northern sea oats (*Chasmanthium latifolium*), creeping bluestem (*Andropogon stolonifera*), bluejoint (*Calamagrostis canadensis*), and bush grass (*Calamagrostis epigejos*), which may range from 2 to 6 feet tall. 🌱

Fragrant Grasses

Q **I'm interested in fragrant plants and wondered if there were any scented grasses.**

A Several ornamental grasses give off appealing fragrance when their leaves are rubbed or broken. They include lemongrass (*Cymbopogon citratus*), citronella grass (*Cymbopogon nardus*), and sweetgrass or vanilla grass (*Hierochloe odorata*). When dried, sweet vernal grass (*Anthoxanthum odoratum*) is fragrant, as well. Sweet flag (*Acorus calamus*) is a scented grasslike plant, but not a true member of the grass family. 🌱

BLADES OF COLOR

The most common fall color for grasses is a warm tan, but there are also some that are as bright as autumn leaves. Plant them where they'll show up: the pale ones backed by dark evergreens, stronger shades where they will blaze against the pebbles of a courtyard or the open sky.

Yellows include many of the molinas, especially *Molina caerulea* cultivars, and *Phragmites australis*.

Shading more toward orange and red are the big bluestems (*Andropogon gerardii*) and switch grasses (*Panicum virgatum*), especially the variety 'Haense Herms.' Indian grass (*Sorghastrum nutans*) does double duty, starting out yellow and shading toward orange as the season progresses.

For darker reds, consider *Miscanthus sinensis* 'Graziella,' which has warm brown undertones; the purplish *Hakonechloa macra; Imperata cylindrica* 'Rubra'; and *Miscanthus sinensis* 'Purpurascens.'

Winter Grasses

Q **What type of ornamental grass would provide interest to my garden throughout the winter?**

A The best grasses for winter interest are those that are quite sturdy, able to stand up to rough weather, including the feather reed grasses (*Calamagrostis* spp.), Ravenna grass (*Erianthus ravennae*), little bluestem (*Schizachyrium scoparium*), and those that have decorative seed heads, such as Indian grass (*Sorghastrum nutans*) and cat tails.

For the prettiest effect, they should be planted in groups of varying heights or where they will be set off by evergreens, garden sculptures, or other structural elements that give them a context. If you just dot them here and there, they tend to look like something you forgot to clean up. 🌿

Dividing Grasses

Q **My ornamental grasses (mostly *Miscanthus* and *Pennisetum*) were planted two and three years ago. So far they all seem to be doing fine. When will I know it's time to divide them, or should I not wait for signs that the plant is no longer thriving?**

A Grasses will let you know they need division by flowering less and/or dying out in the center of the clumps. Be on the alert for the start of these symptoms and divide the grasses then. You want to get in there before things get ugly, but there's no need to divide plants that show no signs of needing it. 🍂

Grasses for Cold Climates

Q **What grasses are cold hardy for my zone 4 New England garden?**

A Many of the most popular ornamental grasses are very hardy, including *Miscanthus sinensis* cultivars such as 'Morning Light' and 'Purpurascens'; midsize favorites like the feather reed grass *Calamagrostis arundinacea* 'Overdam'; yellow foxtail grass (*Alopecurus pratensis*), which seldom grows taller than a foot; and its even shorter cousin, *A. alpinus* ssp. *glaucus,* a 4-inch charmer with very blue leaves.

The Minnesota Landscape Arboretum conducted a large study of cold-hardy ornamental grasses and has published the results in North Central Regional Publication No. 573, "Ornamental Grasses for Cold Climates." The booklet, which includes pictures and helpful descriptions, can be ordered at (608) 262-3346. 🍂

Tall and Spectacular

Q **I saw large clumps of the most beautiful tall (6 feet or more!) ornamental grasses placed intermittently throughout a field on Long Island. They were spectacular. Do you have any idea what they could have been?**

A There are several tall perennial grasses that might thrive in bright sun and well-drained soil in zone 6 or 7. If they had long, bushy, plumelike flowers, they were probably some kind of *Miscanthus*. If the flowers were looser and spikier, they might have been young Ravenna grass (*Erianthus ravennae*), which can eventually grow 10 to 12 feet tall. If the flower heads were very slender, the spectacle could have been feather reed grass (*Calamagrostis* × *acutiflora*).

It's also distantly possible that you were seeing clumps of pampas grass (*Cortaderia selloana*). This gorgeous, albeit sharp-edged grass has huge, billowing silvery flowers that make it a classic specimen plant—indeed, it's almost a cliché. But it isn't usually hardy much north of zone 8, so unless the field had a particularly mild microclimate, dotting it with pampas grass would mean the owners were replanting the clumps each year. 🍂

Cutting Grasses Back

Q **In nature, nobody cuts down grasses, so do I have to cut back the ones I've planted in the small, semi-wild (unmowed) area between my garden and the treeline that divides my house from the neighbors'? I don't mind seeing the new growth coming up through what's left of last year's brown stems.**

A In nature, the open areas where grasses grow are periodically renewed by the cleansing effects of fire. In the absence of this very efficient remover of dead material, you would be well advised to cut back your grasses.

The best time to do it is in early spring, after the grasses have done winter landscape duty but before the new growth starts. Wearing gloves (many grasses have sharp edges) and using hedge clippers if the clumps are large, cut off the dead stalks right above the ground. This will not only open up the plants, bringing light and air to the centers and thus forestalling disease, but it will also remove a potential fire hazard. 🍂

Growing Gunnera

Q **I saw *Gunnera manicata* growing in Costa Rica and loved it, but I've had no luck germinating seeds; is there a secret for doing so?**

A The elephant-size leaves of *Gunnera manicata*— typically 4 to 6 feet across—are real showstoppers. Although these herbaceous perennials, native to southern Brazil, will grow in either sun or partial shade, they need to be in a sheltered spot with rich, constantly moist soil.

Constant moisture also makes seed germination more likely, although in general gunnera (pronounced GUN-ur-rah) is difficult to start from seed, which must be planted as soon as it is ripe because it quickly loses viability. Propagation by division is more reliable, and this is the method used by most commercial growers.

Gunnera manicata will not reliably winter over anywhere north of zone 7, and even zone 7 is sometimes chancy. Gardeners there should take the precaution of piling a dry mulch over the crown after it goes dormant for winter. 🌑

A Wee Bit of Heather

Q I'm thinking of planting some heather on a slope on my property. Will it survive below-zero temperatures? If so, are there any colors other than purple, and when could I expect them to bloom?

A Hardiness varies, but in general *Calluna vulgaris*, the true heather, is a tough plant that can take subzero temperatures, especially with ample snow cover for protection. The slope sounds promising—heather needs good drainage. It also requires acid soil and regular pruning.

The blooms, which will be abundant if the plants are kept sheared, usually appear in late summer and last for six to eight weeks. There are 16 colors to choose from, if you use the list recognized by The Heather Society, the largest international organization of heather enthusiasts. Options include amethyst, beetroot, lilac, lavender, mauve, ruby, shell pink, and salmon.

You can expand both palette and bloom season by planting heaths, which are closely related to heathers; and you can also get a lot of color from the heather plants themselves. There are hundreds of varieties available, many of which have very showy new growth in spring, brilliant yellow summer foliage, or leaves that turn scarlet or orange in winter.

For more information, consider joining the North American Heather Society, 2299 Wooded Knolls Drive, Philomath, OR 97370; you can find them on the Web at *www.northamericanheathersociety.org.* 🌑

Perennials in Particular

A Bed of Heather

Q **I'm a Scotophile and dream of lying in a bed of heather in my kilt, writing poetry. Which variety should I plant?**

A You'd better have both a tough posterior and some tough heather before you try the kilt trick, but to quote David Small, president of The Heather Society, *Calluna vulgaris* is "tough and wiry and will tolerate the odd person lying on it," though it "would not tolerate constant trampling."

Several heathers are named for malt whiskies and a number are named after parts of Scotland—either of which might create an inspirational atmosphere for your poetry writing. For best results, though, focus on height, not nomenclature. Among the mauves, for instance, 4-inch-tall 'Heidepracht' is likely to make a more comfortable bed than 'Macdonald of Glencoe,' which can approach 2 feet. 🌰

Not a Rose

Q **Blooming in a friend's garden recently was a beautiful plant she called Lenten rose. Its flower time overlapped with a plant she called Christmas rose. Can you tell me about them?**

A Neither the Lenten rose nor the Christmas rose is a true rose. Each is a hellebore, an exquisite perennial member of the buttercup family, and superb for growing in areas with part shade, like a city backyard or the edge of a woodland.

While their large, dark evergreen leaves brighten the garden through winter, hellebores are treasured for their somewhat bell-shaped blooms. The colors range from creamy white and pale green, through pink to shades of maroon.

As their common names suggest, hellebores are cold-season bloomers—either the earliest or the latest flowers of the year, depending on what zone you're in and whether you go by the calendar or the spring equinox. The Christmas rose (*Helleborus niger*) may start anytime from November through January. The Lenten rose (*H. orientalis*) gets going

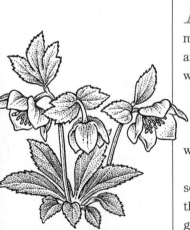

Lenten rose
(*Helleborus orientalis*)

later, in February or March. Both species have an unusually long season of bloom, typically six weeks or more. 🌿

Getting Hellebores to Bloom

Q **I have read that hellebores are good plants for shade, so I bought several, in different colors, and planted them near a clump of rhododendrons at the border of our property, where shade from several of our neighbors' trees limits the flowers I can grow. The hellebores (*Helleborus* × *hybridus*, according to the nursery label) seem to have taken well, but they don't bloom. Any idea why?**

A Hellebores are indeed good plants for partially shaded locations, but your hybrids, based largely on the Lenten rose, *Helleborus orientalis,* are among the ones that will bloom more profusely if they get quite a bit of sun, preferably in early spring when it's more about light than heat.

In fact, dappled shade is hellebore territory largely because they like cool temperatures and consistently moist—but not wet!—soil that is rich in organic matter. So even without those burning rays, hot, dry weather could make them sulk, especially if the soil is poor.

Patience is important, too. Hellebores are touted as quick to grow, but they do resent disturbance and can sometimes take a while to get established; if you've only had them for a short time, that could be the problem. Unfortunately, it's also possible that the soil is too acid.

Although they are fairly tolerant in the soil pH department, most hellebores prefer neutral to slightly alkaline conditions. If the acid-loving rhododendron is doing well, the hellebores underneath it are probably destined to find life a struggle.

Choose a new location for them, away from the rhododendron root zone, and where they will get morning light. Test the soil for acidity, amend with lime if necessary, and when early fall arrives, move the hellebores into their new home. It sounds like a bit of a production, but hellebores are very long-lived plants. Set them up where they will be happy and they will brighten your early springs for many years to come. 🌿

Hens-and-Chicks

Q **Several times I've tried baby cuttings of what is known in the Midwest as mother hens-and-chicks, but they always die. Can you help?**

A The handsome whorls of hens-and-chicks are old-fashioned favorites, both in the garden and as houseplants. The profusion of offsets (baby plants) they make is the source not only of their common name, but also of their botanical one. They belong to the genus *Sempervivum,* which means "live forever," and their full handle is *Sempervivum tectorum,* "live forever on the roof," because they often grew on the thatched roofs of European cottages.

These members of the stonecrop family do best in well-drained, gritty soil and full sun. Normally, hens-and-chicks are rather easily grown garden plants; their only weak spot is an intolerance of steady dampness, so assuming your "cuttings" are actually rooted offsets and not just wisps of stem, the most likely problem is overgenerous watering. 🍂

A Hesitant Hibiscus

Q **My hardy hibiscus 'Disco Belle,' although tall and lush with foliage, produced no buds at all this summer. Last summer it bloomed profusely. What's the problem?**

A How was the weather at your place this year? A rainy, cool season is no impediment to vegetative growth, but it's discouraging for heat and light lovers like fruits and warm-weather flowers. If your tomatoes also delivered a questionable performance, chalk up the balky hibiscus to circumstances beyond your control.

If, on the other hand, you did have plenty of warmth and sun, your healthy but monochromatic plant is probably the product of too much high-nitrogen fertilizer. Did you perhaps reward it for last year's splendors by feeding it overlavishly? 🍂

Tiny Hostas

Q **I have a small shady corner where I'd like to grow hostas, but I have only seen monster-size plants. Can you suggest some small ones?**

A Although hostas are noted mainly for their large, bold leaves, there are a number of small and small-leaved plants, several of which bear fragrant flowers that vary from lavender to creamy white.

Diminutive varieties include 'Venusta Variegated,' which grows about 5 inches tall. Its lance-shaped foliage is mostly white with green streaks. 'Emerald Skies' has wide, somewhat heart-shaped, dark green leaves that reach to about 6 inches. 'Chartreuse Wiggles' grows about 3 inches tall and has narrow, ruffled gold leaves, while 'Blond Elf,' another gold-tone plant, has 8-inch-high heart-shaped leaves. One of the tiniest is 'Thumbnail,' whose frosted green leaves grow only a couple of inches tall. 🍂

Dividing Hostas

Q **I have a hosta plant that is several years old and has developed several new shoots. I understand that I may separate it and plant these shoots as individual plants. When and how is this done?**

A Spring is the best time to divide hostas, but it's easier to go for clumps than for solo shoots. There's less damage to the roots that way, and a faster return to the mound shape that makes hostas so attractive. Single shoots make sense only if you are trying to increase a wonderful but very expensive cultivar (of which, admittedly, there are many).

To divide your hosta, start by taking a look at the emerging shoots. Sometimes they come up in groups so distinct that you can remove one or more of the outside ones without digging up the whole plant. If this looks likely, gently scrape away enough surface soil so you can see where the root mass seems to divide naturally. Use a sharp-edged spade or a large knife to cut the separatee away from the parent mass. Then dig it out and move it. Fill in the hole left behind with good garden soil.

To divide a whole plant, dig it up and shake off the dirt. Quite often the plant will fall apart—or start falling apart—all by itself. If it doesn't, pull it gently into multistem clusters, each of which has plenty of fleshy, healthy-looking roots. You can do all this with just your hands if the plant is on the small side. If it's large and the roots are all knit together, you'll need a sharp knife to cut apart the clumps. While you're at it, cut away and discard any roots that are woody, diseased, or dried up; then plant the divisions, and water them well. 🌿

Iris Foliage

Q **With the iris blooms gone, my garden seems awash with awkward spikes. How soon after they've bloomed may the iris leaves be cut? I read that there's a six-week waiting period for daffodils.**

A According to the American Iris Society, one of the most frequently asked questions about irises is "When do I trim the foliage?"

Their answer is "Never," with only a few exceptions. These occur when the foliage becomes brown on the tip; and the gardener wants to trim off those tips; when the foliage becomes unsightly because of leaf spot (a fungus disease); or when iris borers have come calling and drastic measures are called for.

In all cases, trim as little as possible. While daffodil leaves are essential only for a while and then fade away naturally, iris plants continue to feed through their leaves as long as the leaves are alive

To learn more, contact the American Iris Society, P.O. Box 2968, Baltimore, MD 21229; *www.irises.org.* 🌿

To Beard the Iris

Q **I have a large walled-in bed of bearded iris. It is beautiful, but I'm afraid the weeds are winning. I have had to dig out all the plants, divide them, and carefully weed the entire space before replanting—three times in the last 11 years. I don't think I can face doing that again.**

Bearded
iris

A It's easy to be seduced by bearded iris. Between the fetching old-timers and the modern hybrids, restraint can be difficult.

But if you have a large collection, you're in for it in the digging department no matter what you do about the weeds: the plants multiply rapidly. As they get crowded, they put out fewer blooms and become more vulnerable to disease. To prevent this, they must be lifted and divided every three to five years.

So you've been doing just the right thing for the iris, and by now you should be gaining on the weeds as well. There will always be some, even in an enclosed area, but they will diminish over time if you remove the roots of perennial weeds, and get rid of any blooming ones before they set seed. 🍂

BEARDED IRIS

As hard as it may be to maintain an iris bed, the urge to expand it can still be irresistible, especially if you fall under the spell of "Bearded Iris," Cornell Extension Bulletin 112, first published in 1925. The booklet, which has been reprinted by the Historic Iris Preservation Society, gives detailed descriptions of more than 100 irises, including not just color but also fragrance—with lemon, clover, and honey among the enticing possibilities. Write to the HIPS publication chairman at 312 Dryden-Harford Road, Dryden, NY 13053; *www.worldiris.com.*

Dividing Bearded Irises

Q **When is it too late to divide my bearded irises? I know it should be done after they finish flowering.**

A Dividing shortly after flowering is done gives the plants the most time to recover before fall, but you should have no problems as long as you do it well in advance of a hard frost. At the 70-year-old Presby Memorial Iris Gardens in Upper Montclair, New Jersey, for instance, (where there are 4,000 varieties to look after), curator Elizabeth Buckno and her volunteer crew don't finish up until early August, and those plants do just fine.

The important thing is to remember that bearded irises like to be divided about every four years. The presidential elections make a good reminder.

How Not to Be Bored

Q The bulbs of my irises are being eaten by fat white grubs over an inch long. Is there anything I can do, or should I replace the plants?

A There is a lot that you can do, and if you don't do it, there's no point in replacing the plants. The grubs are iris borers, a special bane of the bearded iris. They will invade in force unless you take action.

And they don't just eat. Sooner or later, they will open the way for soft rot, a foul-smelling bacterial infection that kills more plants than borers do.

Start by digging up the rhizomes and cutting out the borers. Discard badly damaged rhizomes. Cut back leaf fans (on the good ones) to 3 or 4 inches. Before replanting, use a metal rake to comb the soil and remove those borers that have already left the plants to pupate in the ground.

After pupating, the grubs' next move is to emerge in autumn as nondescript brown moths. They lay their eggs in dead iris leaves and other debris. So *your* next move is to wait until hard frost kills the moths, then remove every scrap of material that might harbor eggs.

You will miss some, no matter what. In spring they will hatch into tiny larvae, climb up the new iris leaves, then eat their way down toward the rhizomes from inside the leaf tissue. Watch for ragged edges, browning tips, and little tunnels. Oftentimes, you can kill the borers in situ by squeezing firmly at the lower end of the tunnels.

Some experts advise killing the borers biologically (with microscopic worms called beneficial nematodes) or chemically (with strong systemic insecticides), but both of these methods require near-perfect timing and ideal conditions, so they seldom do enough good to justify the time and money (and in the case of insecticides, ecological damage) they entail.

In practice, the best control is the simplest, cheapest, and least toxic: just clean up.

Colorful Offspring

Q **Last fall I bought some pardancanda (orchid iris) plants. They have thrived and are stunningly beautiful, but I can't find any more. The tags said "*Pardancanda* Dazzler series 'Candy Lily.'" Any information about them would be welcome.**

A *Pardancanda norrisii* is an iris-family flower child created in the 1960s by an avid home gardener named Samuel Norris. It took him a great many tries, but he finally mated a hybrid version of *Belamcanda,* which always has purple-spotted orange flowers, with a lavender-flowered plant called *Iris dichotoma* (*Pardanthopsis dichotoma*). The offspring had flowers in a whole paintbox of colors: pink, purple, yellow, orange, white, and red, many of them spotted or with multicolor petals.

The flowers of *Pardancanda,* like those of *Belamcanda,* last only one day, but each plant produces lots of them so the show lasts a month or more. And you still get the pretty clusters of shiny fruits that gave belamcandas the common name blackberry lily (at least they gave it the "blackberry" part; the "lily" remains a mystery).

Pardancandas do best in bright sunshine, enjoy fairly heavy feeding, and will (where happy) gradually form large clumps. These can be divided in late summer after the foliage has started to turn yellow, or in early spring before the new growth starts.

You can also raise new *P. norrisii* plants from seed, and get all sorts of interesting surprises. Seed-grown pardancandas will vary from 10 inches to 3 feet, and they will bloom over a longer season because they won't all be ready at once. 'Dazzler,' a hybrid available only as a plant, is uniformly 15 to 18 inches tall, and its flowers all bloom in more or less the same time frame. You get one big show and then that's it. ✿

Jerusalem Artichokes

Q **I like the taste of Jerusalem artichokes and have just learned they are related to sunflowers. Are they pretty? Can I plant them in New Jersey, use the flowers, and still get a good crop of tubers?**

A mature Jerusalem artichoke (*Helianthus tuberosus*) plant is 8 to 12 feet tall and about a yard wide. It has narrow leaves and, in late summer, lots of bright yellow flowers 3 or 4 inches across.

The plants are weedier looking than ornamental sunflowers (*H. annuus*), but more important, they are weedier acting, notoriously invasive. Once you plant Jerusalem artichokes, you won't be able to get rid of them, so it is wise to site the patch well away from the garden.

H. tuberosus is an undemanding perennial that grows from zone 3 to zone 9. Given good drainage and plenty of sun, it will persist for decades even in poor soil.

Jerusalem artichoke
(*Helianthus tuberosus*)

But there is a difference between persistence and productivity. If you want abundant crops, plant the tubers in well-drained, fertile soil. Keep the area weeded until the plants are established, after which they will shade out competition.

Plant as soon as the danger of frost is past, so the plants will be as large as possible when shortening days tell them to send their energy into the tubers. Cutting the flowers is fine, but don't harvest tubers until frost kills the plants. 🌶

No Souvenirs

Q In the mountains of western Maine, I fought the desire to dig up a pink lady's slipper, a species I have not seen in southern New England for years. Will these plants flourish in a home wildflower garden?

A It's good you resisted the urge. Far too many of these lovely orchids, both pink lady's slipper (*Cypripedium acaule*) and showy lady's slipper (*C. reginae*), which is pink and white, have died after being transplanted from the wild to gardens that do not meet their specific needs. A much better bet is to enjoy them in the wild.

C. acaule is very difficult to propagate from seed and raise to flowering size. The reason is that the seeds establish a symbiotic relationship with a fungus in the soil. This relationship apparently ends when the plant develops enough roots and leaves to make all its own food. But as a mature plant it still needs highly acidic conditions (pH 4.5 to 5), constantly moist yet well-aerated soil, and dappled shade. Even then, many fail.

There seems to be some special combination of soil chemistry that either exists or doesn't.

C. reginae is larger and has slightly different requirements, preferring neutral (pH 7) to slightly alkaline soil that is moist to boggy. It needs a couple of hours of early or late direct sun, and dappled shade the rest of the day.

While lady's slippers are not on the endangered species list, it is illegal in some states to take them from the wild. One company, Vermont Ladyslipper, 56 Leduc Road, New Haven, VT 05472 (*www.vtladyslipper.com*), has figured out how to raise both species from seed and sells laboratory-propagated mature plants. The plants are shipped only when dormant, in October and April. 🌿

Lady's slipper (*Cypripedium acaule*), left; showy lady's slipper (*C. reginae*), right

Lady's Mantle

Q **I recently purchased an unusual chartreuse-flowered perennial called lady's mantle. How did it get that name? Does it need special care?**

A The graceful lady's mantle (*Alchemilla mollis*) has scallop-edged leaves thought in the sixteenth century to resemble the Virgin Mary's cloak or mantle, which likely gave rise to its name. Its botanical name is from an Arabic word for alchemy, and may allude to the magically appearing drops of rain or dew that are caught on its leaves. The drops were considered essential for mystic potions.

In the garden, lady's mantle ranks among the most rewarding and carefree of perennials, thriving in a wide range of soils, in sun or light shade. It needs no special fertilizer but definitely does better in soil that is consistently moist. In late spring the billowy clouds of chartreuse flowers on slender stems rise above the silvery green foliage, where they remain into early summer. The distinctive rounded leaves are softly furry to the touch.

Large plants can be floppy and tired looking by late summer, but if you lift the outer leaves you'll see fresh new growth underneath. Cut away the old leaves and the new ones will rapidly expand to take their place.

Although it could hardly be called invasive, this hardy perennial does tend to self-sow with some abandon unless you cut off the spent flowers before they make seeds. If you don't like where the young plants have placed themselves, you could easily transplant them to where you want them—or share them with friends. 🍂

Blue Lady?

Q Have you ever heard of the wildflower called lady's smock or cuckoo flower? I understand it naturalizes well and might be a wonderful blue woodland carpet, but I don't know anything about it.

A Lady's smock (*Cardamine pratensis*), a member of the mustard family, is a perennial that grows easily in shade and enjoys moist, somewhat boggy soil. The leaves form low rosettes, then send up flower stalks about 18 inches tall. The simple, four-petaled flowers bloom from late spring through early summer in white or a range of pale purples.

The cultivar 'Edith' is shorter, has double flowers, and blooms in pink, fading to white before the petals fall. 'Flore Pleno,' the most abundant bloomer and most willing spreader, is also short and double, on the lilac side of pink.

Any of these plants would indeed form a handsome carpet, assuming your woodland is damp enough, and somewhere in zones 5 to 8, but their bloom season is fairly short and none of the flowers will be blue. 🍂

In Love with Lavender

Q Lavender is my favorite plant, but it seems every year another one is killed off over the winter. Is there anything you can tell me about what varieties I should look for when I'm replacing it?

A It depends on what aspect of winter is causing the problem. Cold is the most likely culprit. Most lavenders don't make it north of zone 6, and even *Lavandula angustifolia,* the comparatively hardy species that includes such favorites as 'Hidcote' and 'Munstead' (both named for gardens in England, which tells you something), is frequently done in by the zone 5 temperatures it is supposed to be able to withstand.

If you are near the northern part of lavender's range, you can look for the deep-purple-flowered hybrid *L.* × *intermedia* 'Grosso,' a cross between *L. angustifolia* and *L. latifolia* (zone 6), and tougher than either parent. But even with tough varieties, it's worth paying special attention to the planting site. Place your lavenders where they will be warmed by winter sun and protected from winter wind. (A dry straw mulch will also help; remember to remove it in very early spring.)

Cold will also be a problem in zone 6 if you are trying to plant French or Spanish lavender, *L. sytoechas*. These tender beauties are strictly zone 8 to 9 material.

That said, consider also the damp. Lavender needs very well drained soil. It will die if its roots are kept wet no matter how warm it is. 🍎

Embrace of the Lespedeza

Q **Two years ago, I planted two small bush clovers (*Lespedeza thunbergii*). Last summer they grew well over 6 feet tall and produced gorgeous purple blossoms in August and September, drowning a rose bush next to them. This spring, all those branches are dead and new growth is coming up from the base. Will it be just as huge this summer? If so, should I move the rose bush or can I trim back the lespedeza?**

A With any luck, your plants will indeed be just as large this year. Or maybe a bit larger. Other than that, expect the same performance. Whether it's too big a show for the rose depends on the rose, and on your appetite for crawling around at the base of the lespedeza.

If the rose bush is small or prone to fungus, the lespedeza is likely to overwhelm it, and it should be moved. If the rose is medium to large, and robust, it probably won't suffer long-term harm from a late lespedeza embrace, especially if those loving arms are fewer than nature intended.

In other words, the lespedezas should be thinned rather than trimmed. When the shoots appear in spring, remove up to a third from each clump, cutting them off right at the base. If the cut shoots keep growing, cut them again. The less-dense lespedezas will still be tall and weep gracefully over their neighbor, but they'll be too light and lacy for any serious smothering.

LESPEDEZA, THE GOOD AND THE BAD

Just the mention of the word lespedeza (bush clover) can terrify anyone familiar with the highly invasive Chinese lespedeza (*Lespedeza cuneata*), or the equally agressive *L. striata* and *L. stipulacea,* all of which have been widely planted as green manures, erosion controls, and cattle food—often to the sorrow of farmers who then cannot get rid of them.

But there's no reason to be afraid of their beautiful cousin *L. thunbergii,* which, though admittedly quite vigorous, is seldom threatening to the surrounding countryside. It's also inclined to be more tender than generally advertised, though individual plants have survived as far north as Maine.

In zones 6 to 8, *L. thunbergii* will become a lax shrub that responds well to hard pruning in spring. In zone 5 it dies to the ground each fall. Either way, it will make a 4- to 7-foot fountain of willowy stems, and these will be covered in late August or September with small white, pink, or purple flowers—a welcome burst of bloom in a season when perennial flowers are in relatively short supply.

Leery of Loosestrife

Q **In late summer I planted loosestrife. Am I asking for trouble? Will it take over my garden?**

A It depends on which loosestrife you planted, where you live, and what you mean by trouble. Purple loosestrife, *Lythrum salicaria,* may or may not take over your garden, but it has taken over so much native wetland that many states (22 at this writing), have made planting it illegal.

Other loosestrifes are somewhat less of a problem, but *L. alatum* and *L. virgatum* (winged and wand loosestrife,

INVASIVE CHARACTERS

In theory, nurseries and seed companies stay abreast of what's invasive and will refuse to supply the means of garden ruin or ecological destruction; but in practice, that's asking a lot. The line between "trouble free" and "invasive" is often a fine one, and just as realtors often mean no plumbing when they describe an old house as unspoiled, catalogs often mean "invasive" when they say "rapidly forms an excellent ground cover." Catalogs are hampered by commercial needs (upbeat attitude, simple descriptions, national audience), while the best knowledge about which plants are doing what is always local, always evolving, but not always cheerful, and not always explicable in one or two sentences.

That being the case, there are two keys to a clear conscience—and an easy mind about future weed problems. One is the USDA watch list of plants that have been deemed invasive in at least one state (*www.aphis.usda.gov/npb/statenw.html*). It is updated regularly and provides valuable early warnings, but it is also enormous, not applicable everywhere, and in some cases, subject to dispute. So call Key No. 2—your local extension service—for more finely tuned advice.

respectively) have also made it onto the list of plants that at least one state has banned as "noxious weeds." 🍂

Sowing Like the Lupine Lady

Q I have tried several times to gather lupine seed from wild plants and sow it in a field near my house, sprinkling it around the way Miss Rumphius did in the children's story. It never works. Is the seed planting just a story, too, or am I doing something wrong?

A Lupines can be sown this way if conditions are right, but that's a big if. The seed must be mature but fresh, it must find an open niche, and it will have the best chance of thriving in well-drained, neutral to slightly acid soil that gets plenty of sun.

Collecting seed is the first challenge. Seeds in the lowest pods on the stalk ripen first, and they are often disbursed by the bursting pods (or eaten by insect larvae) before those in the upper pods are ready.

To get the largest seed harvest, choose several healthy plants and keep an eye on them. By mid to late summer they should have lots of well-filled seedpods, and those at the bottom should be starting to turn black.

Cut the stems, put them in a large paper bag, and staple it closed. Poke a few small holes in the bag to promote air circulation and leave it someplace cool and dry. The almost-ripe seeds will continue to mature and the bag will catch them when the pods split, in a week to 10 days or a bit more.

Next comes sowing, preferably in early fall or, as a fall-back, early spring. The seeds must make good contact with the earth in order to take root and grow, so flinging them into an established field means gambling that they will find a spot that's not already occupied. You'll have better luck if you clear small patches here and there, scratch open the earth, and press the seeds into it.

After that, all you need to do is wait, possibly for quite a long time. Lupine seeds have very hard coats, and in the wild it often takes several years before they germinate. You can speed the process along by soaking the seeds overnight before planting (or nicking them lightly on the round side with a razor blade). But once the seeds are jump-started this way, they must be planted extra carefully and watered until they're well up.

Don't forget that left to their own devices, only a small percentage of wildflower seeds make it to planthood (that's why plants make so many seeds to start with). Gather industriously and sow lavishly for best results. ❧

Moving Lupines

Q **There is a beautiful bed of lupines in front of an old barn on our new property. I would like to move them into the garden but our neighbor says they cannot be transplanted. Is she right?**

A Probably. Young lupines can be moved around without much difficulty, but the plants develop deep taproots that make them hard to transplant once they've become established. ❧

Mysterious Mandrake

Q **Strange stories abound concerning mandrake. Is this plant real? If so, I'd like to grow it.**

A Tales about this nightshade family member, also known as Satan's apple, are plentiful. A marginally hardy perennial, sometimes rated to zone 5 though often chancy north of zone 7, *Mandragora officinarum* bears small, bell-shaped greenish flowers cupped inside large, malodorous clumps of leaves that look like horseradish.

During the Middle Ages, mandrake's leaves were used in ointments. But it was the fleshy, branching taproot that was said to be imbued with special powers, in particular as an aphrodisiac, partly because the roots resemble the lower half of the human body. (According to the herbal Doctrine of Signatures, expounded by the sixteenth-century physician Paracelsus, a plant's form is the clue to the areas it helps.)

But *M. officinarum* does contain alkaloids with mildly narcotic and hallucinogenic properties, and while it is unlikely to kill you, eating any part of the mandrake is not a good idea. The flowers are quite pretty, and have the merit of blooming in the "off season" (late autumn to early spring), but the plant is seldom grown as an ornamental because its form is squatty—the flowers are stemless—and the fruits have an unpleasant odor.

If you're determined to give it a try all the same, mandrake is fairly easy to grow given the right conditions. Start plants from seed or root cuttings, and transplant them while still small to a sheltered spot, perhaps at the base of a wall, in full sun. Soil should be fertile and very well drained; the roots will rot out over winter if it remains wet. Mandrake resents disturbance, so don't try to move established plants. 🌢

Marshmallow Plants?

Q **Is there a connection between the marshmallows that children like to eat and the garden plant of that name?**

A The perennial herb marsh mallow (*Althaea officinalis*) is a naturalized European that grows wild on the sunny edges of marshes and damp meadows from Virginia to Connecticut. It is closely related to the many species of mallows (genus *Malva*) that grow in gardens. In late summer the marsh mallow has pale pink flowers an inch and a half across, growing in clusters along stalks that rise 3 to 5 feet tall.

The tapered, fleshy white root of this plant has strongly mucilaginous qualities, and as usual with species named *officinalis,* it has a long history of medicinal use. The botanical name *Althaea* is from the Greek word *altho,* "to cure," which it did in soothing syrups and lozenges for sore throats, stomach ulcers, and related complaints.

Many food encyclopedias say marsh mallow was the original base for the puffy white confections of the same name, acting as both filler and stabilizer, but none of the standard references cite period recipes so it's hard to say for sure. It may be that the candies were named for the plant simply because they had a similarly gooey quality.

In any case, modern marshmallows do not contain *A. officinalis.* They are stabilized with gelatin or gum arabic.

Marsh Marigold

Q **Is the plant that is called marsh marigold really a marigold?**

A No, it is a cousin of the buttercup, which is what its flower looks like. The marsh marigold is a hardy perennial native to North America, where it grows wild from the Carolinas to Alaska. It has no connection whatever to the tender perennial called the French or African marigold (*Tagetes patula* or *T. erecta*), which, despite their common names, are natives of Mexico.

The marsh marigold (*Caltha palustris*) has yellow blooms about an inch wide that brighten the edges of swamps, bogs, and wet woodlands in early spring. Its glossy, heart-shaped leaves vary in height up to about 2 feet, but they disappear in summer when they enter a resting period and die back to the ground.

Faltering Montauk Daisies

Q **Why are my Montauk daisies yellowing, even with good sun and regular watering?**

A Yellowing foliage is often a sign of nutrient deficiency, but Montauk daisies are tough plants that don't usually need fertilizer—in fact, they tend to do better without it. In this case the problem is more likely to be soggy soil: Montauk daisies don't like wet feet. Try watering them less often, or if the soil in which they're planted doesn't drain well, move them to a drier spot. 🌶

Making Your Montauk Daisy Behave

Q **I need information on pruning my Montauk daisy. It's about 3½ feet tall. I assume I should prune it in early spring, but where do I make the cuts?**

Montauk daisy
(*Nipponanthemum nipponicum*)

A Early spring is too early to prune Montauk daisy (*Nipponanthemum nipponicum*). Wait until you see the new growth visibly swelling, sometime in mid to late spring. Then whack the plant back, almost to the ground. It will sprout plenty of new growth, and in fact should be cut again by half at the end of June. Cutting twice will give you a more compact, shapely plant that won't fall open in the middle from its own weight and lie sprawling across its neighbors. 🌶

Replanting Peonies

Q **When and how do I transplant my peonies? I planted them a year ago, and they have already far overgrown their location in my raised-bed garden in upstate New York.**

A Autumn is the best time to plant peonies, whether they are newly purchased or simply being moved. You can start whenever the weather cools but should stop at least six weeks before the expected date of frozen ground—that gives you roughly September 1 through November 1 in the Northeast. (Newly planted peonies won't mind early fall's icy mornings because the soil below the surface is still warm, but they must have plenty of time to make new roots before growth stops for the winter.)

Start by choosing a location where they can grow undisturbed for the foreseeable future. Peonies are long-haul plants, not at their best until they have been in place for some years.

Test the soil in the planting spot to be sure it has a pH of at least 6, although 6.5 to 7 is better; amend it with dolomitic limestone if necessary. If you're moving the plant, cut off and discard the spent foliage. Dig up and handle the roots carefully as they are quite brittle.

Dig planting holes roughly twice as deep and wide as the peony roots. Prepare the soil by working in a few shovelsful of compost and a bit of greensand or another long-term source of phosphorus.

Set the roots in the prepared holes, making sure the budlike eyes are no more than 2 inches below the ground. Backfill gently; don't tamp down around the plants. Water them in, then top off with additional soil if necessary.

After the ground is frozen 3 or 4 inches down, add a protective blanket of straw, shredded leaves, or bark mulch. Do not fertilize until spring, when a generous application of compost will be welcome. 🌢

Peonies Yet to Come

Q I read that you should not cut more than a third of your peony blooms or you will have fewer flowers the next year. Does this mean you should not deadhead? The dead flowers look so unattractive.

A Plants get nourishment through roots and leaves and use it to make flowers and fruit. The flowers are takers, not givers, as far as the plant's resources are concerned, and you could cut every one without hurting the plant a whit. In fact, when flowers are removed, perennials can use the strength that would have gone into making seeds to do things like fight disease, put out replacement foliage, and build up their underground resources.

Peony garden hybrid

The one-third business probably got started because peonies have short stems. When you cut them for the vase, you usually take a lot of the foliage, too, and a plant does need its leaves to stay healthy. So leave the leaves, take the flowers, and don't forget the "get rid of it" rule: even healthy-looking peonies usually harbor fungus spores that should not stay nearby or be composted. Send all peony cut-offs to the landfill, bury them a foot deep, or burn them. 🍂

DISBUDDING FOR BIGGER FLOWERS

Many plants will make unusually large flowers if they're forced to make fewer of them. The technique is called disbudding because it's most commonly applied to peonies, chrysanthemums, and roses, all of which have clusters of serially developing buds on each stem. But disbudding is really just a form of pruning, and it can be used on almost any flowering annual or perennial.

The lead bud is usually the largest, even if you do nothing. Removing the flowers that would have come after it enhances the effect by permitting the plant to put more energy into fewer blooms.

Disbudding is especially popular among exhibition growers, who are usually after that one perfect cut flower, rather than well-balanced plants or full-looking borders. As they have discovered, even spire-formers like delphiniums will make bigger leading spires if all the incipient secondary inflorescences are removed from the stem. If you want the blooms to be *really* gigantic, limit the number of stems in each clump and be sure you have those stakes handy.

Limiting the number of stems as well as the number of flowers will also work with summer phlox (*Phlox paniculata*) and astilbe, but it won't help with globe thistle, Joe Pye weed, or hardy asters. When in doubt, experiment. Assuming you don't go hog wild with stem removal, this kind of extreme disbudding will have no lasting ill-effects on the plant.

Ailing Peonies

Q I discovered mottling and discoloration on my 10-year-old peony bushes. They flowered beautifully, but I've been told this may be a virus for which there is no cure. What are my choices?

A "It sounds to me less like a virus and more like a nutri-ent deficiency—probably magnesium," said Roy Klehm, president of the Klehm Nursery in Barrington, Illinois, a company famous for three generations of work with these plants. Viruses often cause streaking, not mottling on the leaves. And because magnesium helps plants use the available nitrogen, phosphorus, and sulfur in the soil, not having enough of it can lead to a variety of other nutritional problems.

To correct a magnesium deficiency, Mr. Klehm suggested feeding alternately with fish emulsion and a balanced rose fertilizer that contains trace elements. Follow package directions for application. Another source of magnesium is dolomitic limestone, or dolomite, a mixture of magnesium and calcium carbonate. Scratch the dolomite into the soil around the base of the plant.

It may take a while before you see the effects of these improvements—all the way until next spring if you don't act until mid summer, after the plants have stopped making new growth. But if the problem persists, the plant may indeed have a virus.

Since most peony viruses are highly contagious, don't wait for the plant to die. As soon as you can clearly see that it's sick and not just hungry, dig it out and discard it, including all the roots with adjacent soil. Afterward, sterilize your shovel by dipping it into a solution of water and household bleach, and do not replant that area with peonies. ❧

Hard-to-See Enemies

Q **Last year when my peony buds were all petrified at about the size of a small pea, a horticulturist noted that the problem might be thrips. She suggested an insecticide, which I used this year. But still no blooms!**

A Though someone knowledgeable pointed the finger of blame in their direction, thrips are unlikely to be your problem unless you live at the southern edge of peony territory (in zone 8, for instance). The culprit is probably a disease, the fungus botrytis blight.

Botrytis can—and will—wilt stems and leaves, but often it first shows itself by shriveling the developing buds. Being a fungus, it spreads through microscopic spores, which are easily transferred from the soil or from other plants. It is far and away the most common affliction of peonies, and even has a species (*Botrytis paeoniae*) targeted right at them.

Once botrytis strikes it is difficult to cure, even with strong fungicides, so prevention is the best defense. Be sure to remove and dispose of all diseased buds, leaves, and shoots as soon as you notice them; every afflicted piece of plant is potentially infectious. Dip pruners in alcohol after you use them, and try not to use your spore-covered hands on clean parts of the plants.

Remove and burn or bury not only the dead peony foliage, but also any weeds or other plant material nearby (the spores could overwinter on it). Cleaning up in the fall is also essential. Bury or burn all top growth, including shed leaves. Never add it to the compost, even if it looks like it's fine.

Fertilizing with cow manure is often blamed for botrytis problems. This manure can cause damage if it's fresh, but will be okay if it's well composted. Nevertheless, be sure to keep it well away from the stems. In fact, keep everything away from the stems: good air circulation always helps when you're fighting fungus diseases.

Botrytis thrives in cool, wet weather and can cause a lot of unsightly damage, but it seldom kills peonies outright so there's always next year. If all else fails, start over in a new spot with new plants. 🌿

Ants in the Peonies

Q I'm looking for information on what relationship, if any, ants have with peonies. It seems you hardly ever see a bud without ants on it. I have heard many conflicting stories. Some people say that the ants kill the blooms, while others say that the peony flower buds have a waxy coating and can't bloom until the ants eat it off. My own theory is that the ants make absolutely no difference to the peonies, but I am curious as to the actual facts.

A The answer is none of the above. Ants are too busy to climb peonies just for the view, and certainly do not wish them harm. But there is a good reason, as there always is when you see effort exerted in nature.

Peonies have tiny nectaries, specialized tissues that secrete nectar, at the edge of their bud scales (delicate leaflike structures covering the bud). Nearly microscopic and amorphous in shape, the nectaries go unnoticed. Even if you look carefully, you'll see the ants and the beads of nectar, but not the nectaries. The nectar, however, is a highly nutritious blend of sugars, proteins, and amino acids, and it attracts the ants to the flower buds.

But peonies aren't Mother Teresa. In exchange for the nectar, the ants provide protection for the buds. Any bud-eating pest is attacked, beaten, and thrown off. Since some ants can bite from one end and sting or spray acid from the other, they make formidable foes. The ants may just be protecting their food supply, but the peonies are getting well-armed guards.

Don't spray the ants with poisons or water—the peonies know what they need better than you do. ☙

Peonies from Seed

Q **A friend in western Pennsylvania moved onto a property that has some rare peony plants. The 3-inch, starfish-shaped seedpods are filled with dark red berries. What kind of peony is it? Can it be raised from seed?**

A What kind it is is anybody's guess. The characteristics you describe fit a great many peonies. But regardless of its identity, the best way to raise a new one is to start with a root division.

Even if you take only a small clump with just one or two eyes (underground growth buds), it will produce a blooming plant in half the time it would take a seed to deliver. More important, using a division ensures that the plant you'll get will be just like its parent.

Typical peony
seed head

Most peonies are complicated hybrids that do not come true from seed. Yours would have to be a pure species type to reproduce itself that way. Nevertheless, many gardeners do plant seeds just to see what develops. To try this, choose seeds that have become firm and black; those that stay red are infertile. Sow the seeds in autumn, in moisture-retentive but well-drained soil, about an inch deep and a foot apart. Wait for signs of growth. You might see something the next spring, but the second spring is more likely and it may even take until the spring after that. Make sure the soil doesn't dry out while you're waiting.

The seeds must have a warm, moist period to sprout, then a cold one to begin rooting, then warmth and moisture again before they start thinking about making growth buds. Sometimes, for reasons best known to peonies, they think about it for another year just to be on the safe side.

Eventually, most will send up shoots. In the fall, transplant the young peonies to their assigned growing places. Wait some more. If all goes well, you might get flowers the third year after transplanting, but don't be surprised if it takes longer. ❧

Quick! Divide and Conquer

Q **Four years ago I planted a whole swath of phlox because they were sold as trouble free. They were beautiful until last year, when I noticed fewer flowers, and that some of the flowers were quite pale. It is certainly not unhealthy—this spring there is more of it than ever. How do I get back to the original color?**

Garden phlox
(*Phlox paniculata*)

A Cancel your lunch plans and get out the digging fork. *Phlox paniculata* is "trouble free" in being difficult to kill, but that same robustness means it needs frequent division, or flowering will diminish.

It also needs scrupulous deadheading (or equally scrupulous weeding). If left on the plant after they fade, those big flowers set lots of seeds, which form new plants on the skirts of the old ones. Soon you're running a phlox farm. But plants from self-sown seeds are seldom as pretty as their parents, and if you leave them in place it won't be long before they take over. ❧

Pokeweed Warnings

Q **I have a beautiful plant that grows to 5 feet, with neat leaves and red stems. In autumn, it bears lovely bunches of black berries that make a beautiful purple dye when crushed. I was told it is swamp milkweed (*Asclepias incarnata*), but I checked some books and swamp milkweed looks different. Can you help?**

A There's no way to say for sure without seeing the plant, but it sounds as if your prize is pokeweed, *Phytolacca americana*, a gorgeous but pernicious perennial weed that grows all over the country but is most common in the East and South. Pokeweed seedlings are easy to pull when small, but they soon form a tenacious taproot, which will grow huge (and very hard to remove) if left in place for years.

The tender young shoots that rise from established roots each spring can be boiled to make the classic foragers' food called poke salad. But before you try it, be warned that the root itself is poisonous, and so are those pretty red stems, neat leaves, and colorful berries.

Only the very young shoots are safe, and even they should be boiled and drained twice, using fresh water each time, before they are eaten. (The "salad" in poke salad comes from *sallet,* the Old English word for cooked greens.) 🌿

Pokeweed
(*Phytolacca
americana*)

A Woodland Poppy

Q I've heard there's a yellow poppy that's good for shade. Can you tell me what this might be?

A Very likely the plant you've heard about is one of the beautiful and easily grown celandine poppies, whose bright yellow blooms appear in spring. Its three species do best in the woodland conditions of dappled shade with some protection from the afternoon sun, and soil that is generally moist.

Two of the poppies are native to China (*Stylophorum lasiocarpum* and *S. sutchuenense*). The third is a native American (*S. diphyllum*) that often has a longer season of bloom, flowering well into summer. Its flat-topped blossoms are followed by somewhat hairy-looking seedpods that decorate the plant for weeks, and the blue-green leaves are handsome even when the plant is not in bloom.

Be sure to leave at least a few of the seedpods; celandine poppies will self-sow if conditions are to their liking. 🌿

Showy Matron

Q At a nursery, while looking for fall-blooming plants to mix into my garden, I found *Hylotelephium* 'Matrona,' a purple-foliage sedum I have never seen before. Can you give me any information about it?

Hylotelephium 'Matrona'

A 'Matrona' is a relatively new hybrid between *Hylotelephium telephium* ssp. *maximum* 'Atropurpureum' and *H. spectabile*. Both parents are winners of the Royal Horticultural Society's Award of Garden Merit, and 'Matrona,' bred in 1990 in Germany, was Hardy Perennial Plant of the Year for 2000 in several European countries. It is also popular in garden centers in the United States because it combines so well with other late-blooming perennials and shorter ornamental grasses.

At 20 to 24 inches, 'Matrona' is taller than most other sedums. Its thick, sturdy dark red stems keep it matronly upright and show off the large heads of delicate pink flowers with darker pink stamens. The eye-catching contrast between the flowers and the fleshy, succulent purple-veined and purple-tinged leaves works much better in person than it sounds in words.

The umbrella-shaped flowers turn bronzy as the weather gets colder. Even dry, they retain their garden interest into winter. Like other sedums, 'Matrona' prefers full sun and average, well-drained soil, and a prominent place to show off. ✿

A Shooting Star

Q I've seen pictures of the wildflower called shooting star and have fallen in love. Is this a difficult plant to grow?

A If you have moist, rich soil, you should be able to grow almost any one of the 14 species of *Dodecatheon,* known collectively as shooting stars. These are members of the primula family, and like many primroses, they hold their flowers well above a basal rosette of leaves. Many shooting stars grow in the open, others are woodlanders, but almost all of them appreciate some shelter from the mid-afternoon sun.

The plants are small, ranging in size from 8 to 18 inches tall, 6 to 10 inches wide. Depending on the species, flowers will be pink, violet, or white. All have the characteristic shooting-star shape, with sharply reflexed petals and long, pointed styles. They bloom in spring or early summer, decline, then rise refreshed the following spring. ✿

PERENNIALS FROM SPRING TO FALL

In the world of perennials, there are about a gazillion choices, so any list based on something as broad as order of appearance must, by definition, be arbitrary in the extreme. And it must be arbitrary twice—both by choice and by time assignment—given that many popular genera offer an assortment of species and cultivars, not all of which bloom at the same time.

Day lilies (*Hemerocallis* spp.), for instance, are available in early, mid-season, and late varieties, extending the flowering time of this one perennial from June to September in zone 5, and even beyond where it's warmer. Same story with monkshood (*Aconitum* spp.), some of which bloom in mid July, while others wait until September is almost over.

Nevertheless, it is helpful to have at least a starter menu:

Very Early to Mid Spring: small irises (*Iris histrioides, I. reticulata*); hellebores; pasqueflower (*Anemone pulsatilla,* aka *Pulsatilla vulgaris*); forget-me-not; coralbells (*Heuchera* spp.); bleeding hearts (*Dicentra* spp.); bloodroot (*Sanguinaria canadensis*); vinca; Virginia bluebells (*Mertensia virginica*)

Late Spring to Early Summer: blue flax; campanulas; columbines; delphiniums; foxgloves; geraniums; peonies; the little phloxes (*Phlox divaricata, P. stolonifera,* and *P. subulata*); pinks; poppies; primroses; spurge; sweet woodruff; thrift (*Armeria* spp.); violets

Summer: astilbes; bee balms; campanulas; filipendulas; hollyhocks; hostas; Joe Pye weed (*Eupatorium* spp.); lobelias; lupines; malvas; meadow rue (*Thalictrum* spp.); garden phlox (*Phlox paniculata*); salvias; scabiosa; yucca

Late Summer to Mid Autumn: boltonia; chrysanthemums; rudbeckias; Japanese anemones, New England asters and Michaelmas daisies; perennial sunflowers (*Helianthus angustifolius, H. maximilianii,* and *H. salcifolius*); sedums; snakeroots (*Cimicifuga* spp.)

Snapdragons? Absolutely

Q **I am trying to find perennial snapdragons for my home garden but can't find anyone who sells them. Do they exist? Can I find them in the southern Delaware area?**

A No problem. Although it's always called an annual, the common snapdragon (*Antirrhinum majus*) isn't really an annual at all. It's a short-lived perennial that can overwinter anywhere temperatures stay above 10°F, so at least in theory, any snapdragon grown in southern Delaware (zones 8 and 9) has the potential to return for a number of years.

Unfortunately, getting through the winter is only half the battle. Snapdragons are susceptible to numerous fungus diseases, including snapdragon rust, anthracnose, and botrytis. Broadly speaking, if the cold doesn't get 'em, disease will, so it makes sense to think of them as annuals in spite of their true nature.

To give them their best shot at survival, plant them where they will be protected from strong winds. Avoid southern exposures, where the plants may be subjected to repeated freezing and thawing in winter.

As summer progresses, take care of your snapdragons by keeping them weeded, removing spent flowers, and getting rid of any foliage that looks diseased. Don't fertilize after mid August; you want the plant to concentrate on toughening up, rather than making new growth.

A winter mulch helps protect the roots but it also increases the chance of rot. If you use one, be sure it doesn't touch the stems and remove it as soon as the danger of hard frost is past. 🌶

Washing with Soapwort

Q **I've heard there's a plant that forms a soapy lather when mixed with water. Do you know what this is?**

A Very likely this is the hardy perennial soapwort (*Saponaria officinalis*), also known as bouncing

Soapwort
(*Saponaria
officinalis*)

Bet or wild sweet William. A native of western Asia, it has naturalized at the edge of woodlands in the eastern United States, where its clusters of inch-wide pale pink or white flowers bloom all summer.

Soapwort readily grows to the height of a foot and a half, in full sun or light shade and in any well-drained soil. But since the species self-sows easily and can become a pest in the garden, it's better to grow one of the tamer cultivated forms like *Saponaria officinalis* 'Flore Pleno' or *S. o.* 'Caucasica.'

BOUNCING BET WAS ONCE THE NICKNAME FOR A WASHERWOMAN

It's easy to make soap from soapwort, *Saponaria officinalis,* as long as you're content with the liquid kind. The saponins that make the bubbles are present in all parts of the plant, most strongly in the roots (which are available dried), but also in the stems and leaves. All you have to do is put some crushed soapwort in a nonreactive pan, pour boiling water over it, then simmer over very low heat for about 15 minutes. Leave the mixture until it cools, then strain.

How much water? How much wort? That will depend on your plants—saponin content varies with the cultivar, its age, and growing conditions—and on how much you need for present use. Soapwort solution doesn't keep; it's only good for about a week.

To experiment, start with 3 cups of water for a loosely packed cup of chopped leaves and stems (or 2 tablespoons of crushed dry root). This should make a gentle soap that is particularly recommended for delicate linens or dry hair, but use it carefully the first time out; saponins can be irritating to sensitive skin.

Tough Sunflowers

Q **I love sunflowers, but I hate having to plant the seeds in well-prepared garden soil every year. Are there any perennial varieties tough enough to survive in a rather dry, semi-wild area?**

A As long as you don't mind smaller flowers, you'll be pleased with *Helianthus maximilianii,* a multi-branched, bright-yellow-flowered 8- to 10-footer native to the Midwest. It's a vigorous grower that should do fine without much care or water—after it gets established, anyway—and you'll be doing the garden a favor if you put it somewhere else. All parts of the plant (especially the seed hulls) exude a substance that can inhibit the growth of other plants.

This discouraging property, called allelopathy, exists in all sunflowers and has therefore gotten a lot of press, but in most cases it is quite weak. *H. maximilianii* has more of it than the familiar annual species, but it has no effect on grasses so your semi-wild garden should be fine. 🌶

Swamp Sunflower

Q **I planted several swamp sunflowers last spring and would like any information you can give me on them.**

A A delightful member of the daisy family, the swamp sunflower (*Helianthus angustifolius*) grows wild in moist soils from Florida to southern New York, and west to Missouri and Texas. The plant is a perennial, and one of some 70 species of a native American genus whose yellow blooms light up the landscape in late summer and early fall.

The swamp sunflower has rough, hairy stems that may reach 7 feet tall. They prefer full sun, but will tolerate some shade, where they will be taller but produce fewer blooms. Keep the plants well fertilized; as the name implies, constant soil moisture is a must.

Propagation is by seeds, cuttings, or divisions. But beware: this is a rapid spreader, and with time many small flowering plants will develop around the base. Unless you want nothing else in your garden, remove the new growth. 🌶

Hardy Sweet Peas

Q **I love old-fashioned sweet peas and plant them every year, but they never seem to do well in my garden. I've heard there is also a perennial type. Is it easier to grow? If so, would it be hardy on Long Island?**

A *Lathyrus odoratus*, the old-fashioned annual sweet pea, would rather be in England. It needs slightly alkaline soil, plenty of rain, and a long season of cool weather to thrive. And no matter where they are growing, flowers must be picked constantly. Plants will stop blooming if they are permitted to form seeds.

L. latifolius (the most common perennial sweet pea) is an entirely different story. Unlike their annual cousins, the plants prefer warm weather; flowering doesn't usually start until July comes around. They will slack off if the heat gets really brutal, but as long as it cools off at night they'll keep blooming for months.

These perennial sweet peas are much more drought-tolerant than the annuals, far more resistant to pests and diseases, and as a rule, far larger. A single mature plant can cover an area 2 or 3 feet wide and 8 or 9 feet high. They're hardy, too, even in New England.

On the down side, perennial sweet peas come only in pink or white, so they don't offer the wide color range of the annuals. And you will not have perfume: old-fashioned varieties of *L. odoratus* live up to their name; *L. lati-folius* is scentless in comparison.

Perennial sweet peas aren't popular in the nursery trade, possibly because they grow deep roots and long vines before flowering. But they grow easily from seed, although it takes two or three years for them to start blooming. 🌱

Perennial sweet pea
(*Lathyrus latifolius*)

Purple Turtles

Q **At a local nursery recently, I came across a beautiful purple-flowering plant called turtlehead. What is it, and what does it need to grow well?**

A The turtleheads are native American perennials with curved, tubular flowers that resemble turtles' heads. There are a number of species and hybrids available, all of which do best in moist, acid soil and semi-shade. If the plant you saw was tall, it was probably *Chelone lyonii,* which grows to about 4 feet and is hardy all the way from zone 3 to zone 8.

C. obliqua, its swamp-dwelling cousin, is shorter and wider. It makes a fine garden subject if your garden resembles its wet woodland home, but it is less tolerant of sun and dry soil than *C. lyonii.* It is also quite a bit less tough, rated hardy only to zone 5. 🌱

Yes, Wolfsbane Exists

Q Horror movies refer to a plant called wolfsbane. Is there such a plant? Or is it a facetious creation? If it exists, I'd like to grow it for a lark.

A Wolfsbane is the common name for *Aconitum lycoctonum*. Like its cousins, the garden monkshoods (*A. nepellus*), wolfsbane contains aconite, a very strong poison (though it is no threat to anyone who doesn't eat it).

Wolfsbane is the tallest monkshood, stretching as much as 6 or 7 feet, though there are shorter plants among its numerous subspecies. Flowers are usually a creamy white or pale yellow. There is also a lavender-flowered one, but wolfsbanes don't offer the brilliant blues and deep purples for which garden monkshood is famous.

Like all aconites, wolfsbane does best in partial shade in moist, fairly rich soil, but it will tolerate sun if it has to. ✿

A Plant of Many Faces

Q I recently heard on the radio that yarrows are excellent garden plants. There was yarrow all over my grandmother's farm, but that was a straggly weed with strong-smelling leaves and dirty white flowers, so the speaker must have been talking about something else. What was it?

A "It" was undoubtedly "they"; there are dozens of worthy yarrows available to gardeners. All are long blooming, hardy, and drought tolerant, and easy to grow as long as you have well-drained soil in full sun.

Many of them are improved cultivars of *Achillea millefolium*, the weed you remember. The fernlike foliage is still pungent, but the flowers are far more colorful, as names like 'Cerise Queen,' 'Terra Cotta,' and 'Paprika' suggest.

Cultivated millefoliums tend to be on the short side, about 2 feet. The bright colors fade as flowers age, and the plants themselves are often as weedy looking as the species. These defects mean millefoliums work best in the cutting garden.

You can also tuck them into the border, where they will be supported by more interesting plants. Or you can choose a more statuesque yarrow like *A.* 'Coronation Gold,' a 3- to 4-foot hybrid with larger leaves and broad yellow flower heads, or the 5-foot *A. filipendulina* 'Gold Plate.'

Perhaps you need something petite. In that case try *A. tomentosa,* the woolly yarrow. Its mats of fuzzy gray-green leaves are seldom more than a foot tall.

Most of these yarrows have deeply cut foliage and flat flower heads, but *A. ptarmica,* one of the oldest and best loved, has bladelike leaves and ball-shaped white flowers. Its common name is sneezewort because the roots were once used as snuff. *A. ptarmica* is a rampant grower, notorious for its invasiveness (though it's not all that hard to pull out). But it is a handsome plant, a dependable source of cut flowers, and very nearly unkillable. ❧

Yarrow
(*Achillea millefolium,*
left; *A. ptarmica,* right)

Planting Yarrow

Q We recently planted yarrow according to instructions, digging a hole as deep as the pot, putting in peat moss, and filling it with water. As suggested, we removed about an inch and a half of the dirt on the bottom of the plant in order to open the roots. All the plants turned brown. Can we still save them?

A Yarrows are famous for being tough to kill, but it sounds as if you may have managed to do it anyway. You might want to turn your attentions to the planting instructor next.

Some of the advice you were given was fine. You did want to set plants as deep in the ground as they were in the pot, and ample initial watering was essential. But the peat moss was unnecessary and possibly deleterious. Though it's often recommended as a soil improver, it contributes no nutrients, and must be thoroughly moistened before use or it will repel water instead of absorbing it. Assuming the soil did need amendment—by no means a given—compost or leaf mold would have been a better choice.

As for opening the roots, a slight teasing apart should be more than enough unless they are very tightly packed.

Although you'll be better off starting over, salvation is remotely possible. Cut the plants back to a joint where tiny green shoots in the leaf axils suggest there is still life, replant in loose garden soil, and apply a dose of transplant fertilizer. Keep well watered, and hope for a stretch of cool weather. ❧

CHAPTER THREE

Roses

Memories of a Favorite Rose

Q When we lived in New York City, my husband and I used to admire the lovely pink roses that grew in Union Square Park. These wonderful bushes seemed to bloom from June into November. What were they, and could they be grown in our zone 4 garden in upstate New York?

A The rose you speak of is 'Betty Prior.' If the real Betty Prior was anything like her floribunda namesake, she might have been that pretty girl in high school we all loved to hate.

The clusters of single flowers are simple and lovely, pink with white centers, reminiscent of dogwood blooms. A prolific bloomer, it is often the first to flower in summer and the last to quit. It is a perfect blender, welcome in any garden, getting along well with annuals, perennials, and evergreens.

While 'Betty Prior' is reasonably tolerant of cold, heat, disease, and amateur gardeners, zone 4 is chancy at best. Winter protection and a sheltered site may work, but you would be better off with a rose from the Canadian Explorer or Parkland series, hybrids with the hardiness of rugosas

Roses

and the prolific, long bloom periods of modern roses. 'Betty Prior' may be good, but she's not perfect. 🌹

Rose Petal Search

Q **My Greek mother used to make a delicious rose jam from rose petals. The roses bloomed in May in Long Island, New York, but we cannot identify the plant from which the jam was made. Can you help?**

A "Very likely, this rose was a variety of Mediterranean origin," said Stephen Scanniello, the rosarian at the Brooklyn Botanic Garden. He thought it may have been either a damask rose, possibly *Rosa damascena trigintipetala* (also found as 'Kazanlik'), or a gallica like *R. gallica officinalis* (aka 'Apothecary's Rose'). Both damasks and gallicas have fragrant petals and flower in the Northeast from mid May through June. Both also have a long history of use, both in jams and in medicinal conserves. A recipe for the latter was described by the British herbalist John Gerard in 1597. 🌹

A TASTY FRINGE BENEFIT

The fruits of the rose (better known as rose hips) have a lightly floral taste and are rich in vitamin C. They can be eaten raw, but since they are quite sour, they're usually made into jelly or jam.

For an easy jam, heat 2 cups of rose hips and 2 cups of water. Simmer, stirring, until the fruit is soft, then put it through a food mill. Measure the pulp and add 1 cup of sugar for each cup of fruit. Simmer until a jam consistency is reached, and store sealed in sterilized jars.

Dried rose hips also make a tasty, light pink tea. You can just gather hips that have dried on the plants, but for the best flavor, harvest them as soon as they are ripe and either dry them on screens in the sun, or string them on button thread and hang in a warm, dry, airy place. To make the tea, put a small handful of hips in the pot, cover with boiling water, and steep for a few minutes before pouring.

The tastiest hips come from the sweetbrier or eglantine (*R. eglanteria*); *R. rubrifolia* (aka *R. glauca*); and the rugosa rose (*R. rugosa*). Rugosas produce the largest rose hips, and usually the largest crops of them.

The Bloom's Off the Rose

Q My *Rosa rugosa* blooms for a couple of weeks in late spring and then quits. I do not deadhead the spent flowers because the hips are attractive and because they feed wildlife. I've seen other rugosas in bloom in late July, even into August (with hips on the same plant). How can I get a longer bloom period?

A Many rugosas will rebloom even if they are not deadheaded, according to Suzy Verrier, a rugosa expert, but you're more likely to get summer flowers if you remove at least some spent blossoms. It will also help to fertilize lightly after the first bloom is over.

"In August it's hot and dry, so they bloom less," noted Ms. Verrier, who has written two books on rugosas and now runs a rugosa nursery, North Creek Farm in Phippsburg, Maine. Give them plenty of water, and mulch heavily to conserve moisture and keep roots cool. But culture might not be enough. The problem could be the variety, she said. 'Agnes,' for example, doesn't rebloom.

If that's your trouble, only a new plant will solve it. Two of the longest bloomers are 'Jens Munk,' a fragrant double pink, and 'Polareis' (sometimes sold as 'Polar Ice'), a semidouble white with pink edges. They don't form hips, and seem to be sterile, said Ms. Verrier, which may account for their exuberant bloom.

Rosa rugosa
'Jens Munk'

They are also exuberant growers, making dense, vase-shape shrubs 6 or 7 feet tall. And they're very thorny, though she said this is not a problem because the thorns are not barbed—you just get puncture wounds instead of long, deep scratches. ☙

Roses' Other Beauty Part

Q I like the way rose hips look—there's just something about those round red fruits that's very cheerful to me. But I have been told it's important to keep my roses deadheaded. Is this really important or is it just for the sake of neatness?

Not all roses have big hips.

A That depends on the rose. The kinds that bloom only once can be left to make hips in peace, but if you don't deadhead repeat-bloomers as soon as the flowers fade, you will reduce the number and quality of additional blooms.

Fortunately, it's also important to stop deadheading as summer draws to a close; the formation of hips tells the rose it's O.K. to prepare for winter. Stop cutting about six weeks before the first expected frost, and you should still get hips to enjoy as part of the autumn show.

They needn't be all round and red, by the way; different species of rose have distinctly different hips. Most are more or less globe shaped, but some are flattened and others look like little bottles. The majority are reddish orange, but some are yellow and others are nearly black. They vary in size, too, from smaller than blueberries to hunky as cherry tomatoes. 🌸

A Quartered Rose

Q What exactly is a "quartered" rose? Old garden books mention them, but there's nothing at my favorite local nursery that looks like it has four parts, although they carry a large selection of roses.

A Quartered roses show their stuff when they are almost fully open. Looking into the face of the flower, you see a cup of larger petals and within them, dozens of smaller ones. The small petals are arranged in distinct whorls, and there are usually four of them, though there might also be three or five.

Quartered roses have been around for at least a millennium, but the fashion for high-centered shapes, i.e., the classic hybrid tea, pushed them off the desirables list more than a century ago. They are too lovely (and in many cases, too fragrant) to have ever disappeared completely, but they did recede into the catalogs of those nurseries specializing in old roses like 'Comte de Chambord,' 'Reine des Violettes,' and 'Souvenir de la Malmaison.'

But look again before you dismiss your local suppliers. If they are truly well stocked, they will carry a good selection of David Austin's English roses. These modern hybrids have been bred to recapture the charm of old roses, including, in many cases, quartering of their multitude of petals.

Fragrant examples include 'The Prince,' a deep crimson; 'The Pilgrim,' which is a rich yellow; and 'Gertrude Jekyll,' a strong medium pink.

One caveat: English roses do best in zones 6 to 9, though they can also perform pretty well in the warmer parts of zone 5. If your nursery is out of that range, a failure to carry these beauties may simply mean that the folks who run it are as focused on your long-term success as they are on their own short-term profits. 🌹

A "Real" Rose Garden

Q **I'm planning to turn my side yard into a rose garden, but my husband (who is big into roses) says it won't be a "real" rose garden because I'm planning to put a lot of other plants in it, too. So will it be a rose garden? Or does it have to have only roses in order to qualify?**

A Qualify with whom? Is your husband refusing to help if you don't go the all-roses route? Mixing roses with other plants started (slowly) gaining legitimacy in the late 1800s, and is by now an accepted practice in all but the most hidebound circles; so unless you're trying to re-create a historical landscape of some sort, your rose garden is a rose garden as long as the roses in it command more attention than the other plants.

That said, it should be noted that classic rose gardens *are* devoted entirely to roses, though they may have low hedges of something else—boxwood, for instance—around the beds. Apart from the formal aesthetic appeal, this scheme does make some practical sense. Keeping the ground clear of all but the roses makes it easy to clean up in fall, add organic supplements such as manure in spring, and keep the soil moist and tidy looking with a summer mulch. 🌹

Rose Replacement

Q **I want to replace a row of climbing roses with a *Rosa rugosa* hedge, but I want to avoid rose-replant disease. What steps should I take?**

A For starters, there's no such thing as rose-replant disease. "It is a term I sometimes hear from home

Roses

gardeners," said Michael Ruggiero, curator at the Peggy Rockefeller Rose Garden at the New York Botanical Garden. "I guess it refers to concerns about replanting in the same soil year after year."

While this is a problem for plants like tomatoes, it's not a problem for roses. "This is because rose diseases are typically sited in the leaves and stems, not in the soil, so roses can stay in the same place for hundreds of years," Mr. Ruggiero continued. "Remove diseased leaves, and don't compost them, and don't mulch with them. Sanitation is very important."

When Mr. Ruggiero replants, he does so with disease-resistant rose species, and as it happens the rugosas are among his favorites. "They're beautiful, tough, and rarely bothered by insects or diseases." 🌿

Care for Climbing Roses

Q I planted some climbing roses this summer for the first time. They flowered nicely, then halted their growth in mid August, about halfway up my 6-foot trellis. I generally prune my roses almost to the ground in fall. But if I want the climbers to go to the top of the trellis next year, should I leave them alone? Do they require any special treatment to protect the vines over the winter?

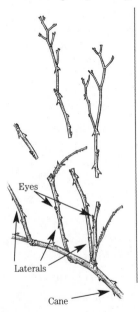

Eyes

Laterals

Cane

A Climbing roses will bloom for years if given a good start. The first few years should be devoted to building a basic structure of long, flexible canes. The flowers will bloom on side branches, called laterals, that grow from these canes, so don't prune them back. But do protect them, bearing in mind that in areas where winters are cold but not mind numbing (average coldest temperatures in the range of 10 above to around zero degrees Fahrenheit), the enemy is not so much the cold itself as it is alternations of freezing and thawing combined with drying winds.

If you're sure the temperature will stay above 5°, leave the canes in place (shielded with a wrapping of burlap if the exposure is extremely sunny or very windy). If you think it will fall to 5° or below, you'll need to give young canes extra protection for their first few winters.

To protect the canes, loosen them from the trellis and gather them into a bundle. Carefully bend the bundle so it's lying (more or less) on the ground, then cover it with about 6 inches of insulation. Old-timers insulate with soil, but some modern experts prefer wood chips because prolonged contact with a wet mound can cause canes to die back. After the plant is well established, it won't need complete burial, but you should continue to insulate the base, up to about 16 inches.

Now then, pruning and training. In spring, after the weather has settled but before strong growth starts, remove anything dead, weak, or twisted. Severely cut back any laterals that bloomed the previous year, leaving two or three "eyes" (the buds that will bring forth blooming stems). Long canes usually put most of their energy into growing straight up. Bend them toward the horizontal to encourage the production of additional laterals. The plant will continue to send out new long canes. Let one or two of them grow each year, so you'll have replacements when, in five years or so, you start removing old, unproductive wood.

Too Late to Prune?

Q **Is December too late to prune my roses? Two plants in my modest backyard plot grew very long shoots this season, and I never got around to pruning. I'm concerned that these will hinder new growth in the spring, but don't want to damage the plants so late in the season with a raw cut.**

A Unless you live south of the Mason-Dixon line, pruning cuts made so late in the season will not heal, and that is almost a guarantee of winter dieback—as much as a foot or two beyond the cut.

The dieback will not kill the cane or the plant, but you will have to prune more in the spring to get rid of it, so you might as well wait and prune only once. When the buds have swollen and growth is clearly under way, take your pruners and get to work.

In the meantime, tie those long canes in so they won't whip around in the winter wind.

THE ROOT OF THE MATTER

Most garden roses are hybrids that will not come true from seed, which means they must be propagated through the use of living tissue. There are several ways to do this, but the most common is bud grafting, a technique that joins a single growth bud from the desired rose to the stem and roots of a carrier plant (the understock, or rootstock).

Bud grafting allows growers to make many new rose plants from just one parent. But they can also make new plants by taking a piece of rose stem and getting *it* to grow roots. This process is often used for the largest, most vigorous types, but because it yields fewer plants and takes longer to do it, "own-root" versions of anything else can be hard to find.

Why bother to look? Two reasons. The first is that an own-root rose has greater powers of rejuvenation. It can come back as itself when all the top growth gets killed right to the ground. Grafted plants will come back as the understock.

The second is that understock roses often present problems of their own. It's not a bonus to have your prized beauty sitting on top of *Rosa multiflora,* a bully that tends to take over unless vigorously policed. And northern growers find little to love in the most commonly used understock, a dull red climber named 'Dr. Huey.' It's rated hardy to zone 5, but it isn't really happy north of zone 6, and neither are the zone 5 roses that are grafted to it.

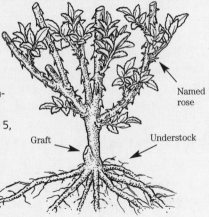

Named rose

Graft

Understock

Strange Sprouts on Roses

Q **I have some old hybrid tea roses that have sprouted long canes with small leaves, much like those found on climbers. Is there some mutation that takes place in hybrid teas that accounts for this, and what can I do to prevent it?**

A What you are seeing is not a mutation but a takeover by the understock, also called the rootstock, the foundation plant on which your hybrid tea was grafted to make it sturdier. It's likely the new canes and leaves resemble a climber because they are a climber, and it's likely that climber is 'Dr. Huey,' a very vigorous rose that holds up a great many of its more fragile kin. If in fact these shoots, which are called suckers, are from 'Dr. Huey,' they will eventually bear his semidouble red blooms.

If you look closely at the offending new canes, you will find they are sprouting from below the graft point, which looks like a bulbous knot and should be right above or right under the ground. To prevent them from overwhelming the hybrid tea, simply cut them off at the point of origin. 🌰

Black Spot Control

Q **I think my roses may have black spot, but I don't want to use toxic chemicals. Assuming it *is* black spot, what can I do?**

A Black spot is a nasty fungus (*Diplocarpon rosae*) that attacks roses, causing circular black spots with fringed margins to form on the foliage. Infected leaves eventually turn yellow and drop, leaving the plants severely damaged and nearly nude. Because the spores are spread by splashing water, the fungus is worse in periods of rain or high humidity.

Preventive sprays made from nontoxic ingredients (see the box on page 158) can help quite a bit. You can also try to control the fungus by keeping the foliage dry between rains (water only at the base of the plant), pruning off infected canes, and removing diseased leaves from the soil.

Leaf cleanup is especially important in autumn, since the fungus spends the winter on infected leaves and canes. 🌰

Reluctant Roses

Q **I have two 'Queen Elizabeth' climbing roses on a west-facing wall that gets sun all afternoon. The bushes are about five years old. They have lush foliage but have produced only one flower between them in all these years. I have cut them back severely; I have also let them grow. The canes get 12 to 14 feet long but do not bloom. I give them rose food in the early spring, hoping that if I'm good to them they will produce, but no luck.**

'Queen Elizabeth'

Roses

A Try a little benign neglect. 'Climbing Queen Elizabeth' blooms only on old wood, so no matter how long they get, those canes have to winter over before they will produce their medium pink flowers.

In early spring, as soon as new growth appears, remove any wood that's obviously dead. A couple of weeks later, go back and cut off anything that looks sickly, cutting back beyond the point of weakness and dipping the pruners in alcohol between cuts. Don't cut anything else. Apply the eats and stand back. 🌿

HOMEMADE FUNGUS-PREVENTION SPRAY

There are many variations on the recipe below, all of them based on baking soda, which is environmentally benign if used in small quantities. It works because fungus diseases such as black spot and powdery mildew need acid conditions to thrive. Baking soda, being alkaline, neutralizes leaf surfaces and keeps the fungus spores from taking hold.

Adding a spoonful of detergent helps the soda cling to the leaves. Adding summerweight horticultural oil increases the fungus-preventive punch while also helping the spray to stick. It's important to have the spray come out as a fine mist, so use a garden sprayer, not an ordinary squeeze bottle.

Make a fresh batch of mixture each time you spray. Be sure you get the whole plant, including the underside of the leaves. Spray in the early morning; horticultural oil applied when temperatures are high can damage sensitive plants, and wetting leaves in the evening is counterproductive when you are dealing with black spot.

Finally, spray often. The mixture does not last long and its effects are entirely preventive. This isn't a cure, so if you wait until you have problems, you will have waited too long.

Ingredients:
1 gallon water (not chlorinated)
1 tablespoon baking soda
1 tablespoon summerweight horticultural oil (optional)
1 tablespoon detergent (dishwashing liquid works fine)

Salting the Roses

Q I read somewhere that I should put Epsom salts around my rosebushes. Is this a good idea and if so, how much should I use, how often, and when during the year?

A While Epsom salts belongs on every gardener's shelf, its primary use is in the gardener's bath after a hard day of bending and digging.

There are many gardeners who swear by the salts for their roses or spinach. And perhaps it does help sometimes, because Epsom salts contains magnesium and sulfur, two essential micronutrients. Magnesium is found in chlorophyll, which helps plants turn sunshine into food, and sulfur is used to make several proteins. If your soil were deficient in one of these elements, Epsom salts might do some good, but most specialists in plant nutrition say that average garden soil contains enough sulfur and magnesium in forms that are readily available to the plants to keep everyone happy and healthy. 🍂

The Old Rose Cottage

Q I don't ask much for my property, just a shrub that keeps its blooms from spring to early winter in zone 5. Someone suggested fairy roses. I don't want an English manicured look for my rustic cottage, but I was told fairy roses don't look like real roses. True?

A False from start to finish (although you are no doubt being humorous about the modesty of your request). Roses and cottages go together like bagels and cream cheese. The English look, at least as imitated in this country, is usually crowded, informal—anything but manicured. And if we define "real" as original or old-fashioned, individual fairy roses look more like real roses than the uptight hybrid teas at the florist.

But individual roses are not the point. 'The Fairy,' which is technically a polyantha, is famous for covering itself with long, loose clusters of pale pink flowers from late spring until hard frost. The many-petaled blossoms are small, round in bud and flattish after they open. The foliage is dense; leaves

'The Fairy'

Roses

are shiny and dark green. 'The Fairy' is comparatively cold hardy and disease resistant, so it's no surprise that it has been a big seller ever since it was introduced in 1932.

But before you fall in love, bear in mind that in this case, "shrub" refers more to shape than size. 'The Fairy' usually grows no taller than 2½ feet. And don't expect any fragrance. You'll get more perfume from 'Carefree Beauty,' a tough, generous bloomer with bigger, darker pink flowers on a bigger bush. And if after all you go for the classic rose-covered bower around the cottage door, try doing the covering with 'Autumn Sunset,' a hardy, repeat-blooming climber whose fragrant flowers glow apricot-gold. 🌸

WHY WON'T THEY BLOOM?

1. They're thirsty. Which means they're also hungry. No matter how fertile the soil may be, roses that don't get enough water can't absorb the nutrients they need.

2. They're overfed. Too much chemical fertilizer can harm plant roots, leading to general ill health. Too much nitrogen, even from organic sources, promotes the growth of leaves and stems at the expense of flowers.

3. They're in the dark. Most roses must have at least six hours of sun in order to bloom at all, and even the ones that can get by with less do better if they get more.

4. They're just babies. Young plants need to establish a good root system and send out strong canes well covered with foliage before they can turn their attention to flowering.

5. They're hurting. Plants weakened by disease or insect attacks cannot produce the large amounts of healthy foliage necessary for abundant flowers.

Operation Transplant

Q **I have a number of shrub roses that are several years old and have been doing quite well. Unfortunately they are directly in the path of a brick walkway we would like to install. When is the best time to transplant them, and am I likely to be successful?**

A The best transplanting time depends on where you live. From the warmer parts of zone 5 on south, the shrubs will do best if moved in early fall, though early spring is also a possibility. In colder climates, the preference is reversed: it's best to move the roses in spring, as soon as the ground can be worked, but you can also move them in the fall if you do it at least six weeks before hard frost is expected.

Assuming you move them to an area that has good soil, good sun, and good air circulation, relocation should be no problem. But digging up and moving plants does always create some stress, so for best results:

- If possible, choose an overcast day for the transplanting operation.
- Water the roses thoroughly two days before you plan to move them.
- Be sure to prepare the new planting holes *before* you dig up the roses; the less time the roots spend enjoying the light of day, the better. Err on the side of generosity when deciding how big to make the new holes; filling in one that turned out to be too big is a lot easier (on the rose, anyway) than last-minute expansion of a hole that turned out to be too small. It's also wise to have dampened burlap handy to cover the roots if they are going to be exposed for longer than a few minutes.
- If you're transplanting in spring, take the opportunity to remove weak growth and prune for shape. But if you are transplanting in the fall, wait until the following spring before pruning anything unless it has been injured. 🍂

Bundling Up

Q Many of the roses I'm tempted by are described in the catalogs as being hardy to zone 6, or zone 5 "with protection." I live in zone 5. Can you explain how I should provide the protection?

A Start by choosing a protected site: on the south side of a rock wall, for example, or in an enclosed courtyard, or on the leeward side of an evergreen hedge.

If the rose has been grafted, plant it with the bud graft (the lump at the base where the named rose was joined to the roots of something else) 3 inches below the surface of the soil. This will probably mean a slower start into growth each spring, but it will also help protect the graft section from frost damage.

The fun part takes place each fall (or winter). Wait until the plant is completely dormant and the ground is frozen down 2 or 3 inches, then mulch the whole area above the roots with 3 to 5 inches of straw, wood chips, or small evergreen branches. This will prevent the alternate freezing and thawing that can heave the roots from the ground.

Once the ground is mulched, protect the base of the canes from winter sun and windburn with a mound of sandy earth (don't use clay soil), wood chips, straw, or coarsely shredded leaves (not oak) that covers at least the bottom foot of the plant. More is fine, if you can bear it. The canes often die back to the mound and sometimes even farther, so the bigger your heap of insulation, the better.

Burying the bud graft

In fact, if it's really cold you'll need to use the ultimate protection, accurately known as The Minnesota Tip. Starting about a foot from one side of the rose, dig a trench as wide and long as the rose is wide and tall. Make sure the trench is deep enough so you can bury the rose halfway. Save all the soil you dug out and have more insulation handy.

Go around to the other side and dig up half the roots. Tilt the rose over so it lies in the trench, then heap the reserved soil over the exposed roots and as much of the rest of the bush as possible. Add additional insulation until you have the whole thing completely covered.

Mounding mulch over the rose bush

Your garden is now decorated with a pretty serious looking heap (or heaps). Hope for snow to turn them into interesting earth sculptures.

When the danger of hard frost is past, remove the protection (and return the plants to their former position if they were tipped). The roses will send out new growth as soon as the ground thaws and the soil starts warming, and that new growth should emerge into the light of the sun.

Minnesota tip

Note: Some garden centers sell styrofoam "rose cones," which supposedly simplify the protection process. They probably do some good, but not enough. And you'll have to look at them all winter. ✿

Why Roses Fail

Q Roses seem to have been increasing exponentially in my neighborhood, but it seems that everyone is growing the same four or five varieties. I am attracted to the more unusual roses, but so far have had miserable luck growing them. Is it simply that there are only a few varieties that can really thrive without constant care?

A Yes and no. There are certainly some roses that take more care than others; hybrid teas are famously fussy, rugosas are equally well known for being nearly trouble free, and there are a few modern roses bred to be as reliable as modern petunias—which, unfortunately, most of them tend to resemble (covered with flowers, scentless, and graceless), except that they're loaded with thorns.

The more complicated but more honest answer is that whether a given rose will thrive in a given situation depends on many factors, including but not limited to: hardiness, disease resistance, and tolerance to such environmental factors as wind and shade.

Variety-specific information about these characteristics is widely available, so it seems as though it should be easy to make wise choices. But no amount of research can protect you from the two most common causes of failure.

The first is the identity problem. Since most commonly sold roses are grafted, only half of the plant you buy is the plant you are buying by name. The roots are something else entirely, something that may or may not be happy at your house.

The second is that it's possible you've simply gotten bad plants. Bad roses used to happen to good gardeners quite often; right up until the late 1990s, much of the most widely used rootstock was infected with a slowly destructive virus.

You can avoid the identity problem by purchasing own-root roses. The virus is a greater challenge. It is less common than it once was but it is still around, so if you have roses that seem to stay sick no matter what you do, get rid of them and plant the replacements somewhere else. 🍏

Roses

EVEN MORE LOCAL THAN POLITICS

There are hundreds of roses available to home gardeners, all of them rated for hardiness, and most rated for disease resistance as well. But this information is, at best, only a rough approximation of reality.

Roses vary remarkably in their reaction to soils, microclimates, locally endemic diseases, and particular insects, so something that flourishes in zone 5 (south coastal Maine) may do horribly in zone 5 (south-central Kansas). And vice versa.

This being the case, nothing can replace local knowledge when it comes to what will thrive in your specific area. Amplify the information in books, magazines, and catalogs by talking with the neighbors and with the nearest extension service. Visit public gardens. And consider joining the American Rose Society, which has branches all over the country, all of them full of rose enthusiasts eager to share their knowledge. You can contact the American Rose Society at P.O. Box 30,000, Shreveport, LA 71130-0030; (800) 637-6534; *www.ars.org*.

A Rambler or a Climber?

Q **What is the difference between ramblers and climbers? Do they have different requirements for care? I'm looking for something that will rebloom and won't require a lot of work.**

A Technically, they're both just long-caned roses, but the following (oversimplified) distinctions are commonly used.

Ramblers have thin, very flexible canes that bloom most profusely in their second year. Many new canes come up every spring, and older ones sometimes send out long shoots, called laterals, that also bloom the year after they form. Almost all ramblers are once-a-year performers, and their red, pink, yellow, or white flowers are usually small. But they produce multitudes when they're in bloom, which may be for as long as six weeks.

Climbers have heavy, stiff canes that live longer than those of ramblers. Their flowers are formed on laterals that grow from canes at least two years old. Climbers can be almost any height, and they offer a great range of flower colors, sizes, and stem lengths. Many of them rebloom, sending out repeated flushes of flowers from late spring until hard frost.

Ramblers take very little care; most are vigorous and thorny, able to scramble up trees or trellises pretty much on their own. Just guide them where you want them to go and keep cutting out the deadwood.

Climbers are fussier. They usually need to be attached to the framework on which they will grow, and once the desired height is achieved, the canes that form the basic structure must be trained to grow outward. Climbers also require more pruning. In addition to normal maintenance, laterals need to be cut back in spring. And once the plant is well established, the basic structure must be renewed from time to time.

There are hundreds of reblooming long-caned roses, but many of them are quite tender, so it's best to read the menu starting with the climate zone. Since the parenting wood must survive the winter, hardiness trumps all other factors when you go to make your choice. 🍂

Shade Lovers?

Q I saw in a catalog that 'Gruss an Aachen,' a floribunda, will flower in shade. Is this true? Are there any other roses that will flourish in the shade?

A It depends on what you mean by flourish and what you mean by shade. 'Gruss an Aachen' is justly famous for producing flowers with less than the usual minimum of six hours of bright sunlight a day. It can get by on three or four hours, and will even bloom (modestly) where the light it gets is somewhat filtered at all times.

But it will not be anywhere near as glorious as it would be if it got more sun, and that is equally true of other shade-tolerant roses such as the gallicas, the albas, and the hybrid musks. If your site is especially challenging, try the pink-and-white single called 'Ballerina.'

Catalogs tend to call a rose shade-tolerant if anybody, anywhere, ever got the thing to bloom in low light, so be skeptical when reading. Keep in mind that disease resistance is as important as flowering ability; fungal afflictions flourish in shade. And be sure that whatever you choose is fully hardy in your zone; shade-grown plants are usually weaker than those that get full sun.

Finally, keep the shade source in mind. If the gloom is being cast by an inconvenient wall, a shade-tolerant variety may grow well enough to bloom, but when a rose must compete with shallow tree roots for every morsel of food and water, lack of sun is likely to be the least of its problems.

Coddling Topiary Roses

Q I love the topiary-like tree roses, but somehow they look like they would be difficult to care for. Are they?

A Alas, yes. Tree roses, also known as standards, are not for the casual gardener. It takes a lot of coddling to keep these delicate creatures in good health, largely because they are constructed from three different plants: one for the roots, one for the interstem (that long, straight trunk), and the pretty named variety blooming away on top.

That's two grafts, one at the base and one where the branching starts. Each makes the plant more vulnerable than a rose grown on its own roots, and the upper one is especially in danger from freezing, wind damage, or whatever strain your personal environment offers.

So unless you live in a mild climate where breezes are always gentle, you have to protect your tree, which many do by keeping them in pots, in itself a high-maintenance proposition except in the case of miniatures. You also have to prune carefully (and often) so the top stays shapely and keeps putting out new blooms.

Feeding Roses

Q When and what should I feed my roses? Are organic fertilizers better than chemical ones?

A As a general rule, organic fertilizers are better than chemical ones because they are gentler to the plant, contain many important trace nutrients, and contribute to soil health. But an occasional booster of balanced rose food won't do any harm as long as you—and the plant—don't get dependent on chemical quick fixes instead of fertile soil.

Although every rosarian seems to have his or her own special formula, and some strongly favor equal amounts of these three basic nutrients, most experts advise going somewhat heavy on the nitrogen, quite light on the phosphorus, and medium on potassium (18-6-12 and 15-5-13 are typical formulations).

When to feed and how much to apply varies with the quality of the soil and the type of rose being fed. Other things being equal, fast-draining, sandy soils need supplementation more often than rich, moisture-retentive loams.

As for the type-of-rose aspect, it's simplest to say that the more frequently a plant blooms, the hungrier it is likely to be. Most roses that flower only once a year need little more than good soil to grow in, while repeat bloomers like grandifloras, floribundas, and hybrid teas usually do better if each bloom cycle is supported with another meal.

In practice, this means one feeding in early spring for everybody, then follow-up feedings at six-week intervals for heavy bloomers only. It is easiest to start out with dry fertilizer, then follow up (if necessary) with foliar feeding.

Many rose growers also give their plants a good shower of seaweed extract in early midseason. Others swear by vitamin potions that are not themselves fertilizers but do stimulate healthy growth. 🍂

A Hedge of Thorns

Q **I would like to have a hedge of roses in my yard. What would you recommend? Is it too much to ask for a reblooming hedge?**

A Not at all. Finding a rebloomer is easy; just leaf through any good catalog, where you'll find many roses, both old and modern, that will make bushes large enough to fill your bill. Or you could simply plant a rugosa.

Rugosas and their hybrids are hardy plants that make thick, thorny barriers that need only minimal care. Most of them bloom enthusiastically in late spring, intermittently throughout the summer, and then modestly in fall. As a rule, they drop their petals cleanly, and some make beautiful hips, as bright and cheerful as flowers.

Among whites, the best-known and most consistent performer is 'Blanc Double de Coubert,' a fragrant near-double about 5 feet tall that makes up for its scanty hips with better than average fall color.

Similarly famous (and alas, similarly shy in the hip department) is 'Roseraie de l'Hay,' a 6-footer with large, loose, dark pink to magenta flowers that have a very strong scent. For plenty of fruit, choose the slightly darker violet-pink 'Hansa.' It grows 4 or 5 feet tall and wide, makes many, highly scented double flowers, and holds on to its hips. ❧

Rose of the Year

Q Is the Rose of the Year worth planting? I've seen them advertised in my local nursery the past couple of years and am wondering if this is a marketing gimmick or if they are indeed worth trying.

A The Rose of the Year is indeed a marketing device. There are rules about how it's used in Britain, but in the U.S. the phrase means little, and American gardeners are better off putting their trust in the title AARS Winner.

All-America Rose Selections is a nonprofit, industry-sponsored organization that tests new roses before they are released for sale, putting them through two years of trials in public gardens all over the country. Experienced rose judges score the contestants on 15 relevant characteristics, including vigor, growing habit, flower form, and color.

The roses are anonymous during the AARS judging process. Scores are collated, which tends to cancel out regional differences and differences of taste; and only the roses with high scores make the AARS grade. There are no rules about numbers of winners, so some years there are several and other years, only a couple.

On the downside, the idea *is* to move lots of roses; only one year has been winner-free since the Selections started in 1938. And the AARS winners are picked from a pretty limited field—new introductions from those companies that choose to participate. Even when they are truly splendid, they're only a tiny speck in the spectrum of wonderful roses. ❧

BLOOMS IN THE VASE

Ideally, long-lasting rose bouquets start two days before you make them.

Day 1. Water the plant well.

Day 2. In the mid to late afternoon, cut flowers that are just starting to open. Bring them into the house and remove all leaves and thorns that would be under water in the finished arrangement.

Fill a deep, clean bucket with warm water. Add commercial floral preservative at the recommended strength, or stir in 2 tablespoons of sugar and 1 teaspoon of bleach per gallon.

Put the roses in the bucket, recutting each stem at an angle while it's under the water. Once they're standing up, the roses should be submerged almost to their necks (it's okay to submerge leaves and thorns that will be out of the water at arrangement time). Put the bucket in a cool, dark place overnight.

Day 3. Fill the vase with tepid fresh water and add preservative as before. If you are using floral foam such as Oasis, let it sit in the vase for half an hour before you start inserting flowers. Again recut the stems under water and then place them in the vase.

All this will be in vain if you keep the arrangement in bright sunshine or under hot lights. If that kind of stressful exposure is essential, don't forget to store the bouquet somewhere cool and dark when it is not on view.

Rose Rejuvenation

Q My rosebushes look devastated from a long, cold, snowless winter. Can they be rejuvenated by cutting them way, way back, as I did with several of my winter-weary shrubs?

A Climbers and large shrub roses will get a second childhood all right; but since these classes don't bloom much before becoming adolescent, you'll have to wait a couple of years before you see many flowers. Hybrid teas, grandifloras, and floribundas, on the other hand, should recover more quickly.

But those distinctions don't matter much now that the damage is done, and all you're really doing is a more drastic version of what you should do every spring: cut back to the point where the plant is strong and healthy.

Roses

Dead is dead, so there's no point in leaving *that;* and wood that is weak or sickly is likely to fall prey to disease. Even if it doesn't get sick, it will sap plant energy that would be better spent building healthy new canes.

Make lemonade from your sour situation by taking this opportunity to prune for a good basic structure. The classic description is "vase-shaped," which means the canes should rise out and up in an evenly widening circle (or fan, if the rose is a climber).

Cut away any canes that are growing toward the center of the plant. Where there are two strong canes right next to each other, remove one. The survivor will get better air circulation, and is more likely to send out balanced new growth.

One warning. If the top growth of a grafted rose is dead all the way down to the bud union, that swollen joint where the named rose meets the rootstock of a different plant, your rose is history. Dig up the roots, get rid of them, and start over. 🌿

"THE WORLD'S MOST EXPENSIVE ANNUAL"

This sobriquet is often applied, with a great deal of justice, to the gorgeous hybrid teas that beckon from garden centers in springtime. But why *not* just enjoy them for a single season? A containerized hybrid tea does cost more than a six-pack of petunias, but so what? It costs less than a long-stemmed dozen from the florist, and for your money you get a bush that can flower all summer, sending out one beautiful bloom after another for three months or more. As a bonus, once you accept that it's annual, you can get rid of it with a clear conscience as soon as it starts to flag.

Outdoor Houseplant

Q A friend gave me a miniature rose in a fancy pot as a birthday gift, but the truth is I hate houseplants. Could I plant it outside somewhere? (I live in Colorado.)

A Probably, but with one caution. Though most miniature rose varieties are by nature easy to care for and comparatively hardy (usually to zone 5), plants like yours have never lived in anything like a garden. They are raised in greenhouses, heavily fertilized, and repeatedly doused with strong biocides to keep pests and fungi at bay.

This means that they're in no shape to brave the real world when they first leave the tender care of their sellers. To turn your gift horse into one that will show well in the garden, you will have to proceed slowly.

You can plant it out anytime from the date of the last frost in spring to six weeks before first frost in fall. But not right away! For the first few days, just set the pot in the shade for three or four hours, and then bring it back in.

After that, start putting it out in the shade in the morning and bringing it in at night. After about a week of this treatment, it should be ready to get morning sun; and after a week of *that,* it should be ready for anything. Including being planted where it is to grow. 🌸

Quenching a Thirst

Q **How much water should my rosebushes get? So far, I have let nature take its course and they seem to be doing very well despite the fact we have had very little rain this summer.**

A It's possible they are doing well because you have highly water-retentive soil, in which case you will be in trouble as soon as the rain resumes (roses hate wet feet). Otherwise, you should provide the water that nature is withholding.

Roses do best when they grow in soil that is consistently moist—but not wet—for most of the root zone. Established plants with large root systems can survive longer in dry conditions than newly planted ones, but survive is about all you can say. No rose can grow or bloom well if it's thirsty.

The standard expression of moisture requirement is "1 inch of water a week," meaning "as much water as the rose would get if there were an inch of rainfall," but this ignores important differences between soils. A rose growing in sandy ground that's low in humus might need twice as much water as one growing in rich loam over clay.

To figure out how much your roses need, turn on the watering system you plan to use (drip, sprinkler, or hose) and let it run for 10 minutes, then turn it off and do something else for a half hour or so.

When the half hour is up, dig a test hole next to the rose, right outside the root zone, and see how far down the water has penetrated. Adjust the watering time as necessary to get moisture all through the root zone, then wait three or four days.

Dig again. The top inch or two of soil may be dry, but things should still be damp farther down. They can be less damp than they were on watering day; in fact they should be, but if you're looking at soil that is dry at 3, 4, or 5 inches underneath the surface, get ready for watering twice a week (and get some more organic matter into the soil before you do any more planting). 🍂

Old Rebloomers

Q My husband and I were besotted with the old roses we saw on garden tours this spring, and would like to plant some in the yard. Are there any old roses that rebloom?

Some modern roses have been bred to look like heirlooms.

A The Bourbon, China, and Damask classes include many remontant roses, as those that bloom more than once a year are called. But although they do bloom repeatedly, they don't do it with the enthusiasm of roses that came after 1867, the year hybrid teas appeared to mark the great divide between "old" and all that has come after.

If you're willing to settle for the look of the thing instead of the thing itself, you might like to explore some of the modern roses that have been developed to look— and smell—like the old ones, while blooming much more frequently. David Austin's English roses are the most famous, but there are also the Romanticas, bred by the well-known French House of Meilland, and also from France, the Generosa series, a trademarked collection developed by the Roseraie Guillot.

When making your choice(s), be particularly attentive to hardiness and skeptical about claims that something can be grown in Zone Whatever "with protection" against winter cold. Not only is providing protection time-consuming (and unattractive), it is by no means a guarantee that the rose, having survived, will thrive. 🍂

PERFUMED ROSES

For many gardeners, it isn't a rose if it doesn't smell sweet, and somehow word has gotten around that only old roses are fragrant. Happily, that isn't true; there are quite a few modern roses with very strong perfumes.

When you listen to rose experts describe fragrance, it's clear that a rose is not always a rose. Some smell of cloves, many, famously, of tea, others of lilies or lilacs or fruit. Like fine wines, some roses have faint hints of tobacco or fallen leaves. Much of this, however, is subjective, so don't be surprised if you don't pick up the same nuances that the rosarians do.

Potted roses can easily be put to the sniff test. But if you are mail-ordering, you might like to try one of the following, all of which are highly reliable in the fragrance department:

'Félicité Parmentier' (Alba) Very double flowers, almost flat when open; pale pink with silver tones. Spring bloomer.

'Mme. Isaac Pereire' (Bourbon) Enormous, rather floppy, deep pink double flowers; a large shrub where happy. Remontant.

'Margaret Merril' (Floribunda) Ruffled double flowers of pale pink to white, with golden stamens. Plants are short but rebloom is good.

'New Dawn' (Climber) Buds reminiscent of hybrid teas open to somewhat loose double flowers; pale pink, darkening in cold weather. Remontant.

'Perfume Delight' (Hybrid Tea) Deep pink, classic hybrid tea form on long stems. Recurrent.

'Rose de Rescht' (Portland?) Extremely double, reddish magenta fading to purple pink. Remontant.

'Apothecary's Rose' (*Rosa gallica officinalis;* Gallica) Semi-double, light red, spring blooming; petals retain fragrance when dried. Remontant.

'Sir Thomas Lipton' (Hybrid Rugosa) Double white with copper stamens that show when flower is fully open; bush is large and very thorny. Remontant.

'The Prince' (Austin) Large, dark red-magenta flowers that look like cups full of petals. Remontant.

'Zéphirine Drouhin' (Bourbon) Bright pink, semi-double flowers in spring and fall; a climber; slow to get started but will grow large once established. Remontant.

Note: Even very fragrant roses sometimes have only faint perfume in cold weather, when growing conditions have been stressful—or occasionally, out of sheer cussedness.

Roses

10 (COMPARATIVELY) EASY ROSES

O ther things being equal, species roses are tougher than hybrids, and roses on their own roots are more forgiving than those that have been grafted. Once-blooming shrub and climbing roses are almost always easier than rebloomers, and everything else in the world of roses is easier than hybrid teas.

For maximum grief-avoidance, gardeners in zone 5 and north should concentrate on hardiness; those in zone 6 on south should bank on disease resistance.

'Autumn Sunset' (Climber) Very cold hardy and disease resistant. Semi-double, fragrant flowers in apricot-gold or very pale orange, depending on how you see these things.

'Betty Prior' (Floribunda) The plant is short and the fragrance delicate, but the single, true pink flowers are abundant and charming and well set off by the darker pink of the buds.

'Bonica' (Shrub) Good foliage and repeated flushes of double pink flowers on a bush that may reach 4 by 5 feet. Lots of small orange hips. Functionally fragrance-free.

'Carefree Beauty' (Shrub) Large, loosely double pink flowers opening from narrow buds. Moderate fragrance and good cutting stems on a bush large enough to have presence without overwhelming its neighbors.

'Knock Out' (Shrub) Phenomenal disease resistance, near constant flowering, and plenty of medium green foliage on a well-rounded, 3-foot bush. Not fragrant, not graceful, not easy to integrate with other colors; masses of single flowers are a screaming scarlet-magenta euphemized as cherry red.

Rosa rugosa alba (Species) Hardy and disease resistant, with deeply wrinkled foliage and high pink-tinged buds that open to very fragrant single white flowers. Good recurrence, though nothing like the tireless bloom most modern roses strive for. Huge orange hips, and frequently good foliage color in autumn.

'Scarlet Meidiland' (Shrub) More like a ground cover than an upright bush. Low and wide, and well covered with loosely doubled, clear red flowers borne in large sprays. Small, rather shiny, medium green leaves. Negligible fragrance.

'The Fairy' (Shrub) Very nearly unkillable. The 2½- to 3-foot bushes are covered from early summer to mid fall with large clusters of small, very double, light pink roses that have only a slight fragrance and tend to fade in the sun.

'Thérèse Bugnet' (Hybrid Rugosa) Huge bush, as much as 6 by 6 feet. Very cold hardy, and strongly fragrant. Though described as blooming continuously, the very double, medium pink flowers often take breaks between flushes.

'William Baffin' (Climber) The hardiest repeat-blooming climber, according to most; it's rated to do well without protection as far north as zone 3. The deep pink, semi-double flowers are not fragrant, but you can't have everything.

Remontant or Recurrent?

Q What is the difference between roses that are remontant and those that are recurrent? Is one more prolific than the other?

A Remontant is an older term, brought into the English-speaking rose world from the French in the late nineteenth century. It refers specifically to roses that bloom at least twice, with distinct rest periods between flowerings. The word recurrent can also be used for those same roses, but it is more commonly applied to roses that bloom in overlapping flushes, with no clearly discernable hiatus between the blooming times. ✿

Growing Bare-Root Roses

Q There is very little choice at my local nursery, so I've been intrigued by a catalog company that sells a huge selection of bare-root roses. Do they take a lot longer to establish than container roses? I am eager to get going.

A Potted roses do offer instant gratification, and if the ones you buy are in flower, you can smell them and check their color (and be sure they haven't been mislabeled). But that's about the extent of the advantages.

Assuming you plant them as soon as the danger of hard frost is past, Grade 1 quality bare-root roses will soon catch up with containerized stock. After all, the stuff in the containers was bare-root when *it* was planted, and that should have been just a couple of months before it was trotted out for sale. (Roses that have wintered over in containers are sometimes available, but they are generally unwise buys; roots can't develop properly in such extreme confinement.) ✿

Bare-Root Roses On Hold

Q We ordered quite a few new bare-root roses before we realized we'd be going away for a vacation shortly after they arrive. I'm not sure we can get them all planted before we go. Is there a way we can keep them on hold until our return?

A Bare-root plants should go in the ground as soon as possible, but newly planted roses need frequent watering. Your best bet is to temporarily "heel them in" when you receive them, and then plant them in their final location when you get back.

Remove the plants from their wrappings, trim damaged roots, and soak the roots for several hours in cool water. Dig a V-shaped trench deep enough to hold both the roots and the bud union, the lumpy place at the base of the stem where the named rose was grafted onto the rootstock. Keeping the plants separated so the roots don't tangle, lean them against one side of the trench and backfill loosely; don't tamp the soil down hard. Water thoroughly.

If the soil is moisture retentive and the trench is in shade, you can probably get away with leaving the roses unattended for about three weeks. (Mulch the ground over the roots with a thick layer of straw or shredded bark, making sure none of it touches the rose canes, and hope for rain.) If your soil is sandy and/or the trench has to be in the sun, bury—or at least shade—the canes, and prevail on the neighbors to come and water at least once or twice while you're gone.

Harvesting a Friend's Roses

Q We are house-sitting for a friend who has many rosebushes. She said I was welcome to cut flowers for the house, but I'm not sure how. If I take stems as long as the ones from the florist, the bushes will be devastated. Where do I cut to be sure I don't hurt her plants?

A The best place to cut is individual to each bush, but following these general rules should keep you both in roses and out of trouble.

First, be sure your pruners are sharp. Second, use common sense. You can cut long stems from large, healthy plants; small plants mean short bouquets. Third, always cut above a leaf stem with at least five leaflets. And finally, cut as you would prune: immediately above an outward-facing bud or a small stem, at a 45-degree angle that slopes down toward the center of the plant.

On hybrid teas, you can usually count on a stem of 6 to 10 inches. On cluster-blooming bushes, the stem could be 3 to 9 inches, or even longer.

Flowers cut in early morning or late afternoon last better than those cut at midday. But the most important key to long vase life is to recut the stems under water after you get them indoors.

Caution: Reblooming roses will keep flowering well into the fall, but since the new growth encouraged by cutting needs time to toughen for winter, harvesting should stop a month before the first expected frost. 🌰

Always cut right above a five- (or more) leaflet leaf stem with an outward-facing bud in the node.

CHAPTER FOUR

Bulbs

Bulbs in General

Timing Their Spring Appearance

Q **I'd like to have a long show of spring-flowering bulbs. When do the different ones bloom?**

A The actual date of spring bloom for bulbs varies with the region and microclimate. Crocuses planted in a city balcony or patio container in full sun, for example, will bloom before those planted at the edge of a sheltered country lane.

A few favorites, in their approximate order of spring appearance, are the winter aconite, snowdrop, crocus, dwarf iris, squill, miniature daffodil, botanical tulip, grape hyacinth, and daffodil. These are followed by the single and double tulips, the Triumph and Darwin tulips, and hyacinth. Later bloomers include the parrot and lily-flowered tulips, wood hyacinth or Spanish blue bell (*Hyacinthoides hispanica*), fritillaria, quamash (*Camassia cusickii*), and *Allium giganteum.* ☙

IT'S A CORM! IT'S A RHIZOME! IT'S A TUBER! IT'S A BULB!

In common usage and catalogs, all these dry-surfaced lumps of underground energy-storage are called bulbs, but in reality there are significant differences among them.

Bulb: Overlapping scales of tissue, each capable of forming a leaf, attached to a basal plate from which the roots grow. Flower buds for the next growth cycle are formed in the center and are already present when the bulb starts growing in spring. True bulbs are the only plants that pre-form the flower in this way. Examples: allium (including onions), daffodil, tulip, lily.

Bulbs (narcissus, tulip)

Corm: An enlarged, solid stem base, with a growth bud at the top and a basal plate on the bottom. Examples: acidanthera, crocus, freesia, gladiolus.

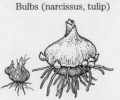
Corms (crocus, gladiolus)

Rhizome: A thickened length of underground stem, with growth buds at intervals along it, and a horizontal growth pattern. Examples: bearded iris, canna, ginger.

Tuber: A thickened piece of underground stem, more variable in shape than a rhizome, with growth buds variously distributed on top, along the sides, all over, or in the case of dahlias, clustered at the end where the tuber is attached to the parent stem. Examples: anemone, tuberous begonia, dahlia, potato.

Rhizome (iris)

Tubers (begonia, dahlia)

Up Too Early?

Q **The weather has been crazy this winter—cold one day, then warm the next. It's only the beginning of February, so there's a lot of cold still to come, but yesterday I noticed that many of my spring bulbs were starting to break the surface of the dirt. I am very scared that these new leaves are going to freeze and not be productive. Is there anything I can do to save my spring flowers?**

A No, there's nothing you can do, so you'll be relieved to know there's nothing you need to do, either.

Those leaves are tough, able to withstand many freezes and thaws without suffering lasting damage. And even if the leaves do succumb, fear not; they are just advance scouts, not the blooming army.

The flower buds for your daffodils, tulips, and hyacinths were formed last year (fed by last year's leaves) and are now safely tucked inside the bulbs, waiting for their pre-determined rest time to pass.

It takes more than a few warm days to trick the buds into premature growth, and although they are a bit more delicate than the leaves, they, too, can stand quite a bit of cold. ✑

SUMMER SPLENDOR:
TENDER BULBS FROM THE TROPICS

The plants known as summer bulbs are like spring bulbs in that they use a wide assortment of true bulbs, corms, rhizomes, and tubers for energy storage. But unlike spring bulbs, they are not frost hardy. Gardeners in temperate zones must plant them each spring and—if they don't want to keep buying new ones—must also dig them up in fall and store them over the winter.

Although this didn't bother the Victorians, who were big summer-bulb fans, over time these tender beauties gradually fell out of fashion. Fortunately, fashion is ever changing, and summer bulbs are again a hot item, with new introductions constantly entering the market.

The big four—which never really went away—are cannas, dahlias, gladiolus, and tuberous begonias, but they are just the start of a list that also includes acidanthera, sometimes called the peacock orchid (*Gladiolus callianthus*), which has tubular white flowers with a deep purple throat; the Mexican shell flower or tiger flower (*Tigridia pavonia*), whose iris-shaped, spotted flowers come in many bright hues; the Peruvian daffodil or ismene (*Hymenocallis narcissiflora*), which has fragrant white or yellow daffodil-like blooms; and agapanthus, which has lush clusters of narrow leaves and starry clumps of blue or white flowers.

Want more? How about the bright yellow, orange, and orange-red wands of *Crocosmia ×crocosmiiflora* and its several close relatives; the tall, fragrant, white-flowered *Galtonia candicans,* sometimes called summer hyacinth; and perhaps most fragrant of all, the tuberose (*Polianthes tuberosa*).

All these and more are easy to plant, easy to love, and readily available, but to be sure of the widest selection, consult specialty catalogs as well as your local garden center.

Acidanthera
(*Gladiolus callianthus*)

SPRING BULBS THAT SPRING ETERNAL

Not all spring bloomers have great staying power. Hyacinths, for instance, are notorious for their tendency to dwindle over the years. The flamboyant large fritillarias behave similarly; and outside of the species types, there are very few tulips that will stick around for long. But if you have sunny, well-drained ground, and at least some winter (they need the rest period), there are many spring-flowering bulbs that will become permanent fixtures in the landscape.

Tops on the list are narcissus, often listed as daffodils, especially the multi-flowered Triandrus group, the Jonquilla group, the flat-faced, fragrant Poeticus group, and the old-fashioned Trumpets.

Species crocuses, including *Crocus chrysanthus, C. sieberi,* and *C. tommasinianus,* are reliable colonizers. Large-flowered crocuses do almost as well.

Other good choices include glory-of-the-snow (*Chiondoxa* spp.), scilla, and rock garden irises including *Iris bucharica, I. histrioides,* and *I. reticulata.*

Big, gaudy alliums often fade over time, but small ones such as *Allium cernuum, A. moly,* and *A. triquetrum* can naturalize so enthusiastically that they cross into the weed class, and the same is true of common grape hyacinths, *Muscari armeniacum.*

Summer Bulbs

Q **When do I plant summer-flowering bulbs? I know they aren't supposed to freeze, but is it O.K. to plant them in cool soil? The season here in Vermont is so short; I want to get them in as soon as possible.**

A Summer bulbs are tropical types that want summer conditions. They will start sprouting when the soil is still less than toasty, but if it is downright cold, they'll sulk, and if they sulk in soil that is damp as well as cold, they're likely to rot.

So people in short-season areas have two options: the first is simply to wait for warm weather and then wait for flowers; the other is to give plants like crocosmias, acidantheras, and dahlias a short head start indoors.

Since you don't want to have to worry about providing greenhouse conditions, wait until it's near the frost-free date, then plant your summer beauties in a free-draining seed-starting medium like Pro-Mix. Water well, then set the pots (or for small bulbs, plug flats) where they will be warm but not hot, 60° to 65°F. Add water only as necessary to keep the soil barely moist, and do not fertilize.

It should take a couple of weeks before sprouts show above the soil and start needing light, by which time the weather should be warmer. Set the pots outside in a sheltered spot where they will get plenty of sun but be protected from cold winds, and be prepared to move them indoors if the temperature threatens to go below 55°. Once you're sure the weather has settled in a warm direction, transplant into the garden. ☙

Blue Mold on Bulbs

Q **Some bulbs I received by mail for fall planting have a powdery blue mold on them. Should they be planted or returned?**

A Wipe the mold off with damp paper towels and plant the bulbs. This *Penicillium* mold, a cousin several times removed from the mold that makes penicillin, is a surface mold and is not a serious problem. Bulbs contain moisture, and keeping them in a closed package allows a buildup of humidity, which encourages the mold. ☙

Speedy Growers

Q **I'm only in my Maine garden for July and August. Are there any summer-flowering bulbs I can plant and see bloom in that time frame?**

A Not many, if you're starting with unsprouted bulbs. The only sure thing is ismene, or Peruvian daffodil (*Hymenocallis* spp.), which blooms anywhere from three to six weeks after the bulbs meet the soil. Early-blooming gladiolus, planted on the first day of July, take longer, but they might just make it to flower before you leave. Calla lilies are worth a try on the same basis.

Fortunately, garden centers usually sell summer "bulbs" such as tuberous begonias and dahlias that have been growing for some time and are already in bloom. Cannas that are well on their way, if not yet in flower, are increasingly available too, as gardeners become more and more interested in these dramatic old favorites.

And of course there are lilies, summer-blooming bulbs of the most splendid sort. They are not "summer bulbs," because they are frost hardy, but they do flower in

Ismene
(*Hymenocallis* spp.)

July and August when you will be there to enjoy them. Dormant lily bulbs are only available in spring and fall, and they don't store well out of the ground, so unless there is someone to plant your lilies before you get there (or after you leave), you'll have to buy started plants.

Buying potted lilies will limit your choices and strain your purse, but if you plant them carefully—and don't cut more than a third of the stem if you insist on cutting the flowers—you'll have the pleasure of more and more with each succeeding year. 🌰

Container Bulbs

Q **Is there any reason why I can't plant tulips, or other bulbs, in the whiskey tubs on my property? There is good drainage on the bottom, but will they be more susceptible to mice and other animals that might look upon them as food?**

A As long as you choose hardy bulbs, and the tubs are large enough (or well-enough insulated) so the soil in them doesn't repeatedly freeze and thaw over the winter, whiskey barrels should work as containers for spring-flowering bulbs. But you are right to worry about rodent damage; mice and voles are clever sleuths where sources of food are concerned.

To foil them, use tight-mesh metal screening. Nail one piece to the bottom of the tub and place another over the top, weighted down with bricks or rocks. Remove the top screen in early spring as soon as you see the first green shoots. 🌰

Tolerating Wet Soil

Q **Everything I read about growing bulbs and their ilk includes the phrase "well-drained soil," but the only space I have to garden in is wet, almost marshy. It isn't particularly heavy, and there's lots of organic matter in it, but dampness is definitely a factor. Are there any flowering bulbs (or bulb-like plants) that will do well in these conditions?**

A As long as your damp area gets plenty of sunlight and isn't too acid, you should be able to grow the native American *Camassia,* which comes in several species. All bear starlike flowers on tall stems, rather like slender hyacinths, and come in a range of cool colors from blue to pale purple to white.

If it *is* acid, you can grow streamside iris, *Iris laevigata,* which also comes in shades of blue, and the striking, flat-faced Japanese iris, *I. ensata,* aka *I. kaempferi,* which is taller and offers a broader range of colors.

And if it is warm as well as wet and sunny, you're set up for cannas. They can take quite a bit of moisture; some will thrive even when their roots are constantly wet, as long as the wetness in question is not stagnant.

Let Those Leaves Alone

Q **I recently saw a garden where all the dying bulb foliage had been neatly braided. I have never seen this before. Is it a good idea?**

A The best thing to do after bloom time is to let things alone, allowing the foliage to die at its own pace. When asked about braiding and bundling bulb foliage before it goes completely yellow, Dr. William Miller, a bulb specialist at Cornell University, said, "Unequivocally—don't. Now you never have to ask again."

Until that last drop of chlorophyll is gone, food is being made. Compulsive neatening reduces carbohydrate production because sunlight cannot get to all the leaf surfaces. Cutting prematurely is even worse. If you really need to braid, grow garlic.

Hiding Dying Bulb Leaves

Q **Every autumn, I plant a lot of spring-flowering bulbs. They are gorgeous when they come up, but then there is the inevitable dying foliage to look at. I've tried planting summer-blooming day lilies to help screen unattractive spent leaves. Would other plants work as well without coming up so early that they would interfere with the blooms?**

A As a reward for not cutting down the bulb foliage before it yellows (which would deprive the bulbs of all the food-making ability they need to prepare for next year's bloom), here are a few suggestions for plants that will serve

184

as great-looking minglers while hiding the dying bulb foliage: astilbe, Siberian iris, the pale pink *Geranium macrorrhizum* 'Ingwersen's Variety,' or any of the medium-size hostas, including 'Emily Dickinson,' 'Dorset Blue,' 'Happy Hearts,' 'Bright Lights,' and 'Gold Edger.' You might also try *Stachys byzantina* 'Countess Helene von Stein,' also known as 'Big Ears' (the plant, not the countess). 🌿

Seeking Bulbs with Attractive Foliage

Q **Are there any spring-flowering bulbs with attractive foliage that would be an asset to my perennial garden? The foliage that is, not the bloom.**

A It's a nice thought, but the answer is no. Though the leaves of early-summer bloomers like iris can be an effective accent, almost all spring-flowering bulbs have foliage that starts turning yellow and unattractive shortly after the flowers fade. And those that stay green for a while longer—grape hyacinths, for example—are too small to have much impact. 🌿

Leaving Bulbs Undisturbed

Q **I want to plant perennials to screen the dying foliage of my spring bulbs, but I can't figure out how to do so safely. How do I dig holes for the plants without impaling the bulbs?**

A Start with perennials that are young, or with small divisions of old plants, so you have only a small root system to deal with. That way you can make small, comparatively shallow planting holes above and between the rising bulb shoots.

You have to be patient: baby perennials won't do much screening in their first year, but they will be sending their roots out over the bulbs, building size and strength. They'll be large enough to do a good hiding job by the next spring and will probably be even larger the year after that.

Eventually, of course, they'll need dividing. But since by then the bulbs will probably need dividing too, you can just dig extra-deep and bring up the whole tangle without hurting anything. 🌿

An Unencumbered Lawn

Q **Are there any bulbs that don't need their foliage beyond the time that the flowers bloom? I would like to plant spring-blooming bulbs in my yard but would also like to be able to mow after the flowers are past.**

A All bulbs need their green leaves to manufacture food for winter storage. There are none that will come back year after year without a chance to stock up this nourishment, so gardeners who don't want to deal with foliage in the grass have two options.

The first is simply to replant each year. The fact that bulbs *can* be perennial doesn't mean they have to be, and many mail-order companies offer bulbs in quantity at very reasonable prices. There is more labor involved, of course, but that may be a price you're willing to pay for an unencumbered lawn.

Alternatively, you can concentrate on the smaller-flowered charmers that come up very early, just when winter has lost its grip and spring is still mostly a promise.

Although there are occasional years when the grass starts coming up with them, as a general rule these little beauties are so far out in front of it that they're all set for their summer sleep before it's time to mow.

Examples include snowdrops (*Galanthus*), glory-of-the-snow (*Chiondoxa*), species crocuses—the giant ones bloom later—and Siberian squill (*Scilla*). If you don't mind being careful for just the first two or three mowings, you can add those large later crocuses, dwarf irises including *Iris danfordiae, I. histrioides,* and *I. reticulata,* and early narcissus like 'February Gold' and 'Rip van Winkle.' 🌰

Glory-of-the-snow (*Chiondoxa*), top; *Iris reticulata,* middle; snowdrops (*Galanthus*), bottom

R & R for Bulbs

Q **My question pertains to hyacinths and paperwhites that have been forced in jars. Can I reuse the bulbs in either the forcing jar or my beds outdoors in Michigan? Should I let them dry out and rest? Do I cut off tops and roots?**

A The paperwhites are a one-time thrill, but you can reuse the hyacinths outdoors. Don't cut off anything but the dead flowers, and whatever you do, don't let them dry out.

The first thing most bulbs need after blooming isn't rest—it's recuperation, a chance to grow plenty of the energy-gathering leaves that will feed next year's flowers.

You need to keep the hyacinths growing until you can get them outdoors, so move them, roots intact, out of the jars and into pots filled with potting soil. Bury them up to the neck. Feed once with houseplant fertilizer, diluted to a bit less than half-strength, and allow them to grow in a cool, sunny place until the danger of hard frost is past.

When the weather is settled, transplant to the garden, setting the bulbs at normal depth (which will mean burying some greenery), and proceed as with any spring-flowering bulb.

After a winter, or maybe two, you'll have flowers again. For the first few years, the hyacinths will have only a few widely spaced bells, and they will probably never be as tightly packed with florets as they were in their first year. But they will still be pretty and they will still be fragrant.

Bulb Planting in Late Fall

Q **When is it considered too late in autumn to plant bulbs that flower in spring?**

A It's difficult to say just when late becomes too late. But although spring bulbs are best planted early, as long as the soil is still workable, you can continue planting right through November and even into early December.

Dig a hole two or three times as deep as the bulb's diameter, and position the bulb root-end down. Cover with soil and water well.

FALL: THE THIRD BULB SEASON

Though the list of fall-flowering bulbs is short, the pleasure these late bloomers provide is a long-lasting one. Where happy, they will come back year after year. The biggest trick is finding them: because fall-flowering bulbs do not store well out of the soil, they're not a garden-center item; and because they are mostly known to connoisseurs, mail-order companies do not stock endless quantities. Order early for the best selection.

Colchicum: Though they are often called meadow crocus, colchicums are actually members of the lily family. Fall bloomers include the widely planted *Colchicum autumnale,* with large flowers in white, rose, or lilac; the fragrant, raspberry-pink *C. speciosum;* and numerous hybrids including 'Waterlily,' which looks like its name.

Crocus: There are a *lot* of crocuses; the fall ones mostly make their grasslike leaves in spring, then vanish until the flower spikes appear to cheer the autumn. Specialty catalogs offer as many as a dozen fall-blooming species, the best known of which is the saffron crocus, *Crocus sativus,* whose red stigmas are the source of the world's most expensive spice.

Lycoris: The lycorises, which are actually members of the amaryllis family, make leaves in spring, rest over the summer, then shoot up bright flowers on naked stalks in fall. The bright red-flowered *Lycoris radiata* is not hardy north of zone 8, but the fragrant pink *L. squamigera* (also known as magic lily and rain lily) is fine right through zone 5.

Sternbergia: Like lycorises, these are members of the Amaryllidaceae. The flowers of the fall-blooming one, *Sternbergia lutea,* are bright gold, so the plants are sometimes called autumn daffodils, even though the blossoms look more like crocus than they do narcissus. Unlike the lycorises, they bear their long, narrow leaves in the fall.

Digging for Bone Meal

Q **How can I keep the skunks from digging up spring-flowering bulbs after I plant them? This fall I tried hot peppers, but no luck.**

A Skunks are carnivores. Bulbs are vegetables. Hot pepper won't protect the bulbs because skunks don't eat them; something else in the same hole is calling those skunks to dinner. Occasionally, that's grubs or worms, but usually it's bone meal. As cinnamon is to apple pie, so bone meal is to bulb planting; almost everyone uses it whether they need it or not.

Bone meal, a by-product of cattle processing, is rich in phosphorus, which is important for plant strength and flower quality, and it is an ideal source of this element because it is slow, gentle, and very easy to use—even if you apply too much it won't hurt anything.

Chemical sources such as superphosphate, on the other hand, are quick-acting but very strong, so they must be used carefully. If they touch the roots, they can damage or even kill plants; they unbalance the microscopic life of the soil; and because they're highly soluble, they dissipate rapidly, often washing out of the earth and into the nearest waterway, where phosphorus is a pollutant.

Given these problems, it's no wonder that bone meal has long been the gold standard for phosphorus supplementation. Recently, though, concern about mad cow disease has caused some to ask if humans could become infected by inhaling bone meal from infected cows. The scientific jury is still out, but meanwhile, there are two alternatives.

The first is to just say no. If your soil is rich in organic matter, all that supplemental phosphorus is probably unnecessary.

If stunted growth, decreased flowering, or a soil analysis tells you that you *do* want to add phosphorus, you can use rock phosphate instead of bone meal. It's very slow-acting, but it's also very safe, and not attractive to skunks. 🌺

Feeding Bulbs

Q **I'll be planting my spring bulbs soon. Should I also be adding food now?**

A If you want many seasons of bloom, it's a good idea to work in a bit of rock phosphate at planting time. But it's not necessary to fertilize spring-flowering bulbs when you plant them. Assuming you've bought quality bulbs, next year's bud is already inside and your first season of bloom is assured. Just work the soil thoroughly, so it's friable and drains well.

When the leaves appear in spring, sprinkle some compost or well-rotted cow manure around the base of the plant, or water once with a high-phosphorus soluble fertilizer, diluted to half-strength. 🌺

Endangered Bulbs

Q I want to order some spring bulbs, but I've heard there are many endangered species being collected in the wild. How can I be sure that I am not buying them?

A You can start by buying from dealers who state that their bulbs are not collected in the wild.

Faith Campbell, the director of the plant conservation project of the Natural Resources Defense Council in Washington, advised that shoppers who do their buying from local nurseries question the owner and look for bulb packages that bear the words "grown from cultivated stock."

When buying plants, ask for specifics if you see the label "nursery-grown." It can sometimes mean "gathered from the wild, then potted and grown on by the nursery." 🌸

Bulbs in Particular

Winter Aconite

Q While a student in Michigan, I used to marvel at golden flowers blooming with the winter's first thaw. They were called winter aconite. Is there any trick to growing them in Pennsylvania?

Winter aconite
(*Eranthis hyemalis*)

A These spring bloomers are truly a marvel. Botanically, their genus name is *Eranthis,* Greek for "spring flower." They are tiny members of the buttercup family and one of the earliest flowers to herald winter's end.

The two most commonly planted winter aconites are *E. hyemalis,* a native of western Europe, which will only survive where the soil stays moist, and *E. cilicica,* a native of Asia Minor, Syria, and Greece, which is more tolerant of dry summers.

Both are being overcollected in the wild, so be sure any tubers you purchase have been propagated in a nursery.

Winter aconites should be planted as early as possible in fall, in groups or drifts, much as you might plant crocuses.

In Pennsylvania, as elsewhere, they prefer light shade and do best in a rich, well-drained soil that has good moisture through spring. 🌱

An Autumn Surprise

Q **In Japan I saw a beautiful, bright red flower growing on the edge of rice fields. It is called higanbana—equinox flower—and its appearance coincides with the equinox holiday. Could you tell me its scientific name and whether it is available here? I'd like to have it in my garden.**

A Higanbana is *Lycoris radiata,* known here as spider lily or, less commonly, hurricane lily. It is a member of the amaryllis family.

In winter, the bulb sends up a clump of strappy, dark green leaves. These die in spring and the plant goes dormant. When the weather cools in autumn, up come the spectacular flowers, 4 inches of vivid color on a naked stalk.

They bloom for about 10 days, then die down, and new leaves appear to begin the cycle once more.

That's in Japan. In the American South, where these plants also thrive, they bloom slightly later, usually in mid October at the height of hurricane season.

The bulbs are available by mail order, but you'll have to grow them as houseplants if temperatures in your garden go below 20°F. In that case, consider planting *L. squamigera,* the hardiest lycoris. Unlike *L. radiata,* it offers fragrance, and it does fine all the way north to most parts of zone 5. 🌱

Spider lily
(*Lycoris radiata*)

Sharp Allium

Q **I was at Mohonk Mountain House in New Paltz, New York, in early July and saw a flower that stood about 2 or 3 feet high. The petals were violet or purple, and they were as sharp as little needles. (The inside was a different color.) The area they were planted in probably got full sun. Do you have any idea what this flower could be?**

A It's difficult to say for sure without information about other plant parts like leaves and stems, said John Van Etten, the former grounds superintendent at Mohonk Mountain House, who was in charge of the gardens when you saw them. But he added that since you saw the flower early in the season, he guessed it was an allium.

"The deer don't eat them," he continued, "so we grow many different varieties—*christophii, schubertii,* 'Globemaster.' And we have a lot of them—in the cottage garden, the alpine garden, the butterfly gardens, even some seasonal display beds."

Allium christophii, also known as *A. albopilosum* and sometimes called star of Persia, has clusters of particularly needlelike pale purple petals, each cluster radiating around a green center, but all of those listed by Mr. Van Etten are possibilities.

The easiest way to know for sure is to check out a good fall bulb catalog. Once you do, you'll probably want to plant lots of alliums even if none of them are the flower you're trying to identify. 🌰

For Deer to Turn Up a Nose

Q **I like the idea that ornamental alliums are not attractive to deer, but the ones for sale at my garden center all have flowers that look as stiff as a ball on a stick. Are there alternatives, and if so, where do I find them?**

A One good thing you can say for the deer is that they are slowly building a market for unusual bulbs. Many graceful alliums that were obscure just a decade ago are now available by mail order, if not yet at the garden center.

One of the most striking is the deep pink *Allium schubertii*. It too makes a ball of short-stemmed florets, but these florets are loose, uneven, and only part of the story. The rest is a set of long-stemmed stars that shoot out among them like fireworks.

If you can't bear stars, even shooting, consider *A. bulgaricum,* recently reclassified as *Nectaroscordum siculum* ssp. *bulgaricum*. Its flower is an umbrella of white bells heavily marked with pink and green.

Other choices include the delicate *A. flavum,* which offers relaxed yellow florets set off by long threads of leaf, and *A. cernuum,* the nodding onion, its dark green stems topped by drooping clusters of deep magenta bells. 🌰

Nectaroscordum siculum ssp. *bulgaricum*, left; *Allium schubertii*, right

BULBS FOR DEER COUNTRY

Tulips and lilies are out—deer will go to almost any lengths to eat these flowers. Only the flowers, so you can have lots of great expectations as leaves grow and buds develop. Then, just when the buds start to color, boom!—a garden full of naked sticks.

Fortunately, the list of bulbs that deer leave alone is longer. Alliums, colchicums, narcissus, hyacinths, grape hyacinths, and fritillarias are almost never bothered; and our antlered friends must be hungry indeed before they show any interest in anemones, chiondoxas, scillas, or crocuses.

Autumn Amaryllis

Q What is the autumn amaryllis?

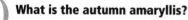

A Autumn amaryllis is one of several common names for *Lycoris squamigera,* also called magic lily or resurrection lily, whose aromatic, trumpet-shaped pink flowers brighten the early autumn garden. These large bulbs, natives of Japan, were once known as *Amaryllis hallii,* and they are members of the amaryllis family.

The common names are a good description of the plant's habit of suddenly sending up flower spikes that reach their full height of about 2 feet within a week or two.

The smooth gray-green, narrow leaves of lycoris first appear early in spring, and then vanish during their resting period in summer. All is quiet above ground, but the roots are still active below the soil, preparing to send up the surprise flower on its naked stalk.

Magic lily
(*Lycoris squamigera*)

L. squamigera bulbs are considered hardy at least to southern New England (zone 5). They are planted in summer, about 5 inches deep, in fertile soil in either full sun or light shade.

Quality bulbs will sometimes bloom the first year, but this species doesn't like to be moved, so they usually take a year or two to begin flowering. Don't despair; once established they will continue to startle you every autumn for years. 🌰

Anemone Anomalies

Q **Some authorities say anemones de Caen are hardy for zones 5 to 9; others say Zones 7 to 10. I live in zone 6. Do I need to lift the bulbs in the fall?**

A Anemone de Caen is the single-flowered group of *Anemone coronaria*. It blooms in red, blue, purple, pink, white, or combinations thereof. It comes from the Mediterranean, and is hardy through Zone Stay Tuned.

Standard sources say zone 7 with protection, or zone 8. But the last two winters in Ithaca, New York (zone 5), have not fazed the coronarias in Cornell University's flower-bulb research program, which is devoted to answering questions like yours.

Dr. William B. Miller, professor of horticulture at Cornell, said that two years is far from definitive, so the zone question is not yet resolved. But so long as the soil is well drained and you put on a good layer of mulch, your bulbs—tubers, actually—should come through fine. 🌸

Anemone de Caen

Seeking Anemone Flowers

Q **Every year I plant many anemones as soon as the weather warms, and every year I get lots of foliage but very few blooms. My garden soil is fertile and well drained and the area gets lots of sun, so why don't I have more flowers?**

A Most likely you are planting them too late. Though there are anemones, primarily the Japanese ones, that produce their flowers in fall, most of these beautiful buttercup relatives are spring bloomers. To set flower buds, they have to form a strong plant while days are cool and short. That's why hardy types such as Grecian windflower (*Anemone blanda*) and pasqueflower (*A. pulsatilla*, aka *Pulsatilla vulgaris*) are usually sold for fall planting.

Since you are planting yours in spring, they are probably the more tender florist's anemone (*A. coronaria*), and with these there is a greater likelihood of getting low-quality stock; if the tubers are very inexpensive, they may not have been given the pre-chilling that encourages bloom, or they may simply be too small. *A. coronaria* tubers don't usually produce flowers until they are about 4 centimeters in circumference, but bins at the garden center are full of examples that would be lucky if they measured 3.

Yet no matter what kind of anemone you're growing, the size at planting should only be a first-year problem. Tubers that produce healthy leaves should grow large enough the first season to bloom the following spring. Could it be that you're tilling the soil each fall, grinding up the next spring's anemones without realizing it?

If not, it's likely that they are down there somewhere; most anemones are hardy to zone 5, and even the more tender coronarias can sometimes survive zone 5 winters as long as the plants are well mulched. If your garden is in the right zone for the species you're trying to grow, and you have not been aggressively tilling, take another look at the soil. It may not be as well drained as you think, and anemones do hate wet feet. 🌰

Help on Windflowers

Q I have tried several times to grow Grecian windflower (*Anemone blanda*), with no success. I even tried planting the bulbs in wire baskets, which convinced me that gophers weren't causing my failure. I admit I cannot detect which end of the bulbs is up, so I planted them vertically, hoping the roots or shoots would figure it out.

Grecian windflower
(*Anemone blanda*)

A *Anemone blanda* bulbs are actually tubers, enigmatic collections of bumps that look more like fossilized animal droppings than anything else. Though many have a slightly flattened quality that might lead you to think there is something vertical going on, it doesn't mean anything.

Fortunately, this is one case where you don't need to know which end is up. It does not matter which way they are planted; commercially, they're just dropped into the soil.

So it isn't orientation that stands between you and a spring carpet of daisylike white, blue, and pink flowers. The culprit is probably poor drainage or clay soil, either of which can lead to rot. According to Dr. William B. Miller, professor of horticulture at Cornell University, "Wet soils are the single most important cause of failure with flower bulbs."

Climate must also be considered. Year-round heat won't do; anemones need a period of cool winter dormancy. And bitter winters would be just as bad. Authorities differ on just how cold-hardy *A. blanda* is, but it does best in places where Fahrenheit temperatures do not fall much further than 0° to 10 below. ❦

Name That Anemone

Q We used to own an old farm near Amenia, New York, where every spring a large patch of the land was carpeted with tiny white *Anemone nemorosa,* and what seemed to be a close relative—same size, same foliage type, but with a frilly, powder-puff center. Now many years after we sold the property, I find I miss those flowers. Can you tell me what they were?

A It sounds as though the anemone relative was a close one indeed, almost surely the double *Anemone nemorosa* 'Vestal,' which has a cluster of tiny upright petals at the center.

On the other hand, it may be that your memory is playing a trick, and that the powder puff was not inside but was instead the flower itself: *A. nemorosa* 'Bracteata Plenifora.' 'Bracteata Plenifora' has a distinctive collar of leaves under a semi-double ruff of petals. The outer row of petals is green, sometimes with a touch of white, while the inner petals are white with occasional flashes of green. The centers are open and flat, but the overall effect is distinctly frilly and does suggest a powder puff, especially when seen from above.

'Vestal,' and 'Bracteata Pleniflora' grow more slowly than plain *A. nemorosa.* Both will, however, eventually spread, if not into carpets, at least into mats, as long as they have the rich moist soil and the filtered shade that gave *A. nemorosa* its common name, wild woodland anemone. ❦

Anemone nemorosa
'Vestal'

Starting Begonias

Q I planted two hanging outdoor begonias about two weeks ago, yet still no sprouts. How long does it usually take? How should they be started?

A It takes forever—or so it seems—for that first sign of life. In fact, the sprouting time can vary from a couple of weeks to well over a month. You just have to be patient and avoid overwatering; the soil should be barely moist.

For plants that are ready to set out in late spring, start the tubers indoors in early April. Plant them about 1 inch deep, in fast-draining soil, concave side up, since that's where the sprouts are.

Once growth starts, keep plants in bright light, and turn them frequently to encourage a well-rounded shape. They like warmth, not heat: 75°F is an optimum temperature indoors and out. Begonias are famous for blooming well in filtered light, but as long as the sun is not scorching they can take a fair amount of it. 🌶

A Mysterious Beauty

Q We just bought an old house with a yard full of blooming spring bulbs. We recognize all except one. It has a ring of white petals with a tuft of yellow threads in the center. Its leaves are roundish and broad, with wavy edges. The plants are about 8 inches tall. Can you tell us what they are? Will they return next year?

Bloodroot
(*Sanguinaria canadensis*)

A It sounds as though you have lucked into a stand of bloodroot, *Sanguinaria canadensis,* a wildflower native to the woodlands of eastern North America. The plants do not grow from true bulbs, but from thick underground stems called rhizomes. Scratch one and you'll see the bright orange-red sap that gives the plant its name.

Bloodroot's lovely flowers are in bloom for only about 10 days, and the equally handsome leaves are usually gone by mid summer. It will not only return next year but spread—as long as it has the light summer shade and moist, slightly acid, humus-rich soil that remind it of home.

You can extend the bloodroot season by planting
S. canadensis 'Multiplex', also known as *S. canadensis*
var. *plena*. It blooms later and lasts longer, but its blooms are
fluffy doubles, far less elegant than those of its wild sister. 🌿

Subterranean Attacks

Q The autumn before last, I planted about 50 English bluebells
(*Hyacinthoides non-scripta*) and 25 crocuses on our wooded property
in Massachusetts. A few of the bluebells came up and none of the crocuses.
Last autumn, I planted 200 bluebells and 50 daffodils. The daffodils came up,
but not the bluebells. It is very discouraging; I would very much like to have
a bluebell woods. I suspect rodent damage. Is there a solution?

A Oh, to be in England, where having a bluebell woods
is easy once you have the woods, and where the delicate, fragrant *Hyacinthoides non-scripta* is the bluebell
you get to have. The taller and scentless, but otherwise similar Spanish bluebells (*H. hispanica*) are more common
in the United States. Though both species are widely sold
in this country, anecdotal evidence suggests the Spanish
ones are more likely to thrive. Cold winters and hot summers both discourage the British from colonizing.

But it sounds as though yours never had a chance to
get discouraged. It's possible that the soil is too wet; most
bulbs need good drainage. Alternatively, as you suspect,
something may be eating them. If so, the something is probably voles. These mouselike rodents adore many bulbs,
including crocuses, and they are impossible to get rid of on
a woods-wide scale.

The best way to find out what's wrong and what to do
about it is to conduct a simple study. Plant small groups of
each species three ways: without protection, and with the
two different protections described below. Plant them 4 or
5 inches deep, all the groups close enough to each other so
that they're growing in more or less the same soil. Be sure
to make above-ground labels.

Protection Method 1: Coat the bulbs with an animal
repellent like RO-PEL or Deer-Off. (Wearing rubber gloves,

put the bulbs in a bucket of the repellent and get them thoroughly covered; let them dry before planting, and wear the gloves for that, too.) These repellents work well, but only in the first year.

Protection Method 2: Plant each group of bulbs surrounded on all sides by a 2-inch layer of tooth-defying gravel. A gravel vole barrier doesn't work quite as well as repellents, but it lasts several years.

Next spring, make note of what comes up. If it's nothing at all, your problem is probably the soil. If you get bluebells, notice which group or groups they belong to, and plant accordingly in the future. 🌶

A Calla Experiment

Q I simply love our callas, but soon my husband will have to dig them out and store them in the basement. He's tired of the annual transplanting and wants to know if our area, near Philadelphia, is warm enough that we can just leave them in the ground. They are near a corner of the house, protected from both north and west winds.

A Zantedeschia, popularly known as callas or calla lilies, are natives of South Africa and can be left in the ground only where they are safe from frost and where cold temperatures are fleeting. Though the large, white-flowered *Zantedeschia aethiopica* 'Green Goddess' is reputedly somewhat tougher than the spotted-leaved hybrids with colored flowers, all of them are better suited to Los Angeles than to Philadelphia.

If your protected corner is very unusual—warmed by proximity to the basement, for example—you could try leaving a couple of plants in the ground and piling an enormous heap of insulating mulch (leaves, straw, old mattresses) over an area large enough to keep the soil they are in from freezing. This would probably be more work than digging them out, and then you would have to look at that mulch pile. But it's worth a try; if it doesn't work, you're not out much. At the worst, you'll have an excuse to try a few new ones. 🌶

Keeping Caladiums

Q The caladiums in my garden gave me such joy this year that I would like to keep them going indoors over the winter. If that isn't practical, can you tell me how to store them for next summer's garden?

A Either way, caladiums are amenable. They can be left in the garden into fall so that the leaves can continue working and the tuber can continue to grow larger. However, once frost is in the forecast, don't stand on ceremony—just dig, taking up the whole plants or only the tubers.

To winter over a caladium, put the tuber into storage immediately or pot up the whole plant and place it in a brightly lighted windowsill. By late January, the caladium is going to look tired and will need to rest before the tuber is repotted in the spring or planted in the garden after the soil has warmed up. Chop off the foliage, knock off the soil, and let the tuber dry at room temperature. Any condensation will encourage bacterial rot. Store the tuber in dry vermiculite or in a mesh bag (like an onion bag) in a dry place, ideally at 70° to 75°F but never below 50°, making sure there is good air circulation. Did I mention it should be stored dry?

Caladium is an extraordinary foliage plant. Its leaves can be white with narrow green borders or combinations of white, green, and rosy pinks, in pale to outrageous patterns that approach a third grader's first attempt at stained glass. Most caladiums are hybrids of *Caladium bicolor* or *C. picturatum,* native to the tropics of the Americas and the West Indies. Plants can be costly, but tubers are inexpensive so you can just say goodbye at frost time if you like. ❧

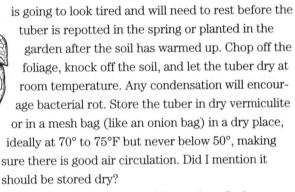

Caladium hybrids

Diseased Cannas

Q The new leaves and flower buds on several of my cannas are black, and some older leaves are distorted and sticky. What's going on here?

A Cannas are vulnerable to a number of different blights and wilts that would cause the symptoms you describe. They are spread by insects, rain, and watering, and are especially troublesome during damp summers. If allowed to spread unchecked, they often kill the plants, and once they take hold they can be difficult to get rid of.

Start by keeping the foliage dry by avoiding overhead watering. And water early enough in the day so that splashed drops disappear before evening.

Good air circulation helps, too, so don't crowd your plants. You can also try controlling the bacteria's spread by snipping off the infected portions as soon as you see them. Be sure to sterilize your pruners afterward in a solution of 1 part household bleach to 10 parts water, since infected tools will also spread the disease.

Unfortunately, these diseases often remain on the rhizomes that are stored away during the winter dormancy, and they also can remain in the soil. If you cannot cure your plants, it's best to remove and discard them, along with the earth that surrounded the rhizomes. And just to be on the safe side, don't plant cannas in the same spot again next year. 🌶

Settling In?

Q Ever since we bought our old house, I have enjoyed the small patches of crocus that come up near the front walk. There aren't many, though, so last fall I planted 200 more bulbs nearby. Now the older crocuses are almost done blooming, but there is no sign of the new ones. Do crocuses take a long time to get established or did I plant a bunch of duds?

A If they were duds, you probably would have noticed soft spots, mold, or other signs of trouble when you were planting them. And though crocuses don't always multiply quickly, they are reliable first-year bloomers.

They do sometimes bloom a bit later the first year than they do in subsequent ones, but the likeliest explanation for the no-shows is that you bought giant Dutch crocus (*Crocus vernus*), and that they are simply waiting to come up when they should, in mid to late spring.

Dutch crocus has the biggest, showiest flowers and is, in our big-show-loving country, the most widely planted type. But the previous owner of your house might have preferred others that bloom earlier.

Possibilities include the small-flowered snow crocus (*C. chrysanthus*), which comes in a wide range of purples, yellows, and bi-colors, as well as white; cloth-of-gold crocus (*C. susianus,* also called *C. angustifolius*), which is actually closer to bronze; and Tommies (*C. tommasinianus*), which come mostly in an array of rich purples. All of these start showing their colors three weeks to a month sooner than their Dutch cousins.

Giant Dutch crocus
(*Crocus vernus*)

Tommies (*Crocus tommasinianus*)

In other words, it sounds as if you were trying for a crocus panoply, but planted a crocus parade instead. 🌿

Saffron in the Garden

Q **Last fall I read about a farmer who grows a few acres of saffron crocus to harvest and sell locally. How easy is it for a home gardener to grow saffron for personal use?**

A That farmer is earning his money. Saffron, the dried orange-red flower stigmas of the fall-blooming *Crocus sativus,* must be harvested by hand because machinery would damage the leaves, which are needed to produce food for the plant. So it's stoop way down—crocus flowers are only a couple of inches above the soil—and carefully pick the flower, take a step, then stoop, and pick again.

It takes about 4,000 crocuses to yield the 12,000 or so stigmas needed for a single ounce of saffron. And every single crocus bulb has to be planted (by hand, bent over) and then harvested, and then lifted (by hand, bent over) every second or third spring to divide the daughter corms; and then each of the daughter corms has to be planted (by hand, bent over). Close your eyes and imagine doing that for a single row, let alone a few acres, and you might not begrudge the farmer his profits.

Saffron crocus
(*Crocus sativus*)

But if your back is strong and your desires can be satisfied with just a few dishes flavored with home-grown saffron (it takes the stigmas from 15 to 20 crocuses to make a single pinch), all that's needed is a perfectly drained, full-sun site that bakes dry during the summer so the bulbs can lie dormant until fall. Plant saffron crocus in early September and the flowers will be ready for harvest in October or November. Air-dry the stigmas after separating them from the flowers (by hand, bent over the kitchen table). 🍎

Transplanting Daffodils

Q **Three years ago, I planted clumps of daffodils here and there in the lawn. They're a gorgeous sight right now, but mowing around them is a nightmare—and my husband says, possible grounds for divorce. I'd like to keep both him and the daffodils; when can I transplant them?**

A The ideal time to dig up daffodils is about eight weeks after flowering, when the foliage has just started to yellow. But given the urgency of your reasons, you can move them as soon as bloom is finished—and while you're at it, you might as well divide the large-flowered ones. Small-flowered types can be left alone indefinitely, but most large-flowered daffodils must be divided every three to five years or you'll end up with nothing but leaves.

Dig the new planting holes before you start, figuring that each old clump is probably getting overcrowded, should be divided, and so will need about three or four times as much space in the new location(s). Have extra soil and sod ready to fill in the old holes. Choose an overcast day, or work in the evening. Using a digging fork, putting it deep into the soil, cut a line around the clump about 2 inches from its outside edge. Keep working your way around, loosening and lifting, following the line you cut, until the whole clump is free. Lever it out, gently break it apart, and then work the sod away from the stems and set it aside for lawn repair.

Separate the bulbs, letting them fall naturally into smaller clumps that still have dirt attached. Don't tear the roots by trying to be too thorough. Plant in the prepared holes, and water well. Don't fertilize until next fall. (If you wait the eight weeks, you can hose off the roots, disentangle them, and do a more thorough job of dividing.) 🌰

When to Feed Daffodils

Q **Can I help my daffodils next year by fertilizing them when they are in bloom?**

Daffodils don't need food when they're in bloom.

A Save the fertilizer for fall. By the time daffodils (genus *Narcissus*) bloom, their leaves are almost finished transferring the carbohydrates they've made into the bulb for storage. As the chlorophyll breaks down and the leaves turn yellow, the plants need only sunlight, air, and water to finish up.

If you need to fertilize daffodils, do it in early spring just as new growth pops up, or in the fall when roots are growing and daughter bulbs are being formed. Use a balanced fertilizer or well-rotted compost to maintain nutrition in situations where the bulbs are crowded or are permitted to set seed, which takes a lot of energy.

Many gardeners also hedge their bets by mixing a bulb booster into the bottom of the hole when planting bulbs, because it is high in phosphorus, which does not move much in the soil. Phosphorus encourages root growth, the first order of business for a newly planted bulb. 🌰

Multiplying for a Spectacular Display

Q **A neighbor of ours has a spectacular display of daffodils each spring. I am madly planting, hoping that someday my yard, too, will be full of blooms. Will the bulbs I'm planting now multiply?**

A Assuming you have moderately fertile, well-drained soil, and plenty of sunshine when their leaves are growing and storing energy, most daffodils will multiply, though they will do so at very different rates.

If you are after quantity as quickly as possible, plant the bulbs far enough apart so each has plenty of room to make more before the children get overcrowded. Enrich the planting soil with compost and rock phosphate. And choose varieties that are noted for their spreading habit; catalogs usually describe them as "good for naturalizing."

There are dozens of candidates. Examples include good old 'King Alfred,' a sunny clear yellow with a long trumpet; the fragrant 'Carlton'; short-stemmed, orange-cupped 'Jetfire'; and the Poeticus narcissus called 'Actea,' with round white petals and a very short yellow cup decorated with a red band. ☞

Bloomless Daffodils

Q **In our postage-stamp-size garden, some daffodils produced foliage but no blooms; others didn't produce anything at all. Could rodents have eaten them?**

A One good thing about daffodils is that rodents don't usually eat them. And daffodil bulbs come with buds enclosed, so you should have gotten blossoms at least in the first year. It sounds as though you may have soil that does not drain well enough, in which case the bulbs would have rotted.

You may also be short on light. Even a bulb with a flower inside will fail to deliver it if there isn't enough sun. You could dig up the bulbs that made leaves and move them to a sunnier spot, but it's easier to just buy new ones and start them out right. ☞

Outdoor Bound

Q **A party guest brought me a pot of blooming 'Tête-à-Tête' cyclamineus narcissus, a small daffodil variety. May I keep the plants in a sunny window until the foliage dies back, and then plant the bulbs outdoors? If so, when should they be planted?**

'Tête-à-Tête' narcissus
(*Narcissus cyclamineus*)

A Invite that person back again. The small but mighty 'Tête-à-Tête' is one of the best for naturalizing after it has been forced. The sunny window is a good idea, especially if it is in the coldest part of the house. But the narcissus should be planted outdoors as soon as the danger of hard frost is past; don't wait for the foliage to die. And don't worry about burying part of the leaves, which you will probably have to do in order to plant the bulbs at the proper depth. The bulb bases should be about 4 inches from the surface. 🍂

Keeping Dahlias Over the Winter

Q This summer, for the first time ever, I planted dahlias in my garden. What a delight! Now that fall is almost here, what's the best way of storing them so I can enjoy their profusion next year? I understand they do not overwinter well and should be taken up.

A Dahlias will not winter over in places where the ground freezes, but they are easy to store if you have a cool place to keep them. Start by making labels while the plants are still blooming, so you remember which color is which. Wait until frost kills the top growth, then as soon as there is a dry day, cut off the dead foliage, leaving stubs 2 inches long. Use a digging fork to lift the tubers. Turn the clumps upside down.

Let the tubers dry a few hours, then gently remove as much soil as possible. Don't wash them off, as the last thin layer of clinging soil will help protect them from shriveling. Line a large box with a plastic bag; then add a 4-inch layer of coconut fiber, dry shredded leaves, styrofoam packing peanuts, or sawdust. Place tubers stem side up on this bed, keeping them well separated. Nestle the labels into the clumps.

Completely surround the tubers with additional packing material, and loosely close the bag. Store in a dark place, ideally at 35° to 45°F. When storage temperatures climb to the mid 50s, the tubers will start sprouting. Ignore short sprouts; they'll be buried when you plant. Clumps that come from storage with long, pale stems, however, should be hardened off before being set out into the garden (see the next Q & A). 🍂

Healthy-Looking Eyes

Q The dahlia tubers I stored over winter look kind of discouraged. They are wizened and limp compared to their plump appearance last fall. Will they recover if I plant them?

A As long as there are a couple of healthy-looking eyes (the buds from which the plants grow, located up near the old stem), even rather shriveled tubers will make decent-size plants.

If shoots have started to grow, evaluate them before planting. If they are still small (less than 2 inches long), just bury the tubers as you would normally, a couple of inches below the soil.

If the shoots are long and pale, they will be too far along to bury completely; they'll also be brittle and vulnerable to sunscald, so handle carefully. Toughen up the shoots by putting the tubers with their new growth in the shade for a week or so before planting. Plant the tubers at the normal depth, with the long shoots above ground, and continue to protect the shoots with a light sprinkling of straw for the next week or 10 days. The idea is simply to shade the bleached growth until it turns green, so don't smother it with a heavy layer of mulch. 🌰

Decorative dahlia
(*Dahlia × cultorum*)

Long-Lost Dahlias

Q I bought several different types of dahlia bulbs this spring, but never did anything with them. They have sprouted, and I wonder if I should throw them out since it is already July.

A Run, do not walk, to the nearest empty spot in your garden and plant the dahlias. A dahlia tuber (it's not a bulb) isn't like a seed, which has the ability to wait in a dormant state, even for years, until the environment is right for germination. They may not look like it, but under normal conditions tubers constantly change. Their physiological processes respond to temperature changes, and they do what they are programmed to do.

When the biological clock goes off, roots or shoots, depending on the circumstances, start growing. The back of your closet or a basement shelf may not be ideal places for growing, but the tubers try to do the best they can until they finally shrivel up and die.

The tubers need as much time as possible for leaves to grow and convert sunshine into nutrients they can store for the winter. Dig them up after a killing frost blackens the leaves, and store them over the winter. Next year they will be fine—assuming that you remember to plant them. 🍎

Dahlia Disaster

Q **For 12 years, I grew a bed of dahlias with great success and profuse bloom, storing the tubers indoors over the winter. But three years ago a disease appeared: yellow margins on the lower leaves, which withered and died, with progressive deterioration. This year has been a disaster. The plants are severely stunted and there are almost no blooms. Please advise.**

A If you have not been restoring the soil with compost—or at least using an all-purpose fertilizer—it's possible that your soil has developed a deficiency. But it's more likely that the bed has been colonized by nematodes, which carry several diseases that could cause the symptoms you describe.

Nematodes are threadlike microscopic animals, sometimes called eelworms or roundworms, which live in the soil and burrow into buried plant tissue. You can't see nematodes, but their presence can be established by a soil test performed by your county extension service.

Some nematodes can be controlled biologically, through the use of specific parasites sold by companies that specialize in such controls, but the best way to get rid of nematodes is to let them get rid of you. Purchase new tubers next spring, and move your dahlia planting bed to another part of the garden.

One other possibility, ventured by Mac Boyer, president of the American Dahlia Society, is a viral disease. Viruses remain in the tubers from year to year, causing progressive deterioration; again, the solution would be to purchase fresh tubers and plant them in a fresh place. 🍎

A Flower as Big as a Dish

Q **We were at a party the other night and overheard someone talking about dinner-plate dahlias. What are they? Do you eat them?**

A No. They eat you, or look as if they could. Dinner-plate dahlias are named for their size, 10 to 12 inches across or more. To get them, enthusiasts start with giant varieties, labeled AA, and then ruthlessly remove most of the stalks and buds, forcing the plant's energy into just a few obscenely huge blossoms.

Most gardeners simply plant the tubers and let them rip. But you will get larger flowers and better stalks for cutting if you do a little pruning. To get lots of branches, start by pinching out the tips of the growing shoots at a leaf axil, when the shoots are about a foot long. Repeat with the first set of side branches. Then as side buds form on each branch, remove them, leaving only the terminal bud. The plant will thus be bushy, but not *too* bushy. (This advice does not apply to dwarf or bedding varieties, which bloom like mad but are not bred for cutting.)

This pruning will result in fewer but larger flowers, growing in clusters of two or three. To get big single flowers—at least salad-plate size—remove any smaller buds that form below the lead bud on each flowering stem. 🌿

Big Bloomer for Spring

Q **Last spring I saw a tall purple flowering bulb called fritillaria, which I'd love to plant myself. Does it need anything special, and where might I buy it?**

A The genus *Fritillaria,* part of the lily family, comprises about 100 species. They are natives of the region around Israel, Jordan, and southern Turkey, and grow wild along rocky slopes.

Typically, fritillarias have long, narrow leaves and their flowers are mostly pendulous and bell-shaped. Colors include mahogany red, orange, yellow, purple, and white, and may be solid or intriguingly patterned, as in the checkerboard of *Fritillaria meleagris*. They range in height from less than a foot tall to more than a yard, and bloom, depending on the species, from spring to early summer.

The one you saw was probably *F. persica,* which bears dozens of small, plum-colored blooms along stems that reach 2 or 3 feet tall. Though seldom offered at retail garden centers, it is widely sold by mail-order bulb special-ists. It is easily grown in full sun or light shade in moder-ately rich, well-drained soil. It should be planted flat side down, in a hole as deep as one and a half times its diameter below the ground. Be warned that like fancy tulips, *F. per-sica* tends to dwindle as the years go by. 🌺

Forcing Hyacinths

Q **I love the fragrance of hyacinths. When is it too late to force them?**

A October is probably your last chance to mail-order hyacinths, but if you can find the bulbs (try a local nursery), you can begin forcing them right up until mid December.

They need a cool period of at least 14 weeks to form roots and prepare for blooming, so pot them up (or put them on forcing jars) and keep them in cold darkness (35° to 45°F) until the rest period is up. If you have no other place that provides these conditions, you can use the refrigerator. Just be sure to keep the pots as far as possible away from the crispers. The ethylene gas that some fruits emit inhibits bulb development. Keep them in this retreat for about ten weeks, and be sure to mark your calendar so you'll remember to remove them.

At the end of the cold period, move the potted bulbs to a cool, shaded part of the room for a week or two. As the flower buds begin to emerge, gradually expose the plants to ever brighter light. A bit of direct sun is useful, but fortu-nately it is not imperative. 🌺

A Mass of Hyacinths

Q **I have heard that there are hyacinths that will produce multiple flowers from one bulb when forced, rather than just a single stem. Is this true? If so, how do I go about forcing them for winter flowering?**

A A single multiflora hyacinth bulb provides a double show—a crowd of spikes holding loose, fragrant white, pink, or blue flowers above, and a tangle of bold white roots below. But for a winter display, these spring bulbs will have to be convinced that winter has already come and gone (see "Forcing Hyacinths," opposite).

The bulbs must be chilled at least 14 weeks. If you pull them out of the cold too early, you may get flowers, but they will stay tucked way down.

Some hyacinths for forcing are sold as "prepared." A prepared bulb has been given a short cold treatment by the grower, but it is never enough. This kind of preparation lets you reduce the cold treatment you have to give the bulb by a week to a month, depending on the cultivar. Typically, 10 weeks will do for prepared bulbs. 🌸

Oriental Lilies

Q **I planted Oriental lilies for the first time this spring. The catalog led me to believe that they would bloom in August or September, but they started before the end of July. What happened? Can I prevent this next year?**

A The category Oriental lily is large, including many hybrids and several species, and although they are all late bloomers, some are a lot later than others. *Lilium auratum* (goldband lily) and *L. speciosum* can be relied on to hold off until at least mid August, and *L. formosanum* seldom gets going before September. The popular hybrid 'Stargazer,' however, may begin blooming in mid July, especially if it's in a sunny situation.

For the best display, plant deeply and keep the ground cool with mulch, a planting of ground covers, or shallow-rooted perennials. Classic lily locations include lightly shaded areas such as the edge of woodlands and the back stretch of deep mixed borders. If your lilies are in the open, they're likely to bloom at the early end of their range no matter what you do.

One solution is to move them in fall, working very slowly and carefully (there's a long, brittle stem below ground before you get to the bulb, and the bulb is not always directly under the flower). Be sure to take as many of the roots as possible, and replant promptly. But why not just plant more? You can't have too many lilies. 🌸

For More Canada Lilies

Q **Can Canada lilies (*Lilium canadense*) be rooted from cuttings of the stalk?**

A If you're going for grace and glory combined, it's hard to beat a good-size patch of these native lilies, each 5- to 6-foot stalk festooned with delicate yellow-orange bells.

But there are two problems with using stem cuttings to get them, said Edward A. McRae, president of the Species Lily Preservation Group, an affiliate of the North American Lily Society.

The first is that it almost never works. The second is that stem cutting is a vegetative process, which means that any lurking viruses (and these lilies are prey to many) will be transmitted to the new plant.

Growing from seed is by far the best way, according to Mr. McRae. As he described the process, all you need is a lot of patience. It's also wise to internalize the phrase "moist but not wet"—seedlings must never dry out, but they will die if the soil is soggy.

Start by collecting seeds from the strongest and prettiest plants. Cut off the seedpods as soon as they turn brown, then let them dry at room temperature.

Remove the seeds and store them in a plastic bag in the freezer until the following August or September, then plant them about a quarter inch deep and an inch apart in a sterile, freely draining potting mix that is moist but not wet.

Keep the pots at room temperature, maintaining this moisture level, until seeds sprout in 10 to 14 weeks. Check for sprouting by gently parting the soil and looking. Canada lilies are hypogeal, which means that the seed leaves, the first sign of life, stay underground.

Canada lilies
(*Lilium canadense*)

Next, put the pots containing the sprouted seeds somewhere cool but not freezing—in the refrigerator, for example. Keep them there, still moist but not wet, for another 12 to 14 weeks. At the end of that time, you should have tiny bulbs.

Mr. McRae gives the babies another year of coddling in pots, but you can also just keep them refrigerated until the danger of a hard frost is past, then plant them where they are to grow, in weed-free, fertile, well-drained soil that is close to neutral in pH. (If you test the soil when you start the seeds, and promptly amend it as necessary, it will be ready at the same time as the bulbs.)

True leaves will appear shortly after planting. So will slugs and weeds, both of which must be kept at bay, especially the first year.

Be patient. Your lilies will start flowering two or three years after planting. And because they are virus free, they should grow larger and stronger for many years to come. 🍐

Round, Hard Somethings

Q **I am attempting to grow lilies in my perennial garden for the first time. Along the main stem where each leaf begins, the plants have a small, round, hard "something" on them. What can you tell me about this?**

A Although alien-looking growths on plants are seldom good news, in this case the "somethings" are not hostile invaders but natural progeny. They are baby lily bulbs, called bulbils, designed by nature to fall to the ground and make new plants.

Each bulbil sends out an exploratory root, usually right around the time it lands on terra firma. The root seeks a bit of penetrable soil, bores in, gets a grip, then pulls the bulbil in after it. Pretty neat—until you realize that your perennial bed is full of incipient lilies that have to be weeded out.

You didn't say what kind of lilies you have, but if you've got bulbils they are likely to be either tiger lilies (*Lilium tigrinum*, aka *L. lancifolium*) or a hybrid with a lot of tiger lily in it.

Tiger lilies with bulbils on stems

Before you let whatever it is spread itself around, you should know that although the hybrids are unlikely to cause problems, *L. tigrinum* itself is lily non grata to many experts. It can be a host to viruses that don't hurt the tigers but wreak havoc among more susceptible types.

If you want to plant delicate species lilies like *L. canadense* and still keep your spotted friends, be sure they are separated by at least 100 feet. 🍎

FOR LILY LOVERS

Though bulb catalogs offer hundreds of lilies, most of them are hybrid Asiatics and Orientals, splendid flowers to be sure, but only a taste of the genus *Lilium,* which comprises close to a hundred species.

And with lilies, unlike with bulbs such as tulips and daffodils, the species varieties are in many cases just as spectacular as the hybrids: tall, brightly colored and/or fragrant, truly commanding plants.

To learn about the many beautiful species lilies that are unknown to ordinary commerce, and to have an opportunity to buy seed-grown bulbs, which are the best guarantee of healthy stock, consider joining the Species Lily Preservation Group. Check the Web site *www.lilies.org/slpg/index.html,* or write Species Lily Preservation Goup, 336 Sandlewood Road, Oakville, Ontario, Canada, L6L 3R8.

Saving Easter Lilies

Q **I work in a nursing home where many patients get Easter lilies as gifts. Everyone just throws them out when the flowers are finished. I think that's a shame, and I would like to take them home and plant them in my garden. Will they grow? Will they flower again next Easter?**

A Don't take the Easter part of the name too literally. This best-loved member of the lily family, *Lilium longiflorum,* actually blooms in mid summer when it has its druthers. But since more than 11 million are forced into early bloom and sold all potted up and decorated, this lily and Easter are forever entwined.

Forcing a bulb takes a toll, and it can't be counted on to force again for the following Easter; but given a year to rest up in your garden, Easter lilies can recover and will bloom next summer and for years to come.

So gather them up (they look much better when planted in groups anyway) and care for them inside until after the last frost date in your area. Knock each bulb out of its pot, trying hard to keep the soil around the roots. Plant it with the base 8 inches deep in a sunny, well-drained spot, leaving the foliage and flower stem intact. The flowers will be finished, but the shiny green leaves should remain all summer; they play an important part in providing food to help the bulb regain its strength.

Planting the lily so deep allows the part of the stem that is below ground to develop roots and protects the bulb over the winter. Unlike many other bulbs that grow roots only from the base of the bulb, *L. longiflorum* is a stem-rooter, growing roots along the buried stem as well as from the bulb's bottom.

Don't cut the stalk down until the leaves turn yellow, and fertilize once a month between now and then. A 3-inch winter mulch is a good idea.

Next Easter will come and go without a peep from your lilies, but the mother bulbs will be hard at work, developing new flower stems for the Easter-in-July show. 🌿

Flowering Lily of the Valley

Q **I have a lot of mature trees and have tried planting lily of the valley as a ground cover underneath them. The plants have made leaves, but in four years they have scarcely spread at all, and they don't make many flowers. I thought they would grow naturally in this situation but that doesn't seem to be happening. Do I need to feed them?**

A Possibly—a 1-inch layer of compost in spring and fall certainly wouldn't hurt—but other problems are more likely. The soil may not be acid enough; lilies of the valley do best in a pH range from 4.5 to 6. They also prefer moist soil, so the area may be too dry (mature trees suck up a lot of water).

And there may not be enough sun. Though lilies of the valley are famous for flowering in shade, the truth is that they need quite a bit of light to flower well.

They also need a cool winter rest. Like lilacs, they are a northern thrill and pretty much out for gardeners who live south of zone 7. 🌿

Lily of the valley
(*Convallaria majalis*)

Bringing Lilies of the Valley Indoors

Q I have heard that it is possible to force lily of the valley to bloom indoors in the winter. I have them in my garden, and I wonder—can I just dig them up and bring them inside or is there more to it than that?

A More, but not a great deal. Dig and lift the lily-of-the-valley rhizome and cut pieces about as large as a thick finger, making sure that each piece contains a distinct bud, or eye. Those pieces are called pips. To grow and bloom, pips need to go through a cooling period of eight weeks at soil temperatures no warmer than 45°F.

The pips should be wrapped in barely moist peat moss, put in a plastic bag, and placed in the coldest part of your refrigerator—low and in back, near those forgotten leftovers. Some bulbs and rhizomes can have their flowering inhibited by ethylene gas, so you may want to first eat all your apples, pears, and cantaloupes, which produce ethylene.

Once they have been through the cooling period, the pips can be potted up just below the surface in a rich, well-drained medium. Since lilies of the valley do well in low light, they can then grow in an east or west window. They should bloom in about three weeks.

If you want to save your refrigerator for food, you can try to guess when the ground is going to freeze. Since the pips don't care where they get their cooling, you can wait until the last minute to dig them. As long as the soil temperature stays below 45°, the time counts toward the eight weeks. 🍎

Propagating Narcissus

Q I recently forced (on pebbles) some Chinese sacred lilies from a garden center. To my surprise, one turned out to be a double, which I've never seen before. Have I a chance of propagating this oddity? I usually throw these bulbs out.

A Your bulb could be a unique mutation. But it is far more likely that somewhere between the grower and you, a true double was mixed in with the singles.

To propagate it, plant the bulb in a pot, in well-drained soil, as soon as it has finished blooming and while it still has its green leaves. Put the plant where it will stay cool but not cold (50° to 60°F) and get the brightest light possible. Feed with half-strength fertilizer every two weeks or so until the foliage starts to die back in late spring.

When the foliage dies, cut it off. Quit watering, and store the bulb, still in its pot, someplace where it will be warm (77° to 86°F). Leave it there for four months to simulate a Mediterranean summer. In the fall, water and start again.

The central bulb will flower next year if its nutritional needs are met; the daughter bulbs that form around it will take two to four more years to grow large enough to bloom. 🌿

A Narcissus by Another Name

Q **I enjoy forcing Chinese sacred lilies, but I have wondered about their name. What's the story?**

A The Chinese sacred lily probably arrived in the Orient from somewhere in the Middle East, said Dr. August De Hertogh, a professor of horticultural science and a flower bulb specialist at North Carolina State University in Raleigh. "The reason it's sacred is because it's for New Year's," he said. "New Year's is a big flower day in China."

The reason it is called a lily is less clear, unless the name comes from its powerfully sweet fragrance. Like paperwhites, these flowers are actually a type of tender narcissus (*Narcissus tazetta*) sold for indoor forcing. They are slower to bloom than paperwhites, bloom less profusely, and flop more, but they smell much better. 🌿

Divide and Multiply

Q **A friend gave me some snowdrop bulbs years ago, and I planted them under a dogwood tree. They have grown into clumps large enough to divide. When is the best time? And how can I be sure I won't harm the roots of the dogwood?**

A With most bulbs, you need to wait for the foliage to yellow before dividing; snowdrops, however, should be dug, teased apart, and replanted immediately after they flower but while the leaves are still green.

Protect the dogwood's roots by digging slowly and carefully, so you see the roots before your trowel gets down far enough to cut them. (Gently pry them aside if necessary to pluck out the snowdrops.) 🌶

To Trick a Tuberose

Q Whenever I'm in Mexico, I buy masses of tuberoses. Can they be grown in the Northeast? Where can I find them?

A The bulbs of this powerfully fragrant flower (*Polianthes tuberosa*) are seldom sold in garden centers, but many catalogs carry the double form, and some also sell singles.

Once you have the bulbs, you must make them think they are still in Mexico. They need a long season of strong sun and steady warmth at night, so in zones 4, 5, and—to be on the safe side—6, they should be started indoors around mid April, in a light, fertile growth medium like Pro-Mix.

If you want to transplant your tuberoses to the garden later, give each bulb its own small plastic pot. If you don't want to bother with transplanting, use larger clay pots, and plant the bulbs in uncrowded groups. Keep the pots in a warm place, and keep the growing medium moist but not wet. As soon as shoots emerge, put the pots in the sunniest spot in the house.

In June, or whenever you can count on nights warmer than 60°F, transplant the plants (or sink the pots) outdoors in the sunniest possible spot. From then on, they need little care other than regular watering and a couple of light feedings with a balanced fertilizer.

The plants form polite, low humps of strap-shaped foliage, perfect for the front of the border, until the flower stalks start in late August or early September. Doubles are supposed to be shorter than singles, but both can sometimes be tall—2 feet or more—and spindly. They almost always need staking and cry out to grow up through something that will hide their nakedness. 🌶

Tuberose Generations

Q After digging and storing them for several years, I have more than two bushels of tuberoses, single and double. Most have a larger center bulb surrounded by 10 or 20 bulblets. Though I plant them early, they make very few flowers, so I think they probably should be divided. How is this done?

A When you plant a large tuberose bulb in spring, it spends most of its energy producing a stalk of flowers. Anything left over goes into the creation of daughter bulbs, the ones around the edge, while the main bulb usually either dwindles in size or else splits in two.

As with most bulbs, energy for next year's flowers is gathered by this year's leaves, but it takes a very long, warm growing season—think in the 70s in November—for one year's leaves to restore the strength of that hard-working central bulb. And because the daughter bulbs have fewer leaves, they take at least a couple of long-summered years to reach blooming size.

Unless you live in zone 8 or warmer, your bulbs are probably finding it hard to bulk up enough to bloom, and their crowded conditions are, as you surmised, making the situation worse.

Nevertheless, if you don't mind running a tuberose farm and have plenty of patience, you can rebuild the central bulb and grow out the bulblets without starting them early indoors. Under optimum conditions, most will reach or recover blooming size in two or three years.

Separate all the bulbs from each other and sort according to size, then plant them after the weather has warmed, in well-drained, highly fertile soil. The small bulbs from the outer ring should be about 2 inches deep and 3 or 4 inches apart; the larger ones 3 inches deep and 6 inches apart. Let the tuberoses grow undisturbed all summer, being sure to water regularly, then dig them up in fall before the greens are destroyed by frost.

Brush off the extra soil and set the plants indoors where they will be warm and dry. Let the leaves wither, then cut them off. Store the dormant bulbs in wood shavings or shredded coconut fiber in a dark place, at about 60°F.

TULIPS TO THE MAX

Tulip lovers stretch the season by planting lots of different species and cultivars. Though each only blooms for a short time, the tulip parade can last two full months if you plan it carefully.

Early: The first tulips are low to the ground, including the wide-leafed Kaufmannianas, sometimes called water-lily tulips because of the shape of the flowers, and Gregii's, known for their mottled leaves. Soon after them come Emperor, aka Fosteriana, tulips, the earliest of the (sort of) long-stemmed types; Single Early, which is usually slightly taller than Emperor; and Double Early, ditto.

Mid season: Once the days lengthen and weather warms up, you'll get Triumphs, first of the truly long-stemmed florist's types, which come in a wider range of colors than the early birds. Also Peony-flowered tulips, known for their lush doubleness; and Giant Darwin, the florist's tulip on steroids.

Late: This is the season for Darwin tulips, also known as Single Late, the classic tall-stemmed cups of color that first come to mind when you hear the word tulip. It's also the time for exotica: huge Parrot tulips, with their twisted and ruffled petals; urn-shaped Lily-flowered tulips; Viridifloras, with flames of green rising up the outside of the brightly colored flowers; and Fringed tulips, sometimes listed as *Tulipa crispa,* their petal edges frilled with narrow teeth that glow when the light shines through.

Species: There are dozens of species tulips available, primarily through mail order. Smaller and more delicate than garden tulips, they are mostly mid-season bloomers, with a few earlies, such as the tiny white *T. biflora,* and a few members of the late show, such as the bright red *T. wilsoniana* (*T. montana*). The available array keeps growing, so it is best to buy from a purveyor who is clear about blooming time in the catalog.

Repeat each year until the bulbs are at least the size of ping-pong balls, by which time they should be ready to flower. 🌸

Return Tulips

Q **I love tulips, but I don't love replanting them each year. Is there any way to have them come back the way daffodils do?**

A Large-flowered tulips will never equal daffodils in the return department, but you can get them to come back for several years if you focus on Single Earlies and Giant Darwins, and give them the right conditions: neutral, well-drained soil that gets quite dry in summer, plenty of sunshine for the growing leaves, and freedom from competition with densely rooted perennials such as day lilies.

The other alternative is to plant "wild," or species tulips, which are (or should be) wild only in the sense that they still resemble the delicate wildlings from which they have been cultured, selected, or hybridized. These tulips are far smaller than the common varieties, and although some, such as *Tulipa wilsoniana* (aka *T. montana*), a bright red 6-incher, do look like miniatures of the big guys, others, such as the twisted-petaled *T. acuminata* and the multiflowered, star-shaped *T. turkestanica*, most emphatically (and charmingly) do not. 🌰

Helping Tulips

Q Last year, the tulips I planted the previous fall gave a spectacular show. I left the foliage until it yellowed, even though it looked terrible and I was constantly tempted to cut it down. But this spring's show wasn't as good. Any idea why not? Should I have planted them deeper?

Tulips with daughter bulbs

A Tulips should be thought of as annual replacement bulbs: either you help the bulb replace itself or you have to replace it. Planting deeper makes no difference.

Even though it's a labor of love, it takes nearly everything the bulb has to make a flower. The bulb uses its energy reserves to create daughter bulbs. By the time it flowers, the mother bulb is ready to die, giving whatever resources it has left to the daughter bulbs, but unequally. Only one or two of them will become large enough to flower.

This takes more than sunshine and the occasional splash of water. Besides well-drained sites to keep them from rotting, all these bulbs need feeding. Fertilize right after shoots emerge in the spring, and again in October. These are also the times when regular watering is essential, but they do like it dry in the summer.

Leaving the foliage up (remove when yellow) to continue making the nutrients that are stored in the bulb is important no matter how awful it begins to look. None of us looks great while giving birth, but it's a well-earned tiredness. 🌰

What's French About Them?

Q I often buy French tulips at the florist. In my bulb catalogs I never see a category called French tulips. Can you give me a source for them?

A The Royal General Bulbgrowers' Association in the Netherlands recognizes 15 groups of tulips, but French isn't one of them. The tulips you want are Dutch-produced bulbs grown in southern France (also northern California) for the cut-flower industry. The most prominent are 'Avignon,' 'Menton,' 'Maureen,' 'Renown,' and 'Mrs. John T. Scheepers.'

All of them are in the tulip group Single Late, and all have very long strong stems, very large shapely flowers, very good vase life, and very healthy profit margins. "French tulip" seems to have more cachet than "California tulip" or "Dutch tulip."

The growing environment, and the way the bulbs are treated, produce these beauties earlier and larger than elsewhere. In catalogs, you can find Single Late tulips, including some with French names, that are not grown for the trade. They are all good garden performers, but as with backyard grapes, you may not get quite the same results. 🌿

Single Late "French" tulips

Hunting the Black Tulip

Q I've heard there's a black tulip and would like to try it this year, if such a thing exists. Where do I look?

A There are no truly black tulips, but there are several that are so dark they are often listed as such. One favorite, 'Queen of Night,' might best be described as a velvety-looking purple-black. It's a Single Late, or Darwin, type, with long stems and large, squarish flowers. There is also a double sport of this cultivar, called 'Black Hero,' sometimes listed as a Peony-flowered variety. A third option is 'Black Parrot,' a deeply fringed, highly ruffled late bloomer, larger than 'Queen of Night,' with deep reddish undertones instead of the Queen's purple. 🌿

PART TWO

The Landscape Garden

CHAPTER FIVE

Vines

Vines in General

Shady Fencing

Q **I have a tall privacy fence in a shaded area. Can you recommend a perennial climbing plant to camouflage it?**

A Assuming your fence is a solid material like wood or stone, the climbers to choose are those that have tiny suction-cup-like disks or small aerial rootlets along their stems.

This group includes such shade-tolerant stalwarts as Boston ivy (*Parthenocissus tricuspidata*), Virginia creeper (*P. quinquefolia*), English ivy (*Hedera* spp.), and wintercreeper (*Euonymus fortunei*). Two flowering vines are climbing hydrangea (*Hydrangea anomala petiolaris*), which will bloom in light shade, and trumpet creeper (*Campsis radicans*).

The reliably deciduous, slender-stemmed Virginia creeper might be the best bet if your fence is wood, which will of course be more prone to rot if it has a moisture-retentive covering on it all year round. 🍂

Quick Covers

Q I've just moved to a new house with a trellised porch and too-close neighbors. Please suggest a quick-growing perennial vine.

A There are good reasons vines have been called nature's drapery, and privacy is certainly one of them. For trellis growing, there are two types of plants to choose from: those that climb by twining around their support, and those that climb by attaching small tendrils or leaf stalks.

Hardy perennial twiners to consider are the silver vine (*Actinida polygama*), a relative of the kiwi with silvery leaves and white spring flowers, and Dutchman's pipe (*Aristolochia durior*), which has large heart-shaped leaves. Dutchman's pipe can take a couple of years to get established, and it does not leaf out until fairly late in spring. But once it gets going, it makes a beautiful wall of green.

Vines that climb with tendrils include grape (*Vitis* spp.), which you can also grow for its fruit, and clematis, of which there are hundreds of species and cultivars that offer a mind-boggling assortment of flower colors and shapes. 🌿

Looking for Height

Q I have an established perennial garden against my house and need some height in the back. What kind of vine can I plant that is eager enough to grow behind the garden but not so eager that it will take over after it has taken hold?

A If you're going for the green look, Dutchman's pipe is a good choice. It's obscenely vigorous, but most species don't send up many runners, and those that do appear are easy to remove. For maximum control (and minimum sight of ugly bare stems), cut it down to a foot from the ground in late fall, after it has gone fully dormant.

If you're eager for flowers, how about a nice clematis like an early-flowering *Clematis alpina*? There are some very pretty blues in that group, including 'Helsingborg' and 'Pamela Jackman.' Or you could choose one of the large-flowered hybrids, like the late pink 'Comtesse de Bouchard.'

The "nice" is not rhetorical, by the way; vigorous species like *C. montana* and *C. terniflora* will be increasingly hoggish neighbors as they settle in.

There are also several annuals that should do fine if they are started in pots (with stakes to climb) so they have a bit of height when they arrive behind the perennials. Scarlet runner beans, morning glories, and Spanish flag (*Ipomoea lobata*) are possibilities, and this is an ideal spot for the canary bird vine, *Tropaeolum peregrinum,* which has wonderful, lobed medium green leaves, feathery bright yellow flowers, and an unfortunate tendency to get naked knees as the season progresses. 🌿

Protecting Shingles

Q **I have a shingle house and would like to grow vines up on a trellis against it. Do I have to worry about the vines damaging the shingles?**

A There are three dangers to watch out for: vigorous shoots (of wisteria, for instance) that jump the trellis and pry behind the siding; rot-promoting moisture held against the building by a heavy covering of leaves; and the heartbreak attendant on destroying a large, beautiful vine when it's time to paint or do repairs.

To mitigate—you can't avoid—the first two, build your trellis at least a foot from the wall. That way, the house will have breathing room and the vines will have water (most roofs have overhangs that divert rain away from the foundation.)

As for the heartbreak problem, there are two solutions. The first is to choose a vine that makes a rapid recovery: hops, for example, or Dutchman's pipe. Once their roots are well established, these vines can grow 20 feet or more in a single summer.

Virginia creeper has flexible stems.

Alternatively, you can make a trellis that's hinged at the base, so the vines on it can fold down out of the way. This won't help with plants like wisteria, which make rigid, woody trunks. But it will work with more flexible characters like Virginia creeper. 🌿

Vines in General

ONWARD AND UPWARD

Though "clinging" and "vine" seem like a wedded concept, only a few vines really do hold on that way, using aerial rootlets that act as suction cups to attach themselves to their support. These rootlets are very strong and enable even very heavy vines to rise high on flat walls. Examples include climbing hydrangea, Boston ivy, and English ivy.

More commonly, vines are inclined to twine, wrapping their main stems around the nearest available support and circling it as they grow. Examples include beans, morning glories, bougainvillea, hops, hoya, and wisteria.

Climbing hydrangea

The other large group are tendril-climbers, which send out specialized, leaf-less stems that wrap tightly around any adjacent object that's thin enough to get a grip on. Examples include peas, cup-and-saucer vine, grapes, passionflower, and porcelain vine.

The specialized stems that do the holding on can also have leaves, in which case they're called petioles. Clematis are the best-known petiole users, but asarinas also climb this way, and so do those rare nasturtiums that genuinely climb.

Morning glory

But not all vines do genuinely climb. Some just head for something supportive and grow on, around, over, or through it, sending out a tendril or two, applying a rootlet, or twining a bit without behaving in any recognizably organized way. Expect to provide some guidance if you plant these and have a particular direction of growth in mind. Examples include trumpet vine, silver-lace vine, and some of the jasmines.

Asarina

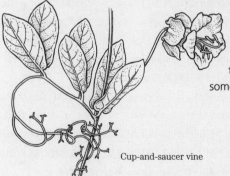

Cup-and-saucer vine

Tying Vines

Q Does it matter how I tie my vines up along my garden fence? I'm growing morning glories, sweet peas, moonflowers, and clematis.

A You don't have to tie up any of these vines. They'll hang on by themselves as long as they have string, netting, or something else thinner than a fence post to embrace.

In the case of morning glories and moonflowers, which climb by twining around their support, even a fence post will do as long as it's not more than 3 inches in diameter and the surface is rough enough for them to get a grip.

Sweet peas and clematis, on the other hand, both require supports that are no more than about a quarter inch wide. The sweet peas hang on with delicate tendrils, the clematis by wrapping their leaf stems (petioles) around the nearest narrow object. Both are determined climbers; they'll entangle themselves in their own stems if nothing else is at hand, but they don't have what might be called a broad reach.

Most vines will climb the comparatively smooth bamboo stakes sold in garden centers. But they will be happier—and more inclined to go straight up—if you provide twigs with the bark on, rough sisal twine, and/or something else with texture.

Preparing for Winter

Q How (if at all) do I winterize my vines? I have a hydrangea vine, several clematis, and wisteria and live near Ann Arbor.

A Assuming you've chosen the tougher varieties, these are all hardy plants that should come through without much special attention. To help them along, don't add any fertilizer after mid summer. You want new growth to slow down and the wood that's there to toughen up before serious cold arrives. But don't stop watering—the plants are still using their roots to store energy for the winter.

After the ground freezes to a depth of 2 or 3 inches, apply a thick but lightweight mulch of straw or small evergreen boughs to help prevent the repeated thawing and refreezing that heaves up the roots.

And next time you plant, choose protected sites where the vines will not be subject to drying winds or direct southern sun in winter. Avoiding the sun sounds strange, but hot bark splits when cold nights fall. 🌤

House of Flowers

Q Someone told me about a wonderful children's project that involved making a house of sunflowers and morning glories. How exactly is this done?

A Sunflower houses are not an exact science, which is a great part of their charm. All you need are the flower seeds and a patch of open ground that gets plenty of sunshine.

Choose a sunflower that grows tall but also makes some branches, rather than an old-fashioned type that goes straight up and then hangs its heavy head. 'Giant Sungold,' 'Soraya,' and the pale-flowered 'Moonwalker' are good bets. Make sure the morning glories are the climbing sort; it's hard to beat good old 'Heavenly Blue' in this situation.

Wearing gloves, use agricultural lime to draw the shape of your house on the grass. (Don't make it too small. When the plants are full grown, the walls will be about 3 feet thick.) Following the line, remove a foot-wide strip of sod. Enrich the exposed soil with some compost and well-rotted manure.

After all danger of frost is past, plant sunflowers about 3 feet apart, arranging a triangle of seeds at each location and spacing the seeds in the triangle about 2 inches apart.

When the sunflowers have four leaves, cut off the weaker extras. You should now have single, strong plants, spaced evenly around your perimeter. Wait until they're 2 feet tall, then plant morning glories every 4 inches or so in the spaces between them. When the vines sprout, use thin twigs to train them toward the sunflowers.

Resist the temptation to fertilize. Sunflowers that grow tall too quickly are prone to falling over; and morning glories that get lots to eat make leaves instead of flowers. 🌤

Old-Fashioned Vines

Q I'm intrigued by the idea of using vines to give my late-nineteenth-century house some old-fashioned atmosphere. Can you suggest quick growers that also flower?

Hyacinth bean
(*Dolichos lablab*)

A It does seem that no Victorian home was considered properly attired that was not festooned by flowering vines. Wisteria was often the plant of choice, but quick-growing alternatives can be found among the annuals and tender perennials.

An easily grown plant that should add old-fashioned atmosphere in a hurry is hyacinth bean (*Dolichos lablab*), a tender perennial whose purple and lavender flowers are followed by decorative purple seedpods. Hyacinth beans grow to about 12 feet and do best in full sun.

The balloon vine, also known as love-in-a-puff (*Cardiospermum halicacabum*), is an annual with delicate, finely cut leaves. It grows about 10 feet in sun or part shade and has small white flowers that are followed by fluffy, pale green seed capsules.

There's also cup-and-saucer vine (*Cobaea scandens*). Its unusual pale green flowers mature to a purple hue. This tender perennial vine is a vigorous grower that should reach 15 feet at least, as does the moonflower (*Ipomoea alba*). The moonflower's vase-shaped, pure white blooms perfume the air as dusk approaches.

For greater mass and covering power, consider the bottle gourd (*Lagenaria siceraria*). The Victorians wouldn't have chosen it, but as long as it has full sun and warmth, it will grow very large, very quickly, and produce silky white flowers. If the growing season is long enough, the fruits will become the gourds that give the plant its name.

A Bittersweet Harvest Wreath

Q I'd like to make a harvest wreath using all natural materials. What is the simplest way to do this?

A One of the easiest wreaths to make is a simple circle of bittersweet stems festooned with their bright yellow-orange berries. For best results, cut when the berries are still mostly unopened; they'll open by themselves after the wreath is made. (You can cut just about anytime, but the more fully opened the berries are, the more prone they are to falling off.)

Cut eight to ten stems, each about 4 feet long, and strip away any leaves. Line the stems up on the ground in a staggered pattern of uneven lengths, allowing about 3 feet of each stem to be parallel with all the others.

Next, tightly twist the parallel stems. A few fruits and side stems will get crushed—that can't be helped. Just clip off anything that gets in the way.

Form the rope into a ring, letting the loose, staggered ends stick out past the joint, one set above it and one set below. Tie the joint with twine to hold the ring shape in place, then weave the staggered ends in and out among the stems to hold the whole thing together.

Let the wreath dry for several days. It should shrink and tighten enough to let you remove the twine, but that doesn't always happen. If it doesn't, just wind a few stems of berries around the twine or replace it with ribbon, raffia, or a tie made out of a thin piece of vine. 🍂

Putting together a bittersweet wreath

Vines in Particular

Hanging Black-Eyed Susan

Q I've seen porch baskets loaded with trailing vines that have beautiful bright orange flowers with very dark centers. What are they and will they survive in Maine? I'd like to grow them up a trellis if they would get tall enough.

A It sounds as though you've fallen for *Thunbergia alata*, aka black-eyed Susan vine. That Halloween color combo is the most common, but you can also get a dark-centered white ('Alba'), and there is a stunning all-white variety called 'Baker' (sometimes 'Bakeri'), as well.

T. alata is perennial, but only in very warm climates. It's usually sold as an annual and will certainly merit that designation in Maine.

Start plants indoors at least six weeks before the last frost, or buy seedlings at a garden center, but don't rush the season. After the weather is settled and warm, plant in rich but well-drained soil, in full sun, protected from strong winds.

Maximum length is about 8 feet, which the plants can achieve in one season if the ground is fertile, the weather hot, and the summer at least three months long. Note that's *length,* not height; *T. alata* is a weak climber. Plan to weave it through or tie it to a trellis, or it will just flop around. 🍂

SHADES OF BOUGAINVILLEA

Although only a few species are cultivated, the bougainvillea hybrids that are available come in many shades of white, yellow, orange, pink, purple, and crimson. As with the poinsettia, the vibrant colors of the bougainvillea are a result not of its flowers—which are hardly worth a mention—but of the petal-like bracts that surround them.

Bougainvillea in Winter

Q **I was recently given a bougainvillea. Can you tell me how to care for it through the winter in New Jersey?**

A This tropical climbing shrub from South America (named for Louis Antoine de Bougainville, the French navigator of the late eighteenth century) is easily grown in almost any kind of soil. But you'll have to treat it as a houseplant; it won't survive outdoors anywhere north of zone 9.

Bougainvillea can take a bit of shade when it's in its proper tropics, but as a houseplant it needs full sun all day, and through the winter it must have cool nighttime temperatures, typically as low as 55° to 60°F.

Starting in fall, reduce the watering. Soil should be allowed to get quite dry without drying out completely. In early February, as growth starts with the approach of

Bougainvillea

Vines in Particular

spring, water more frequently and start feeding regularly with a diluted liquid fertilizer that is high in phosphorus.

Bougainvillea blooms mostly at the ends of the branches, so prune it only once a year before new growth starts in spring, and plan on giving the long stems something to twine around. 🌶

Propagating Clematis

Q Is it possible to propagate clematis? I put pieces I cut from the stem in water, and buds are opening, but nary a root is evident. Should I have used rooting hormone, then put these cuttings directly into soil? Or is there a better way?

A Clematis can be difficult to propagate from cuttings, but layering is fairly easy. Just as new growth begins to harden but before growth stops, bend a year-old shoot to the ground, make a small wound in it, and bury a section of 6 to 8 inches (including the wound) 3 to 4 inches deep, with the rest of the shoot above ground. Keep the area moist. Carefully dig it up in three or four months, cut the shoot below the newly formed roots, and there you are.

Cuttings are another story altogether. A cheerful attitude is critical because about 90 percent of the cuttings will rot before they root. Large-flowered species are more difficult than small-flowered, but the technique is the same. For large-flowered species, take a tip cutting while the wood is still soft, before flowering. For small-flowered species, wait until late June or July, when the wood is semi-hard.

Cut a tip about 6 inches long, including at least two leaf nodes. Cut cleanly with a sharp knife. Remove all but one leaf, dip the cut end in rooting hormone, and put it 2 to 3 inches deep in an equal mixture of perlite and vermiculite. One node should be buried. Keep the cutting moist but not sopping, in bright but not direct light, and wait. As long as the leaf doesn't wilt, there is hope. After six weeks, give a gentle tug. If roots have grown, there will be resistance. If not, wait awhile longer and try again. 🌶

Want more?
Try layering.

CLEMATIS: TO PRUNE OR NOT TO PRUNE

Clematis come in such wide variety that pruning them is a famously vexed question, yet most can be treated exactly like flowering shrubs. You prune them according to whether they flower early, on last year's wood (Group 1), or later, on this year's new growth (Group 3).

It's Group 2 that tends to make people crazy, because Group 2 flowers both ways. To complicate matters further, individual cultivars (and individual plants!) vary in their response to pruning.

This being the case, it's nice to know that all clematis will bloom even if you never cut anything. The ones that should have been pruned will simply produce fewer, smaller flowers, and they will be high on the plant.

At the other extreme, clematis is tough. If you do severely prune something you shouldn't have, it will recover—eventually—and will probably be all the stronger for the experience.

Finding out which group your plant belongs to should be easy, since most authorities label varieties by pruning group: either 1, 2, and 3, as above, or A, B, and C. Unfortunately, they don't always agree on which hybrid goes where, so it's wise to buy from a specialist and go with its group assignment.

If you have inherited a clematis and don't know its name (or group), prune just one stem as though for Group 3, then watch to see what happens to that stem as compared to the stems you left alone. The plant will tell you what you need to know.

Group 1: This group comprises plants that flower on old wood. Some examples: *C. alpina, C. armandii, C. chrysocoma, C. macropetala, C. montana,* and the cultivars 'Edo Murasaki' and 'General Sikorski.' No pruning is necessary, but if you want to limit size, cut back stems that have produced flowers as soon as they finish blooming. Don't cut any trunks, and leave the larger, woody stems unless you need to radically reshape the plant.

Group 2: This group comprises plants that have large flowers on old wood in late spring, then smaller flowers in late summer on the current year's growth. Some examples: 'Duchess of Edinburgh,' 'Guernsey Cream,' 'Henrii,' 'Lanuginosa Candida,' 'Will Goodwin.'

In very early spring, before any new growth starts, cut back to the topmost pair of strong buds. This may be all that is needed, but to be sure, try an experimental second pruning. As soon as the first flush of bloom is over, cut one or two stems down to strong buds that are about 2 feet from the ground. If this produces good results, prune all of them that way next year.

Group 3: This group comprises species and their hybrids that bloom on new growth, anytime from mid June to fall, some flowering repeatedly all summer long. Some examples: *C. integrifolia, C. tangutica, C. terniflora, C. texensis, c. viticella, C. ×jackmanii.*

In early spring, before any new growth starts, take a deep breath and chop 'em down. Way down. Down to a pair of fat, healthy buds that are about 12 inches from the ground (15 to 20 inches if the plant is an old, thick one).

Combating Clematis Wilt

Q For three years I've watched my clematis rise from its planter and climb aggressively up its trellis, only to wilt and die once it gets 2½ or 3 feet tall. The soil appears to be good. The plant gets full sun until about 1:00 p.m., and I feed and water it regularly. What can I do to keep this from happening?

A It sounds as if your plant is afflicted with a fungus disease called clematis wilt, which has no cure. But it also sounds as if you've got a tough plant because it isn't dead yet. To reward its perseverance, start by getting rid of every trace of the diseased foliage. Then repot it in new soil, burying it about an inch deeper than before. Don't feed it until next spring, and then only sparingly until it is well along. Be sure the soil stays barely moist, not waterlogged.

The standard wisdom on clematis is "head in the sun, feet in the shade," because the plants appreciate cool soil around the roots. Since yours is in a container, there's a good chance that as the season warms up the soil is doing the same, and at just the time the plant most needs cool roots, they are instead being fried. This can be a problem particularly if the container is on a stone patio or in another hot spot. Dark colors absorb heat, too; so be sure to choose a pale container when you repot the plant. 🌿

The Dutchman in Winter

Q Last spring I planted Dutchman's pipe and morning glories for an instant privacy screen. Growth was vigorous beyond expectations. I realize that they are completely intertwined with each other and that only the Dutchman's pipe is a perennial. Should I pull up the morning glories now? Cut back everything next spring?

A The usual advice on Dutchman's pipe is to prune it in early spring, but if you are the tidy type, you don't have to wait that long. Just cut everything to about a foot from the ground as soon as the vine is completely dormant, which will probably be sometime in late November. You won't have to look at a bunch of brown stems, and the

Dutchman's pipe, which is not so much perennial as immortal, will have less of a head start next year.

On the other hand, you could just do nothing. Giving the Dutchman's pipe a head start on next year obviously has advantages in the privacy department, and though a lacework of brown stems is less lovely than a wall of green, it does offer some winter protection from prying eyes. (Morning glories will pretty much rot away by spring, so you don't have to worry about cutting or pulling them).

ANOTHER USE FOR DUTCHMAN'S PIPE

Though best known for its summer coat of large green leaves, Dutchman's pipe can also be beautiful when it's bare, if you cut lengths of dormant vine and bring them inside.

The long, dark, fancifully curled stems add interest to flower arrangements, and—if you wait to cut them until late winter or early spring—they can be forced into graceful and delicate growth. Put the cuttings in a jar of tepid water and put them in a cool area, away from bright sun. Change the water every few days. After two or three weeks, the buds will swell into perfect green hearts, summer leaves in miniature.

Sometimes that's it, but with luck there will also be flower buds, and right along with the leaves there will be blossoms, the jazzy little brown-and-green saxophones for which the plant is named.

Happy Wanderers

Q While in Tasmania last August (the end of winter and the beginning of spring there), I saw a bush with a profusion of small purple trumpetlike blooms. My guide said it was called happy wanderer. I also saw a vine that shared the same name and appearance. What is the botanical name, and is it available in North America?

A The botanical name of the plant Australians call happy wanderer is *Hardenbergia violacea.* In the United States *H. violacea* is known as coral pea, and 'Happy Wanderer' is a named variety, sold at some garden centers. Other purple-flowered varieties of *H. violacea* are available, as are white and pink forms of the same plant.

The vining form of *H. violacea* is a rampant grower in its native haunts, but it can be grown only as a houseplant in most parts of the United States. Although it will grudgingly survive an occasional dip to the mid 20s, anything colder will kill it.

Even in very warm areas where it can live outdoors, this vine tends to be well behaved, said Kathy Musial, a curator at the Huntington Botanical Gardens in Los Angeles. It is far more polite, she reported, than the wisteria it otherwise brings to mind.

Coral pea sets flower buds in fall and blooms from December through March. If you want lots of flowers, plant it early in the spring so it can put on size all through the summer before it stops enlarging and starts blooming.

Getting Ipomoeas to Fill In

Q Can I pinch the end of the cypress vine to encourage side shoots to develop? I am growing it on a tent-shaped form in a large pot and the vine has reached the top, but it has not filled in the spaces below. I also want to know the same thing about a morning glory that I grow on a fence. Should I pinch it to encourage side shoots?

A The cypress vine (*Ipomoea quamoclit*) and the common morning glory (*I. tricolor*) are cousins. Both are vigorous climbers that shoot up before they start filling out, and they often remain rather skimpy at the base even when the tops are lush.

Pinching the tips to encourage side branches works best when the plants are still quite small. Once they get going, they'll branch heavily all by themselves—forget pinching and think more about applying a machete—but most of those branches will start a couple of feet from the ground. You could bend down some of the side branches and fasten them to the base, but their urge to grow up is so strong that this seldom works as well as it seems it should.

At this point, the easiest way to get fullness at the base of your tent arrangement is to plant a second crop in among the growing vines. If you soak the seeds overnight to loosen their tough coating, ipomoeas sprout and grow quickly in hot weather. Pinch out the tips of the new plants when they've got about four or five leaves, then pinch out their first branches the same way. 🌶

The Gloriosa Lily

Q **Last summer, a friend grew a climbing lily. Now I would like to try. Just what is it and what does it need?**

A The botanical name for the climbing lily, *Gloriosa superba,* translates as "glorious proud," an apt description of this stunning and most unusual flower. A native of South Africa, it is also known as flame lily for its large, twisted petals that are typically a dark scarlet-red edged in gold. Cat's claw, yet another common name, hints at the way this peculiar plant climbs by wrapping the tips of its leaves around a string or the twigs of nearby plants.

Gloriosa lilies do best in rich, well-drained soil with dilute feedings every other week or so. Full sun is best, but in some gardens they have managed well in light shade. They also need an object to scramble over to reach their potential height of 6 to 8 feet.

In zones 10 and 11, this tender summer bloomer needs no protection after it disappears underground in autumn for a period of winter rest. Gardeners in zone 9 should provide mulch, however, and those in zones 8 and north must take the tubers indoors as soon as temperatures start to fall. Gloriosas should never see the thermometer dip below 50°F.

To keep them over the winter, store in dry peat moss or vermiculite, at 55° to 70°. (If you grow them in pots, you can simply let the soil dry out, leave the tubers in place, and store them pot and all.)

Bear in mind that all parts of the plant are highly toxic if eaten, and that just handling the tubers can irritate bare skin. 🌶

Polite Honeysuckle

Q I'd like to have a honeysuckle vine near the house, where I could smell the flowers on a warm night, but I've heard that honeysuckle is very hard to control. Are there "polite" varieties that would not be invasive here in Delaware?

A How about the common woodbine, *Lonicera pericly-menum*? Though sufficiently vigorous to escape cultivation, it's far less invasive than the notorious Japanese honeysuckle, *L. japonica.*

Woodbine is hardy to zone 5, grows to about 20 feet, and blooms in mid to late summer. The fragrant flowers are either cream or white, and can have streaks of red, as in the variety 'Belgica,' or red-purple, as in 'Serotina,' which is sometimes called late Dutch honeysuckle.

Another possibility is *L. × americana.* It's slightly less hardy than woodbine—zone 6 is its outer limit. But it should do fine in your area, especially planted near a house, which will give it some protection. It, too, is a late summer/fall bloomer with highly perfumed flowers, but the colors are more intense: yellow rather than cream, with lots of deep maroon streaks. ❧

Woodbine (*Lonicera periclymenum* 'Serotina')

Considering Hop Vines

Q I am thinking about planting a hop vine, but I have not seen them at any of the many garden centers that serve this part of Ohio. Before I start looking in mail-order catalogs, can you tell me if there's a reason hop vines are not more common?

A There are thousands of beautiful, comparatively trouble-free plants that never show up in garden centers. The reasons for their absence are as various as the sellers who don't stock them (and the wholesalers who don't supply them), but whatever the problem is with hops, it's not that they are hard to grow.

Common hop (*Humulus lupulus*) is hardy in zones 4 to 8, and thrives in almost any well-drained soil of moderate fertility. The vines want sun but will climb to find it, so you can plant them in partial shade if you don't mind scantily clad stems in the lower regions. Their main vulnerability is to fungus diseases, so don't plant hops where they will be crowded, and be sure they get good air circulation.

There are lots of varieties to choose from, though many have subtle differences interesting only to brewers. From the ornamental standpoint the big choice is between the green-leaved sorts and the cultivars that have golden foliage. There is also an ornamental hop, *H. japonicus* 'Variegatus,' with variegated foliage in green and white.

The cone-shaped flowers of the female hop plant are pretty as sculpture but not especially showy or colorful, and they have a strong odor some people find unpleasant. You'll need a female if you do want the flowers—for viewing, brewing, or putting in hop pillows to promote peaceful sleep. Otherwise, get a male; it too has flowers, but they are much smaller.

You don't mention the planting site you have in mind, but it should be one with lawn around it and a tall, strong trellis (or sturdy tree) on which the hop can grow; these vines tend to run both immense and amok. The immensity is mostly straight up, and amok is easy to control by mowing, but beware of putting a hop at the edge of uncultivated land. Once the roots are well established, new shoots can come up 15 feet—and more—away from the parent plant. 🌿

Keeping Climbers at Bay

Q **There is a creeping plant next to my front porch that a neighbor tells me is a climbing hydrangea. If this is so, I'm afraid it will get too big for the location (the porch rail is only a few feet high). But I think I read somewhere about a Japanese "creeping" hydrangea. Do you know about such a thing? How big is it likely to get?**

A Whether you have a true climbing hydrangea (*Hydrangea anomala* ssp. *petiolaris*) or its near look-alike, the Japanese hydrangea vine (*Schizophragma hydrangeoides*), growth—30 feet or more—is in the cards.

Long considered the best climbing vine for its combination of large beautiful flowers, wonderful three-dimensional structure, and lustrous dark green leaves, climbing hydrangea is nearly unlimited in its ability to creep over, scamper onto, or climb up anything that its little aerial rootlets can glue themselves to.

Schizophragma is very similar in appearance and behavior to the climbing hydrangea, differing mainly in its hardiness (zone 6), in its details of flower construction, and in its more relaxed, yet still elegant, way of holding its flowers. In addition to the straight species, it is available in several cultivars, including the silvery-leaved 'Moonlight' and the rosy pink-flowered 'Roseum.' Schizophragma shares climbing hydrangea's shaggy bark, which gives it winter appeal, although to a lesser extent. And it blooms after a couple of years, while climbing hydrangea often takes several years to bloom.

Both of these vines will probably grow too large for your space, but they can be pruned to keep them shorter. They bloom on short spurs emerging from last year's growth, so prune them in summer soon after they flower.

Japanese hydrangea vine
(*Schizophragma
hydrangeoides*)

Controlling the size of your vine will be an annual chore, and you will probably tire of it long before the vine tires of growing. It would be better to move it to a location where it can stretch out and wow you. 🌿

Climbing the Wall

Q I'm trying to cover the wall of my terrace with English ivy. I bought two big clumps with vines about 2 or 3 feet long, which are tied to sticks to make them stand upright. I planted the ivy in a big container next to the wall. Now what do I do? Should I untie the ivy from the sticks and hope it clings to the wall? It looks as if it will just flop down if I do. Should I get a trellis? Or are there ways to get the ivy to stick to the wall—with brick-piercing staples, hooks, bubble gum, or something?

A You'll have to introduce the ivy to the wall, but once you do, they'll become fast friends—so fast you may not want to do this (see the next question). If you decide you *do* want to proceed, the key to success is knowing that only new growth produces the aerial rootlets, called holdfasts, that help ivy cling. The 2 or 3 feet of stem you bought won't cling, so you'll have to help hold the plant up while new growth develops.

Bubble gum would work, but the pink globs would cost you style points. Masonry staples are O.K. if they don't crush the stem. Soft putty is perfect, as are glued ceramic disks with bendable wire holders that are sold for this purpose at garden centers. On a wooden fence, use thumbtacks staggered at 6-inch intervals along either side of the stem.

The ivy should be planted 4 to 6 inches deeper than it was in its original container in order to force dormant buds to grow. Pinching the top of the plant will force new side shoots. If the new growth is kept close to the wall, it will send out holdfasts that will attach themselves.

You will need a large container (say, half a whisky barrel, with companion plants covering the bare soil), both to give the roots room to grow and to keep them from being killed over the winter. There's nothing sadder than dead ivy clinging to a wall. 🍃

Destructive Ivy

Q **Is English ivy destructive and dangerous to trees and houses? Even if it pulls off a little bark or some mortar, are bricks unaffected? Or does it destroy masonry and sap the life out of a living tree?**

A Slowly but surely both the tree and the building will be sorry they couldn't move to get out of the way. Ivy won't pull off tree bark unless you try to remove it by brute force, but as it spreads upward and throughout the canopy, it shades out the tree's inner leaves. None of those leaves are there just for decoration—the tree needs all the food they can make. A trunk covered by ivy can also make it hard to see structural damage from other sources. It isn't that ivy attacks in the way that twining vines can strangle a tree; ivy does its damage inadvertently.

We may think ivy is beautiful on buildings, but the Ivy League grounds and buildings managers at Harvard and Yale agree it's a problem. Ivy grows small rootlets, appropriately called holdfasts, which make a glue that dissolves some of the mortar between bricks. Worse, the ivy traps moisture, dust, and debris next to the building. Between acid rain and the decomposition of the debris, the acidity next to the building increases. That causes further damage to mortar as the carbonates in it dissolve. All buildings with mortar eventually need repointing (replacing worn mortar). Ivy makes it happen sooner.

Parthenocissus tricuspidata, commonly called Boston ivy because it was used to cover Harvard's brick buildings, is at least deciduous. In the winter, snow and ice are able to drop off and the walls can dry out. But because English ivy is evergreen, it never takes a break. 🍎

THE AARGH! LIST

There is no bright line between "easy-to-grow" and "invasive spreader"; almost all of the best garden vines can be pests if the environment is welcoming. But the ones on this list are so aggressive—at least in some areas—that unleashing them on the neighborhood can be an antisocial act. Before planting these bullies, please consult your state's Department of Conservation.

Five-leaf akebia	*Akebia quinata*
Porcelain berry	*Ampelopsis brevipedunculata*
Trumpet vine	*Campsis radicans*
Oriental bittersweet	*Celastrus orbiculatus*
Climbing euonymus	*Euonymus fortunei*
English ivy	*Hedera helix*
Japanese honeysuckle	*Lonicera japonica*
Kudzu	*Pueraria lobata*
Wisteria	*Wisteria floribunda* and *W. sinensis*

A Blanket of Ivy

Q We have a number of tall trees on our property. The ivy I planted around them has grown too dense. Can I get rid of it with a lawn mower?

A It sounds as though the ivy is one of the hardy evergreen English ivies (*Hedera* spp.), which do become
invasive if unchecked. But it is unlikely that a lawn mower's
blades are powerful enough to cut through their thick
stems. Also, these plants are so close to your tree that you'll
risk injuring its bark.

A better method would be to use lopping shears. These
pruners, normally used to trim small limbs on shrubs and
trees, have heavy curved blades and long handles that provide good leverage. Sever the ivy stems as close to the
ground as possible, and be prepared to do so repeatedly
because they will continue to reappear. This is going to be a
long, tedious process, but the plants will eventually become
so weak that the roots will die. 🍎

Sheltering Jessamine

Q When I lived in Alabama, we had a wonderful jessamine vine. I miss it
horribly now that I live in Philadelphia, and would like to plant another,
but everyone says it isn't hardy here. Is there any chance I might be successful
if I put it in a sheltered spot?

A The short and probably true answer is no. Carolina
jessamine, *Gelsemium sempervirens,* is not considered hardy anyplace north of Virginia.

But gardening is as full of improbable thrills as it is
of disappointments, and city gardens can be a full zone
warmer than those in the surrounding countryside. Plant
your vine against a southeast-facing stone or brick wall,
in the most protected spot possible (a courtyard would be
ideal). Wherever you plant it, mulch the roots generously
in late fall.

And don't get too invested. A young vine could survive
for several mild years and then, just as it's starting to bloom
in earnest, be killed by a normal winter.

Alternatively, you could build a greenhouse. Jessamine
does quite nicely under glass and was once a popular con-
servatory plant. 🍎

Purple Lablab

Q **I have seen a beautiful purple-flowering vine called lablab. Can you tell me something about growing it?**

A The lablab vine (*Dolichos lablab*), also known as hyacinth bean, is a twining perennial native to the tropics, where it is appreciated for its edible pods. But Thomas Jefferson is believed to have grown it, and so can you, as a decorative annual on a trellis, fence, or arbor. It makes a quick-growing, attractive summer screen. Its purple or white 4- to 6-inch flower spikes are lined with ¾-inch butterfly-shaped blooms that look exactly like all other bean and pea flowers. These later develop into 2- to 4-inch beanlike pods, typical of the pea and bean family, Leguminosae, whose botanical name comes from the ancient Greek word for bean.

Lablab grows best in full sun and fertile, moist soil. Gardeners with long, hot summers can plant it like other beans, but those in the North will have better luck starting seeds indoors, in peat pots, four to six weeks before the expected date of the last frost. 🌶

Raising Moonflowers

Q **I have had two failures (no germination) with moonflower. I nicked the seed coat, soaked it in water, and waited for warm weather to plant seed. Any suggestions?**

A The surest method is to presprout the seeds before planting. Soak the seeds overnight, and then place them between layers of damp paper towel in an unsealed plastic bag. Keep the bag out on a kitchen counter where you'll remember to check on it. Some seeds will sprout in three or four days; others may take weeks. Plant the sprouts ½ inch deep in 4-inch pots of a soilless medium, keep them in a warm sunny spot, and be sure the soil stays barely damp but not wet.

Moonflower
(*Ipomoea alba*)

Moonflowers are slow to take off and should not be planted outside until the soil—not just the weather—is thoroughly warm, so Northern gardeners should expect to grow them in those pots for about a month. No matter where you live, don't be in a hurry. They really love it warm. Having patience until it's time to put them out, and again until it's time for them to bloom, is one of the subtler joys of summer. ✿

MOONFLOWERS

What the morning glory is to the day, the moonflower is to the night. This twining vine produces lovely heart-shaped or lobed foliage, and later in the season it begins to send out what look like tightly furled umbrellas that get longer each day. Finally, one late afternoon, one or two uncoil before your eyes into 6-inch-broad, green-tinged white flowers with deep throats—landing pads for night-flying moths attracted by the sweet, light fragrance. Collapsed by morning, the old flowers are replaced by new ones that unfurl each afternoon until cooler days stop them.

Saving Morning Glories

Q I have morning glories that bloom beautifully planted along a fence. Should I cut them down this fall, or will the flowers bloom on these vines again next year?

Morning glory
(*Ipomoea purpurea*)

A The common morning glory (*Ipomoea purpurea*) is a quick-growing tropical annual that will not survive another season and must be grown anew from seed next year. You could harvest and save seeds from your present plants, but if they are hybrids, it is unlikely that next year's blooms will be as large or as colorful as this year's. Unless you are certain your plant is not a hybrid, the only way to be sure of having the flower color and size you like is to buy fresh seeds and sow them each spring.

Still, popular morning glories do include the famous 'Heavenly Blue,' a crimson-rose variety called 'Scarlett O'Hara,' and a white-flowered vine called 'Pearly Gates.' These are usually assigned to the species *I. tricolor*, though some sources list them as *I. nil*. Any of them will come true from seed as long as it is the only one you grow and there are no other morning glories in the neighborhood. ✿

Scrawny Glories

Q Every year I grow morning glories in tubs on my city roof. For the last few years, the vines have had the same problem: after they've gotten quite tall and started flowering, the bottom leaves turn yellow and drop off. New growth doesn't re-cover the naked stems. The tops of the plants look healthy, but the whole effect is less than pretty. Is there anything I can do?

A Attrition of the lowest leaves of annual vines is normal— they're just relatively old. But if the problem extends up more than 2 feet or so, and it has been more than three years since you changed the soil, plan to empty and wash the container, then use fresh earth next year. (In addition to providing fresh nutrients and well-aerated soil, this will get rid of possible problems such as disease spores and the buildup of fertilizer salts.)

Meanwhile, try to be consistent about watering; plants under drought stress often drop their lower leaves. Consider using an organic mulch like compost, which will conserve moisture, help keep roots cool, and protect against the distant possibility that a fungus like verticillium is being splashed from the soil onto the leaves.

There is also a chance your plants are suffering from ozone damage, though the discoloration it causes is usually whitish, not yellow. If your roof is in a high-traffic area, exhaust rising from the hot streets could be bothering your morning glories as much as it is bothering you. 🍂

Morning Glory Proclivities

Q I was tempted to grow morning glories in a hanging basket, but was afraid they wouldn't flower if there was no place for them to climb. Would it work?

A They're going to be a bit confused and frustrated, but they will flower anyway. Climbing vines like morning glories are simply trying to get up where the sun shines and the pollinators fly. They evolved amid taller competition and developed a drive to climb in order to get their share of the good things in life and produce seed.

Don't be surprised if a few stems find the wires the basket hangs from. The rest will twine around each other looking for support—and may end up looking like a tangle of yarn after three cats have finished with it. 🌿

Name Games

Q Last year we saw a beautiful vine with bright red flowers and very delicate, feathery leaves. The owner told us it was cypress vine, and that the botanical name was *Ipomoea quamoclit.* We ordered seeds for *I. quamoclit* from a catalog that called it cardinal climber, figuring that since the botanical name was the same, the plant would be, too. It isn't. The leaves of our vine are much larger, and they are saw-toothed. What is the name for cypress vine, and how can we be sure that's what we're getting?

A The name of your feathery friend is *Ipomoea quamoclit.* The vine you got is a hybrid of *I. quamoclit* and *I. hederifolia,* called *I. × multifida* by botanists and *I. quamoclit* by just about everybody else. It is a more robust plant, with thicker stems, longer growth (to 20 feet), and slightly larger flowers.

The confusion comes because botanists are not of one mind about whether these vines, members of a group of about 20 that have narrow, tubular flowers, are morning glories (*Ipomoea*) or a separate genus called *Quamoclit.* If they did have their own genus, cypress vine would be *Quamoclit pennata,* the vine you got this year would be *Q. multifida,* and so on.

Dr. Daniel Austin, a botany professor at Florida Atlantic University in Boca Raton and a morning glory specialist, said that the separate-genus theory got its big boost in 1830 and ruled for a long time, but that "they're not really that different—the tubular flower shape is just an adaptation to the pollinators, hummingbirds and butterflies." And differences in the number of seed capsules don't matter either. "Molecular genetics supports reuniting *Quamoclit* with the rest of *Ipomoea.*"

This merger appears to be almost complete, but if there is any doubt, it's best to ask because the common-name situation is a mess. Your *I. × multifida* is sometimes called cypress vine; *I. quamoclit* is occasionally known as crimson glory; and both are sold as cardinal climber. The safest route is to order from a catalog that offers both and shows pictures. ☙

Passionflower Survival

Q Last year I was given a small passionflower plant. It survived through a Michigan winter's snows, and this summer it grew about 4 feet up a trellis. How should we protect it this winter? It's in a sheltered spot.

A The plant world is ever full of surprises, not the least of which occurs when warm-weather species like passionflowers succeed in surviving the cold. Most of the showiest varieties are very tender tropicals, and even maypops (*Passiflora incarnata*) and blue passion-flower (*P. caerulea*), the hardiest of the common types, will usually winter-kill anywhere north of zone 7. (The snow probably helped yours survive by insulating the ground beneath.)

Since you have nothing to lose by further experiments (if you don't want to dig up the plant and take it indoors), you may as well mulch the roots with an 18-inch layer of fluffed-out straw. You might also try protecting the stems a bit by untangling them from the trellis, laying them on the ground, and covering them with mulch in the same way. Pray for another mild winter and maybe you'll be lucky again. ☙

Blue passionflower
(*Passiflora caerulea*)

Beware the Porcelain Berry

Q On vacation in New Jersey this summer, I noticed a vine with lovely blue-and-white berries. Do you know what this is?

A Don't be seduced by the beautiful porcelain berry (*Ampelopsis brevipedunculata*), notable for its clusters of blue-and-white late-summer berries that do look like porcelain. Readers have written in with a passion, calling it a "rampant, vicious, invasive plant" that "has become the scourge" of New York, New Jersey, and Connecticut, "covering trees and bushes the way a haunted house's furniture is draped with dusty sheets." Oh, dear.

Porcelain berry used to be safe in cold climates (like northern New York State or northern New England), where nature controlled its rampant growth. But we seem to be in a warming trend, and many southern plants, bugs, and diseases are being found considerably north of their usual range. So it's better to err on the side of caution. 🍎

The Pet Snail Vine

Q A friend purchased a snail vine in California, brought it home, and planted it. The blossoms are blue and curled up, hence the snail name. What is it, and will it grow and overwinter in Oklahoma?

A The snail vine, *Vigna caracalla,* is a kind of bean. It used to be called *Phaseolus caracalla* and is still sometimes referred to that way. The seeds are edible but slow to form, and most gardeners grow the plant for the unusual, highly fragrant flowers.

In its native South American tropics and similarly toasty climates, the snail vine is a perennial. Growers in places that see frost are usually advised to dig up the tubers in fall and store them as they would dahlias. This works fine but only if you *get* tubers, which is by no means guaranteed, especially in the first year. A safer alternative is to keep your plant in a big pot and bring it in and out as the seasons dictate.

That's what they do at Monticello, where the snail vine is a particular pet and very popular with garden visitors, said Peggy Cornett, director of the Thomas Jefferson Center for Historic Plants at Monticello. Thomas Jefferson didn't grow it, but he wanted to. In a letter to Benjamin Hawkins, one of his garden suppliers, Jefferson wrote that the snail vine was "the most beautiful bean in the world," then went on to say, "I never could get one of these in my life."

The snail vine was a popular greenhouse plant in England by 1786, when Jefferson visited Kew Gardens, and the Thomas Jefferson Center thinks that that is probably where he saw it. Later Americans had better luck. The snail vine was common here by the mid nineteenth century, and it was a florists' favorite in the high Victorian 1890s.

UNCOMMON THRILLS

Branching out beyond the tried and true is easiest for Southerners; something there is about a vine that loves tropical climates, and people in zones 9 and warmer have a wealth of choices. But even in the chilly zones there are uncommon thrills, especially if you grow annuals—or build a greenhouse.

Chilean glory vine (*Eccremocarpus scaber*): Tender perennial in zones 10 to 11, annual or greenhouse farther north. Small, shiny leaves on interesting four-sided stems. Long racemes of very showy red and/or orange flowers, which cover the plant all summer and into the fall.

Climbing snapdragon (*Asarina erubescens, A. scandens,* and *A. procumbens*): Perennial in zones 7 to 11, annual or greenhouse farther north. Delicate-looking but strong vines grow to 10 feet and are eventually covered with thick mats of graceful heart-shaped leaves. Flowers are borne individually but otherwise resemble small snapdragons in red, pink, or white.

Hop (*Humulus lupulus* and *H. japonicus*): Herbaceous perennial, zones 4 to 8. Vigorous vines put on 20 feet or more of growth each year. Broad palmate leaves with serrated edges come in gold ('Aureus') and mottled green-and-white ('Variegatus'), as well as the better-known dull green. Only female plants of *H. lupulus* produce the large flowers used for brewing and in floral arrangements. Can be invasive if it is allowed to spread.

Perennial pea (*Lathyrus latifolius*): Herbaceous perennial, zones 5 to 9. Late to appear, the vines make 10 to 15 feet of growth each season. Leaves are bluish green. The waxy white or pink, sweetpea-like flowers are borne on long racemes (good for cutting), and bloom from early summer to hard frost. Seldom bothered by pests or diseases, but alas, not fragrant.

Potato vine (*Solanum jasminoides*): Evergreen in zones 8 to 10, annual or greenhouse farther north. The clusters of delicate white or purple flowers are pretty, and lightly fragrant in some varieties. But this is one to grow for the cascades of shiny, narrow leaves, which come in dark green, light green, or a variegated green and yellow. Excellent in window boxes and hanging baskets; tolerant of shade.

Purple bell vine (*Rhodochiton atrosanguineum*): Perennial in zones 9 to 10, annual or greenhouse farther north. Ten-foot vines with heart-shaped leaves. The striking flowers are pale magenta bells with long, very dark purple clappers.

Scarlet kadsura (*Kadsura japonica*): Evergreen, zones 7 to 10. The scarlet refers to the berries, which show up well against the wall of green made by this very vigorous, trouble-free vine. Also available in variegated forms. Can be invasive in the southern part of its range.

Silvervein creeper (*Parthenocissus henryana*): Zones 7 to 10. Similar to its cousins, Virginia creeper and Boston ivy, but less rampant—and less hardy. The medium green leaves have three to five lobes, saw-toothed edges, and beautiful white veins that show up best when the plant has some shade. Good red color in fall.

Then it fell out of fashion, and it is only now reappearing. You'll find seeds from some of the specialty seed companies and plants from specialty nurseries. The color is somewhat variable. The flowers are often more purple than blue and may have a lot of yellow in them as well. 🍂

The Name of the Vine

Q **In Bidos, Portugal, I saw a beautiful vine with fragrant purple-and-white flowers growing on a stone wall. It was identified as *Trepadeira caracoleira*, and said to be rare. I'm having trouble finding it. Can you help?**

A Your first move is to look skeptically at that capital T. Once you know that *Trepadeira* is *not* a botanical genus but simply the Portuguese word for climber, you're very close to learning that you're looking for the snail vine, *Vigna caracalla* (sometimes identified as *Phaseolus caracalla*).

V. caracalla is a tender perennial bean that traveled to Portugal via Brazil. You can obtain plants from some nurseries, or you can grow them from seed. Before you order, be warned that the snail vine is part lizard. It wants to bake itself on a hot wall and will not grow as lushly as it does in Portugal unless it gets similar growing conditions. 🍂

Sweet Potato Preserver

Q **Please tell me how to save the tubers of 'Blackie' sweet potato. I don't want to lose this gorgeous plant to frost.**

A Sweet potato tubers are difficult to save. They must be cured for two or three weeks at 75° to 80°F (in high humidity) before they can be stored, and storage temperatures should stay between 55° and 60°. But even when all this is done correctly, the tubers are short-lived and likely to rot before spring.

Fortunately, sweet potatoes are easy to grow from rooted cuttings. Just clip a few healthy stems and remove the lower leaves. Put the stems in water or in a small pot of planting mix (not potting soil), being sure that at least one leaf node is covered.

The stems will root in a week or so. Pot each in a 3-inch pot, and keep the plants in a sunny window where temperatures do not fall below 60°. Fertilize very sparingly, and be sure the soil stays moist but not wet. The plants won't look great—sweet potatoes need lots of light, more than they ever get indoors—but they will grow, though slowly.

By March or April, the new plants should be well branched. If you have as many as you want, just transfer them to larger pots and wait until all danger of frost is past to plant them out. If you want more, take cuttings as you did in the fall. By May you will have plenty of healthy young plants to set out in the garden. 🖎

THE SWEETEST SWEET PEAS

*L*athyrus odoratus is well named, as the original sweet peas were powerfully fragrant. According to legend, that's what attracted Father Cupani, the monk who first adopted them from the wild. He found the plant in Sicily, in 1696, and collected it for his garden. Three years later, he sent seeds to a friend in England, where the sweet pea flourished. Word spread quickly, and Father Cupani's little purple-and-blue flower was being offered commercially by the early 1700s.

New varieties appeared from time to time ('Painted Lady' came along about 50 years after Father Cupani's efforts), but there wasn't much change on the sweet pea front until the early nineteenth century, when a flurry of breeding greatly widened the color range. The flowers remained quite small, however, compared to modern varieties, and they continued to smell as sweet as ever.

Revolution came in the 1870s. From then on, the flowers got larger and larger, the stems longer and longer, the plants taller and ever more tall. But the fragrance grew less and less strong. These days, many of the most gorgeous cultivars have no perfume at all. (Catalog-reading tip: "light fragrance" means "don't expect any.")

Fortunately, several sources sell "antique" varieties. They are not only fragrant, but also much easier to grow than the big British "exhibition" cultivars. And if you want to grow Father Cupani's original variety, it is still being sold today, sometimes as 'Cupani' and sometimes as 'Matucana.'

Sweet Peas on the Roof

Q **Is it possible to grow old-fashioned sweet peas in containers? I have a large, sunny planting area on the roof of my loft building, and have been fairly successful with other annuals.**

A They'll grow, no problem. Whether they'll give you much in the way of flowers is another question. Sweet peas (*Lathyrus odoratus*) bloom best where long, cool springs are followed by mild summers. And they must get plenty of water, so coaxing them to do well on a city roof is going to be a challenge.

Begin by selecting heat-tolerant modern varieties such as the Spencer hybrids. Then maximize your portion of cool spring weather by starting seeds indoors, in individual peat pots, in late February or early March. Plant about 1½ inches deep, and keep the soil evenly moist but not wet. They will germinate and grow best at 60° to 65°F.

Sweet peas need to start climbing early in order to form robust plants. They'll sulk forever if they're denied support in their youth, so when they're about 4 inches long, insert 10-inch twigs (or bamboo skewers) about a half inch from the stems. You can set plants outside as soon as nighttime temperatures usually stay at 40° or above—late March or early April. Once they're acclimated to the outdoors, light freezes won't hurt them.

For their rooftop home, choose a container at least 10 inches deep, and fill it with rich, slightly alkaline soil. The outside of the container should be white or another pale color that will not absorb heat, and it should be placed where it will be lightly shaded in the afternoon.

Set the plants 2 inches apart in each direction, and give them 5-foot strings or something similar to climb. You can be creative about this, but don't ask them to embrace uncoated wire, which would turn hot in the sun. 🌱

Sweet pea
(*Lathyrus odoratus*)

Attack of the Trumpet Vine

Q I live in Massachusetts and notice that a vine, which looks like some sort of trumpet vine, is invading the lovely seaside rugosas in front of my house. In fact, they seem to be making headway all over town. What, if anything, can we do? (I will not use toxins of any kind.)

A If it looks like a duck and it walks like a duck . . . From your description, chances are good that the invader *is* trumpet vine, also known as trumpet creeper

(*Campsis radicans*). This well-loved and widely planted ornamental is also a native weed, and it appears to be gaining ground, creeping upward from south to north all over the eastern half of the United States. (It's hardy at least to zone 5, but it used to be quite well behaved in the colder parts of its range.)

Trumpet vine spreads through its winged seeds, by sprouts from the roots, and by stems that will root wherever they touch the ground. It's not fussy about soil and will grow in sun or shade, though it flowers better in full sun.

Trumpet vine is deciduous, but the woody stems persist and can eventually reach 30 feet long.

Farmers are routinely advised to use herbicides, but you can keep the vine at bay by cutting off everything you see at the base, using loppers for the thickest stems. The vines will re-sprout at least a few times, and lots of times if they're well established, thanks to those root sprouts. But if you keep after them faithfully and don't let them put on enough growth to nourish the roots, they will eventually become exhausted and give up. While clipping, familiarize yourself with the leaf shape so you can recognize and remove seedlings. It's much easier to dig out the babies than it is to kill off adult plants. ❧

Trumpet vine
(*Campsis radicans*)

Propagating Wisteria

Q **Last fall, when my neighbors pruned their beautiful wisteria vine, I gathered some of the seeds. Do they need any special treatment to sprout? How long will it take a new vine to start bearing flowers?**

A Don't hold your breath. The wisteria next door is probably an import, either Chinese (*Wisteria sinensis*) or Japanese (*W. floribunda*), though it might be one of the less common, less hardy, but less unpleasantly rampant natives like *W. frutescens*. In theory, any of them will bloom from seed, but some plants may take 10 or 15 years before they get around to it, and some will never make much of a show. Knowing the origin of your seeds is no guarantee of loveliness because wisteria seeds do not come true, or duplicate the parent plant.

It's easy to make new plants from cuttings or divisions, easier still if your neighbors will let you layer a shoot. First, choose a flexible young branch that can be bent to lie along the ground. Scratch a shallow trench and cradle a few inches of the branch, including a couple of leaf nodes, in it. Allow at least a foot of the growing tip to stick out. Pile 3 or 4 inches of soil on the trenched part, and pin or weight it if necessary to be sure it stays buried.

By fall, the buried section will probably be well rooted, but to be safe, let it winter over. Next spring, sever the new baby from the main plant and transplant it to its new site. Figure at least three or four years before the first flowers appear.

If you still want to use seeds, soak them overnight or pour boiling water on them to soften the seed coat, and plant them before they get dry. They should sprout in a few weeks and bloom sometime before Social Security runs out. 🍂

Slow Wisteria

Q **I have had a wisteria for two years. It is growing nicely with a lot of leaves, but there are no flowers at all for some reason. My local nursery suggested giving it 5-10-5. Please help by telling me what I should do before my husband cuts it down.**

Wisteria takes a long time to bloom.

A It is likely that your wisteria simply isn't old enough yet and that it will flower when it's ready, regardless of your husband's threats. It should not be given any more fertilizer, however, since lots of nitrogen in the soil causes plants to forgo flowering and grab the opportunity to grow tall. Keep feeding it and you may have to go to the third-floor windows to really appreciate it when it finally blooms.

Assuming that your wisteria is in full sun all day, a definite requirement, you can also encourage blooming by properly pruning it. Just after it has bloomed (anytime from late May through mid June if yours isn't cooperating yet), cut back all the side shoots to just six or seven leaves. Any subsequent shoots that develop from the pruned side shoots should be cut once they have two leaves. On the main branches, those that you train to the support, leave a single shoot at the end to serve as a leader.

In late winter, prune back half of the new growth on the leader shoots, and prune the side shoots you pruned the previous summer to just an inch or two from their bases. That way the overall growth can be controlled, and the side shoots will become flowering spurs instead of a tangled, leafy mess.

Wisteria is not a plant to be lazy about pruning. It has no shame and will cover whatever is standing still in its path. Or neighborhood. 🍎

CHAPTER SIX

Ground Covers and Lawns

Ground Covers in General

What Is a Ground Cover?

Q **It might seem like a silly question, but what is a ground cover? I see references to ground covers all the time, but nobody says what they are, except that they're not grass.**

A That about covers it. A ground cover is any low-growing plant or group of plants that will make a living blanket over the area in question, crowding out weeds while providing visual interest. Most of the more common ground covers are rapidly spreading, long-lived perennials with soft stems, such as pachysandra, but low-growing woody shrubs like spreading junipers are often used also. 🍐

Ground Covers in General

OVEREXUBERANT GROUND COVERS

Beautiful, easy, quick to spread. When you read these words in the catalog, they sound very enticing. But be careful what you wish for. Many of the most common ground covers are actually hell-bent on covering the earth. Once they have taken hold in the garden, they are very hard to eradicate, and there's a good chance that they won't stop when they reach the property line.

Bishop's weed, or goutweed	*Aegopodium podagraria*
Creeping bugleweed	*Ajuga reptans*
Crown vetch	*Coronilla varia*
English ivy	*Hedera helix*
Houttuynia	*Houttuynia cordata*
Indian strawberry	*Duchesnea indica*
Mint (especially spearmint)	*Mentha* spp. (*M. spicata*)
Spotted dead nettle	*Lamium maculatum*
Vinca, or periwinkle	*Vinca minor*
Wintercreeper	*Euonymus fortunei*

Ground Covers for Shade

Q **I would like to add a ground cover to unify the space beneath some shrubs. What do you suggest for partial shade?**

Epimediums are among the best ground covers for shade.

A Among the hardy herbaceous ground covers that are superb for shade are the European wild ginger (*Asarum europaeum*), which has rounded, glossy evergreen leaves and grows about 6 inches high, and barrenwort, or bishop's hat (*Epimedium* spp.), which has semi-evergreen leaves that seem to flutter over its wiry stems.

Consider also lilyturf (*Liriope muscari*), with grassy evergreen foliage, and sweet woodruff (*Galium odoratum*), whose starlike leaves are, as its name suggests, fragrant; and an assortment of hostas.

There are a number of low-growing woody plants that are also good ground covers, including bearberry (*Arctostaphylos uva-ursi*), whose tiny evergreen leaves often turn red in autumn; several herringbone-patterned cotoneasters (including *Cotoneaster horizontalis*) and *C. dammeri;* and the St. John's wort called Aaron's beard (*Hypericum calycinum*), whose yellow flowers dot its dark leaves through late summer. 🍎

Covering Hot, Stony Ground

Q **Can you suggest a very low ground cover that will thrive between large fieldstone pavers? I tried moss, but the area gets full afternoon sunlight and the moss dries out in the heat.**

A When you say hot, dry, and stony, you're describing the perfect environment for creeping thymes. There are dozens of these gracefully spreading, tiny-leaved plants, many with strong scents other than that of the classic herb.

Choices include lemon-, coconut-, caraway-, and lime-scented varieties. Or if you don't want to grow hungry every time you take a step, there is the well-named woolly thyme, which has only a light fragrance. It forms a very low mat of silver-green fuzz that makes you want to stoop down and pet it. 🍎

Carpeting a Tree

Q **There's a large dogwood in my front yard. I'd like to plant a ground cover beneath it but don't know which one to choose. Can you suggest something that will set off the dogwood attractively?**

A Garden writer Alan Lacy, who has a special interest in the subject, suggested you think of ground-cover plants as a small garden, rather than as something that will simply cover up the dirt.

In his New Jersey garden, Mr. Lacy is experimenting with a mix of evergreen and deciduous ground covers, "playing with leaf textures, colors, and forms." His goal is to arrange them in a tapestry-like design, rather than a "boring carpet" of only one species.

He suggested that in the dappled shade of a dogwood, such a tapestry might include deciduous plants like lungwort, *Geranium sanguineum,* and Japanese painted fern.

261

Evergreen accents could be provided by the European wild ginger (*Asarum europaeum*), which has glossy, somewhat rounded leaves, or *Arum italicum pictum,* which has arrow-shaped leaves marked with silvery gray and cream. Especially elegant is lilyturf (*Liriope*) 'Silver Sunproof,' which is striped silver and green, and its cousin, the maroon-bladed mondo grass (*Ophiopogon planiscapus* 'Nigrescens'), usually sold under the name 'Ebony Knight.'

According to Mr. Lacy, most of these plants spread steadily, but their expansion is in neat clumps, not the sprawl of English ivy or vinca. 🌢

Beneath a Beech

Q **A huge beech tree shades most of our yard. I can't get grass to grow there but don't want bare dirt. What ground covers can you recommend?**

A Beeches (*Fagus* spp.) are handsome trees, but their surface roots and dense shade do make underplanting tricky. The plants to try are those that are relatively shallow rooted and tolerant of shade: spotted dead nettle (*Lamium maculatum*), wild ginger (*Asarum* spp.), ground ivy (*Glechoma hederacea*), Boston ivy (*Parthenocissus tricuspidata*), hardy English ivy (*Hedera helix* 'Baltica'), barren-wort (*Epimedium* spp.), violets (*Viola* spp.), and small ferns. Most of these plants are tough characters, which is why they have a chance under the beech, but that toughness means they can be invasive, so be prepared to root them out if they start to spread too agressively. 🌢

Spotted dead nettle
(*Lamium maculatum*)

Shady Challenge

Q **I have a mature holly tree about 25 feet tall, and I'm having trouble getting ground covers to take hold under it. Does the soil have to be reconditioned?**

A If the tree is growing well, the soil is very likely fine. But you can make the area beneath the tree more hospitable to ground covers by improving the surface soil. Mix a couple of shovelsful each of manure and compost with several handsful of perlite. Scratch open the top inch or two of soil and work the mixture into it. The manure will help enrich the soil, while the perlite will lighten it sufficiently for new plants to become established more easily. ❧

Plants for Mean Streets

Q **Please recommend some street-hardy ground covers for urban tree pits. I've been considering creeping juniper, lilyturf, and vinca, but I cannot find any information about how these and other ground covers hold up under the tough conditions between sidewalk and street, including foot traffic, salt, and dogs.**

A Even on the blackest of Mondays, no Wall Street trader ever faced the kind of stresses found every day in a typical street tree pit: compacted soil, insufficient water, shadows from buildings, pollution, and salt, all topped off by the innate insensitivity of neighborhood dogs.

In an ideal world, trees would prefer a simple 3-inch layer of mulch to help hold water, not compete for it. But ground covers usually need people to tend and water them, a bonus to a tree that must otherwise depend on rainfall, and sharing is better than no bonus at all.

English ivy and vinca are probably good choices, but because the growing environment for plants on some streets is worse than it is on others, these plants may not thrive everywhere. And keep in mind that ivy and vinca don't have to be plain green. Try cultivated ivy varieties such as 'Buttercup' or 'Galaxy' for variegated or distinctive leaves. Or look for *Vinca minor* cultivars that are a nice change from the typical lilac-blue, like 'Gertrude Jekyll,' with small leaves and white flowers; 'Alba,' with white flowers; and 'Atropurpurea,' with purple flowers. The vinca 'Sterling Silver' has beautiful creamy variegated leaves. Or try some of the more prostrate forms of wintercreeper (*Euonymus fortunei*), such as 'Minimus' or 'Longwood.' Lilyturf (*Liriope muscari*) can handle the street pit, but it needs to be cut back in late winter; creeping juniper is a full-sun plant and isn't likely to survive on a typical city street. ❧

FALL COLOR AT YOUR FEET

Ground covers are a frequently neglected part of garden design. How else to explain the overwhelming use of *Vinca minor,* English ivy, and pachysandra when so many other choices are available?

Instead of thinking only of very low-growing evergreen selections, broaden your possibilities to include other plants that can be massed to tie together areas of the garden. The relationship between a ground cover and its location and use should determine the appropriate height, not some limiting idea that anything more than 4 inches tall cannot qualify.

Fall color is an important part of garden design, and it should be part of your ground-cover selection process, just as it is for trees and shrubs. Here are a few plants to think about as ground covers:

Fragrant sumac (*Rhus aromatica* 'Gro-Low'): The glossy, deciduous leaves, which are aromatic when bruised, turn a fiery orange-red in the fall. The wide-spreading shrub grows to 2 feet tall and works very well, even on a slope, in full sun or partial shade.

Bigroot cranesbill (*Geranium macrorrhizum*): This mound-forming semi-evergreen perennial has leaves with a distinctive medicinal scent that turn reddish in the fall. It grows from 12 to 15 inches tall and spreads well through a thick, rhizomatous root structure. It is easy to grow, and is both heat and drought tolerant. Different cultivars have different spring flower colors.

Leadwort (*Ceratostigma plumbaginoides*): Fall color and flowers occur at the same time. The shiny green leaves turn strawberry tints, then bronze-red in fall, while the cobalt blue flowers last from late summer until frost. Cut back the bare wiry stems in late winter.

Leaves appear in late spring, just after you're convinced it is dead. Grows 8 to 12 inches tall. It works well in full sun or shade, but colors up better in the sun.

Siberian carpet cypress (*Microbiota decussata*): This wide-spreading evergreen grows to 2 feet tall, with arching, scaly, feathery foliage that turns bronze after a frost. It's unusual in that it is an evergreen that tolerates shade. It really is from Siberia, and very cold hardy.

Rockspray cotoneaster (*Cotoneaster horizontalis*): The dark, shiny deciduous leaves turn orange-red, complementing small red berries growing along the stems. This densely branching woody shrub grows from 2 to 3 feet high, spreading to 6 feet. Its arching habit makes it look like the perfect refuge for rabbits or chipmunks as it covers and cascades down a bank. Lower-growing cultivars are also available.

Weed or Wildflower

Q **We recently bought an old farm in Vermont and are discovering many garden plants hidden among the weeds. One of them is a ground cover, or at least we think it is. There's a big patch of it at the edge of the lawn under a bunch of untended shrubs. It seems healthy, but miniaturized. The leaves are only about an inch long. They are oval and slightly fuzzy, growing in pairs on long, wiry stems. There are lots of spires of pretty blue flowers, but the flowers are tiny. What is it? If we rescue it, will it get bigger?**

A Time to get out the magnifying glass. Do those tiny flowers have four petals and two stamens? Does one petal appear to be narrower than the other three? If the answers are yes, you have some kind of speedwell, a member of the genus *Veronica.*

There are well over a dozen species that grow in the Northeast, but the location and those flower spires mean yours are likely to be one of the following four: If the leaves look almost like felt and are growing on little stems, it is probably common speedwell (*Veronica officinalis*). If the leaves are quilted with veins and grow right out of the stalk, the beautiful little bird's-eye speedwell (*V. chamaedrys*) is a more reasonable guess.

Both of these perennial speedwells have flower spires with nothing but flowers on them. If the spires have tiny leaves tucked in between the flowers, your plants might be one of the annual forms, either corn speedwell (*V. arvensis*) or field speedwell (*V. agrestis*).

All of them prefer well-drained soil, along with very light shade, and thrive in open areas such as lawns, roadsides, and clearings in the woods, where they can spread into large colonies like yours.

Speedwell
(*Veronica* spp.)

Whether you call them ground covers, wildflowers, or weeds, they have certainly found their niche and are perfectly happy in it. They don't need rescuing, and moving them won't make them appreciably bigger. 🌿

Winter Ground Covers

Q **Are there any shade-tolerant ground covers that can be planted in fall? I don't want to wait until next spring if I don't have to.**

A Quite a few shade-tolerant plants are perfectly happy to go into the ground after it has cooled off. You can plant the following hardy species anytime through autumn and even into early winter—as long as the ground is not frozen and is not expected to freeze for at least a month or so.

Lilyturf (*Liriope muscari*) is especially accommodating, and there are lots to choose from, including several with variegated yellow-and-green leaves. A handsome cousin is the maroon-black mondo grass (*Ophiopogon planiscapus* 'Nigrescens'), which is frequently called only by its descriptive cultivar name 'Ebony Knight.'

There are also European wild ginger (*Asarum europaeum*) and the hellebores, also called Lenten and Christmas roses, with their sturdy, long-lasting serrated leaves.

Other useful shade-tolerant ground covers that can be planted in fall include two low-growing shrubs: wintergreen (*Gaultheria procumbens*), an American native that is related to the blueberry and rarely exceeds 6 inches in height, and Aaron's beard (*Hypericum calycinum*), which roots wherever it touches the ground.

There's also wintercreeper (*Euonymus fortunei*). The cultivar 'Emerald Gaiety' has small, oval green-and-white leaves that sometimes last all winter and, when they do, add a hint of pink to their bright color mix.

Instant Color: A Constant Battle

Q **Many years ago, I used to see advertisements for a wildflower seed mixture. The promise was that just scattering the seed would create a meadow. Is this still being sold? Does it really work?**

A Instant meadows are still being sold, and people are still scattering seeds and dreaming. Predictably, the results are proportional to the amount of work, not the amount of dreaming.

Although some wildflower mixes include a wide range of plants, the ones that promise an instant carpet of flowers are made up primarily of annuals. They will bloom (and die) the summer the area is seeded, assuming the seeds land on bare soil and that they germinate and grow in the face of stiff competition from weeds.

To get something like the pictures on those packages, you'll have to first kill and remove any plants already growing on the site. After they're gone, lightly open up the bare soil with a steel rake, spread the flower seeds evenly, use a roller for good seed-to-soil contact, and lightly mulch with straw to retain moisture and keep the birds from finding all the seed.

Keep it moist, pull up a chair, and enjoy the summer riot of color. Unfortunately, the following spring you'll find that many of the annuals didn't reseed themselves enough to prevent fall's weed seeds from taking hold. So you start all over again. An annual meadow is an annual job. 🍎

Perennial Meadow

Q **I have been trying to establish a wildflower meadow, but have failed twice. Before I try it yet again, can you recommend a wildflower mix that will actually work?**

A While the lilies of the field may not toil, those who put them there sure have to. It just isn't easy to build an entire ecosystem from scratch. You need to assemble a stable mixture of annual and perennial wildflowers and clump-forming grasses, all appropriate for your site and climate, all able to get along with each other.

A mixture that's just right for your conditions will have the best chance of long-term success, but no prepackaged mix can offer that level of specificity. The only way to get that is to assemble it yourself. Look around at what is already thriving in the neighborhood, then ask local experts for advice. The extension service will be glad to help, and so will the people at the soil and water conservation district office, usually listed in the phone book under State Government.

A custom mix will improve your chances, but bear in mind that there simply are no instant, maintenance-free meadows. It takes two or three years before most of the perennial plants will reach blooming size, and you will still have to weed a bit, especially at first, no matter how carefully you prepare the soil. 🌸

Wildflowers vs. Weeds

Q **I planted a "conservation wildflower mix" that was supposed to be right for the upper Midwest, but instead of a good mix of flowers, I got a field that was weedy the first year and even weedier the next. I was careful to till the ground before I planted, but that doesn't seem to have helped at all.**

A One tilling is only a single battle won. Many weed seeds remain viable for decades; many have delayed sprouting strategies, so they don't all germinate in the same year; and all the time, year in and year out, wind, animals, and birds are busily bringing in reinforcements.

Gradually, however, you will have a meadow that blooms—though there won't be many annuals in it. If you keep after the perennial weeds, each year the perennials you planted will grow more roots, eventually forming an interwoven mass that chokes out almost everything else, including annual weeds (and what's left of the annual flowers).

To thwart the natural succession that would eventually fill it with trees, the meadow should be mowed or burned (check with your fire department to see that it's legal) each fall, or before spring growth begins. 🌸

Ground Covers in Particular

The Way of the Bunchberry

Q **I have tried many times to transplant bunchberry (*Cornus canadensis*), to no avail. Now I have found some plants with red berries. Will they contain seeds I can plant? Is fall the right time to pick them, and what are my chances of success? There is a corner of my yard where a carpet of bunchberry would be lovely.**

A Collecting wildflower seed is much less destructive of native stands than the gathering of plants, and in the case of bunchberries it's also more likely to lead to success, according to Cheryl Lowe, horticultural director of the New England Wild Flower Society in Framingham, Massachusetts. The society has had a lot of experience with these lovely little plants, which, at about 6 inches tall, are the shortest native dogwoods. Ms. Lowe recommended the following method of propagation.

This fall, gather the berries as soon as they are soft and part readily from the plant. Crush them lightly. Then cover with cool water and soak them for a week or so to loosen the clinging pulp. Strain, and then work the mush between your fingers to free the seeds. Rinse them.

Fill a planting flat with sterile potting mixture and plant the seeds ½ to ¾ inch deep, 2 inches apart in all directions. Water thoroughly from the bottom. Choose a partly shaded spot outdoors and sink the flat so the top is level with the soil surface. Cover with a porous plant cover like Reemay, to keep animals out and prevent splashing. Leave for the winter.

Start checking for seedlings in early spring and remove the cover when they appear. When the seedlings have four leaves, transplant to a flat filled with potting soil that has been mixed with a small amount of aged bark. Sink the new flat as you did the old one. Keep the little plants moist but not wet.

Leave the plants in the nursery flat for another year; then transplant to their final location, which should be partly shaded, cool, and damp. Remember that bunchberries thrive in Greenland and will do best where chilly.

"The farther north you go, the better they do," Ms. Lowe said. "They really don't like hot, humid summers. Our best spot here is a north-facing slope where a seeping spring keeps the ground cool all summer."

Bloomtime for Creeping Jenny

Q **I have a creeping Jenny that is in full sun. The plant flowered all through the spring into early summer. At that time, it lost all of its flowers. Is there anything I can do to bring back the bright yellow flowers?**

A *Lysimachia nummularia,* often called creeping Jenny because of its ground-hugging, spreading habit, does best in locations that range from damp to soggy to downright wet. (In fact, it can do so well it becomes invasive. Be careful about planting it near areas where it could go wild.) *L. nummularia* likes plenty of sunshine but prefers cooler temperatures.

Since it must have moisture to thrive, it's likely that your plant suffered from summer's heat and drought. All you have to do for flowers is to wait. And do be a bit skeptical about unreasonable claims. *L. nummularia* is often described as blooming from May to September, and it does flower intermittently long after it puts on its initial spring show. But as a rule, the only plants that bloom all summer are bedding annuals (like petunias), geraniums, and tropicals (like fuchsias). Everything else takes a rest from time to time. 🍎

DAY LILIES AS GROUND COVERS

Day lilies offer a lot more than beautiful flowers. They also help control erosion, holding the earth, even on slopes, with their tenacious roots. It may take a while to get them established in difficult situations (poor soil, dry soil, weedy roadsides), but once they have taken hold, they will not only stay put but spread, covering the area allotted to them with a summer-long sea of green fans and a month or more of bright bloom.

For best results, use the old-fashioned orange-flowered *Hemerocallis fulva* 'Europa'; it's the most aggressive spreader. Plant in clumps at least 4 inches in diameter, spacing them no more than 18 inches apart. For the first couple of years, provide plenty of water and remove the most invasive weeds. After that, your lily carpet should do fine on its own for a decade or more. Eventually, flowering will dwindle if the day lilies are not divided, but with any luck, that will be more of a bother to your children than to you.

Looking for Epimediums

Q   I have two species of epimedium that are doing very well in deep shady edges of my perennial garden in northern New York State, and I'd like to plant more. Are there many different kinds?

A   Epimedium is an underused ground cover that by all rights should put pachysandra on the compost pile. The plants thrive in all types of shade and compete well with tree roots, growing where little else has a chance but preferring moist, well-drained soil.

Some epimediums are clump-forming and slow to spread, and look good in small, intimate groups or planted in wide swaths or as a border edge. Others, like *Epimedium pinnatum, E. × perralchicum* 'Fröhnleiten,' and *E. × rubrum,* spread faster and make better ground covers.

Species and hybrids range from 6 to 12 inches high, with heart-shaped foliage that is tinged red in the spring on some species and often turns bronze in the fall. In early spring, shy, columbine-like flowers that may be rosy pink, yellow, white, violet, or bicolor, depending on the species, are held aloft on wiry stems.

Cut down old foliage in the early spring before new growth begins, so that the flowers may be seen more easily. Epimediums should be planted or divided after flowering when the foliage is mature, or in the fall. 🍐

Growing Wild Ginger

Q **Would it be easy to grow wild ginger (*Asarum arifolium*) as a ground cover in a garden near Boston?**

A Asarums are easy to grow if conditions are right. Soil must be very well drained yet moist, and rich with organic matter. They need shade but also require good air circulation; those beautiful leaves are vulnerable to fungus diseases. And slugs love them. Other than that—piece of cake.

There are dozens of species of asarums, each more attractive than the last to the connoisseurs who collect them. Far more various than hostas, their leaves may be arrow-shaped or round, dark or light, plain or mottled and stippled with silver.

The equally lovely flowers grow hidden beneath the leaves, so blossom enthusiasts usually grow their asarums in pots. Which is just as well. Easy is not the same as swift, and many of the most exquisite cultivars are very slow growing.

Canadian wild ginger (*Asarum canadense*)

For fastest spread and best hardiness, you would be better off with *A. canadense,* native from New Brunswick to North Carolina, than with *A. arifolium,* which is naturally found from Virginia southward. Though *A. arifolium* is often rated hardy to zone 5 and will usually come through as long as it gets good snow cover, it isn't as tough as its northern cousin and doesn't spread as quickly in the colder regions. 🍎

Lawns

Practical Lawn Care

Q **Would it be practicable to replace a home grass lawn with a short perennial ground cover that would need much less care, water, and pesticides than grass?**

A Let's start with the happy news that grass lawns do not "need" pesticides or herbicides. They can get by on the water nature provides, and they will be fine without coiffeurs that suggest they have joined the army.

What low-maintenance lawns do require is careful planning, judicious use of fertilizer, regular mowing, and, most important, reasonable expectations.

Start with good soil: loose, rich in organic matter, slightly acid to neutral in pH. Choose a mix of grasses appropriate to the location; and plant the seed—generously, so you get a thick stand—in early fall, the best time to establish or rehabilitate turf.

Feed sparingly. Overfeeding pushes growth so you have to water and mow more often, and the pushed growth is likely to be weak, hence vulnerable to disease.

If you take these steps, you should have a lawn that is not constantly needy. It will not be absolutely weed free, which is where the reasonable expectations come in (a few dandelions never hurt anybody), and it may go brown for a while if there is a prolonged drought. But most of the time it will be smoothly green, soft and inviting to human use, which is what a lawn should be.

Lawns

Children can't roll around on ground covers. You can't have picnics on them or lie on them and look at the stars. On the other hand, if the only thing you do with your lawn is look at it, a mix of handsome low-growing plants—no more pachysandra, please!—may be a sensible alternative. ✿

A New Lawn, Beset by Weeds

Q **Our large new lawn is being overwhelmed by crabgrass, broadleaf plantain, and wild violets, but we don't want to use chemical herbicides. Are there organic solutions other than hand-weeding?**

A Organic gardeners avoid problems by building healthy systems. They tolerate some diversity (even healthy turf isn't completely weed free), and they see serious infestations—whether of weeds, pests, or diseases—as symptoms of illness, rather than as illness itself.

Start by examining the patient from the ground up. Is the soil compacted? Does it lack organic matter? Has it been saturated with fertilizer or, conversely, starved? Any of these is an invitation to weeds.

So is sparse seeding or a choice of grasses not suited to local conditions. And so, unfortunately, is drought. New lawns need consistent moisture to build the thick web of roots that helps keep weeds under control.

If none of the above applies, it's likely you'll see gradual improvement simply by providing good care as your lawn matures. A smooth expanse of grass is no more natural than a flower bed, and it needs the same kind of continuing attention if it is to do well.

Lawn with plantains rampant

For detailed guidance, consult your local extension service, which is also the best source of help with specific problems. In the short term, concentrate on the plantains. They are the most likely to persist if allowed to establish themselves now. Don't let them set seed, pull as many plants as possible, and treat the rest with a flame weeder. ✿

FIVE STEPS TO A NATURALLY WEED-RESISTANT LAWN

1. Prepare the soil.

Though they are seldom thought of that way, expanses of mown grass are actually very intensive gardens. Loose, fertile soil of the right pH is even more important for good lawns than it is for tasty tomatoes or lavishly blooming shrubs.

2. Invest in the best seed, use enough of it, and plant it at the right time.

The first defense against weeds is a turf that is thick enough to prevent them from getting the light they need to sprout and grow. The grass won't be thick if you're stingy with either quality *or* quantity, and it won't fill in properly unless you give it a proper start.

3. Think long term.

Be sure the seed mixture comprises grasses that will be long lived, such as red fescues and bluegrasses. There should be only a very small amount of rye grass, if there is any at all.

Rye grasses grow quickly, helping the lawn to look good fast and preventing the growth of some weeds. But because they are up so quickly, they steal nutrients, water, and light from slower-growing but more durable types. As a result, newly established turf has a lot of rye in it. This is fine for a short while. But even perennial rye dies out within a few years, and when it does it leaves a whole lot of room for weeds to move in.

A sprinkling of rye can be used if you are the impatient type. But you'll have better long-term weed control if you go for the slow stuff and hand-weed for the first year or so while the good grasses are settling in.

4. Adjust the mower to the season.

No matter what height you like your lawn, letting it get a bit shaggy in summer— a good 3 inches tall—will cut down on weeds. The taller grass provides more shade, keeping the grass roots cool and healthy while making it harder for weed seeds to sprout and find the light.

5. Don't water if there's a drought.

This may seem counterintuitive, and it isn't entirely true: if you have an endless supply and can water the lawn thoroughly, by all means go ahead. But if water is limited, you're much better off letting the lawn go dormant than trying to give it "just enough to stay alive." Grasses naturally lie low and turn brown during droughts. They aren't dead—they're just sleeping. A small amount of water won't be enough to keep grasses green, but it will keep the lawn green, because the watered weeds will thrive.

Corn Gluten for Grass Care

Q I understand that there is finally an organic "weed and feed" product for lawn care. What is it? Does it really work?

A The long-hoped-for panacea is corn gluten meal, a by-product of corn milling. It is quite high in nitrogen, which makes it a good fertilizer for grass. And it will prevent weed seeds from growing.

But—there's always a but—that's it. Corn gluten kills by drying up the baby sprouts as soon as the seed cracks open. It has no effect on perennial weeds (other than to encourage them) or on annual weeds that are already growing (ditto).

Furthermore, it must make good contact with the weed seeds in order to kill them, not a problem on bare soil but a tricky proposition if the grass is reasonably thick. It works best when the soil is warm, by which time many annual weeds have long since been up and about. And it lasts for only about six weeks, so you have to apply it frequently.

All that said, corn gluten is a relatively benign fertilizer, and it can help control annual weeds if you use it faithfully, from spring to fall, for a couple of years. It is nontoxic and, in home-garden quantities, safe for the environment. 🌶

Zoysia: A Wonder Grass?

Q I saw an ad recently about a "wonder grass" called zoysia. Is it really as wonderful as they say?

A The zoysias are frequently touted (especially by those who sell them) as miracle grasses—phenomenally quick spreading, hardy all the way to New England, tough enough to withstand salt spray, able to thrive in both sun and shade and in a wide range of soils.

All true. Unfortunately, zoysia grasses are also deeply uninterested in being green unless the temperature stays well above freezing, both day and night. They're *alive* when the daffodils are blooming and when the falling leaves are scarlet, but brown is not a background color that sets off these things to their best advantage. 🌶

Lawns

A Lawn for the Children

Q Our children love to play on the grass, but we would love to get out of the lawn-care rat race. It seems like we spend every weekend feeding, weeding, or mowing. Is there anything besides grass that's tough enough for children to play on?

A Rubber is good. You could try a thick layer of straw. And sand, of course, is traditional. But nothing living is as good as grass for what grass is good for: playing tag, running around in circles until you fall down laughing, and, when you are older, playing croquet.

There are a few other plants that have been used as lawns, chamomile probably being the most famous (except in California, where they plant dichondra). But none of the alternatives is trouble free, and all of them, including chamomile and dichondra, are better suited to sedate strolling than the rough-and-tumble play of energetic children.

Fortunately, grass need not be as much of a time hog as you've let yours become. The children will be perfectly content if you grow what's called a yachtsman's lawn: "He mows what grows."

Just rake off the leaves in fall, or, even better, mow them with a mulching mower. In early spring, before the lawn greens up, broadcast a generous sprinkling each of compost and corn gluten (a natural fertilizer that suppresses the sprouting of annual weeds).

Repeat the gluten every six weeks or so, stopping at the first sign of frost. Keep your mower sharp, and don't use it too much; the grass will be happier if it isn't being whacked every other minute.

Lawn Holes

Q On golf-course lawns, I sometimes see rows of small triangular holes about 3 inches deep from which the soil has been removed. What are they?

A Although that grid of tiny aeration holes looks like it would be harmful, the holes, which fill in quickly, are benefiting the lawn. Aerating turf creates spaces for oxygen to penetrate, which stimulates soil microorganisms and root growth. It also decreases the potential of problems from thatch buildup.

Lawns should be aerated yearly, and twice yearly is a good idea where the lawn is green year-round. You can do it at any time. There is no rule about the season, and no need to do it all at once. Handheld spiking tools for aeration work fine on small areas. If the lawn is large, a power-driven aerator will make the task easier. 🌿

A Mysterious Visitor

Q This summer and last, our lawn has been torn apart every night. Large areas of grass are cut almost in a circle, with a hinged area at the rear. It has been suggested that the marauder may be a skunk, groundhog, or chow. The lawn was treated for grubs in early spring. Can you suggest a way to destroy the attraction for the intruder or to repel the animal?

A If you had a groundhog that confined itself to digging up the lawn, you'd be Lady Luck's own tot. And dogs are daylight destroyers; if a chow were making those holes, you'd see it in action. Your busy visitor is either a skunk or, possibly, a raccoon. The hinges point toward raccoon, but the frequency of the visits is more suggestive of skunk.

Both of these animals dig for grubs, and while it's tempting to say there are lots of holes because whatever it is can't find enough of them and has to keep looking, grub removal does sometimes help.

But if the culprits are skunks, you're still stuck. They eat earthworms, too, and you certainly wouldn't want to destroy *those* harbingers of healthy soil, no matter how many diggers they attract.

The only effective repellent is a large dog. Since you don't have one, there are two options: you can call a professional (look in the Yellow Pages under Pest Control or Animal Control), or you can just relax and do nothing.

Skunks are beautiful and quite shy, disinclined to make trouble unless provoked. They improve the garden environment by eating yellow jackets and wasps—a skunk will wipe out a whole nest of these pests overnight. Most of their digging is done in late summer and fall and will not do permanent harm to the lawn.

Raccoons, on the other hand, though beautiful, are not what most gardeners would call an improvement. But if all they can find at your place is what they can dig out of the lawn, they won't hang around for long. The world is full of other people's ripening corn, seed-filled bird feeders, unsecured garbage, and bowls of pet food, and these are the things that encourage raccoons to move in. 🍂

When to Fix the Lawn

Q **Can you replace grass in the summer in South Dakota?**

A Fall and spring, in that order, are the right seasons for starting or renovating a lawn, and considering the number of spring chores most gardeners face, it's especially comforting to know that putting it off until the fall isn't procrastination but proper planning.

The lawn grasses typically grown in the North are cool-season plants, so the heat of June, July, and August is hardest on them, and those months are the worst time to establish new growth. Spring's cool weather is better, but even so, the warming encourages more leaf growth at the expense of root growth.

In the fall, as early as September, cooler temperatures and more frequent rain work to encourage root growth and nutrient storage, giving the plants better preparation for winter and a faster start the following spring. 🍂

Pray for Snow

Q **The new addition to my house is destroying our small back lawn. By the time the contractor has finished, it will be late December and too late to put in a new lawn. Any suggestions?**

A Early, deep, and lasting snow would hide the problem until spring. And since you can't count on that, sod, if you can find it, can still be put down as long as the ground beneath isn't frozen. Late December, however, will be far too late for seed to germinate and establish a strong enough root system to avoid being heaved out or damaged by the freezing and thawing cycles of winter.

Dr. Martin Petrovic, professor of turf grass science at Cornell University, said seeding is best done from September into October when the heat of summer is over, the soil is still warm enough to encourage growth, and there is a lack of competition from weed seeds. Spring is the next best time to seed, although the grass will face competition from germinating annual weeds, as well as the summer heat, before its roots are fully established.

To eliminate that new-construction look this winter, put down an inch of straw, anchored with string or cord in a grid pattern to keep it from blowing away. If you prepare the site and broadcast seed before putting the straw down, the seeds will germinate as soon as spring warms the soil. Remember to take the grid off before the first mowing, although the straw can stay. 🍎

Snow-Seeding

Q **I told a friend I have to reseed some of my lawn, and she said I should have snow-seeded during the winter. What does that mean?**

A Snow-seeding is a form of dormant seeding, in which grass seed is scattered on top of the snow. Too cold to germinate, it waits until the snow melts and the soil temperature reaches about 50° to 55°F.

If this sounds like a work-free lawn, it's not. The soil still has to be prepared. So if you cleared down to bare soil and scratched up the surface last fall, you could have flung your seed onto the snow cover with confidence. Snow-sowing is best done just before (or during) another snowfall, to keep hungry birds at bay. And ignore the stares from your neighbors. 🍎

Lawn-Mowing Dangers

Q **I understand that if the lawn-mower blades are not sharp, they will tear the top of the grass and make it vulnerable to disease because the open edges are rough and fungus can enter. Is this true?**

A Mowing a lawn is not exactly like giving a haircut. Cutting living tissue is stressful under the best conditions, but using a dull blade adds insult to injury, especially on a rotary mower, which cuts by brute force, whacking instead of scissoring neatly like a reel mower.

The problem isn't just the direct ability of disease organisms to enter the wound, although that plays a part. Even with a sharp blade, the loss of leaf surface means reduced photosynthesis and reduced ability to take up water. These stresses make the plant weaker and less able to fight off diseases, and they slow down root growth. When the cut is ragged and torn, the increased surface area open to the air means a 10 to 15 percent additional water loss through evaporation, and a longer time to heal. Diseases find it easier to enter a host with weakened defenses.

It is also important to avoid mowing when the grass is wet with dew or rain. Not only are fungal populations higher when it is damp or humid, but the water on the grass impedes the lawn-mower blade, leading to a poorer-quality cut. Again, rotary mowers are bigger offenders than reel mowers under these circumstances.

Cutting grass right also means cutting it the right height. While grass may prefer never to be cut and we may prefer that golf-course-greens look, the best compromise for a healthy, good-looking lawn is to cut it 2½ to 3 inches high year-round. 🌶

Grass Stripes and Pinstripes

Q How can I make my lawn look like the Yankee Stadium outfield? I want that striped look. Is it in the cutting, or is it different kinds of grass?

A You can have that ballpark look by doing what the Yankees' groundskeepers do. George Solano, who helps keep the Bermuda, blue, and rye grass in the outfield in top shape through dry springs and hot summers alike, said the trick is in the cutting: a metal bar is attached to the front of the mower to bend the grass as it is cut, leaving it at a slight angle. After being mowed in alternating directions, the grass strips reflect light differently, giving the effect of lighter and darker stripes.

But to see the stripes, you'll have to put a video camera up a tree and watch your lawn on television. The effect is really just an optical illusion. The small amount of contrast between stripes is enhanced by the angle of view and the camera. 🍂

Raking vs. Mulching

Q We've been using a mulching lawn mower regularly for several years now. When leaves start to drop in fall, we mulch and leave them in place as well. Our lawn is one of the better looking and healthier ones in the neighborhood. Why do the majority of homeowners insist on the removal of grass clippings and leaves from their lawns?

A Don't brag about your lawn; it just sets the neighbors to dumping more fertilizer on theirs. Just mention that according to studies done at Michigan State University, the nutritive value of mulching and leaving grass clippings saves 20 to 25 percent of the fertilizer one would ordinarily use. And then talk about how improved your golf game is since you've been spending more time with a club and less with a rake.

And if they start talking about thatch buildup, inform them that a three-year Cornell University experiment found no difference in thatch thickness or quality of turf between areas where 6 inches of fallen leaves, both oak and maple, were shredded by a mulching mower and left on the grass, and areas where the leaves were raked off. (Thatch is the dead, dying, and decaying organic matter, mostly old turf stems, that accumulates in a layer just above the soil.)

But weekends can't be all golf. You do have to either rake or run the leaves over with a mulching mower. You can't just leave them there because they'll block the light and eventually kill the grass, along with your neighborhood reputation. 🍂

Lawns

The Tread of Little Feet

Q I love looking at the bird feeder outside my kitchen window when I'm having my morning tea, but I don't like looking at the lack of greenery on the ground below. Are there any plants that can withstand the constant foot traffic under a bird feeder? This one is in a perfect place, so I don't want to move it.

A Unless you're fond of splotches and splatters, broad-leaved plants under the feeder will not be a visual improvement. You are much better off with grass. It not only makes life easy for ground-feeding birds like juncos, sparrows, and mourning doves, but also hides the droppings of those that do their eating on high.

Discarded hulls and uneaten seeds will make it difficult for the grass to grow if they are allowed to pile up. So either learn to love frequent raking or try switching to hull-less sunflower seed. It costs more, but it is a labor-saving product.

Alternatively, you might consider changing your mind about the feeder's location. If you install the kind that clamps right against the window, you won't see what's underneath unless you are outdoors. 🍎

It's Not Funny

Q I've seen the term "ha-ha" used with reference to English gardens. Is this some joke, and can you explain?

A The ha-ha is a deep, wide ditch that physically separates lawn from pasture while leaving them visually integrated. Its purpose is to keep livestock from wandering over to cultivated areas, and it was popular in eighteenth- and nineteenth-century naturalistic gardens in England, since it was virtually invisible from the manor. It did not mar the view of the distant landscape because it was constructed with a low, concealed retaining wall on the garden side and a sloping, grassy gully on the pasture side.

Though certain coarse types might be amused if they watched an inattentive promenader fall over the edge, in this case "ha-ha" is meant simply to evoke surprise. It's supposed to be the sort of thing you'd say when you come upon one and realize you've reached the end of the line. In the eighteenth century it was sometimes written as "haw-haw," or "ah-ah," or "ha," and all of those variations are considered (by the Oxford English Dictionary) to have come from the French. ✿

Live and Let Live

Q **We had a few tufts of wild onion (miniature bulbs sprouting chivelike stems) last summer but assumed that our lawn-care specialist's chemicals would take care of them. This spring, the problem is worse. A neighbor told us the only solution is to dig them out. In many hours of weeding, I noticed that each tuft was rooted by a hive of tiny bulbs, impossible to clean out completely, making me fear a similar predicament next spring. What can we do to get rid of these things?**

A Wild onions (*Allium canadense*) and their equally obstinate relative wild garlic (*A. vineale*) pop up in early spring and can be 8 inches tall and really obvious before you even think of cutting the lawn. There are no effective so-called natural controls, like insects or grubs that feed on them, or pinpoint chemicals that have no effect on anything else. Digging them out is unlikely to completely solve the problem since it is inevitable that a few small bulblets will get away.

The best solution is to reread Rachel Carson's *Silent Spring* while you let the growing grass hide the onions and wait for them to die back in the summer. Kept from going to seed, they do not spread aggressively. All environmentalism is local, and begins with understanding that it's time to rethink our ideas of lawns and gardens. Forcing a human sense of perfection, order, and beauty on nature often comes at a high price. ✿

CHAPTER SEVEN

Shrubs

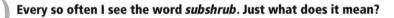

Shrubs in General

What *Is* a Subshrub?

Q **Every so often I see the word *subshrub*. Just what does it mean?**

A The term is a source of a certain amount of disagreement among horticultural authorities. But in general, the word is applied to those low-growing plants whose upper portions are similar to herbaceous perennials in that they have soft stems that appear anew each year, but whose lower portions are woody and shrublike and do not die to the ground at the end of the season.

Among the plants that might be considered hardy subshrubs are the thymes, some artemisias, candytufts, santolinas, and chrysanthemums. Plants that are tender subshrubs include Mexican heather (*Cuphea hyssopifolia*) and lantana. 🌰

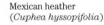

Mexican heather
(*Cuphea hyssopifolia*)

Cultivar or Variety?

Q **Please explain the difference between cultivars and varieties.**

A In the eighteenth century, when Linnaeus invented the naming system that is still used in biology and botany today, he expected that every plant would have a unique and universally recognized two-word name: the first (genus) capitalized and the second (species) not. *Spiraea japonica* refers to the same plant the world over.

But sometimes differences arise, as a result of natural mutation or uncontrolled cross-pollination. These differences may be important but not unique enough to justify a new species name. Such plants are called varieties, and their differences are likely (but not guaranteed) to reproduce well from seed. Varietal names, in italics, are not capitalized and simply follow the species name, sometimes set off by "var." *Spiraea japonica albiflora* is smaller and paler than its parent.

Cultivars (a contraction of "cultivated" and "variety") are plants that have been bred or selected for desirable characteristics. They are propagated vegetatively, from cuttings rather than seeds, because their seedlings generally do not reproduce the parent. Cultivar names are capitalized, enclosed in single quotes, and not italicized. *Spiraea japonica* 'Goldflame,' with bright yellow leaves and bright pink flowers, is considerably more colorful than *Spiraea japonica*.

All this helps to assure that everyone—no matter what language they speak—can speak the same language when they want to identify a plant. 🌰

CAVORTING IN THE SHRUBBERY

When people refer to shrubbery these days, they usually mean simply a number of shrubs. But in the eighteenth and nineteenth centuries, the shrubbery was a special garden, densely planted with things like collections of rare rhododendrons. Thick hedges of privet or yew were frequently part of the shrubbery, which was designed to be viewed from within as you strolled on narrow walkways that took numerous turns. It was dark in there, and it was ideally private . . . the walkways were paved with gravel, so you could hear if someone was coming.

Pistillate Flowers

Q I recently came across the word *pistillate* in the description of a sea buckthorn plant. Can you explain this term?

A Although most flowers are hermaphrodites, which means they contain both male and female parts, this is not true for every plant species. Some plants have separate male and female flowers, and these are referred to as staminate and pistillate, respectively.

Sometimes the separate flowers are borne on the same plant, as is the case with vegetables such as cucumbers and corn. Sometimes the separate flowers are borne on different plants, as is the case not only with buckthorns but also with willows, hollies, and many others. Buckthorns described as pistillate have female flowers, and they are the ones that bear the colorful orange berries. 🌰

New Shrubs from Old

Q I have a camellia that I would like to propagate to share with friends. Can you tell me an easy way to do this?

A An easy—and some say virtually foolproof—way to increase the number of shrubs, trees, or vines is by a propagation method known as layering. This technique guarantees the creation of a plant with flowers, fruits, or leaves that is identical to its parent. Layering entails placing part of an attached living stem or branch of a woody plant in the ground until it roots. Summertime, when soil temperatures are high, is the ideal time to do this.

The first step is to make a slanted cut or slit about a quarter of the way through the part of the stem that will be placed in the soil, but not so deep that the branch will break. (It is a good idea to treat this wound with a root-inducing hormone.) Make a trench several inches deep and long near the plant to be layered, and bend the slit stem down, placing the cut area under several inches of soil. Firm the soil well around the stem, which can be kept in place with an inverted V-shaped twig, a rock, or a bent piece of wire.

To layer camellias, be sure to use young, flexible branches.

Leave the layered stem in place for a full season, then tug gently to see if roots have formed (robust new growth on the outer side will also be an indicator of success, but since the stem is still attached to the parent plant, its message can be ambiguous). When you are confident that roots have formed, clip the new plant away from its parent, dig it up, and transplant it to its new home. ✿

Pruning and Pruning

Q **Can you tell me the difference between "pruning hard" and "pruning deadwood only"?**

A Pruning hard has different meanings depending on the plant being pruned, but it always involves cutting away a fair amount of living tissue. For example, hard pruning might be done to rejuvenate an overgrown rosebush (as the canes grow old and woody, they put out less bloom). It might be done to reshape a straggly-looking forsythia, to keep wisteria from eating your house, or to improve fruit quality by limiting the output of a grapevine.

Pruning deadwood, on the other hand, isn't really pruning at all; it's just cleaning up. Deadwood is removed to keep plants looking good and to keep them open to light and air. (Pruning to fight disease is another story altogether.)

Most summer-flowering shrubs and deciduous trees are pruned while the plants are still dormant. Although it's easier to see what's dead and what isn't after growth has resumed, it's easier to remove deadwood without damaging anything else when there's no new growth in the way.

Hard pruning should be done early in the season. Letting the plant make lots of stems and leaves right before you cut them off wastes the energy it took to produce them.

When in doubt about what's dead and what's not, scrape off a bit of bark with a fingernail or knife. Living branches will be green underneath. ✿

WHEN THEY BLOOM TELLS YOU
WHEN TO PRUNE

Most deciduous flowering shrubs need regular pruning to stay shapely and blossom-laden. But no one wants to prevent this year's flowers in order to ensure next year's, so it's important to do the job at the proper time. Fortunately, there's an easy rule. All you have to remember is that "prune comes after bloom." Although there are exceptions (such as rhododendron), most shrubs don't set buds for next year until this year's show is over.

Spring bloomers, including forsythia, beauty bush, lilac, mock orange, viburnum, and weigela, build their buds for next year during the summer. The buds then wait through the winter, ready to burst forth from the "old wood" as soon as the season starts. Prune this group in late spring or early summer, as soon as the flowers fade.

Summer bloomers like butterfly bush, crape myrtle, peegee hydrangea, beautyberry, and Japanese spirea, on the other hand, bloom on "new wood," the growth of the current year. You want them to make lots of new wood, so they should be pruned in early to mid spring, after the danger of heavy frost is past but before new growth has started.

It takes a bit of mental gymnastics to think of spring as coming "after" summer, but if you start counting from when the plant blooms, the formula works.

A Time to Start Over

Q It was a brutal winter, and several of my shrubs appear to be dead though everything else has at least started to leaf out. When should I assume they've had it?

A An unusually cold winter can leave dead plants and major branch dieback in its wake, as well as widespread leaf discoloration among evergreens. Marginally hardy shrubs are especially hard hit, as are any other plants, shrubs, and trees under duress.

If a damaged plant shows a hint of new growth, it can be coaxed along by trimming it extensively, keeping it well watered, and feeding it (sparingly!) with a diluted solution of a balanced fertilizer.

But don't agonize over plants that can be easily replaced. Add to the compost heap those that show no significant signs of life by lilac bloom time, when even plants that are late to leaf out should at least be showing green buds. Also discard those that require so much pruning as to be rendered unrecognizable.

Spring is the time to renew gardens by starting over with something vigorous and new, possibly experimenting with something never grown before. In small gardens especially, each plant is important. But the gardener's psyche is important, too, and a healthy new specimen can do wonders. 🍂

Can These Shrubs Be Tamed?

Q **We recently moved into a city neighborhood with many large houses built in the 1920s. The foundation plants consist of very old yews, Japanese andromeda, junipers, and some azaleas. They've been allowed to grow quite high and have been "shaped" with a hedge trimmer. Many are obstructing the light coming in the ground-floor windows. I'd like something more interesting, and am inclined to replace many of them. On the other hand, I wonder how they would fare if I simply chopped them off at an acceptable height and allowed them to grow in.**

A As you suspect, not all shrubs can be arbitrarily chopped off successfully. While your yews would probably be fine after many years of recovery, the junipers would be iffy. The Japanese andromeda (actually *Pieris japonica*) would never recover its grace or beauty and, if cut too far down, would die. The azaleas, however, would respond well to pruning, even if you took them down to only a foot tall for a major renovation.

If the andromeda and yews are 8 to 10 feet tall, you may want to try pruning the shrubs up from the ground, turning them into small trees. The view through their trunks is bound to be more interesting than looking into thick foliage.

If you decide to replace them, think before you act. Practically every garden-worthy shrub has many named cultivars available, including ones that are shorter than the typical species. Visits to libraries or botanical gardens, and an evening spent with a few gardening catalogs, should be your first steps. 🍂

Blooming Branches

Q **I would like to force some garden shrubs to bloom indoors. Which plants should I choose, when should I cut them, and how long will it take before they flower?**

A Virtually any spring-flowering shrub or tree can be forced into bloom in a bright room indoors, assuming the plant set its buds properly last summer and these buds have gone through a chilling period long enough to tell them they've gone through a winter.

Though chilling periods vary, as a general rule you can start forcing in mid February. The time needed for the flowers to open depends on a number of variables, including the amount of cold the plant experienced through the winter and the amount of water or rain it received through summer and autumn.

Plants to cut and take inside include Chinese or Japanese witch hazel, forsythia, deutzia, redbud, quince, pussy willow, crab apple, rhododendron, azalea, mountain laurel, Carolina silverbell, viburnum, and magnolia. 🌿

Nurturing Young Evergreens

Q **I have planted some new evergreens, but I'm afraid it will take a long time for them to fill in to match the surrounding plants. Can you suggest a fertilizer to speed up this process?**

A Though you might be able to do it by using an overdose of nitrogen, pushing your plants into unnaturally fast growth isn't a good idea. The new growth that has been forced this way is tender and succulent, highly vulnerable to insects, disease, and winter damage.

Newly planted evergreens often appear to "sit still" for the first year. They're spending their energy underground, getting their roots established. That is as it should be; treat them well now, and you'll be rewarded with more (and more rapid) growth in the future.

Make sure they get plenty of water. Feed them once in early spring, with a balanced fertilizer formulated for acid-loving plants; and mulch the ground underneath them so weeds do not compete.

If the gaps are very wide, you can plug them with tall annuals or inexpensive deciduous shrubs. These plants will provide the immediate lush effect you want without competing with the evergreens. When it's time to get rid of the fillers, cut them down to ground level rather than digging them up; you don't want to hurt the roots of the finally large-enough evergreens. 🍎

Surviving Winter's Bite

Q **While I was out walking after a recent storm, the thought struck me that trees and shrubs take whatever winter throws at them. Since all living things are mostly water, why don't plants freeze solid and die?**

A Sometimes they do die, but that mostly happens when people push their luck and try to grow something that isn't hardy in their area, or when winter becomes extraordinarily cold for an extended period or shows up too early. But under normal circumstances, plants don't just sit there wishing they could go inside—they acclimate in stages.

As summer days grow shorter, plants begin "freezing acclimation" by producing hormones that slow growth and induce dormancy. By the first hard frost, they are ready for freezing temperatures, and for beginning the second stage of their preparation.

The year's first below-freezing temperatures freeze the water found between plant cells. Since there is now more liquid water inside the cell than outside, osmotic pressure draws some of the water out of the cell, where falling temperatures cause it to freeze as well. Inside the cells, the concentration of cell parts increases as more water is drawn out. The more concentrated the cell parts, the lower their freezing point. So down to a particular temperature, different for each species, the cells themselves won't freeze, and the plant will survive. Below that temperature, the plant will suffer dieback, starting in its branch tips because they are thinner and more exposed to the cold. But branches are expendable. The soil and any snow cover insulate the roots somewhat; if the roots survive, so will the plant. 🌿

Bitten Bark

Q **Some of my shrubs look as if the bark has been chewed away in several places around the base. What's happening here?**

A A number of small mammals, including rabbits, mice, and rats, feed on bark in winter when food is scarce. Among the plants they consider especially delectable are evergreens such as yew, rhododendron, and juniper, and deciduous shrubs and trees such as apple, dogwood, crab apple, and hawthorn.

A few bites are tolerable, but plants will not survive being completely girdled (when a strip of bark is removed in a circle all around).

Along with keeping weeds and ground covers (in which rodents like to hide) well back from the trunk, preventive measures in winter include wrapping the tree's base with aluminum foil or with several layers of burlap or other heavy cloth, or encircling it with fine wire mesh.

Don't forget to remove the wrappings when spring comes. 🌿

No Real Deer-Proof List

Q **Our property is mostly open, with a long sweep of meadow between the road and the house. We tried fencing the perimeter, but deer are still getting in somehow. I don't mind making a fortress around the vegetable garden, but we want a more natural look for the grounds around the house. Please suggest some attractive shrubs that deer will never eat, preferably something other than holly and bayberry.**

A Long, unhappy experience has taught garden advisors to speak always of plants deer "seldom eat" or "rarely destroy," and there are two reasons for this. One is that they will eat anything if they get hungry enough. The other is individual differences, occasionally from deer to deer, but mostly from species to species within plant genera and sometimes, vexingly, even from plant to plant.

Roses, for instance, appear frequently on lists of things that deer adore and also on lists of things that the deer-bedeviled can safely plant. Although that's partly because the list makers are not in complete agreement, it's primarily because deer love most roses but seldom eat sweetbriers (*Rosa eglanteria*), hedge roses (*R. multiflora*), or the thornier rugosas. The huge rhododendron clan also has more- and less-vulnerable members.

So with that caveat in mind, here's a short list of shrubs that deer tend to find less delicious: if hostas and azaleas are chocolate cake, this group is boiled rutabaga. Abelia, American boxwood, buckeye (*Aesculus* spp.), buddleia, callicarpa, Carolina allspice (*Calycanthus floridus*), forsythia, Harry Lauder's walking stick (*Corylus avellana* 'Contorta'), kerria, leucothoe, mock orange, Oregon grape holly (*Mahonia aquifolium*), pieris, privet, smokebush (*Cotinus coggygria*), spicebush (*Lindera benzoin*), spirea, sumac, viburnum, and witch hazel. 🌢

Undoing What the Deer Did

Q **The deer have decimated my yews and rhododendrons this winter. Nary a leaf is left. Will the plants come back? If so, is there anything I can do to help them along?**

A Both of these plants can withstand severe pruning, so if they were well established and healthy last fall, there's a chance they might survive. Much will depend on the weather. A long, cool, moist spring augurs better for recovery than an early return of summer heat.

As soon as the snow is gone, spread a 2-inch layer of compost over the root zones and prune off anything damaged. Once the extent of loss is clear, cut back to strong growth buds.

After they leaf out, spray the plants with diluted seaweed extract to give them a boost. Be sure they don't dry out, but be careful of overwatering. 🌢

Shrubs in General

HERE, BIRDIE BIRDIE

When it comes to attracting birds, any shrub is better than no shrub. Birds need places where they feel safe, as anyone who has put a feeder in a bare yard well knows. But some shrubs are better than others because they offer food as well as shelter. To get the largest assortment of birds, plant an assortment of shrubs. And don't forget that many (if not most) fruiting shrubs are dioecious: plants are either male or female, and you need both if you want berries.

Proven performers in the bird department include blueberries, cotoneasters, elders, firethorns, hollies, honeysuckles, junipers, and viburnums.

Shrubs for Shady Spots

Q **There are several tall trees around my new house, most of them near the property line. The previous owner had nothing but lawn in the very large yard, but I would like to add some shrubs. There isn't really any sun, but it's not dark, either.**

A The conditions you describe sound similar to the dappled shade of the woodland edge. Quite a few shrubs do enjoy this light, but before you plant, take time to enrich the soil with the organic matter that is also typical of a forest border—compost if you have it, along with shredded leaves and well-rotted cow manure.

Begin by ensuring year-round interest with combinations of broadleaf evergreens, including mountain laurel, Japanese holly (*Ilex crenata*), rhododendron, azalea, and the graceful *Leucothoe fontanesiana*.

Then position deciduous shrubs for contrast. Those that appreciate filtered sun include summersweet (*Clethra alnifolia*) 'Pink Spires,' which bears spires of pale pink flowers in late summer; the Korean dogwood (*Cornus kousa*), whose white early-summer flowers are followed by bright scarlet fruit; enkianthus, which has strings of bell-shaped blooms in early summer; and witch hazel (*Hamamelis × intermedia*) 'Arnold Promise,' whose spidery yellow flowers appear as winter ends.

The cut-leaf Japanese maple (*Acer japonicum dissectum*), which has delicate fernlike foliage, is also tolerant of

Witch hazel, a shade-tolerant early bloomer

dappled shade, as are the star magnolia (*Magnolia stellata*), whose fragrant white flowers appear in April, and the semi-evergreen daphne 'Carol Mackie,' an aromatic spring bloomer whose leaves have cream-colored edges.

Filtered shade is also preferred by the oak-leaf hydrangea (*Hydrangea quercifolia*), which bears its large white flowers in late summer; *Kerria japonica*, with its bright yellow spring blooms, and the maple-leaf viburnum (*Viburnum aceri-folium*), which has black fruit and purple autumn foliage.

Remember to keep this woodsy area well watered through the worst of summer's heat. 🍐

Sand Shrubs

Q **I recently bought a summer cottage in a coastal area where the soil is quite sandy. Are there any shrubs (other than beach plums) that will grow well there without a lot of help from me?**

A Among the shrubs that have generally proven amenable to life in sandy soil are rugosa roses, glossy abelia, blue-beard (*Caryopteris* × *clandonensis*), cotoneaster, shore juniper (*Juniperus conferta*), and tamarisk. 🍐

Short and Formal

Q **I would like to use a hedge as a formal outline for a part of my garden, but I want this outline low. What plants can I use, and how should I do this?**

A A good hedge begins with good spacing, and that in turn depends on the rate of growth and size of the plants used. The farther they are apart, the longer it will take for a hedge shape to form. Even though they are more expensive than bare-root plants, it is best to start with con-tainer-grown or balled plants, which are easier to plant and less likely to die. To ensure a neat, formal line, use stakes at each end and run a taut string as a guide when planting.

Plants that can be clipped severely enough to keep a formal hedge low include yews (*Taxus* × *media* 'Hicksii' and *T. cuspidata* 'Nana'), arborvitae (*Thuja occidentalis* 'Little Gem'), English boxwood (*Buxus sempervirens* 'Suffruticosa'), Japanese quince (*Chaenomeles japonica* var. *alpina*), dwarf Japanese holly (*Ilex crenata* 'Convexa'), *Viburnum opulus* 'Nanum,' dwarf Alberta spruce (*Picea glauca* 'Conica'), and lavender. 🍂

A Living Fence

Q **I'm planning to put in a pool, and that means I must also put in a 4-foot fence. I am truly worried that it will spoil my yard. Could you suggest a shrub that could be planted around the fence, one that would hide it fairly quickly and create an appealing enclosure. Nothing too expensive, please; I'm going to need a lot of them.**

A There are several shrubs that will hide the fence, and a few of them are even comparatively inexpensive, including boxwood, yew, privet, spirea, honeysuckle, and forsythia. But before you choose one, a couple of things should be considered.

To start with, a screen of shrubs is a wide item: informal plants that are 5 feet tall will be almost that wide or wider; and formal ones, which can be pruned to a narrower profile, require enough walking space in the rear so you can get back there to prune. Furthermore, shrubs will hide the fence from only one side. Assuming it's the view from the house, you'll still have to do something to keep the swimmers from feeling like they're in jail.

You can solve that problem by planting shubbery for the house side and climbing roses and/or fence-covering vines like clematis on the pool side. Alternatively, you can have a good-looking, slender, less-formidable barrier by giving up the shrub idea and going directly to the embellishment-on-fence solution. (This means the fence itself must be attractive, but why shouldn't it be?)

As you ponder shrubs vs. vines-on-fence, and indeed, pool placement itself, bear in mind that no matter what the fence is made of or hidden with, you're still going to have a box in the middle of the lawn unless you think about integrating the pool enclosure with the rest of the landscape.

Finally, remember that barriers are just that: they not only keep people away, they also prevent air from moving freely in and out. To the extent this means less windchill, fine, but if your fence is on the solid side and the enclosure is any smaller than, say, a basketball court, you could end up with a stagnant pool in a stifling little room. 🍂

Avoiding the Early Haphazard Look

Q I have a colonial house, built new to look old. When I have some time, I would like to do the research and plan a colonial-style landscape. Meanwhile, the house is on a builder's lot and is screaming for me to plant something. What shrubs could I put in right now that would fit with a period scheme when I get one figured out?

A Everybody knows that if you move in before the house is finished, you'll probably never get around to completing the cabinetwork; and the same is true of the period garden— or indeed of any garden that's planted before it's designed. You put in a shrub here, a shrub there, and pretty soon you *do* have a garden—from the Early Haphazard period.

Such gardens tend to be unsatisfying, but they are difficult to rip out, especially if the plants in them are healthy. In the long run, it will be much better to just let the place scream until you have at least the rough outlines of a plan. The noise should be a good incentive to get to work on it sooner rather than later.

You can get still get a head start, however, if you establish your own little nursery in an inconspicuous spot. Just buy some small shrubs, plant them in widely spaced, orderly rows, and let them grow larger on site. This will accomplish three things. It will save you money (large shrubs are expensive). It will give you a chance to see how well particular cultivars adapt to your soil and climate. And it will give you a chance to be sure you like summersweet as well in real life as you do in the catalog picture.

There are many shrubs known to have been used in the colonial period—usually as the species, or "common," form of the plant. Fancier varieties tend to be later introductions.

Mountain laurel (*Kalmia latifolia*) was grown in colonial gardens.

The list includes, but is by no means limited to, chokeberry (*Aronia* spp.), common boxwood (*Buxus sempervirens*), common lilac (*Syringa vulgaris*), common smokebush (*Cotinus coggygria*), common winterberry (*Ilex verticillata*), common witch hazel (*Hamamelis virginiana*), European red elder (*Sambucus racemosa*), mock orange (*Philadelphus coronarius*), mountain laurel (*Kalmia latifolia*), New Jersey tea (*Ceanothus americanus*), Piedmont rhododendron (*Rhododendron canescens*), red buckeye (*Aesculus pavia*), shadblow (*Amelanchier canadensis*), strawberry bush (*Euonymus americanus*), steeplebush (*Spiraea tomentosa*), summersweet (*Clethra alnifolia*), sweetbrier and gallica roses, and swamp azalea (*Rhododendron viscosum*). 🍏

British Isle Bloomers

Q Driving through Ireland recently, we were overwhelmed by an evergreen covered with yellow flowers growing wild along much of the coast. I was told it's called furze there. What is its name, and is it available here?

A The plant is also called gorse, or whin, and botanically it is *Ulex europaeus,* said Betty Scholtz, director emeritus of the Brooklyn Botanic Garden. Having led tours through the British Isles, she has seen many a tourist similarly captivated. The fact that it seems to be ever in bloom somewhere in the British Isles has led to a favorite adage: When gorse is in flower, kissing is in season.

A member of the pea family (Leguminosae), gorse is a spiny, densely branched, somewhat weedy deciduous shrub. It grows from 2 to 7 feet tall, and its bright yellow flowers appear through late winter and spring.

Gorse is grown in the United States in mild coastal climates (zones 6 to 8) and can be a useful seaside plant since it thrives in sandy, acid soil. But it is also very invasive where conditions are hospitable. Check with your local extension service for warnings before you plant. 🍏

Shrubs in Particular

Andromeda Damage

Q There are granulated brown specks on the undersides of the leaves of my andromeda (*Pieris japonica*), and the top is mottled gray. Are bugs causing this? If so, is there an insecticide I can use?

A What you're seeing is the work of the andromeda lace-bug, a destructive insect whose cousins feed on azaleas and rhododendrons. Lacebugs spend the winter as eggs on the leaves. After hatching in spring, the insects suck the sap from the leaves and excrete the droplets. This activity causes the upper sides of the leaves to appear speckled yellow, gray, or pale brown. Although the leaf damage you see from the top resembles that inflicted by mites and leafhoppers, only lace-bugs leave the sticky residue underneath.

The safest approach (for you and your garden) is to spray the undersides of the leaves thoroughly with a solution of insecticidal soap, which will help destroy next year's brood and wash away the droplets. Next spring, start a soapy spray program early and continue weekly into the summer. If the soap does not seem effective, try a horticultural oil spray, which is a slightly heavier gun. It may take a full year—or more—for these low-impact solutions to work, so don't reach for a stronger poison until you're sure you really need it. 🍏

Azalea Companions

Q I have a number of azaleas and would like to add several shrubs or small trees that would be good companions. What would you suggest?

A Among the deciduous shrubs or small trees that do well in similar conditions—partial shade and moist, somewhat acid soil—are summersweet, shadbush, redbud, Japanese maple, Carolina silverbell, sourwood, fothergilla, oakleaf hydrangea, and Burkwood viburnum. Appropriate evergreens include glossy abelia, Oregon grape holly, American holly, hemlock, aucuba, and yew. 🍏

GOING FOR THE GOLD

It's a look that can easily be overdone, but plants with golden foliage do make striking accents when paired with contrasts like purple smokebush, sand cherry, or the black-green needles of deeply colored evergreens. In theory, they're also wonderful for lighting up dark corners, but in practice they usually need full sun to keep their sunny color. Planted in shade they tend to fade toward bright green.

With that caveat in mind, go forth and shop. For year-round effect, there are evergreens. From arborvitae through spruces to yews, most of them come in ever-gold as well. The genera *Chamaecyparis* and *Juniperus* are particularly rich in gold-foliage cultivars, with offerings from several different species and a large assortment of sizes, shapes, and degrees of hardiness.

Among deciduous shrubs, you can choose from golden alder (*Alnus incana* 'Aurea'), golden elder (*Sambucus canadensis* 'Aurea'), golden Japanese barberry (*Berberis thunbergii* 'Aurea'), golden mock orange (*Philadelphus coronarius* 'Aureus'), and yes, you are seeing a pattern. If it says 'Aureus' or 'Aurea,' something about that plant is going to be yellow.

There is also golden ninebark (*Physocarpus opulifolius* 'Dart's Gold'), golden privet (*Ligustrum × vicaryi*), several spireas including the pink-flowered 'Gold Mound,' and if you want to go all out, yellow-berry cranberrybush (*Viburnum opulus* 'Xanthocarpum'), which has golden twigs and berries as well as golden leaves.

Azalea Leaf Loss

Q Is a soil deficiency causing the leaves of my evergreen azaleas to yellow and drop off? Although it is only early October, the plants are about half denuded.

A Autumn yellowing and leaf loss in azaleas and other broadleaf evergreens may indeed indicate a soil deficiency, but it's more likely that the problem is insufficient moisture through the hot days of summer and beyond. It is not unusual to have lengthy periods with no rain in late summer, and early autumn is often on the dry side as well. All that thirst takes a severe toll on these shallow-rooted species. This problem is especially likely in sunny areas or those with insufficient mulch.

If there has been heavy rain lately, fine. Otherwise, give them some water. The roots should go into the winter moist but not soggy. With any luck, your plants will recover nicely and produce good new foliage after flowering next spring.

Since it's also possible that the problem is one of the many fungus diseases that attack these plants, be sure to rake away and destroy all of the fallen leaves. If the plants are watered properly next year but the problem still persists, take a few of the damaged leaves to your local cooperative extension service for diagnosis. 🌿

The Elusive Bayberry

Q I have several bayberry plants that have not borne fruit since I planted them in my Cape Cod garden two years ago. Might there be separate male and female plants? Would this account for the lack of berries?

A The plants do have separate sexes, and if you have planted male plants exclusively, you will have no fruit. It's only on the young stems of female plants that you will find the waxy gray berries of the aromatic bayberry (*Myrica pensylvanica*). This semi-evergreen native shrub grows wild in coastal areas from North Carolina to Newfoundland. While every part is fragrant, it is the handsome berries that are used for decoration and bayberry candles.

Bayberries are known for their ability to grow in dry, poor soil within reach of salty ocean spray. But since they're not easily transplanted from the wild, it's best to buy from a reputable nursery that has labeled the sexes clearly. 🌿

Bayberry
(*Myrica pensylvanica*)

Boxwood Background

Q Having seen exquisite boxwood planters in Williamsburg, Virginia, I want to grow some myself. Can you tell me about this plant and which ones survive the cold?

A The Moors edged their harem gardens with boxwood. Ancient Greeks used its finely grained wood for musical instruments. And the Bible has many references to the plant that boxwood expert Mary Plowden-Wardlaw calls "man's oldest garden ornamental."

There are more than 30 species and numerous varieties in the genus *Buxus,* she explained. All "grow slowly and differ significantly enough to warrant planning ahead before purchasing." Dwarf plants rarely exceed 2½ feet, while the arboreal forms may reach 25 feet or more.

Ms. Plowden-Wardlaw's own Massachusetts garden, which contains plants started in 1918 by her mother (the horticulturist Sarah Chapman Francis), has been an informal testing ground for many varieties.

Among the cold-tolerant plants she suggests are *Buxus sempervirens* 'Rotundifolia,' a large shrub whose dark, shiny leaves keep good color through winter; *B. s.* 'Newport Blue,' which stays under 3 feet and has blue-green leaves; and *B. s.* 'Vardar Valley,' a somewhat spherical plant native to the Balkans. *B. microphylla* var. *japonica* has a pyramidal form and makes a fine hedge.

For additional information, contact the American Boxwood Society, P. O. Box 85, Boyce, VA 22620; *www.boxwoodsociety.org.*

And the Winner Is . . .

Q I understand the Pennsylvania Horticultural Society's Gold Medal Plant Award winner for this year is a boxwood called 'Green Velvet.' What does this award mean (if anything)? And what is the plant like?

A Unlike the Oscar, Emmy, and Tony, not all awards go to the famous. Since 1988, the Pennsylvania Horticultural Society has made Gold Medal Plant Awards to bring attention to underused woody plants.

Nurserymen, horticulturists, and amateur gardeners nominate plants that they feel are outstanding. Three specimens of each plant, all landscape size and from the mid-Atlantic region, are evaluated by a committee of professionals who choose the winners. By introducing these plants to a wider audience, the society hopes to encourage more diversity in garden planting and to increase the number of growers and retailers offering these plants.

The boxwood *Buxus* 'Green Velvet' has gone from humble origins to become one of the society's Gold Medal Plant Award winners. In 1973, adjacent rows of *B. microphylla,* a Korean species, and *B. sempervirens,* an English species, planted at Sheridan Nurseries in Ontario, accidentally cross-pollinated and produced a boxwood with the best traits of both its parents but none of their bad habits.

'Green Velvet' has the deep green foliage of its English parent and the cold hardiness (zones 4 to 7) of its Korean parent. The combination has produced a boxwood 3 feet high and 4 feet wide, with rich, lustrous, deep green foliage, giving an appearance of depth and health. As welcome bonuses, *Buxus* 'Green Velvet' tolerates drought and is also highly resistant to deer predation. 🍎

Hold That Lopper

Q I have large butterfly bushes in my yard that attracted record numbers of butterflies and hummingbirds this summer. I know they need to be cut back very hard in the spring, but I was wondering if there is any reason it should not be done in the fall. I would like to tidy up for the winter.

A Why would you want to look at a row of stumps? Butterfly bush is semi-evergreen, holding on to its foliage well into winter. Besides, tidy for the winter may mean disappointment in the spring. In areas where winters are cold, butterfly bush (*Buddleia davidii*) often suffers significant dieback. If pruned hard in the fall, dieback would occur close to the plant's crown, and you could lose the plant. That would leave a hole in your garden, and a lot of swallowtails would be scratching their heads, wondering where their next meal was coming from.

Cutting back in early spring, just as the leaf buds are beginning to swell, gives you the option of cutting your buddleias back to 12 to 18 inches above the soil or just above the highest surviving buds, giving you a taller shrub more quickly.

Fall cleanup brings extra energy to gardeners, and the urge to whack everything down is strong. Whether it's a desire for a neat closure to the growing year or revenge after a season of limited success taming nature, be selective. Other plants that shouldn't be cut back until early spring include artemisia 'Powis Castle,' caryopteris, perovskia, lavender, santolina, Montauk daisy, and candytuft. 🍎

Butterfly bush
(*Buddleia davidii*)

Shrubs in Particular

What Ails Camellia?

Q My mother has a camellia plant that is about 49 years old. It has buds all over it every year. The buds, however, open only about halfway, then the petals turn brown and the buds fall off the plant. Why does this happen? Any suggestions?

A If your mother's plant is a *Camellia japonica,* the most common kind, and it is growing somewhere near the northern edge of its range (in southern New Jersey, for instance), it may simply be getting blasted each year by frost.

But if it's living in the so-called camellia belt—a warm zone that starts in southern Virginia, goes all through the Deep South, and then snakes along the country's perimeter until it winds up in the Pacific Northwest—the problem is probably a fungus disease called petal blight, which is epidemic through that area.

There are three ways to deal with petal blight.

1. Clean up. If you can rake away and discard or burn all fallen blossoms and buds as soon as they drop, you may be able to prevent reinfection. But the spores also travel on the wind, so you won't get far unless the neighbors for at least half a mile around are also sanitation-minded.

Camellia japonica,
often prey to petal blight

2. Live outside the camellia belt. The fungus isn't a problem where winters are cold.

3. Plant a fall-blooming species, which would be less prone to blight. Japonicas are spring bloomers, with flowers that come anytime between January and May. Fall bloomers flower between September and December. They include *C. sasanqua,* which is almost as hardy as *C. japonica; C. × hiemalis,* which is a bit more tender; and most of the varieties developed by Dr. William Ackerman, who worked with these plants for many years at the National Arboretum in Washington, D.C. His introductions, including white 'Polar Ice,' pink 'Frost Prince,' and pinkish lavender 'Winter's Star,' are among the hardiest, capable of surviving as far north as Long Island, New York, and the southern New England coast. ❧

Caper Bush

Q **While visiting Greece, I saw the caper bush growing wild. Can this be grown in a sheltered garden just outside Chicago?**

A The caper bush (*Capparis spinosa*) is one of several hundred members of the caper family, and is the species whose pickled flower buds brighten salads and other dishes. A rambling, spiny, 3- to 4-foot-tall deciduous shrub, it bears white flowers and grows naturally throughout the Mediterranean.

Unfortunately, the caper bush isn't hardy; anything colder than a light frost will do it in. In theory, you could grow it as an annual or pot it up in a tub and bring it in for the winter, but in practice these plants just don't thrive unless they're clinging to rocky hillsides in climates that resemble home. 🌰

Curious About Cocaine

Q **As a gardener I am curious about the cocaine plant. (I assure you I have no intention of growing it.) Can you tell me about it?**

A The cocaine plant is one of 90 tropical and subtropical woody species of its genus. Its botanical name is *Erythroxylum coca* (not to be confused with *Theobroma cacao,* the cocoa plant which is used to make chocolate).

The cocaine plant is believed to be native to Peru, although it also grows elsewhere in western South America. A humid atmosphere and high elevation are required. In the early 1900s the plant was introduced into India and Ceylon with seeds from Kew Gardens in England. The shrub has leathery leaves 2 inches long, in pairs at the end of slender reddish brown branches, and grows 6 to 18 feet tall. Clusters of yellow flowers grow beneath the leaves on wood of the preceding year. 🌰

Hiding Hazel Leaves

Q **After years of admiring a beautiful contorted hazel that I see only in winter, I decided to buy one. But at the nursery I discovered that the leaves are ugly. Could I plant morning glories to cover them?**

A The leaves of the contorted hazel, *Corylus avellana* 'Contorta,' are less than lovely, but their major fault is that they hide the corkscrewed branches that make the naked plant so compelling. In winter, you have a fantastic sculpture decorated with dangling catkins; in summer, just a green mound.

But a flowering blanket thick enough to hide that mound would kill it. The best way to screen the hazel is to plant it at the far edge of the garden, behind something big and bushy like Joe Pye weed or globe thistle. If you want the hazel closer, plant a distraction nearby. As long as you choose something large like a clump of plume poppies, or something gaudy like double day lilies, you won't really see the hazel until you want to. 🌰

Contorted hazel
(*Corylus avellana*
'Contorta')

Crape Myrtle for Yankees

Q **On motor trips in Virginia, I have noticed a shrub with beautiful red blossoms. I've been told it is crape myrtle, and that it requires a milder climate than New York City's. Even in Brooklyn, however, I have seen blossoming shrubs that resemble those I admired in the South. Has a more cold-resistant strain of this shrub been developed?**

A Although crape myrtle is primarily a Southern plant, hardy to zone 7, it can survive in zone 6 if there is a sheltered microenvironment that keeps plants from getting too cold for too long.

The National Arboretum began breeding crape myrtles in the late 1950s, introducing its first hybrids in 1978. The main goal has been disease resistance—especially to powdery mildew—not hardiness. But as luck would have it, the arboretum's introductions seem a bit more like zone 6 plants than traditional crape myrtles are. The hybrids, named for American Indian tribes, include 'Natchez' and 'Tuscarora.' Both are large, up to 30 feet tall. There are medium-size, multistem shrubs like 'Acoma' (10 feet tall and wide), and even 2-foot-tall miniatures ('Pocomoke' and 'Chickasaw'). More information and good color pictures of crape myrtle can be found on the National Arboretum's Web site: *www.usna.usda.gov.* 🌰

Silver Curry

Q **Last summer I saw a garden edged with a lovely silver-leaved plant that had a curry-like scent. Can you tell me what it was and where I can find it?**

A The plant you saw, *Helichrysum italicum* ssp. *serotinum* (aka *H. angustifolium*), is called the curry plant because of the aroma that you noticed. But strangely enough, its fragrant, narrow, and extremely handsome silver leaves are not an ingredient in the spice blend known as curry powder.

The curry plant is a tender subshrub native to the Mediterranean, hardy to zone 7. It is one of some 500 species in the daisy family whose cousins include the popular strawflower. Although it is a true sun lover, as its botanical name suggests (*helios* is Greek for "sun"), the curry plant is undemanding and needs only well-drained soil.

If left untrimmed, this dainty plant ultimately reaches a height of about a foot and bears clusters of small yellow, daisy-like blooms. Like rosemary, which its leaves somewhat resemble, individual curry plants can also be trained into lollipop-shaped topiaries known as standards. 🌿

Seeing Red in Winter

Q **This past spring I planted two red-twig dogwoods. One had some new growth, so we have had a few brilliant crimson branches to enjoy during the winter months. Next winter I would like more of the red color and have heard that you should trim the shrub down quite a bit. But when?**

A The subtle whites, browns, and grays of the winter landscape have a quiet beauty, but some days you just need something that shouts. Whether they are in your garden or just off the side of a road, the bright red stems of *Cornus alba* or *C. sericea* and their cultivars, or the yellow-green stems of *C. stolonifera* 'Flaviramea,' can jolt you right out of your winter blues.

But as with people, the young are the most colorful. As the stems get older they turn duller and darker, so late-winter pruning is necessary to keep the display bright red. By cutting the 3-year-old stems every year, right down to

6 inches above the ground, you force the plant to keep sending up new growth, and you always have two-thirds of the shrub—the 1- and 2-year-old stems—providing showy winter color. ☙

The Nifty Winged Wahoo

Q **When we planted our hedges of *Euonymus alatus*, I expected they would have bright red fall color. Instead, they are very blah. I read that they are pH adaptable. Does that mean that I will get better color if I acidify the soil?**

A Euonymus color does not react to soil pH the way *Hydrangea macrophylla* does. The straight species, *E. alatus,* is variable in its fall color, ranging from a soft peachy rose with hints of yellow through bright pinks and dark rosy reds. Unfortunately, the fact that it is adaptable to a range of soil pH and propagates so easily from seed has allowed it to escape from cultivation and become invasive in the woods and prairies of parts of the East and Midwest.

Distinctive corky-winged branches give this shrub the nifty common name winged wahoo, and brilliant fall reds give it another: burning bush. Since yours appears to have its fire put out, it sounds as though the variety planted is not one of the more colorful ones.

If brighter is better, try some of the cultivars that have been selected for color: 'Nordine' (red with orange tones), 'October Glory' (brilliant magenta red), or 'Rudy Haag' (pinkish red). ☙

A Sporting Chance

Q **I have a 20-year-old euonymus plant whose leaves are green with an off-white border. Recently, I found three branches with solid green leaves—and no border. What is the explanation?**

A There is no particular cause; it's just a matter of odds. If you grow enough variegated plants long enough, you're bound to see this happen sooner or later.

The leaves on the ancestor of your euonymus were solid green. At the growing point of every branch are three well-organized cell layers that contribute to the growth of leaves, stems, and fruit. A random genetic mutation in the middle layer, which controls production of chlorophyll, resulted in a sport—a branch that differs from the rest of the plant. An observant plant breeder took cuttings and propagated the branch, resulting in a variegated euonymus.

Interestingly, the new sport, showing a reversion to all green, is not the result of another mutation. Dr. Dennis Werner, a plant breeding expert at North Carolina State University in Raleigh, said that occasionally in a branch, the lower cell layer (with normal genes) swaps places with the middle layer, and the leaves go back to being all green. Perhaps the switch is just a reaction to the boredom that comes with doing the same job day after day. 🍎

Flies to Euonymus's Flame

Q **I have a set of three euonymus 'Manhattan' shrubs, just like the ones I see in Central Park, and they have grown fairly tall, about 5 feet. They get a lot of sun and have a lot of flowers in late summer. When they are blooming, hundreds of flies and some bees swarm the shrubs, landing on the flowers. I have tried to research the shrub but found nothing about flies. I can't believe this happens all over Central Park.**

A The flies are there at the request of the euonymus, which views them not as pests but as pollinators, and there isn't much you can or should do about it. Many plants, including favorites like hollies, hawthorns, and willows, attract flies rather than bees, moths, or other insects. Most flowering plants have more than one pollinator, just in case. One type may get preferential treatment—bees, for example, may be lured with bright colors and sweet aromas—but being pollinated is more important to the plant than how it is done. In general, and there are lots of exceptions to the rule, flies are major pollinators if the flowers are white, pale yellow, or greenish; if they are more wide open than tubular; and if their aroma is more musky than sweet.

With everything else that happens in Central Park, who'd notice a few extra flies? 🍎

DOUBLE-DUTY PRUNING

Most spring-flowering shrubs bloom on young (one- or two-year-old) wood, so it is important to cut them back regularly, thus encouraging new growth. If you want to leave the flowers on the bush, "prune right after bloom" is the standard rule (see page 288).

If you want the flowers for forcing, though, the time to prune is in late winter or early spring, just as the very first buds begin to swell. Not only do you get the flowers, you also get a chance to prune while the bush is bare, which makes it much easier to see what you're doing.

That being the case, be sure to do a thorough job of it. Remove elderly stems at ground level, eliminate crossing branches, and force growth outward by pruning right above outward-facing buds.

Not everything that needs removing will be good vase material, but after you've done the pruning part you can tell which branches to keep by looking carefully at the buds. Flower buds are usually at least a little rounded, and they often appear in clusters. Leaf buds come to a sharper point.

Forcing Forsythia

Q **We are renting a property with a long, bushy forsythia hedge. Can I cut some branches for forcing without hurting the plants?**

A Yes, indeed. Forsythia is a rampant grower, so you will not damage the plants if you cut judiciously. If you want only a few stems, look for branches that should be removed anyway (those that are sticking out at odd angles, for instance), and cut them off almost but not quite flush with the parent wood.

If you want armloads, take this opportunity to renovate the bushes by removing a few—not more than a third—of the oldest stems, which will look woodier than the others. Cut them off at ground level so you keep the fountain effect. (Shrubs like forsythia, kerria, and spirea are most attractive when the basic architecture is of long stems that arch gracefully.)

Forsythia

Bring in your harvest, recut the stems at an angle, and submerge the branches overnight in cool water (use the bathtub for long ones).

Then stand the stems in a bucket of water and keep them in a cool place. Change the water every few days. When the buds show color (in one to three weeks), cut the stems again, arrange them in a vase, and keep the flowers away from heat and bright sun. 🍂

Natural Barbed Wire

Q **A large old shrub on my property bears fruits that resemble small oranges. But its bright green branches have long, sharp thorns. Can you tell me what this might be?**

A It sounds as though your shrub is the trifoliate orange (*Poncirus trifoliata*), which is sometimes called the hardy orange. Formidable and rather vicious thorns make it an excellent natural alternative to barbed wire. It is a native of northern China and a cousin to the true orange, although its fruit is more decorative than tasty.

This sculptural plant, which can grow to nearly 10 feet, is especially striking in spring, when the large, fragrant, five-petaled white flowers are in bloom, and again in autumn, when it is dotted with fuzzy lemon-yellow fruit. The intricate twigs remain bright green all winter.

The plant's botanical name is from the French *poncire*, a kind of citrus. But this shrub, which grows as far north as Pennsylvania and southern New York, is hardier than any true citrus. 🍂

New Hollies from Cuttings

Q **Please tell me why the holly branches I cut are not growing roots, even though they have been in water for three months. The water has been changed regularly, and their leaves are still green. What can I do to help them grow roots?**

A Very little. Most shrubs are not like willows, where a casual glance at a glass of water will prompt cuttings to grow roots. Cuttings have to be taken at the right growth stage: for hollies, use 4- to 6-inch cuttings of semi-hard wood (the current year's, after it is no longer new-sprout soft). Remove the lower leaves so that just two to five leaves remain. Remove a thin slice of bark along the lowest inch or two of the stem. Dip the stem in rooting hormone powder, covering the new wound, and stick the stem in a moistened growing medium of half sphagnum peat, half perlite. Cover the pot with a plastic bag, seal the bag to keep it humid, and place it in bright light but not direct sun. Wait six weeks before gently tugging to see if there are roots. If there aren't, wait longer.

Holly Buddy

Q How close must a male holly be to a female for her to have berries? Does only the female produce berries?

A A single male can pollinate more than one female within a range of about a quarter mile. As a rule of thumb, if you can see one plant from the other, it will work. But whether you have a male or a female, it will have to be in bloom at the same time as its new companion or it is all rather pointless. With sex, as with comedy, timing is everything.

Telling the Holly Boys from the Girls

Q I have a new house with a mature holly. All summer I waited for the red berries to develop, but they never did. I have since found out that hollies are either male or female, and that you need both to get berries. How can I tell what I've got? I don't want to buy a holly of the same sex and again end up without berries.

A You'll have to put off buying another holly until yours is in bloom in May or June. Then you can examine the flowers to find out what you've got. The small, nearly inconspicuous, creamy white flowers, single or in small clusters, are found in the leaf axils (the joint between leaf and branch).

The flowers, unfortunately, are similar at first glance, with four or five stamens (short stalks, each topped with

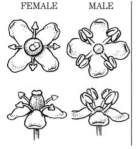

FEMALE   MALE

a small pollen sac) surrounding a single pistil (a small glob-ular structure containing the ovary). In the male flowers, the stamens are prominent, rising above the shrunken pis-til. In the female flowers, it's just the reverse. The stamens are sterile and smaller, and the pistil is swollen and healthy-looking. If the gender isn't obvious, take a few flowers to a nursery and compare them to blooming hollies that are tagged with the plant's sex. ✿

Fragrant Winter Flowers

Q We recently moved to a new home near Cincinnati and discovered a wild-looking shrub. Although it is still early spring and most of the trees around here are just starting to leaf out, this plant is already producing sweetly scented whitish blooms. Could you say what it might be?

A Although many gardeners are familiar with the twin-ing honeysuckle vines, some of which can be rampant weeds, few realize that this genus also includes a number of shrubs. What you've discovered in your new garden is quite possibly the winter honeysuckle *Lonicera fragrantissima.*

This intensely fragrant honeysuckle is a native of China that, depending on location, produces its flowers in late win-ter or early spring. And they perfume the garden for weeks.

Winter honeysuckle is hardy to zone 5. It grows easily in any soil, in either sun or part shade; in summer it pro-duces a crop of blue-green leaves, which can remain well into winter. It can be an exuberant grower, though, and demands control, so prune the shrub in late spring after the flowers fade. ✿

Hydrangea Mystery

Q When I bought my house in Newton, Massachusetts, seven years ago, my hydrangeas produced large blue flowers. At the end of the season I would cut the shoots to the ground. After two or three years, the shrubs grew foliage but no blossoms.

So I experimented. I did not cut all of them down at the end of the season. I found that in spring the old shoots did not leaf out, although the new growth was healthy. I therefore believe that my hydrangeas are the type that do not produce

from old wood. Is there something I can do to cause them to flower again? Although I am no expert, I believe the shrubs are called Nikko Blue.

A Grab a cup of coffee: you might have to read this twice for it to make sense. 'Nikko Blue' is a cultivar of *Hydrangea macrophylla,* one of the hydrangeas that do bloom on old wood—sort of. Each year new shoots arise from the plant's crown. They are easy to spot because they don't have any side branches. The following year, in late summer, they produce flowers both from terminal buds and from side shoots that grow during that summer. So the flowers are on new wood that comes from year-old wood.

The years you cut them down and they still bloomed, you most likely cut them some distance above the soil, leaving some short year-old stems that could produce new side shoots. Then you may have gotten a bit neater, pruning right to the soil. Since there were no year-old shoots, there were no flowers the following summer.

It all sounds complicated, but pruning these hydrangeas isn't that hard. As soon as the flowers become disreputable-looking, prune the stems that had flowers right down to the ground (they'll die anyway in another year or so). Prune only stems that have side branches. Those without side stems are the ones that will branch and flower next year; unless you need to control size, don't prune them even part way. Leaving them whole encourages both food production this year and larger flowers next year. 🍂

Getting Hydrangeas to Bloom

Q **I have a lush hydrangea in deep shade that bloomed three years ago but nothing since. I have never pruned it. Is that the problem?**

A There are several different hydrangeas, each with different pruning needs. All of them do benefit from pruning, but yours should have had at least a *few* blossoms, even in its unpruned state.

Since there were absolutely none, your problem is probably the site. Has the shade by any chance been deepening over time, as would happen, for instance,

Oakleaf hydrangea
(*Hydrangea quercifolia*)

as a large tree got even larger? Hydrangeas will bloom in dappled shade, but they do need some light in order to flower well. They also need good but not super-rich soil; too much nitrogen will encourage stems and leaves at the expense of flowers. 🌰

Nailing Down the Truth

 Is it true that "planting" nails around the roots of hydrangeas makes the flowers blue?

A No, it isn't. The old rusting nail trick is a favorite of gardeners, but what they are adding when they use it is iron, which has no effect on hydrangea flower color. Leaf color is another story. If leaves turn yellow, they may be telling you that they don't have enough iron to make chlorophyll. Should that be the case, burying a few nails, a piece of an old skillet, or any other uncoated iron item would eventually remedy the situation. But it won't turn the flowers blue no matter how long you wait. 🌰

Hydrangea Color Tells All

I need an answer to the issue of hydrangea color. With indicator dyes, pink is common for acid conditions and blue for basic conditions. But a gardening friend says that for hydrangea flowers to be blue, you need acid soil—which seems backward. My soil usually needs to be acidified to keep my azaleas happy, yet the new lace-leaf hydrangea I put in was the most wonderful, heavenly blue. Please set me straight. Are there other plants whose colors change with acidity?

A Many indicator dyes do turn red in acid and blue in alkali, but the hydrangea flower's color response is unique. Research shows that the flower color is not directly affected by acid or alkaline conditions; rather, the key factor is the availability of aluminum. Acidic conditions convert the aluminum compounds normally present in the soil into a form that the shrub can absorb, resulting in a blue flower. In alkaline soil, the aluminum remains tied up in insoluble compounds. Result? Pink flowers. No other garden plant is so insistent on telling it like it is. 🌰

Drying Hydrangeas

Q **I love hydrangeas and would like to preserve their beautiful blossoms. What is a simple way to dry them for arrangements?**

A Hydrangeas are dried the same way you would dry most flowers harvested for that purpose. Wait until they are almost fully open, then cut them off the plant, keeping a good-size stem. Hang them upside down in a warm (not hot) airy place, out of strong sunlight.

While small-flowered plants such as baby's breath can be hung together in bunches of several stems, hydrangea flowers are so densely packed, they are likely to rot if bunched. To ensure good air circulation, it's best to hang individual stems and keep them well apart. For maximum color retention, hang them in a place that does not get *any* direct light. 🍂

Those Old Conifer Blues

Q **How do I get more of the blue color in my 'Blue Rug' junipers, which are now dark green?**

A It's a question of light. Dr. Kim Tripp, director of the botanic garden at Smith College in Northampton, Massachusetts, said ground-cover junipers, including your 'Blue Rug,' are full-sun plants.

Some evergreens are not satisfied to produce food through photosynthesis; they also make a protective, waxy blue substance. But to do this requires a lot of light—six to eight hours each day of uninterrupted full sun. If they are already in full sun, she says, they may be younger plants, which typically show less blue than mature ones. If so, they just need a few more years to start showing off their color.

But some evergreens change color in the winter and then change back in the spring. That happens when the cold causes a chemical change that is reflected in the coloration. Siberian carpet cypress (green to plum) and some Eastern arborvitae (bright green to dull brownish green) are two examples of this change. Spring warmth brings back the normal color—sort of the same effect it has on people.

'Blue Rug' juniper, along with some other cultivars, including 'Blue Chip' and 'Saddle River,' hold their blue color during the winter, while others, like 'Blue Horizon' and 'Prince of Wales,' turn purply bronze. The 80 or so cultivars of ground-cover junipers are hard to tell apart, and Dr. Tripp said that what is labeled 'Blue Rug' frequently turns out to be something else. 🌰

Spring Shrub Overhaul

Q I have an overgrown kerria that blooms sporadically and is a big mess. But I love it and don't want to lose it. What should I do?

A Pruning is the key to keeping kerrias looking their best and blooming well. Once the flowers have faded, cut to the ground one-third of the oldest canes. Also trim to the ground all the very weak and spindly shoots. This will enable light to reach and strengthen the new and developing limbs.

Next year, and the year after, repeat the procedure. After that, remove all three-year-old canes each year, after the plant has flowered. 🌰

Cut Lilacs That Last

Q I would like to cut some lilac branches for display inside the house, but even though I always smash the stems, I haven't had good luck getting them to last more than a day or two. How can I have long-lasting lilac bouquets?

A Long lasting and lilacs don't go together, no matter what you do, but here's how to have them look good for at least four or five days.

Start by getting up early—lilacs cut before the day warms last longest. Select flower trusses that are about half open, and use a very sharp pruner to cut just above a leaf node. Because next year's flowers will form on this year's terminal branches, try to leave as many of those as possible.

Cutting the highest flowers first will encourage a nice full shrub with lots of bloom down where you can enjoy it. Use a ladder if necessary.

Once back on terra firma, remove lower leaves from the stems. Fill a vase with warm water and add commercial flower preservative.

Hold the bottom of the stems under warm water, and recut at a 45-degree angle. If the stems are thick and woody, use a sturdy knife to slit the bases a couple of times. Otherwise, just leave them as is. The smashing that many of us grew up learning to do is no longer recommended; badly crushed cells can't take up water. Put the cut stems in the vase while they are still wet.

Display the lilacs in a cool place, out of direct sun and away from the fruit bowl (the ethylene gas given off by apples, bananas, tomatoes, and other fruits hastens the decay of flowers). If you have room in the refrigerator, store the bouquet in it each night when you go to bed.

Don't forget to keep an eye on the water level (lilacs drink a lot), and to change the water every other day so decay-causing bacteria won't build up.

Shivering Lilacs

Q The recent hot weather has made my lilacs send out flower buds far sooner than normal. I'm afraid they'll be destroyed by frost before they can bloom. Can I do anything to protect them?

A "As long as the flower buds are pretty well closed, there won't be a problem with frost," said Brad Roeller, display garden manager for the Institute of Ecosystem Studies at the Mary Flagler Cary Arboretum in Millbrook, New York, which has a large public collection of lilacs, including French hybrids and species types. "I've never had a problem with flower buds," he continued. "The young, tender leaves are actually more likely to be damaged." And even if they are, the tree itself is unlikely to suffer lasting harm.

An Embattled Lilac

Q The lilac by my cedar fence is being overgrown by a 12-foot hemlock next to it. I pruned back the hemlock in March, trying to give the lilac more room, but it still looks crowded and is growing up and out in a narrow, treelike fashion, rather than a rounded shape. Should I try to move it to a better location? When is the best time?

A Between the fence and the hemlock, the lilac should get a lot of credit for being any shape at all. It will never thrive unless it has more breathing room. But before you get out the shovel there are a few things to consider.

To start with, this divorce involves two trees. If digging up the lilac will damage lots of the hemlock roots, it might be better to just chop it down and start fresh. It's not hard to find 8-foot common lilacs at well-stocked garden centers, and as a bonus you'll have one hole to dig instead of two.

If the lilac is rare or otherwise special, you could either move it or cut down the hemlock. If you decide to move it, do so in very early spring before growth begins. You can prepare this year by cutting down with a sharp spade where you will be digging next year, a process called root pruning.

Cut only a third of the way around; that's as much damage as the plant can suffer in any one year. (Extremely valuable trees go through a 3-year root-pruning rotation before they are moved.) Don't make any prying motions with the spade or remove any soil. You're just forcing the lilac to make some new roots closer to the plant, roots that will come in handy when close-to-the-plant is all it has. 🍎

Tending Lilacs

Q Would you tell me how to prune my lilacs? My two 15-year-old bushes had only two flowers each this spring, so I suspect I do not know how to prune them properly.

A Lilacs have to grow for a few years before they start flowering. After that, they bloom in spring on year-old wood, the stems that grew from the older branches during the previous summer.

Pruning consists mostly of removing elderly trunks and clipping off seed heads within reach. But if you want to cut back young growth, the proper time is right after flowering. It should be done as soon as possible, and no later than three weeks after petal fall.

If you are not pruning too late or cutting off all of the new growth, you might be using too much fertilizer, which could push vegetative growth at the expense of flowers.

Otherwise, your problem is more likely to be a lack of light than a lack of knowledge. Lilacs need plenty of sun to flower well, and shade is the most common culprit when mature bushes fail to bloom.

Or is this the first year of scarcity? If so, and there was plenty of young wood that should have been flowering, the difficulty could be last year's drought. Lilacs start building buds for next year's bloom shortly after they flower, and they need water as well as sun to do it. ✿

Lilac's Last Blooms

Q I was given a lilac four years ago. It bloomed its first year and has never bloomed again. It's in a sunny spot and appears healthy. I've read that some lilacs don't bloom for several years, but I'm confused because this bush did bloom once. Any ideas?

A According to Jack Alexander, the chief plant propagator at the lilac-magnificent Arnold Arboretum at Harvard University, your plant is behaving normally—it just has the usual transplant sulks.

Most spring-flowering shrubs, lilacs included, form flower buds the previous year. That initial display was set when the lilac was still comfortably at home in the nursery. When it was moved, the disturbance set it back. Give it a bit more time, and whatever you do, don't move it again.

Common lilacs (*Syringa vulgaris*) and the French hybrids based on them are especially sensitive in this regard. If you're the type who likes to move the furniture around, try planting 'Miss Kim' (a cultivar of *S. patula*). She's a bit less fussy about an occasional relocation.

'Miss Kim' is easy to find at nurseries, as are a good number of *S. vulgaris* varieties and cultivars. But for the widest selection of colors, fragrance, and bloom times, mail order is the way to go. 🌰

Petal Edges Make It Special

Q Can you tell me what kind of lilac I have at the house we just bought in Richmond, Vermont? The bush has obviously been here for years, and is very tall because it struggles with 70-foot pines for sun. Each petal is medium purple, with a narrow rim of white. No one I've asked at all the local nurseries has ever seen such a bush.

Syringa vulgaris
'Sensation'

A Your struggling survivor is almost surely the French hybrid (*Syringa vulgaris*) called 'Sensation,' introduced in 1938 and quite popular ever since, though it is not especially fragrant, heavy-blooming, or otherwise distinguished except by flower color. As your bush has demonstrated, 'Sensation' is hardy and willing, so you might as well leave it be. But no lilac should be asked to perform well in the acid soil and deep shade suggested by those giant pines, so if you decide to get any more, be sure to plant them in a sunny spot with soil that is close to neutral or slightly alkaline. 🌰

Mock Orange Memories

Q When I was a child in Illinois in the 1940s, we had a wonderful flowering shrub called a mock orange. The fragrance in spring filled the whole yard. I would love to plant one, but my garden is small and I'm afraid there isn't room—I remember the thing as enormous. Can I prune one to a smaller size without losing all the flowers?

A The heavenly perfume of mock orange is, for many, an American madeleine—one sniff and you're back in a gentler, more spacious past. What children don't notice, however, is that *Philadelphus coronarius* is wonderful only when it is blooming, a grand total of about three weeks.

After that, it is undistinguished, without strong architectural interest, autumn color, or attractive winter bark. Even more than lilac, it's a one-trick pony. And now that gardens are smaller (and gardeners more demanding), it is no longer widely planted.

But you can still have one and make it behave, either by pruning it every year right after it blooms or by choosing a smaller variety. Or ideally, both. Mock oranges bloom on year-old wood, so no matter what kind you have, cutting out old stems regularly will help it flower freely.

P. coronarius will grow 9 or 10 feet tall and, if left unpruned, become a thicket 8 or 9 feet wide. The double-flowered hybrid 'Minnesota Snowflake' is shorter, about 6 feet, and has the merit of staying well filled out all the way to the ground. There are other white-flowered hybrids, single and double, of roughly the same size. And if 6 feet is still too big, there is 'Miniature Snowflake,' a fragrant double, which is only 3 or 4 feet tall. It won't look anything like your childhood friend, but if you close your eyes . . . 🌰

Mountain Laurel

Q On a garden tour in Virginia, I saw a lovely pink-flowered shrub that I thought was some kind of rhododendron, but the owner said it was mountain laurel. I'd like to plant a group of them near the edge of my property. Would they survive the winters in Massachusetts? If so, will they grow in the sun? (The one on the tour was in a shade garden.)

A The mountain laurel (also known as the calico shrub) is an extremely tough American native that grows wild from Florida to Ontario. Its botanical name, *Kalmia latifolia,* honors Pehr Kalm, a Swedish botanist who collected plants in North America in the late eighteenth century.

The mountain laurel's leathery evergreen leaves show a distinct resemblance to its cousin the rhododendron's. And like that cousin, mountain laurel does best in part shade, with moist, rich, well-drained soil. It will grow in full sun where summers are cool, but it won't be particularly happy about it.

The clusters of numerous small flowers range from white to purple or red, varying with the cultivar and the flower's age. The red buds of the cultivar 'Heart's Desire,' for example, develop into cinnamon-and-white blossoms; 'Ostbo Red' has red buds that become red-and-white flowers; while the diminutive 'Elf' has light pink buds that mature to white-and-lavender. 🌰

Success with Tree Peonies

Q For three years I have bought tree peonies from my local discount center in the spring. Each year they fail. Any advice?

A One definition of insanity is doing the same thing repeatedly, expecting a different result. Start by planting at the right time of year. After a winter in cold storage, no fine feeder roots are left. Fall planting, at least six weeks before the ground freezes, gives these roots time to grow.

Tree peonies (actually a woody shrub) are usually propagated by being grafted onto a piece of herbaceous peony root. The root nurses the tree peony along for two or three years to develop its own roots. Specialty growers wait until the plants can be sold on their own roots, but discounters may sell younger plants with the herbaceous peony root still attached. They have a hard time surviving, and sometimes the herbaceous peony puts up its own stems.

Plant tree peonies 10 to 15 inches deep in perfectly drained, slightly acidic soil with protection from the sun during the hottest part of the day. But planting in the right season is the real key to success. 🌰

Tree peony
(*Paeonia suffruticosa*)

Pine Eaters

Q My once-beautiful mugho pine was attacked last June by legions of loopers. These inchworms ignored adjacent trees and shrubs. They shredded the needles into fine green dust. They clustered on the denuded branches and began rhythmically and synchronously undulating like The Wave at a ballgame. I tried hosing them off and crushing them but could not keep up. Finally, I guiltily massacred them with an insecticide. My neighbor told me that he lost all his long-needled shrubs to inchworms while away on vacation a few years ago. Now I'm beginning to see them again. Are there environmentally friendly remedies I can use?

A One of the more entertaining insects, European pine sawflies eat only two- and three-needled pines, and mugho pine seems to be especially delicious.

The stand-up-and-sway behavior is defensive. They are extremely gregarious, always eating together, and when one member of the group raises the alarm, they all join in to scare predators away.

Unfortunately, you are late for environmentally friendly methods this season. But there are two good times to beat these pests. During late fall or winter, you can individually remove any needles with telltale rows of pale yellow egg cases (now, there's a way to kill a long afternoon). In the spring, watch for the larvae when they are still very small. When they emerge, the ends of the needles where the eggs were laid look like curled straw. At this time it is easier to shake or brush them off the branch and into a pail of soapy water.

And while you're waiting to take proper action, don't fret. All is not lost. European pine sawflies eat just last year's needles, so they won't kill your mugho pines. The damage is only aesthetic. Whatever killed your neighbor's shrubs, it wasn't those guys. 🌶

Privet Pests

Q I have a 40-foot-long hedge of shrubs whose name I don't know. The leaves are roughly oval and shiny. For the last couple of years I have noticed little white spots on the bark. Then this summer, around mid July, I noticed that the leaves were starting to drop in one section about 6 feet wide, and eventually those bushes lost all their leaves. Their stems and branches were coated with white, which I was told was scale. One thing or another delayed me from addressing the problem over the summer, and now that it is fall, I wonder if it's too late to do something. Is it O.K. to prune the diseased branches back?

A Your privet hedge, and possibly any neighboring lilac, ornamental cherry, or plum, is being attacked by white prunicola scale, an insect that comes with armor plating. Fighting it can be a bit trickier than fighting other insects.

For most of their lives, when they are eggs or feeding adults, or are quietly passing the winter, scales stay put right where they are, protected by a hard outer shell. There's not much of a view, but as real-estate agents say, location is everything. Because scales are soft-bodied insects, the shell serves them well against predators, including sprayer-wielding homeowners.

The key to controlling scale insects is to get at them when they are in their vulnerable crawler stage, looking for a juicy branch to settle on, erect a scale bungalow, and lay a few eggs. That means late April to early May for the generation that overwinters on the branches, and mid July to early August when the second generation's crawlers emerge to look for their own spot.

Horticultural oil (see the label for the proper dilution, depending on the season) is very effective against crawlers because it both smothers them and is absorbed by their cells, where it wreaks havoc with their metabolism. But when they are under their covers they just laugh off anything you throw against them. Don't waste your efforts (or your horticultural oil) right now; wait for next spring.

Pruning should wait until late March or early April, before new growth begins. During the winter the insects are dormant, so no further damage is being done. 🍎

Privet Hedge Control

Q I have 8-foot-high privet hedges that line my driveway and act as a beautiful natural fence. Because of their height, they are now unmanageable. I would like to cut them back to 5 or 6 feet. To do so, I would be cutting established branches that are ¼ to ½ inch thick. What is the best time of the year to cut privet hedges back so drastically?

A Ideally, major privet renovations should be done just before new growth begins in the spring, in order to give the plants the best opportunity to heal their wounds.

While cutting back 2 or 3 feet may sound drastic, it isn't. Privet hedges can be cut back to 18 inches above the ground and will do just fine if they are cared for afterward—fertilized, mulched, and watered during summer dry spells.

That kind of total renovation may be necessary if improper pruning, or no pruning, has resulted in a hedge with foliage at the top but sparse foliage at the base.

To let light into the whole shrub, promoting foliage growth all the way down, be sure to prune with a taper so the top is slightly narrower than the bottom; this will prevent the upper section from shading the lower parts.

When you do your maintenance pruning in the spring, including the shortening, shear off half of last year's growth on the sides as well as the top to continue promoting a dense wall without bare areas all the way down. Go over the hedge lightly in mid July just to keep it neat. And smile while you prune. With a 5-foot hedge, you will have a different relationship with your neighbors. 🌰

Exotic Proteas

Q **Recently my florist has stocked an extraordinary flower called a protea. Can I grow this in upstate New York?**

A Certainly not in a Northeastern garden, although possibly in a greenhouse. Proteas are tender plants, usually rated hardy only through zone 9. They belong to one genus in the family Proteaceae, an ancient group that dates back more than 300 million years and includes some 1,400 species of shrubs and trees in 60 genera. Most are native to Australia, South Africa, and Central and South America, although a number are now being cultivated commercially in California.

The first proteas arrived in Europe early in the eighteenth century. They were named by the Swedish botanist Carl Linnaeus for the Greek sea god Proteus, who was known for the ability to change his form at will. It is believed that this choice of name was an allusion to the extraordinarily varied flower forms of the many different species. The giant *Protea cynaroides,* or king protea, for example, has huge white, pink, or red flowers that resemble artichokes. The daintier *P. nana,* or mountain rose, has small, pendulous, cup-shaped reddish flowers with needle-like leaves. 🌰

Proteas are too tender to grow outdoors in the North.

POINTERS ON PRUNERS

Pruners come in two basic styles, anvil and bypass. With anvil pruners you have only one sharp cutting blade, which closes against a dull bed (the anvil) to sever whatever. Bypass types are more like scissors, with two sharp blades, one of which secures the branch while the other moves past it, cutting as it goes.

Anvil pruners cannot be brought as close to the cut as bypass types, but they do have two advantages: Only one sharp blade means only one blade to sharpen, and the mechanism does give a bit more leverage. Though this can make a difference if you want to use a small pruner for very thick or very hard wood, it's usually easier to use a bigger pruner for heavier jobs and stick with bypass for everyday use.

Bypass pruners come with all kinds of blade lengths and angles, with and without ergonomic handles, and in special versions for lefties. They also come in a wide price range, with the best-made costing two or three times as much as the cheapos. Fortunately, even the most expensive pruners cost less than dinner and a movie for two, so there is no reason to stint. Just remember the old saying: good tools make all tasks go lightly.

In fact, it's best to have at least two pruners, one saved for rough work (at ground level, for example, where you might hit gravel) and one used for delicate operations like removing spent lilac blossoms.

This will let you go a bit longer between sharpening sessions. But those sessions are as important as the pruners themselves because it is *absolutely essential* to make clean cuts when you are pruning shrubs. Wood that has been torn or crushed, as is guaranteed to happen if the pruners are not sharp, is (literally) an open invitation to disease.

Just as it's better to plant a five-dollar tree in a ten-dollar hole than the other way around, it's better to have a pair of sharp cheap pruners than to work with quality tools that have been allowed to get dull. If you don't want to sharpen them yourself, be sure to have them sharpened regularly by a professional—your local nursery or garden center can usually recommend someone. Keep your tools clean and oiled between uses so they don't rust, and they should serve you well for years.

The Firethorn's Berries

Q **My pyracantha doesn't always bear well, but when it does it has orange berries. I would rather they were red. Is there anything I could put on them that would change the color?**

A Fertilizers or soil amendments won't help any more than you could eat your way from blue eyes to brown. Berry color, like so many other plant and animal characteristics, is determined by genetics. Your firethorn (genus *Pyracantha*) will always be orange; except, of course, when the two main enemies of pyracanthas, fire blight and apple scab, blacken the berries and leaves.

Pyracantha could be seen more often in the landscape as an informal hedge, in foundation plantings, or as espaliers, since it offers spectacular clusters of red, orange, or even yellow fruit that persist well into winter and has narrow, glossy dark green leaves. Unfortunately, its vulnerability to disease and poor winter hardiness have limited its use. Until recently, that is.

Two cultivars introduced through the breeding program directed by Dr. Elwin Orton, research professor at Rutgers University, offer a high degree of resistance to the two diseases, as well as improved hardiness. 'Fiery Cascade,' a low-growing pyracantha at 3 to 4 feet tall and 5 feet wide, can handle winter temperatures as low as zero degrees Fahrenheit. It produces a large number of berries, which are orange in late summer but *do* turn bright red in the fall. 'Rutgers,' the other variety, has orange berries and grows 4½ feet tall and 5 to 6 feet wide. 'Rutgers' is even hardier, surviving to –5°. Both might suit places in the garden where a taller pyracantha won't work.

Quince Malady

Q **My flowering quince is blooming gloriously. Early spring is wonderful. But every August, I am ready to yank the shrub because it looks dead. The leaves have dropped off, and it looks awful. It is under an ailanthus tree in my New York City garden and gets some sun during the day. I water the garden during dry spells. Do I need a dormant oil spray? The leaf dropping has been going on for about three years. It's pitiful to see the struggle. Any suggestions?**

Japanese flowering quince (*Chaenomeles japonica*)

A Like some great entertainer, flowering quince puts it all on the line for spring visitors to nurseries and garden centers and then collapses backstage after the show. The branches are easy to force into bloom, so they are common at florists' from late winter into spring, helping seduce gardeners into wanting their own.

Unfortunately, because of a widespread malady, quince is dependable only as a one-season shrub: those spectacular but short-lived white or orange-to-red flowers, and the bronzy leaves that are just emerging when the flowers appear, are about all it has to offer. Once the leaves turn dark green and the flowers fall, you could pass it by without noticing, until sometime in July or August when it begins to defoliate. It is best planted out of the way so that branches can be clipped to bring in for forcing, but it is not the ideal front-and-center shrub.

Horticultural oil won't help because the problem is caused not by an insect but by the same fungus disease that attacks English hawthorns. The fungus is spread by rain and survives the winter on the fallen leaves. If there are English hawthorns in the area, the disease will be difficult to control. If there are none, and you don't want to use a fungicide that is labeled for this problem, a good fall cleanup could reduce the severity, but rainy springs can bring it right back. Some battles are just not worth the fight, and this may be one. 🌰

Nonblooming Rhododendrons

Q **My rhododendrons grow in partial shade in good, peaty soil. I feed them Miracid from late spring through summer. The leaves are beautiful but the plants won't bloom. What's wrong?**

A Most likely, the problem is your feeding program. Miracid is a useful fertilizer that does help maintain the level of soil acidity needed by rhododendrons. But if you look carefully at its label, you will see that its formula is 30-15-15, which means that it contains a high percentage of nitrogen. While this proportion is useful for encouraging good foliage growth—and you say you have beautiful leaves—the nutrient needed to promote good bloom is phosphorus.

For this reason, try switching from Miracid to a high-phosphorus fertilizer, one where the middle number of the trio on the label is the largest, something like 15-30-15. This proportion is high in phosphorus but also supplies the nitrogen needed for good foliage development and the potassium for good root growth.

You also might consider feeding a bit less often. As long as the soil is good, two or three feedings per growing season should be plenty. 🌰

MAINTAINING SOIL ACIDITY

Increasingly (unfortunately), acid rain is supplying more than enough extra to meet the needs of acid-loving plants in the East (where soils tend to be acid to start with), but if you happen to live in the West, or on a limestone seam, you may need to add acidifying agents in order to keep plants like rhododendrons and blueberries happy.

That doesn't mean you need to buy those agents, however—you can use the leftovers of your caffeine habit if you drink coffee or tea every day. Just work the spent grounds or tea leaves into the soil around the plants. Since both these amendments are strongly acid, one family's recyclings should be enough, but if you have a lot of ground to cover or need to make major changes in pH, your local coffee shop will probably be delighted to help out.

Dying Rhododendrons

Q **Recently, we lost several rhododendrons to a disease identified as** *Phomopsis,* **and it was recommended that we spray the remaining plants. Can you tell us more about this disease?**

A Although rhododendrons are generally pretty tough, they are subject to a few nasty problems. Two of them are canker diseases (caused by *Phomopsis* and *Botryosphaeria* fungi), which kill stem tissue. Branches wilt and eventually die.

Both diseases attack plants that are under severe stress, said Margery Daughtrey, a plant pathologist with the Cornell University Long Island Horticultural Research Lab in Riverhead.

Ms. Daughtrey suggested pruning away all affected branches as soon as they are noticed. Prune at least several inches below the wilted area, low enough so you're cutting in healthy tissue; but as extra insurance, dip the pruners in a weak bleach solution between cuts. Because these canker diseases are neither highly contagious nor present through-out the plant's vascular system, Ms. Daughtrey said, it is possible to isolate the problem areas and just "throw the bad parts out."

Be sure, too, through periods of heat and drought, to keep your plants well watered. This will help bolster their own defenses. And since moisture and darkness are ideal conditions for fungal growth, water early in the day so that all foliage will dry by dark.

Because the infections have already occurred and prevention of future stress is a more important tactic now, fungicides will probably not be of much help. 🌶

Summer Rhododendrons

Q I love rhododendrons—can't get enough of them. Someone told me recently that there is one that actually blooms in mid summer. Is this true? Is it as beautiful as the ones that bloom in the spring?

A If you measure beauty by a flower's size and its ability to blind through brightness, as so many rhododendron lovers seem to, then the good news is tinged with bad. The really showy rhododendrons seem to bloom themselves out in spring.

But if you don't need that much candlepower to be impressed, and you remember that azaleas are rhododendrons, you can extend the flowering season by turning to some of the more subtle, delicately refined native azaleas. They belong to the same genus, but their side of the family hasn't been bred into circus clowns. In addition to offering more variety of bloom time, the deciduous azaleas add great fall foliage color.

Sweet azalea (*Rhododendron arborescens*) is a large, informal shrub with lustrous dark green foliage and, from June into July, fragrant flowers in white to light pink. It's hardy all the way to zone 4. Other forms have smoky pink or yellow flowers. The exceptionally sweet-smelling Florida hammock sweet azalea (*R. serrulatum*) flourishes from zone 7 on south, but can survive much farther north if conditions are to its liking. It also blooms from June into July, with small white to pale pink flowers. August brings the small orange-red to red flowers of plumleaf azalea (*R. prunifolium*). 🌶

PRUNING RHODODENDRONS

Rhododendrons, unlike most shrubs, have no painless window for pruning. They start forming the buds for next year's flowers before this year's have even opened, and by the time bloom season is done, those buds are well advanced.

It's difficult emotionally to cut off any of next year's flowers, but if you continually avoid pruning, you may be even more devastated. In fact, you could end up having to cut the rhododendrons to the ground and start all over again.

Pruning rhododendrons requires imagination as well as sharp secateurs. Dr. Richard Lighty, the director of the Mount Cuba Center for the Study of Piedmont Flora in Greenville, Delaware, advised that you try to visualize what the shrub *should* look like. Reach your goal by critically selecting strong outer branches that, when pruned back, will expose smaller inner branches in the right position to fill in. Once exposed to light, these inner branches will begin to grow.

As the flowers fade, trim no more than 15 to 20 inches off the strong branches. Where should you prune? Where the strong branch is near the tip of an inner branch that has a whorl of glossy leaves surrounding the buds, your signal that the inner branch is healthy. If the shrubs are still too big, reprune in two years.

To make sure the plant has stored enough food that it can easily handle pruning, fertilize in late fall the year before you intend to prune. If you fertilize after pruning, it will put out long, leggy growth.

Although it is better to stay on top of your regular pruning chores, rhododendrons can be cut down to 12 to 15 inches from the ground if necessary.

Cut back to expose strong inner branches.

The plants have buds at their base that will generally send up new shoots. But there won't be any flowers for two or three years.

Rose of Sharon

Q **When should I prune my rose of Sharon, which has become rather messy looking?**

A The rose of Sharon (*Hibiscus syriacus*) is a summer-blooming shrub whose flower buds develop on the new twig growth made in spring. It should be pruned very early in spring, just as the grass begins to green up and before leaf buds start swelling. 🌰

The Sumac Story

Q I'd like to plant a clump of sumacs at the back of our lawn near the edge of the property. They seem to be everywhere, so I can't believe they're hard to grow, but none of my local nurseries carries them. Can you suggest a source? Any tips on care?

A It happens every autumn. Huge sweeps of straggly, undistinguished shrubs that grew unnoticed in unkempt fields are suddenly, gloriously, ornamental.

The long, almost palmlike fronds of leaves shine bright red with hints of yellow and orange. The branches spread like candelabra, holding up huge crimson fruit clusters that keep glowing long after leafdrop, when all the world is gray. No wonder gardeners think about bringing them in from the wild.

Unfortunately, as you point out, sumac grows *everywhere,* all the way from zone 2 to zone 9. It grows in dry soil, poor soil, moist soil, near-bog, bright sun, and part shade. It spreads by seed and by underground runners that can travel 20 feet or more in search of a good spot to make a new clump of sumac. But if there is also a lawn on the other side of your border, there will be adequate local control as long as everybody keeps mowing.

Smooth sumac (*Rhus glabra*) is the most common roadside attraction. It's fuller and more readily clump-forming than staghorn sumac (*R. typhina*), named for the velvety down that covers every branch. Smooth sumac tops out at about 8 to 10 feet, staghorn at 12 to 16 feet.

Fragrant sumac (*R. aromatica*) is shorter, at 3 to 4 feet, and bushier, more like a garden plant. No matter which type you choose, you will need both male and female plants if you want fruits. Sumacs are available through nurseries that specialize in native plants, and some large garden centers will order them for you if you ask. 🍎

Smitten by the Scent of Viburnum

Q We moved to a new home last spring and were delighted by the amazing scent of a viburnum the previous owners had planted near the entrance gate. It was absolutely delicious to walk past it in bloom. Well, this spring it's dead, I think maybe because we had an unusually cold winter. I'd like to replace it with another that is just as fragrant. Can you recommend one that is cold hardy in zone 5?

A Just how "unusually" cold was it? Zone 5 is expected to go down to −20°F, so if you want a viburnum that can withstand colder temperatures than that, you'll have to choose one rated at least to zone 4.

But let's not give up on the original just yet. Are you sure it's dead? A very cold winter might kill back a great deal of the top growth, yet leave living wood at the base of the bush. Check for swelling buds on the lowest branches; they are often protected by snow and thus survive when all else freezes. Try scraping off a small piece of bark. Green tissue underneath means the viburnum is still alive.

If so, wait until it leafs out before cutting off all the deadwood. Since there will not be much living wood left, don't prune any of it this year; the viburnum needs all the leaves it can get to recover before it's reshaped. Next year, prune right after bloomtime to start restoring a good-looking structure.

Of course, viburnums do leaf out early, so there is also a good chance that yours is as dead as it appears. In that case, look for signs of disease or insect damage. It's possible that it was already sick or infested with borers when you moved in. If so, you should wait a couple of years before putting another viburnum in the same place.

Finally, if it is indeed dead of cold, the replacement of choice will be a cultivar of *Viburnum × burkwoodii*. The white-flowered 'Fulbrook' is reputedly the most fragrant, though the pink-budded 'Mohawk' can run it a close second. There are other viburnum species at least as—or even more—fragrant, but none of them is as tough (*V. × burkwoodii* is rated to zone 4). For zone 5, there's Korean spicebush viburnum, *V. carlesii.* And if you ever move to zone 7, plant *V. × bodnantense.* Perfume city, and strikingly lovely; it blooms on the bare branches. 🌿

WHAT'S THAT PERFUME IN THE AIR?

Flowering shrubs can provide some of the sweetest perfumes in the garden. The trick is to be sure the one you choose will deliver as promised. Though a fragrant cultivar—say *Daphne × burkwoodii* 'Carol Mackie'—can be counted on to smell good, the 'Carol Mackie' you buy now and plant 10 feet away from the one you planted five years ago may or may not be just as delicious as Carol No. 1.

And thanks to genetic variability, such differences are even more likely in shrubs that are not named cultivars but are simply members of the species. (Named cultivars are usually clones, and *ought* to be identical even if they aren't.)

The solution? Buy plants in bloom, if possible, so you can give them the sniff test. They will improve a bit once they settle in, but only a bit, and if there is an unpleasant undertone—some calycanthuses, for instance, smell like grape bubblegum—don't expect it to go away.

With that warning in mind (and a nice clear nose, which can be tricky in allergy season when most of them are blooming), consider Carolina allspice (*Calycanthus floridus*); chaste tree (*Vitex agnus-castus*); clove currant (*Ribes odoratum*); daphne; fothergilla; glory bower (*Clerodendrum* spp.); fragrant honeysuckle (*Lonicera fragrantissima; Leucothoe fontanesiana;* lilac; mock orange; seven-son flower (*Heptacodium miconioides*); summersweet (*Clethra alnifolia*); sweet azalea (*Rhododendron arborescens*); many, but by no means all, viburnums; Virginia sweetspire (*Itea virginica*); winter hazel (*Corylopsis* spp.); and witch hazels.

Carolina allspice
(*Calycanthus floridus*)

Viburnums Under Attack

Q In my western New York garden I used native viburnums, partly because they are supposed to be more pest-resistant. Now I find that my arrowwood and cranberrybush viburnums are being attacked by something. The leaves look like lace tatting, and underneath some of them I'm finding small larvae. If native shrubs are more pest-resistant, why are they being attacked? Is there something I can do about it?

A Native shrubs and trees are normally better adapted to the resident pests as well as to the climate, but the viburnum leaf beetle (*Pyrrhalta viburni*) is a stranger, originally from Europe, who has come to dinner in an increasing number of places on this side of the Atlantic.

The larvae skeletonize leaves in May and June, starting from the bottom of the plant and working their way up, and the adults finish up any leftovers from July till October. Eggs are laid in slits on the underside of the tips of young branches in nice, straight lines that appear as dark brown bumps. And that's the key to their control.

Prune and remove any branch tips that have eggs laid in them, anytime from mid October, when the adults finish depositing them, to early May, when the larvae hatch.

Left untreated, heavy infestations can kill vulnerable viburnums in two or three years through repeated defoliation. Plants too large to prune can be treated with insecticides. Call your county cooperative extension service for the names of control products labeled for use against the viburnum leaf beetle. 🌰

Viburnum and its leaf beetle

AVOIDING THE VIBURNUM LEAF BEETLE

The viburnums most vulnerable to the viburnum leaf beetle (*Pyrrhalta viburni*) are arrowwood (*Viburnum dentatum*), European cranberrybush (*V. opulus*), American cranberrybush (*V. trilobum*), and, to a lesser degree, Sargent viburnum (*V. sargentii*).

Hybrids and cultivars of *Viburnum* × *burkwoodii*, *V. carlesii*, *V.* × *juddii*, and *V. rhytidophyllum* resist the beetle.

Show Me the Flowers

Q Two summers ago I planted a double-file viburnum 'Shasta,' whose label promised the white flowers pictured on it and described berries. Why has it never bloomed and never had any of those berries? It looks healthy and gets light sun in the latter part of the afternoon.

A When plants refuse to bloom despite all begging and pleading, there's always a good reason. In the case of your *Viburnum plicatum* var. *tomentosum,* there are probably two.

First, it needs at least six hours of full sun, so you may need to move it to a sunnier spot. Second, the plant normally grows 6 feet tall and 10 feet wide, and if you have been shearing or pruning it at any time other than just after flowering, you have probably been cutting off the following spring's flower buds along with the branches. Since it takes flowers to make berries, solving the flower problem will also solve the berry problem.

A failure to bloom as pretty as the picture is a common complaint, with a variety of causes. Late frosts can kill flower buds, and overfertilizing can promote vegetative growth at the expense of flowers. Sometimes the problem is just that the plants aren't old enough to flower, and the only cure is time. Many plants need to outgrow a juvenile stage, become well established, and grow to a particular size before they are ready to expend the energy to produce flowers, seeds, and even berries. Clones (like your viburnum 'Shasta'), which are propagated from cuttings taken from mature stock, are less likely to go through a juvenile stage than plants grown from seed. But patience is always a virtue when gardening. ◢

'Shasta' viburnum

Berryless Viburnum

Q Last year I fell in love with and purchased a Sargent viburnum 'Onondaga.' The shrub is doing fine, but after flowering it doesn't produce berries. Do I need a second Sargent viburnum nearby to get berries, or does this cultivar not make fruit?

A There is a lot to love in a *Viburnum sargentii* 'Onondaga': those wonderful dark maroon young leaves, that hint of color retained by the mature leaves, and the perfectly color-coordinated reddish flower buds that open into flat-topped white flowers with traces of pink on the back of the petals. For all those characteristics, thank the National Arboretum in Washington, D.C., which introduced 'Onondaga' in 1966 as part of a large plant-breeding program that has released 19 cultivars into the horticultural trade.

Unfortunately, berries didn't seem to come with the other fine attributes. Maybe plants have a built-in modesty that limits them as to how great they can be. You should get a few berries here and there, but not enough to attract any but the most enterprising birds.

Many self-fruitful plants—those that don't need another to complete pollination—will produce more fruit if a compatible plant is close enough to cross-pollinate them. Adding another viburnum with an overlapping bloom period may bring a few more berries, but not very many. 'Onondaga' just doesn't make fruit dependably. It isn't that the National Arboretum doesn't like berries: *V. s.* 'Susquehanna,' a much larger relative, produces berries galore. Of course, it has plain green leaves—but you can't have everything. 🍂

Winterberry

Q **I see bare branches covered with red berries at the florist's. The florist says that they are hollies, but I thought hollies were evergreen.**

A Holly always calls forth an image of glossy, spiny evergreen leaves with red berries. The majority of native American hollies, however, are not evergreen, and that includes *Ilex verticillata*, or winterberry, a deciduous shrub that is widely distributed through most of the eastern half of the country. Winterberry is hardy to zone 4, where temperatures can go as low as –30°F.

There are cultivated varieties and hybrids differing in height (3 to 15 feet), berry color (bright reds to reddish orange and yellow), and berry size (¼ inch to ½ inch in diameter). The berries are long lasting if you cut the branches and bring them into the house, but do not put them in water. Outside, berries last as long as the birds allow.

Winterberry
(*Ilex verticillata*)

To grow winterberries, remember that a male is needed for the females to produce berries, and that the male and females have to bloom at the same time for pollination to occur. One of the best berry producers is the female cultivar 'Winter Red,' with long-lasting, intense red berries. 'Apollo,' 'Raritan Chief,' and 'Jim Dandy' are good pollinators because they bloom long enough to pollinate many common cultivars. 🍂

HARVESTER, HOLD THOSE SHEARS!

A thicket of branches, each laden with bright red berries; a wide patch of wildflowers carpeting the mowed verge; lilies growing in thick clumps on the banks of a drainage ditch . . . these roadside beauties seem to be saying, "Come and get me. I'm yours for the taking."

The temptation is especially strong when the land is clearly untended, even stronger when there appears to be plenty for everyone. But it is almost always ill-mannered (and often illegal) to give in.

Private property is just that, of course. You're not supposed to take it. And whether the land is public or private, there is a good chance that the plant in question is protected by law. Both of those considerations aside, think how ugly the roadside would be if everybody did take "just a little" of the things that are attractive.

Legal protection varies from state to state, but New York is fairly typical in having laws that forbid cutting, digging up, attacking with herbicide, or in any other way disturbing several classes of plants. In ascending order of worry, the classes are: rare, exploitably vulnerable, threatened, and endangered.

In each class there is a list of dozens of plants, many of them old friends. Among the exploitably vulnerable, which can be defined as "O.K. for now but not if people keep picking so damn many," are things like winterberry and mountain laurel, Canada lilies and bloodroot, princess pine and all her relatives (the native clubmosses, *Lycopodium* spp.), as well as most trilliums, and every native orchid in the state.

You can find out what's protected where you live by calling your state's department of environmental conservation or by doing a Web search for the classes listed above. But between obeying the law and simply being a good neighbor, it's easier to assume that those roadside beauties are best enjoyed right where they live.

An English Winter Wonder

Q In a memoir of growing up in England in the 1880s, there is a description of an early-blooming shrub with mauve-and-yellow blossoms that is called chimonanthus (wintersweet). Could you tell me if this plant is available in the United States, and whether it would do well in central Connecticut?

A It is and it wouldn't. *Chimonanthus praecox*, fragrant wintersweet, is available in the United States, but it isn't hardy enough to thrive in zone 6, or even the northern parts of zone 7.

339

Wintersweet
(*Chimonanthus praecox*)

Wintersweet is probably the earliest-blooming shrub. Its translucent, waxy flowers, pale yellow with purplish centers, begin opening in December or January, long before the leaves on this 8- to 10-foot shrub emerge. But that's only in the southern sections of zone 7—most of Long Island and southern New Jersey—and warmer areas. And just to rub it in a bit, the fragrance (very unusual in an early-winter bloom) is a delicious lemony spice. 🌿

SHRUBS FOR COLOR, NORTHERN DIVISION

Gardeners in zones 6 and north can only look in envy at most winter-blooming shrubs—witch hazel is about all they get. But winter color is certainly possible in colder areas; you just have to find it in stems instead of flowers.

Two groups that offer a good range of colors are the shrubby dogwoods and the willows. Among the dogwoods, stem colors include chartreuse (*Cornus stolonifera* 'Falviramea'), orange (*C. sanguinea* 'Winter Beauty'), and bright red (*C. stolonifera* 'Cardinal'). Willows offer an even wider variety of stem colors, including a warm orange-red (*Salix alba* 'Chermesina'), purplish (*S. purpurea*), and wine-black (*S. melanostachys*).

For a Bushy Yew Hedge

Q **I started a yew hedge last spring and want to keep it bushy. Should I trim it before winter or wait until next year?**

A A naturally bushy evergreen like yew is best sheared toward the end of winter or in very early spring, just before the soft, light green foliage emerges.

The best time to trim is after a rain or in the early morning when the plants are damp with dew. This minimizes the browning of the sheared ends, a temporary discoloration that occurs when the plants are cut dry. Though it's not usually a good idea to prune plants when they're wet because it can spread disease, in this case the danger is minimal (unless, of course, your yews are having problems). 🌿

Reshaping a Yew

Q I have a yew about 5 feet wide next to the deck of my swimming pool. It is blocking part of the deck so we cannot pass by. Can this be trimmed from the front? It looks as if all I will have is the inside branches left, a rather ugly sight. But if I can do it, when is the best time?

A It sounds as if you may secretly hope there is nothing to be done, so before we get to the pruning part, please consider being brave and saying goodbye to the thing. Though it goes against a gardener's grain to kill a healthy shrub, why keep one where you can look forward to two or three years of bare spots followed by a lifelong commitment to time-consuming maintenance?

If you are determined to keep it, there are two alternatives. The yew can be trimmed from the front, but it will be ugly, and not just while the inside branches are putting on new growth. No matter how green it gets, the shrub will always look like it has been sliced in half.

A more attractive alternative is to reshape the whole plant. Cut back a little bit (6 to 9 inches) all around each year, pruning individual branches to slightly different lengths rather than shearing along the face. It will take longer to prune than to shear, but the result will be a tall, narrow, vaguely columnar shrub that won't look as though it belongs in a cemetery.

No matter what shape you choose, the best time to start cutting is early spring before the plant puts out new growth. This gives you maximum green to cover the exposed bare spots, and gives the plant maximum time to harden up before winter. 🍎

Shear Madness

Q What is the difference between pruning and shearing?

A Pruning means cutting off a part of a living plant, and covers everything from snipping a twig to reaching deep inside a tree canopy and sawing off a major branch. Shearing is a particular kind of pruning, one in which only branch tips are cut, and they are cut as a group rather than individually.

The goal of shearing is to force lots of small outer branches while creating a smooth outline. The result—if it is successful—is that the sheared plant loses its natural identity and becomes a formal shape. The most common example of the technique is the flat-faced wall of a sheared hedge, but people also shear plants into mounds, pyramids, graduated balls on sticks, or (in a few extreme cases) things like chess pieces and leaping dogs.

Shearing at the simple hedge level *seems* as though it should be easy: just hold the shears at the proper angle and clip away. In fact, it takes patience, practice—and strong arms—to see where you need to cut and then do the cutting properly.

Electric hedge trimmers promise to relieve you of much of the work, and they do make it go faster. But they are heavier than hand shears, their speed increases the chance of mistakes, and they have a regrettable tendency to tear everything they touch instead of cutting cleanly. ✿

CHAPTER EIGHT

Trees

Trees in General

An Eon Here, an Eon There

Q **I am interested in planting a tree from seed. Starting a yew (which might grow for 1,000 years) or a sequoia (which might grow for 3,000) seems an easy way to achieve immortality. How would I go about this?**

A With a tree's long view of life, it shouldn't be surprising that their seeds are remarkably patient. Growing trees from seed isn't like growing annuals or vegetables, where everything happens in a single summer.

In nature, seeds germinate only when they and the world are ready for each other. Some seeds are not fully mature when they leave the tree and need a warm or cool period to finish developing. Others need both warm and cool periods, and in the right order.

Some seeds have a hard coating that needs to wear away before moisture can enter and germination can begin. Years of rain, being blown over rocky terrain, or a trip through an animal's digestive system can do the trick. But gardeners speed things by scarification (sanding, nicking, or filing down the seed coat) and stratification (controlled periods of moist warmth or coolness).

Tree seeds are more of a commitment than marigolds, so be sure to get advice on the seeds' needs when buying. Of course, plant only trees suited to your climate. 🍎

Finding Champion Trees

Q I've heard of huge "landmark" trees and would like to see them. How can I find out where they are?

A "The National Register of Big Trees" has been published every other year since 1940. Sponsored by the Davey Tree Expert Company and published through American Forests, a private group founded in 1875, the registry contains the location, height, and diameter of each of these magnificent specimens.

For purchasing information, write to The National Register of Big Trees, c/o American Forests Association, P.O. Box 2000, Washington, DC 20013, or call (800) 873-5323. 🍎

Remembering Grandmother

Q I want to plant a tree as a memorial to my grandmother. Could you tell me which species suitable to the Northeast are the longest lived?

A It isn't the length of the life that counts, it's the quality and meaning the life contains. The best species of tree might be the one she swung on as a little girl, or the one your grandfather proposed under, or even the one she planted to commemorate your birth.

If you don't know which tree she would have preferred, you'll have to balance longevity against other factors to make the right decision. Canadian hemlock (*Tsuga canadensis*) can live more than 600 years, with the record being more than 900, but an insect, the hemlock woolly adelgid, is wiping out hemlocks at a frightening rate.

Eastern white pine can live longer than 400 years, but it is susceptible to insects and diseases and won't tolerate road salt well. *Ginkgo biloba* can live to more than 300 years, and it doesn't have any natural enemies or diseases in North America, but it doesn't appeal to everyone and the female produces fruit that has an unpleasant odor when it ripens and drops off.

Because all grandmothers are beautiful, a beautiful tree like a white oak (*Quercus alba*), a sugar maple (*Acer saccharum*), a white fir (*Abies concolor*), or a European beech (*Fagus sylvatica*) might be a terrific choice. Each can live to at least 200 years, but more important, each would be a stunning memorial: stately, sheltering, and strong, looking better as it gets older. Of course, if your grandmother didn't like squirrels, forget the oak. 🍎

Trees for Privacy

Q **We live on 2½ acres bordered by woods and wetlands, which are soon to be lost to a housing development. On one side we have a shady, sandy area where holly and rhododendrons are growing, and there is plenty of space to plant. What trees will thrive and provide privacy?**

A Will the area still be shady when they cut down the woods? It will almost surely be less moist and more windy. On the other hand, there will be fewer deer, and even a slight increase in sunlight will greatly expand your options.

For best results, plant a ribbon of shrubs and trees two or three deep. Compared with a single row of trees, a stepped-down assortment of sizes and species keeps out more sound. It makes the wall more interesting, and it helps prevent the buildup of pests and diseases.

You could, for example, plant tall evergreens like hemlocks and arborvitae near the property line. Then, coming toward the yard, add Chinese dogwoods or native shadblows, followed by more rhododendrons; clethra, for its fragrance; and a collection of highbush blueberries for spring flowers, summer fruit, and bright color in the fall.

If woods removal gives you a bit more sun at the border, you can add white pines and some varieties of spruce to your list of tall trees. The next layer might include witch hazels, the earliest bloomers of all, and oakleaf hydrangeas, as beautiful for their leaves and bark as for their white flowers.

There are hundreds of possibilities. One good way to see them is to tour local parks and arboretums, notepad in hand. 🍎

Trees in General

LATER BLOOMERS

Here are 10 trees that will flower after the big springtime show is past.

Autumn-flowering (Higan) cherry (*Prunus subhirtella* 'Autumnalis'): A double delight, this small tree (to 25 feet) flowers in both spring and fall. There are several varieties, and you can have any flower color you like as long as it's some shade of pink. Not reliably hardy north of zone 6, though it's worth a try in zone 5 if you have a protected spot.

Ben Franklin tree (*Franklinia alatamaha*): A good choice for smaller yards, this medium-slow grower seldom gets more than 15 to 20 feet tall. All the better to enjoy the large, fragrant, camellia-like white flowers that bloom toward the end of summer, shortly before (sometimes even while) the bright green leaves turn red-orange for fall. Zones 5 (in the warmer parts) to 9.

Southern catalpa (*Catalpa bignonioides*): With these quick-growing, wide spreaders, you get a big tree (to 50 feet) in a (comparatively) big hurry. The handsome leaves are usually mid to deep green, but there are also yellow-leaved forms. All offer abundant, bell-shaped white flowers in mid summer, followed by long, dark seedpods. The tree is also known as Indian bean, though the pods are not edible. Zones 5 to 8.

Southern catalpa
(*Catalpa bignonioides*)

Golden raintree (*Koelreuteria paniculata*): The leaves themselves are a colorful show, reddish pink when young, green in mid summer while the many-branched panicles of golden flowers are blooming, then a rich and lovely yellow before they fall in autumn. As a bonus, this 30-footer is a tough cookie, able to thrive in poor soil and drought, as long as the soil is on the alkaline side and there is plenty of sun. Zones 5 (in the warmer parts) to 9.

Japanese pagoda tree (*Sophora japonica*): In spite of its name, this late-summer bloomer is more spreading than pagoda shaped and will take up quite a bit of territory (as much as 100 by 70 feet) when it is full grown. The fragrant white, pea-like flowers are small but showy, borne in panicles that can be up to a foot long. Zones 5 to 9.

Japanese tree lilac (*Syringa reticulata*): These are the latest and tallest lilacs, blooming in early summer about a month after common lilacs and growing to a mature height of 25 to 30 feet. The fragrant flowers are a creamy white, with small florets in very large bunches, on multibranched panicles. The species takes several years to get established and start blooming abundantly; plant the much smaller cultivar 'Ivory Silk,' which tops out around 12 feet, if you're in a hurry. Zones 4 to 7.

Linden (*Tilia* spp.): The most common distinction is between the bigleaf linden (*T. platyphyllos*) and the littleleaf (*T. cordata*), but there are a great many species in commerce, ranging in size from 25 feet tall to over 100 feet, and in shape from broadly pyramidal to rounded to upright and almost columnar. All have round to oval leaves, and myriad small yellow, mid-summer flowers that are famous for their haunting perfume. Zones 3 to 9, depending on species. The most fragrant, *T. tomentosa*, is chancy north of zone 6.

Sourwood (*Oxydendrum arboreum*): This mid-size tree, 30 to 50 feet tall at maturity, can be somewhat straggly in shape, so plan to do a bit of creative pruning when your sourwood is young. After that you can just sit back, enjoying the huge, graceful sweeps of white flowers that appear in mid to late summer, then the spectacular

Sourwood
(*Oxydendrum arboreum*)

fall foliage show of red, yellow, and purple, all quite bright and all at once. Zones 5 to 9.

Stewartia (*Stewartia* spp.): Some stewartias are evergreen shrubs, others small deciduous trees. All produce large, open-cupped white flowers that spring from the twiggy shoots in mid to late summer. The Japanese stewartia (*S. pseudocamellia*) has the added distinctions of a strong columnar shape—to 70 feet—and beautiful, peeling bark, but those without a lot of space need not be without a stewartia. The mountain species (*S. ovata*) tops out at 20 feet or less. Mostly zones 5 to 8, though there are also more tender species for zones 6 to 9.

Japanese stewartia
(*Stewartia pseudocamellia*)

Yellowwood (*Cladrastis lutea*): This early-summer bloomer just squeaks in. Its long, fragrant panicles of white flowers appear very shortly after the big spring show is over. But "after" is the operative word, so the wisteria-like blossoms do shine brightly among the clear green leaves. Yellowwoods are graceful trees, upright to about 40 feet and spreading nearly as wide. They are hardy to zone 4, but they're also somewhat brittle (plant yours in a sheltered spot, where it will be safe from strong winds and heavy snows).

Trees in General

What Makes a Fall?

Q All summer I heard that the drought was going to ruin the fall color display in the Northeast, but this autumn was as beautiful as any. Since the drought didn't affect the colors, why was there such a dire prediction? What exactly determines the quality of a tree's display?

A The most beautiful autumn displays, the ones that cause a sharp intake of breath when rounding a bend on a New England back road, happen when we are very young or very old, the times when we are most observant and most willing to be thrilled. In the years between, the quality of displays is up or down, with the credit or blame going to the vagaries of weather.

True, summer droughts cause many problems, but the weather that matters for fall color is the weather of the moment. The perfect display is a balancing act: enough rainfall just as autumn begins, temperature and sunlight during the period when lengthening nights initiate the process that gradually closes off the leaf petiole. Cool temperatures reduce chlorophyll production, and as it breaks down, the yellows and oranges of other chemicals show through. No matter what you've heard about a certain Jack, frost is not essential for color; in fact, it is actually a problem. Freezing temperatures produce muted colors and can kill leaves. Bright, sunny days encourage the production of red chemicals in some trees. But the most important ingredient for a perfect display is a four-year-old on her first trip north. 🍎

Unwrap That Root Ball

Q I'm going to be planting trees in a few weeks, so I am wondering what's the latest scoop on planting. Specifically, is it really O.K. to just leave all that burlap around the root ball?

A Like other things in life that aren't what they used to be, burlap has changed. Whether for the better depends on your point of view. A single layer of plain old untreated burlap, now almost a thing of the past, rots away nicely and lets roots wander freely out of their soil ball. But you are just as likely to run into a plastic burlap-like material, or into burlap that has been treated with a rot-resistant chemical.

Both are popular in the horticultural industry for the same reason: they stay intact longer, through sunshine and waterings, as the tree makes its way from its growing site to you. But that perseverance presents problems for growing roots trying to find their way into new surroundings. Rot-resistant burlap takes years longer to decay than untreated does, and even untreated burlap presents a formidable boundary if wadded down in layers and left in place.

In both cases, these barriers restrict the diameter of the roots as they grow out. In some cases, the tree may even die. At that point, you can dig it up and use the original wrapping to take the dead tree to the dump.

To avoid such problems, after placing the tree in that nice extra-wide-but-no-deeper-than-the-ball hole, untie the twine around the trunk and cut away the burlap. 🍂

Prudent Pruning?

Q I live in an eight-year-old community where there are many trees that I estimate are 11 or 12 years old. They are growing nicely. This fall, however, a tree company was hired to "thin them out" by pruning good-size healthy branches. Is that a good idea?

A Seeing healthy branches fall is alarming, but there are plenty of circumstances in which pruning makes sense. You might remove the lowest branches ("limb up") to open up the space beneath the tree, or prune away unbalanced growth to make a more graceful shape. To maintain tree health, you'd be wise to get rid of potential problems like crossing branches or limbs with weak angles of attachment. And you might occasionally thin the canopy to allow more light to come through.

There's no way to judge the wisdom of this particular pruning without knowing more about these particular trees. And now that the deed has been done, your worries about it are moot, at least for the short term.

Trees in General

It is likely that the trees will look fine as soon as they leaf out. But if you still have questions about them, the best person to ask is your community's landscape manager. He or she should be able to reassure you that the tree company is run by trained arborists. There are plenty of cut-rate "tree companies" that are no more than a couple of cowboys with chain saws and a pickup truck, but they usually prey on individual homeowners. Middle managers whose heads will roll if something bad befalls all the trees are usually willing to pay the higher prices that skilled workers command. 🍂

Mulch Measurement

Q I'd like to put a layer of mulch underneath my trees, but am not sure how deep it should be or how widely it should be spread.

A Three or 4 inches deep is enough; anything deeper could interfere with soil aeration. But do spread the layer out widely. In a tree's idea of a perfect world, the mulch would start about a foot away from the trunk (to give it breathing room) and extend all the way to the edge of the leaf canopy.

A tree's first line of defense is its bark. Mechanical damage, the euphemism for the destruction caused by people and their wayward mowers and string trimmers, opens up bark wounds to pests and diseases. A wide ring of mulch should warn away even the most inattentive mower. 🍂

Is Mulch Good for Trees?

Q My impression is that the heavy mulching of trees started as a way to put some distance between tree trunks and aggressive lawn trimmers, but that we've now been persuaded that lots of mulch has an aesthetic or even growth-nurturing purpose. Time and again when I pull the mulch back, I see bark softened by too much moisture and damaged by beetles. Aren't all the mulch maniacs setting the stage for widespread tree disease and death?

A The problem is not with the mulch but with its overcozy relationship to the tree, which needs a bit of personal space to be comfortable. Aesthetic questions aside, almost all trees and shrubs benefit from a moisture-conserving, weed-discouraging blanket over their root zones, while none (except swamp dwellers) is happy when moisture is conserved right up against the wood.

Problems with the mulch-against-trunk condition include damaging fungus diseases, insect infestations, and (especially in winter) bark-eating mice and voles. But all of these will be no problem as long as the mulch maniacs leave a bit of open ground between the mulch and the tree.

While we're on the subject, don't forget to be equally respectful of your vegetables and flowers; soft-stemmed plants need their space, too. 🍎

TO FEED OR NOT TO FEED

When it comes to the wisdom of feeding trees, expert opinion is sharply—in some cases acrimoniously—divided, but the weight of modern practice is increasingly in favor of the dictum that less is more.

A small amount of fertilizer is fine. It will help compensate for the absence of natural fertility that tends to distinguish lawns (where all the leaf litter gets raked up and there is no understory to speak of) from woodlands (where the trees are nourished by lots of decayed plant material).

But before you go out and buy tree food, remember that the small amount needed is likely to be already present as a by-product of fertilizing the lawn. Once you get into adding more than that, it's likely you will do more harm than good—if you do anything at all. The harm comes because fertilizer pushes the tree into making lots of tender, soft growth. It's lush, it's green, it's very impressive, and it's also highly vulnerable to insect attacks, climate stress, and the myriad fungus diseases that would be thwarted by tougher tissue.

The doesn't-do-anything-at-all situation results from putting the food where the tree can't get at it. Most of a tree's feeder roots are in the top 10 to 18 inches of soil, and most of them start near the outer edge of the canopy (the drip line) and spread outward from there. That means using an injector to put the eats down deep is not going to do much except pollute the groundwater. And spreading the tree's meal close to its trunk will be just as fruitless.

The bottom line? Keep feeding to a minimum unless the tree is in a container (or a tree pit) where it cannot possibly find nourishment on its own. And if you do use fertilizer on a landscape tree, spread it in a wide band that works out from the drip line.

Caring for the Trunk

Q My community hires a landscaping company to take care of gardening for all residents. There are many trees 8 to 10 years old, and they pile dirt about 10 inches high around the trunks. My question is, is that a good idea?

A No. Covering a tree trunk with soil, like covering it with mulch, frequently leads to problems. Soil retains moisture, and if the trunk is constantly damp the bark will eventually weaken and rot. When the moist bark freezes and thaws in winter, it expands, contracts, and eventually splits. Both the rotting and the splitting let insects and diseases invade the tree.

Piling soil on can also lead to another problem. Roots, which we usually think of in their role of water and nutrient absorbers or as anchors so the tree doesn't fall over, also absorb oxygen that filters down through the soil from the air. Every tree has an optimum depth for its roots: deep enough to protect the roots and let them anchor the tree, while shallow enough to get both the air and the water it needs.

By the time a tree is as old as yours are, it has established itself and gotten comfortable. Pile extra soil on, especially over the area where the roots meet the trunk, and it no longer can get all the oxygen it needs. You won't hear gasping or choking sounds, but gradually its health and vigor decline, reducing its ability to fend off diseases and increasing its susceptibility to insect attack. It may die, or it may just suffer in silence, depending on how sensitive the species is. Maple, beech, oak, and willow are especially resentful of being smothered. ❧

Protecting Trees from Builders

Q We're building a garage near several fine trees that I do not want to lose. How can I protect them?

A First, install a temporary fence at a distance around the trees that corresponds to their drip line (that is, the area below the outermost portion of their limbs). Besides preventing damage to the trunks themselves, this fence will discourage workmen from piling soil or debris too close to the trees.

More important, it will keep trucks and other heavy machinery at a distance and thereby prevent the soil compaction that such vehicles cause. When soil is compacted, air and moisture cannot penetrate to the roots; this is often the cause of serious damage to (and even the death of) trees at construction sites.

Be careful to guard against stress by making sure that there's ample water through the growing season.

If paving is required within the drip-line area, use only gravel or open stonework. Do not add an impervious blanket of concrete or asphalt. 🍂

Strangler Fig

Q On a recent trip to Florida, I heard about a "strangler fig." I can't imagine such a violent name for a plant. Kindly explain.

A Strangler figs are among the more peculiar members of the plant world, appropriate for a sci-fi movie. Although they don't attack humans, they are lethal to trees.

This strange plant begins its life on a branch or in a crevice where its seeds may have been dropped by a fruit-eating bird. During its early days, which are spent as an epiphyte, or tree percher, the plant takes nourishment only from rain and surrounding fallen leaves, and does no harm to the host plant.

But as it matures, the strangler fig develops roots that grow downward and establish themselves in the soil. These are soon followed by lateral roots that develop from the vertical ones. As both sets of roots multiply and thicken, they tighten around the supporting host plant in a basketlike weave. This cuts off the host plant's flow of sap. At the same time, the fig's branches and leaves grow upward, blocking the host plant's light. This combination of events eventually leads to the host plant's death.

Figs are members of the mulberry family, and two strangler fig species that are native to southern Florida are *Ficus aurea* and *F. citrifolia. F. aurea,* which can grow to about 60 feet in height, has thick, leathery-looking oval leaves about 3 to 4 inches long. *F. citrifolia* has whitish bark, broader leaves, and decorative edible fruit. 🍂

Unnecessary Staking

Q As I walk around the city or suburbs I see newly planted young trees with everything from no support stakes to as many as four stakes. Is it necessary to stake newly planted trees? If so, how should it be done?

A Stake only when necessary, not as a general practice. Trees that are container grown or balled-and-burlapped can usually stand on their own after being planted and don't need staking. If your new tree has too large a canopy compared to the size of the root ball and won't stand up, or if it will be in an unprotected site where strong winds are common, use one or at most two stakes for support. Using three stakes, so that nothing less than a hurricane can move the tree, prevents it from undergoing the stresses from everyday winds. Trees respond to those stresses by growing thicker, better-tapered trunks and stronger root systems. An overprotected tree grows up to be a wimp that isn't prepared for the real world when the stakes are removed.

Use a tie that spreads out the pressure and has some give, such as inch-wide plastic webbing, rubber hose, or inner-tube sections. Never tie a stake directly to the trunk, because the constant shading causes uneven growth. The stake should not be a permanent fixture. Remove it as soon as its job is done, and never leave it for more than a year. 🍎

Scouting Long-Horned Beetles

Q Now that most insects are disappearing for the winter, is there anything I can do with regard to watching for the dangerous Asian beetles that were spotted in Manhattan? I have read that they may spread and would like to be as wary as possible.

A Asian long-horned beetles attack and kill primarily maples, but also horse chestnut, elm, willow, poplar, ash, box elder, and rose of Sharon trees. As recent invaders, they have no natural enemies in the United States except you. With fall here, it would be easy to let your guard down and stop looking for them.

But don't. Although the adult beetle—an inch to an inch and a half long, black with white spots and huge antennae—

dies after laying eggs, the larvae overwinter in the holes the beetles make in trees. The distinctive holes are only slightly smaller than a dime, perfectly round, and have smooth edges. They are found singly or in scattered groups. As the larvae bore through the vessels that bring water and nutrients up from the roots, the tree quickly withers and dies.

Information and updates on the Asian long-horned beetle problem, including photographs of the insect, can be found at the United States Agriculture Department's Web site: *www.aphis.usda.gov.* 🍎

SAVE THAT STREET TREE

They may seem as tough as elephants, but street trees often need a human friend, especially in summer, with its cruel heat and paltry rain. Yellow or burned-looking foliage and dropped leaves are sure signs of trouble, but even before such symptoms show up, it would be a good idea to consider adopting a tree near your home.

Start by checking the soil. If it is so compacted that it resembles concrete and rainwater runs off, stab it several times with a garden fork to loosen it so that air and water can penetrate. (Don't move it around, though; that would hurt the tree roots.)

Then begin a regular program of deep, slow watering. A twice-weekly minimum of 8 to 10 gallons of water is generally suggested for each tree. Administer it slowly, so the moisture penetrates to the bottom roots. More water may be needed by young trees, especially when the heat is intense and the rain is minimal. Keep in mind that the point is not just to dampen the top inch of soil, but to have the water reach the lowest roots. Helping your street tree thrive means helping improve city air as well as city ambiance. Every leaf counts.

Tree's Revenge?

Q **Several years ago, I had a large and healthy silver maple tree in my yard taken down because it had been planted too close to the house. The 4- or 5-foot-wide stump was ground down to a few inches below ground level. Now, every fall my lawn gets covered with some kind of mushroom that I believe is coming from the roots of the removed tree. Short of digging up and removing the tree roots, is there anything I can do to prevent these mushrooms from sprouting every fall? They make it very difficult to use or maintain the lawn for the last month or two before winter. I guess I'm being punished for taking down a healthy tree.**

A Perhaps the person who should be punished is the one who either planted the tree or built the house there, depending on which came first. Let it be a caution for the future: small trees become larger, and large trees spread out. Both eventual height and width need to be taken into consideration when purchasing and siting any tree.

As the roots continue to decay the problem will lessen, and the mushrooms should be gone in another two or three years. In the meantime grab your golf clubs and play driving range. 🌰

Stumped

Q **I have a tree stump that's as large as a seat, and I wish it would rot. Will pouring salty water on it help?**

A Crying isn't going to help matters, and neither is bathing the stump in vinegar, kerosene, or any of the other commonly available liquids recommended by folk wisdom. Burying it in a heap of manure will speed things up slightly, but not enough to justify having a heap of manure in the yard.

There are commercial preparations that claim to dissolve the lignin that binds the cells of the wood, thereby hastening decay, but the only truly efficient method for getting rid of a stump is to hire a tree company with a stump-grinding machine. In less than an hour the stump will be gone, replaced by a pile of wood chips for mulch.

The alternative is to think positively about this stump, at least for a while. Since it is as large as a seat, why not use it for one? Or if you don't want to sit on it yourself, set a large planter on it. (Be sure the planter and its contents are in proportion with the size of the stump; a little pot on a big platform is not a pretty sight.) 🌰

Tree Cracks

Q **I've noticed long vertical scars on the bark of several of my trees, all of them on the same side. None of them has scars all the way around, but some of them do have more than one scar. Is an insect up to some mischief here?**

A Probably not. Your description sounds more like the scars of cracks caused by frost damage. In the winter, tree trunks freeze when the temperatures dip. But on intermittent warm days, parts of the trunks of trees grown in open or exposed areas may thaw, typically on their south or southwest sides. At sundown, when the temperature drops suddenly to below freezing again, severe stress can occur. This in turn results in a vertical splitting of the trunk.

Some growers suggest wrapping the trunks of young trees with kraft paper or burlap for winter. This may help protect them until they become established. But with older plants, not much can be done to prevent splitting caused by frost. 🍅

Spare That Tree

Q **How do I keep the neighborhood pooches from relieving themselves on my trees?**

A For starters, make sure everybody knows what's going on. Dog owners may not realize that damage is being done—especially if they are law-abiding types who scoop up and discard the solids. A simple sign along the lines of "ALL Animal Wastes Kill Plants—Please Curb Your Dog" may be enough to make a difference.

If that doesn't work, you can move on to fencing. Open wirework admits light and air, and is better for the plants than boards, concrete, or other solid materials. The fence doesn't have to be very tall; like the signage, it's more a method of communication than an unbreachable barrier. But that also means it won't speak to everyone, so hedge your bets by spraying the fence with a dog repellent (available at the hardware store). Renew the repellent at frequent intervals; even the "waterproof" ones wear off. 🍅

Trees vs. Vines

Q **I'm alarmed at the rate at which English ivy and other vines are taking over trees around town. Some trees seem perilously close to suffocation. Don't the vines damage them?**

A It depends on how the vine climbs and how vigorous it is. Plants like English ivy, which attach themselves to the surface of the bark with aerial roots called holdfasts, do no damage to the tree until they get so huge that their weight breaks branches and their leaves block out too much light. Plants like wisteria, which wrap themselves around the trunk, are a bigger hazard. As these vines grow, they can strip and then strangle the tree, eventually killing it.

Because English ivy adds a handsome green winter cloak, it can be allowed to stay as long as you keep it confined to the lower trunk, where it won't lie on the branches or interfere with the tree's sunlight. But climbers like wisteria or honeysuckle, which can grow as much as 20 feet a year, should be removed altogether or cut back as close to the ground as possible. Winter is the easiest time to do this cutting. 🍎

Nail in a Tree

Q My son built a birdhouse and hung it on a nail he had driven into a honey locust. Will this hurt the tree?

A As long as the house is a lightweight single-family dwelling and not some monster condo that will drag the nail down through the wood and create a big wound, don't worry. "In due time, the tree will grow over the nail the way it grows over the stubs of branches that have fallen off," said Dr. John Seiler, a professor of forest biology at Virginia Tech in Blacksburg, Virginia.

He added that after a decade or so the tree is likely to engulf the nail and push the birdhouse right off. "You can remove the nail whenever you want," he said. "A hole that small will probably heal over within a year, with most of the closure taking place after the tree resumes its growth in spring."

There is no need to use tree-wound paint, which almost always does more harm than good since it thwarts the tree's efforts to heal itself. 🍎

Twinkling Trees

Q Our apartment building has a lovely garden. There is a restaurant over-looking it that used to have tiny clear lights on some of the larger trees. Our landscape architect told the management that the lights would kill or at least stunt the trees' growth. How can this be? Tavern on the Green uses many more lights on their trees. The manager said he would like to put the twinkle lights back. Is the landscape architect right?

A Lights in trees, twinkle or otherwise, do not affect a tree's growth as long as they are not wrapped too tightly. Unlike poinsettia, kalanchoe, Christmas cactus, and chrysanthemum, which require a certain number of hours of total darkness to start flowering, trees are not sensitive to the level of light from even the gaudiest display. It's easy to forget, however, that the wire connecting the lights will not stretch as the tree's trunk and limbs grow thicker. Left unchecked, wrapped areas can become girdled, which can certainly damage or even kill them. Twinkle lights may not be part of the landscape architect's grand vision for the garden, but if you and the manager prevail, be sure that the wires are loosely wrapped and checked every year or two.

Why Trees Weep

Q Recently I purchased a weeping cherry and find it strange that the limbs really do grow downward, not up toward the sun like other plants. Why?

A The weeping tree form is a mutation, and scientists don't really know why it happens. What they do know is that most "normal" plants have a single growing tip that remains dominant, and this is what causes the trunk to head in a vertical direction.

In the weeping tree, this dominant control mechanism is somehow disrupted. Instead of developing an upright trunk from the vertical growing shoot, the weeping tree develops a downward form by superimposing one layer of horizontal growth on top of the previous one. The process by which weeping plants assume their pendulous position, deviating from the vertical, is called plagiotropism.

Missing Snow

Q My father and I have noticed that trees in the park seem to melt the snow right around their trunks, baring the ground up to a foot or two away. My father has heard that there's some enzymatic activity around tree roots that makes the soil above them just a teeny bit warmer. But if this is so, why wouldn't the ring of melted snow be as wide as the tree's root spread, which is surely on average larger than two feet?

A Your father has the right idea but the wrong plants. Dr. Tom Whitlow, an associate professor of plant physiological ecology at Cornell University in Ithaca, New York, said that there are some plants (Jack-in-the-pulpit, for example) that release enough heat as part of their respiration process that they not only melt surrounding snow as they begin to grow in the early spring, they can actually feel warm to the touch.

But this respiration process is unusual and is not shared by any trees that he knows of. Instead, he continued, the melted snow you notice is probably due to a combination of the sun's heat being absorbed and then radiated by the dark bark, and the runoff of water from snow melting on the branches. Mixing water with snow does more than just help melt the snow, it also makes the snow wetter, and wet snow is a better conductor of the radiated heat than is powdery, dry snow.

Next time you see a tree with a bare trunk, look around it and see if there is more snow melted on the south side than on the north. Since there is more sun from the south, the melted circle shouldn't be symmetrical.

Ben Franklin's Tree

Q I have heard that a tree was named for Benjamin Franklin. What does it look like, and where does it grow?

A The Franklin tree (*Franklinia alatamaha*) was indeed named for Benjamin Franklin, a friend of father-and-son botanical explorers John and William Bartram. The two discovered the plant in 1765 near Fort Barrington on the Altamaha River, near what is now Darien, Georgia. In 1773, on a second journey, William Bartram collected seeds.

Descendants of those plants still grow in Philadelphia at the edge of the Schuylkill River in Historic Bartram's Garden.

The plant has not been seen in the wild since 1903, and "it is believed that all Franklinias today growing anywhere in the world are descended from those propagated by the Bartrams," said Martha Wolf, the executive director of Bartram's Garden.

This handsome deciduous tree has silver-gray striped limbs and can grow slowly to a height of 20 to 30 feet. It is hardy as far north as southern New England, but north of New York City it tends to be shorter and more shrublike because of the cold. From late summer to frost, it bears clusters of white camellia-like flowers. These develop into round, woody fruits, and eventually zigzag-shaped capsules. The long, shiny leaves turn a brilliant orange-red in the fall. 🍂

BARKING UP THE RIGHT TREE

Though trees are seldom chosen for the splendor of their bark, it's a design detail that deserves attention, especially in any climate where winter is leafless for longer than about five minutes.

Possibilities range from the rich coppery colors of Amur cherry (*Prunus maackii*) to the dark ridges on Amur cork (*Phellodendron amurense*), from the scrolling sheets of glowing amber that peel from the milk-chocolate paperbark maple (*Acer griseum*) to the ghostly silver sheen of sycamore (*Platanus* spp.).

These beauties do not appear until the trees are several years old, so you can't go by what you see at the nursery. Photographs can help, of course, but for best results, take a few field trips to arboretums where you can see mature specimens.

While you're there, keep an eye out for paperbark cherry (*Prunus serrula*), katsura (*Cercidiphyllum japonicum*), lacebark pine (*Pinus bungeana*), and shagbark hickory (*Carya ovata*). And don't be shy about asking for hints. People who spend their days caring for trees tend to notice subtleties that a quick tour might overlook.

Bark for Canoes

Q **If it's harmful to strip bark from trees, how did early American Indians make their birch bark canoes?**

A The boat builders in question were careful—in some cases worshipful—of the world around them, but that doesn't mean they were unwilling to kill trees. When they needed a birch for canoe material, they took it down.

Small amounts of the thin outer bark can be removed without harming the tree; it naturally sheds patches. But to build a canoe you need all the bark layers, including the cambium that is essential for life, and you want all the layers in one piece. The fewer seams you have to caulk (with spruce resin), the more watertight your vessel will be. 🍂

Which Tree Grows in Brooklyn?

Q **Just what is "the tree that grows in Brooklyn"?**

A The tree that grows in Brooklyn is that ubiquitous denizen of vacant lots, *Ailanthus altissima,* or tree of heaven. The Brooklyn connection is the result of the classic book *A Tree Grows in Brooklyn* by Betty Smith, about a young girl who is inspired by an ailanthus. As Katherine Powis, librarian of the Horticultural Society of New York, said, "No matter where its seeds fall—boarded-up lots, neglected rubbish heaps, or cellar gratings—it manages to grow lushly, survive without sun, and reach the sky." (Many gardeners consider it a pernicious weed.)

According to Ms. Powis, the ailanthus is a native of China, and seeds were apparently sent to France in 1751 by Pierre d'Incarville, a missionary. Seeds were then brought to Philadelphia in 1784 by a William Hamilton, who had seen the tree growing in the garden of the physician to King Louis XVI. 🍂

Breathing Trees

Q **Is it true that trees "breathe" through their bark?**

A It is true that gases, including oxygen, pass through the outer bark to and from the living cells of the inner layers of a tree. This is a form of respiration, or breathing. The gases move through stem pores called lenticels, whose function is equivalent to that of stomata, or breathing cells, found on leaves.

The shape, distribution, and size of lenticels vary with the kind of tree. If one looks closely, lenticels can be seen fairly easily on trunks of young trees, or on species such as cherry or birch, which have smooth bark. They appear either as somewhat raised transverse streaks, or as scattered bumps or small dots that at first glance may be mistaken for scale insects. But in many species, the roughness of a trunk's maturing bark eventually obscures them. 🍂

Trees in Particular

Not for Wine Bottles

Q I thought cork trees were from the Mediterranean and would not grow in New England. But I have a friend in Maine who has a beautiful Amur cork grown from a seed taken from the Arnold Arboretum in Boston. Is this a special hardy strain, and if so where can I get one? (My friend's tree doesn't make seeds.)

A Amur cork is hardy, all right, down to about −40°F. But it is not related to *Quercus suber,* the commercial cork, which you correctly link to the Mediterranean. Amur cork is from the Amur River region in northeastern China. Its botanical name is *Phellodendron amurense.*

Dr. Peter Del Tredici, director of living collections at the Arnold, said that on its home grounds Amur cork is an extremely valuable timber tree, prized for its hard, highly figured, deep golden wood.

In the United States, however, it is usually planted as an ornamental. The trees are 40 to 50 feet tall, with a gracefully spreading shape, deeply ridged bark, and rich green leaves that put on what Dr. Del Tredici described as "a striking display in early fall; they turn a beautiful clear yellow that really shines."

The Amur cork is easy to grow. It's tolerant of a wide range of soils and is seldom bothered by insects or diseases. The trees are male or female, and you need both to get the beautiful blue-black berries. People don't eat them, but birds do and thus spread the trees, which have become dangerously invasive in disturbed woodlands. Amur corks hog openings that otherwise could go to native species.

You can't count on having a female tree stay lonely for the 100 years it might live (and can't be sure a single tree is

Amur cork
(*Phellodendron amurense*)

as lonely as it looks. The two sexes can be quite widely separated and still be close enough to cause trouble). So the best way to have both an Amur cork and a clear conscience is to plant a known male, ideally one of the special selections like 'Macho' or 'His Majesty,' developed for garden use.

Retail nurseries seldom stock them, and even the young ones are too large to be suitable for mail order. But they are available to the trade, and if you ask in early spring, a full-service garden center should be able to order one for you. 🍐

Planting Under a Beech

Q I have volunteered to replant an area in my co-op's garden that is directly under a 75-year-old beech tree, but all the books I've read warn against planting under a beech because of the dense shade and shallow roots. This is a very formal garden, so I am hoping for a low hedge similar to boxwood, with taller holly plants at each end that I can shape into pyramidal columns. In front of these I want borders of perennials and annuals. Any suggestions?

A While you're at it, why not hope to win the lottery, live forever, and bring about world peace? Unfortunately, the books were right, but beauty is well within reach if you work with what you've got.

Rather than planting in the soil, consider containers that can be switched back and forth. The holly columns (have fun pruning) will grow well in deep, formal boxes, preferably boxes on legs so they don't smother the roots underneath them.

Plant four hollies. Put two of them under the beech and the other two where they get bright, diffused light but not all-day sun. Switch them roughly every month.

Sun-loving annuals can be treated the same way if you don't mind moving them every 10 days or so. Most perennials are likely to be more trouble than they're worth, but you can plant lots of early-spring flowering bulbs like crocus, snowdrop, and scilla, as long as you're careful of the beech roots. (Bulbs that flower later in the season will not get enough sun on the foliage to bloom in subsequent years.) Use a narrow bulb planter, and watch where you punch it.

Since you want a low hedge, it sounds as if the view beyond the tree is pretty—or at least not ugly. Could it become an asset if it were framed with ornamental fencing? Does the tree shelter a spot where a good-looking bench might be welcome?

And what's up with the venerable beech itself? These handsome trees don't usually need setting off; they're beautiful all by themselves. 🍎

Birch Borers

Q We've been told that a white birch we love has borers and might live only a few years. Is there anything we can do this fall, or must we just watch it die?

A No, you shouldn't just watch it die, but you should be aware that even the most vigorous rescue efforts may not work.

The bronze birch borer (*Agrilus anxius*) is the larval stage of an olive-to-reddish-brown beetle that lays its eggs in the bark during summer. After hatching, the yellow-white larvae feed by tunneling into the wood. This activity stops the flow of nutrients and water, causing the decline and death of leaves and branches.

As soon as you can, cut out and destroy the dead or dying branches. The borers tend to work from the top down, so it may not be possible to get all of them. Also cut out small wounds in the bark where a trail of sawdust shows there's a borer inside.

If the trees are healthy, they may start to recover once the threat has been substantially removed, but if they are stressed by poor growing conditions or weakened by injuries, the prognosis is poorer.

Start now to increase your tree's strength with a program of regular watering, especially important in the dry periods of summer and early fall. Fertilize in mid spring with all-purpose tree fertilizer, following the label's directions. Then in autumn, after all the leaves have fallen, fertilize lightly again, following the label's directions.

Although pesticides are sometimes recommended, they are seldom successful. Good care and watchful management may save your tree, but if they don't, learn from your experience and plant a more resistant variety next time. Though most birches are vulnerable to one extent or another, white birch is the worst. 🍎

BLACK WALNUT BLUES

Black walnuts have a long history of cultivation on American farms and, to a lesser extent, in gardens all over the East and Midwest. They are beautiful trees, with upright trunks and wide canopies. They bear delicious (though hard to crack) nuts, and they are very valuable as timber trees—a single straight trunk can be worth thousands of dollars.

Unfortunately, black walnuts are not completely garden-friendly. The extensive surface roots compete with anything planted over them, the thick leaf cover produces dense shade, and all parts of the tree exude a chemical called juglone, which inhibits the growth of a great many plants.

Vegetables in the solanaceous group—tomatoes, peppers, eggplants, and potatoes—seem particularly sensitive to juglone, as are many perennials, including columbines, peonies, and chrysanthemums. Hydrangeas appear to hate juglone. So do rhododendrons and azaleas, lilacs and lilies. Ditto pines and birches, apples and blueberries.

Because juglone-laden feeder roots extend far beyond the tree's canopy, and juglone-containing leaves and nut hulls also tend to get spread around, none of the plants listed above is likely to do well unless it's *at least* 50 feet away from the drip line of a black walnut and 100 or more feet away from the trunk.

So what's left? Quite a lot. Kentucky bluegrass and black raspberries actually seem to thrive when planted near (but not under) black walnuts. If the soil drainage is good and other growing conditions are right, gardeners have also had success with cucurbits (squash, melon, and cucumber), as well as beans, beets, and carrots.

The list of possible flowers is longer, starting with spring-flowering bulbs (except crocus) and woodland wildflowers such as Jack-in-the-pulpit, sweet woodruff, and cranesbill. Many hostas appear to be up to the challenge, and asters, day lilies, coralbells, and Siberian iris are also likely bets. Euonymous usually does O.K., and so do Japanese maples, viburnums, redbuds, and hemlocks.

Black walnut
(*Juglans nigra*)

One warning: As the recurrence of words like "seems" and "possible" suggests, these pros and cons are based on observations, not controlled experiments. And to complicate matters further, the amount of juglone in the soil can vary considerably, depending on such factors as soil type, drainage patterns, soil microorganisms, and the age of the tree.

So if there's something you're dying to try under a black walnut, try it. But watch carefully. Affected plants will quickly show signs of stress and should be moved before they start dying, too.

The Fruits of Catalpa

Q I have a catalpa tree. Is the bean-like fruit useful for anything?

A You could paint it gold and hang it on the Christmas tree, but that's about it, although you are far from the first to wonder about those long pods. Almost every part of the catalpa has been used for medicinal purposes at one time or another. Tea made from the seeds supposedly soothed asthma and bronchitis, and wounds were dressed with poultices made from the leaves. The bark was closest to multipurpose: tea made from it was used as an antiseptic, a sedative, and a cure for snakebites.

But don't try this at home. Instead, enjoy your catalpa for its handsome shape and beautiful flowers—and for all the healthy exercise it gives you when you rake up the pods.

Cedar-Apple Rust

Q I've noticed brown growths about 2 inches in diameter on my red cedar. Are they harmful?

A Yes and no. The round growths are one stage of a peculiar disease called cedar-apple rust, which causes more damage to apples that it does to cedars.

It is caused by a fungus that requires two groups of host plants to complete its development. One group includes certain species of native cedars (which botanically are junipers, in particular *Juniperus virginiana* and *J. scopulorum*). The other group includes the apples or crab apples (*Malus* spp., including among many others the apple varieties 'Jonathan' and 'Rome' and the crab apple varieties 'Bechtel' and 'Parkman').

The junipers first become infected in late summer and autumn by wind-borne spores from the apple leaves. The following spring, the growths begin developing on the junipers as minute green swellings. By autumn they have reached the full 2- or 3-inch-diameter growth you saw and are a greenish brown.

With the warm rains of the following spring—the second year after infection—the growths swell and develop bright orange hornlike projections. Spores from these orange horns are then carried by wind back to the apple trees, where they infect both leaves and fruit.

By mid summer, rusty orange spots appear on the apple fruit as well as on the upper surface of the leaves. By summer's end, the spores are once again released, and the cycle continues.

The growths can remain on the juniper leaves for a year or more, even though they and the twig may have died. The best disease control is to prune off and destroy infected branches as soon as you see them. Avoid planting apples and junipers within a mile of each other.

Strangely enough, the cedar-apple fungus does not spread from apple to apple or from juniper to juniper, but must alternate between the two host groups. In apple-producing areas the disease can take a severe toll, and the planting of junipers may be restricted or prohibited by law. Call your local extension service to find out if such rules are in force where you live. The extension service can also recommend disease-resistant apple varieties appropriate for your climate. 🍎

Reblooming Cherries

Q I love flowering cherry trees and have heard that there is one that actually blooms in autumn as well as spring. Can you tell me about this plant?

A The tree in question is Higan cherry (*Prunus subhirtella* 'Autumnalis'), which does indeed flower in spring and again in fall.

A native of Japan, it is also known as the rosebud cherry and the winter- or autumn-flowering cherry. It is distinguished by its gray bark, slender arching limbs, and pale pink semidouble flowers that measure about ¾ inch. Its small black fruit ripens in early summer. 🍎

Improving Chestnuts

Q I have a cookbook that is a few years old. Along with the recipes, it talks about breeding programs to develop American chestnuts resistant to the blight that nearly wiped them out. Supposedly, the nuts are at least as tasty as the Italian chestnuts I buy. Were the programs successful? It would be great to be able to buy American chestnuts.

A The American chestnut, *Castanea dentata,* is truly a native North American tree, dating back more than 30,000 years. In the late 1800s, the fungus that causes chestnut blight entered the United States on imported Chinese chestnut (*C. mollissima*) and Japanese chestnut (*C. crenata*) trees, two species that had developed resistance and so could carry the fungus without being affected by it. At the time, American chestnuts made up more than a quarter of all deciduous trees in Eastern forests, which included huge stands of chestnuts alone.

The blight was first noticed in New York in 1904, on trees that lined the avenues at the Bronx Zoo. By 1950 American chestnuts had died out except for the few trees that early settlers had carried beyond their normal range and therefore beyond the range of the fungus.

The nuts are indeed delicious, but quite small. At 60 to the pound, they are hardly worth the effort it takes to peel them, especially when compared with modern chestnut hybrids, which yield a dozen to a pound. The real value of the American chestnut is as a timber tree.

American chestnut
(*Castanea dentata*)

The Chinese and Japanese chestnuts produce large but not very tasty nuts, and are not very good for timber. They are valued for their blight resistance.

Chestnut breeding programs today have two aims. Breeders who are interested in chestnuts as a food crop produce hybrids that are mostly Asian, with a touch of American for flavor. Programs like the one at the Connecticut Agricultural Experiment Station in New Haven, the oldest chestnut breeding program in the country, are interested in timber trees and produce hybrids that are mostly American with a touch of Asian for disease resistance.

European chestnuts (*C. sativa*) like the ones you buy from Italy are terrific, but unfortunately they are suscepti-ble to the blight. ❧

Christmas Tree Survival

Q **I have purchased a live Christmas tree and want to be sure it survives the holidays for planting outside. How should I do this?**

A To keep your tree healthy, begin by storing it outside in an area protected from both wind and sun, and spray its needles with an antidesiccant. Water the root area well, and cover the entire root ball with heavy burlap or old blankets to keep it damp and to prevent freezing.

When you are ready to move the tree indoors, stand it in the coolest spot you have, away from a heater, fireplace, or sunny window. Keep the plant in a large waterproof tub so you can moisten the roots again without ruining the floor. And most important, do not keep your evergreen indoors any longer than three or four days.

When you're ready to move it outdoors, gradually rein-troduce your tree to the cold by keeping it for several days in a shady spot protected from the wind. If freezing weather makes planting impossible, keep the root ball moist and wrapped in blankets as before. With proper care, a hardy evergreen can survive this way for months.

Once the tree is in the ground, firm the surrounding soil to eliminate air pockets, and water well. Mulch the area with bark chips or hay, and if the area is windy, stake or tie the plant to prevent it from being blown down. If there is no rain or snow, remember to add water during extended thaws, and spray with an antidesiccant again in February.

Remove the stakes in spring so the tree can learn to stand up on its own. ❧

RECYCLE THAT TREE

No longer magical with ornaments or lights, Christmas trees are too often tossed unceremoniously onto the curb right after the holidays. But there's no reason holiday evergreens can't be allowed to serve long after the merry-making is over.

For a splash of instant green, cut the branches of pine, fir, spruce, or other needled evergreens and add them to barren window boxes.

You can also use branches to protect dormant plants. A thick cover of ever-green limbs helps keep the surface layer of soil moist, and also helps to stabilize soil temperature, reducing the rapid cycles of frost and thaw that can heave perennials and shrubs from the ground and rip their roots.

Christmas greenery also can be used as tracery on trellises and arbors. Held in place with plastic ties or string, cut boughs give plants like climbing roses, and vines like grapes or clematis, a good-looking shield from drying winter winds and sun.

In addition, leftover evergreens are useful for augmenting the natural foliage around a bird feeder or bath. Wild birds like protection and aren't choosy whether their evergreen screen is living or dead.

There is an art to denuding a Christmas tree, though, and pruning shears or loppers are a must. Heavy gloves make it easier to handle the rough bark and the needles. If you must cut up the tree inside, cover the floor with a plastic sheet to prevent a mess of needles and sap.

Remove the evergreen boughs from gardens and planters when the tips of early spring bloomers, like crocus or snowdrops, have pushed about an inch out of the ground. Where no bulbs are planted, leave the branches until mid April or whenever spring seems securely in place.

Lights on Live Christmas Trees

Q **We're having a live Christmas tree this year. Is it all right to use lights, or will they dry it out too much?**

A Stay away from large bulbs, but minilights should be O.K. They don't put out much heat, and they'll be in use for only three or four days—which is as long as a living evergreen can survive indoor conditions. And of course, be sure the wiring is well away from the root ball, which should be kept damp but not wet. 🍂

THE BEST LIVE CHRISTMAS TREE

Every year, readers ask "What is the best live Christmas tree?" And every year the answer is the same: The best live Christmas tree is the one that is happily growing outdoors, where it belongs. It's the one that was planted at the right time (early fall) and has never suffered the multiple stresses of indoor-decoration duty (heat, drought, lots of handling, huge temperature swings).

From the tree's point of view, the whole process is sheer torture, and the fact that some of them manage to live through it is only proof that some trees are extremely tough.

But what's the alternative? Whether you are an avid gardener or simply a lover of natural beauty, it seems wrong to kill a whole tree just to have what amounts to a big bouquet. And there is justice in this aversion when the tree is wild. Now that the forest itself is precious, who wants to murder a piece of it for something so transient?

Nobody, natch. But nobody has to. Although you can still buy wild trees, which are usually recognizable by being straggly and ill-shaped, farmed Christmas trees are widely available and they are every bit as domestic as a head of broccoli. It takes them longer to grow, but they are still agricultural products, planted and cared for with the intention that they will be harvested.

So if you want a Christmas tree in the house, go ahead and buy a farmed one. If you want a *live* Christmas tree, decorate one that is in the yard. Like everyone else, living trees want to be home for Christmas.

Blooming Too Early

Q Since we had such a warm autumn and have had a mild winter so far, several of my crab apples developed blooms a few weeks ago. Will they flower again when spring comes?

A Possibly, but not as well as they might have. Woody plants that normally produce very early blooms (forsythia is another example) develop the buds for these blooms during the summer of the year before. There is only one set of flower buds each year, so if too many open early, that's it.

All you can do now is wait and hope that not all the buds broke—and they rarely do. To encourage the formation of the flower buds next season, fertilize in very early summer with an all-purpose blend that is high in phosphorus (the middle number of the three on the package). Follow package directions. 🌢

A Bud Off the Old Block

Q We have a large crab apple tree with white flowers and tiny apples in late summer. We have pictures showing that it was already mature over 50 years ago, but sadly, it is not in good health now. Last summer a large bough died, and the bark on the trunk doesn't look good. If it dies I have no way to order a new one, because I have no idea what variety it is. I wonder if I can propagate a new small tree to replace it. Could you suggest how I might do this?

A Call your county cooperative extension service to find someone familiar with propagating roses or fruit trees, for which bud grafting is commonly done, and hire him or her to do it for you. That would be the best method, according to Tom Simpson, whose Simpson Nursery in Vincennes, Indiana, has bred some favorite crab apples, including 'Indian Magic,' 'Brandywine,' and 'Centurion.' Starting a cutting from a branch would be difficult at best, requiring a greenhouse, a misting system, and luck. Many varieties just won't root, and without knowing what you have, Mr. Simpson didn't think that trying would be worthwhile.

Bud grafting takes practice. A leaf bud (the small tissue structure from which a leaf grows) is carefully cut away and then inserted just under the bark on the trunk of a closely related tree, like an apple or another crab apple. This tree, called the rootstock, is chosen for its hardiness and provides support and a root system for the grafted bud, which grows up to be just like your original crab apple. 🍎

Choosing the Best Crab Apples

Q This is a tale of two crab apples, and I hope you know a happy ending. Both trees were on the property when we bought our house last year, so I don't have any information about them. This summer the backyard tree has lost all its leaves. The front tree looks fine, but I am afraid that it will also succumb. What steps can we take to help the remaining tree?

A Don't cut down the leafless tree—it isn't dead. Crab apples, lovely as they are, attract not only humans and birds but also a whole host of fungi. Your backyard tree almost surely has apple scab, which wet, cool weather will encourage. But if it hadn't been scab, it might have been cedar-apple rust, fire blight, or powdery mildew.

When buying one of the trees, the previous owner of your house may have fallen in love with a pretty flower and forgotten to ask about disease resistance. Considering everything there is to decide when choosing a crab apple—such as size and shape of the tree when mature; size, color, and persistence of the fruit; single or double flowers in red, white, or pink; and whether it's an alternate-year bloomer—she or he may have just been awestruck in the middle of all those trees in glorious flower at the nursery.

Scab is a surprising disease. You may not notice the dull, smoky, or sooty area on new leaves, or even the irregular olive-green or brown velvety spots. But you certainly notice when all the leaves fall off in mid summer. Rake up and destroy those fallen leaves because the fungus overwinters on them and can reinfect the tree next year. Spraying an entire tree every eight to ten days with fungicides to prevent scab is not just difficult, it's absolutely silly when disease-resistant crab apples are available everywhere.

Resistance does not mean invulnerability, and a summer of perfect fungus weather can overcome the most resistant of trees, so some cultivars are clearly better than others. High on everyone's list are 'Adams,' 'Adirondack,' 'Donald Wyman,' 'Harvest Gold,' 'Indian Summer,' 'Professor Sprenger,' 'Prairifire,' 'Snowdrift,' and 'Sugar Tyme.' By the way, all of these have excellent resistance to cedar-apple rust, too. 🍎

Dogwood Control

Q I have a dogwood tree that is getting overgrown for the small garden it's in, and I want to prune it radically. Is it true that the "bleeding" that results won't hurt the tree? And will such radical pruning be harmful?

A Flowering dogwoods (*Cornus florida*) do "bleed," or produce runny sap when pruned. But Richard Weir III of the Cornell Cooperative Extension in Nassau County, New York, said, "Once in a while such bleeding is O.K., although the sap can sting." The best way to keep a dogwood in bounds in a small space is to begin by removing the dense inner branches, he continued. Then trim some larger limbs and twigs, cutting them back to where they branch or fork. Avoid removing only the twig tips; this will destroy the natural shape of the plant. Your goal should be that of a "good haircut," making it appear as if nothing has been removed. 🌰

WHY WON'T IT BLOOM?

When flowering trees fail to flower, the first question to ask is How old is this plant? It always takes at least a few years—sometimes 10 or more—before a tree leaves the juvenile stage and is mature enough to spend some energy on reproduction.

Other reasons for flower failure:

- **Overfertilizing,** which can push excessive foliage growth, burning up all the carbohydrates before it is time to set flower buds.
- **Excessive shade.** In most cases, four to five hours of full sun is enough, but more sun usually means more flowers.
- **Frosts or drought** at the wrong time.
- **Pruning** the flower buds right off because you didn't understand a plant's life cycle.

Waiting for Dogwood Bloom

Q I planted a skinny 4-foot dogwood hybrid (*Cornus* 'Constellation') about three years ago. The young tree seems to be doing well and receives about four or five hours of direct sun a day, but has never bloomed. Is it likely to flower as it ages?

Hybrid dogwood 'Constellation'

A Profusely. Your dogwood is one of a series of recent hybrids between *Cornus kousa* (Korean dogwood) and *C. florida* (flowering dogwood) bred at Rutgers University. Each member of the Stellar series (including 'Aurora,' 'Galaxy,' and 'Stellar Pink') has sterile flowers. Because no energy is devoted to making seeds, they produce a heavy complement of flowers every year, unlike their parents, which bloom in alternate years. But these hybrids flower only when they become adults, which can take four to eight years. Before that, they are in a juvenile stage, just like

375

humans, when rapidly growing tall and strong is more important than sex. Your tree was probably just a year or two old when you planted it, so it may take a few more years. 🌰

Finding Special Trees

Q **I am often frustrated by the lack of availability of certain interesting plants. It took me ages to find a *Davidia involucrata* (dove tree), for example. Why don't more nurseries carry this plant?**

A Why is such a spectacular tree so hard to find? Because it doesn't fit with the instant-garden mentality that the current generation of garden owners seems to have.

Dove tree, or handkerchief tree, requires patience and plenty of it. It gets its common names from the two spectacular bracts that accompany its small flowers. The bracts are large but delicate white or creamy white specialized leaves that highlight the flowers and move in the slightest breeze. The larger bract can be 8 inches long and the smaller one about 4. Although it is in full flower for only two weeks in mid May, davidia is unforgettable. But it is slow growing, taking at least 10 years to bloom, and usually has its best display in alternate years. 🌰

Eucalyptus Hardiness

Q **Can you give me information about growing hardy eucalyptus in Iowa? I bought a small plant by mail, but there were no instructions.**

A There are some 500 species of eucalyptus, or gum tree. Virtually all of them are native to Australia and Tasmania, so the word "hardy" here seems misleading. Full sun is essential, and night temperatures should not go lower than about 50°F. The plants tolerate drought and a wide range of soils. In California and some areas of the Southwest, several species are popular in gardens or as street trees; but in colder climates, eucalyptus must be grown indoors as pot plants. By all means, give your plant a summer vacation outdoors as soon as it is warm enough to plant annuals. But be sure to move it inside before a frost. 🌰

Socrates' Hemlock

Q **I have a hemlock in my yard and wondered if this is the plant used to kill Socrates.**

A It's unlikely that you are growing the philosopher killer, which (outside of the classics classroom) is almost always identified as poison hemlock. Your hemlock is almost surely one of the many handsome evergreen trees in the species *Tsuga canadensis,* a member of the pine family. The poisonous plant used by ancient Greeks to put people to death is an unrelated biennial herb in the carrot family, *Conium maculatum.* Its common names, winter fern and poison parsley, are apt descriptions of its feathery foliage, which also resembles dill.

Although every part of *C. maculatum* is highly poisonous, it is believed that the Athenians used a decoction of the fruit to kill Socrates. The plant is native to Europe and Asia, but patches of poison hemlock now grow wild along American roadsides, streams, and meadows, where it might tempt the unwary into mistaking its leaves for wild carrot or parsley and its roots for parsnips. 🍂

Hemlock Havoc

Q **My hemlocks have been dropping their needles. There seems to be some sort of white cotton fungus. Is this the problem? And what safe product can I use to eradicate it?**

A The "white cotton" certainly is the problem, only it's not a fungus. What you see lining the branches at the base of the hemlock needles is the telltale sign of *Adelges tsugae,* the hemlock woolly adelgid. These tiny, dark, soft, aphid-like creatures cover themselves with white or gray waxy protective threads that resemble cotton.

The adult insects begin laying their eggs in late winter (mid February in the New York City area), and the first brood begins feeding about six weeks later. This cycle repeats at least once and sometimes more, with each generation sucking more life out of the tree. The first year of attack the insect may go unnoticed, but you will definitely see problems in the second year, and by the third, the tree may be dead.

The safest sprays are the horticultural oils, which are deemed about 95 percent effective if applied at least three times. The first application should be in April, the next ones at six-week intervals after that. Insecticidal soaps are also safe, but work better if the cycle is started about two weeks later. It is essential, in either case, to cover the insects thoroughly and use sufficient pressure to penetrate their protective coat, so a professional may be needed if you have tall hemlock trees.

Fertilizer applications usually worsen the infestation and should be avoided, but do be sure the trees are kept watered and free of aggressive weeds; they need to be in the best possible health to fight off the adelgids.

Monitor carefully for live insects; the cottony fluff may persist on the branches even after the villain beneath it is dead. 🍂

Blotchy Leaves

Q **Last summer the leaves of our neighborhood horse chestnuts turned brown and became dry and brittle. We have had enough rain this year, but I'm beginning to see the same thing starting again, so it isn't a lack of water. Whatever it is, it is getting more serious. Is there anything I should be doing?**

A Horse chestnut leaf blotch, a disease that affects several species of *Aesculus* (horse chestnut and buckeye), is more ugly than it is dangerous. What at first appear to be small, water-soaked areas on a leaf soon turn reddish brown, frequently with a yellow edge. Eventually the areas enlarge out to the leaf edges, drying and curling them and generally looking like blowtorch leftovers.

The good news, if there is ever good news associated with diseases, is that it doesn't get bad until well into the growing season, when the leaves are nearly finished making the year's food supply. The leaves look awful, but the trees don't seem to care much. Horse chestnuts can get leaf blotch every year (and frequently do) without serious consequences.

Horse chestnut
(*Aesculus
hippocastanum*)

The disease spores spread two ways. Once the outbreak occurs, rain releases spores that travel along the wet leaves. The thick, leafy crown typical of a mature horse chestnut doesn't dry quickly, and the disease easily takes hold.

Spores also overwinter on the fallen leaves and are carried aloft the following spring when the air is full of moisture. On foggy spring days the spores may travel a quarter mile. Cleaning up all the leaves in autumn helps, but with such adventurous spores the cleanup needs to be a neighborhood affair. 🍎

Katsura Conundrum

Q Five years ago, I had a nursery plant a 12-foot katsura tree on my lawn in Columbia County, New York. I have fertilized it as recommended and watered it as much as possible. Last spring I noticed that the bark appeared to be coming off. The nursery didn't have an answer, and it suggested wrapping the trunk with a lightweight paper wrap.

Subsequently, a tree pruner advised removing the wrap because of potential insect or fungus problems. The condition, however, has continued and now affects about 30 percent of the tree.

Someone suggested that deer may have been chewing at the bark, so this summer I added a wire mesh around the trunk to negate the deer problem. A friend also pruned the tree so that the reduced strength of the trunk would have to serve fewer limbs on top.

Can you tell me what I should be doing to try to save this tree? I fear it may be dying.

A It is surprising, and more than a little disappointing, that of all the people you talked with about your katsura tree (*Cercidiphyllum japonicum*), none realized that a certain air of genteel shagginess from the peeling bark is not only normal as the tree ages, but usually considered desirable. Only the arborist who advised removing the wrap gets a little credit for being right. Consider yourself lucky that no one suggested a chain saw as a way of preventing this so-called problem from spreading.

Just in case a walk around the neighborhood should uncover other trees with exfoliating bark (peeling, flaking, splitting, loose, or falling off in big plates), please identify them and look them up at the library before taking action. You may find a shagbark hickory, which, compared with your katsura, will look positively disastrous. Others include kousa dogwood (rounded, irregular flakes of gray, tan, and brown), cornelian cherry dogwood (muted gray-and-tan pieces flake right off), parrotia (the bark peels off in gray, green, and tan pieces), and sycamores and London planes (large plates come loose and drop off). In most cases, the bark on younger trees is smooth, and the exfoliation occurs as they get older. Unlike people, trees are proud to show their age. 🍎

Magnolia Planting Time

Q **I wanted to plant a magnolia this October, but my nurseryman said magnolias shouldn't be planted in the fall. Why not?**

A For most trees, fall is the best time to plant. The soil is warm but not waterlogged the way it can be in spring, and trees without leaves make fewer demands on their roots to provide nutrients.

A few trees, however, including magnolia, birch, hawthorn, black gum, tulip tree, and most oaks, get downright cranky when planted in the fall. No one knows for sure, but researchers think that there is something that prevents the root structure from taking up enough water to overcome transplant shock, and that winter comes before the tree is ready for it.

Studies by Dr. Nina Bassuk at the Cornell University Urban Horticulture Institute in Ithaca, New York, show that transplanting these trees when they are smaller increases the success rate for fall planting. She has had much better results with trees that measure less than 2 inches in diameter at a point 6 inches above where the trunk emerges from the roots than she has had with larger trees. Be sure to water that new tree in well. Whether it has leaves or not, it needs water.

Watering also settles the soil and helps eliminate any air pockets. Dormant trees planted in October or early November should need only that one deep, soothing watering to last them the winter. But all that said, it is still better to plant magnolias in spring. 🍎

BAD BALANCING ACT

Some ideas are harder to kill than crabgrass. One of them is that when a tree is dug up to be sold, the branches should be removed to compensate for the loss of roots. The rationale is to balance root loss with the removal of an equal amount of top growth. The tree is then thought to be better balanced and better able to withstand transplant shock.

As logical as this sounds at first, it just doesn't hold up. The human equivalent might be removing the right arm of someone who has just lost her left leg in an accident.

Transplanted trees need all the food they can produce to support the regrowth of those lost roots. The food comes from leaves doing their thing, so the more leaves, the better. The only branches that should be pruned are those that are dead, diseased, damaged, or rubbing against other branches.

A Tree from Home

Q **I was born in the South and have been raised to love and adore the Southern magnolia, *Magnolia grandiflora*. I would like to find cold-hardy varieties that will grow at my Pennsylvania home, in zone 6. What varieties do you recommend?**

A Of the many species of magnolia, the evergreen *M. grandiflora* is the one that puts a Southern lilt in your voice and a julep in your hand with its striking large, deep green patent-leather leaves, its breathtaking fragrance, its waxy white blossoms in June and July and sporadically throughout the summer.

There are some cultivars that are hardy in zone 6, including 'Bracken's Brown Beauty,' an upright 25-foot tree loaded with flowers, and with smaller leaves that have heavily brown-felted undersides. Others include 'D. D. Blanchard,' 'Poconos,' 'Victoria,' and 'Edith Bogue.'

Not all zone 6 sites are created equal, however. Dr. Kim Tripp, vice president of horticulture at the New York Botanical Garden in the Bronx, said that microclimate is everything, and that the garden's *M. grandiflora* does well because it is in a protected courtyard.

Cold winters mean that the best place for a hardy Southern magnolia is near a wall, which will reflect winter warmth and provide shelter from cold winds. High, light

Southern magnolia
(*Magnolia grandiflora*)

shade from bare trees nearby will help keep the winter sun from desiccating the leaves.

The same cautions apply to the soil. Your memories may be of magnolias growing in clay, but in the North, clay soils stay too wet and too cold for too long, so magnolias need moist but well-drained, humousy, acidic soils.

If you're really crazy about magnolias, you may want to join the Magnolia Society to exchange Southern reminiscences and pick up some Northern advice: 6616 81st Street, Cabin John, MD 20818; (301) 320-4296; *www.magnoliasociety.org.* ☙

Slow Betty

Q I have several plants on my property, 110 miles upstate from New York City, that have literally not grown since I bought them four years ago. One is a magnolia 'Betty.' I thought that perhaps the trees were not quite hardy enough for the zone, but my nurseryman contends that if they survive each winter, that's not the problem. He suggests fertilizer, but most of my other plants are thriving. Any suggestions?

A Magnolia 'Betty' is one of the Little Girl hybrids, a group that consists of 'Ann,' 'Betty,' 'Jane,' 'Judy,' 'Pinkie,' 'Randy,' 'Ricki,' and 'Susan,' all bred at the National Arboretum. These small trees grow 10 to 15 feet tall and are hardy in zones 4 through 7.

Kris Bachtell, director of collections at the Morton Arboretum in Lisle, Illinois, said it's likely that the tree's roots have never grown out of the (now imaginary) container it came in.

Container-grown trees and shrubs are often in the containers long enough that their roots grow to the edge and begin circling around the perimeter, forming a dense, impenetrable mass. If the soil ball isn't scored and some roots pulled outward and away from the ball before planting, the tree doesn't realize that it is in a new home, and the roots continue to grow round and round, never going into the surrounding soil. This limits the amount of water and nutrients that can be taken up, slowing growth to a standstill.

Mr. Bachtell's advice is to dig up the plant carefully next spring (magnolias are among the trees that should not be planted in the fall) to look at the root ball and see if the roots need to be loosened and spread out. 🌶

Frostbitten Magnolia

Q **An April snowstorm destroyed the pink magnolia (*Magnolia* × *soulangiana*, we think) that was here when we bought our property. We'd like to replant but want something that will not keep getting blasted by frost the way the old one did. Can you suggest a variety that will bloom reliably in the Hudson Valley?**

A Is there, perhaps, a note of pique in this question? From the sound of things, your old plant *did* bloom reliably. Then, in the fashion of spring magnolias, it sometimes lost blossoms to frost. Since early splendor is the whole point, risk comes with the territory.

Nevertheless, we took your problem to Stephen Tim, vice president for scientific affairs at the Brooklyn Botanic Garden. He recommended 'Elizabeth,' a *Magnolia acuminata* × *M. denudata* hybrid that's one of the garden's own introductions. It's a beautiful plant: hardy, floriferous, and very late, so it almost always escapes blackening frost. Its only flaw is that it can be difficult to find.

And it's yellow. If you'd prefer to stick with pink, Roger Gossler, whose family nursery in Oregon has one of the country's largest collections of magnolias, suggested 'Spectrum,' a hybrid from the National Arboretum, or the similar 'Galaxy.' He also thought highly of 'Forrest's Pink,' which blooms over a long season and will make new buds if the first ones are lost. All are deciduous and bloom on bare branches. For dark green leaves framing huge, fragrant, creamy white flowers, plant the hardy evergreen 'Edith Bogue.' 🌶

Reblooming Magnolia

Q **I live in Park Slope, Brooklyn, where there are many wonderful magnolia trees. During the past three years I've noticed that a few of them have a second flowering in July. My question is, why is it only a handful of trees? The trees have white-and-pink blossoms, and they don't look any different from the other trees that have similar blossoms.**

A When you can bloom like a magnolia, it's natural to try to get in a few extra flowers later in the season. The magnolias you are seeing are most likely *Magnolia × soulangeana* or some of its many cultivars.

Pat McCracken, who breeds magnolias in North Carolina, said that ones that have *Magnolia liliiflora* in their background, like *Magnolia × soulangeana,* characteristically love to try to push a few of next year's buds into bloom early. They're just showing off, especially if the trees are healthy and have had a good growing season—enough sun and water, and temperatures to their liking. Some of the cultivars and hybrids are more insistent than others, which is why some will rebloom while others do not, even under identical growing conditions.

To a magnolia connoisseur, this second flush consists of second-rate flowers—slightly misshapen and usually smaller—but to the rest of us they are just as welcome as the big show earlier in the spring.

Magnolia × soulangeana

If you prefer your magnolias to bloom in the summer or you want to trade one big spring show for a month or more of flowers later on, there are a number of choices among the hundreds of cultivars and hybrids of magnolias commonly found in cultivation. The Little Girl hybrids of *Magnolia liliiflora,* and the *M. grandiflora* cultivars 'Bracken's Brown Beauty,' 'Edith Bogue,' and 'Victoria,' are all hardy in zone 6 and bloom or rebloom during the summer.

Choosing a magnolia is a delicious problem. 🌰

Keeping a Seedling Safe

Q What is the best thing to do with a 20-inch silver maple seedling in a pot as its first winter approaches? The seed fell from a tree in my yard this spring, and I would eventually like to have it take a place along the street.

A It needs to be outside so it can have its normal winter dormancy, but it also needs to be planted. Its roots need the earth's insulation to protect it from cold damage.

Since the roots are not going to grow much over the winter, planting with or without the pot is up to you. It will grow quickly next year, but may be vulnerable to snowplows this first winter, so find a spot in the garden, away from the curb. In the spring, before the leaves begin to grow, replant it in its final location. 🍂

A Desert in a Maple's Shade

Q **We can't get anything to grow under the good-size maple tree in our front yard. A few years ago, we had some limbs removed to let in light. Still no grass. The roots are quite large, and there is very little topsoil. Several attempts to add topsoil and grow grass have failed. Even pachysandra fails to flourish. I think the tree will eventually have to come down because it is perilously close to the house, tightly wedged between our driveway and front walkway. What can we do?**

A It would probably be best to thank the maple, say goodbye, and hire a trained arborist to remove it. Pretend you just got the place and decide whether you want a tree in that spot. It is quite likely that you will be happier with shrubs, perennials, or simply the grass that has eluded you for so long. If not— you might need the shade, for instance—the arborist should be able to suggest several other trees more appropriate to the site.

This solution is neither painless nor inexpensive, but it seems to be looming regardless. If you can afford it, you might as well have the maple removed in late summer, so you can plant in early fall. Whether you go for a new lawn, a new tree, or anything in between, the sooner you get your new plantings in, the sooner they will replace the maple in your affections as well as in your yard. 🍂

Maple trees need plenty of room.

Saving a Damaged Maple

Q How much do I owe a large maple tree that was badly damaged by an ice storm? It lost most of its wide branches and now looks like a telephone pole. I think it should probably be removed, but I hate to cut down a 50-year-old tree. Will it recover, and if so, how quickly?

A It is likely to be a long time—at least a decade—before your badly damaged tree will recover much of its visual appeal. And that's assuming the tree is still basically healthy, which is a daring assumption if it has lost more than two-thirds of its branches.

Maple trees don't usually have just one straight trunk with branches sticking out the sides; instead, they tend to divide into multiple large limbs that form a more or less oval structure. A tree that retains a good part of this structure can begin to look promising as soon as dormant buds on and near those limbs spring into vigorous life.

So if you can see the start of a good-looking new framework in the skeleton that remains, give it a chance to leaf out before doing anything irrevocable. Sometimes things aren't as bleak as they first appear.

But don't be misled by lots of twiggy new growth. A damaged tree can sprout suckers galore, everywhere it has been wounded. But as Dr. Art Ode, the director of the Cox Arboretum, in Dayton, Ohio, explained: "This new growth will not be well attached. If the tree has lost its main structural branches, the sucker growth is likely to be vulnerable to future storms. Unless there is a sentimental attachment, it would be better to put the time and effort into nurturing a new tree."

Miniaturizing a Red Maple

Q Early in the spring, I cut down my red maple, leaving a 4-inch-tall stump about 8 inches in diameter. In the summer, it put out new growth around the circumference of the stump. It looks very healthy. The tree was planted in a confined area with protection south, east, and west, and with some northeast exposure. There is adequate water. I'd like to grow the tree now as a small bush—not more than 4 feet high. What do you suggest? Is there any hope for my little red maple?

A *Acer rubrum,* the red maple, is a very vigorous tree. Your healthy new growth is a bunch of water sprouts, every one of which wants to be the only 100-foot maple on the block. Each is fully capable of putting on 6 or 8 feet—straight up—each year, so you've got your work cut out for you if you want a 4-foot bush. The sprouts will not grow evenly, so shaping will take skill as well as effort, and plenty of both at that.

If you are determined to give it a try, expect to make multiple pruning cuts on each sprout every year, working always in deep winter when the tree is fully dormant (maples tend to bleed profusely if pruned during active growth).

At the end of all this, it is unlikely that the bush will be very attractive. And thanks to the dead stump at the center, it may be unhealthy as well. It would be better to remove the stump and plant something better suited to your needs.

Red Japanese maple
(*Acer palmatum*
'Atropurpureum')

A dwarf Japanese maple, for instance, offers beauty of form as well as foliage. Several, including *Acer palmatum* 'Bloodgood,' the weeping *A. palmatum dissectum* 'Crimson Queen,' and *A. palmatum* 'Atropurpureum,' have foliage that remains more or less red throughout the season.

Hold On Tight

Q **Why is it that many oak trees keep their leaves through most of the winter even though the leaves are dead? They seem to shed the leaves little by little, so that they have to be raked several times. Are there other deciduous trees that do this?**

A This is one of those interesting little phenomena that apparently are not interesting enough to have prompted a definitive scientific study. Beeches and chestnuts also hold on to their leaves, and are in the same family as oaks, the Fagaceae.

What is known is that young trees, and young branches that sprout from old stumps, seem to hold on to their leaves longer than mature trees do. Why they hold on is a mystery, but there are at least two possibilities as to how they do it.

When fall comes, deciduous plants move all of the carbohydrates from their leaves back into their woody parts—trunk, branches, and roots. A hard tissue called the abscission layer is then formed at the point where the leaf stalk meets the stem, effectively closing the door between leaf and plant, and causing the leaf to fall off. It may be that the abscission layer in oaks and beeches isn't as thick as it is in other trees, and the leaves just hang on longer, hoping that the tree will hear them knocking and open up, or at least send out a warm sap toddy.

Another possibility is that the bundle of vascular tissue between the leaf stem and the twig is larger or stronger in these trees and that it just takes more time and effort to break it.

Either way, these trees are always stubborn, always the last to let go of last year. 🍂

Urban Oaks

Q I would like to plant an oak—or maybe even two—in the large garden area behind my city brownstone. Are there any that will survive urban growing conditions?

A It depends on which city you live in, of course, but if it is in zone 5, 6, or 7, you have your answer in the true oaks planted all over New York City. Many of the 15,000 trees planted each year by contractors for the Parks and Recreation Department are pin oaks, red oaks, swamp white oaks, sawtooth oaks, and English oaks.

These trees have, in addition to their beauty, the qualities city trees need to survive. They hold up better under drought conditions than many other trees. They are relatively free of insect and disease problems, are long lived, and tolerate a wide range of soil conditions. There are many different trees because ecological diversity, on the streets or in your yard, reduces the chance of a massacre by a single pest or disease.

Just as important, they will in time provide large canopies with a large leaf mass, shade, fresh oxygen, and a lovely rustling when a breeze blows through. When they reach maturity, you might even forget where you are for a moment. 🍂

Oak Leaf Breakdown

Q **I know it's nice to have leaves in the foundation plantings, but oak leaves don't compost or rot in one winter, and it takes fast work to pull them off the ground when the crocuses come up. Do I give up spring skiing and start uncovering in March?**

A You are absolutely right about oak leaves taking their time to decay. "Oak leaves are unique in that they decompose at a far slower rate than other tree leaves," said Bruce C. Van Duyne, the Passaic County agricultural agent with Rutgers University in New Jersey. "A couple of inches of oak leaves can take about two years to decay. Used around trees or large shrubs, this is fine. But it can be a problem when oak leaves are piled high over areas planted with bulbs or perennials."

In these places, Mr. Van Dyne suggested chopping up the leaves in order to achieve more rapid decomposition. You don't need a special shredding machine. Just rake the dry leaves into small piles and run a lawn mower over them. If necessary, repeat until the pieces are no more than a couple of inches across. Once they're that small, they should break down over the course of one winter. ❧

Oak Galls

Q **Our pin oak tree has several oak galls. Are they harmful?**

A Many different plants can be afflicted with galls, peculiar-looking raised growths on leaves, twigs, branches, or trunks. The culprits behind (or in) them are tiny wasps or flies. The females lay eggs on their favorite plant part, and these eggs hatch into legless grubs. The gall forms around them as the insects feed and develop. They finally leave, in spring, to start life anew.

Scientists believe the gall growths may be a reaction to chemicals the insects secrete or possibly inject while feeding. In any case, each insect species causes its own uniquely shaped gall, either round, flat, spiny, or star shaped.

But you needn't worry. Very rarely do galls damage the tree, though the growths do not disappear once the insects

Trees in Particular

leave. If the problem is severe, you can try to reduce the gall-making population by trimming off and destroying the affected limbs. Do it early in the season, before the adults emerge. 🍂

No Olives Up North

Q I would like to locate and plant an olive tree. I live in northern Westchester County, New York.

A True olive trees (*Olea europaea*) are located, and planted, in the countries that border the Mediterranean, and in other places where the climate and soil are similar. Northern Westchester does not qualify. But if it's any consolation, neither does Virginia. Thomas Jefferson tried several times to bring the olive to his native turf, and it didn't work out for him, either.

It's not enough to have warm weather—you also need gravelly soil and a mostly dry climate. Jefferson kept sending trees to southern Georgia, where they did survive for a time. But between the clay soil and the humidity, they weren't the happiest of trees, and since they did not bear good crops, their owners let them die.

If you wanted the tree as a curiosity rather than as a significant source of olives, you could (with some difficulty) grow it as a container plant, trucking it outside each summer and bringing it in when the weather turned cold. Of course, you could also move to southern California . . . the culture shock might be extreme, but the culture of olives, at least, would be attainable. 🍂

Of Wreaths and Berries

Q I'm always attracted to seasonal pepper berry wreaths that I see in catalogs and at florists. My gardening books don't show anything about pepper berry. Are they the same as red peppercorns in gourmet shops? When I finish with my wreath, should I save the berries?

A Better to enjoy the wreath while it lasts and let it be a happy memory. Pepper berry, the name florists and wreath makers use, is actually pepper tree. There are two species that find their way into wreaths, the dusty rose berries of the California pepper tree, *Schinus molle,* and the dark red berries of the Brazilian pepper tree, *S. terebinthifolius.* These poison-ivy relatives have become highly invasive weeds in California, Florida, Texas, and other warm, dry subtropical regions. So you can buy these wreaths without feeling guilty about threatening a species. Most states where they run rampant would be happy if you bought a wreath for every door and window.

The Brazilian pepper tree is indeed the source of red peppercorns. However, they are grown as a food crop only on the Indian Ocean islands of Mauritius and Réunion. Those used in the United States for wreaths are probably safe, but they weren't grown, processed, shipped, stored, or sold as food, so you don't know what's happened to them between the tree and your door. In general, it's not a good idea to eat things from the florist. 🌰

Pepper berry wreath

Pruning Evergreens

Q Now that the winter is mostly over, it would be nice to get some yard work done before mowing season begins. How early can I prune my pine trees?

A Are you sure they are pines? To many people, any evergreen tree is a pine, even when it is a spruce or a fir (or even when it is a hemlock, cedar, chamaecyparis, juniper, yew, or plastic Christmas tree).

If it really is a pine (your county cooperative extension office will be glad to help you identify it), you should wait until early summer when the new growth, called candles, is fully elongated. Pinch each candle back by half. Spruces also need to be pruned after growth has started.

If your needled evergreen is not a pine or spruce, do not wait. Pruning should be done before new growth begins, except for damaged or dead branches, which can be removed anytime. 🌰

Forever Green?

Q When I bought a large Eastern white pine late in the summer, it was full and beautiful, but this fall many of the needles turned yellow, then brown, and fell. I watered it regularly. Why did this happen?

A Think of "evergreen" as a marketing term more than a true description. Evergreens lose their leaves or needles like deciduous trees. They just don't lose them as dramatically, all at once every fall.

Eastern white pine needles begin growing in the spring, and by September or October of the next year are ready to die. Since they last about 18 months, and since new ones have meanwhile grown farther out on the branches, it is the inner needles that die. Remember, one year's great growing season means the next year's great brownout.

Other evergreens have other schedules, and not every needle will drop on time anyway. Unlike the leaves on deciduous trees, needles don't die when the tree dumps its food factories and hunkers down for winter. Needles die when their life span is up.

Japanese black pine needles last three to five years, and Scotch pine needles last about three years. Austrian pine needles begin dying at four, but some old codgers will hang on eight years, probably boring the younger ones with tales of how it was when they were young. 🍎

White pine
(*Pinus strobus*)

Deerproofing the Hedges

Q I have just read that hunters can expect to do well this year—the deer population has been prospering lately, and there should be lots of them. We'd like to protect our mixed evergreen hedge but would rather not wrap the trees in burlap. There are a lot of trees, so we would like a low-cost solution, if possible.

A There are a number of low-tech, low-cost repellents, including human hair, soap, hot pepper, and garlic, all of which have some deterrent effect, but none of these household items are as effective as commercial spray-on products, especially the ones with bitter components, which have been formulated to be long-lasting.

These once-a-winter formulations are expensive compared to sweepings from the barber shop, but they cost a lot less than fencing or replacement trees. 🌰

KEEPING DEER-DAMAGED HEDGES

By now, it is no longer news that deer love classic hedging evergreens such as arborvitae, hemlock, and yew. Gardeners are routinely advised to choose deer-resistant plants instead. But what if you already *have* the hedge, and deer have already eaten it? What if your newly purchased home grounds are ringed by 20-foot trees that look like lopsided lollipops?

If space is severely limited, you may have to cut them down and start over with something else, but if you have a strip at least 12 feet wide to devote to the area, you can build a better hedge on the bones of what you have.

After all, it's only the lower regions that need help. Everything above 6 or 8 feet is no doubt fine, and it will only grow lovelier over time. The trick is to go for depth: plant a shorter hedge in front, and you'll screen the naked area from view while adding textural interest, just as you do when you plant a baptisia in front of rust-prone hollyhocks.

For best results, think in three layers: hurt hedge at the back; good-size shrubs or small trees like holly, lilac, and pieris in the middle; short, full items like mugo pine, boxwood, and barberry toward the front.

The most pleasing hedges have rhythm and rest, which cannot be achieved by a hodgepodge of "one of these and one of those," so it will pay to limit your selections and plant multiples of each. But if the deer pressure is extreme, don't do it right away. Instead, plant a test garden of likely candidates and wait a year to see just how deer resistant they actually are. (Deer vary considerably in their tastes, and a plant that escapes unscathed in one place may well get lunched in another.) It's frustrating not to plunge right in, but waiting is worth it when you'll be buying—and planting—large numbers of new shrubs.

Sourwood Trees

Q **Can you tell me something about the sourwood tree, which I gather has spectacular autumn color? And where can I find one?**

A If grown in a spot that gets at least half a day of sun, the leaves of the sourwood (*Oxydendrum arboreum*) do indeed turn a breathtaking scarlet in autumn. In July and August, the twig endings are also covered with clusters of tiny white bell-shaped blooms, much like those of its cousin the blueberry, making this one of the very few summer-blooming trees.

An outstanding American native and member of the heath family, Ericaceae, the sourwood needs a somewhat acid, well-drained soil rich in organic material. And while it can reach as much as 50 feet in height, its growth is reasonably slow, and it's also amenable to the pruning needed to help it fit its allotted space.

The botanical name is from the Greek words for "acid" and "tree," and alludes to the pungent taste of its leaves. The sourwood is not as commonly sold as its merits would suggest, but you should be able to find balled-and-burlapped specimens at a well-stocked nursery. That failing, smaller trees are widely available through mail order. 🌿

Overwhelmed by Spruces

Q I'm told that the best time to shear spruce and fir to improve their growth habit is very late spring or early summer, when they begin to grow from the terminal buds. Shearing then is supposed to stimulate dormant buds to produce growth that "fills in" the tree. I have so many that I may not have time to shear them all during this fairly short window. Since the terminal buds form the previous season, is there any reason not to shear at least some of the trees in winter?

A There is more to a spruce (or any other plant) than meets the eye. The terminal buds may form the previous year, but pruning schedules must take into account the tree's internal chemistry.

Wayne Cahilly, the manager of arboretums and grounds at the New York Botanical Garden in the Bronx, said that pruning the new growth after it has lengthened but before the needles have begun to expand from the twig removes the terminal growing points and stops their production of growth-regulator chemicals. These chemicals suppress growth in lateral or side buds, so reducing the supply enables those side buds to expand, helping the tree to fill in.

Norway (and other) spruces must be sheared at the right time.

Removing the terminal buds during the winter would allow the lateral buds to grow unchecked in the spring because no growth regulators would be present at all. Instead of just expanding a bit, each lateral bud would try to take over as the new terminal. The result would be internal chaos and a tree with a ragged look. Plan a shearing party and get friends to help. Timing is important. 🌿

Serbian Spruces

Q I recently bought what my nurseryman called Serbian spruce trees. I looked in a book for them but could not find the term Serbian spruce. Is this a correct name?

A It is indeed the name of a graceful spruce native to southeastern Europe. Its botanical name is *Picea omorika,* and it has only recently started getting wide distribution in commercial nurseries.

Typically, it has a narrow, somewhat pyramidal shape and its needles are greenish on top and silver-blue beneath. Branches droop as the tree ages, but usually not evenly. The slow-growing tree tends to remain irregular in outline and can (eventually) reach 100 feet.

If yours has long, slender, almost weeping branches, you might have the cultivar *P. omorika* 'Pendula,' which has been selected to droop even more than the species.

Like all spruces, the Serbian ones should grow where they have plenty of air circulation and sunlight. Crowding one in among other trees will make it lose its lower branches and be more vulnerable to pests and diseases. 🌿

Not Quite Magnolia

Q I've been told that our magnolia trees aren't true magnolias, that is, *Magnolia grandiflora,* but are tulip trees, or tulip magnolias. My understanding is that the tall tulip trees without fragrant white or pink waxy blossoms belong to a different genus, *Liriodendron.* Can you please clarify this issue?

A Once again, the joys and confusions of common names. *Liriodendron tulipifera* is called both tulip magnolia and tulip tree. It is a member of the same family as magnolia (Magnoliaceae) but not the same genus (*Magnolia*). It's a relative, but it isn't a magnolia the way *Magnolia grandiflora*, the Southern magnolia, is a magnolia. That's all right, though, because another of its common names is tulip poplar, and it isn't a poplar, either. But it is a worthy tree in its own right, tall and stately, with pale green to yellowish flowers that bloom in early summer.

These trees are often confused with *Magnolia × soulangiana*, the saucer magnolia. "Saucer" because once the flowers open, they form a large, saucerlike cup. I think your friend is calling them tulip magnolias because of the shape the petals form before the flower opens. At that point the pink-based flower buds do resemble a tulip. 🌰

Tulip tree
(*Liriodendron tulipifera*)

Wanting a Willow

Q At the corner of our property we have a French drain that receives water from the sump pump in the basement and some roof and surface water. In the spring, and during a rainy season, it is very wet in the surrounding area (about 25 by 50 feet). I would like to plant a weeping willow tree a few feet from the French drain. Would a weeping willow survive in an area that is dry at least 75 percent of the time, or must it be near water all the time?

A The spring flood conditions near the outlet of your (possibly malfunctioning) drain make it easy to imagine you have the equivalent of a seasonal stream; and from there it's a short swim to visions of weeping willows. But weeping willows on stream banks thrive because their roots are in consistently moist soil.

And if by some chance the tree did survive (willows are pretty tough characters), you are likely to be the one doing the weeping. It is unwise to plant a willow—or any aggressively rooting tree—that close to a French drain, which is essentially a buried trench full of rocks. The drains don't work when clogged with organic material. 🌰

A Yew Run Amok

Q I've got a seriously overgrown yew, which I've chopped back so it's about 8 feet tall and nearly as wide. Nothing but a few straggly weeds grow under there now. Can I surround it with day lilies, both for the flowers and to fill in the gap?

A You can, if by surround you mean plant in a ring at least 6 feet from the trunk (9 or 10 feet would be better).

As you have noticed, even weeds are having trouble in the deep shade under that yew, which in its years of overgrowing has undoubtedly set down a mat of roots that would give pause to anything but the most tenacious ground cover. You may want to settle for a nice, smooth mulch of pine needles.

Ylang-Ylang Tree

Q While visiting Hawaii, I saw a beautiful fragrant tree called the ylang-ylang. Any chance it will grow in southern New Jersey?

A The ylang-ylang tree, whose botanical name is *Cananga odorata,* has pendulous, brittle branches and often a sculptural crooked trunk. It can also grow to more than 60 feet. In tropical areas like Florida and Hawaii, it is used as both a garden specimen and a street tree. But because of its height potential and tropical climate needs, it is not recommended for use as either a greenhouse plant or a houseplant.

CHAPTER NINE

Special Situations

Tempering the Wind

Q **My house is at the edge of a windy meadow, and I desperately need something to temper the winds. What do you suggest?**

A You can't stop the wind, but nothing beats a strategically positioned barrier of plants to help convert those tumultuous gusts to tolerable breezes. A windbreak of sturdy evergreen trees or shrubs can reduce the wind considerably. The plants should be positioned at least twice as far from your house as they will be high when they are fully grown (in other words, a 5-foot plant should be about 10 feet from the building).

When thinking about the eventual height, don't forget that trees block light as well as wind. Your evergreens should not cast shadows on south-facing windows in winter. You'll need to leave gaps between young trees to allow for their mature size, yet these gaps can funnel the wind through at an even greater speed. To plug them temporarily, plant inexpensive, fast-growing shrubs like forsythia or privet, then cut down the shrubs when the trees get large enough to need the space.

Native plants that make good windbreaks include Eastern red cedar (*Juniperus virginiana*), American arborvitae (*Thuja occidentalis*), hemlock (*Tsuga canadensis*), white spruce (*Picea glauca*), balsam fir (*Abies balsamea*), and white pine (*Pinus strobus*). 🌱

RESPECTING THE WIND

Although wind is an important element of the garden climate, it is often overlooked unless it is a blast from the sea or the impressive rush of air that plagues high-rise terraces. Big mistake.

Wind needn't be a delphinium-busting gale to have deleterious effects. Even a moderate breeze can dry out plants as fast as or faster than hot sun. When steady, it will stunt the growth of everything from peppers to pine trees. Bugs and weed seeds use the wind to move into and around planted areas. All of which helps explain why walled gardens can be so lovely and productive.

The Bright Side of Moss

Q Living in a wooded area, we have little sunshine for gardening. I have an open area facing west, which is mostly moss. I want to put in a small garden for shade plants but hear that ground that has moss will not be good garden soil. Is this true?

A That depends on what you mean by garden. At best, you will be limited to plants that grow in what sounds like fairly serious shade—no sun until mid afternoon or later. And if you've got moss, you've got acid soil, which might be too acidic for other plants to thrive in. (The soil-testing kits sold by garden centers can tell you this.) Moss may also indicate compacted or scanty soil, very low fertility, or poor drainage. The fact that there's nothing there but moss may be telling you that nothing else should be.

You can rebuild the area, loosen the soil, incorporate compost and fertilizer, and add lime to counteract excessive acidity. But why not first look carefully at what you've got? Gardens composed only of mosses and a few strategically

GROWING MOSS

The most important ingredient in any recipe for moss is patience: it can take years to achieve that fuzzy carpet. The next item on the list is powers of observation. There are hundreds of different mosses, each suited to a particular ecological niche, and the best way to choose one that will grow well where you want it is to notice what's already growing there or in a similar location.

With any luck, the moss you want will be somewhere on your property or that of a friend, because the next step is to collect some. Taking mosses from public lands is not legal; taking them from private ones without permission is stealing. If necessary, moss starts can be purchased; specialists in bonsai supplies carry them.

Collecting Moss

Collect moss after a soaking rain, or, if that's not possible, water the mossy area thoroughly. Though there are some mosses that will grow on several different substrates, you'll have the best luck if you collect from a surface similar to the one you want to cover (wood, soil, or rock).

Take small, roughly 1½-inch-diameter patches, and never more than two or three from a square foot of moss. If it is growing on soil, make sure you take the patches with soil attached. Keep the patches moist.

Growing Moss from Slurry

This method is mostly used for hard surfaces such as rocks, flowerpots, and concrete. The idea is to coat the object with a mush of ground moss that contains lots of spores. To get it, you simply process clean moss in a blender, combining it with a thick liquid that will hold it in suspension and help it adhere.

Yogurt and buttermilk are thick and sticky—and acidic, which moss likes—and are therefore often used in slurry recipes, but they are not essential. Potter's clay (from the craft store), thinned to thick-milkshake texture with water, works even better because it holds moisture longer. Diluted manure can also be used if you have a blender dedicated to garden purposes.

placed rocks have been treasured in Japan for hundreds of years, and adventurous gardeners here are starting to transplant the idea. Horticultural sophisticates are babying what bits of moss they have and pouring buttermilk over every hard surface in sight, trying to cultivate more of the stuff. Here you have it naturally.

Maybe all you need is to add a bit of variation in terrain—a mound here, a boulder there—to create something lovely, unusual, and nearly trouble free. Do be sure to include a path. Moss can't take much trampling. 🌿

For about 3 cups of slurry, enough to coat roughly 1½ to 2 square feet of surface, you'll need:

1 loosely packed cup of moss pieces, or a bit more
2½ cups of thick liquid: diluted potter's clay, diluted manure, yogurt, buttermilk, or whatever mixture thereof you want to try

Grind the moss in a blender with 2 cups of the liquid. The result should be about the texture of thin pudding. Add more moss (or more liquid) if necessary.

Thoroughly wet the object, paint it with the remaining ½ cup of thick liquid, then paint on the moss slurry.

Keep the surface constantly moist, using a gentle mist so you don't dislodge anything. Once a day will probably be enough if the item is in a damp, shady place, but don't let it dry out. Within six weeks or so you should see the thin green, algaelike filaments that signal new moss is growing.

Transplanting Moss

This method is most often used where the moss will grow on soil, though transplanting will work on any surface as long as it is porous. Before you go out collecting, prepare the site. Remove vegetation (except extant moss, of course). Test for pH and lower it if necessary; most woodland mosses are acid lovers, happiest when the pH is about 5.5. Rake the area smooth and water thoroughly.

Collect the moss patches. Place them on the prepared site, pressing down well, then pin them to the soil here and there with twigs to help them bond with their new home. If you're doing only a small area, you can cover it with the moss "sod," but otherwise, spread the patches out about 8 to 10 inches from center to center. They will grow together, eventually, as long as you keep the soil between them damp and free of weeds. For faster coverage, make some slurry and spread it between the patches.

Water well right after planting and frequently thereafter. The moss should take hold in about a month. Once it's established it will tolerate a dry day or two, but not until then.

Green Moss in Dry Times

Q We have a damp, wooded area where there is a seasonal stream. The rocks there are covered with beautiful moss that stays green almost all year, even when the stream is dry. How does the moss stay green without any water or nourishment?

A Primitive plants going back nearly 400 million years, mosses have survived this long because they figured out how to take advantage of their niche. Instead of the water and nourishment-drawing roots of more advanced plants, they grow a form of rhizoid that is just a holdfast, letting them cling to rocks and other hard surfaces. And their leaves, only one cell thick, absorb all the food and moisture they need directly from the air. 🍎

A Bog Garden

Q **We have a low-lying backyard area with persistent dampness. Lawn grass will not thrive. Are there any trees and shrubs we can plant?**

A Water means life in a garden, although too much of this good thing is a challenge. It sounds as though you have the ideal conditions for a natural bog, a place to combine plants that thrive in continually moist soil. Among the trees that flourish in damp earth are the red or swamp maple (*Acer rubrum*), whose small red flowers brighten in early spring and whose silvery-ridged trunks are especially handsome in winter; the serviceberry (*Amelanchier arborea*), which bears its white flowers briefly in early summer; the river birch, a fast-growing native whose handsome peeling bark is a reddish gold; and the native Eastern white cedar (*Thuja occidentalis*), an evergreen that develops a narrow, pyramidal outline.

Shrubs that do well in moist soils include the sweet azalea (*Rhododendron arborescens*), whose white spring flowers add perfume to the late afternoon; the swamp rose (*Rosa palustris*), with its pink early-summer flowers; the spicebush (*Lindera benzoin*), whose clusters of tiny chartreuse blooms line its limbs in spring; and the Tatarian dogwood (*Cornus alba*), which has red-toned young twigs that color the winter landscape. 🍎

Patience and the Lotus

Q **The 'Momo Botan' lotus in my backyard pond bloomed well (three or four flowers) the first summer after I brought it home from the nursery. But for several summers, it has produced only one or two blossoms. The tubers were divided and repotted last year, but even though it has been hot and sunny this year, there's been only one bloom.**

The pot, which has multiple tubers, gets lots of sun; the growing tips are within an inch or two of the water's surface; and every couple of weeks I push four tablets of aquatic plant fertilizer into the container, as recommended. Should I just give up, dig out the tubers, sauté the blessed things and, like the lotus eaters of old, serenely recall the beauty of those first blooms?

A Often plants rebel if they are too crowded, so make sure the pot is large enough—12 to 15 inches in diameter is best. Maybe it's as simple as that, because everything else you're doing is just fine. The plants are probably taking a breather after being divided, and will bloom more profusely next year with those fragrant, 6-inch-wide rosy-pink flowers. Dividing every two or three years is important, and you'll probably have plenty of tubers to give away.

It's likely that the lotus eaters in Homer's *Odyssey* were indulging in either the opium poppy or wine made from the fruit of its buckthorn relative, *Ziziphus lotus* (reputed to cause forgetfulness and contentment), not your sacred lotus, *Nelumbo nucifera*.

Sacred lotus
(*Nelumbo nucifera*)

Lily Pad Takeover

Q On my small Virginia farm is a spring-fed pond 80 feet across. Whereas once about a fourth of the surface was occupied by pink and white lily pads, now the entire pond has been taken over, and the fish are dying. How best to cut back the lilies?

A Holding your breath and bending over the side of a rowboat to reach underwater and cut them back will gain you a year or so of, well, breathing room before they grow back. Because lilies won't grow in water more than four feet deep, the pond has probably become silted in, making it shallow enough that they can grow all across it. Draining and dredging will help by making the pond deeper. Be sure to check with the state environmental protection department first—a spring-fed pond may be classified as a wetland, and you will need a permit to change it.

Water lilies also prefer still water, so installing a recirculating pump to move water will make them less happy while increasing the oxygen supply for the fish.

Water lilies and ponds can coexist, however, if you take a few precautions. Plant them in pots; use the natural or man-made slope of the pond or sunken platforms to keep the pots no more than four feet deep. Pull up the plants every two years to divide and repot them, cutting off any rhizomes creeping over the pots' sides (heading for pond domination).

Figuring Pond Size

Q I see instructions for water gardens listed in terms of number of pond gallons. How do I figure out how many gallons are in my irregular, free-form fiberglass pond?

A Several simple math formulas will give you the number of gallons in symmetrical ponds. For a square or rectangular pond, multiply length by width by depth, and that number by 7.5. For an oval pond, multiply length by width by depth, and that total by 6.7. For a round pond, multiply the diameter by the diameter, that number by the depth, and then that number by 5.9.

The easiest way to compute gallons for a free-form pond is to use the formula for an oval, said William Uber, president of Van Ness Water Gardens in Upland, California. Mr. Uber added, "While it's important to know the number of gallons when adding chemicals, for planning the number of fish, the surface area is really more important."

He suggested the following for computing pond surface area in square yards. For a square or rectangular pond, multiply length by width and divide by 9. For an oval pond, multiply 3.14 by one-half the length, that number by one-half the width, then divide by 9. For a round pond, multiply one-half the diameter by one-half the diameter, that number by 3.14, and then divide that by 9.

Again, a free-form pond can be measured as though it were an oval, but use common sense. Whether you are adding fish or chemicals, it's better to err on the side of caution.

Indoor Water Garden

Q **I have a 10-gallon fish tank. Please advise on setting it up as an "underwater garden."**

A Start by adding a fluorescent aquarium grow light, more easily controlled than the sun. Provide an anchor for your plants with 2 inches of coarse aquarium gravel. Choose handsome underwater species, combining different shapes and textures as you might in a traditional garden. Possibilities include *Cabomba caroliniana,* which has lacy, dark green leaves; *Myriophyllum,* with its fine, dark, hairlike foliage; and *Vallisneria americana,* whose ribbonlike foliage is a medium green. Underwater plants can be purchased at aquatic nurseries and tropical-fish stores. 🍂

A Water-Garden Barrel

Q **I would like to have a water garden on my rooftop terrace but don't have much space. How do I do a barrel?**

A Start by being sure the hoops are tight and the bottom is not warped. Because wood shrinks as it dries, a barrel that has been in storage for a while may have gaps between the staves, which means it will leak. Not to worry. Pour in as much water as it will hold (it might not be much), and let it sit. A day later, add more. As long as there is some water in the barrel, the staves will absorb it and swell. Once they are thoroughly soaked, the barrel should be watertight.

As soon as it will hold water to the top, fill the barrel and let it stand for several days. Then siphon the water out and scrub the inside with a stiff brush and mild detergent. Rinse it thoroughly several times.

If you prefer, you can just line the barrel with heavy plastic. Fold the liner over the rim and staple it; or staple it close to water level, and then use silicone aquarium caulk between liner and barrel to seal the edge.

Choose a permanent place for the barrel near a load-bearing wall (water is *heavy*), and fill it. Let the water sit a day or two so the temperature can stabilize and any chlorine can escape, then add the plants. Two or three pots of aquatic plants should suffice, so the hardest part will be choosing among the many temptations, which include floating hearts (*Nymphoides* spp.), with their tiny, dainty flowers and small floating leaves; dwarf papyrus (*Cyperus haspan*), whose 2-foot stems are topped with graceful bunches of grassy leaves; water irises; water caladiums; and water cannas.

Standing water provides a breeding ground for mosquitoes, but these are easily foiled by "mosquito donuts," compressed disks of the bacterium *Bacillus thuringiensis* var. *israelensis,* available at garden centers. It's toxic to mosquito larvae but will not harm plants, birds, fish, or beneficial insects. 🌿

Fish in a Barrel

Q I'd like to make a small water garden in a whiskey barrel and understand that I can even keep goldfish in it! Are there any tricks I need to know before I set it up?

A There are only two things to keep in mind. First is that old whiskey barrels contain residues that can be toxic to fish. If you want to get going right away and don't mind the look of plastic, line the barrel with heavy-duty pond-lining material (available at large garden centers). If you'd prefer a more rustic look and are willing to wait for it, fill the barrel with water and let it sit for at least three months to leach the residues out. Change the water every two weeks or so.

Once you have the barrel ready, fill it with chlorine-free water and whatever else you plan to put in. Be sure to include some oxygenating plants like anacharis or parrot's feather. These underwater purifiers will keep the water from getting stagnant and help keep it clear. Add don't forget to fend off the mosquitoes (see the answer to the previous question). 🌿

Seashore Plantings

Q I live at the beach, and now that it is high summer and I'm outdoors all the time, I notice the lack of greenery. Can you help me with some plants that will survive in a very sunny garden with very poor soil that is mostly sand?

A The first key to survival is improvement of the soil. Although no amount of amendment will turn your place into English border territory, if you choose a few planting pockets (or build raised beds) and add lots of organic matter to them, everything you plant in those favored spots will show its deep gratitude. Since it's much too hot and dry right now to plant anything, you've got time to add compost and composted manure before cooler temperatures and autumn rains usher in the next planting season.

Since you're at the shore, it will be easy to add seaweed to the mix. Just rake up that storm-delivered eelgrass and spread it for mulch. You don't need to dig it in or wash the salt off. Plan to use a balanced fertilizer at planting time. Compost, manure, and seaweed are wonderful soil builders, but they use nutrients while decaying and are not rich enough in primary plant foods to correct the severe deficiencies you describe.

Next, do some rubbernecking. Your neighbors almost surely have conditions like yours, so the things that are thriving for them will probably thrive for you, too. Finally, start your wish list.

Rosa rugosa should probably be near the top. These seashore classics thrive in dry, sandy soil and salt air, putting out a fragrant billow of magenta, pink, or white flowers in spring, flowering intermittently in summer, and holding their big orange-red hips well into fall. The crinkled medium-green leaves are resistant to most rose diseases, and the plants themselves quickly grow into handsome shrubs.

You can stop with just one, but rugosas look best when planted in sweeping drifts that lead the eye toward a focal point: a garden folly, an elegantly contorted pine, or, of course, the deep blue sea.

Silver- or gray-leaved plants like artemisias, sages, and lavenders are usually drought resistant. And don't forget succulents. Their water-storing leaves are designed for situations like yours. Sedums offer strong shapes that look good surrounded by sand and stone, and portulacas willingly spread mats of blazing color over soil so poor and dry even dandelions won't grow. ❧

Rosa rugosa,
a seaside classic

Visual Clues

Q I'd like to design a small garden that uses very little water, but I'd like to make my choices by eye, rather than going to the nursery with a list of recommendations. Do the plants themselves provide clues or will I have to do a lot of reading tags and asking questions?

A It isn't foolproof, but there are a few visual cues you can use, based on the ways plants have devised to conserve water. Thick flesh is one: sedums, aloes, cactuses, and portulacas all store water in those swollen tissues. Narrow leaves are another. Plants like rosemary, coreopsis, and sea buckthorn don't give away much in evaporation.

Hairiness is another clue; it, too, slows the rate at which water leaves the leaves. Examples include borage and lamb's ears. Which brings us to silver, a famously drought-tolerant color exemplified by artemisia, dusty miller, and silver sage (which is also hairy).

When a Northern Gardener Heads South

Q I'm moving from Minnesota to Florida and would like some information on gardening there.

A You are wise to look for specialized information because the Florida climates (of which there are several) contrast markedly with your present area, and much of the soil is sandy, quick to dry, and virtually devoid of nutrients.

"Gardeners move here and think they can do business as before," said Larry Pardue, a former head of the Horticultural Society of New York transplanted as the executive director of the Marie Selby Botanical Garden in Sarasota. "Roses, for example, require Florida root stock. You won't find that on mail-order plants from Oregon, and you have to make adjustments. Also, petunias grow here in winter, and sweet alyssum is a perennial."

Without winter cold to kill them off, all sorts of tender things will thrive—and so will all sorts of exotic bugs and diseases. So before you design your garden, before you plant *anything,* contact the cooperative extension service in your new hometown. The experts there will be glad to help you learn a whole new way of growing things. 🍎

August: Not for Planting

Q **I have just moved into a new home. There is room for planting in front, and I would like something colorful there, but what can I plant in August? Anything would be better than the bare dirt we have now.**

A Assuming you want it to thrive, the only thing you should plant in August is a dream for the future. Lawns, perennials, shrubs, and trees will all get a far better start in the cool, rainy weather of fall.

Instead of rushing out to plant, spend what's left of the summer touring your new neighborhood, noticing what's healthy and pretty. Don't forget to check out the parks. Then scout local nurseries for good supplies of the things you want.

This is also the time to order and spread generous layers of topsoil and compost to improve that bare dirt. (The fact that it does not even have weeds suggests it needs some help.) Once armed with good soil and good ideas, you'll be ready to dig right in when the fall planting season arrives. 🍎

Autumn Bloomers

Q **I seem to have missed the boat for fall when I did my spring planting. Is early July too late to add flowers for late-season color?**

A Providing you have a well-stocked local nursery to supply you with established plants, there are many annuals and perennials that can be set out in early summer. (Tip the plants out of their pots to make sure they are not badly rootbound. Plants have a hard time getting settled in when it's hot and dry, so you need to use material that can be transferred with minimal shock to its roots.)

Among the long-lasting annuals are browallia, lantana, globe amaranth (*Gomphrena globosa*), ageratum, cigarflower (*Cuphea ignea*), and cleome. Perennials include Japanese anemone (*Anemone hupehensis* and *A.* × *hybrida*), Joe Pye weed (*Eupatorium purpureum*), Michaelmas daisy (*Aster novi-belgii*), toad lily (*Tricyrtis* spp.), plumbago (*Ceratostigma plumbaginoides*), and sedums such as *Hylotelephium spectabile* 'Autumn Joy.' Of course, there are chrysanthemums in countless shapes, sizes, and colors. 🌰

Hylotelephium (aka *Sedum*) *spectabile* 'Autumn Joy'

Winter's Consolations

Q My Philadelphia garden looks so barren this winter, I wondered if you could suggest plants to add in spring to make it look better next winter.

A More and more, it seems, gardeners are thinking of winter as something other than the dreary season between autumn and spring. Clever plant choices help create fine silhouettes, intriguing shadows, and handsome frameworks for outdoor spaces.

While you're in the mood to improve things, keep your eyes open for pleasing gardens in your neighborhood and keep your notebook handy.

For tone and texture, consider adding gold-sword yucca, which has yellow-striped evergreen leaves; lacebark elm (*Ulmus parvifolia*), which has orange-brown exfoliating bark; red-twig dogwood (*Cornus alba* 'Sibirica'); or an edging of lilyturf (*Liriope* and *Ophiopogon* spp.), with narrow evergreen leaves.

Many grasses, including the *Miscanthus* cultivars, linger through winter adding their feathery plumes, while colorful berries endure on firethorn (*Pyracantha* spp.), winterberry (*Ilex verticillata*), and Japanese dogwood (*Cornus kousa*) until they are stripped by the birds. Winter flowers are borne on witch hazels (*Hamamelis* × *intermedia*), cornelian cherry (*Cornus mas*), and hardy jasmine (*Jasminum nudiflorum*). 🌰

Fillers for Cracks

Q On visits abroad I've seen plants used decoratively in the cracks between paving stones. I'd like to try this but don't know what plants to use.

A There are many plants that will thrive between pavers, sending leaves and flowers through the cracks as they spread their roots under the protective mulch of the stones. Which ones you choose will depend on the size of the spaces between the stones, and on whether you want just a bit of green fuzz or something more like a rock garden.

In the latter case, you might like to try old-fashioned pinks, *Dianthus deltoides*. In early summer, this long-lived perennial sends up green wands topped with fragrant flowers in shades of red, pink, and white. But they're equally valuable for their sturdy tufts of narrow, dark green leaves, which start early in spring and stay good looking for a long time. An alternative is sweet alyssum, an annual that self-sows so reliably that it's effectively perennial. Alyssum can have a somewhat weedy appearance; the stems are lax and the leaves are pale, but its fragrant white, pink, or purple flowers will keep coming all summer as long as you shear it back from time to time.

If you want the low, mat-like look and would like to have fragrance to boot, choose Corsican mint (*Mentha requienii*), which has tiny, round, intensely fragrant leaves, or one of the various creeping thymes (*Thymus serpyllum*). *T. s.* 'Coccineus' has crimson flowers and dark foliage, while *T. s.* 'Albus' has lighter green leaves and dainty white flowers in early summer.

Don't forget that not all paved places are created equal. Where conditions are hot and dry, the pinks and thymes will thrive, the alyssum will be O.K., and the mint will fade away. Should the pavement be in damp shade, on the other hand, the mint will be happy, the heat lovers won't, and you could also think about using moss. It is a slow grower that will take much longer than plants to fill up the spaces, but if conditions are right for it, the effect can be beautiful. 🌿

Decorating Rocks

Q I recently built a rock retaining wall in a sunny spot. What flowering plants will grow in the spaces between the stones?

A Plants for a rock garden, which is what you're really making here, include a great diversity of species. Some plants like having their roots protected by the damp conditions naturally found beneath stones. Others enjoy the heat the rocks store when exposed to the sun. And still others prefer the fast drainage that gravelly soil allows.

Among the vigorous and undemanding perennials to consider are basket-of-gold, which has yellow flowers; rock-cress, which has white flowers; thrift, which has pink flowers; snow-in-summer, with its distinctive silvery green foliage and white flowers; cheddar pinks, with pink, cream, or crimson blossoms; creeping gypsophila, which has white or pale pink flowers; soapwort, with its lavender pink flowers; and the always-enticing sedums and thymes. ❦

A Lichen Challenge

Q I would like to duplicate a rock wall I saw covered with lichens as well as ferns. What growing conditions do I need for lichens, and how do I arrange for them to move in? A friend suggested looking for a "spore bank." Is this hopeless?

A Yes—or at least you're pushing the limit of possibility. Lichens are complicated organisms consisting of two separate symbiotic growth forms: green algae and colorless fungi. Some prefer dry rocks, some moist rocks, and some trees in moist forests.

Hundred-year-old gray-green lichens endure in profusion on rocks surrounding the Mohonk Mountain House near New Paltz, New York. Ruth H. Smiley, a botanist and member of the family that owns the hotel, has observed them there for more than four decades. She said these lichens arise naturally on the conglomerate rock when conditions suit them. They are thought to flourish in direct proportion to the purity of the air.

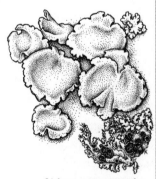

Lichens are two growth forms in one, and cannot be moved at will.

There is no way to buy them, they cannot be transplanted, and although the fungus part does make spores when temperature and humidity are right, there is no "spore bank" that you can readily access.

Plants to Edge a Path

Q I have a stone path in my backyard and would like to line the path with plants that will soften the edge. What do you suggest for a partly sunny area?

A Plants that rise a bit before draping down are the best choices, since if the path is a well-traveled route, it's likely that anything too sprawly will suffer from being stepped on.

Lady's mantle (*Alchemilla mollis*), which has softly scalloped foliage and chartreuse flowers in early summer, works well assuming you prune the spent flowers so they don't flop. Ornamental strawberries are a lower-profile alternative. They will send runners into the path, but that will just make things prettier (they don't set much in the way of fruit, so you needn't worry about jam underfoot).

Other choices include hardy geraniums and hardy gingers, hostas, ferns, trollius, and the smaller forms of astilbe.

Fooling the Eye

Q I read a short article about a small garden where a winding path made the area seem larger. What other design tricks help?

A Fooling the eye seems to be a continuing goal of small-space gardeners, and a serpentine path certainly helps, especially if it's also slightly narrower at the far end of the garden. Another method of achieving a false perspective is to plant species with large leaves, like hostas or rhododendrons, close to the window or viewing point, and those with small leaves, like liriope or cut-leaf maples, toward the rear. This is a favorite device in Japanese gardens. Artfully positioned mirrors also help make gardens feel larger.

Wall Decoration

Q **I have a narrow path next to a dreary wall. Other than vines, what can I grow here that's decorative?**

Pear espalier, pretty and delicious

A A superb way to improve a lackluster wall is with an espalier, a plant pruned and trained to grow flat, with its branches creating formal shapes such as fans, candelabra, or a plaidlike weave. Species amenable to training for espaliers include rock-spray cotoneaster (*Cotoneaster horizontalis*), firethorn (*Pyracantha* spp.), and yew (Taxus spp.), as well as many fruit trees such as apple, pear, and quince. 🌿

Adding an Arbor

Q **I have a small garden and would like to add an arbor for roses or clematis. I know it's easy to buy them, but does do-it-yourself have to be a big project or is there an easy way?**

A Depends on your definitions of "big" and "easy." A simple arbor of bent saplings that will last for three or four years and support clematis (but not roses, or at least not for long) can be erected in an afternoon (assuming you have access to the saplings).

A long-lasting structure that's sturdy enough to hold up roses, on the other hand, will have to be made of something like rot-proof wood posts, ideally anchored in cement footings, combined with rot-proof crosspieces. Think "two weekends plus basic building skills." And forget metal. A wrought-iron arbor is easy to buy, but only professional metalworkers are going to think of constructing one as a backyard project.

Given that your garden is small, a hybrid may be the best answer. Purchase a very simple wood arbor (be sure to get one that comes with some kind of anchoring device). Then gussy it up to make it unique. Paint it with bright-colored enamel, or if you like architectural antiques, be on the lookout for old moldings or other decorative details that you can attach to the frame. 🌿

Mirrors and Trelliswork

Q **My small backyard is fairly dark. I've heard that mirrors and trellises will help. How does it work?**

A Trelliswork is indeed an effective and practical way to add an illusion of space, especially when designed with the false perspective known as trompe l'oeil. The secret of trompe l'oeil trelliswork lies in diagonal lines that appear to radiate from an imaginary vanishing point—much like the perspective of railroad tracks. Because mirrors add brightness as well as the illusion of depth, nothing beats a mirror-trellis combination when it comes to improving a small, dark garden.

You can build a simple wall trellis yourself by using a horizontal and vertical grid, or attempt a more elaborate plaid of double slats, diagonal or diamond patterned (don't forget that you'll have to paint whatever you build). If your talents do not lie in the area of construction, look for prefabricated panels at local garden centers or hardware stores, and in mail-order catalogs.

To weatherproof a mirror for use outdoors, with or without trelliswork, glue it to marine-grade plywood and seal the edges with silicone caulking. ❧

Night Light

Q **I would like to add night lighting to my backyard garden. Is this hard to do?**

A Not anymore. Formerly, the only fixtures available were 110-volt, so a licensed electrician had to install the lines outdoors. But now low-voltage kits, with transformers that reduce the system to 12 volts, allow exterior lighting that is both safe and easy to install.

For dramatic night design, illuminate trees or shrubs from the bottom up, not the other way around. Use light to accent sculptured limbs or unusual plants by putting the fixtures close to the soil and aiming the beams skyward. Backlighting is also effective: putting a light behind a dense plant turns its outline into a silhouette; backlighting an open one reveals internal patterns.

Outdoor systems and lamps are sold at hardware stores and large garden centers. These ready-to-use kits contain all the basic items, including a transformer, a 50- or 100-foot weatherproof cable, and several lamps. Choose a system with a timer to operate the lights.

Solar-powered lights are widely available, as well. They are simple to set up, and they work well as path lighting. But they are not powerful enough for artistic effects. 🍎

Changing Levels

Q **I have a steeply graded garden area where I would like to add some steps. What do you suggest?**

A Wood is a glorious material, especially for informal stairs, although it will eventually rot and need replacing. Treated wood like railroad ties lasts longer than ordinary logs, but not much longer than more benign alternatives such as cedar and locust.

Possibilities include using log sections or railroad ties for risers, with planks, gravel, or brick for treads. Materials for garden steps that need no preservative include slate, millstones, concrete pads, and flagstones.

Whatever material you choose, you would be wise to have the steps installed by a professional. While it is certainly possible to do it yourself—building supply centers are full of books that give detailed instructions—it isn't as easy as it looks, especially on steep slopes. And if you botch it, you're in big trouble. Badly constructed steps aren't just ugly and inconvenient—they're dangerous. 🍎

A New Weather Vane

Q **I was certain that I wanted an antique weather vane to put on top of my barn but have found them to be pricey. If I do decide to splurge for one, do you think it will hold up reasonably well or am I better off buying a new one? I have a nineteenth-century house and have tried to avoid using any reproductions.**

A All early weather vanes were made to go outside, including the ones that were expensive even when new. But time has turned many of them—even the less well made ones—into objets d'art, and their patina is an important component of their value. If you repaint or regild an antique to protect it from the weather, the patina is gone and so is a lot of the charm (to say nothing of a substantial part of your investment).

If you don't protect it, it may continue to provide service for many years, gathering yet more patina in the process. It may also gather gunshot wounds, a frequent fate of rural weather vanes. Or it may be gathered up by enterprising thieves; weather vanes, like garden sculptures, are increasingly vulnerable as the market for them heats up.

So all in all, you're better off with a reproduction. If you get a good one, its position way up there on the barn should enable it to blend right in. 🍎

Deck Privacy in Shade

Q My patio is in full view of the neighbors, so I would like to plant a privacy screen on either side of me. My yard is tiny and entirely under the the thick shade of red maples. Any suggestions?

A It is time to think good thoughts about building a fence. Then think good thoughts about vines, shade-tolerant life forms that need little root room and can flourish in narrow spaces where hedges cannot.

If there is at least a bit of light, your choices include Virginia creeper (*Parthenocissus quinquefolia*) and Boston ivy (*P. tricuspidata*), either of which will turn as red as the maples in autumn. And for truly crepuscular conditions, there's English ivy (*Hedera helix*). Don't roll your eyes; if you plant several varieties, shifting patterns of leaf shapes and colors will rescue your privacy screen from cliché.

An alternative is to use the fence to support a collection of pots. They can sit on shelves or nestle in hangers, and contain summering houseplants or brilliant shade bloomers such as begonias, impatiens, and fuchsias.

Paint the fence, use handsome pots, and you'll have a living sculpture that provides privacy and presents nothing to prune. Paradise (although you will have to water it a lot). 🌱

Rock Garden Plants

Q I am intrigued by the whole idea of rock gardens, and would like to establish one in my tiny backyard. Could you suggest some easy plants that I can get started with?

A "First, you should be aware that rock garden plants demand perfect drainage," said Lawrence B. Thomas, of the North American Rock Garden Society. (His own rock garden is on an eleventh-floor terrace.) "To achieve good drainage, you should incorporate copious amounts of chicken grit or perlite into your soil."

Once the soil is ready, and assuming you have good sun, some easily grown species suggested by Mr. Thomas are *Androsace sarmentosa*, which has clusters of pink spring flowers on short stems; American bluets, also called Quaker ladies (*Houstonia caerulea*), which sow their own graceful pale blue–flowered progeny in unexpected places; *Draba rigida*, a mustard family member that forms tight mats and bears brilliant yellow flowers in early spring; and *Saxifraga cotyledon*, which forms tight mats of small silver-edged leaves.

Other compact, easily grown favorites include creeping baby's breath (*Gypsophila repens*), whose multitudes of dainty pink flowers last for many weeks through late spring; candytuft (*Iberis sempervirens*), which has mounds of white spring flowers; the Carpathian bellflower (*Campanula carpatica*), whose violet-blue blooms last through much of the summer; and the yellow flax (*Linum capitatum*), which freely bears its bright sunny flowers in late spring.

Contact the North American Rock Garden Society at P.O. Box 67, Millwood, NY 10546; *www.nargs.org.* 🌱

Slow Growers

Q Can you suggest several slow-growing plants requiring little care that I can use in a semi-shaded area around a cemetery plot?

A Assuming that this area has dappled shade, there are a number of plants you can combine. Flowering perennials that do not demand much tending include the dwarf astilbe (*Astilbe chinensis* 'Pumila'), columbine, sweet woodruff (*Galium odoratum,* aka *Asperula odorata*), hardy begonia, lily of the valley, fringed bleeding heart (*Dicentra eximia*), epimedium, European ginger (*Asarum europaeum*), coral-bells (*Heuchera sanguinea*), and violets.

Among the diminutive, slow-growing shrubs that might be appropriate are the small-leaved cotoneaster (*Cotoneaster microphyllus*), Somerset daphne (*Daphne* × *burkwoodii* 'Somerset'), and many creeping or dwarf-needled evergreens including junipers, yews, and hemlocks. A rose called 'The Fairy' has small, pale pink flowers that will bloom freely if it gets at least a half day of sun.

But before you plant anything, be sure it's O.K. with the management. Regrettably, more and more cemeteries are making rules against this.

Sweet woodruff
(*Galium odoratum*)

Special Gardens

Victoriana

Q I live in a nineteenth-century house and want flower beds in the Victorian style. What plants do you suggest?

A Since you want style rather than substance, why not emulate the gardens at the Mohonk Mountain House in New Paltz, New York (first planted in 1888), where the Victorian spirit is maintained to perfection. "We aim for effect, not historical accuracy," said head groundskeeper Chet Davis.

One year Mr. Davis used the annuals heliotrope 'Marine,' cosmos 'Sensation,' cleome 'Rose Queen' and 'Helen Campbell,' and nigella 'Miss Jekyll.' All supply bold, bright, and trustworthy color. The tall ageratum 'Blue Horizon' is similar to the tall nineteenth-century form of ageratum. And he recommended love-lies-bleeding: "Look at this plant and you can almost imagine ladies in bustles."

The Victorians were also partial to bold or exotic foliage, Mr. Davis continued, plants like elephant's ear caladium, castor bean, and canna lilies. One year Mohonk's formal area had, as its centerpiece, a symmetrical bed featuring an agave, or century plant, whose exotic leaves are some 5 feet long. It was surrounded by geometric patterns of germander and santolina. Victorian-style carpet bedding like this, in vogue in the nineteenth century, was inspired by Oriental rugs. 🐚

Keep Your Timex

Q I have been trying to find information about Victorian clock gardens. The flowers were planted around a sundial and opened at various times during the day. I only know of four-o'clocks, and moonflowers that open in the evening.

A Before modern distractions, everyone who lived with flowers recognized that some of them opened or closed at about the same time each day. Linnaeus, the father of modern plant classification, was one of the first to publish a list arranging common flowering plants in an order that could be used as a clock. After all, sundials do not work on cloudy days, and mechanical timepieces were expensive in the eighteenth century.

Floral clocks work in any weather because the photo-sensitive plants that reflect day length actually take their clues from the length of the night, not the day. But no one understood this until much later, and Linnaeus's list happened to include some day-neutral plants, such as dandelions, which couldn't care less about punctuality and which change their schedule throughout their blooming season. Most of Linnaeus's timekeepers are weeds, but his interest was in getting people to work on time, not in having them admire the clock. Whether you want bindweed, thistle, and hawkweed (5, 7, and 8 a.m. in Uppsala, Sweden, where Linnaeus lived) in your garden is up to you.

The summer sun rises earlier and sets later the farther north you are, and flowers open and close earlier, too. Unfortunately for the Victorian-era gardeners who were using his plant lists, Linnaeus lived farther north than all of Britain, the United States, and most of Europe. Consequently, floral clocks rarely produced useful results. Many Victorians ended up including sundials, simply arranging their plants according to whether they opened in the morning or afternoon. Perhaps if Linnaeus had lived in Geneva with the rest of the clockmakers, his list might have been more useful. 🍎

Historic Plants

Q I am renovating an older house. I would like to use some plants that may have been grown between 1800 and the early 1900s. Could you recommend a good source of information?

A You're asking about a long and very busy period in American horticulture, during which enormous changes took place in landscape design, and there was a huge increase in the assortment of plants available to home gardeners. Fashions varied from place to place, and of course with the economic status of the gardener.

So if you want what might have been grown in your very own garden, one of the best ways to get started is to visit local historic houses. Authenticity outdoors is still a relatively new and underfinanced concept, so the plantings currently on view may or may not be the real deal. But garden restoration is a growing trend, so the conservators are likely to have useful information, even if they haven't had a chance to use it yet themselves.

Another way to find local experts is through the historic landscape committee of the American Society of Landscape Architects, 636 Eye Street N.W., Washington, DC 20001; (202) 898-2444; *www.asla.org.* 🍎

Designing a Mix

Q Walking through a nursery recently, I overheard gardeners discussing their designs for "mixed borders." Could you clarify this term?

A The mixed border is a section of the garden, often only a few feet wide and usually many feet long, that includes every type of plant commonly grown in gardens, including bulbs and vines, and herbaceous species and woody ones.

Although they can be simple rectangles, mixed borders are often more like beds, irregular in outline, and themselves bordered by paths or lawn. They are anchored by a backbone of shrubs, below which wind ever-changing ribbons of shape and color created by flowering annuals, perennials, and bulbs. 🌰

White on White

Q I've heard about all-white flower gardens in England and would like to make one myself. What plants do you suggest?

A Although the most famous white garden in Britain is the one created by Vita Sackville-West around 1949 at Sissinghurst Castle, as early as 1918 the American gardener Louise Beebe Wilder wrote about her ideas for a white garden.

Easily grown plants you might begin with include baby's breath (*Gypsophila elegans*), candytuft (*Iberis amara*), *Cleome spinosa* 'Helen Campbell,' woodland tobacco plant (*Nicotiana sylvestris*), *Browallia speciosa* 'Silver Bells,' summer hyacinth (*Galtonia candicans*), *Clematis* 'Henryi,' goatsbeard (*Aruncus dioicus*), and *Veronica spicata* 'Alba.'

If you like the effects you're getting, move on to white lilies, white roses, and white-flowered varieties of shrubs such as lilac and hydrangea. 🌰

The Menu for Monarchs and Swallowtails

Q How do I attract monarch and swallowtail butterflies? What do they feed on?

A Monarchs and swallowtails feed on different plants at different stages. There are four distinct stages in a butterfly's life cycle: the egg, the caterpillar or larva, the chrysalis or pupa, the adult butterfly. Only the second and fourth stages eat, and the caterpillars do most of it.

Monarch caterpillars specialize in various species of milkweed, whose bitter juice makes them distasteful to predators like birds. In its butterfly stage, the monarch may also drink the nectar from goldenrod, thistle, cosmos, butterfly bush, lantana, and lilac.

During its caterpillar stage, the Eastern black swallowtail dines on members of the carrot family, which includes Queen Anne's lace and parsley. During its butterfly stage, the swallowtail prefers nectar from flowers such as thistle, phlox, clover, and purple loosestrife. 🐛

COUNTING SUNNY HOURS

A sundial makes a charming garden accent and, like a birdbath, actually serves a purpose beyond mere ornamentation. But whether it is a common horizontal type (meant to be mounted on a pedestal) or the less common perpendicular form (for wall mounting), a sundial must be placed with care.

- It seems obvious, but make sure the spot gets unobstructed sun all day.
- The sundial will be a focal point no matter where you put it, so put it where a focal point makes sense—in the (wide) intersection of two paths, for instance, or at the end of a long axis.
- The mounting spot must be level, and it must be accessible; if you put the sundial in the middle of a flower bed, nobody will be able to read it.
- Don't forget about daylight savings time when you set it up. The sundial should tell the true (sun) time, even though it's likely to be used mostly in the summer.
- To avoid mistakes, place the sundial provisionally, without affixing it to the spot, and check it every few hours for a couple of days.
- Just in case you're fond of crossword puzzles, the part that casts the shadow is called the gnomon.

Appealing to Butterflies

Q I would like to have lots of butterflies in my garden. Can you suggest ways to attract them?

A Watching these ethereal creatures is surely one of gardening's great pleasures, but since baby butterflies, aka caterpillars, eat the leaves of garden plants, you may want to limit your garden's attractions to the nectar-producing flowers on which the adults feed.

If you do this, you won't have nearly as many butterflies (they don't stick around long if there is no place to lay

Special Gardens

eggs), but you will also have less of a problem with the raggedy-leaf look.

Alternatively, you can plant flowers for the adult butterflies in your garden, and beyond the garden's borders leave the weeds that caterpillars are fond of. Of course, weeds don't stay put, so plan to be vigilant about incursions if you decide to go this route.

Plants for butterflies: butterfly bush (*Buddleia davidii*), bee balm (*Monarda didyma*), lilac, black-eyed Susan (*Rudbeckia* spp.), cosmos, lantana, gayfeather (*Liatris spicata*), phlox, goldenrod, and globe amaranth (*Gomphrena globosa*).

Weeds for caterpillars: clover, wild fennel, milkweed, nettle, Queen Anne's lace, Bermuda grass, sorrel, and thistle.

Garden plants caterpillars adore: parsley, lupine, hollyhock, mallow, dill, fennel, cultivated milkweed. 🌢

Gayfeather
(*Liatris spicata*)

Attracting Fireflies

Q **I have information on planting to attract butterflies, but are there any plants or flowers that will attract lightning bugs?**

A The best thing to plant is nothing, said Dr. James Lloyd, a professor of entomology at the University of Florida at Gainesville and a specialist on Lampyridae, the family to which fireflies belong.

"Let everything go back to nature," he advised. What North American lightning bugs really like best is woodlands, marshes, old fields, and similar minimally disturbed habitats. They spend most of their lives as larvae, at or below ground level, and are not directly attracted to plants and flowers because they are all more or less carnivorous.

Members of the green-lighting genus (*Photuris*) will eat berries from time to time, but that's about it. The many *Photinus* species (yellow light) feed largely on earthworms; and *Pyractomena*, which tend toward orange in the illumination department, dwell in damp places and eat slugs and snails. 🌢

CATERPILLER KILLERS

If you are keen on butterflies, be extra careful about how you apply pesticides, including environmentally benign ones like Bt (*Bacillus thuringiensis*). As far as the pesticide is concerned, a caterpillar is a caterpillar whether it's a cabbage looper or a monarch-in-waiting.

Fortunately, caterpillars are comparatively fussy eaters. Those cabbage loopers eat many plants, but only in the cabbage family. They don't eat carrot family members like the parsley and dill that baby swallowtails dote on.

If butterfly plants are growing close to something you absolutely must protect with pesticide, don't use a dust, which will spread. Use a liquid, and paint it on the plant with a brush (sprays drift, even on still days).

Fragrant Night Bloomers

Q **I love fragrant plants, but I don't like bees. Is there anything I can grow that will perfume the garden without attracting insects?**

A Perfume that doesn't attract insects would be a horticultural oxymoron: putting out the come-hither for pollinators is a flower's raison d'être, and perfume is a large part of the mating dance. But you can have a fragrant garden that's low on bees by using night-blooming plants.

Choices range from the small, inconspicuous, but mightily perfumed annual known as night-blooming stock (*Matthiola bicornis*) to the many cultivated varieties of *Brugmansia*, a tropical tree that can grow to 10 feet or more and has been showing up in nurseries under the name angels' trumpets. All parts of the brugmansia are highly poisonous, but there's no denying the plant's appeal. Its huge flowers blare tropical sweetness from dusk until almost sunup. White is the most common color and usually the most fragrant, but brugmansia also comes in yellow, orange, peach, and pink. Like Chinese hybiscus, mandevilla, and the many other tropicals sold by nurseries in temperate climates, brugmansias are not frost hardy and must be overwintered indoors.

Brugmansia's trumpets lift up at night.

If you want to stick to annuals, there are plenty to choose from—nicotiana, for example. You'd never know it from the modern cultivars, which lost fragrance when they were bred to stay open during the day, but old-fashioned flowering tobacco (*Nicotiana alata*) has a very strong night perfume, and so does its much taller, architecturally splendid cousin *N. sylvestris*.

Other candidates include moonflower vines, night-blooming jasmine, evening primrose, and oddball day lilies like 'Pardon Me,' which don't get going until the sun goes down. 🍃

PART THREE

The Kitchen Garden

CHAPTER TEN

Vegetables

Vegetables in General

Reasons for Rotation

Q **I had my first vegetable garden this year and it was laid out perfectly. Do I really need to rotate my crops?**

A Rotation is useful for two reasons. It helps prevent the buildup of pests and diseases specific to particular plants or plant families. And it maximizes the use of soil nutrients.

Although there are some equal-opportunity scourges—slugs come to mind—that will attack everything in the garden, they are in the minority. Many of the nastiest mosaics, for example, attack legumes (peas and beans) but have no interest in nightshades (tomatoes, peppers, potatoes, and eggplants). Similarly, earworms are a real problem in corn but couldn't care less about lettuce. By moving their favorite targets around, you make it harder for these bad actors to establish themselves.

While you're foiling the pests, you're also managing the soil. Corn and squash require a lot of nitrogen. Peas and beans *make* nitrogen (or, more accurately, *fix* the nitrogen from the air into a form that roots can use). By alternating one with the other, you can reduce the amount of supplemental fertilizer you'll have to add.

Unfortunately, corn will always be a lot taller than beets, so where space is at a premium and crops must be closely planted, it will always be wise to put tall crops to the north of short ones so they don't cause shade problems. One more reason people who have large gardens in full sun have an advantage over those who don't. 🌢

GOOD COMPANIONS

The interactions between garden plants have not been extensively studied in carefully controlled trials, so there isn't much hard scientific data on the abilities of different species to help (or hurt) each other when they're grown close together. But over the years, gardeners' observations have formed a body of advice that's impressive enough to be worth some consideration.

A lot of the tried and true is just common sense. Plants with strong odors—such as basil, rue, marigold, scented-leaf geraniums, and garlic—repel or confuse many insects that rely on smells to find their targets. Herbs and flowers loved by bees—such as borage, thyme, and bee balm—help attract these pollinators and thus improve fruit-set on many vegetables, including summer and winter squash, tomatoes, peppers, and beans.

There are also many specific combinations that are famous, at least in folklore, though as the diet advertisements say, "results may vary." Much will depend on climatic conditions, the nature of the soil, and the overall health of the plants in question. Nevertheless, more than a few gardeners swear by rules like these:

- Plant parsley near asparagus to improve vigor.
- Radishes grown near lettuce are more tender.
- Petunias help repel bean beetles.
- Beets interplanted with onions will help stifle weeds.
- Carrots will grow larger if interplanted with chives.
- Dill or caraway will help repel cabbage moths.
- Tomatoes hate fennel; keep them apart.
- Beans don't do well near alliums (garlic, onions, chives).
- Nasturtiums attract aphids and deter cucumber and bean beetles.

Don't Break Out the Tiller

Q **The soil in my vegetable garden is rich and loose, not at all densely packed. Is there any reason to cultivate it?**

A Depends what you mean by "cultivate." No amount of rich looseness will prevent weeds, so at least until the plants are large enough to be surrounded by mulch, you'll still have to hoe (cultivate) to keep the competition from taking over—unless your garden is small enough for you to hand-weed.

But if you are talking about major soil disturbance like rototilling, reason is on the side of abstaining. The top 6 to 8 inches of healthy soil are filled with pores that allow the passage of water and oxygen, essential to the health of plants, and they also contain a fantastically complicated web of life-forms that are equally important.

Tilling won't utterly flatten the pores or destroy the web, and it is just about essential when you are incorporating green manure or breaking new ground. But once the soil is loose, open, and fluffy, the less you do to disturb it, the better. 🌶

Transplant Techniques

Q **By the time I buy vegetable seedlings they're a potbound lump of roots. What can be done to help them flourish?**

A You don't say why you are forced to buy plants that have stayed in their pots too long, but if there is anything you can do to locate healthier stock, that would be your best option. Though it may take a bit of shopping to find a nursery that offers new batches of seedlings periodically through the planting season, the results will be worth it.

Whether they are true annuals like lettuce or tender perennials like peppers, most of the vegetables sold as seedlings are plants that are genetically programmed to go from seed to fruit in a single season. When their roots get crowded, they don't know there's more room to come. They just figure the soil they've got is all they're going to get, and they respond by switching their energy from plant formation to flowering.

Peppers and eggplants get stunted; lettuces and cabbages bolt toward flowers instead of making heads. Among common vegetables, only tomatoes can really recover from seriously crowded roots.

That said, the method for transplanting seedlings is the same regardless of how crowded the roots are. Begin by treating the seedlings—before transplanting—to a thorough drenching with water laced with a quarter-strength solution of any water-soluble plant food. Let them drain a bit. Loosen them from their plastic tray by squeezing it gently, then ease them out. If the roots are crowded into a ball, tease them apart.

To minimize the shock of the move, transplant either in the evening or on a cloudy, relatively windless day. Water the seedlings well, and be sure to shade them from the sun for the first couple of days. 🍅

Wood for Raised Beds

Q **For convenience and a neat appearance, I would like to build wood-framed raised beds to use in my garden. Can I make them out of ordinary pine boards, or must I spring for cedar?**

A That depends on how much you enjoy the small amount of carpentry required for bed-building. Pine is the least expensive choice, it's easy to find and easy to work with, and it will give anywhere from four to seven years of service before the moisture in the soil rots it beyond use. But then you will need to build new beds.

Eventually cedar will go, too, but because it is rot resistant, it will last about twice as long as pine. Since cedar costs about twice as much as pine, the cost of materials tends to even out over the long run. Only the amount of labor changes.

If you want to build one set of beds that will last more or less as long as you do, you can use the woodlike "lumber" made of recycled plastic. It costs more than either natural wood and does not weather to an equally lovely patina, but it never needs replacing and is not objectionable looking once you have it filled with plants. 🍅

DIVERSITY MATTERS

In nature plants are gregarious, living in complex communities. Short, early bloomers share space with tall species that leaf out and flower late; shallow-rooted types cozy up to deep-rooted neighbors. Heavy feeders benefit from association with plants that make more nutrients than they themselves need.

And because each piece of ground hosts a diversity of species, pests and diseases (which tend to target particular groups of plants) are naturally limited; there's never enough of any one thing to support major infestation.

Vegetable gardens can't be as intricate as the natural patchwork, but they can take a lesson from it, and the more diversity they support, the more productive they will be.

- Plant vining crops like squash in the corn patch; the sprawling vines will provide a living mulch that conserves surface moisture (corn has shallow roots) and keeps down the weeds. Don't plant the squash until the soil warms and the corn is about a foot tall. Corn likes toasty toes, and baby plants will be smothered unless they get a head start.
- Plant heavy feeders like squash, cucumber, corn, and celery next to—or right after—peas and beans, which fix nitrogen through their roots, improving the fertility of the soil under and around them.
- Once summer heat strikes, plant greens like lettuce and spinach on the shady side of tall pea and bean rows. The soil will be cooler there, and the extra nitrogen in the soil will help the leaves grow swiftly.
- Instead of planting a large bed of one crop, consider planting alternate rows. Bush beans work well with members of the cabbage family, for instance, and carrots get along well with determinate (short-vined) tomatoes.

Technically Organic

Q **Is my garden technically organic if I use chemical fertilizers?**

A It's not technically organic. It's not philosophically, socially, morally, or economically organic, either. But it may still be a very good garden and not damaging to the environment *if*—and this is a very big if—you are careful to do two things.

The first is to be very sparing about the fertilizer you use, to minimize the danger of its leaching out into groundwater. The second is to keep adding lots of organic matter so the soil structure is maintained, micronutrients remain available, and the health of soil-dwelling organisms is not excessively compromised by the presence of the chemicals.

If you use chemical fertilizer but avoid chemical pesticides and herbicides, you can call your garden "low toxicity." It's not as melodious as "organic" but it's a much healthier place to be—for you and every other living thing—than the conventional alternative. 🌶

From Barbershop to Garden

Q **I have read that human hair is beneficial to soil and to vegetables when they are first planted. Can hair that is dyed be used, or is it toxic?**

A Dyed hair should not be used in the garden. There are too many products involved for blanket pronouncements about toxicity, so the rule on strange chemicals applies: when in doubt, leave it out.

In hair's natural state, however, it brings two nice presents to the garden party: it contains quite a bit of fertility-boosting nitrogen, and it sometimes repels deer.

To use hair as fertilizer, put it in the compost pile where it can decay in private. (Hair is not pleasant to encounter while harvesting dinner.)

To repel the more timid among your deer, put hair in cheesecloth or mesh bags and hang them close to the vulnerable vegetation. 🌶

Exotic Fertilizer

Q **Is it safe to use exotic manures in the vegetable garden? I'm talking about bat guano and the things like elephant poop that zoos sell to raise money.**

A All manure used in the vegetable garden should be treated—by simple aging, active composting, heat- and air-drying, or sterilization—to kill pathogens. The packaging of exotic excretions doesn't always mention how the contents have been cured, but you don't usually have to worry about anything that has been shipped over a long distance. It has almost surely been dried, because manure that still has moisture in it is heavy and smelly. 🌶

One-Stop Fertilizing

Q Is there an all-purpose fertilizer that can be spread over the entire vegetable garden to help everything grow, or do I need to have special mixtures to nurture each individual crop?

A Compost. Compost is the all-purpose answer to everything, and if you have enough of it you won't need much of anything else. Though different crops have different needs, they will be able to serve themselves from the smorgasbord provided by healthy soil with plenty of compost in it. Once you start adding specific fertilizers, you start having to pay close attention to each individual diet.

Salad greens, for example, want lots of nitrogen to promote the fast growth of leafy tissue. Peppers, on the other hand, are more eager for the potassium that promotes flower and fruit development. Although they too need nitrogen, they'd make great big green leafy bushes with nary a pepper in sight if you gave them a lettuce-appropriate dose.

And major nutrients like nitrogen and potassium are just the beginning. There are dozens of micronutrients, such as boron, calcium, and copper, that plants must have— in different amounts—to thrive.

In practice, it can be hard to create soil so fertile that no amendment is necessary, especially when growing vegetables in a small space. But before you break out the fertilizer cookbook and start concocting special meals for all the crops you want to grow, make sure the soil is "in good tilth"—well drained and well aerated—and that the pH is between 6 and 7 (the best range for most vegetables). Ensuring these such conditions exist may be all you need to do. But even if you need to do more, this is the place to start. If the soil is bad or the pH out of whack, it won't matter what you put on the table; the vegetables won't be able to eat. 🍎

To Avoid Double-Digging

Q This fall, after the vegetable harvest, I will relocate two 3-foot-by-6-foot-by-10-inch raised beds (soil and all) to sites that are currently covered by grass. Is there anything I can do to the new sites now, in early summer, to ease (or eliminate) turf removal, soil double-digging, and other preparation chores?

A You can eliminate turf removal by covering the area with something thoroughly opaque: heavy black plastic or a solid 5-inch layer of paper (old telephone books and thick stacks of newspaper work well). As long as no light gets through for at least three months, the grass will be killed. This is the easiest course of action, but all you'll get out of it is dead grass, which probably won't become useful compost until it has been under the bed for a while.

Alternatively, if you're willing to work a bit, you can substantially improve the soil and still avoid the heavy labor of double-digging. Start by removing the sod, which is not a big chore if your spade is sharp, then flip it over and replace it grass-side down. Cover the exposed roots and earth with a 3- or 4-inch layer of composted manure, then a 12- to 14-inch-thick blanket of loose straw. Keep the pile moist but not wet.

Within three months or so, everything except the top layer of straw should have decomposed, enriching and loosening the earth underneath. When moving day comes, just rake away whatever loose straw remains and put the old bed on the new one. Then with all that energy you've conserved, mix the soil you've built with the soil you've moved to bring it new vigor. 🥕

Bargain Seeds

Q An inveterate yard-sale shopper, I bought a box full of leftover vegetable seed packs last fall, some more than a year old. Now that spring is coming, I've started to wonder if they are still good. How long do vegetable seeds last? How can I tell if these are still O.K.?

A How long seeds remain viable depends not only on the type of seed, but also on how the seed was stored. The combination of warmth and humidity is the biggest enemy. If the temperature and relative humidity add up to less than 100, your seeds will last longer.

For example, your house may be a comfortable 70°F, but as the humidity approaches 25 to 30 percent, the seeds begin to deteriorate. Similarly, a refrigerator stays at 40° but the humidity can be too high. Best solution? Store seed packages in the refrigerator or other cool place in closed glass jars, with a teaspoon of dry powdered milk or a commercial desiccant to absorb excess moisture.

You can test seeds for viability by putting a dozen between sheets of damp paper towels in a plastic bag at room temperature. Check every two to three days to see if the towels are still damp. If half the seeds germinate in the time listed on the seed pack, they are probably O.K. to plant. However, older seeds may germinate and then grow poorly. 🍂

VEGETABLE-SEED LONGEVITY

W hen stored under ideal conditions—airtight, in a cold, dark location— vegetable seeds can remain viable for the following periods of time. But as the ideal is seldom met, use these times as rough guides, not gospel.

One year: onions, parsley, parsnips

Two years: sweet corn, leeks, okra, peppers

Three years: beans, broccoli, carrots, celeriac, celery, Chinese cabbage, kohlrabi, peas, spinach

Four years: beets, Brussels sprouts, cabbage, cauliflower, Swiss chard,

chicory, eggplant, fennel, kale, mustard, pumpkin, rutabaga, sorrel, squash, tomatoes, turnips, watermelon

Five years: cardoon, collard greens, corn salad (mâche), garden cress, cucumber, endive, muskmelon, radishes

Six years: lettuces

Too Many Seeds

Q I have a good-size city plot, but there are just too many seeds in most of the packets I buy. Any suggestions?

A Figuring out what to do with leftover seeds is a common challenge for gardeners with a little space and a lot of temptation. If you have no neighbors or friends who have gardens, one possibility is to look for a local horticultural society, botanical garden, or group of greenspace activists who would be interested in donations of seeds for community gardens, children's plots, or other projects.

Charlotte Elsner of Philadelphia, whose vegetables regularly win prizes from the Pennsylvania Horticultural Society, sometimes stores her leftover seeds in tightly sealed jars in the refrigerator. But longevity varies considerably.

The best solution, she said, is to avoid the problem altogether by buying from suppliers who sell small packets of seeds. A bonus of smaller packets is that you save money. Ms. Elsner added that there is a consolation when none of the above works: "Nature, after all, produces millions of unused seeds. So if gardeners throw some out, it's no worse than that."

Seed Saving 101

Q We are beginning vegetable gardeners eager to save our own seeds. We know we must avoid hybrid varieties. Can you provide any other tips?

A To start with, start slowly. Seed saving isn't difficult, but it does add one more class to your course load at Food Grower's U. There are significant differences between the reproductive systems of common vegetables, and you'll have the best luck if you confine your first efforts to the simplest ones.

That means self-pollinating annuals, like tomatoes, beans, and peas. They flower and set seed in one season, you can still eat some fruit from the seed-bearing plants, and they do not require wide separation from other varieties (or elaborate segregation techniques) to make seeds that are true to the parent type.

You can grow, then save the seeds of as many different varieties of these (self-pollinating) species as you want, as long as plants of the same species are about 25 feet apart. That's enough to prevent most accidental interbreeding.

Once you've chosen which varieties to save, get ready for the fun part: fine-tuning them to suit your situation. Notice which 8 to 12 plants are the healthiest, and mark them with a twist-tie. Use another color twist-tie to mark the earliest producers. Choose a third color for tastiness, and a fourth for heavy crops. By the time of peak harvest, you should have at least one or two plants that sport multiple ties. Save the seeds from those. After a few seasons, you'll have a custom-tailored garden no amount of money could buy off the shelf. 🌶

Healthy Heirlooms

Q I'm a bit confused about heirloom vegetables. I've heard a lot about how much better the taste is, but I'm assuming that some of the new and improved varieties were developed to make the plants more pest resistant. I have enough problems with pests—will I have more if I start planting heirloom varieties?

A Bioengineering has brought some short-term pest resistance to field crops like feed corn and cotton, and there are a few oddball items like 'Fly Away,' a hybrid carrot that is (comparatively) unattractive to carrot rust fly. But from the home gardener's point of view, most of the improvement in "new and improved" is in resistance to diseases, not pests.

Disease resistance can help with the pest problem, however, because illness invites attack. Other things being equal, a garden filled with unhealthy plants is likely to be filled with pests as well, while a garden that is thriving will remain more or less unbothered.

Because plant health is vital to pest resistance, it's important to note that heirloom plants are not necessarily more prone to disease than modern hybrids. Although some of the tastiest varieties *are* on the delicate side, many others are tough cookies. And when the environment is challenging, heirlooms can outperform hybrids, many of which must have ideal conditions in order to produce well. 🌶

OUR VEGETABLE INHERITANCE—AND LEGACY

Among food and garden lovers alike, the current buzzword for value is heirloom, a very good description of open-pollinated vegetable seeds. Unlike hybrids, heirlooms can be saved year after year, and although we always think of the word as extending toward the past, it's just as relevant to the future: heirlooms aren't just what our great-grandparents grew, they are also the varieties we can leave to our great-grandchildren.

Heirlooms are most famous for offering great flavor and for enabling the gardener to "grow your own" from start to finish. But they offer a lot more than freedom from the need to buy seed each year.

Adaptability, for instance. Heirlooms are the special province of individuals and of small, regional seed companies, who do not need to sell zillions of packets in order to make a profit; and that means they tend to be better attuned to specific local conditions (drought in the Southwest, humidity in the Southeast, cold in the North) than "one size fits all" hybrids.

Hybrids are created through carefully controlled parentage, and as a result they are uniform. Every plant will be about the same size, and it will bear its fruit in the same narrow time frame. These characteristics are important to the mechanized operations of commercial growers, but they don't do much for home gardeners.

And though hybrid varieties are often disease resistant, they are identically so. If a disease strikes that they cannot resist, every single plant will suffer.

Heirlooms, on the other hand, are individuals. Even when they are grown from seeds that came in the same packet, each plant is subtly different from every other. They grow and ripen unevenly, so you get a longer harvest period. And they are unevenly vulnerable to diseases. When trouble strikes, some plants will no doubt be afflicted, but others may come through.

All this is not to say there's no place for hybrids, but hybrids are not in danger. It's heirlooms that rely on home gardeners for their continued survival, heirlooms that offer independence, and heirlooms that give gardeners a chance to do their part for the preservation of genetic diversity.

To learn more, and to gain access to a huge assortment of delicious possibilities, consult the *Garden Seed Inventory,* available from Seed Savers Exchange, 3076 North Winn Road, Decorah, IA 52101; (563) 382-5990; *www.seedsavers.org*. It explains, eloquently, why heirlooms are important. And it is the source of sources, listing very nearly all the open-pollinated (nonhybrid) vegetable seeds available commercially in the United States, along with the names and addresses of the companies that supply them.

Basement Nursery

Q Last year, in an effort to improve on my usual method of growing seedlings in a sunny window, I installed a fluorescent fixture with grow lights in my basement. The resulting seedlings were weak. I set a timer for 18 hours of light. Where did I go wrong? Could the problem be proximity to the oil burner?

A You were right to move the seedlings into an environment where the light can be controlled and the day and night temperatures don't fluctuate wildly. Even the sunniest windows rarely offer more than a few hours of really bright light each day, and that doesn't count the losses because of cloudy days or, no offense intended, a light covering of dust or dirt on the window glass.

But even with the fluorescent lights on for 18 hours, the seedlings probably weren't getting enough light. While a fluorescent light looks bright to us, it is a poor substitute to a seedling expecting to bask in the sun. To provide enough light, use two 4-foot-long, two-bulb shop fixtures (available at any hardware store), suspended just 2 to 6 inches above the seedlings.

Special grow lights aren't magic. Often, there is just a blue coating on the inside of the tube. The overall amount of light is reduced, and the seedlings think they have sunglasses on. A mix of warm white and cool white tubes will give the right kind of light, and more of it.

A small fan is needed nearby to move the air, helping to prevent fungus diseases and to flex those little seedling stems, enabling them to grow stronger and thicker (just like going to the gym). But don't get carried away trying to make little Arnold Schwarzenpeppers.

Most seedlings like it comfy—temperatures in the 60s and room to grow. If they are too crowded, or if that furnace is overheating them, they will become stretched and spindly. Perhaps they are trying to grow up quickly and get away.

Buy your seeds early while there are lots of choices, but don't start them too early. Look on each package for the right timing, and mark your engagement calendar. 🍎

How Much Potting Up?

Q I'm in the early stages of the annual rite of starting a number of vegetables from seed, transplanting the seedlings to small pots in a few weeks, transplanting these to larger pots in a few more weeks, and finally setting my plants in the garden. Numerous gardening books recommend this ritual, yet plants don't seem to mind the final transfer to the garden, a very large pot indeed. Why can't I immediately transplant each seedling to a fairly large pot, saving time and avoiding excess plant handling?

A There are a couple of reasons to go through the ritual. One is that it conserves space. Whether on the windowsill, under lights, or even in a greenhouse, most home gardeners have only a limited area where the light is bright enough for good seedling growth, and they don't want to waste it on empty pot surface.

The other reason to keep the plant in proportion to its container is the danger of damping-off. This fungus disease, which is encouraged by large expanses of bare, damp soil, attacks the tender stems of baby plants and can kill them overnight. The spores are everywhere, so damp-off is a danger even when you start out with a sterile potting mix.

You might want to compromise by skipping the middle step-up for fast growers like tomatoes. And if you have lots of growing space, there's nothing to prevent you from trying it with everything you grow. Start a larger than usual number of seeds, then hold back a few seedlings of each variety in the original starting pots. If the transplants do suffer damp-off, they'll probably do it fairly soon, and you'll have backup seedlings. If the transplants do well, all you've lost are those few extra seeds. 🍎

Growing Food in the Shade

Q My yard is surrounded by large trees and is shady for all but five or six hours a day. I'd love to have a vegetable garden but know there isn't enough sunshine. Other than maple syrup, is there anything I can grow to eat?

A The answer, in a word, is salads. Go for edible leaves: spinach, sorrel, arugula, cress, mustard, and leaf lettuces (the heading kinds need a fair amount of sun). Chard is a good bet, and so are parsley, tarragon, chervil, and mint.

All those trees mean the soil in your yard is likely to contain lots of nutrient- and water-grabbing roots, so for easiest planting and best results, build raised beds on top of the existing sod. (Line them with eight or nine sheets of newspaper before filling to help kill the grass.)

Be sure to leave plenty of room between plants for air circulation; foliage dries slowly in shady locations, and fungus diseases can be a problem. 🌰

Partial shade? Grow salad.

Degrees of Shade

Q You told a questioner that the only food that would grow in the shade was salad. We've heard that carrots and beets and even broccoli are possibilities. What gives?

A Shade comes in degrees: partial, filtered, light, heavy and total (aka give it up). The easiest way to figure out what will produce in your particular situation is to think about the distance from leaf to food.

Plants whose leaves are eaten need less sunshine than those that use their leaves to convert sunshine into something else. Salads require at least five or six hours of sunshine a day. For root-makers like carrots and beets, figure on six to eight hours. Broccoli and other edible flowers need at least eight hours, and crops that must flower and then make fruits, such as tomatoes, squash, or beans, must have a minimum of eight to ten hours and do better with more. 🌰

Gallon Jug Waterers?

Q This summer's drought and underwatering may be causing very poor cucumber and tomato production from my raised beds. For a simple irrigation system, a friend suggests cutting holes in the bottoms of gallon water jugs, inverting them, poking the tops 3 or 4 inches deep into the soil, 6 to 8 inches from the stems of the plants, and filling the jugs with water. What do you think of this method?

A Not much. It sounds good on paper, but in practice you end up with a garden full of plastic jugs. This does make a sort of sculptural statement but not one that's especially handsome or space-efficient. As adjacent plantings grow, foliage covers the jugs, which makes them hard to fill. Dirt falls into them when you weed. They tend to get deposits of dead bugs, fallen leaves, and other debris, and will eventually support a nice growth of algae.

And they have the same drawback as all single-point drip-irrigation systems; plant roots go where the easy water is instead of spreading down and out. This makes for weak, poorly anchored plants that are overdependent on the irrigation source. Go away for a week or just plain forget to fill those jugs, and your plants are toast. Soaker-hose systems take longer to set up, but they are less obtrusive and better for the plants. ✿

Coping with Drought

Q **I have always had a substantial vegetable garden in my yard in New Jersey, but I am worried about this year's drought-fighting water restrictions. Should I put a cover crop in that space this year, and if so, do you have any suggestions?**

A Cover crops are good for the soil, and buying vegetables directly from local farms is good for agricultural preservation, so you won't go wrong planting only "green manure" this year.

But you could also take the advice of Dr. Michael Hayes, the climate-impact specialist at the National Drought Mitigation Center in Lincoln, Nebraska. He suggested that you hedge your bets by planting a cover crop on half the space and devoting the rest to vegetables.

"Summer could be wet enough for you to get a crop, even if you can't water," he said. "There have been plenty of droughts where timely rain enabled crops to do well."

No matter which option you choose, be sure to plant the cover crop as soon as the weather is right for it. Even drought-tolerant stalwarts like cowpeas need moisture to become established, and moisture is more likely in spring than later.

If you go for half and half, plan to use copious mulch on the vegetable side, which should feature fruit crops like tomatoes, peppers, and melons rather than moisture lovers like lettuce and peas.

Your plants will need some water to grow and to set fruit, and drought will diminish yields, but the fruits themselves will still be tasty if they are a little thirsty at ripening time. They may even be tastier, thanks to the concentration of flavors.

For the best suggestions on cover crops, consult your local extension service. There are many factors to consider, including soil type, whether you want a harvest from the cover crop, and the tools you will use to plow the cover in at the end of the season. Buckwheat, for instance, is fairly easy to mix into the soil by hand, but cowpeas are rototiller territory. 🍂

Late Vegetables

Q I was unable to get an early start on my vegetable garden this year. Are there any crops that you would suggest for late sowing? We don't usually get frost until mid October, so I'm hoping there is still time to plant.

A When it comes to gardening, rarely is it too late to find something to enjoy. And if your garden receives full sun well into autumn, you can add a crop of late vegetables in mid summer.

Around the end of July, for example, you can still plant seeds of cucumbers, snap beans, carrots, Chinese cabbage, head and leaf lettuces, and peas, and you can transplant seedlings of late-maturing cauliflower. Until mid August you can plant seeds of beets, endive, kale, and Bibb lettuce, and transplant seedlings of late broccoli. And until the beginning of September, you can plant leaf lettuce, spinach, and turnips, and transplant seedlings of early-maturing broccoli and cauliflower.

Because the soil is quite warm in mid summer, the seeds should germinate quickly. Remember to loosen and prepare the planting area first, and keep the young plants well watered through the late-season heat. 🍂

A Cricket-Free Garden

Q For several summers, I have been plagued by hundreds of crickets in my vegetable garden. I do not want to use a pesticide. Is there a natural or environmentally safe alternative?

A A pesticide is any substance that's used to kill pests, so getting rid of the latter without using the former tends to be a tall order, but chickens work pretty well, and ducks work even better. Toads, snakes, spiders, and skunks are all helpful accomplices, too, particularly if you don't want to keep poultry.

Assuming there are no perennials to protect, you can also use winter to break the cycle. In late fall, remove all organic debris to the compost, then turn the soil. Cricket eggs will thus be exposed to hungry animals and freezing temperatures. Let the ground freeze hard, leave it for six weeks, then mulch to prevent erosion.

If you are willing to use a pesticide, you can try insecticidal soap, boric acid, or formulations based on neem (*Azadirachta indica*). None of them is perfect, but all are natural and comparatively safe, environmentally. Pretend you have grasshoppers and follow the instructions on the label.

Who Ate the Leaves?

Q For the last two years, I noticed large pieces missing from the leaves of our edible-podded peas as they began to grow. I couldn't find any bugs, nor any traces of slugs. I recently observed some sparrows or finches biting the plants. They seem to be the culprits. Is this a recognized problem? If so, what are the best organic ways to prevent it?

A Birds are most likely to pull up new plants (they know there's a big seed underneath), or to bite chunks out of peas and beans shortly before they're ready to pick. In the latter case, it's usually moisture they're after, and putting out a birdbath with clean water in it often solves the problem.

Leaf-eating birds are not a common complaint, and as a general rule, neither finches nor sparrows are interested in vegetables. Perhaps the birds you saw were thirsty or, in the case of the sparrows, going after small bugs that weren't readily visible to you.

Was the damage to the leaves confined to young, low-growing plants? If so, you might have voles. Or more accurately, you might have a vole. Anything more than one and there wouldn't have been any leaves left to take chunks out of.

The only reliable organic vole remover is a cat, though mousetraps baited with peanut butter work pretty well. (Be sure there are no skunks around if you go for the traps—skunks are very fond of peanut butter.)

If you are sure it's the birds, the best defense is to tent young plants with the bird netting sold at garden centers. Ugly bird-scare devices (there is a wide variety of them, from fake owls to flapping silver strips) are readily available and might be worth trying, though the results they deliver are mixed. But on balance, birds in the garden do more good than harm, so it's better to keep them around. 🥕

Outsmarting the Intruders

Q I've had it with deer invading my vegetable garden and am building a new fence. How high do I have to go to absolutely prevent them from entering? And while you're answering, please tell me what to do about the rabbits and woodchucks. They are less of a problem than the deer, but they do invade from time to time.

A "Absolute" critter prevention would require fencing that you could sell to the nearest maximum-security prison when you got tired of looking at it. But if you can live with keeping them out almost all of the time, here's a checklist. It does not consider aesthetics, and while we're on the subject, don't forget that whatever you build is only as good as the gate.

Deer. The fence should be 8 feet high if the fence is vertical, 6 feet if it slopes outward at a 45-degree angle (they don't like broad jumps). Neither fence needs to be solid; all you need is some kind of

An 8-foot fence will deter deer.

barrier (wires are the easiest and least expensive) running horizontally from post to post, at intervals no more than a foot apart. Electricity is optional, but recommended for the 5-foot level. Bait it with peanut butter so they get a warning shock that tells them to avoid the fence.

Rabbits. Galvanized 1-inch wire-mesh fencing or chicken wire, at least 2 feet high and at least 10 inches under the ground (they're good burrowers). No power needed.

Woodchucks. Galvanized 1-inch wire-mesh fencing, at least 2 feet high and at least 10 inches straight down, with an additional 8 inches bent forward underground, making an L-shape (with leg of the L on the garden side)—woodchucks make rabbits look like pikers in the burrowing department. No power needed.

All three. Start with galvanized 1-inch wire-mesh fencing, the 5-foot size. Bury the bottom 18 inches of fencing, as described under woodchucks. Above the fencing, string wire at 4 feet high, and then at 1-foot intervals up to 8 feet high. If you're not worried about raccoons, you can string wire at 4 and 5 feet, then run a band of black plastic netting between the 5-foot wire and the one at the top. If you *are* worried about raccoons, electrify the 4-foot wires and bait them as above under deer.

Well, you asked. 🍎

Reading Yellow Leaves

Q **The leaves on some of my tomato and bell pepper plants are starting to turn yellow. The plants get plenty of sun and water each day. What am I doing wrong? Is there something I can add to the soil to help the plants along?**

A Chlorosis, a shortage of chlorophyll that results in yellowing leaves, can happen to a wide range of plants. The yellow leaves are the plant announcing, "I don't feel well," and could be caused by just about anything, including a panoply of diseases. But if it is happening slowly and there are no other symptoms (curling, spots, brown edges, wholesale leaf-drop), it's likely that your plants are either waterlogged or hungry. They might also be suffering from an iron deficiency, though this is less common than was once thought.

Since you are watering every day, start by assuming that's the problem. If your soil is heavy clay, frequent watering could be drowning the roots. If it's sandy, chances are that constant watering is leaching nutrients from the soil. Either way, the solution is simply to cut back on the water a bit; it's O.K. for the surface soil to dry out, and the root zone should be moist, not wet.

It will also help to give your plants a foliar spray of soluble, all-purpose plant fertilizer or, even better, a fish- and seaweed-based organic mix. After that, observe them for ten days or so. If they don't green up, purchase some chelated iron (available at garden centers) and apply it— very carefully—according to directions. 🍂

Vegetables in Particular

Adding Artichokes to Your List

Q **I have been trying to grow artichokes for two years, but all I get are huge leaves. I can grow almost any vegetable, but I am about ready to admit defeat. Can you help me?**

A Artichokes are the unopened flower buds of *Cynara scolymus,* a tender perennial thistle native to the Mediterranean basin. Mature plants are 4 to 6 feet tall and a yard wide, so the huge leaves are to be expected.

So are your initial failures if you live in the Frost Belt. Artichokes don't flower until the second year, but they won't survive that long where freezing winters are the norm. They don't much care for hot summers, either, which means there are only a few places, mostly on the West Coast, where the plants do well. But that said, you can still add them to your list of vegetable accomplishments, getting meaty artichokes in only one year from seed, as long as you are willing to fuss around with them a bit.

The trick is to start small plants in comparative warmth, then fool them with a fake winter before their "second" spring. The most reliable variety for this treatment is 'Imperial Star,' but you can also use it with 'Green Globe' or 'Violetto.'

Start the seeds about eight weeks before the last expected spring frost. Soak them overnight in cool water, then plant in moistened soilless mix and keep them at 70° to 80°F until the plants have their first true leaves. Transplant to individual 4-inch pots filled with potting mix like Pro-Mix. Grow in bright light, with day temperatures of 60° to 70° and night temperatures of 50° to 60°, for six to eight weeks.

Now comes the interesting part. The little plants must have at least two weeks of "winter" temperatures between 40° and 50°. (If this describes spring at your place, plant them outside about a yard apart, in well-drained, loamy soil.)

Otherwise, improvise. Move the pots to a cool spot outdoors in the morning, then set them in a garage overnight. Or keep them in an unheated sunroom and use an air conditioner to dispel unwanted solar heat. At the end of the cold fortnight, plant them outside.

Once they are in the garden, treat the plants the same way you do other fruiting vegetables. Make sure they get enough water, feed sparingly, and keep an eye out for pests. The artichokes should be ready to harvest about three months after setting out, and each plant should yield anywhere from five to eight of them.

An Artichoke That Isn't

Q I've been dreaming about a scrumptious vegetable I ate last summer, Jerusalem artichoke. But I was told it was not really an artichoke. So what is it and where do I find it?

A It's true that the Jerusalem artichoke, also called sunchoke or girasole, is not an artichoke at all but a sunflower. The Jerusalem artichoke (*Helianthus tuberosus*) belongs to a completely different botanical genus than the globe artichoke (*Cynara scolymus*).

The part of the Jerusalem artichoke that you enjoyed eating is the tuber, a potato-like, swollen underground stem. Typically it is about 3 to 4 inches long and 2 to 3 inches in diameter. (The portion of the globe artichoke that is eaten is the immature flower head.)

A vigorous-growing, multistemmed, flowering native American perennial, the Jerusalem artichoke can grow to 10 feet tall. Like its sunflower relatives, it bears bright yellow blooms and is at its best in full sun with well-drained soil. The tubers may be planted early in the spring, as soon as the ground can be worked, or seedlings can be planted after the last frost.

Jerusalem artichoke
(*Helianthus tuberosus*)
tubers

Seeds and tubers are widely available via mail order.

Warning: Jerusalem artichoke is highly invasive, and difficult to eradicate once well established. Be sure to plant your patch away from other garden areas. ✇

Almost Arugula

Q **At a fund-raiser, I bought a small plant that was labeled perennial arugula. Now that it's about 6 inches wide, I'm afraid it's something else. The leaves are smaller, shinier, and darker green than arugula from the store. They are also much narrower than regular arugula. Is it really the same plant?**

A It isn't the same plant (it isn't even the same genus), but it is very similar in flavor and is often called wild arugula. The botanical name of your new friend is *Diplotaxis tenuifolia* or, according to some sources, *D. erucoides.* True arugula, on the other hand, is *Eruca vesicaria* ssp. *sativa.*

If you taste them side by side, the differences will be clear right away: the wild kind is almost hot, decidedly more pungent than garden arugula, though it is also sweeter. To many palates, it also has a cleaner, less old-radishy flavor, and it holds up better when cooked.

The two arugulas have similar growing habits. They thrive in the cool of spring; then, as the weather warms, they become stronger flavored and shoot up flowers that are also edible. At that point, they part company. True arugula flowers are white with a hint of lavender, and once they show up, that's pretty much it for the leaves, which become tough and disagreeably strong. Wild arugula flowers are yellow, and you can enjoy them, then cut the plants back, and get another crop in the fall.

Like garden arugula, the wild kind will self-sow. Let it go to seed this summer and you'll have babies by late autumn. Lots of babies. And babies galore next spring. Be sure to get rid of excess plants as soon as you see them. They're easy to weed out when young, but mature plants have long, fleshy roots and are difficult to remove. 🍎

Growing Asparagus

Q **About five years ago, I planted asparagus roots from the farm store. Finally last year, I had a bumper crop. This year, out of 48 plants, I have 5! What exactly does asparagus need to grow and thrive? Soil, fertilizer, pH, mulch, sun, companion planting? I always let it go to seed after the harvest.**

Healthy asparagus crown

A What asparagus needs, for starters, is plenty of time to get established. While some experts feel it's O.K. to start harvesting the second year after planting, most still go with the old rules: cut for two or three weeks in the third year, four to six weeks in the fourth. In subsequent years, you can keep harvesting as long as the plant continues to send up thick spears. When they start getting thin, it's time to stop. Overcutting will always weaken plants and, taken to extremes, can kill.

If your patch was planted in heavy clay, the death toll may be due to rot. Asparagus prefers well-drained sandy loam that's right around neutral in the pH department. Just slightly acid is ideal, though slightly alkaline is also fine. There should be at least a half day of sun. Fertilize in early fall, then again in late spring after the harvest is over.

Mulch is a plus as it keeps roots cool and suppresses weeds. There is no good companion plant. Asparagus roots are heavy feeders that grow close to the surface, and they should be free from all competition, including the baby asparagus plants being formed by those seeds.

Seed making also takes energy that would otherwise go to spear production; but you're right to let the plants grow all season and die naturally.

How do you let the plants mature without getting seeds? Sexism. Asparagus plants are either male or female. When you replant, choose root divisions from a modern, mostly male cultivar like 'Jersey Giant' or the widely adapted (and widely available) 'Jersey King.' ☙

Asparagus Ailments

Q **I planted rust-resistant asparagus in my Maine garden four years ago. Last summer, the first spears were normal but later ones had blotches. Some spears started to grow but did not develop normal foliage and soon dried up. Even those with normal foliage had blotches on the stems. Some that had died back put out new shoots and foliage in the fall. Did they have rust? What should I do this spring to prevent its return?**

A They probably do not have rust. Dr. Stephen Garrison, a specialist in vegetable crops with Rutgers University Cooperative Extension in Bridgeton, New Jersey, said that if rust were the culprit, you'd see problems on the mature ferns in fall.

"It sounds to me like it may be more than one organism," he said. The blotches might be a fungal disease called purple spot, but purple spot doesn't kill the stem. "Dieback is more typical of a root problem," he offered. Overharvesting combined with drought could also cause dieback. And if you had asparagus in the same place before, there's a chance that the problem is fusarium wilt.

This summer, harvest lightly so as not to stress the roots. After the ferns die in the fall, cut them down and discard them. If there is no improvement within two years, start a new patch in new ground. Good choices for the Northeast include 'Jersey Knight,' 'Jersey Giant,' and the new 'Jersey Supreme,' all developed at Rutgers—Asparagus Central for your quadrant of the country. ☙

Misbehaving Beans

Q **I planted bush beans this spring. The ones that made plants are doing all right, but several seeds behaved in a very odd way. They came up but they never made leaves; all I got were small stems with the original beans split at the top. Eventually, they dried up. Should I get seeds from a different supplier next time?**

A The odd behavior isn't caused by defective seed but by the depredations of the seed-corn maggot, a voracious little creature that will, in spite of its name, munch out the germ of beans, peas, squash, cabbage, and just about any other large vegetable seed you might be thinking of planting. In most cases nothing emerges from the soil, leading gardeners to assume the seed has rotted, but beans often have just enough strength left to come out of the ground and cause confusion.

Seed-corn maggots are a problem only in the cold, damp weather characteristic of early spring, when softened seeds sit in the ground long enough to attract their notice. The easiest cure is simply to wait until the cold, damp weather passes before planting. If kept well watered, bush beans can even be sown in the hot weather of mid summer. Unlike spring-planted bush beans, which are usually done by the end of July, this late-planted group will keep on producing until killed by frost.

Saving Bean Seeds

Q **This year we grew 'Provider' bush beans. We're ready to pull up the plants as part of our garden cleanup, but I notice there are many fat pods that we somehow overlooked. The beans inside look almost like dry beans, but they are still soft. Can I dry them and save them for seed?**

A The basic criteria have been met: 'Provider' is not a hybrid (hybrids do not come true from seed); and if you grew only one kind, you've avoided the small chance it could cross with a neighboring variety. As long as the beans are fully mature and have not been damaged by frost or mold, you can save them for seed.

But before you start what could become a long-term relationship, you might want to re-evaluate your intended. Though 'Provider' is early, reliable, and prolific, it isn't particularly tasty.

More flavorful alternatives, including 'Blue Lake Bush,' 'Kentucky Wonder Bush,' and 'Tendergreen Improved,' are easy to find in garden stores. Specialty catalogs offer dozens of others, each more interesting and delicious than the last.

That said, if you're keen on 'Provider,' by all means proceed. Pull the plants up roots and all, shake off the dirt, and hang them upside down in a warm, dry place. When the pods are crisp, remove the beans. If they're wrinkled, put everything in the compost bin and add bean seeds to the shopping list.

If the beans are plump, smooth, and hard enough to break when hit with a hammer, you're in business. Pack them in airtight jars and freeze for a week to kill any lurking bean weevils, then let the jars return to room temperature unopened. Store in a dark, cool, dry place. 🍎

'Blue Lake Bush' beans

Beet Bonanza

Q I am having trouble planting beets correctly. Last year they were too crowded, and thinning them took forever. This spring I spaced the seeds much farther apart, almost 2 inches. There are a few empty spots, but in general the plants are still as thick as weeds. How do I prevent this?

A You don't, because beet fruits are built like pineapples, as bonded clusters of single-seeded units. They don't come apart even after they dry, which means the things in the seed packet are clusters, not separate seeds.

Not every seed in every cluster will sprout (when none does, you get empty spots), but usually enough come through to make thinning unavoidable. 🍎

A Different Cabbage

Q I frequent Chinese restaurants and enjoy the green-and-white cabbage called bok choy. Can I grow it myself?

A You can easily grow the beautiful bok choy (*Brassica rapa chinensis*) in containers or in the ground. This fast-growing, hardy biennial is also known as Chinese celery cabbage.

The plant consists of a loose head of some dozen glossy green leaves with contrasting smooth, light stalks and veins. All parts, including the flowering shoots, are edible, although the younger the plant, the more tender it is.

Bok choy does best with full sun and the cool temperatures of spring and autumn, in rich, slightly alkaline soil that is kept evenly moist. Varieties range in size from a squat 3 to 4 inches up to a robust 24 inches or more. Depending on the type and the season, bok choy may be harvested within a month and a half after sowing. One easily grown variety, 'Mei-Qing,' is table ready in about 45 days; another, 'Lei-Choi,' in 47 days. 🌶

Harvesting Broccoli

Q I've gone to a lot of work to protect my broccoli from invasions of one sort or another. Now can you tell me the best way to harvest to get the most out of my plants?

Cut right above a leaf node . . .

. . . and secondary shoots will grow larger.

A The central head is always the largest, but many varieties of broccoli also make numerous small side shoots. If you leave them—and continue to care for the plant—your broccoli bounty will be increased.

First, keep your eye on that central head. You want it to grow as large as possible while remaining firm and tightly packed, with no sign of the expanding buds that signal imminent flowering.

As soon as it stops enlarging and/or the buds begin to swell, cut it off, locating the cut right above a leaf node where a secondary shoot is forming.

The ideal spot for decapitation can be anywhere from 4 to 9 inches down, depending on the season. Hot weather makes broccoli bolt, and although it doesn't mind light frosts it will be killed by hard ones. So if the main head reaches harvest size in mid spring (for early varieties) or early fall (for main crop types), cut it short. Leaving most of the plant behind will give you the most side shoots. If the main head isn't ready until the weather is about to turn, you might as well cut it with a longer edible stem and enjoy it while the enjoying's good. 🌱

SPROUTING BROCCOLI

The large-headed broccoli common in both stores and gardens is not the only source of delicious spears and tender florets. You can also grow the heirloom variety 'Di Cicco,' or sprouting broccoli. This one also makes a large plant, but instead of offering one large head and several much smaller ones (which are ready much later), sprouting broccoli skips the big production in favor of a smaller central head and a steady supply of side shoots that, while by no means huge, are larger (and earlier) than the side shoots of traditional broccoli.

For More Brussels Sprouts

Q **I'm confused about when and how to harvest my Brussels sprouts. The plants are good sized and I see lots of baby sprouts, but they are much smaller than the ones in stores. I'm told that removing the leaves will make the sprouts grow larger, but I'm not sure how many to remove or when.**

A Leaf removal works by driving the energy of the plant into sprout growth, but there are two ways to do it, with very different results.

The home-garden way (minimal leaf removal) gives you more sprouts over a longer season, but only a few at a time on each plant. The commercial version (off with its head!) yields fewer sprouts, but they are uniform in size and ready all at once.

To go commercial, watch until the sprouts at the bottom are ½ to ¾ inch in diameter. Then remove the top of the plant, including the growing point and the top rosette of leaves with its tiny sprouts. The plant will now concentrate on the sprouts at hand, which will be ready in about a month.

For the home-garden approach, just remove the bottom two or three rows of leaves, cutting or snapping them off carefully so you don't damage the sprouts in the axils. Harvest the bottom sprouts as soon as they are about an inch in diameter. Then, as each successive sprout reaches harvestable size, remove the leaf below it and cut or twist off the sprout, leaving a small spur of stem on the plant. In a long, mild fall, these spurs sometimes produce another crop.

As long as it has its growing point, a plant will put out new leaves and sprouts until daytime temperatures stay below around 45°F. It will yield small harvests every 10 days or so for two months or more, and the sprouts, which are improved by light frosts, will be at their tastiest. 🍐

VEGETABLES AGAINST CANCER

Many plants contain compounds called phytochemicals, which show promise in the fight against cancer. As is often the case when discoveries are being made rapidly, just which chemicals are most helpful, and to whom, is by no means clear; but the beauty part with vegetables is that you can't lose. They're high in vitamins, minerals, and fiber, they're low in fat, and eating them was a good idea long before the first phytochemical was ever identified.

CHEMICAL	ACTION	VEGETABLE
Carotinoids	antioxidant	carrots, winter squash, sweet potatoes, parsley, spinach, kale
Flavonoids	block receptors for hormones that promote cancer	broccoli, eggplant, peppers, cabbage, carrots, cucumbers, parsley, squash, tomatoes
Indoles	help prevent DNA damage, decrease influence of estrogen	broccoli, Brussels sprouts, cabbage, collards, kale
Lycopene	fights cell damage from carcinogens	tomatoes, watermelon
Phenolic acids	increase activity of cancer-fighting enzymes	broccoli, cabbage, carrots, eggplant, parsley, peppers

A Hungry Eye for Cardoons

Q I have an Italian cookbook that has recipes for cardoons. They sound delicious, but I can't find them for sale. Can I grow them in western Pennsylvania, and if so, how?

A The cardoon (*Cynara cardunculus*) is a kind of thistle, closely related to the artichoke. It's a bit easier to grow, far lovelier when growing, and equally delicious, with a taste somewhere between artichoke and chestnut.

But it sure isn't instant. Cardoons take about six months from seed to table. And although even a beginner can count on gorgeous plants and beautiful, if heroic, material for the vase, it's a major project to grow cardoons you can eat.

The plants start with a basal rosette and grow quickly into a clump of thick-stemmed, silvery green, saw-toothed leaves that may be 4 to 6 feet tall. The flowers are large and purple, like artichoke flowers, but in this case you don't *want* flowers. Cardoons are grown for the leaf midribs, which will become tough and bitter if the plant reaches blooming age—about eight months—or is forced to bloom by summer heat.

Actually, they tend to become tough and bitter anyway, so full-grown cardoons are tenderized and sweetened by blanching before harvest. Blanch them when the weather cools, in late September, by loosely tying the outer leaves around the center, then heaping leaves or straw around the plants to exclude light and protect from frost. They'll be ready to eat in four to six weeks.

Still game? Seed should be started indoors in February, in individual 3-inch pots. Give the seedlings lots of light but don't let temperatures rise above 75°F. Set young plants out in fertile, well-drained soil as soon as the danger of hard frost is past; cardoons grow best in cool, damp weather. Make sure they get plenty of water. Feed with a balanced fertilizer shortly after you set them out, and again in late August. But beware: if the plants are allowed to bloom, they can be invasive. 🍎

'Romanesco': A Temperamental Beauty

Q **Our vegetable garden is on the small side so we have never bothered to grow broccoli, but we are thinking of taking a flyer on 'Romanesco' because it looks so beautiful. Does it taste as good as it looks? Is it hard to grow?**

A It is impossible to gaze unmoved at the rococo turrets that form a head of 'Romanesco,' which in spite of its green color and common name is a cauliflower, not a broccoli.

The minutely studded celadon spirals look sort of like minarets, sort of like seashells, and sort of like bra cups that might have been worn by Carmen Miranda. And when the plant has been well grown, the taste is just as spectacular, sweet, nutty, and faintly sharp, with none of the sulfurous quality that haunts even the best broccoli.

But as you could guess from the fact that this marvel is seldom offered for sale, 'Romanesco' is not easy to grow. It takes almost five months from seed to harvest, and all of that time must be spent in bright sunshine and cool temperatures.

So gardeners in the Northeast have two choices. Either start plants indoors, six weeks before the last frost, and then hope for a terrible summer, or else (the preferred method), start in mid summer and hope for the early arrival of a very long fall.

The garden soil should be nearly neutral to slightly alkaline and highly fertile; the large plants are heavy feeders. Use a thick layer of organic mulch such as straw, to help keep the soil cool and moist. And be sure to water regularly. 'Romanesco' is very sensitive to drought and reacts badly to large fluctuations in soil moisture. 🌶

Carrots Under Attack

Q Help! Our organically grown carrots were beautiful when we started harvesting them six weeks ago, but now they're full of blackish, horizontal lines, and some have worms in them. Should we just abandon the crop? How do we keep this from happening?

A Welcome to the wonderful world of the carrot rust fly, a very common pest. Adults lay eggs on the soil around the crowns of carrots, parsnips, and related plants. The newly hatched maggots tunnel into the roots, eat for a month or so, then return to the soil to pupate; a few weeks later they turn into the next generation of flies.

The only way to stop further damage is to harvest the carrots, trim off the nasty parts, and eat or preserve the rest. But whether you eat the carrots or not, don't just abandon the crop. And don't put any of it on the compost pile. If the infected carrots are not removed and destroyed, maggots and pupae can overwinter in them or the soil near them and make things worse next year.

Prevention is tricky. Start by planting next year's crop as far from this one as possible. Try planting late: flies lay their first eggs in May or June, so if you plant in mid June you can sometimes sneak by them (it takes carrot seeds a couple of weeks to germinate). Be sure to harvest early as well, since the second generation of flies lays its eggs in mid August.

Alternatively, you can use floating row covers to prevent egg laying. Be sure to bury the edges in the soil so no flies can get underneath, and leave them on from planting to harvest. 🥕

Disappointing Carrots

Q We were looking forward to superior flavor from our home-grown carrots, but so far the ones we have harvested taste worse than the ones from the store. I know they are fresh: we're picking them as soon as they are ready. Can there be something wrong with our soil?

A Carrot flavor is almost entirely genetically determined, so your problem is probably not in the soil but in your choice of variety, or in that otherwise tasty phrase, "as soon as they are ready." 'Amsterdam' and 'Nantes' carrots are sweeter and juicier than 'Chantenay,' which are the best storage types, or 'Danvers,' which have only durability to recommend them. But no matter what kind you grow, maturity is all; those little guys sold as "baby" carrots are full-grown miniatures (or, in some cases, pieces of big carrots).

Sugars are the carrots' winter energy supply, and they don't start building it up in quantity until after the roots are full size. Before this happens, the carrots have developed most of their genetic allotment of turpenoids, the compounds that give them their characteristic taste. There is a reason the word sounds like turpentine, and until sugar balance is achieved, turpenoids are something only a carrot could love.

The only readiness test is taste (pull the roots in the evening as they build up sugar during the day), but you don't have to harvest them all at once. Carrots will keep in the soil for weeks after their best flavor is attained, especially if the weather is cool. They won't keep improving, though, and will eventually become woody. They may also fall prey to a late generation of the carrot rust fly; be sure to harvest promptly if you've had rust fly problems in the past. ✿

Timing the Carrot Harvest

Q Is there a good rule of thumb for determining whether carrots are ready for harvesting? It breaks my heart to pull them from the soil and find that they are not ready.

A The short answer is no. A test carrot is the only way to tell whether the group is ready, but you shouldn't need very many tests if the carrots have been well spaced so that all grow at the same rate. (You *did* thin them, didn't you? Crowded carrots always mature very unevenly.)

The best way to avoid heartbreak is to be patient; carrots don't taste good until they're mature, so there's no point in pulling up babies. The seed packet should tell you approximately how many days it will be to harvest, and since those estimates tend toward the optimistic side, there's not much point in checking until the allotted time has elapsed. ✿

Chard, Pretty and Plain

Q Last year I planted 'Bright Lights' chard. This spring, I was amazed to see that it survived and was growing again. I assumed I would have more chard, but now the plants aren't making leaves and have started sending up seed stalks instead. Can I save the seeds?

A You can save the seeds, but don't expect them to produce as handsome an assortment of strong reds, yellows, corals, and pinks as the one they came from. 'Bright Lights' is an assembled variety, blended from seeds that came from fields of single-color plants. Each color is grown in chard isolation, very far from others that might cross with it and muddy its looks.

Your colors, on the other hand, have been intimate, freely mixing their genes. Their seeds will produce edible chard plants, some of which will be pretty. There is even an outside chance that one or two will be gorgeous. But most will simply be on the dull side, more like conventional chard, making you wish you had bought another packet of 'Bright Lights' seed instead.

And although the tall, colorful stems have a certain weedy splendor, chard has flowers that only a seed saver could love. So you might as well pull it up and put it on the compost. 🌶

Edible Chrysanthemums

Q **I've been eating fresh chrysanthemums in salads in restaurants, but often they're bitter. What chrysanthemum do you recommend that is both edible and palatable?**

A It all depends on how much chrysanthemum you plan to eat. A few petals of any kind lend an agreeable fragrance to tea, but only the leaves of the small-flowered "chop suey green," *Chrysanthemum coronarium,* are mild enough to use in any quantity. Even then, the quantity should be small.

When using the flower petals, it is important to cut off the white or sometimes greenish-colored heels by which they are attached. This is the portion that produces a bitter taste. (And not just in chrysanthemums—you'll want to remove it from rose petals, too.) 🌶

Ornamental Corn

Q **I would like to grow colored corn for use in fall decorations. Is it a diffi-cult plant?**

A Anyone with a few feet of sunny space can grow several stalks of ornamental corn, also known as Indian corn. Unlike the sweet yellow or white corn, which is eaten directly off the cob, the ornamental kinds with their kernels of red, yellow, rust, or blue are traditionally ground for cornmeal and flour. They are also dried whole and used in autumn decorations.

Ornamental corn

Ornamental corn has the same growing needs as sweet corn: highly fertile soil, plenty of sun, and regular irrigation. Like sweet corn, it should be planted in a block rather than in long rows, to help ensure the pollination necessary for well-filled ears. 🍏

SWEET, SWEETER, SWEETEST CORN

The sugar in ordinary sweet corn, whether heirloom or hybrid, is fleeting—rapidly turning into starch as soon as the ear leaves the stalk. That's why so many old recipes tell you to put the kettle on the stove before you go out to pick.

But now there are several alternatives to ordinary corn, all identified by initials that describe how the sweetness gene has been modified—by conventional breeding methods, not biotechnology.

Ordinary corn is **su,** or "normal sugary." The next step toward sweet is **se,** for corn that has one "sugary enhanced" parent and one su parent. After that comes **se +,** for corn that has *two* se parents.

And after that comes **sh2,** the corn known as supersweet (the *sh* comes from "shrunken," a description of the dried kernel). This corn is in a class by itself, extremely sweet when harvested and much slower than other types to turn starchy in storage.

Many corn lovers feel that supersweet corn is *too* sweet, unpleasantly saccharine and lacking in true "corn" flavor. It is also much harder to grow. It will not germinate in cool soil, it's quite fussy about water and fertilizer, and it must be grown in isolation—if an sh2 variety crosses with any other corn, the kernels of both will be tough and starchy.

How do you tell when you're buying seeds? Ordinary corn doesn't usually get any special billing, but se, se+, and sh2 varieties will (or should) have those initials listed right after the variety name.

Corn by the Numbers

Q I tried to grow sweet corn several years ago and failed miserably. I have heard that you need a certain minimum number of plants so that they can cross-pollinate, a necessity for the plants to yield corn. Is this true?

A Your informant is on the right track but not great on the specifics. Cross-pollination usually means between two varieties of something, but with corn, crossing varieties often results in starchy, bland kernels and should be prevented. Separate different strains by planting them *at least* 500 feet apart or by choosing varieties that ripen at different times.

With corn, it's cross-pollination between plants of the same variety that's essential, because corn is not self-fertile. Although each plant is both male and female, the two parts reach sexual maturity at slightly different times. The ear is the female part. Each kernel on it is attached to a strand of silk. A grain of pollen from a tassel, the male part, must fall on the silk in order for that kernel to develop. Just to make matters more complicated, pollen grains are very short lived. Although the pollen is shed over a period of several days, individual grains are viable only for about four hours. So the trick is to be sure the pollen gets good, wide distribution.

You can't call in the bees for help; corn is pollinated by a combination of wind and gravity, and that's where the "minimum number of plants" comes in. It's not so much a matter of numbers as it is of how they're arranged: the rows should be in blocks, not strung out in narrow lines.

Plants should be 10 inches apart in rows 36 inches apart. The recommended minimum is four rows, giving you about 40 plants in a square that's 9 feet on each side. If you take advantage of prevailing winds, you can get away with something smaller, but since two ears per stalk is average, you probably won't want to.

Time to Plant the Corn

 I always get my peas in the ground before St. Patrick's Day. Is there a "best time" to plant corn?

A Folk wisdom says to plant corn "when the oak leaves are the size of a mouse's ear," because by that time the danger of frost should be well past and the soil should have warmed up. Corn does best when planted in warm soil and grown in hot weather. Then ideally, just as the ripening starts, nights will begin to cool off. Heat is great for vegetative growth, but the plant will produce ears that have more carbohydrates (including sugars) when temperatures are moderate.

Cancer-Fighting Crucifers

Q **I've been reading about the cancer-preventive benefits of broccoli and other members of the cruciferous family. What are the other members?**

A The mustard family, Cruciferae, is a large group that includes several hundred genera of annuals and perennials.

Cruciferous flowers have a crosslike arrangement, with four petals and four sepals (the outer covering of the flower). At the table, the most commonly found crucifers are in the genus *Brassica,* which includes kale, cauliflower, cabbage, Brussels sprouts, kohlrabi, Chinese cabbage, mustard, and turnip. Horseradish (in the genus *Armoracia*) is also a crucifer.

The preventive agents are mostly compounds called indoles, which help inhibit DNA damage, and there are more of them in broccoli sprouts than in any other crucifer. 🌶

Bitter Fruit

Q **Sometimes my cucumber harvest tastes disappointingly bitter. Why?**

A Cucumbers that have been stressed by lengthy periods of hot temperatures and poor or dry soil may develop a bitter taste in late-season harvests. Sometimes the bitterness is only in the stem end, but other times it affects the entire fruit.

You can't do much about the weather, but you can keep your plant well watered during periods when rain is minimal, and maintain a summer mulch to help conserve soil moisture. Cucumbers are heavy feeders, so if your soil is on the poor side, add a side dressing of 5-10-5 (or similarly balanced) fertilizer when the plants are about six weeks old. 🌶

CANOLA: A COUSIN OF BROCCOLI

Canola oil comes from *Brassica napus,* another member of the crucifer family. The name canola, which has replaced the common name rapeseed, comes from an amalgamation of Canada oil low acid. Why Canada? It was Canadian scientists who helped test and breed hundreds of strains of the plant to prove it was beneficial in the human diet.

No Second Helpings on Cukes

Q My cucumber crop is really outstanding, so I want to save some seeds for next year. Does the size of the cucumber left to ripen matter? These are kirby, but I don't know if they're hybrid or not.

A If your cukes were Kirby with a capital letter, you could save them. But that old-fashioned nonhybrid strain fell from the list of varieties sold for home gardening in the late 1980s. The kirby name now applies to any short, fat pickling cucumber with sweet flesh, a small seed cavity, and thin, warty skin. There are hundreds of these lowercase kirbys, some hybrid and some not.

Only nonhybrid varieties can be counted on to come true from seed, and then only when each variety is prevented from cross-pollinating with others. Since you don't know what you have, saving and planting these seeds is a gamble that is unlikely to pay off. It would be better to wait until next year and then, if you want to improve your garden by saving the seeds of vegetables that do particularly well there, be sure to choose nonhybrid (aka open-pollinated) varieties. ☙

Kirby-type cucumbers

Cucumber Leaf Woes

Q A whitish-looking covering is spreading over the leaves of my cucumber plant, and the affected parts seem to be dying. What can I do?

A As the summer heat intensifies and humidity levels rise, the leaves of a number of garden plants begin sporting the white coat of several closely related fungi called powdery mildew. This name aptly describes this disease, which saps plant nutrients, causing yellowing, the death of some leaves and fruit, and in severe cases the death of the entire plant.

Since powdery mildew spores are spread by the wind, start by picking off all the diseased leaves and fruit and discarding them. (Bury or throw them out in the garbage; don't recycle them on the compost pile.) Then thin the remaining stems or leaves a bit, to increase the air circulation around each plant. Keep the plant well watered and fertilized to reduce stress.

Next year, plant your cukes in a different spot and choose a mildew-resistant variety such as 'Diva' or 'Celebrity' for slicing, or 'Conquest' if you're after pickles. 🌶

CUCUMBER FIRST AID

The best way to get sweet cucumbers is to plant sweet varieties and harvest them when they are young, but in an emergency, you can remove some bitterness by salting the cucumber. Slice or chunk the cukes, sprinkle liberally with salt, and allow to sit for 30 minutes to an hour. Pour off the liquid and rinse. Cucumbers will be slightly wilted but still crisp—and milder.

Growing Garlic

Q I would love to try growing garlic myself but don't know how. Is it difficult, and when should I plant it?

A It's so easy to grow garlic (*Allium sativum*) that it's surprising more gardeners don't grow their own.

"Garlic is a bulb, like the tulip, and needs the cold-winter treatment that Mother Nature provides," said Patricia K. Reppert, the owner of Shale Hill Farm in Saugerties, New York, who started the annual Hudson Valley Garlic Festival. And like tulips, garlic can be planted almost anytime in autumn as long as the ground is workable.

The bulbs, which come in clustered segments, must be separated before planting. The segments are then placed pointed side up about an inch below the ground in rich, well-drained soil. Full sun is best, but garlic can manage as long as it gets six hours of sun a day.

The hardest part seems to be finding a good garlic farmer from whom to buy cloves for planting. "You can't use what you find in the supermarket since much of that garlic has been treated to keep it from sprouting," Ms. Reppert said.

Organic garlic will sprout just fine, but it's still worth buying locally if possible because local garlic will be adapted to your area. Whether it's organic or conventional,

Softneck garlic

most widely distributed commercial garlic comes from one of the softneck varieties, a group that does best in areas with mild winter temperatures and comparatively even day lengths year-round. Softneck is fine if you live in zone 7 or warmer, and it usually does all right in zone 6, but from zone 5 north it will not do as well as hardneck varieties. Hardnecks are sometimes sold in farmers' markets or specialty stores, and like softnecks, they are readily available through mail order. 🍎

A Yen for Garlic

Q **Although it is mid December, the ground in my Warwick, New York, garden is still soft. Can I plant garlic or is it too late?**

A Theoretically, it's too late, but this is an odd year because temperatures have been so much warmer, so much later. Garlic cloves should be planted early enough to build a strong root system before the ground freezes, late enough so they aren't tempted to make green tops instead. In your area (southern end of zone 5 to northern end of zone 6), neither too early nor too late is usually defined as sometime between mid October and mid November. But there is a lot of warmth stored in the earth right now. Help keep it there with an 8-inch layer of dry mulch like straw or shredded leaves. Remove the mulch in early spring; the garlic will be as eager to see the sun as you are. 🍎

Growing Real Gherkins

Q **I've always made pickled gherkins from pickling cucumbers, carefully harvesting the baby ones while they were still very small and firm. Now I've been told that "real gherkins" are actually a different vegetable. Is this true?**

A Real gherkins are really cool cucumbers, not a different vegetable but a different species. Standard slicers and picklers are both *Cucumis sativus;* gherkins are *C. anguria.* They're often called West India gherkins, a reference to their route here from Africa. They're also known as bur or burr gherkins, a very good description of the small, oval fruits, which are covered with soft spines. They have thin, pale green skin, lots of tiny seeds, and an agreeable, distinctive flavor clearly related to that of cucumbers yet not exactly the same.

Fresh gherkins almost never show up in stores or at farmers' markets. If you want them, you have to grow them, but they are as easy to cultivate as any other cucumber. Easier, maybe, since the vigorous vines seem to be somewhat less tasty to cucumber beetles than those of *C. sativus.* Gherkins need lots of heat to flourish, and don't be stingy with the water or you'll get bitter little pills. 🌰

A Bottle of Birds

Q We planted birdhouse gourds this summer in our vegetable garden, to have some interesting birdhouses for the wrens and other small birds. Are they edible and prepared in the same way as acorn squash, say? How do we go about turning these large veggies into birdhouses?

A Edible, meaning it won't kill you, is a pretty minimal standard. Gourds in the genus *Lagenaria* are classified informally by shape as dipper, snake, kettle, or bottle, which is the shape used for birdhouses. Of the more than 20 varieties of *Lagenaria siceraria,* or bottle gourd, a few have rinds that can be used to flavor soups when the gourds are immature, but most are simply too bitter.

Harvest birdhouse gourds after a light frost withers the leaves. Leave a couple inches of stem on the gourds and hang them to dry at room temperature, with good air circulation, until you can hear the seeds rattle around. Small gourds take about six months, and larger ones can take up to a year. For maracas, just paint and shake. For birdhouses, drill a hole and scoop out the dried pulp and seeds.

Birds need enough room to move around and raise their chicks, but not so much that it is hard to keep warm, so the size of the bird that will use the gourd depends on the size of the gourd. A 6-inch-diameter gourd with a hole 1 to 1½ inches in diameter will appeal to a variety of wrens. An 8-inch gourd with a 1½-inch hole is fine for chickadees, tufted titmice, downy woodpeckers, and nuthatches. Be sure to place the hole high enough to keep the youngsters from falling out. 🌰

Bottle-gourd birdhouses with a flowering vine

Winter Plans for Kale

Q We are really enjoying the kale we planted this year. It has withstood several frosts and seems unaffected. How much longer can we expect it to keep growing? Is there anything we can do to help it survive? We have a lot left to eat.

A Once the days are short and cold, you can't expect kale to keep growing. But you can help it survive almost indefinitely. The trick, which also works for Swiss chard and other hardy greens, is to keep the soil around the roots from freezing.

If you don't already have one in place, start by applying a thick blanket of organic mulch—straw or shredded leaves. That will be enough if you are in zone 7 or the warmer parts of zone 6. If it's colder, use bales of straw and old windows (or clear plastic) to build a lean-to cold frame.

Place a row of bales close to the long side of the kale row. They should be to the north if the row runs east–west, to the east if it runs north–south. Put another row on top so you have a wall about 3 feet high. On each short side, make a sloping wall by butting single bales firmly against the back wall, then topping them with partial bales.

Now use the windows (or clear plastic sheeting) to cover the front, making sure the cover does not touch the plants. At the top, windows can just lean against the straw. Plastic should be draped and held in place on top of the bales by rocks or a heavy board. At the bottom, where the cover touches the ground, mound on a few inches of soil to hold it and seal out drafts.

At this point, you should have a structure whose sloping, clear roof faces south or west. Use loose straw to fill in any gaps in the walls. That's it. Throw a heavy blanket over the cover when night temperatures are predicted to fall below 20°F; and open the frame at the top on warm, sunny days or you'll cook your kale before you bring it indoors. Don't try this with root crops; mice and voles will colonize the bales of straw if you feed them beets and carrots. 🌰

'Ragged Jack' and 'Lacinato' kale

Vegetables in Particular

The Life of the Leek

Q Some of my leeks were too small to harvest so I left them in the ground last year, and now they are about to flower. Will they still be good to eat after flowering? I don't want to harvest them now. I want to enjoy the flowers. But it would be nice if I could eat the leeks afterward.

A Biennial members of the same family as onions, shallots, and chives, leeks have their own agenda. They spend the first growing season stocking up on energy and storing food in their thickened stem base—the part of the leek that we eat. By harvesting during the first fall, you are the beneficiary of the leek's efforts. If you wait until after flowering, during the second growing season, the leek is the beneficiary. It uses up that energy as the plant devotes everything to setting seed before it dies.

As its second spring arrives, the leek begins to create its flower stalk. To support the flower, the center of the edible portion becomes woody and inedible. Taking energy from storage to produce a flower reduces the size of the leek and gives it a sharper flavor. The best-tasting overwintered leeks are harvested early in the spring.

Not all leeks are winter hardy, so if you intend to leave your leeks in the ground to overwinter, choose a hardy variety like 'Bleu Solaise,' 'Siegfried,' or 'Laura,' and mulch them after the ground freezes. 🌰

Harvest leeks in fall or early spring.

Hot Lettuce

Q I would like to grow lettuce but have heard it doesn't like warm weather. Are there any kinds I can try?

A Since lettuce often does poorly in mid-summer heat, it is usually grown as a cool-weather crop: sown in spring and grown through early summer, then sown in late summer and grown through early autumn. But there are many varieties specifically bred to withstand summer conditions, and most catalogs identify them as such.

For best results, try out a few different heat-tolerant selections. All are likely to fare better than spring and fall varieties do in the summertime, but some will probably do quite a bit better than others, depending on the specific conditions in your garden.

You might want to start with those tested by the Cornell Cooperative Extension in a trial of several heat-resistant varieties in summer gardens in Queens and Staten Island in New York City. The researchers found that the varieties 'Oak Leaf,' 'Slobolt,' 'Butter Crunch,' 'Kagran Summer,' and 'Parris Island' did not bolt, or go to seed, until very late in the season after producing plenty of edible leaves. They also had no serious disease or insect problems.

Some lettuces can take the heat.

"If you only have room for one, try 'Parris Island,' since it yielded the most for the space," advised Charles Mazza, the extension's New York program leader. "Each plant occupied about 10 inches of ground but had edible leaves that were 15 to 18 inches high."

A Mâche Farm at Home

Q I am trying to grow mâche, an expensive green sometimes called lamb's lettuce or corn salad. I have tried sowing it in the ground and also in Jiffy-7 peat pellets, with abysmal results. How do I do better?

A Mâche (*Valerianella locusta*) is delicious, delicate, and nutty. It is pretty, too, a multitiered rosette of small, rounded leaves. Yet it is not well known or widely grown, which may explain the expensive part.

Price notwithstanding, mâche is a weed. It once grew wild in European grainfields, and it will do the same in your garden if you let it go to seed. But first you have to get it to germinate. It dislikes disturbance and does best in cool weather, so plant seeds directly in fertile, well-drained garden soil, in full sun, as soon as the ground can be worked.

Keep the ground moist but not wet, and be patient. Mâche takes longer than most greens to sprout; 10 days to two weeks is not unusual. Thin the young plants so they stand 6 to 8 inches from center to center.

Repeat sowings until the weather heats up, then resume in autumn. Mâche is very winter hardy, and the last of the fall crop can be left to become first taste of spring.

LETTUCE LOVE

Want a dizzying variety of tastes, textures, and forms of beauty? Want 'em quickly and in a small space? Welcome to the wonderful world of lettuces. There are hundreds of varieties available, choices that meet every growing need. But they all break down into four main types:

- **Leaf lettuces.** These lettuces do not form tight heads. No matter how large they get, they are always loose collections of leaves, bound together at the base. Leaf lettuces are the quickest to mature and also the best for cut-and-come-again harvesting—just cut only the outer leaves and the plants will keep making more.
- **Butterheads.** The heads may be loose or tight, baseball to volleyball size, but they are always composed of leaves that are softer and—if well grown—sweeter than those of other types. Most butterheads are very heat sensitive and produce well only in spring and fall.
- **Crispheads.** As their name makes clear, crisphead lettuces form tight heads of very crisp, juicy leaves. This is the class to which iceberg belongs, but don't let that keep you from trying it. Homegrown crispheads are delicious; but they do take longer to grow than other types, and they are the pickiest about good growing conditions.
- **Cos.** These are the heading lettuces with the tall profile, also known as romaines. Although they eventually form tight heads, they can be grown as cut-and-come-again, and although they are both crisp and juicy, they are somewhat easier to grow than classic crispheads.

Making Mushrooms

Q **I love mushrooms but don't know much about how they grow. Any suggestions on how to raise them?**

A Mushrooms have no chlorophyll and do not use sunlight or the process of photosynthesis to make their own food. Most of these fleshy, spore-bearing fungi are saprophytes, which means they derive their food from dead or decaying matter; but some are parasites, which feed on living hosts.

Mushrooms appear outdoors naturally from spring to late autumn, but because some of the wild ones are highly poisonous, it is essential to learn from an expert before attempting to harvest them.

Fortunately, there are a few cultivated types, such as shiitake, that do not pose the danger of wild ones and that can be started indoors from kits sold in catalogs, at garden centers, and over the Internet.

Commercial button mushrooms require complete darkness, but most of the gourmet mushrooms grown indoors need some indirect light, said Paul Stamets, author of *Growing Gourmet and Medicinal Mushrooms.* When asked how much light is enough, Mr. Stamets answered, "If there's sufficient light to read the instructions on a mushroom kit, there's enough light to grow them."

The growing medium of choice is wood or straw, which must be kept evenly moist. Air temperatures typically range between 50° and 80°F. With a bit of luck, mushrooms from kits will appear in about two weeks.

Watching the process is a lot of fun, and most kits will yield a small crop, but growing your own is not a way to save money on mushrooms. If you plan to eat them often, you'll still be buying most of your supply. 🌶

Haute Nasturtium

Q **I know you can eat nasturtium flowers and leaves, but someone told me you can also eat the seeds. When do you pick them, and how are they prepared?**

A What you eat are the green seedpods, which are tastiest when they are young, and about the size of large peas. At that stage they are juicy and crisp, with a nose-tingling bite somewhere between horseradish and watercress. (As the pods swell they get less pungent, but they also get tough and dry.)

Just a few go a long way; nasturtium pods are a condiment, not a vegetable. To enjoy them raw, chop coarsely and sprinkle over cold sliced beef, or stir into potato salad. Cooking makes them milder, so if the hotness is disagreeable, try tossing about half a cup of pods into a four-portion-size pot of cooked rice or a summer stir-fry of zucchini, snap beans, and onions.

Pickled nasturtium pods are tasty in their own way. To make them, boil up a strong brine of six tablespoons pickling salt in a quart of water. Let it cool. Put the nasturtium pods in a glass, stainless, or china bowl; cover with the brine; and put a saucer or plate on top to hold them under the liquid.

Let the pods soak for three days at room temperature, then drain them and transfer to sterilized jars. Cover with white vinegar, add a bay leaf, and refrigerate. Let sit another week before using. They keep indefinitely. 🍃

Nasturtium's edible
leaves, flowers, and pods

Growing Okra

Q We like to try new vegetables and attempted to grow okra last year. It tasted great, but we didn't get much. A lot of the seeds never came up, and the plants we did have didn't make pods until late in the summer. Is this delicacy just too Southern to be grown in the North?

A Delicacy? That's a matter of opinion, but it certainly is beautiful to look at in the garden. Okra (*Abelmoschus esculentus*) is a close relative of hibiscus and is similarly decorative, with broad, more or less palmate foliage and large cream-colored flowers with red throats.

An okra harvest is a sometime thing in Northern climes. The seeds need warm soil, the plants need heat to grow well, and fruiting won't start until the days are less than 15 hours long.

Start seeds indoors in peat pots to get a jump on the season; they need very warm soil to germinate. And they have tough coats, so soak overnight or nick them with a file to encourage sprouting.

Don't be in a hurry to get the seedlings into the garden. Gradually acclimate them to outdoor life while they're still in their pots, and wait until it's warm both day and night to plant them—preferably in the sunniest, most sheltered, richly fertile spot you've got.

Give them a good dose of liquid seaweed or other transplant fertilizer at planting time, and fertilize lightly again when they start to flower. Don't give them too much nitrogen or you'll have leaves instead of fruit. Keep the pods picked, even if you don't intend to eat them, or the plant will consider its job done and stop flowering. Some okra varieties grow to 8 or 9 feet tall, but the best ones for the North are shorter: the widely available 'Clemson Spineless'; 'Blondy,' the most cold tolerant; and 'Burgundy,' which has red stems and maroon pods. 🌶

Okra, beautiful and delicious

SHEDDING SOME LIGHT ON ONIONS

Onion plants switch from making green tops to making fat bulbs in response to the length of daylight, so for best success it is important to choose varieties appropriate to your location: long-day types for Northern gardeners, short-day onions for those in the South.

- **Short-day onions.** Most of the sweet onions like Vidalia, Texas Sweet, and Maui fall into this class. They not only form bulbs in the shorter days of the South, they also prefer the low-sulfur soils more typical there than elsewhere. Short-day onions do not keep as well as long-day types; and although they seem sweeter, they aren't. What they are is mild. Long-day onions have more sugar, but it is masked by their greater pungency.
- **Long-day onions.** Most storage onions like Yellow Spanish and Stuttgarter belong here. They have denser flesh and a higher sulfur content than short-day onions, both qualities that help them keep longer. Walla Walla, the sweet onion from Washington State, is an exception that proves the rule. It is a long-day onion that grows large and remains mild, but it does not keep any better than Southern onions do. Long-day onions mellow over time, so they are usually sweetest right before they come to the end of their storage life.
- **Don't-care onions.** There is only one so far, a hybrid called 'Super Star.' It is day neutral (not sensitive to day length) and can be grown wherever it can be planted in spring, which is to say anywhere except the Deep South. 'Super Star' is a mild white onion, similar to the old standby 'White Sweet Spanish' but larger, milder, and earlier to mature.

Last-Minute Onions

Q We want to try planting onions this spring. Since we're beginners, should we stick to sets? They look easier than seeds, but they don't offer much variety compared with what we see in catalogs.

A The big thing to know about onions is that the switch from green growth to bulb building is brought about by day length, not by temperature or by the age of the plant. You need lots of big leaves at the magic moment to get large, sound onions.

Northern varieties head bulbward in the long days of late spring. If you sow seeds outdoors in March, they should grow to respectable size in time; but if it's later than that it would be smarter to plant the tiny onions called sets, or else prestarted plants.

Sets are convenient, but that's about it. Because they are grown the year before planting, they must be long-storage types, which tend to be more durable than delicious. If you do want to plant them, be sure to use small ones—sets larger than a half inch in diameter often split or send up flowers instead of making sound bulbs.

For sweeter, larger, more interesting onions, prestarted plants are the way to go. The choice among commercial ones is paltry compared with that for seeds, but it's a lot wider than for sets.

Whatever you choose, plant it early. Onions grow best in cool weather. 🍎

Onion-Spacing Quandary

Q The 100 onion plants I bought came with instructions to space them 6 inches apart, but if I do that there won't be room for them all. Can I plant them closer together and pull up the extras to eat as if they were scallions?

A You could, but you shouldn't—for two reasons. The first is that onions send their roots out, not down. If the seedlings are close together, their roots will soon intertwine and it will be impossible to pull up the green ones without hurting the main crop.

Even more important, onions must grow quickly in spring if they are to wind up as large, firm bulbs at harvest-time in mid summer. Competition slows them down, whether it comes from weeds or from short-lived siblings.

For best results, make a separate small bed for the extras. As long as the soil is fertile, they can be planted just an inch apart since you will be pulling and eating them before crowding becomes an issue. 🌰

Harvesting Onions

Q **Though the tops of our onions are still partly green, most of them have fallen over. The skins are brown in places. I say it's time to harvest. My husband says we should leave them until the tops are completely dry. Who's right?**

A Both of you. The onions will continue to gain weight—albeit not much—until all the leaves are down and brown, but leaving them that long is chancy. If the weather is hot and humid, they may fall prey to disease; if it's rainy, they may resprout. They'll also have a some-what shorter storage life.

Sweet onions like Walla Walla and Sweet Spanish can be left in place; they don't store well, anyway. But if you planted strong-flavored keepers like Stuttgarter (the most common onion sets), hoping to put them under the Christmas roast, lift them now. Spread them out in a warm, dry place, protected from strong sun, and let them cure until the necks are dry and tight, a week or two.

Harvest onions when their tops fall over.

At that point, you can braid the tops (braid in a length of twine to give the finished rope hanging power) or cut them off. Either way, store the onions where they will be cool and dry and get good air circulation. 🌰

Cut or braid tops—
your choice.

Walking Onions

Q I've heard about a "walking onion." Can you tell me what it is?

A Members of the onion family have been in the garden for so long that their origins are obscure. The onion dates at least to Alexander the Great, who came across them in Egypt in the fourth century B.C. and introduced them to Greece.

The walking, or Topset, onion (*Allium cepa* var. *viviparum*) has graceful, 3-foot-high stems topped with clusters of little bulbs called bulbils. Because of the weight of the bulbils, the stems invariably bend over and the tops root in the soil, inspiring the nickname walking onion as they move across the garden.

The bulbils are quite strong flavored, like yellow onions when first formed and almost as intense as garlic once they have matured. Seeds should be planted in spring; bulbils can go in almost any time (walking onion plants are hardy through zone 4). Locate the patch in full sun and expect to renew it every three or four years. 🌱

Scouring for Skirrets

Q I've heard about an unusual edible plant called skirret. Can you provide any information on finding and growing it?

A Skirret (*Sium sisarum*) is a perennial distantly related to parsnips. Its fleshy, creamy yellow roots have been grown as winter crops in Britain since at least the sixteenth century and are similar in taste to parsnips, though they are a lot skinnier.

Skirret does best in a rich, moist soil, preferably in full sun, although it will tolerate light shade. It can be started from seed or from root divisions, but seeds are more widely available. They are sold by several companies that specialize in unusual or heirloom vegetables. Plants grow about 2 feet tall and bear white flowers in summer. Like its cousin, skirret tastes sweeter after a frost. 🌱

Skirret
(*Sium sisarum*)

Table-Worthy Pea Flowers

Q We plan to experiment with edible flowers this year and thought sweet peas might be a good place to start. There are so many varieties available. Do some sweet peas have better flavor than others?

A Probably, but please don't do any taste testing. Although they are less dangerous than was formerly thought, sweet peas (*Lathyrus odoratus*) can cause paralysis and are still appropriately classed as poisonous. For edible pea flowers, grow edible peas (*Pisum sativum*), including English (or shelling) peas, snow peas, and snap peas such as 'Sugar Snap.'

Most of these have white flowers, but the snow pea variety 'Carouby de Maussane' has beautiful purple-maroon flowers that fade to blue-purple as they age. It's a vigorous vine that grows to 6 feet or more and produces a large crop of very large pods.

Bean flowers offer a similar effect: scarlet runners are a striking crimson that hummingbirds love, and purple-podded beans like 'Royalty,' 'Royal Burgundy,' and 'Trionfo Violetto' have lavender-to-purple flowers. 🍂

Harvesting Pea Vines

Q At a chic restaurant recently, I tasted tendrils from a pea vine. Can I harvest the tips from the plants in my garden and still have peas later on?

A Gardeners afflicted with woodchucks know it's possible to prune severely and still get a crop of peas. In fact, since pruning forces the vines to branch, you might even get more peas than ever. But pruning sets back growth and delays flowering, so there is some risk. If the weather turns hot before the vines reach full size, you could end up with a smaller crop or no crop at all.

To grow for tendrils, start by deciding which kind you want to end up with. Trendy American chefs favor what might be called pea scribbles, tangles of tightly curled tendrils that come from plants known as afila peas. Marketed under such cultivar names as 'Godiva' and 'Novella,' afilas make tendrils instead of leaflets.

Asian chefs prefer the vine tops of snow peas such as 'Oregon Sugar Pod' and 'Snowflake.' Though less dramatic looking than afila tendrils, snow pea vines are tastier and more tender. (The vines of regular garden peas are edible but tend to be fibrous and bland.)

Sow seeds as soon as possible, following the directions on the packet. When the plants are about 14 inches tall, cut off the top 6 inches—4 inches for afila types—making the cut right above a leaf node. The plants will branch where you made the cut and resume growing to the height normal for the variety. Depending on the weather, flowering will be about a week to 10 days later than on unpruned plants. 🌶

Sugar Snaps for Fall

Q **I want to plant a fall crop of 'Sugar Snap' peas. But how can I plant a cool-season crop in the hottest part of the summer? It doesn't sound as if it would work.**

A It doesn't always, but you can usually get a fall crop of peas by choosing the right variety, then keeping the seeds and seedlings cool when they are first starting out. In order to get snap peas, plan to plant one of the newer, shorter cultivars instead of the classic tall-vined 'Sugar Snap.' The short ones are more disease resistant (this is especially important in hot weather), and they mature more quickly.

None of them is as delicious as the original, but several are good enough to be welcome as season-extenders. These include 'Sugar Lace,' which has more tendrils and fewer leaves than 'Sugar Snap'; 'Sugar Bon,' which is very short and very quick to bear; and 'Sugar Sprint,' a new entrant on the shorter-and-easier list.

The trickiest part is providing cool soil and moderate temperatures in August. Be generous with the water, provide shade with a tent of screen, and be sure to add a cooling mulch of straw as soon as the seedlings are up. To find the right planting date, subtract the days to maturity on the packet from the date of the expected first frost, then go a week further back to allow for slower growth as the days shorten. 🌶

Potted Black-Eyed Peas

Q **Next spring, I want to try to grow black-eyed peas in large flowerpots or similar containers. Can you provide some tips?**

A Black-eyed peas, or cowpeas (*Vigna unguiculata*), are also known as field peas—and a field is the best place to grow them—you won't get many meals' worth if your back 40 is a flowerpot. On the other hand, cowpeas don't mind the heat and drought that often smite container-grown vegetables, especially those on terraces and roofs. In fact, a Southern-style summer of hot days and warm nights is almost essential for success.

Just one warning: drought resistance is owed in part to a long taproot with many side rootlets. Pots should be at least 16 inches tall and 10 inches wide at the base. Bigger would be even better.

Wait until the weather is in the 60s at night. Fill the pots with sandy soil or a light potting mix. Plant the seeds an inch deep, about 6 inches apart. Black-eyed peas can grow from 3½ to 6 feet long and are handsome enough to pass for ornamentals, with dark green leaves and small cream, yellow, or purple flowers. They aren't true vines because they can't climb, but they can't really stand up, either. Plan to tie them to a support or the suburbs will have nothing on you in the sprawl department.

Harvest the pods as soon as the peas swell, and the plants should continue to produce for at least a month.

Finally, prepare for frustration. Even if you grew only one plant of each variety, you wouldn't have room for them all. Black-eyes are the best-known version of *V. unguiculata*, but there are dozens of tasty choices in red, brown, black, cream, and speckled. ❧

Black-eyed peas
(*Vigna unguiculata*)

Growing Chiles

Q **Although we live in Minnesota, we cook a lot of Mexican food and use a great many dried chiles: pasilla, cascabel, etc. Can we plant the seeds from these instead of buying by the packet?**

A You can certainly plant them, but there are two caveats to keep in mind. First, if the original plants were hybrids—or were grown where they could cross with other peppers—the seeds probably won't come true (reproduce the characteristics of the parent plant).

Second, most commercially grown hot peppers come from the Southwest, and of course the growers choose cultivars that thrive in Southwestern conditions. So even if you do get plants that are just like the parents, they may not prosper in your more challenging climate. 🌶

Peppers Indoors

Q Our habañero pepper plants were productive all season, and we decided to winter them over in our home just north of New York City. The plants seem healthy and have lots of flowers, but only three peppers. The flowers drop off too easily. What do I do to get more peppers? Do I need to pollinate the flowers by hand?

A Your peppers should be able to pollinate themselves with no help from you, though you could compensate for absent breezes by shaking the plants gently every other day. It certainly wouldn't hurt. But it's not likely to help, either, because the problem is most likely poor fruiting conditions.

While a healthy pepper plant will keep right on making flowers for quite a while after it has been brought indoors, it's making them with energy stored up from its season in the sun. That's enough for flowers, but not for fruit, and the energy is bound to run out as the plant adjusts to indoor conditions.

Peppers are perennials that can indeed flower and fruit all year if conditions are right, but that's a big "if" unless you have a heated greenhouse.

Small-fruited peppers like habañeros do better indoors than the large-fruited bell types. Naturally small plants, like 'Firecracker,' a very hot-fruited ornamental that is well suited to pot culture, do even better.

Regardless of size, however, all of them grow and fruit best when they get lots and lots of sun, and day temperatures between 68° and 78°F. Nights can be a bit cooler, as long as they don't go below 60°. It sounds easy, but in most homes there's a built-in problem: peppers tend to drop their flowers if stressed by wide swings in temperature, and such wide swings are common near the sunny south windows that are most likely to provide enough light.

Indoor life presents other stresses that can cause flower drop. Peppers prefer consistent moisture, but potted plants often alternate between the desert of neglect and the overwatered swamp of remorse. Aphids are likely to be a problem as well—peppers are among their favorite plants.

What all this means is that most Northern gardeners are content to see their peppers simply live through the winter. Having a mature plant ready to put outside in early summer will give you a much longer season than if you had started from scratch, and it is reason enough to keep your habañeros growing, even without winter fruits. 🌶

Jalapeño Harvest

Q **I have a great crop of jalapeño peppers. What is the best way to dry them for winter?**

A Jalapeños are delicious fresh, as flavorful as they are hot, with thick, crisp flesh that is as juicy as a sweet bell pepper's. That texture, which is lost in drying, is a great part of their charm, and it makes jalapeños harder to air-dry than thin-walled peppers, such as cayennes and Thai hots. Traditionally jalapeños are preserved by canning.

It may be best to share your bounty while it is at its peak, but if you do go the drying route, use one of the inexpensive home food dehydrators sold at housewares stores. 🌶

The Elusive Piquillo

Q **I'd like to try to grow the piquillo peppers from Spain that have been showing up in so many hip restaurants, but I can't find seeds. I can't find fresh peppers, either—all my searches lead only to roasted peppers in cans. I know the chefs think these are fine, but I'd really like to grow my own. Can you help?**

A Piquillos are probably an old-fashioned seed saver's variety, unique to Spain and best adapted there, so finding them in the United States could be near impossible. Dr. Paul Bosland, a hot pepper expert and professor in the horticulture department at New Mexico State University in Las Cruces, said that in this country, "Hungarian paprika would be about as close as you can get."

"They're thick walled and sweet," he continued, "but the hotness does vary. Be sure you get one of the mild kinds." Wood-roast one of those, and you'll get something resembling the peppers that the chefs are using.

Resemblance is as far as you'd be likely to get even if you *did* find piquillo seeds, because growing produce is like selling real estate: location is everything. The flavors of vegetables and fruits are genetically determined, but how those flavors are expressed depends a lot on climate and soil. Yours may be excellent for pepper growing, but they won't be the same as those in Lodosa, Spain, the piquillos' home ground.

To get as close as possible, try growing peppers that are described as thick fleshed, sweet, and mildly piquant— Bull Nose would be another good choice. Roast and peel samples of everything, then have a taste test, using canned piquillos as your standard. 🌶

Homegrown Paprika

Q I would like to make my own fresh paprika, but I'm not sure which plant it comes from or how to grow it.

A Paprika is a type of red pepper, one of the many delightful condiments derived from varieties of the plant known botanically as *Capsicum annuum*.

Peppers are cousins of the potato, tomato, and eggplant in the nightshade family, Solanaceae. They are believed to have been first cultivated about 9,000 years ago in what is now Central America. Spanish explorers brought them to Europe around the end of the fifteenth century. From Spain the plants found their way to many other countries, Hungary among them, where (dried and pulverized) they became the culinary spice paprika.

Peppers are annuals or short-lived perennials that can grow to about 3 feet in height. Like tomatoes, they require good sun, rich, well-drained soil, and consistently warm temperatures to flower, set fruit, and ripen from green to red. Some varieties can produce red-ripe fruit in as little as 65 days after six-week-old seedlings are set out in the garden, but the Hungarian paprika types take 80 or 90 days, so you will need a long summer to get a good crop. 🌶

How Many Eyes to a Potato?

Q **How do I cut up seed potatoes for planting? I've heard each piece must contain at least two eyes, but it looks to me as though most of the eyes are bunched together at one end of the potato.**

A That part is called the seed end, and it does have the largest number of eyes. They are also the quickest ones to sprout. But there are eyes all over the potato, and since each planting chunk should weigh at least two ounces, you can usually gerrymander the minimum two eyes into each one. Don't worry about making uniform shapes; as long as the meat is well attached to the eyes, the sprouts will be able to draw nourishment from it. As a general rule, the larger the seed piece, the higher the yield, and it doesn't hurt to allow three eyes, not two, just to be on the safe side. You can leave even more if you want, but too many eyes, like too-close spacing, will result in lots and lots of little potatoes instead of the same weight in larger spuds. 🥔

Each potato chunk should have two or three eyes.

Potato-Beetle Wars

Q **Help! Colorado potato beetles are destroying my potato plants. I've been trying to go the organic route, handpicking them every day, but it's not working. If I don't do something soon, I'm afraid the plants will die.**

A *Leptinotarsa decemlineata,* to give the miserable creature its proper name, is a challenge to control—organically or otherwise—and you'll probably never completely get rid of them if you live in an area where they are well established. But don't panic; potato plants can take a lot of defoliation and still produce a decent crop. And if you take action now, attacking the beetles on several fronts, you can keep populations small enough to prevent major problems in the future.

Start by applying a dose of the organic gardener's friend, Bt (*Bacillus thuringiensis* var. *san diego* or *B.t.* var. *tenebrionis* are the best strains to use). Small larvae die after they eat it—but only the small ones. You're still stuck with the larger larvae and adults. Those can be killed with rotenone, a strong but short-lived botanical poison favored by organic gardeners when they must take extreme measures. Neem extract (Azadirachtin), a combination toxin and repellent, is also on the organic O.K. list. Well-stocked garden centers and farm supply stores will usually have these products.

It's also wise to keep handpicking, which will be especially useful if it includes crushing the yellow eggs hiding under the leaves. Expect to find a lot of them, and look harder if you don't; a single female can have 10,000 descendants by the end of summer.

Hand-picking helps, but should be part of a multi-front attack.

To add insult to infestation, Colorado potato beetles can live a full two years. But they won't stay around where there's nothing to eat, so the final—or first—line of defense is late planting. If they don't find any potato, eggplant, or nicotiana leaves when they emerge from the ground in spring, they'll leave. More will appear, but not so many. 🌶

Seeking Tasty Pumpkin Seeds

Q We have been roasting and eating the seeds from the pumpkin we used for our Jack-o'-lantern this Halloween, but they are not as large and tasty as the pumpkin seeds (pepitas) that I've bought as snacks. Are they the same thing?

A Yes and no. The plant species, *Cucurbita pepo*, is the same, but pumpkins that will produce seeds for eating and pumpkins that will be good for making lanterns each come from specialized varieties. The lanterns have been bred for their looks, while edible-seed types have been bred for large seed size, high oil content, and seed hulls that are easy to remove by machine.

To grow your own, plant a variety like 'Lady Godiva,' called the naked-seeded pumpkin because the seed hulls are so thin you don't have to remove them. (The flesh, like the flesh of jack-o'-lanterns, is worthless: stringy and bland.) 🌶

Children's Seeds

Q I would like to introduce my eight-year-old to gardening using some easily grown vegetable. What do you suggest?

A It depends on how fussy an eater the child is, but if the goal is to get a crop before the attention span wanders, the easiest vegetable to grow from seed is the radish (*Raphanus sativus*), and it is truly magical to see it sprout into being. The numerous radish varieties also have tempting names like 'Comet,' 'Cherry Belle,' and 'White Icicle,' and colors that vary from white to scarlet, red, and yellow. Sow the seeds about half an inch deep in rich, somewhat sandy loam, spaced about 6 inches apart. Keep the soil evenly moist, watering with a fine spray whenever necessary. Germination should occur within five days, and plants should be ready to harvest (and eat) in about a month.

Radishes grow best in cool weather; be sure to start seeds in early spring so they can mature before summer's heat. They must grow quickly to taste good, and they are favorite prey for a number of bugs, so to avoid disappointment—and teach an important lesson about hedging your garden bets—it's a wise idea to plant at least two crops.

Bush beans are a good second choice. They take longer than radishes (55 days or more), but they're just as easy to plant and grow; they will do well from late spring all through the summer; you can eat them right off of the plant; and they're likely to taste pretty good even if growing conditions are less than ideal. 🌶

A Simple Answer

Q I love the idea of making pies from homegrown fruit, but don't love the idea of all the work home fruit growing seems to entail. What is the very easiest choice for someone who can't (won't!) spend a lot of time or money?

A Rhubarb. 🍂

Right Diet for Rhubarb

Q Three years ago I transplanted three rhubarb plants. I smother them with manure early in spring, during the summer, and at the end of the summer. Yet all I get are thin stalks, although they came from a plant that gave my friends wide stalks. What to do?

A It sounds as if you might be smothering them more than they can stand. Rhubarb is a heavy feeder, it's true, and composted manure is a fine fertilizer, especially if you are using what country folk call hen dressing. But too much of a good thing is still too much; one generous application each year should be enough.

Heap it on in late fall after the plants have gone fully dormant, or in early spring before they start active growth. Give them a side dressing of compost in mid spring and a small amount of balanced commercial fertilizer—or more composted manure—when you are almost done harvesting. Be sure to mulch heavily all through the growing season. Rhubarb does best when its roots stay cool and get plenty of moisture.

Thin stalks may simply mean that the plants are young and not yet well established, but they can also indicate overcrowding. Rhubarb plants should be at least 3 feet apart in all directions.

Shade might also be the culprit. Although rhubarb will survive low-light conditions, it must be grown in full sun to produce thick, flavorful stalks. 🍂

A Bonus Crop

Q We planted scarlet runner beans to attract hummingbirds. Now they're making beans. Can these be eaten? They look almost like regular beans, but not quite.

A Scarlet runners, *Phaseolus coccineus,* are close relatives of regular beans (*P. vulgaris*) and, like them are edible at every stage from flower to dried seed. The rough pods are tastiest and least fibrous when comparatively small, about 6 inches long and still completely flat. The beans inside have the best flavor when very large, about an inch wide, but not yet starting to dry out. At this stage they will have leathery, slightly bitter purple-splotched pink skin. Peel it away to reveal the bright green beans underneath; steam or stir-fry them only long enough to heat through, and get ready for a treat. 🍎

Spinach by Another Name

Q This year I tried growing strawberry spinach. The seeds sprouted quickly in my compost, but not one plant ever got larger than an inch and a half. Will they survive the winter cold and grow next summer? Would it be a good idea to let a few winter over with my houseplants? Is compost too "sour" for this species?

A It's difficult to imagine what could have befallen your plants. Strawberry spinach, *Chenopodium capitatum,* also known as strawberry blite, should be 18 to 24 inches tall at maturity, and though it may have been stunted by intense heat or excessive shade, it's a weed at heart. Keeping it from taking over is more likely to be an issue than getting it to grow.

C. capitatum is closely related to Good King Henry (*C. bonus-henricus*) and to lamb's quarters (*C. album*), one of the most common weeds of cultivated ground. All do best in the mild weather of late spring and early summer, and will grow lush if the soil is rich. As long as you harvest them when they are young, tender, and mild, all three are delicious as cooked greens; but only strawberry blite, aka beet-berry, also produces the small, bright red fruits that give it its common names. Although they are edible, that's about all that can be said for them; the kindest noncommercial descriptions feature adjectives like bland and insipid.

Strawberry blite is an annual. It will not winter over, indoors or out, so don't bother trying to save any of this year's reluctant crop. Next year, sow it where it is to grow, and if you plant it in compost, let the compost be a thin layer on top of good garden soil. If this year's compost did cause problems, it was not because it was sour but simply because compost, by itself, is not a good long-term home for plants. Weeds do grow in it, as anyone with a neglected compost pile will testify, but even weeds are happier with their feet in the dirt. 🍎

A Greener Spring

Q **I have some spinach seeds saved and would like to know if I can plant them in the fall. If not, will they be all right next spring?**

A There's a certain sadness about autumn cleanup and shutting down the garden. But one of the things to lighten a gardener's heart is to seed some cold-tolerant varieties of spinach in the fall and let the young plants overwinter. By giving them a head start, you ensure that you will be eating fresh spinach salad next spring while your friends are still waiting for their seeds to germinate. And even better, during the long winter you can occasionally think about it quietly waiting there, and let a faint smile play across your lips.

'Fall Green,' 'Vienna,' and 'Winter Bloomsdale' are varieties recommended for overwintering. Planting them up to the second week of October gives them a chance to develop a few leaves and roots before winter. They don't need to be mulched: the leaves will get ratty through the winter, but the root system will be fine. When spring arrives, new leaves will sprout from the established root system.

If your saved seeds are not one of the overwintering types, you can plant them next spring, but don't hold on to them any longer than that. Theoretically, spinach seeds remain viable for three years if stored cool and dry, but germination rates often start falling by the second year. 🍎

Curbing Squash Vines

Q Help! Winter squash vines are taking over my garden. I thought I had given them plenty of room, but they've spread all over and are smothering the rest of my vegetables. I know you can prune tomato plants. Is it O.K. to cut back squash? If so, where should I make the cuts?

A It's almost impossible to kill healthy squash vines once they get going. But to be sure, we took your question to Rob Johnston, the owner of Johnny's Selected Seeds in Albion, Maine, and a specialist in winter squash.

"A typical squash plant will make 20 pounds or so of squash, and that's all you want to ask of it," he said. "So once the plant sets four or five fruits, you can prune it back." On each runner, leave a couple of leaf nodes past the last fruit you want to keep, then pinch off the growing tip at the next node. If the vine is huge, you may have to cut off quite a bit instead of just pinching. As long as you don't trample the leaves or disturb the main root, you won't hurt the plant or the squash left on it.

"You can also just pick up a vine that's in the way and move it," he said, "even one that has set roots at the nodes. Just loosen the roots carefully, and expect the plant to look a bit wilted for a few days. It will recover." New placement may mean the leaves are no longer upright. Don't fret: they'll turn themselves around.

And next year, if your garden's a small one, consider a bush squash such as 'Table Ace' or 'Burpee's Butterbush.' Because they have far fewer leaves per fruit, they're less tasty than the vining types, but they're very well behaved. 🌱

SQUASH VINE TIPS

In Southeast Asia, squash vine tips are considered a delicacy. Sautéed in a bit of oil with garlic and ginger, they can be very tasty.

But they can also be quite bitter, because squash contain cucurbitacin, the compound that makes cucumbers bitter. The quantity of cucurbitacin will depend on growing conditions as well as the type of squash. To be on the safe side, cook up a couple of leaves and taste them before deciding on squash vines for dinner.

Squash Before the Frost

Q **Our winter squash plants got off to a slow start this year, and I'm afraid the fruits will not mature before frost. Is there any way we can speed them up? Would fertilizer help?**

A You know the party is almost over, but the squash don't. They'll just keep making more vines and baby fruits unless you shout "Last call!" To force the plants to concentrate on ripening what's there instead of growing more, start by clipping off the tips of all vines and branches. Allow each plant a maximum of five large, good-looking fruits and remove the others.

There's no point in fertilizing now, but do have coverings handy. The first frosts are often light. If you can bring the vines through them, you can often get a couple of weeks' additional growing time. 🌱

Saving Sunflower Seeds

Q **I have a sunflower that I have guarded from the deer all season, and I would like to save the seeds from it. How would I do this, and how do I store them over the winter?**

A Forget the deer—it's time to start guarding your sunflower from the birds.

To keep seeds for growing or eating, you have to wait until they are mature. Birds will start lining up just before the petals fall, but the seeds won't be mature until the bracts (the petal-like leaves surrounding the flower) turn brown, and the back of the head turns lime yellow. Depending on the size and thickness of the head, this may follow the petals' falling by three or four weeks. During this time, you can protect the seeds by covering the head with a paper bag. It is a choice between having a peculiar-looking garden and not having sunflower seeds.

Cut the mature heads off, and hang them in a dry spot with good air circulation. Upside down or right side up doesn't matter, but it takes at least two

Sunflower
(*Helianthus annuus*)

weeks for the seeds to dry. They are ready when they come out of the head with a gentle rub. Store at room temperature in a sealed glass jar with a commercial desiccant, because sunflower seeds are susceptible to mold in humid climates.

Seeds from hybrids may not grow up true to their parent. Open-pollinated types will be chips off the old block, as long as there are no other varieties close by to cross with them. ✿

Tired of Green Tomatoes

Q **I live two hours north of Boston, and there are some seasons I feel like my tomatoes don't even have a chance to ripen. I'm tired of recipes for green tomatoes. Can you suggest the easiest and most efficient ways to extend the season?**

A There are two main strategies. One is to plant early varieties, some of which taste pretty good, although none are as tasty as the best of the late types. In your area, 'Stupice,' 'Ruby Cluster,' and 'First Lady' are good choices as of this writing, but be sure to keep checking catalogs and experimenting. You are not alone; breeders continue to work on this problem, and something better may well appear a few years down the road.

It's tempting to try starting the plants early, moving them into ever-larger pots as you wait for warm weather to come. This works fine, but only if you have a greenhouse or a big bank of grow lights. Tomato plants that grow for more than 6 to 8 weeks without sufficient light will be very weak. They'll suffer transplant shock when you set them out and end up no farther along than smaller plants that didn't have to struggle so hard to get going.

So assuming you *don't* have a greenhouse in which to start plants extra early, the next best season stretcher is a clear covering that will create a mini greenhouse right in the garden. Individual coverings such as paper Hotkaps, plastic milk jugs, and glass bells work well in small gardens, but they take a lot of fiddling. If you have a large planting, it's easier and more economical to use hoop-supported tunnels of clear plastic or spunbond polyester. ✿

THE LYING-DOWN TOMATO PLANT TRICK

To help tomato seedlings form the largest and sturdiest plants, bury the youngsters on their sides (removing lower leaves before burying) in trenches as deep as you can make them and still have the the top third of the plant emerge above ground. Roots will form all along the buried stem, and they'll get off to a faster start because they will all be starting in the warmer ground near the surface.

Burying the plants this way means the tops will stick out at an odd angle at first, but in only a day or two they will bend back so they're growing straight up. In two weeks or less the plants should be as tall as they were before, and fruiting won't be delayed at all.

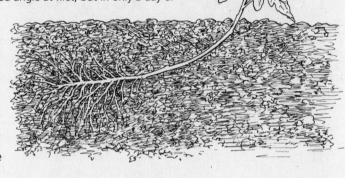

Cherry Tomatoes Rampant

Q My cherry tomato plants grew well all summer and now are so large they are threatening to take over the garden. I love the tomatoes, but I don't want the vines to smother my late crops that are just coming on. Is there a way to prune them?

A The original wild tomatoes were small fruits growing on rampant vines, and most of their cherry-size descendants are similarly exuberant. Many of them are also, like their wild relatives, comparatively blight resistant. While full-size tomatoes are usually slowed down by disease well before they die from frost, cherries are likely to keep on going well into fall.

Some varieties are bred to stay dwarf, but yours are clearly the indeterminate, endlessly growing kind. Their numerous secondary stems, which could have been restricted to two or three in early summer, are probably so hunky by now that they're almost the size of the main stems themselves, and the even more numerous tertiary stems are no doubt quite substantial as well.

Now that it is almost September, pruning would be more work than it's worth, but you could build a makeshift arbor and get them going farther up before they start going sideways, which should help keep them from crowding the neighbors. If there's a tree handy, you can run twine from the lower branches and tie the vines onto it.

Next year, consider growing your cherry tomatoes on a fence or other support system that permits early training. Remove most of the suckers (secondary stems that grow out of the leaf nodes). And don't be surprised when hugeness threatens at the end of the season anyway. Since none of the dwarf sorts are anywhere near as tasty as the best long-vined ones, think of it as the price you have to pay for flavor. 🍅

Blossom-End Rot

Q **Can you tell me what's causing the dark rotting spots on the bottom of the tomato fruit on my terrace?**

A It sounds as if you have a classic case of blossom-end rot, which can take a toll not only on tomatoes, but also on watermelons, peppers, and squash. Blossom-end rot is caused by a lack of calcium. This might be the result of a soil deficiency, but it's more likely that the plant is having trouble taking up the calcium that's already there. This difficulty is common when soil moisture is inconsistent. Keep the soil evenly moist by watering regularly and using a mulch of straw or bark. 🍅

Troubled Tomatoes

Q **Some leaves are curling inward on the tomatoes I'm growing in raised beds. Other than that, they seem fine. What should I do about it?**

A Your tomatoes are probably curling up in self-defense. Faced with uneven watering, from dry spells or busy gardeners who just wave a hose around instead of adequately watering every plant, tomatoes will curl their leaves to conserve water. Exposing less leaf surface to the sun reduces the amount of moisture lost through transpiration.

Temperatures between 85° and 90°F seem to trigger this genetic response, and it usually affects the oldest leaves first. Plum or paste tomatoes are especially prone to leaf curling. Once the problem is eliminated, usually when panic induces the gardener to find the time to water thoroughly and regularly, the leaves uncurl. 🥕

Too Hot to Work

Q My tomato plants look terrific, seem to be healthy, and have produced many flowers, but there have been only a few tomatoes even though the weather is hot and sunny. I water and fertilize, but most of the flowers just drop off. Am I going to get any more tomatoes this year?

A They are just taking a heat break and will start working again once it cools off a bit. Pollen is very sensitive to heat, and it changes chemically if the temperature reaches 95°F or more. For tomatoes, peppers, eggplants, pumpkins, cucumbers, and squash, the change is deadly. The pollen no longer fertilizes the flowers, and they drop off, victims of unrequited love.

Since you can't prevent the heat, apply Wall Street's advice to your vegetable portfolio—diversify and spread your risk. Choose varieties with different maturation times, and stagger the planting so that your garden is producing early, mid summer, and late crops. 🥕

Tomato Heartbreak

Q Each summer, I plant a dozen different tomatoes in my garden in northern New Jersey. They did fine the first few years, but recently, one or two plants per year (differing varieties) have developed the same problem. They set fruit; then the leaves get dark spots and turn yellow. By late summer the plants are dead. This year, only one plant has been spared, yet that plant is going great guns. What on earth is going on? I rotate planting areas on a three-year cycle, and have been watering through the drought.

A There are several diseases that might be causing your problems. But from the sound of things, it seems most likely that you have been conducting field trials, discovering which tomatoes are most vulnerable to early blight, caused by the fungus *Alternaria solani.* It is endemic to the Northeast, mid-Atlantic, and Midwest, striking hardest in warm, humid years.

The spores live in the soil and on plant debris, so rotation planting and rigorous cleanup help keep this blight at bay. But since they also live elsewhere and travel easily, you can't completely get rid of them.

Alternaria prefers stressed, unhealthy plants, so the first step in fighting it is to plant vigorous seedlings. Space them far apart for good air circulation, in fertile, well-watered ground. Mulch as soon as you plant, so rain can't splash spores from the ground onto the lower leaves. (Use landscape fabric if the soil is still cool, and switch to straw when the weather warms.)

Water only at ground level—wet leaves not only spread early blight, but also succumb to it more quickly. If you use a fungicide, be sure it is labeled for alternaria, and apply it preventively early in the season. Once the blight has taken hold, there is no cure.

Plants with small fruits (cherry tomatoes) are somewhat resistant, and late varieties with large vines come through better than early, short ones. 🍃

Barren Tomatoes

Q **My tomato plants seem to be growing well, but they just won't flower and fruit. Why?**

A When healthy, vigorous tomato plants won't flower, the problem is usually that they've absorbed too much nitrogen, most often thanks to a chemical fertilizer with a high first number (10-10-10, for instance).

If too much nitrogen is the problem, all you can do is wait until they use it up, or until plentiful rains wash away the unused portion. Next year, if they need fertilizing, use a mixture formulated to encourage fruiting, either composted manure enhanced with rock phosphate and granite dust, or a commercial formulation labeled 5-10-10.

Shade is the other culprit. Tomatoes will not set flowers if they receive less than six hours of sunlight each day, and the tomatoes won't be very tasty unless they get at least eight. 🍅

When Freezing Is Good for Tomatoes

Q I can tell that I'm going to have a huge crop of tomatoes this year and wondered if you had any thoughts on how I might keep them for use later. I don't do canning.

A It's really easy to preserve your homegrown tomatoes for use through autumn and winter. All you need is a freezer. Just rinse the tomatoes, pat them dry, then set them in single layers on flat pans such as cookie sheets (brownie pans if you have a small freezer).

As soon as they are frozen solid, transfer them to heavy-duty freezer bags. Seal well, label clearly, and return to the freezer.

Stored this way, tomatoes are superb additions to hot winter stews, soups, gravies, and sauces. And there's no need to defrost—just add them directly to a simmering pot. Their fresh flavor will brighten any cooked dish. Unfortunately, frozen tomatoes collapse when they thaw, so they can't be used when you need slices, chunks, or other discrete pieces. 🍅

Seeking 'Big Girl' Tomatoes

Q When we started to garden 30 years ago, we experimented with many varieties of tomatoes. It didn't take long to settle on 'Big Girl'; we thought it stood up to bugs and disease better than others, and we loved the flavor. After a time we found it hard to find seedlings, and now it is almost impossible to get them. Why?

A Take a stroll through the supermarket, looking at how many products say New! and you'll have a good part of your answer. W. Atlee Burpee & Company introduced 'Big

STYLISH PLANT SUPPORTS

A simple row of poles with netting strung between them is the little black dress of plant support, always successful, always appropriate, but it is by no means the only option when it comes to holding up crops like tomatoes, squash, melons, beans, and peas.

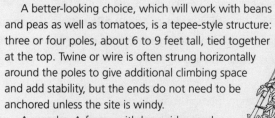

Cage

One of the simplest options, often used for tomato plants, is a cage made of heavy fencing or concrete-reinforcing wire—the kind with widely spaced holes, not the mesh. It should be 2 or 3 feet in diameter and 4½ to 5 feet high, and it should be secured by three stakes driven at least 10 inches into the ground. (The conical wire tomato supports so widely sold in garden centers are too flimsy to work with anything except short-vined, determinate tomatoes, which seldom need any support at all.)

A better-looking choice, which will work with beans and peas as well as tomatoes, is a tepee-style structure: three or four poles, about 6 to 9 feet tall, tied together at the top. Twine or wire is often strung horizontally around the poles to give additional climbing space and add stability, but the ends do not need to be anchored unless the site is windy.

Tepee

A wooden A-frame with long sides made of wood lattice, heavy twine, or wire is best for melon and squash vines. Their heavy fruits can pull down the plants unless each is individually supported, so you need a strong structure to tie the supports to. Old stockings are a favorite support material. Being transparent and porous, they let light and water through, and, being stretchy, they conform to the shape of the fruit (which means it's less likely to fall off).

A-frame

Girl' in 1976, and although it continues to offer that variety, it also continues to keep introducing other tomatoes.

"'Early Girl' has taken over the girl spot," said David Seitz, the director of research and product development for Burpee. He pointed out that commercial growers of seedlings can grow only so many, and that 'Big Girl' just got squeezed out by newer introductions. It may also be feeling the pinch from the other direction. As heirloom varieties become more and more popular, they too are starting to take up space on nurseries' seedling shelves.

To cover your bets, ask your local garden centers about their tomato plans well before planting time. Then, if you have to, you can start your own plants from seed or shop around for mail-order seedlings. 🍅

What's Stealing the Tomatoes?

Q Some animal—we suspect a skunk—ruined a lot of our tomatoes, in one case eating all the way around the middle while rolling the tomato at least 100 feet from the garden. It also took bites out of many tomatoes. If it's not a skunk, what is it and what can we do?

A Raccoons are adept at carrying things and are more partial to takeout than skunks, so if the fruit keeps traveling a raccoon could be the culprit. But it could be opossums, and you might also keep an eye out for porcupines. Though porcupines mostly eat the new growth of trees and are supposed to be indifferent to garden produce, they've occasionally been caught red-toothed in the tomato patch.

Unfortunately, none of these unwanted guests is easy to banish. They rapidly grow used to lights, radios, and any dogs that can't get at them. Predator (or human) urine, promoted as a repellent, is effective only sporadically.

Four feet of wire mesh fence in a tight weave (8 inches buried, the rest above ground) will probably work against skunks, porcupines, and opossums. Raccoons are more of a challenge: add two strands of electric wire to that fence. Or just wait a while. Before long the corn will be ripe and they'll concentrate on that. 🍅

Tough Tomatoes

Q **Last year I attempted to grow tomato plants (six different varieties, including heirlooms) on my twelfth-floor balcony, facing south-southwest. The skin of all the varieties was very thick. Why would this happen? Is there anything I can do differently this year to prevent this?**

A Unfortunately, most fruiting vegetables need a lot of leaf in proportion to fruit in order to develop good flavor, and that means big plants. But big plants (or would-be big plants) grown in pots usually experience considerable stress: lack of root room, overheated soil, and inconsistent moisture, to name three common problems. Stress on the plants means less fruit and poorer quality.

In theory, stress shouldn't affect skin thickness; that's determined by genetics, not growing conditions. But it might well have made the fruit less juicy, and that in turn could lead to the perception of thick skin.

Unfortunately, while you can reduce stress by planting varieties of tomatoes, squashes, and eggplants that have been bred for container growing, you can't solve the quality problem this way. The fruits of these miniaturized versions are almost always as reduced in flavor as the plants are in size.

But don't despair. If you have room for a really big pot—a half whisky barrel, for example—you can get garden-quality taste by growing cherry tomatoes. The most flavorful types, like 'Sweet 100' and 'Sun Gold,' want to make very large plants, but because they aren't trying to make large fruits as well, they aren't as vulnerable to stress as are their full-size cousins.

For best results, don't plant more than two plants per half barrel. Keep them well watered, and feed every six weeks or so with a low-nitrogen fertilizer. If well fed and consistently watered, they will tolerate crowded roots and keep producing well into the fall. Expect to do some pruning, and be sure to provide a tepee of 6-foot stakes or other tall, strong support. 🍃

The tastiest big tomatoes come from big plants.

Cracked Tomatoes

Q I had so many tomatoes that cracked this year. By mid summer many of them had long cracks coming down from the stem end, and later in the season others had cracks going in the other direction, around the stem. What causes that?

A Both radial cracking (from the stem downward) and concentric cracking (around the stem in interrupted circles) are physiological problems caused when the plants take up too much water too quickly. As tomatoes begin turning red, their skin becomes less flexible. Uneven watering or rain following a dry period encourages the plants to take up too much water, cracking the fruit in a radial direction. Later in the season, cool nights combine with uneven moisture to cause concentric cracking.

The smallest and largest (cherry tomatoes and those over 3 inches in diameter) are most susceptible, as are particular varieties, especially older ones. But there are crack-resistant varieties, including 'Ruby Pearl' (a cherry tomato), 'Celebrity,' and any of the Mountain series, such as 'Mountain Delight,' 'Mountain Fresh,' and 'Mountain Gold.'

GROW ANOTHER ROW

Bursting with broccoli? Surfeited with squash? There's no such thing if you see your extra produce as a part of Plant a Row for the Hungry. This program, started in 1995 by the Garden Writers Association, encourages volunteers to grow and donate fresh produce for soup kitchens, homeless shelters, and other neighborhood food programs. While a single bag of cucumbers, peas, or tomatoes may not look like much, the yield can be considerable when multiplied. As of 2002 the program had marshaled more than 1.3 million pounds of homegrown vegetables and fruits, and it still continues to grow.

Of course, you don't have to join anything to share your harvest; just get in touch with the nearest food pantry and find out what they can use. But if you want to be an official part of this group of committed gardeners, contact the Plant a Row campaign, 10210 Leatherleaf Court, Manassas, VA 20111; (703) 257-1032; *www.gwaa.org/par.*

Yellow Tomato Leaves

Q I have been planting tomatoes for seven years. Every year they grow well and yield a nice output of fruit. Then around August 1 the leaves turn yellow, starting at the bottom and moving up the plants, which die in a few weeks. I have been told that the cause is the acidity of the soil. I have applied lime in substantial quantities, but this year the same thing happened.

A Northeastern soils are usually on the acid side, and adding lime to prevent them from becoming *too* acidic is an old farming tradition. But adding large amounts of lime—or any other mineral—without knowing whether you really need it can do more harm than good.

And it certainly won't do anything to prevent the problem at hand, because you are describing a classic case of fungal infection, most likely fusarium wilt, though it might be early blight (*Alternaria solani*).

The spores of these diseases lurk in the ground for years and cannot be removed. To combat them, there are three things you can do:

1. **Move the tomatoes.** Plant next year's crop in new ground (fusarium infects a wide variety of garden plants, so just moving the tomatoes elsewhere in the same garden may not be sufficient protection).
2. **Make a mulch barrier** between the soil and the plants, so disease spores can't splash up onto the leaves. When the soil is still cool, use a thin layer of dark weed barrier. After the soil warms, add a thick layer of straw.
3. **Plant resistant varieties.** They will be identified with initials after their names, with each initial standing for a disease: V is for verticillium wilt; F, for fusarium.

Voraciously Green

Q Late this summer I noticed that one of my tomato plants seemed to be drooping. I was horrified to find a 5-inch-long green tomato hornworm. I picked it off and disposed of it. Where did it come from? Can I prevent a recurrence? It was so big I was surprised I hadn't noticed it before. I make sure not to plant tomatoes where they have been planted before for at least three years.

A Tomato hornworm doesn't really care where you plant your tomatoes as long as you plant enough. Size alone should convince you that tomato hornworms are always hungry and can do significant damage.

The common name for this serious pest is shared by the larvae of several large moths. The moths lay their eggs on tomatoes, potatoes, and other members of the tobacco family.

The egg hatches, the larva eats (and eats) and eventually drops to the ground. It buries itself and pupates over the winter, emerging as a moth the following year. It notices that you've moved the tomatoes, but since it can fly, it doesn't mind.

Careful inspection followed by handpicking is the best tactic. The caterpillar blends in quite well, but by the time it has grown to 5 or 6 inches long, hiding becomes more problematic. Especially since there is less tomato plant to hide behind. 🍃

Tomato hornworm

Indoor Tomatoes

Q I have grown tomatoes successfully in pots, but they have always been outside. This summer, we put seedlings in my daughter's very sunny southern-exposure window shelf, but inside. The plants grew and flowered but bore no fruit. Why?

A Most likely they are suffering primarily from unre- quited love. While tomato flowers are complete, having both male and female parts, the pollen still has to get from one place to another within the flower. Outside, a visiting bee or a light breeze can move the pollen, but indoors it may not happen unless you give them a gentle morning shake when the flowers are fully open, to help transfer the pollen.

Your bright southern exposure is a double problem. While it still doesn't supply enough light for a plant to make the food necessary for a major production like a crop of tomatoes, it does heat up the space between window and plant. Tomato pollen is killed by temperatures above 95°F, so even if the pollen found its way, it might not matter. Only the whiteflies will find the environment to their satisfaction.

Take the plants outside—who knows, there may be enough summer left to get a few tomatoes. And next year, leave them outdoors all season, where they belong. 🍅

Keep Diseased Tomatoes Out of the Compost

Q By the time the frost killed them, our tomato plants were almost dead from some kind of blight. Is it O.K. to put them in the compost?

A Gardening doesn't have many rigid rules, but "Keep sick stuff out of the compost" is one of them. Early blight, late blight, and anthracnose, to name just three of the most common tomato miseries, are all fungus diseases that winter over on bits of infected plant debris. Fusarium wilt, a fourth contender in the gardeners' nemesis sweepstakes, doesn't even need debris to hang around from year to year.

The tiny spores of these destroyers are likely to be with you always. You can't completely eradicate them, but you can minimize their presence by burning affected foliage or sending it to the landfill. Next year, be sure to mulch under the young plants to keep fungus spores from splashing up from the soil to the lower leaves. 🍅

Watermelon Magic

Q How are seedless watermelons propagated if there are no seeds from the fruit?

A We get seedless watermelons from seeds created by plant breeders, working in ways Mother Nature never dreamed of (necessary when you are making plants she would not have any use for).

First, they develop a special variety to be the female seed parents by treating baby watermelon plants with colchicine, a chemical derived from autumn crocuses. If it is applied just right, it stops chromosome division. The seedling becomes a tetraploid, with four sets of chromosomes, not the usual two. The tetraploid plants must then multiply in order to build up breeding stock.

In the next step, the tetraploid females are bred to normal (diploid) males. Though the males are conventional watermelons, with two sets of chromosomes each, they, too, come from stock developed for breeding.

The marriage of diploid and tetraploid produces watermelons that contain the seeds for seedless watermelons. These seeds are triploid: three pairs of chromosomes. But three pairs can't be evenly divided for baby-making purposes, so plants grown from triploid seeds are sterile. Their male flowers can't pollinate anything, and females can't produce seeds.

They can't produce watermelons, either, unless they are pollinated. So some old-fashioned diploid watermelons are planted in every field of the seedless ones. Diploid male flowers are the fathers of the seedless children.

Creating seedless watermelons is laborious and time consuming. Just developing a tetraploid line can take as long as 10 years. Which is about what it would take to give all the details. A fuller explanation is available online at *http://cuke.hort.ncsu.edu.* Click on watermelons, then on breeding.

One final note: Seedless watermelons do have seeds, or at least the partial seeds called initials. They are soft and unobtrusive because they are sterile, but they are there. 🍎

Seedless watermelon (with partial seeds called initials)

Who's There? Ripe Watermelons

Q I am growing a rather small crop of baby watermelons and don't want any wasted by harvesting them too early. Can I tell when they are ripe by knocking on them?

A Only if you have a very good ear. A dull, hollow sound means dense flesh and helps indicate ripeness. But a ringing hollow sound means "not ripe yet"; and unless you spend a lot of time listening to melons, the difference may not be obvious.

For better results, check the following signs:

1. **The vine tendrils** nearest the stem should be dead or nearly so, brown and dry.
2. **The spot** where the melon rests on the ground should be yellow, not white.
3. **The skin** should be dull, not shiny, and it should be tough—you might be able to barely dent it with a fingernail, but it should not cut this way easily. 🍐

I YAM WHAT I YAM

When you eat a tuber that's sweet, white, and fluffy, like Irish potatoes with sugar added, or one that tastes similar but is pale gold, chances are you know perfectly well that these are types of sweet potato, *Ipomoea batatas*.

But what do you call it when the tuber is sweet, moist, and a deep, rich orange? The correct answer is also sweet potato, though nine out of ten would say yam.

'Tain't so. True yams belong to several species in the genus *Dioscorea*, including the Southeast Asian *D. alata*, known as the greater yam or water yam; *D. rotundata*, the Eboe yam, a staple in West Africa; and *D. opposita*, the Chinese yam, which is mostly grown in Japan. They are very important foodstuffs in places other than the United States but all of them are tropical or subtropical, and none of them is grown here although one or another occasionally shows up in specialty markets in large cities.

Yucca or Yuca?

Q What is your guess of the success rate for cultivation of yucca grown in zone 6? I have come to enjoy this imported root staple after introduction by my Peruvian friends. Winters are quite mild in my garden (there is seldom snow for longer than a month or two), so I think it's probably closer to zone 7 than zone 6.

A If you do want to grow yucca—the ornamental with sword-shaped leaves and tall stalks of white flowers—you'll have no problems as long as you choose a variety of Adam's needle, *Yucca filamentosa*.

But it sounds as though you're really hoping for yuca, *Manihot esculenta* (aka *M. utilissima*), a perennial shrub that is widely grown in the dry tropics. Its other names are manioc, cassava, and tapioca, and your chances of success with it are zero.

There are several kinds of cassava, but all of them grow best in warm weather and cannot survive frost. While this is also true of many vegetables that do fine in zones 6 and 7 (tomatoes come at once to mind), cassava takes from six to nine months, all of them toasty, to form storage roots large enough to be worth harvesting. 🌶

A Dearth of Zucchini

Q My three zucchini plants have been flowering for the last several weeks. They have produced only one female flower that resulted in a zucchini. I had the same problem last year and harvested only two zucchinis. There are cucumber, pepper, eggplant, tomato, basil, and parsley plants nearby. Can you tell me what's happening?

A Are you getting female flowers that don't go on to make zucchinis? Or are your plants suffering a gender gap and making only male flowers? The more common problem is female flowers that don't produce zucchinis, but both difficulties are caused by the same sorts of stress, according to Dr. Brent Loy, a professor of plant biology at the University of New Hampshire who has worked a great deal with the squash family.

The three most likely culprits are shade (squash is a sun lover), very hot weather (especially if temperatures do not moderate at night), and unusually wet conditions. "If it was very wet, that might stimulate male flowers," Dr. Loy said, adding that the female flowers can abort at such an early stage, you might not know they had ever appeared. But ending up with all male flowers is a possibility if everything goes wrong enough, and that includes starting transplants and then

Zucchini

FEMALE

MALE

letting them get potbound. "Plants that have been stunted by adverse conditions or by delayed transplanting will tend to produce an abundance of male flowers," he said. Squash plants have to be in pretty good health for the females to form and prosper. ☙

Zucchini Blues

Q Last year, we had zucchini that had some kind of mushy rot at the base of the plant on some stems. It didn't seem to interfere too much with fruit production, but I'm wondering what caused it. I looked for bug burrowing and didn't find any.

A Your zucchini, and many others every year, are the victims of squash vine borer. The borer is actually the larva of a moth that attacks squash, cucumber, and muskmelon, and does exactly what its name suggests. The adult moths have metallic green wings 1 to 1½ inches across and look more like a wasp than a moth. The female glues an egg near the base of the stem; once hatched, the white-and-brown larva (which can grow to an inch long) eats its way inside and upward until the plant simply collapses.

If you are going to rush your zucchini seedlings into the garden in a race to make that first zucchini bread, squash vine borers are a menace. Sometimes they can be prevented by loosely wrapping the lower 6 inches of stem with aluminum foil. If a close look reveals yellowish grains of fecal matter on the ground, or if a shiny ooze is coming from an entry hole, you can use a razor blade or sharp knife to slit the stem upward until you find the larva. Remove and kill it, then bend the stem down and bury it so that all of the cut portion is below ground; new roots may develop, and the plant may continue to grow.

But the best defense is to sidestep squash vine borers altogether by starting seeds later, so that there are no plants in the garden until the summer heat is in full swing. By then, the adult moth has laid her eggs elsewhere, possibly in your neighbor's garden, but your zucchini will produce enough fruit to cover his unfortunate losses. ☙

CHAPTER ELEVEN

Herbs

Herbs in General

What Is an Herb?

Q It sounds like a silly question, but just what is an herb? I've been look-ing at herb books and they seem to include almost everything except Christmas trees, so are there any rules at all?

A Not really. The definition most dictionaries list first is that herbs are plants with no woody structure. Whether annual or perennial, they die to the ground either after flow-ering or at the end of each growing season. By this definition, banana trees are herbs and rosemary bushes are not.

The second, more familiar definition is that herbs are plants that are useful: as seasonings, as medicines, or for other practical purposes such as dyeing cloth. This covers an awful lot of ground and has its own problems—vegetables, for instance, which were included in the old herbals but are seldom thought of as herbs these days. The bottom line seems to be that herbs are a lot like pornography: you may not be able to define it, but you know it when you see it. ✿

IT'S OFFICI(N)AL

A great many plants, not just those commonly thought of as herbs, have as their second botanical name the word *officinalis,* which means the plant in question has (or was thought to have) healing properties. It's derived from "officinal," originally a healer's workshop, laboratory, or storeroom, and later the commercial pharmacy, where medicinal drugs—including herbs—were either kept or sold.

Herbs for Shade

Q **I would like to have a kitchen herb garden but I know herbs need lots of sunshine, and our yard is shady everywhere. There is one section that gets quite a bit of morning light. Will that be enough for basil, my favorite, and parsley and oregano?**

Most culinary herbs do need lots of sunshine, more than it sounds as if they'll get in your yard, but there are a few that should do all right with morning light, assuming the soil is well drained.

Regrettably, basil and oregano are not among them, but parsley will probably be fine. You can also grow chervil, fennel, tarragon, lemon balm, sweet cicely, sweet woodruff, and any of the mints. 🌶

A Different Design

Q **Most of the herb garden plans I see feature pretty patterns made from short plants. But I would like to try something more like a classic perennial border, with short plants in front, taller ones in the middle and back. Other than dill, what could I plant that would give some height?**

A Tall culinary herbs include lovage, *Levisticum officinale,* a perennial that looks and tastes a lot like giant celery and tops out at about 6 feet, and angelica, *Angelica archangelica,* a biennial (or short-lived perennial) that looks a lot like lovage but has a very different taste. The flavor of angelica is vaguely like anise, and as with lovage, a little goes a long way. Still, there are those who like it a lot—in the old days, the candied stems of angelica were used as a confection.

Other tall herbs include fennel and caraway, close relatives of dill that reach the same size and that, like dill, tend to self-sow rampantly.

If you don't mind including herbs that are more for decoration than for daily use, you can include chicory, *Cichorium intybus,* a weedy-looking 5-footer that redeems itself with scores of sky-blue, daisylike flowers, and valerian, *Valeriana officinalis,* which usually grows to 4 feet or so and has clusters of small white or pink flowers that perfume the garden with vanilla. And if you want to really stretch out, consider elecampane, *Inula helenium.* It's an enormous plant, easily 4 feet across, with leaves that may measure 2 feet long and a foot wide. The stalks of its sparse-petaled yellow flowers can reach 7 feet. ❧

The Art of Drying Herbs

Q **How should one dry herbs? How long does the flavor last? Can you tell by the color when they are no longer of value?**

A All herbs can be dried, but not all of them are worth it. Parsley, chervil, chives, and coriander, to name four popular favorites that are widely marketed in dried form, taste more or less like hay that way, no matter how carefully they have been processed.

Most of the others, including basil, dill, thyme, rosemary, sage, and tarragon, come through very nicely—changed, to be sure, but still useful.

If you're not feeling romantic, you can use a commercial dehydrator, which should come with full instructions. If you want the warm sense of accomplishment that accompanies the low-tech approach, all you need is an attic with screened windows or some other dark, dry, warm (but not hot) area that gets plenty of air circulation.

Most herbs have the strongest flavor right before they start to form flower buds. They should be freshly picked, preferably in the morning as soon as the dew has dried. (Basil, however, is an exception. It's more flavorful at the end of the day.)

Hanging herbs to dry

If the herbs have long stems with sparse foliage at the bottom, you can hang them in bunches. Use rubber bands to tie loose bundles of eight stems or so. Hang them in the chosen spot and keep checking. If the herbs have tightly packed leaves (or flowers) that might rot before they could dry, strip them from the stems and spread them on screens. Prop the screens on piles of books or bricks so air can circulate.

No matter which way you dry them, the herbs are ready to store when they are brittle and should be removed from the drying area as soon as this happens. Strip the leaves from the stems, but leave them whole. Store in airtight glass jars in a cool, dark, dry place for up to a year.

Color is indeed a clue. A pale look presages pale taste. ✿

FROZEN FLAVOR

Herbs that have been frozen taste fresher than dried herbs, but only for the first four months or so after freezing. After that, flavor declines rapidly, so freezing should be thought of as an adjunct to drying, not a substitute for it.

And freezing herbs won't help you any if you forget to use them, something it's all too easy to do. As a reminder, post an inventory of frozen assets where you will see it when you reach for the seasonings.

Method 1: To freeze lemon verbena, lovage, marjoram, mint, oregano, parsley, sage, and tarragon, use whole leaves (discard stems). To freeze dill, fennel, and thyme, use tender sprigs. Basil discolors when it is frozen, so if you want it to stay bright green, dip branches in boiling water, just for a second or two, then remove, discard stems, and gently dry the leaves.

Whatever you're freezing should be completely dry. Spread it out in a single layer on a cookie sheet and place it in the freezer. As soon as the herbs are frozen, usually in no more than an hour or two, pack them in heavy plastic freezer bags and put the bags in freezer-safe glass jars (canning jars) for storage.

Method 2: To freeze coriander and chervil, which tend to fade rapidly if frozen whole, combine 1 tightly packed cup of the chopped herb with ⅓ to ½ cup of water in a blender or processor, and process until you have a coarse puree. Freeze in ice-cube trays.

As soon as they're frozen, pack the cubes as described above, in plastic bags in glass jars. Use the cubes as you would the herb (1 standard-size cube equals about 2 tablespoons freshly chopped), remembering you will be adding liquid as well.

Chives are not on the list because they don't freeze well. They don't dry well, either. Use them fresh or substitute green onion tops.

Hardy Scented Herbs

Q I would like to try a scent garden, having seen beautiful gardens for the blind in New Zealand and Virginia. But what plants can I grow here on the Niagara Peninsula?

Tansy
(*Tanacetum vulgare*)

A Quite a few scented plants do well in cool climates, although some may need special treatment, depending on the reliability of the protective snow cover. Fragrant-leaved perennials like lemon balm (*Melissa officinalis*), tansy (*Tanacetum vulgare*), catmint (*Nepeta × faassenii* or *N. mussinii*), sage (*Salvia officinalis*), peppermint (*Mentha × piperita*), spearmint (*M. spicata*), and many thymes (*Thymus* spp.) should survive quite nicely, though a bit of mulch never hurts. Heavy mulching should help with winter survival of oregano (*Origanum vulgare*).

Tender herbs like rosemary, bay, lemon verbena (*Aloysia triphylla*), lavender cotton (*Santolina chamaecyparissus*), and the scores of scented-leaf geraniums (everything from lemon to pine, rose, nutmeg, and coconut) will not winter over in cold climates, but they will thrive outdoors in the summer. Bring them on in when it gets cold, and you can enjoy them as houseplants.

Fragrant annuals include heliotrope, basil, dill, and marigold. 🌰

Homegrown Herb Tea

Q I'm very fond of herb tea and would like to try growing my own. Can you suggest a few choices—nothing fancy or difficult, please—that would grow well in my (zone 6) vegetable garden? It gets full sun, and I have always had success with herbs like basil and parsley.

A Good herbs for tea that should grow well in your garden include chamomile (leaves and flowers), fennel (leaves and seeds), hyssop (leaves and flowers). And for their leaves, you could grow bergamot, aka bee balm (*Monarda didyma*), betony (*Stachys officinalis*), lemon balm, applemint, peppermint, spearmint, and sage. All are hardy at least to zone 5.

Lemon verbena and scented-leaf geraniums should also thrive there in the summer, though they are not frost hardy. (Anywhere temperatures dip below about 35°F, these two will have to spend the winters indoors.)

And don't forget rose hips, raspberry and blackberry leaves, and the flowers of elderberries and linden trees (*Tilia* spp.). Though not usually grown in vegetable gardens, they too are valuable additions to the homegrown tea lover's pantry. 🌢

A Hardy Herb Garden

Q **I would like to plan an herb garden and don't want to be putting in annuals every season. What herbs can I include that will survive winters in zone 6?**

A There are so many hardy herbs fit that bill, you would be wise to refine your plan a little more before you start choosing plants. Is this a culinary herb garden? If so, consider chives, garlic chives, fennel, sage, tarragon, thymes, winter savory, and—as long as you keep its roots confined—mint.

If your interest is more in medicinals, you'll want arnica, catnip, echinacea, feverfew, valerian, and comfrey (which should be used only externally, no matter what you read).

And don't forget that some annual herbs are such rampant self-sowers that you'll have to plant them only once. Borage, dill, chervil, and coriander will come back reliably year after year as long as you let some plants go to seed. They won't necessarily come up right where you want them, but a little untidiness never hurt anybody, and they are easily weeded out if they're really in the way. 🌢

Yummy Flowers

Q **I love the idea of edible flowers but don't know how to use them in cooking. Do they all taste about the same, or are there real differences? It seems like there would be, but I don't know how to tell.**

A The best way to find out how edible flowers taste is to taste them. There can be large differences between different cultivars of the same species, and there are always differences in individual perception.

That said, here's a short course to get you started. Mild-flavored flowers include pansies and their relatives the violets and violas, day lilies, roses, the crimson flowers of scarlet runner beans, and the bright blue blossoms of borage. Nasturtium petals, though often described as spicy, are also delicate enough to be used in almost anything. The strong taste is in the heel of the petals, where they join together, and in the heart of the flower; and nasturtium leaves are spicy indeed, like a cross between mustard and watercress.

Calendulas, marigolds, and chrysan-themums are quite assertive, with an acrid edge that's hinted at in their fragrances. Herb flowers, especially those of lavender, hyssop, thyme, and sage, can vary from bland to very strong, so be sure to taste before using.

Nasturtium, the best-known edible flower

In short, the rule with flowers-as-food is "nibble and you'll know." But don't experiment unless you're *sure* the flower is safe to eat. And remember to look them over care-fully for insects; aphids adore nasturtiums, and more than one inattentive cook has been stung by a bee that was hid-den in the heart of a squash blossom. 🌶

FLOWERS ON THE PLATTER

No summer meal is complete without an appropriate floral accompaniment, but if you want to put the flowers up close and personal with the food, be sure they are organically grown. Flowers bought from commercial florists almost always carry pesticide residues, and the same is often true of flowers from farm-stands and farmers' markets. (When in doubt about growing methods, ask.)

Also keep in mind that a great many flowers are poisonous, to one degree or another, if eaten. Some are positively dangerous; this list includes (but is by no means limited to) azalea, delphinium, foxglove, wisteria, hydrangea, and oleander. Equally to be avoided are sweet pea, daffodil, rhododendron, lily of the valley, cro-cus, and Jack-in-the-pulpit.

In theory, you could drape a few sweet peas across the edge of a large platter that had something dry (like bread) in the middle, but to be on the safe side, never put anything that might be harmful on the same plate as the food.

Free Potpourri

Q In recent years I've purchased packages of potpourri but found them rather expensive. Since I have a small garden, what can I grow myself for potpourri and how do I make it?

A True potpourri (from the French for "rotten pot") is a mixture of aromatics, fermented in salt, that is somewhat tricky to make. But it's easy to create a very good shortcut version that's similar to the packaged stuff: just harvest some colorful flowers and fragrant foliage, dry them, and blend them in a bowl.

One of the best places to find material for potpourri is in the herb garden. A mere sampling of possibilities includes the aromatic leaves of rosemary, scented-leaf geranium, lavender, lemon verbena, mint, lemon balm, and bay, and the flowers of chamomile, rose, marigold, lavender, and salvia.

Whatever you use, be sure everything is thoroughly dry before blending, or you will have problems with mold.

To heighten the fragrance of your potpourri, add to each quart of dried leaves and flowers a tiny drop of an essential oil, such as lavender or rose, or a spice like cinnamon. It is also a good idea to add a tablespoon of powdered orris root, which acts as a fixative. You can find these products at herb nurseries and craft stores. 🌰

Ingredients for potpourri

Herbs in Particular

Allspice

Q What are the plants used to make allspice? I'm pretty sure they're tropical, but I was wondering if I could grow them in my greenhouse.

A Although the word "allspice" seems to imply a peppery combination of several spices—essentially

519

cloves, nutmeg, and cinnamon—the seasoning actually comes from a single tree, *Pimenta dioica* (or *P. officinalis*), whose green berries are harvested in summer and dried in the sun.

Allspice is indeed tropical, indigenous to Central America and Mexico, and hardy in the United States only in zone 10 (southern Florida, Puerto Rico, Hawaii). It is believed to have been used in the kitchens of the Aztecs and Mayans, as well as by tribes of the West Indies, and was introduced to Europe by the Spaniards in the sixteenth century.

Your greenhouse would have to be huge before you could grow your own. A full-grown allspice tree reaches about 40 feet tall and would have to be well on its way up before it started making berries. 🌿

Those Basils of Yesteryear

Q I adore basil. A few years ago, it was a fabulous herb, aromatic and delicious. It had small leaves, and one needed only to brush it to be overwhelmed by its exquisite aroma. Today stores offer a basil that has huge, tasteless, bitter, aromaless leaves. What happened?

A In the beginning, there was basil, and it was good. And instead of resting, breeders hybridized and selected and cross-pollinated and experimented, and it was, perhaps, not so good for Italian culinary use, but terrific for other ethnic dishes (think Thai) and for ornamental use (think tiny or lettuce-large leaves, frilly or wrinkled, green splashed with purple or solid deep purple).

Sweet basil
(*Ocimum basilicum*)

So now there are dozens of variations of *Ocimum basilicum*. The straight species is usually called sweet basil and is still widely grown, but each cultivar has its own idiosyncrasies, fans, and uses. Trying to declare one basil to be the best is just asking for an argument. Try several, and choose the one that suits you (seeds and seedlings are still some of the best bargains around, and many mail-order companies offer special assortments).

Oh, all right. 'Genovese.' 'Genovese' is the best basil for tearing up onto sliced tomatoes or for pounding into pesto. We expect we'll be hearing a few contrary opinions. 🌿

TASTY BOUQUET

Once harvested, fresh herbs keep best when loosely wrapped in damp toweling and stored in the refrigerator. Unfortunately, out of sight is all too often out of mind—and off the menu. To avoid forgotten-herb syndrome, pick a small bunch every week and keep it in a vase of water on the kitchen counter. Even though you know they're as close as the fridge (or a walk to the garden), you'll find yourself using a lot more of everything from parsley and basil to lovage and chervil when there is a beautiful green bouquet of them right in front of you while you cook.

Holding on to Basil

Q I want to grow basil indoors this winter, so I started some seeds in early August. It worked! I now have lovely little plants, but it's starting to get cold at night and I think it's time to bring them in for the winter. Is there anything special I should know about growing basil indoors?

A Give the plants as much sun as possible (or keep them just a few inches under fluorescent lights 14 hours a day), keep them away from cold nighttime window glass, and stand by to combat whiteflies, spider mites, and mealybugs that will then attack everything else in the house.

Even with luck, the basil plants will respond to winter conditions by becoming lanky. And they will be very slow to replace leaves that have been harvested, so unless you have many deep, deep windowsills to grow many plants, don't plan on too many batches of pesto.

Willful Basil

Q Six weeks ago I bought several large potted basil plants from my local garden shop and put them on our sunny, sheltered terrace so I could have fresh basil at my disposal throughout the fall. The plants were doing fine and providing us with plenty of leaves, until we went away for two weeks. When we came back, they had started flowering. I cut off the flowers that were there and have been pinching out the new ones, but the plants are still making far fewer leaves than they used to. How do I restore my potted basil patch to its former glory?

A You don't. Basil is an annual plant. It wants to make lots of leaves, then switch its energy into making lots of flowers, followed by lots of seeds. That accomplished, it wants to die. Keeping the flowers pinched out will stave off the end for a while, but as you've noticed, the plant is determined.

Now that it is in flowering mode, it will focus on flowers until exhaustion puts it out of its misery. It will keep growing for quite a while and will still put out a few leaves, but they'll taste somewhat bitter and flat compared to the sweet leaves of summer. 🌿

Wilting Basil

Q Can you provide some tips on growing basil? I thought I had it all down (sunny spot, good drainage, not too much fertilizer), and my plants did grow well for a while. But then first one, then another started developing brown patches on the stems. Eventually, all the plants wilted and died. I did have them pretty close to each other, more like 6 inches apart instead of the 8 to 10 inches suggested on the packet. Could that have been the problem?

A Spacing the basil too close together probably didn't help, especially if you pinched back the young plants to make sure they were nice and bushy. Closely packed plants full of succulent leaves are slow to dry out after rain or dew, and that makes them vulnerable to mold and disease.

But don't beat yourself up about it. Everything else you did was right, and it's quite likely that your basil would have died even if it had plenty of breathing room. The culprit is a devastating basil wilt, *Fusarium oxysporum,* which is carried primarily on contaminated seeds.

The fusarium became epidemic before the problem was fully addressed, and although there are now resistant strains, the disease is still widespread, in part because it lingers in the soil for years.

For best results, plant next year's basil in a different spot, and don't plant any old or bargain seed. Either choose a resistant variety such as 'Nufar,' or buy from a source that tells you its basil seed has been tested and found to be disease free. 🌿

Bountiful Borage

Q **Last year I planted borage for the first time. There were three plants, all of which were beautiful but very large. They must have spread themselves around because this year I have a whole garden full and it looks like they're going to be enormous—many are already 3 feet wide and show no signs of slowing down. I know I can just rip them out, but before I do, is there anything I can do with it all?**

That's the thing about borage: once you have it as a plant, you more or less have it as a disease. It's one of the most persistent self-sowers known to gardening.

Borage's beautiful little blue flowers are favorite edible garnishes, adding color to everything from salad to cake. The taste is very delicate so you can use lots, assuming you have the patience to pick them.

And borage leaves are delicious, tasting mostly of cucumber with a hint of lettuce sweetness. But the fine white hairs that give them their silvery glow are not so pleasant on the palate. To get around the problem, cooks either use very young leaves in salads, or employ larger ones as removable seasonings—steeping them in white wine punches is classic.

You can also add them to cooked dishes such as chicken soup, since heat destroys the prickly quality. And borage leaves are very tasty prepared like spinach or other tender greens. That sounds like a way to use up your whole windfall: creamed borage all around! Unfortunately, borage deserves its reputation as a natural laxative, so it can't really be used as a solo vegetable. A handful of leaves mixed with other greens is the largest amount that's wise.

What's left? Ruthlessness (rip 'em out) and last-minute presents. The upper sections of full-grown borage plants, sparse of leaf and rich with flowers, make very pretty fillers for country-style bouquets.

Borage
(*Borago officinalis*)

IS THERE A DOCTOR IN THE GARDEN?

There is no doubt that many plants are useful medicinally, just as there is equal certainty that many of them are poisonous. The problem is that these are often the same plants. The vast array of widely available herbal supplements and the equally huge assortment of books on herbal healing reinforce a general sense that natural products are safer than manufactured ones. But the truth is a resounding "Sometimes yes and sometimes no." Herbal medicine is a huge and complicated subject, well worth investigating but by no means something to plunge into incautiously. Things to bear in mind:

- Very few scientifically rigorous studies have been done, largely because almost all such studies are underwritten by drug companies, and herbs, which cannot be patented, could never return the investment involved.
- There is no way for the home gardener to standardize dosage: plants produce different amounts of active chemical agents depending on how and where they are grown, when they are harvested, and the variety characteristics of the particular plant.
- Herbs may interact badly with other drugs, rendering them less effective, or more toxic, in unpredictable ways.
- Like other drugs, many herbal toxins are cumulative. Small doses may produce no adverse symptoms but become dangerous in the aggregate.

The don't-mess-with-it list. A sampling of herbs that have historic reputations as medicinals but are potentially deadly: aconite (*Aconitum napellus*), deadly nightshade (*Atropa belladonna*), foxglove (*Digitalis purpurea*), lily of the valley (*Convallaria majalis*), lobelia (*Lobelia inflata*), May apple (*Podophyllum peltatum*), and pennyroyal (*Hedeoma pulegioides* and *Mentha pulegium* both go by this common name, and the oils of both are toxic).

In addition, many well-known herbs appear to be carcinogenic (sassafras, coltsfoot, and comfrey); cause abnormal heart rhythms and/or violent gastrointestinal symptoms (tansy, broom, and bloodroot); or have other downsides that make freelance experimentation unwise.

The give-it-a-whirl list. A sampling of herbs that are very unlikely to hurt you and may well do some good, assuming you use only small amounts: agrimony (*Agrimonia eupatoria*), catnip (*Nepeta cataria*), chamomile (*Matricaria recutita* and *Chamaemelum nobile*), echinacea (*Echinacea angustifolia*), fennel (*Foeniculum vulgare*), feverfew (*Chrysanthemum parthenium*), garlic (*Allium sativum*), hops (*Humulus lupulus*), peppermint (*Mentha × piperita*), and valerian (*Valeriana officinalis*).

In addition, there are herbs that emphatically should *not* be ingested but do have strong healing properties when used externally. First and foremost is aloe, most commonly *Aloe vera,* which deserves its high reputation as a healer of burns. But arnica (*Arnica montana*) is right up there as an easer of aching muscles, and comfrey (*Symphytum officinale*) does seem to promote the healing of wounds when applied as a poultice.

Chamomile Confusion

Q I recently planted an herb garden that included several plants of chamomile purchased at a plant sale. I thought they would be low-growing mounds with very fragrant little flowers, but instead they are tall and rangy, almost 3 feet, and although the flowers look and smell right, the perfume is faint compared to what I expected. The soil is good, but I am not adding any extra fertilizer, so why are the plants behaving this way?

A It's impossible to know for sure without seeing your garden, but it certainly sounds as though you have planted German chamomile, *Matricaria recutita,* rather than Roman chamomile, *Chamaemelum nobile,* sometimes called *Anthemis nobilis.* The plants are closely related and very similar in appearance, but the German kind tends to be less strongly scented and is much taller and weedier.

German chamomile is also an annual, so the correctness of this diagnosis will be confirmed next spring. It is a vigorous self-seeder, so you may well have plants again, but they will be tiny seedlings. Roman chamomile plants are hardy perennials that would—if you had them—come back as thicker clumps than you had last year. 🌸

Harvesting Chives

Q I would like to line my herb garden walkway with clumps of chives, but I would also like to use them in cooking. How do I harvest them without damaging their looks, and is there a way to get them to rebloom?

A Chives should be harvested by being clipped about a half-inch above ground level. Remove groups of four or five stems from random spots inside the clumps and your cutting will not show.

Pink-flowered common chives (*Allium schoenoprasum*) bloom exuberantly but briefly from late spring to early summer, and sometimes put up a blossom or two again in the fall. Garlic chives (*A. tuberosum*) start producing their starry white flowers in mid summer and keep blooming for almost a month, at the end of which, that's it. There is nothing you can do to encourage either one to rebloom, though deadheading is still a wise idea. Removing spent flowers not only improves the looks of the planting, it also helps prevent the rampant self-seeding that can make chives into weeds.

Warning: The chive border sounds like a pretty idea, but it will not be trouble-free. Garlic chives suffer from weed invasions. Common chive clumps expand rapidly and tend to die out in the middle, so expect to divide your plants every three years to keep them healthy and within bounds. 🌶

Getting Good Cilantro (and Lots of It)

Q **I love cooking Mexican food, so I was thrilled to find cilantro seedlings at my local nursery this June. I bought a dozen and planted them in fertile soil in full sun. They were given a drink of soluble fertilizer at planting, kept weeded, and treated well every way I could think of, but they were very disappointing. They shot up flower stalks right away and I hardly got any cilantro at all. What did I do wrong?**

A Two things. The first is simply that you attempted to transplant cilantro, something that cilantro does not like. The second is that you started in June. The green leaves of cilantro (*Coriandrum sativum*), known in English as coriander, grow best in cool weather; so unless you live in Alaska, it's likely that summer heat made the bolting problem worse. Coriander is easy to start from seed, which can be planted just about any time the ground is workable. It will grow lots of lush greenery in spring, and if you plant a new crop, it will do the same in fall. In between it will make flowers.

The good part is that those flowers will make seeds, and if you let them ripen and fall you can have cilantro as a weed in your garden. It's every bit as reliable as dandelions in the lawn. 🌶

Aromatic Cloves

Q **As the fragrance of cloves filled my home from holiday cooking, I couldn't help wondering what plant they are from. Is there any chance I could grow it in Georgia?**

A The word "clove" is from the Latin *clavus,* meaning "nail." And that's a good description of this aromatic spice, which is the dried, unopened flower bud of the clove tree, *Syzgium aromaticum* (the blooms are bright red when they open).

This handsome evergreen tree originated in the Moluccas, or Spice Islands, in southeast Asia. It grows in sandy, acid soil in tropical maritime climates. Georgia is warm, but not warm enough for you to grow your own. 🌰

Love-in-a-Sandwich

Q After a lifetime of savoring thick-crusted "Jewish corn bread," with its tangy little black seeds, I have discovered their name, love-in-a-mist (*Nigella sativa*). I read that the plant is grown commercially in the Mediterranean, but can I grow it in New Jersey? Where can I get seeds, aside from digging them out of the bread?

Black cumin
(*Nigella sativa*)

A *Nigella sativa* is the right plant, but love-in-a-mist is the common name for *N. damascena,* a popular annual. *N. sativa* is most often called black cumin. To add to the confusion, it is also called black caraway, although true caraway, found on Jewish rye bread, is *Carum carvi.*

Black cumin is an annual, growing to a foot tall, with flowers similar to those of love-in-a-mist but a paler blue. It grows in average soil as long as it gets full sun. Sow in spring and harvest when the seedpods turn brown. Empty the pods and let the seeds dry. Black cumin is used in Indian spice mixes and Mediterranean sweets as well as sprinkled on breads.

Don't ruin your bread digging out seeds: oven heat destroys their ability to germinate. Mail-order herb-seed companies should sell *N. sativa* seeds. 🌰

The Problem with Dill

Q Every year I buy dill plants, and every year they don't survive the move to my garden. Why?

A Dill (*Anethum graveolens*) may be delicious, but it doesn't like being moved. It has a long taproot, and

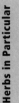

Dill
(*Anethum graveolens*)

can be transplanted successfully only when it is very small. You'll do better if you start from seeds.

To have a constant supply of leaves, sow a crop every three to four weeks all summer, planting the seeds in shallow rows about 10 inches apart. A Mediterranean native, dill is a hardy annual that self-sows easily after flowering. It is best grown in full sun, in moderately rich, well-drained soil, with some shelter from the wind for its tall, hollow stalk.

For the most intense leaf flavor, harvest early in the day and before the plant begins to set its flower buds, snipping the fronds with scissors. 🌿

THE WHEN AND HOW OF HERB HARVEST

The best time to pick herbs for daily use is when it's time to use them. Herbs for storage, on the other hand, should be harvested right before the plant flowers, since that's when the leaves are likely to be most flavorful.

Gather all herbs except basil in mid morning, shortly after the dew has dried. Gather basil in late afternoon; it has better storage properties after a day in the sun.

Washing is not recommended; it bruises leaves and leaches flavor, but that means the herbs must be grown clean—never treated with pesticides, and protected from splash-ups of soil with a layer of mulch. (If necessary, use a soft brush to remove the occasional aphid or crumb of dirt.)

Annuals: Cut stems of branching types like basil by a half to two-thirds of their length, making the cuts right above joints where you see healthy growth buds. Take outer stems of base-branchers like parsley, cutting them right at ground level. You can continue harvesting annuals until frost takes the plants, but be sure to let a few flowers form on chervil, coriander, dill, and borage if you want the plants to self-sow.

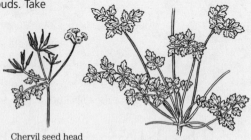

Chervil seed head

Chervil leaves

Perennials: Cut as you would branching annuals, but be sure to stop about six weeks before frost so the plants have time to toughen up for winter. (Taking a sprig or two every now and then won't hurt anything; you just don't want to force a lot of frost-tender new growth.)

Eating for Revenge

Q **Is it true that *Houttuynia cordata* is a culinary herb and can be substituted for coriander? It grows all over the place here.**

A Every so often a plant comes along that gardeners fall in love with, only to discover it's really a menace. And that is just what has happened with the exceedingly invasive houttuynia (usually pronounced who-TOO-nee-ah). At first, this plant, with its sometimes-variegated heart-shaped leaves, appears to be the ideal ground cover for difficult, shady, or moist spots. "But it deserves a warning," cautioned Harold Epstein, president emeritus of the American Rock Garden Society. "It's a plague."

But revenge may be possible. Houttuynia is a culinary herb that is enjoyed in parts of Asia (it's originally from China and Japan). You can improve both dinner and garden by harvesting it roots and all, though only the leaves are eaten. They are quite strong, with a flavor slightly reminiscent of orange. Proceed cautiously until you're sure you like the taste. 🌿

Lazy Lavender

Q **I have a three-year-old lavender plant that produced only a single spike of bloom last year. Now that the growing season is about to start again, what should I do to encourage better flowering?**

A To flower well, lavender must have full sun and soil that is the right pH, which for lavender ideally is slightly on the alkaline side, between 7 and 7.5. It must also have breathing room; if neighboring plants are pushing at it, they could have a discouraging effect. And like most herbs, lavender should not be heavily fertilized. The stories about these plants thriving in poor ground are exaggerations, but it is true that too much nitrogen will encourage them to make leaves at the expense of flowers. 🌿

English lavender
(*Lavandula angustifolia*)

Verbena Tea

Q **On a trip to Paris, I enjoyed an herbal tea from a plant called verveine. Can I grow this myself?**

A While it is possible that you had tea made from the bitter-tasting true vervain (*Verbena officinalis*), a famous herbal sedative, the fact that you enjoyed it suggests you were served the more commonly used *Aloysia triphylla,* whose common names include lemon verbena, lemon-scented verbena, and yerba Luisa.

Lemon verbena is a tender shrub with fragrant, lance-shaped leaves and tiny purple-pink flowers. Native to Chile and Peru, it is not hardy north of zone 8, but you can dig it up, put it in a pot, and bring it indoors for the winter. Don't be upset when the leaves fall off; lemon verbenas typically go dormant in winter. Just move your plant to a cool sill with bright filtered light, and water sparingly.

Move it to a sunny window in late February, prune it back to the larger branches, and begin regular watering. Before long it will start leafing out, and should again be covered with leaves when (after all danger of frost is past) you replant it for the summer.

Of course, you can just leave it in the pot, but if you do, be sure to give it a root pruning every couple of years. Lemon verbena wants to be big (10 by 10 feet) and the plant will suffer if it isn't cut back regularly.

Tea is its best-known culinary use: just pour a cup of boiling water over 2 tablespoons of crushed fresh leaves or 1 tablespoon of dried ones. 🍃

Growing Mint on the Balcony

Q **A few weeks ago, I bought a small bunch of mint at the supermarket. I stored the part I didn't use in a glass of water in the refrigerator and then sort of forgot about it. Now I see a whole bunch of roots coming out of the stems. Can I plant them in a pot on the balcony and get enough mint to use in cooking? I don't know what kind it is.**

A Although almost any mint will root in water, yours is probably spearmint, *Mentha spicata,* the one most commonly sold. It's a frequent star on the mint julep circuit and also the best choice for savory dishes like stuffed grape leaves.

If the fate of the previous bunch is any indication, a large pot on the balcony should provide all the spearmint you need. It will produce all summer and fall as long as it gets plenty of moisture and protection from searing heat.

To help the roots stay cool, use a heavy clay or cement pot at least 8 inches deep and 10 inches wide; anything smaller is likely to be more trouble than it's worth. Plant the mint so the soil comes to about an inch below the rim. Ordinary potting soil is fine. Firm the soil around the stems and water until it is dripping wet, letting the excess water drain away.

Set the pot outdoors, and keep it heavily shaded for at least two weeks. The mint needs time to adjust to daylight after its sojourn in the refrigerator.

After that it can go anywhere, although (being potted) it will need more care if you put it in bright sun. Keep the soil moist but not wet. Wait for a few inches of new growth, then harvest by pinching off the tips, right above a leaf node.

In addition to becoming bushy, your mint will send out runners. Before long they will fill the pot, giving you a good excuse to buy a new bottle of bourbon and a Middle Eastern cookbook. 🌰

Spearmint
(*Mentha spicata*)

Cuban Oregano—
Not for Putting on Pizza

Q I was given a handsome plant labeled Cuban/Mexican oregano (*Plectranthus amboinicus*). The leaves are succulent, velvety, and intensely pungent. However, it is not like any oregano I know, and I wonder if it is truly a culinary herb. My cooking and gardening books do not enlighten me. Should I use it fresh, dry it, or just admire it?

A The real question is: what is oregano, anyway? Plants in the genus *Origanum* go by the common names sweet marjoram, wild marjoram, pot marjoram, and dittany of Crete as well as oregano. But there are plants in other genera that are also called oregano.

Dr. Arthur O. Tucker, a botanist at Delaware State University who specializes in the identification and chemistry of herbs, advised that oregano should be thought of as a flavor, not a plant.

Your *Plectranthus amboinicus*—also called Puerto Rican oregano, Indian borage, and Spanish thyme, just to add a little more confusion—is used in cooking in both Cuba and the Virgin Islands; in Mexico, however, the most common choices for oregano flavor are *Lippia graveolens* and *Poliomintha longiflora.*

Cuban oregano is not on the GRAS list (pronounced grass, this is an acronym for Generally Recognized As Safe) from the Flavor and Extract Manufacturers Association, which tests plants for the Food and Drug Administration. So while it may be consumed in other countries, you should think of yours as an ornamental and enjoy it as part of a summer mixed-container planting, or as a tender annual in the garden.

To most Americans, the plant usually found on top of pizzas and in tomato sauces is the only true oregano. That one, usually but not always called Turkish or Greek oregano, is the white-flowering *Origanum vulgare* ssp. *hirtum.*

What all of these oreganos share is carvacrol, an essential oil that gives them, more or less, the pungent taste we associate with oregano.

There are two lessons here for the culinary gardener. Always taste a leaf of any herb before you buy it for culinary use to see if it tastes the way you think it should. And don't be surprised if your versions of the dishes you had on far-flung vacations don't taste quite the same. ☙

Cuban oregano
(*Plectranthus
amboinicus*)

Seeking Corsican Mint

Q **I have searched in vain for a plant called Corsican mint. Recently I saw an offering for Corsican pearlwort. Is it the same thing?**

A Corsican mint, or creeping mint (*Mentha requienii*), is no relation at all to pearlwort (*Sagina subulata*).

There are some similarities, though, in that both are low growing and matlike. Both are useful between paving stones or along patio or container edges, are easily propagated by division, and are hardy only to zone 6.

But that's where the resemblance ends. Corsican mint has tiny round leaves, as opposed to pearlwort's narrow ones; its flowers are purplish pink, whereas pearlwort's are white, and of course the mint is the one that's tasty, reputedly the original mint in crème de menthe.

Corsican mint grows best in partial shade. Any ordinary soil will do as long as it is kept moist. Like all mints, it will spread enthusiastically where it's happy, but unlike some of the coarser sorts it isn't likely to take over the garden. 🌶

Curly vs. Flat Parsley

Q **I have only a very small patch of garden in which to plant herbs, so which is better, flat-leaf parsley or curly parsley? Are they equally easy to grow?**

A Think of curly parsley, *Petroselinum crispum,* and flat-leaf (or Italian) parsley, *P. crispum* var. *neapolitanum,* as fraternal twins. They aren't identical, but botanically they are very close, and they have the same growing needs. The difference comes later: in the kitchen, where flat-leaf tends to have a stronger flavor (and be much easier to wash); and in the small, tight bouquets called tussie-mussies, where the curly variety is a more decorative choice.

Parsley is easily grown from seed but should be started early since it's very slow to germinate. (Folk wisdom says it must go to the devil and back nine times before it sprouts.) The alternate light freezes and thaws of early spring will help it along outdoors in zones 6 and 7. Indoors (the best place to start it in zones 3 to 5), an overnight soak in cool water before planting will speed germination. Parsley does best in moist, rich, slightly acid soil in full sun. Plants should be about 8 to 12 inches apart, depending on variety.

Seedlings for both kinds of parsley are widely available in the spring, and they will work fine as long as they are very young when set out. But don't make the mistake of buying large ones and then trying to transplant them. The roots are easily damaged, and if they are, the plant will quickly bolt to seed instead of making lots of tasty foliage. ✿

Winterizing Parsley

Q We live near Philadelphia. Our Italian parsley has come through several frosts, including one that was quite severe (26°F), without suffering any damage. Is there a chance we could winter it over if we mulched it well? It has been delicious, and it would be great to have the same plants next year.

A It will winter over if the roots don't freeze, but that will help only if you want to save seed. Parsley is a biennial. As soon as it resumes growth next spring, it will send up flower stalks, and when it does the leaves will become bitter.

Mulch or no mulch, it will probably stay usable at least until the end of December. Just don't touch the leaves while they're frozen, or they will go limp. Let them thaw naturally, in the warmth of midday or in your kitchen, and they will be fine. ✿

White Rosemary?

Q I keep my potted rosemary outside during warmer months and bring it indoors to a southern window when the weather cools. While it thrives outdoors, indoors it gets a whitish deposit on the leaves and soft new stems. Is this common with rosemary? Is the infestation contracted outdoors or inside? How should I treat this problem?

A The deposit is powdery mildew, an all-too-common fungus disease that likes the warmth and low humidity indoors. But don't blame your lilacs, phlox, or roses for passing their powdery mildew along. The fungus has several distinct species, and each has its own preferred host. Most diseases pick on stressed plants, but this mildew attacks the healthiest, so take it as a backhanded compliment. Generally, it is not fatal, and once the plant gets back outdoors, it should be fine.

Picking infected leaves off one by one while you listen to a book on tape may sound like a way to counteract the winter doldrums, but try to control yourself as it just helps spread the fungus spores onto the leaves right below.

Chemical treatment is problematic because you probably use the rosemary in cooking. One control product labeled for use against powdery mildew on food crops is Remedy, based on a bicarbonate formulation. Baking soda, at three teaspoons to a gallon of water, is an effective home remedy. Plan on having to spray the rosemary more than once to make a difference. 🌰

Indoor rosemary is prone to mildew, but will recover.

Season for Sage

Q We just bought a house in the Berkshires with a small, very neglected garden. I was thrilled to find a sage plant, straggly but with some leaves, which I used in stuffing for our Thanksgiving turkey. Unfortunately, the sage didn't taste very good. Could there be something in the soil that affected the flavor?

A Assuming you have the straight species of culinary sage, *Salvia officinalis,* rather than one of its ornamental relatives, chances are your problem is the season, not the soil. Sage leaves taste best when they are young. Tender and delicate in early spring, they get tougher and more aromatic as the weather warms. Flavor is at its complex peak when flowers are just starting to form, and that is the best time to harvest a crop for drying.

To get the tastiest fresh sage, cut early and often, forcing the plant to make lots of new growth. The essential oils that give young leaves their lemony quality are volatile. As they dissipate, the leaves taste more and more like dried sage, a combination of camphor and pine. That sounds like a flavor too tough to kill, but it too fades over time, and the leaves you picked had undoubtedly seen many moons come and go.

Unpruned sage (left); pruned sage (right)

Leave the plant for now. Next spring, watch for the first signs of green, then cut it back severely, leaving 3 to 5 inches of heavily budded wood at the base of each stem. As the plants put out new growth, keep cutting them back, then stop harvesting in mid September so the plant can toughen up for winter.

You can make an exception for Thanksgiving. Late sage won't be as luscious as summer's, but it will be a little better than dried. 🌿

THE LIMITS OF THE COUNTRY LOOK

You've seen the pictures a million times: bunches of dried herbs hanging from the beams in a country kitchen, a beautifully arranged wreath of dried herbs and flowers (or bright red chilies) within snipping distance of the stove. It looks easy and practical, as well as cozy and homelike.

But it's not really a good idea—unless you plan to use up the goodies in a very short time. Dried foods left exposed in a working kitchen will be magnets for grease and/or dust, and their quality will be degraded by light, heat, and steam. The old-time farmers whose kitchens inspired this look had airier kitchens (no insulation) and lower expectations about cleanliness of the food.

Savory Character

Q I have a nice, bushy plant of winter savory that has been in my garden for years. It has provided all the savory I need for cooking, and I have never had any problems with it. But my new boyfriend, who is a chef, says I should be planting summer savory because the winter kind is too strong to use with summer vegetables. I say if it's too strong, just use less. Who's right?

A How cute is he? Does he display keeper qualities? From the gourmet's point of view, he's right. The annual herb summer savory, *Satureja hortensis,* has a more delicate flavor and less of a harsh aftertaste than the perennial *S. montana,* called winter savory for its hardiness.

It's nice to have both, since winter savory (which goes best with dried beans and rich meats like pork) is also a more attractive plant, easy to prune into a lush but compact little bush. The summer kind tends to be weedy looking, no matter how often you cut it back.

But why is he ordering from your garden as though it were a menu? He should be out there helping you plant the savory—and doing a bit of weeding, too, to earn his share of the harvest. 🍎

Soursoup Plant

Q I would like to grow the herb used in soursoup (also known as *tchav*). I think it's chervil.

A *Tchav,* or *shav,* is Yiddish for sorrel (*Rumex acetosa*), which is sometimes called sour grass. Its light green, spear-shaped leaves taste somewhat lemony and are delicious in a number of soups and salads as well as with fish.

Sorrel, a hardy perennial, grows quickly from seed to a mature size of 18 to 24 inches, but you will gain a year of harvests if you start with plants. Sorrel does best in good garden soil in full sun, but it will tolerate part shade and grow in almost any ground as long as it is well drained.

The plants are lushest in spring—like rhubarb and strawberries, they are a symbol of the season—but there is usually another, smaller crop after the weather cools in the fall. 🍎

Sorrel
(*Rumex acetosa*)

Growing Sturdier Sorrel

Q The garden sorrel I planted last year has made it through the winter, and the leaves are a couple of inches long. Can I cut them for salad now, or must I wait until they're larger? Also, what can I do to make them sturdier? I used a standard vegetable fertilizer (5-10-5) and got crisp, upright leaves a foot tall and 3 inches wide. But when I tried to cook them, a whole panful collapsed into a sad little mass of gray-green puree.

A First to come in spring, last to leave in fall, garden sorrel (*Rumex acetosa*) is a hardy perennial that thrives in cool temperatures. You can cut now and keep on cutting right through the season, as long as you leave a quarter of the growth so there's something to nourish the roots.

As the weather warms, your sorrel will make fewer leaves and switch to flowering stalks. Unless you want to save seed, these should be cut off. The plant will go almost dormant in summer, then send up new growth when the weather cools. Again, you can safely cut three-fourths of it.

Sorrel is easy to grow and is seldom bothered by pests or diseases. One mid-spring application of balanced fertilizer (or a mid-winter mulch of well-rotted manure) is all the food it needs. As a plant, it's sturdy.

But the leaves are another story. Old recipes often begin "melt a handful of sorrel" because that's what it does. There is no way to toughen it up and no reason to want to. Sorrel is far too strong-flavored to eat as a vegetable. If you tasted that sad little mass, you know it had enough lemon-bright flavor to season a whole pot of potato soup or a pan of cream sauce. And because it made puree all by itself, it saved you the trouble.

Tarragon from Seed

Q I have tried to grow tarragon from seed but without success. The plants grow, but they don't taste like tarragon should. Is it the seeds, something about my garden, or me?

A Culinary or French tarragon is *Artemisia dracunculus* var. *sativa*, a selection of *A. dracunculus*, or Russian tarragon.

Unfortunately the trade-off for French tarragon's delicate basil-anise flavor is that it doesn't grow as vigorously as the species. It seldom blooms, and when it does bloom, it produces infertile seeds.

Any tarragon seed you can buy will grow up to be Russian tarragon, with a taste that doesn't belong in food. French tarragon has to be propagated vegetatively, from cuttings or divisions. If you want to grow tarragon to use in the kitchen, you have to plant plants.

Taller Tarragon

Q My herb garden is on a hillside right above the Hudson River in Rhinecliff, New York. It is sheltered from the wind and could, I think, be assigned to zone 6. The soil is well drained, and most of the herbs are happy. But tarragon eludes me. I dream of harvesting armloads of it, but my plants, though healthy, never grow more than about 18 inches tall. What's wrong?

A Probably nothing (unless you count misguided ambitions). Culinary tarragon (*Artemisia dracunculus* var. *sativa*) doesn't get much taller than 2 feet unless it is struggling for light or has somehow managed to flower, neither of which is recommended for tarragon that is kitchen-bound.

If your plants are healthy and tasty, that's what you're aiming for, said Holly Shimizu, an herb expert and executive director of the U.S. Botanic Garden in Washington, D.C. "Size is not the greatest measure of success. You want to make several harvests over the season, and that continual cutting back will keep the plant low and bushy."

On the other hand, even though your plants appear healthy, they just might be suffering from borderline malnutrition. People often lump tarragon with Mediterranean herbs like rosemary, lavender, and thyme, Ms. Shimizu said. And tarragon is like them in needing both lots of sun and very good drainage. But unlike those warm-climate favorites, tarragon is a cool-weather lover. And it is at its best only in highly fertile soil; so if you have had your tarragon on a Mediterranean diet, try adding some compost and chicken manure.

Lastly, if you have gotten all your plants from the same place, consider a different source. True French tarragon is always propagated vegetatively rather than by seed, so every new plant is a clone of its mother. If your source is using a short strain, your plants will be short as well no matter what you do. 🌿

Creeping Thyme

Q **I would like to plant creeping thyme between the stones on my terrace. Is this herb edible?**

A Creeping thyme, *Thymus praecox,* is edible but less aromatic and flavorful than the equally low-growing wild thyme, aka mother-of-thyme (*Thymus pulegioides*), which is both edible and tasty. In either case, however, plants you've been walking on are not generally good candidates for slipping into the stew. Consider setting additional plants between the stones of a wall, where (assuming you don't have dogs) they will be safe from contamination. 🌿

Creeping thyme
(*Thymus praecox*)

The Flower of May Wine

Q **I'm interested in the May flower that is added to May wine. How does this plant grow?**

A The delightful plant whose foliage is used to flavor bowls of May wine is sweet woodruff (*Galium odoratum,* sometimes referred to as *Asperula odorata*). When crushed or bruised, the tiny leaves smell like a mixture of vanilla and fresh meadow grasses. (This fragrance is most pronounced when the leaves are dried, though the herb is generally used fresh.)

The plant is a woodland resident. While it is most comfortable in rich, damp, slightly acid soil and the dappled shade of taller plants, it adapts both to drier soil and to sun.

Sweet woodruff is difficult to start from seed, so it is wise to begin with plants. But you don't have to buy many of them—where it is happy, it's a rapid spreader.

THE SECRET OF MAY WINE

The use of sweet woodruff in May wine has roots going back to the late Middle Ages. Medieval churches were often bedecked with aromatic garlands of lavender and sweet woodruff for holidays, and the practice of using sweet woodruff to improve the flavor of May wine is believed to have started in thirteenth-century Germany.

Modern recipes typically call for a bunch of fresh woodruff to be steeped for a few days in a gallon of white wine, usually a Rhine wine. Before serving, a few fresh sprigs and some of the pretty white May flowers are floated as decoration, often along with fresh strawberries. But it is not advisable to eat too many fresh woodruff leaves, since large quantities have been known to cause vomiting and dizziness in some people.

CHAPTER TWELVE

Fruits

Small Fruits

Blueberries in Shade

Q I would like to know if I can plant blueberries in a raised bed in my garden on Long Island, New York. The spot I have in mind is in the shade of a mature oak tree, about 12 feet from the trunk.

A There are three common kinds of blueberry: the wild ones, *Vaccinium angustifolium,* low-growing spreaders that are pretty but not suitable for small-scale home fruit production; rabbit-eye blueberries, *V. ashei,* which do best in the South; and highbush blueberries, *V. corymbosum.*

These last ones would be an excellent choice for a Long Island garden, particularly one with the acidic soil for which the area is famous. (And the same goes for any garden with similar soil in zones 5 to 8.) But it would be best if you could find a brighter spot for them. Although blueberries are often described as able to tolerate some shade, there's likely to be more than "some" only 12 feet from a mature oak.

Sunshine problems aside, the location you have in mind won't be ideal unless that raised bed is really king-size. Most of the reliable, readily available highbush cultivars, including 'Blueray,' 'Patriot,' and 'Bluecrop,' can eventually become shrubs 6 feet tall and almost as wide. You'll need at least two of them—even varieties advertised as self-fertile

Highbush blueberry
(*Vaccinium corymbosum*)

do much better with a pollinator nearby—and while there are some handsome dwarf types that would fit nicely in a raised bed ('Northblue,' for instance, is about 2 feet tall), they are not what you'd call fruit factories.

Of course, that won't matter if you're growing blueberries as ornamentals. Their pretty spring flowers and bright yellow, orange, or red autumn foliage are reason enough to grow them even without fruit—which is what you will certainly be doing unless you protect your crop from the birds.

Catalogs offer a good selection of early, mid-season, and late-ripening fruits, so you can have blueberries for almost two months. You can also end up with bloom times too widespread for cross-pollination, so be sure to ask if the catalog doesn't say when they flower. 🍐

FOILING THE BIRDS

Bush fruits such as blueberries, gooseberries, and currants are magnets for birds, which have no trouble eating the whole crop in about two days.

One of the best ways to foil them is to use small-mesh bird netting, supported by a separate structure that keeps the netting away from the fruit and allows enough room beneath so *you* can get at the fruit without removing it.

For best results, build a decorative arbor over the bushes when you first plant. It will add visual interest while the shrubs are still small. Then, when it's time to foil the flying freeloaders, you'll have a ready-made frame from which to hang the bird netting. Make sure you get the net in place in time; the birds will start on your berries well before they have ripened.

Barren Blueberries

Q Two years ago, I bought a highbush blueberry by mail. The bush seems to be thriving; it's planted in acidic soil and gets five hours of sun, but it has not borne fruit, and I can see no sign of buds again this year. What does this plant need?

A Assuming the soil is satisfactory, the problem of no blooms may be one of age. Mail-order nurseries often ship plants that are two to three years old, but it usually takes four to six years before the plants are mature enough to flower.

Also, highbush blueberries need company to bear fruit—or at least to bear a satisfactory amount of it. Even after your bush starts blooming, it won't start fruiting in earnest until you plant a different variety, one that blooms at about the same time, within bee-flying distance.

These varieties bear flowers in more or less overlapping order, from earliest to latest: 'Bluetta,' 'Earliblue,' 'Northland,' 'Patriot,' 'Blueray,' 'Ivanhoe,' 'Bluecrop,' 'Berkeley,' 'Jersey,' 'Herbert,' and 'Coville.' ☙

The Elusive Cherry Bush

Q I thought I had found the perfect addition to my small yard when I spotted a bush cherry (*Prunus* hybrid) in a museum catalog. It sounded as though I could get lots of cherries for the birds, and even save a few for myself, all from a shrub only 4 feet tall. But the museum's plant division closed, and all the nurseries in our area think I'm cuckoo. Can you help?

A There are several species of bush cherries, all offering clouds of bloom and generous quantities of fruit. But most of the fruit has very sour flesh and not a whole lot of it (big pits). While that is no problem for the birds—or for people who like making jelly—it does mean that species bush cherries are considered landscape shrubs, rather than home orchard material.

Enter the noted plant breeder Elwyn Meader, who crossed two sour-fruit species, *Prunus jacquemontii* and *P. japonica,* and came up with three much tastier hybrids: 'Joy,' 'Jan,' and 'Joel.' These tough little bushes grow only 4 or 5 feet tall. They have pinkish white flowers and good-size, very flavorful, tart fruits that can be eaten out of hand but are probably best when cooked.

Hybrid
bush cherries

Young plants grow quickly in fertile, well-drained soil in full sun and should start fruiting modestly in their second year. By the year after that, you should have enough fruit to invite the whole flock in for pie. ☙

RIBES WARNING

It's strange to think of a fruit bush as being Typhoid Mary, but that is the case with the genus *Ribes,* home of currants (*Ribes nigrum* and *R. rubrum*), gooseberries (*R. uva-crispa*), and jostaberries, a currant and gooseberry cross.

These fruits are alternate hosts for white pine blister rust (*Cronartium ribicola*), a fungus disease that doesn't hurt the ribes much but is lethal to white pines.

Rust spores start growing on the ribes in spring. They spend the summer on the bushes, infecting leaf after leaf; then in fall they move into the pine needles, which provide the protection they need to safely winter over.

Two or three years later, in the spring, the blisters they've formed on the pine needles burst. Rust spores drift out over the countryside, looking for likely ribes plants to settle on and multiply. Meanwhile, back at the pine tree, the fungus is traveling back from the infected branches toward the trunk. When it gets there, it will start destroying bark. And then the tree will die.

The disease cannot spread from one pine to another, so keeping ribes out of the neighborhood will protect these valuable trees—for many years there was a federal ban on planting currants and gooseberries. This ban was lifted some time ago, and there are now many parts of the country where these delicious and time-honored fruits can once again be part of the home garden. *But not everywhere!* Ribes are still banned in many places; the rules change from state to state, and from county to county within states. Be sure to consult your local extension service before planting.

And remember that even if they are not illegal, currants and gooseberries may still be inimical to the health of your prized white pine (or that of your neighbors within a half mile). Where possible, choose blister-resistant varieties, which will be labeled as such.

Old-Fashioned Berries

Q **I would like to grow some old-fashioned currants. What are their needs, and where can I buy them?**

A Like their gooseberry cousins, currants (*Ribes rubrum, R. sativum,* and *R. petraeum*) prefer moist, cool summers and are at their best in zones 3 to 6. In areas where summers are dry or hot, they will benefit from heavy mulching and some shade from the sun.

Currants are quite sensitive to soil potassium deficiencies, typically indicated by scorched leaf edges. But this problem is easily remedied with the addition of greensand marl, potash rock, or hardwood ash. Other than that, they are not fussy and will tolerate a wide range of soils.

Most currants are self-fertile, but like most self-fertile fruits they will do better if there is a cross-pollinator nearby. One warning before you plant: currants, like gooseberries, are hosts to white pine blister rust. They are illegal in some districts, and even where they are not, they should not be planted within half a mile of the pines. ☙

Growing Gooseberries

Q **I thought gooseberries were an English fruit, but now I've been told they are offered in American catalogs. I'm sure the catalogs will make them all sound wonderful, so before I start looking at choices, are some more wonderful than others?**

A Gooseberries, members of the same genus as currants (*Ribes*), are much more popular in Europe than they are here. Too few Americans realize just how tasty, or how beautiful, these light green, red, reddish purple, or golden-yellow berries can be. Unfortunately, many gooseberries are highly susceptible to the powdery mildew that is common in the United States. Breeding for disease resistance seems to be at odds with great flavor, but there are resistant cultivars (remember, resistant does not mean immune) such as 'Hinnomakis Yellow,' 'Hinnomakis Red,' 'Oregon Champion,' and 'Achilles,' which produce great fruit, sweet and juicy, not puckery and tough.

Before you choose anything, though, check with your local extension service to be sure that planting members of the genus *Ribes* is permitted in your area. ☙

Gooseberries
(*Ribes uva-crispa*)

A Monster Gooseberry Bush

Q **Several years ago, I bought a gooseberry bush. It has grown and is now a monster with thorns but no gooseberries. I planted it on a former compost pile (it was originally sickly), so maybe it is getting too much nitrogen? What should I do to get it going in the right direction?**

A You may be right that excess nitrogen in the compost pile is promoting vegetative growth at the expense of flowers and fruit. But there is another possible reason: age. Your gooseberry may still be a juvenile, not yet ready to flower. If so, time will provide the cure.

Since your gooseberry is now well, this spring, before it begins to grow, will be a good time to trim it back and move it from the compost-pile emergency room to a more worthy permanent site, with good air circulation and soil rich in organic material. Full sun is preferred, but gooseberries, unlike most other fruits and berries, will do fine in partial shade. To keep it a reasonable size and at its most productive, prune out canes more than three years old. 🍐

Pruning Grapes

Q **We recently bought an older home, complete with a grapevine on a trellis. A friend told us that pruning grapes is complicated and that we should to do it no later than Washington's Birthday. Can you give me a simple explanation of how to prune grapes?**

A Because grapes bleed if pruned when the sap is running, dormant pruning is traditional, but anytime before the buds break in spring is fine.

Your goal is a nicely balanced plant. Prune too severely, and the plant will respond with leaves, not grapes. Prune too little, and the bunches won't mature. Even worse, too much fruit with too few leaves to supply food can actually kill the vine.

Terrified? Don't be. Within reason, the vine will forgive your mistakes. If you pay attention to the results of your annual pruning, you'll get better at it. There are different pruning techniques to maximize the yields of different grape species, but Dr. Tim Martinson, a viticulture specialist in Cornell University's Finger Lakes Grape Program, said a technique called cane pruning will work well enough on any grapes to let you hold your head high in all but the most competitive company.

Grapes are produced on shoots that grow out of the buds found on year-old canes, which in turn are growing from older wood. The older wood, which has dark, peeling bark, is likely to be the stem and major horizontal branches that grow along the trellis. Growing from these branches are the year-old canes, identified by their smooth tan bark. The most fruitful canes are about pencil-thick, with bud nodes at least 6 inches apart.

Choose four to six canes that are well spaced out so that the plant will look good and the leaf canopy will lightly, but not completely, shade the grapes. Prune the other canes off and prune the chosen few back, leaving no more than 10 buds on each, with a total of 20 to 40 buds on each plant. About three-quarters of each year's growth gets pruned off, so don't be surprised at the size of the pile. 🍇 .

Proper pruning yields well-filled bunches.

The Fruitful Concord

Q **Are Concord grapes just wild grapes that have become cultivated, or is there something special about them?**

A That depends on what you mean by "just" and "special." 'Concord' is a distinct variety, but it was developed from the seeds of wild grapes (*Vitis labrusca*) by a grower named Ephraim Bull, of Concord, Massachusetts. The first cuttings from the parent vine were sold in 1849 or 1850, and a decade later Concords had spread all over the country. The Concord is still special in being extremely good-looking, juicy, and pleasant-tasting, but it is neither as sweet nor as flavorful as 'Catawba,' for instance, or 'Delaware,' or 'Golden Muscat,' or several other table grapes that also have *V. labrusca* ancestry.

As a noted authority, Dr. U. P. Hedrick, wrote in 1944: "This is the most widely grown grape in North America. Black, cluster and berry large; quality good but not the best. Vine characteristics nearly perfect. Very fruitful." All still true, and probably of some of the same vines; Concords are remarkably long lived. 🍇

A Practical Matter

Q On the North Fork of Long Island, it appears that all the vineyards are planted in a north-south direction, thus availing the plants of morning and afternoon sun. Is such planting of vineyards generally the practice?

A Generally, yes, said Dr. Andy Walker, a professor of viticulture at wine central, the University of California at Davis. But a lot depends on latitude and growing conditions.

"On shallow soil, where intense heat might lead to water stress, the ideal might be northwest to southeast," he said, "and the major consideration where it's cool and humid is air circulation, so in that case the vineyard would be sited to catch the prevailing wind."

Finally, he added, there is convenience. "Roads tend to run north to south in agricultural districts, and farmers are practical people." 🍇

Fighting Grape Fungus

Q I planted a two-year-old grapevine about four years ago. Two years later, I had plenty of tiny bunches of grapes on the vine, but they grew only to the size of buckshot. Last year, I had many more bunches. The grapes grew a little bigger, but then quit. Am I going to taste a grape this year, or am I going to be buying my grapes in the supermarket again? Please help.

A There's a reason wine costs so much: grapes can be hard to grow well. The period starting two or three weeks before flowering and lasting until two or three weeks after the fruit sets is fraught with danger. During that time the plants are especially vulnerable to several fungus diseases, including black rot, the disease that is most likely causing your problems.

Alice Wise, a viticulture research specialist at Cornell Cooperative Extension of Suffolk County in Riverhead, New York, said that black rot does not respond well to most low-toxicity fungicides, leaving homeowners with few choices. Copper- and sulfur-based sprays, common treatments for fungus diseases, may work, but they are not always a good answer because many grape varieties are very sensitive to them, and spraying may burn the leaves. If you do choose to use a fungicide labeled for use on grapes, be sure to follow the directions carefully, especially if you intend to eat or make wine from the grapes. 🍐

Junipers and Gin

Q **What species of juniper produces the berries used to flavor gin? Is it hard to grow?**

A If it is gin making you want, the plant you need is the common juniper, *Juniperus communis*. Although the drink is a Dutch invention—the word "gin" is a corruption of the Dutch name for juniper—the British embraced it with great enthusiasm in the eighteenth century and turned it into a major business.

Although common juniper is a single species, this shrubby evergreen varies widely in its growing patterns, from a ground cover to a tree that tops 36 feet. The growing needs of the cultivars are equally various, but almost all of them are tough customers that will adapt to a wide range of soils and climate zones.

Various parts of the pungently aromatic plants have long been used medicinally and are mentioned in countless legends, primarily as aids for warding off evil spirits. But it is the plant's berries that provide an essential ingredient in gin (as well as providing flavoring for marinades and sauces).

Male and female flowers are borne on separate plants, so you must have both if you want berries. The ¼-inch fruit take two years to ripen, turning from green to a bluish purple. Both the immature and mature berries may appear on the plant simultaneously, so take care when you gather your harvest.

Junipers grow easily as long as the soil they are in is well drained. While at their best in dry, sunny spots, they will tolerate light shade. Nobody's perfect, however, and junipers are favorite prey for a number of pests and diseases. Before you buy one that catches your fancy, ask the nursery about its ability to fight off these afflictions. 🍂

HARVESTING JUNIPER BERRIES

Juniper berries should be harvested when they have ripened to a handsome, dark purple-blue. Ripe and unripe berries may be on the plant at the same time, but harvest only ripe ones. Before you add the berries to your soups or stews, air-dry them until they shrivel and turn black.

Good News for Kiwi Lovers

Q **I have been told it is possible to grow kiwis even in far northern climates. We love kiwis and would love to grow them in our garden (near Chicago), but we always thought they were tropical.**

A There are kiwis and kiwis, and none of them is tropical, though the fuzzy kind familiar from the grocery store (*Actinidia deliciosa*) starts getting iffy when temperatures fall to 10°F or so.

Hardy kiwis, on the other hand, take Northern winters in stride. *A. arguta,* the most commonly planted species, will do fine as far north as zone 5, with some cultivars tough enough for zone 4. And *A. kolomikta* 'Arctic Beauty' is rated hardy all the way through zone 3. The fruits of these species are smaller than fuzzy kiwis, about the size of grapes, but they are also grapelike in being smooth skinned—no peeling required.

Argutas are vigorous vines that are seldom bothered by pests and diseases. They will grow in a wide range of soils as long as the soil is well drained, and they ask only two things to produce large quantities of fruit. One is plenty of sunlight; the other is a male kiwi plant. Although there is one cultivar, 'Issai,' that is supposedly self-fertile, it isn't always. And 'Issai' is smaller, fussier, and less hardy than the dozen or so other cultivars available from nurseries that specialize in unusual fruit.

Consider 'Ananasnaja,' for example, which is famous for its flavor as well as its (comparatively) large fruits, or 'Ken's Red,' which is the size and color of a cherry.

If you don't have full sunshine, don't despair; you can still grow *A. kolomikta.* It will tolerate partial shade, and although the vines are not as large or productive as *A. arguta's,* they will still put out plenty of tasty fruit. Assuming of course, that you plant a pair, which in this case is certainly no hardship. Male kolomiktas are highly ornamental, with heart-shaped leaves that are variegated in green and white and pink. 🍎

My Own Mulberry

Q **I want to grow my own mulberry tree and harvest fruit. Is this possible?**

A By all means, try growing a mulberry (*Morus*) if you have full sun and enough space so that fallen fruit won't stain walks or wind up on rugs once it's tracked in. Mulberries are large trees, 30 feet and up, and they are notoriously messy. The juice from the fruit was used as a dye in the Middle Ages.

Three species of mulberry are grown for fruit. The white (*M. alba*) is the toughest, hardy to zone 4, but it is also the least tasty; its fruits, which are pink or red when ripe, tend to be insipid. The black (*M. nigra*) and the red (*M. rubra*) are both hardy to zone 5, and bear sweet fruit that is purple-black when ripe. The black makes the largest berries, but it is also the largest tree, suitable only where there is plenty of room. 🍎

Growing Persimmons

Q **In the last few years I've been eating the flat or round persimmons, which are totally different from the kind with a pointed end. These often have four seeds that are quite large. I planted them and have gotten a green-leaved plant. What will happen as it gets larger? Is it tropical? Should it be brought indoors?**

A Round, flattish persimmons like 'Fuyu,' which can be enjoyed while still firm, are indeed very different from the pointy plum-shaped varieties like 'Hachiya,' which tend to be sweeter when completely soft but are inedibly astringent until that happy day arrives. Yet both of them are the same species, *Diospyros kaki*, the Oriental persimmon. There are somewhere around 2,000 known cultivars of this fruit, most of them developed in Asia, where persimmon trees are widely admired for their beauty as well as their utility.

Height can be up to 30 feet, though it's usually kept much lower by pruning. The shiny leaves start the season pale green, then darken, then turn yellow and red before dropping in fall, and the bright orange fruit often clings long after the branches are bare, to very ornamental effect.

Oriental persimmons require plenty of sunshine and do best in areas with mild winters. They are not tropical—in fact, most require at least a short dormant period in order to bear fruit—but they thrive best in warm places, from the Carolinas on south, and even the very toughest will be killed if the temperature drops to 0°F.

American persimmons, *D. virginiana*, are considerably hardier than the Orientals. They do fine in the mid-Atlantic states, and some varieties can survive as far north as southern Massachusetts. Although their astringent-till-soft fruit tends to be small, roughly golf-ball size, it can be every bit as tasty as that of the Orientals.

Varieties are perpetuated by grafting, since persimmons do not come true from seed, and that means there's no way to know whether your plant will bear fruit that resembles the one you ate. It could be larger, smaller, more or less sweet; even its relative astringency could be different, as this characteristic can depend on weather and pollination as well as genetics.

No matter how the fruit comes out, your tree will be pretty—if it survives. Persimmon enthusiasts in areas where hardiness is borderline sometimes plant the trees in barrels and winter them over in the garage, but they aren't really houseplants. 🍎

CALLING ALL EXPLORERS

Are you partial to pawpaws, keen on hardy kiwis, hungry for hickory nuts? Time to join NAFEX, the North American Fruit Explorers, a nonprofit membership organization devoted, as its literature puts it, "to the discovery, cultivation, and appreciation of superior varieties of fruits and nuts."

That includes everything from pears to persimmons, pine nuts to pecans, and every way of growing them from conventional to organic.

The pages of "Pomona," the quarterly newsletter, are a mad mix of stories, advice, weird discoveries, and breeding and propagation techniques. A great read (for the fruit-obsessed) even if you have no more ground to grow in than a flowerpot on the fire escape.

The more than 3,000 members run the gamut from professional orchardists to backyard gardeners. All you need to join is an interest in fine fruit, a collegial spirit, and the very reasonable dues. Write NAFEX, 1716 Apples Road, Chapin, IL 62628, or log on to *www.nafex.org*.

Raspberry Know-How

Q My raspberries have become a true bramble patch. I've never been sure about how or when to prune them, so I have avoided the whole problem. Can you tell me how and when to prune so I can take back my yard?

A Understanding how raspberries produce is the key to getting the most from them. While their roots are perennial, their canes are biennial, dying after the second growing year. In order to prune successfully, you have to know which canes bear when, and that is a function of whether they are summer bearers or fall bearers.

Summer-bearing raspberries act like true biennials: the first year is for producing leaves, and the second is for flower and fruit production. After that, the dead canes just stand around interfering with berry picking. Every year, raspberries send up new canes, so the penalty for not pruning—rampant sprawl and painful harvests—mounts.

The elegant way to prune summer-bearing raspberries is to cut all the canes at soil level in the summer, after they are finished fruiting, and then prune out all but the strongest four or five new canes in the spring, once they are 8 or 10 inches high.

Know when your raspberries fruit, and you'll know when to prune them.

Fall-bearing raspberries, also (somewhat misleadingly) called ever-bearing, produce fruit twice: at the tops of the canes in late summer or early fall of the first year, and again lower down on the canes during midsummer of the second (and final) year.

Prune fall-bearers in the spring. For maximum yields, completely remove the canes that produced fruit during the previous midsummer (look for old, cracking bark on the two-year old canes). Leave enough of the brand-new canes to produce a late, first-summer crop, while removing as many as necessary to control the size of the plant.

Alternatively, you can simply cut fall-bearing raspberries to the ground each spring. You'll get only the late crop of berries, but you won't have to decide which canes are two years old and which are only one; you simply whack them all back. 🍎

Black Raspberry Pests

Q We have had a large patch of black raspberries along the back fence of our yard for years. Recently, I noticed that the undersides of the leaves of many of the plants were infested with tiny white insects, causing the afflicted plants to turn yellow. They don't seem to attack the fruit, but they're difficult to wash off when they are on the berries. How can we treat these, short of ripping out the whole patch?

A The insects might be glacial whiteflies, white apple leafhoppers, or any of several kinds of aphid, assuming, of course, that they're not some variety of scale.

There are two possible solutions, each of which will eliminate a multitude of pests. One is to spray with dormant oil in early spring, before the canes leaf out. If your predators are overwintering as eggs on the plants, this will probably smother them into submission.

The second solution is radical cleanup, especially important if you have not been cutting out the fruiting canes each year after they finished bearing. Bramble patches that grow untended for long periods often "suddenly" fall prey to diseases or insect infestations that have actually been building up for years.

In the fall, cut all canes to the ground. Rake up everything, and burn or bury it. While you're in housekeeping mode, get rid of perennial weeds like dandelions. After hard frost, mulch around the stubs of the plants with a 10-inch layer of straw, salt hay, compost, composted manure, or any combination thereof. This will protect the roots through the winter and also give the plants a leg up on the weeds when the growing season starts.

Next spring, thin each plant to the three or four strongest canes. When they're about 4 feet tall, cut off the top 8 inches or so to force fruit-bearing side branches. Unlike the red and yellow kinds, black raspberries fruit on year-old wood, so next summer will be berry-free, but the following summer you should get a bug-free bumper crop. 🐛

Weeds in the Raspberries

Q We have bought a house that has a good-size, healthy-looking raspberry patch, but it is infested with dogbane. We have been told that another name for this weed is Indian hemp. Is there any way to get rid of it without using herbicides?

A *Apocynum cannabinum,* named Indian hemp for its fibrous stems, is somewhere between perennial and eternal, hard to get rid of even if you do use herbicides.

But if you are willing to settle for control instead of eradication, the strategy is simple: prevent reseeding and starve out the deep, extensive roots. Don't try to dig it up: any missed bit of leftover root could make a new plant.

Begin by dividing the patch into orderly rows of raspberries. You will be losing a lot of plants, but wide, weed-free paths will lead you to improved fruit quality, easy picking, and triumph over dogbane.

Mark out the rows of raspberries about 2 feet wide, allowing 4 feet between them for the paths. Using a Bush Hog or weed whacker, mow the 4-foot strips down flat. Rake and discard the debris. Spread a layer of aged manure over the mown strips to feed the raspberry roots. Cover with porous landscape fabric, and top the fabric with straw.

Dogbane
(*Apocynum cannabinum*)

Now that you have paths, all you have left to worry about is the dogbane right in the raspberries. The manure will encourage it, too, but it will be easy to clip off at ground level while you are down there pruning out dead raspberry canes. Repeat every time it grows back.

If the patch is large and you have a life, you won't be able to clean it out all at once. Choose a small section, concentrate on getting it as dogbane-free as possible, and just clip off flowers from the rest so they don't make seeds.

It will take a couple of years to get each section clean, and you will have to renew the paths from time to time. But meanwhile the raspberries will be producing—brambles are tough plants by nature, and yours have already had years of practice at getting along with dogbane. ✿

Raspberries grown in full sun have the finest fruit.

Safe for Raspberries?

Q **At the end of last summer, friends gave me four cuttings from their raspberry bushes. I found a good spot for them, but it was previously occupied by lily of the valley. I know that lily of the valley is poisonous, and wonder whether raspberries planted in the same ground would be dangerous to eat.**

A Lily of the valley (*Convallaria majalis*) does contain cardiac glycosides that could be fatal if you ate a lot of them. But as long as you don't eat the lilies themselves, they shouldn't pose any danger.

"Even if the glycosides were excreted into the soil, they would likely be broken down there," said Dr. J. Scott Cameron, the national program leader for horticulture for the Agricultural Research Service of the Agriculture Department, whose research background includes a lot of work with red raspberries. "It's quite unlikely that they would be absorbed by raspberry roots and translocated into the berries."

"There is always something to be said for erring on the side of caution," Dr. Cameron continued, but borrowed toxicity is unlikely to be a problem. "While red raspberry plants are fruiting, they are also attempting to grow new roots and new shoots for the following year's crop. This creates intense competition within the plant for resources, and as a result the building blocks for fruit come primarily from the fruiting wood itself, and less from below ground."

The biggest problem with the site, he said, would not be the lilies of the valley themselves, but the fact that they did well there (if in fact they did). Lilies of the valley like partial shade and consistently moist soil that is not overly fertile. Raspberries require good drainage, full sun, and fertile soil to thrive. 🍎

Monster Bugs

Q **My strawberry plants have lots of berries, but there's something wrong with them. They're small and sort of lumpy looking and a lot of them have hard spots. They taste O.K., but the texture isn't as good as it should be because of the hard spots. The plants look fine. I have been weeding and fertilizing, and there has been plenty of rain. Why is this happening?**

A You could be having pollination problems; rainy weather at blossom time can cut down on bee activity. It's more likely, however, that what you have is tarnished plant bugs, which nothing seems to cut down except heavy artillery.

Tarnished plant bugs (*Lygus rugulipennis*) are true bugs, members of the order Hemiptera, related to squash bugs and stink bugs. As the name implies, they have the color of tarnished metal, greenish tan, with mottlings of black, gold, and silver. They're about ¼ inch long, faintly oval, and (at least compared to beetles) fairly soft-bodied. They feed by sucking, inserting their beaks into the tissues of a wide variety of flowers, including asters, hollyhocks, snapdragons, nasturtiums, and strawberries.

This deforms the flower, naturally, and in the case of strawberries it deforms the berry, too, because the damaged flower parts cannot develop properly. Tarnished plant bugs can sometimes be controlled with handpicking (go out early in the morning when they are still sluggish) or insecticidal soap, but if the infestation is heavy you may have to resort to a pyrethrum-based insecticide. Check the label carefully.

Pyrethrum itself is of comparatively low toxicity, and evanescent, but it is often mixed with other, more worrisome and/or persistent chemicals. In the old days they used DDT, which gives you an idea of what you're up against.

It will help to keep the area around the strawberry bed free of plant debris and tall weeds, both favored hiding places for the bugs when they're not eating your strawberry flowers. This is also where they overwinter, so thorough garden cleanup in the fall and good maintenance in spring will cut down on next summer's problems. ✿

Tiny Cousins

Q **Are Alpine strawberries hard to grow? Do they take a long time to start fruiting?**

A Called fraises des bois in upscale nurseries and catalogs, alpine strawberries (*Fragaria vesca* var. *semperflorens*) are close relatives of the typical hybrid garden strawberries. Too tiny to be worth dipping in dark chocolate, they do have some characteristics that gardeners welcome. Because they are small, beautiful plants that do not send out runners, they are ideal for edging or in containers, window boxes, and hanging baskets. They can handle a little shade, but the best taste still comes with the most sun.

Alpine strawberry plants are tolerant of light frosts, so they can be put outdoors as soon as the ground can be worked. Planted early, they may bear a few berries by the end of their first summer, but generally they begin bearing in spring of the following year.

If you intend to grow them strictly as ornamentals, any alpine strawberry will do. But if you mean to eat them, two things bear remembering when you order seeds or look for plants at the nursery.

Alpine strawberries
(*Fragaria vesca* var.
semperflorens)

First, they produce fruit over a long period, from three weeks to several months, so only a few thimble-size berries are ripe at any given moment on any given plant. Second, not all alpine strawberries are created equal when it comes to flavor. White fruit, while lovely to look at on the plant, has an insipid taste. For the best eating, select cultivars with red fruit such as 'Sweetheart,' 'Alexandria,' 'Baron Solemacher,' or 'Ruegen.' 🍓

Double-Duty Strawberries

Q The 'Pink Panda' strawberries at the garden center are in the perennial aisle, but it looks like they're making fruits! Can we plant these instead of the old-fashioned kind to get beauty and breakfast at the same time?

A That depends on your appetite—and your taste buds. The fruits of this pink-flowered variety are edible, but they're not abundant and not delicious; the plant was bred for its ornamental properties.

Truth is, the only strawberries you can get double duty out of are the far-less-exquisite-than-advertised white or yellow varieties of the so-called "wild" strawberry, *Fragaria vesca*. All varieties of *F. vesca*, including the red ones, make pretty plants and edible berries, but you have to net the red ones to keep birds away, which cuts down considerably on the ornamental aspect. Birds aren't attracted to the pale ones, so they are easier to integrate into a mixed garden (although they don't taste as good).

F. vesca grows wild on several continents, including this one, but the "wild strawberries" commonly served are cultivated versions. The only wild things about them are their hardiness and the small size of the fruit; the berries are about ½ inch long.

Seeds and plants of *F. vesca* are widely available by mail order. Gratification is fastest with plants, but *F. vesca* grows very quickly from seed—you might even get a few fruits the first year—so don't be afraid to try it if you're planning a large patch. 🍓

Tree Fruits

June Drop

Q My apple trees blossom heavily and set scores of fruit, but then the apples fall off and only a few mature. What can I do to get more to stay on the tree?

A From the opening of the first flower bud until picking time, a lot happens that reduces a fruit tree's potential yield. In the end, if 5 to 15 percent of the flowers become ripe fruit, the crop should be considered a good one.

Unpollinated flowers are the first cause of lost fruit. A late frost can damage buds, and strong winds can dry out the stigmas in open flowers, making them unable to receive pollen. Trees that cross-pollinate, like apple trees, need bees to bring pollen from another apple variety. Bees can be scarce in damp weather, hard winters can reduce their populations, and in some areas, bees have been so beset by parasitic mites that there are very few left.

Flowers that are poorly pollinated may set fruit, but the fruit will eventually drop. Trees that require cross-pollination may accidentally pollinate their own flowers in a wind-driven fit of confusion. (Bees that concentrate on a single tree effectively self-pollinate the blossoms.) And sometimes bees, normally experts at their work, may not cover the pistils with enough pollen. In all of these cases, the resulting fruit that sets will have too few seeds or seeds that are not viable, and the tree will drop them.

Finally, some fruit drop is self-protection. A natural thinning, called June drop, can occur from late May into July. Fruit begins to enlarge and then, for no apparent reason, falls. If it all were to grow, the competition for nutrients would prevent any fruit from reaching full size, and the weight would break the branches. So the tree sacrifices quantity for quality. After the June drop, thin out any remaining weak or small fruit by hand until the fruit is sufficiently spaced for optimum ripening. Apples and pears need 6 to 8 inches between the fruits; peaches, 4 to 6 inches; and plums, 2 to 3 inches.

And summer is still ahead. Some fruit will be lost to insects, birds, and neighborhood children. And some disease may yet wipe out the entire crop. Happy harvest. 🍎

Fruit Fall

Q **I have a semidwarf apricot tree that produces many apricots. But in recent years three-quarters of them have fallen off while still immature. Why?**

A It's possible that you are simply seeing a phenomenon called June drop. Most fruit trees do it; they're simply getting rid of fruits that weren't pollinated properly or shedding excess that's more than the tree can bear. This kind of thinning is not only natural but necessary; you'd have to remove excess fruit yourself if the tree didn't do it for you.

But there is a less benign possibility. The cause of the fruit drop may be a pest called the plum curculio, an elusive, hard-shelled beetle that also attacks peaches, apples, and pears. Also known as the snout beetle because of its elongated proboscis, this insect hibernates through winter in leaf litter and begins to emerge in spring. The females lay eggs in the developing young fruit, which provide an ideal feast for the hatching grubs.

If you have curculio damage, there will be telltale crescent-shaped scars on the fruit, easiest to see on the apricots that have dropped. Or you could look for the larvae near the pit or the hole where the larvae burrowed.

Unfortunately, once the larvae are in the fruit, they cannot be killed. So it is essential to work on prevention. Throughout the summer, pick up and destroy all fallen fruit, as close to daily as you can bear. Do the same with all surrounding leaf litter in autumn.

Fanatical hygiene will help in the long term (assuming your neighbors practice it as well), but for the first few years you will probably also have to use a pesticide. Start checking the fruit as soon as it has formed; and as soon as you see the first telltale scar, spray with an orchard formula, preferably one that contains pyrethrin or ryania or rotenone. The label should list curculio as a target.

Follow directions carefully, and remember that these pesticides are equal-opportunity killers, hitting beneficials as hard as they do the curculios. Don't use any of them until the petals have fallen, or you will destroy the pollinators working among the flowers. 🍎

WHAT IS IPM?

Organic gardeners may be the most dedicated, but they are by no means the only ones trying to work in harmony with nature. From backyard flower fanciers to farmers with global reach, more and more enlightened growers are fighting trouble with IPM (integrated pest management).

IPM is described by its advocates at the University of California as "an ecosystem-based strategy that focuses on long-term prevention of pests or their damage through a combination of techniques such as biological control, habitat manipulation, modification of cultural practices, and use of resistant varieties. Pesticides are used only after monitoring indicates they are needed according to established guidelines, and treatments are made with the goal of removing only the target organism. Pest control materials are selected and applied in a manner that minimizes risks to human health, beneficial and nontarget organisms, and the environment."

In other words, it's organic gardening except that chemicals are permitted when everything else fails. This may sound like a contradiction in terms, but in fact the heart of good organic practice is respect for the fantastic complexity (and fragility) of natural systems. Avoidance of chemicals is a result of that respect, not the base on which it is founded.

McIntosh Family Tree

Q **Last year, I picked tart and crunchy "native New England Macouns" at an orchard in Massachusetts, but at another place the owner declared them "a cross between McIntosh and a Cortland type." Given the similarities in taste, coloring, and name, one might suspect a common lineage for Macs and Macouns. But what is the relationship?**

A Like a Kentucky Derby winner put out to stud, the 'McIntosh,' a venerable apple first found around 1800 on John McIntosh's farm in Ontario, Canada, has been crossed with many other apples, often with winning results.

Macoun
apples

Your 'Macoun,' introduced in 1923, is the result of a 'McIntosh' crossed with a 'Jersey Black.'

'Cortland,' introduced in 1915, is a 'Macoun' half sister: a 'McIntosh' crossed with an apple called 'Ben Davis.' Other interesting offspring of the prolific 'McIntosh' include 'Empire' (a 1966 introduction, whose other parent is unknown), 'Jonamac' (1972, from a cross with a 'Jonathan'), 'Spartan' (1936, 'Newtown'), 'Summerred' (1964, 'Golden Delicious'), 'Tydeman Early' (1945, 'Worcester Pearmain'), and 'Liberty,' a 'McIntosh' grandchild, a cross between a 'Macoun' and a 'Purdue 54-12.' ❧

Apples from Seed

Q I wish to grow trees from the seeds of the apples I buy. I have tried several times, with different varieties, but none has germinated. Please tell me how to germinate and grow them. And at what size and age can the young trees be planted outdoors?

A The seeds in an apple are part of life's lottery: a genetic mix that is half the tree they grew on and half whatever apple tree the bee happened to visit last. As in any lottery, there are more losers than winners, and your future apples are not likely to meet your expectations, but hey, you never know.

Fair warning given, there are two steps before planting your seeds. First, apple seeds, like many others, need a cold period, called stratification, before they will germinate: 60 days in a damp paper towel or sphagnum peat moss in the refrigerator (not freezer) should do it. Second, apple seeds are coated with a chemical that inhibits germination. Normally this would come off when the seeds spend a little time in a digestive tract. You could do it that way, of course, but it would probably be better to try washing it off. After the cold period, wrap the seeds in cheesecloth, soak them for an hour, then rinse, using hot water for both—100° to 110°F. Repeat the hot-water soak and rinse several times.

Place the prepared seeds in a damp paper towel in a plastic bag, in light but not in direct sun. They should germinate in about a week. Plant three or four of the germinated seeds half an inch deep in a 6-inch pot, and keep the seedlings in full sun indoors until all danger of frost is past. Plan your timing so that the seedlings will be outside by mid summer at the latest and have time to harden off before winter.

Bury the pot up to its lip, and leave it in the ground until next spring. The seedlings can then be transplanted to your future orchard site (mark them so that no one steps on them). Assuming you have a compatible tree for cross-pollination, you'll have apples four to ten years later—and finally see if you've won the lottery. 🌿

The Apple Tree Blues

Q We have an apple tree that really started having apples last year. This year, there are a lot on the tree, but they look as if they have worms in them, and they're splitting. Also the leaves look very dry. We spray it twice in the spring. The apples are falling off the tree and are not really full size. What are we doing wrong?

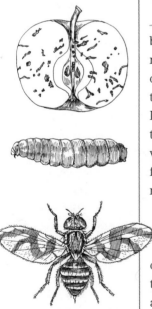

Apple maggot larvae in fruit (top); pupa (middle); adult (bottom)

A Your error is in trying to grow apples, the most pest-prone fruit in all creation. It may take a while for the bugs to notice, but once they get wind of apples in the neighborhood, they come running (also flying, crawling, and doing the hootchy-koo). You may also have made the mistake of living in an area where it has not rained in a while. Drought produces all the symptoms you describe except the worms, which may be apple maggots, codling moth larvae, or just possibly young plum curculios. Since premature fruit drop and multiple worm sightings often indicate apple maggot infestation, let's assume that's what your problem is.

To battle apple maggots, prevent buildup of pupae in the soil by regularly removing and disposing of the fallen apples. Experts recommend doing this at least weekly; once the fruit has fallen, apple maggots migrate into the soil to become pupae in roughly the time it takes to complain about the problem. If it has been dry in your area, water the tree. Come to think of it, water all your trees. It takes longer for them to show signs of stress, but that doesn't mean they aren't thirsty. Stressed plants are more vulnerable than healthy ones to insects and diseases. And trees that go into the winter in a weakened condition are more apt to suffer cold injury.

Finally, plan now to set out sticky traps next spring. Pupae hatch into adult flies in June and look in the tree for something to lay eggs in. They won't notice that those attractive bright red orbs are commercial sticky traps or old croquet balls that you've painted red and covered with a sticky coating like Tangle-Trap. They'll be sorry; you won't. ✐

Fruits and Nuts

Q **I've been told the cashew tree produces an apple that is technically not a fruit, and a nut that is technically not a nut. Botanically speaking, what is a fruit, what is a nut, and where does the bounty of the cashew tree fall?**

A Botanically speaking, a fruit is the matured ovary of a seed-producing plant, including the seeds, their coating, and anything immediately associated with them.

A nut is harder to crack. Technically, it is a hard, one-celled, one-seeded fruit whose seed is enclosed in a woody or leathery coating, and it does not open when ripe. But some nuts, including walnuts, are ambiguous. Because their fleshy coatings split, they fall somewhere between true nuts and the kernels of stone fruits, like almonds, which (technically) are not nuts at all.

But these are models of clarity compared with the cashew, *Anacardium occidentale.* In the cashew's case, the large, juicy, fleshy item (called a "cashew apple" in spite of its decidedly pear shape) is technically a swollen peduncle, or stalk. At the end of the stalk, while it is still small and svelte, a flower grows. From the flower comes the cashew nut, which is technically the fruit of the tree. Once the fruit is formed, both it and the stalk start to swell, and by harvesttime, the stalk, a culinary delight in its own right, is 8 to 10 times bigger than the fruit hanging off the end of it.

There's not much to this "real" fruit except the sweet, meaty kernel we know as a cashew, but it does include a thin, hard shell and a clinging film of brown skin. These are

Stages of the cashew (*Anacardium occidentale*)

both removed before the nut is marketed, and a good thing, too. The cashew, though tropical, is related to poison ivy, and the oils in its shell cause allergic reactions far worse than those inflicted by that odious vine. 🍐

Figs for the North

Q **I have been reading about the health benefits of figs and remembered that when I was a child in Texas, my grandmother had a fig tree in her garden. I live in Connecticut, so I'm not sure I can grow one myself, but if it is possible, I would like to try.**

A Figs are rated hardy only to zone 7, but fig lovers in cooler climates have developed a variety of antifreeze strategies that permit outdoor cultivation as far north as New York City, or even Boston, which is in zone 5. They plant tough varieties—'Brown Turkey' or 'Desert King'—in warm, protected corners. For winter, they either swaddle the trees in multiple layers of insulation or (unbelievably) bury them. To do this, they dig tree-length trenches beside the trees, which may be 12 to 15 feet tall. Then they loosen the roots, lay the trees on their sides in the trenches, and pile big mounds of soil over them. In the spring, the buried trees are exhumed and set upright in time to bloom and bear late-summer fruit.

But figs also perform well when grown in large pots, and although this method is not trouble-free, it's easier than the yearly graveyard routine. It also looks good, unlike the plant-as-mummy trick, which is an aesthetic affront of no mean proportions.

Of course, in this case large *does* mean large; the pot should be at least the size of a half whiskey barrel if you want more than a token crop. Set it on one of those wheeled platforms that makes moving easy. Leave it in a sunny spot right through early fall; you want the fig to get the message that winter is coming so it goes into dormancy. When hard frost threatens, bring it in for winter to a damp cellar or a garage where temperatures remain cold but don't go below freezing.

Ken Durio, whose family-owned Louisiana Nursery in Opelousas, Louisiana, offers 40 varieties of figs, recommends

'Magnolia' for pot culture. It's quite hardy, bears tasty fruit, and has large, deeply lobed leaves that make it worth growing as an ornamental. He also suggests 'L.S.U. Purple,' which is slow to mature but can eventually bear as many as three crops a year under ideal circumstances. 🍎

ORGANIC TREE FRUITS

For the home gardener, organic strawberries and bramble fruits are not much harder to grow than organic vegetables, but organic tree fruits are definitely a challenge. This is partly because plantings are in place for years—sometimes decades—which gives pests and diseases lots of time to dig in. It's also because fruit trees have lots of enemies, many of them widely distributed and many of them extremely tough, thanks to years of natural selection in response to chemical biocides. Nevertheless, fruit trees can be grown organically if you are willing to take the following steps:

1. Start by learning the basics. Never mind how delicious it sounds—is this something that does well in soil like yours, in your climate zone, in your micro-climate? Are there particular cultivars that have built-in disease resistance?

2. Pay close attention to the plants, keeping them in the best possible health. In addition to weeding, feeding, pruning, and applying the prophylactics (such as dormant oil sprays) that ward off problems before they happen, plan to spend plenty of time just watching out for trouble. Organically approved remedies work best when diseases are just getting started and pest populations are small.

3. Keep it clean. Many pests and diseases winter over on fallen fruit, dead leaves, or weed debris close to the target plants, and a lot of the really nasty characters need to spend time on or in the ground in order to complete their life cycles. Rake up fruit as soon as it falls and do the same for leaves, composting only healthy material (burn everything else, or send it to the landfill). Mow the area around the trees if it is in grass, plant a low cover crop such as vetch, or make sure the area is mulched.

4. Accept imperfection, which is nature's way. The goal is to have fruit that tastes good, not fruit that looks like it's made of wax.

5. Take the long view. Just as it takes years to build good soil with a fluffy texture, plentiful nutrients, and the necessary balance of life-supporting organisms, it also takes quite a while to establish the kind of self-policing ecosystem where beneficials are numerous enough to vanquish most pests.

Until this happy state is achieved, there will be many temptations to resort to strong chemical fixes "in an emergency." If you succumb, you'll lose some of the gains you've made in the journey toward balance, and the number of emergencies will not diminish as rapidly as it otherwise would.

Why Fig Trees Are Covered

Q I live in the Bronx and have a fig tree that bears very sweet blackish figs from September until the first really cold days, when there is no more ripening; the rest of the figs stay green and die off. These trees are common around New York. If you look in some backyards, you will see them covered with plastic or other material, usually topped with a garbage can. My grandfather covered his tree, my father covered his tree, and I cover my tree, but I haven't got the foggiest notion why or if it is really necessary. My neighbor doesn't cover his, and it comes back every year.

A You do it for a couple of reasons, not the least of which is to maintain the traditions of generations of Mediterranean immigrants who valued and preserved their figs through New York and Boston winters, both as a touchstone to their homelands and because they knew that the best figs are those eaten in the shade of the fig tree itself. It may be one of the last things you share with your grandfather, and the first that you share with your own children, and that's reason enough.

The more practical reason is that while the Bronx and the Mediterranean may share a lot of surnames, they don't share the same climate. Figs need a long growing season and mild winters. Those that produce fruit most reliably when planted north of their comfort zone are the varieties that would produce two crops each year in a sunnier climate. In cold climates they produce just one, in late summer or early fall. The buds grow to pencil-eraser size, then overwinter, maturing into ripe fruit during the following summer. Protecting those buds through the winter is the key.

Does your neighbor actually get any figs, or does he grow his fig tree as just a shrub? I would bet he gets few compared with you. If his fig does produce fruit, it is probably in a very protected spot, perhaps in a corner with brick or stone walls that protect it from wind and absorb and then re-emit some heat.

So continue to honor your father and grandfather. They knew what they were doing. 🍐

A Winter Coat for Figs

Q When is the proper time to cover a fig tree, and what material should be used? When should the tree be uncovered?

A Bundle the fig into its winter coat in late autumn, when all the leaves have fallen and a hard frost is near. There are several methods of protection, each of which has fierce partisans, but the following is representative.

Tie the branches together in a snug bundle, tucking straw among them so each has a bit of padding. Wrap the bundle in several layers: first, a layer of sturdy paper like the type used for roofing; next, a layer of burlap or heavy plastic; and finally, a layer of old blankets or straw mats. Be sure the wrappings are tied snugly so they don't put weight on the branches. Then encase the entire mass in heavy plastic that drapes to the ground. Try for a tapered shape that will shed snow. Tape the top and side seams well with waterproof tape so that no rain or snow can penetrate.

Remove the wrapping in early spring, when other deciduous trees are just beginning to sprout and a hard frost is no longer likely. This should be done soon enough to ensure there's no danger the tree will smother, and that means a late frost might still nip the buds and baby fruit. Be sure there are blankets or plastic handy in case you need to protect your fig one last time or two. 🍐

Growing Grapefruit

Q There was a sprouted seed in the grapefruit I had for breakfast. The grapefruit was so delicious, I decided to plant the seed. I put it in a small pot of ordinary potting soil. Will it live? What are the odds that it will produce delicious fruit someday?

A As long as the seed did not dry out while you were doing the dishes, the odds are good that it will produce a plant. The plant will have oval, shiny green leaves and be reasonably attractive in a low-key, houseplant sort of way. But unless it can grow to treehood outdoors, don't talk to any bookies about getting grapefruit from it.

Even in an ideal climate (zone 9 or warmer), you would be unwise to bet on breakfast anytime soon. Grapefruit trees that have been started from seed can take a decade or more to bear fruit. They grow 30 to 35 feet tall, mostly straight up, with few fruiting branches, and they tend to be very thorny.

For all these reasons, commercial growers prefer grafted trees, which are more compact, have fewer thorns, bear more heavily, and start producing much sooner.

On the other hand, a mature grapefruit tree grown from seed will yield several hundred pounds a year, plenty for home consumption. If you live where the climate permits and have enough room in the yard, why not go ahead and take a flier? The price is right, and most grapefruits do come true from seed, so all you need to get your payoff is patience and a long ladder. ☙

Cold Is No Friend of the Lemon

Q **I have two lemon trees that I grew from seed nine years ago. Until this winter they were grown in pots, and kept indoors during the winter months and outdoors the rest of the year. Last October, for the first time, I planted them outside. The winter has been unusually cold (it went down to single digits several times). Will they survive? Will they ever bear fruit?**

A No, unfortunately, on both counts; your lemon trees have gone to the great orchard in the sky. All the common kinds of citrus are sensitive to frost, and most lemons, which are among the tenderest, will be killed if temperatures drop below about 25°F.

But even if your trees had gone on living as before, they might not have produced for four or five more years, at which point they would have been between 10 and 20 feet tall. Seed-grown plants are a gamble when it comes to height, while citrus trees sold for pot culture are either naturally dwarf, like the Meyer lemon, or grafted onto dwarfing rootstock.

The beauty of potted lemon trees in the North is shiny green leaves, fragrant winter flowers, and a better chance at usable fruit than sweet citrus like oranges, which need hot summers to develop sugars and seldom bear well in confinement. Lemons, on the other hand, don't mind mild summers, and many varieties will be comfortable in containers as long as the containers are large and the soil in them is well drained.

The downside (there is always a downside) is that indoor conditions frequently make lemon trees vulnerable to scale, red spider mites, and other pests that thrive where plants are stressed by drought and low light. Key limes, kumquats, and sour mandarins, though not immune, are generally less bothered than lemons.

So before you try growing lemons again, consider the alternatives. Kumquats, for example, will give you the same year-round gifts of shiny leaves, fragrant flowers, and delicious fruit while giving you far less grief.

If you're set on lemons, Meyers are probably the way to go. They're hardier than other lemons (down to about 18°F), well adapted to pot culture, and quite generous about fruiting young. 🍎

The Real Mango

Q Last summer, I planted a mango seed in a window box on my terrace and then forgot about it over the winter. This year, to my delight, I have a beautiful plant with pale lilac flowers that close and fall off, leaving a round bulb with points or needles. These bulbs (at least seven or eight) are growing larger in size. Am I growing mangoes?

A Alas, no. You're growing a weed, probably, judging from the lavender flowers and spiny fruit, a datura.

Whatever it is, "it's certainly no mango," said Dr. Richard Campbell, curator of tropical fruit at Fairchild Tropical Gardens, a research center and display garden in Coral Gables, Florida. "Mangoes have whitish or yellowish flowers. They take a long time to fruit, four to ten years. And by then they'll be anywhere from 7 to 30 feet tall, depending on variety and conditions."

Mangoes are tropical, too tender to grow outdoors north of the warmer parts of zone 10, and as Dr. Campbell stressed, they are big trees, "pretty tough to fruit in a container." They make nice foliage houseplants, though, with broad, shiny leaves and a vigorous though somewhat leggy habit. (Mangoes will bush out a bit if pinched, but their main thrust is upward.)

To grow one from seed, start with a domestic mango. Imported mangoes are treated to be certain they don't bring along alien pests like fruit flies, and the seeds of treated fruit won't sprout.

Once you have a likely candidate, remove the leathery coating and plant the seed about ½ inch deep in well-drained potting soil. It doesn't matter whether the seed is lying flat or standing on edge. Put it in a warm place, 75° to 85°F.

Once started, the mango will grow quickly with a lot of bright light and a little neglect. Let the soil dry out almost completely between waterings, and feed sparingly, using only liquid fertilizer diluted to half strength, to avoid burning the sensitive roots. 🌱

Producing Fruit

Q **I have two espaliered pear trees that have borne excellent fruit just once in 14 years. They are fertilized in the spring. Is there something I can do to have fruit more often?**

A Do the trees bloom? They can't make fruit if they don't make flowers. Or, according to Richard Reisinger, orchard manager at Cornell University in Ithaca, New York, if they *are* blooming well, the problem is probably a lack of cross-pollination. "Are they two different varieties?" he asked. "You definitely need to have that for good crops." If they are two different varieties, the problem may be a lack of bees. If that's the case, you can use a small paintbrush to move the pollen around yourself.

Alternatively, the difficulty may be cultural. "People tend to overfertilize fruit trees," he continued, "and that keeps them in a juvenile, nonbearing state." If the trees are not making many flowers or are putting out more than 18 inches of new growth a year, you're probably giving them too much fertilizer.

Another possibility is that you're cutting off the fruiting spurs when you prune your trees. The short, stubby branchlets that produce the pears grow on wood that's two to four years old, so if you're removing most of each year's growth to keep the trees looking shapely, you may be removing your potential fruit as well. 🌱

SELF-FERTILE? YES AND NO

Most varieties of tree and bush fruits will not bear crops unless there is another, different variety of the same fruit nearby for cross-fertilization purposes. So it's very exciting to come across the term "self-fertile," which means the flowers of the variety can pollinate themselves. Unfortunately, although there are a few exceptions, the vast majority of "self-fertile" fruit bearers will not produce nearly as much when they stand alone as they would if they had a lover in the vicinity, blooming at the same time.

Too Many Pears

Q **Last fall, our pear tree was loaded with fruit. The branches drooped very much, especially the low ones. I'm planning to prune it soon. What should I do to prevent damage from heavy crops?**

A While you could cut off some of the fruiting spurs as part of pruning operations, prevention of damage from heavy crops usually comes later, when you remove most of the baby fruits, leaving only a few to grow to full maturity.

Saying goodbye to all that potential fruit is painful at first, but your reward will be larger, tastier pears, the reduction of dangerous weight on the branches, and a tree that bears yearly. (When pear trees produce too heavily, they tend to take a year off.)

Start thinning as soon as the fruits are about the diameter of quarters. Most will be in clusters of two to five. Remove all but the largest, healthiest pear in each cluster. You can cut off the extra ones or pull them away by hand, but whatever you do, leave the tops of the stems attached to the tree so there is no danger of damage to the fruiting wood.

When you finish, the pears should be 6 inches apart. Put the rejects in the compost. Don't leave them under the tree where they could attract pests or spread diseases. 🍐

Pears should be thinned for best quality.

Harvesting Pine Nuts

Q **Do pine nuts come from pine trees? And if so, what type? Can I grow my own here in Klamath Falls, Oregon?**

A You won't be able to grow pignoli, the most famous variety. They come from the Italian stone pine, *Pinus pinea*, a handsome, umbrella-shaped tree that is native to the Mediterranean and too tender for life in Klamath Falls.

Nurseries in your area are more likely to offer assorted cultivars of the much hardier Swiss stone pine, *P. cembra*. This species also yields nuts (as does any pine with "stone" in its name), but it is primarily an ornamental.

Dr. Peter Del Tredici, the director of living collections at Harvard University's Arnold Arboretum, said your best bet is *P. koraiensis*. It is the source of those ubiquitous Chinese pine nuts, and it is a very tough character, able to withstand high winds and temperatures of 20 to 30 below. But before you go rushing out to plant a few, bear the following in mind.

Nut-bearing pine trees tend to be slow growers, and though grafted plants might bring your wait for the first nuts down from 15 or 20 years to something more like five or six, it's going to take a good long time before you see much of a crop. When it comes, that crop will be encased in extremely hard shells. The shells will be tightly clasped in the cones, and the cones themselves will be well fixed to the upper branches of the trees, from which you must wrench them at the appropriate time. (You can't wait for them to fall of their own accord; by that time the blue jays and squirrels will have beaten you to the nuts.)

Has Dr. Del Tredici ever harvested nuts from the well-established specimens at the arboretum? No, he said: "The cones are unbelievably sticky, for starters—just to handle them is a commitment."

Planting the trees is a commitment, too, of space as well as time. Though our pinyon-nut-bearing Southwestern native, *P. edulis*, can take bush form, and some *P. cembra* cultivars are modest in size, *P. pinea* is a big tree, and *P. koraiensis* is huge. Dr. Del Tredici saw some in China that were more than 100 feet high. 🍂

Stone pines are the nut bearers.

PART FOUR

The Potted Garden

CHAPTER THIRTEEN

Houseplants

Houseplants in General

Auxin Powers

Q **It seems my houseplants all lean toward the window. Just what causes this bending?**

A Gardeners who notice what their plants are doing will observe that patterns of growth vary considerably with different light conditions. When sun-loving species are grown with full overhead light, the stems are thick, short, and upright, with leaves closely spaced. That's because the cells are growing equally on all sides of the plant.

But when the light comes from one side only, as in the case of houseplants on a windowsill, the stems on the shady side of the plant grow longer and faster. This physiological process, called phototropism (from the Greek *photo,* for "light," and *tropos,* which means "turn"), is controlled by the plant hormone auxin, which causes the cells to lengthen.

Auxin accumulates in the cells on the shaded side. Since the cells on that side then grow faster than those on the sunny side, the plants bend in the way you've observed. If you rotate

Rotate plants for even growth.

your plants a quarter turn every other week or so, you will minimize this graphic demonstration of auxin power. 🌱

Night Lights for Plants?

Q **Do plants need a period of darkness? I work in a thirty-sixth-floor office lit by several fluorescent ceiling lights and abundant northern light, but virtually no direct sun. Last winter I kept the office lights on at night so the plants had artificial light at night. They seemed to do well, but do they need a period of darkness?**

A It depends on the plants. Christmas cactus, poinsettia, and chrysanthemum need specific periods of darkness to start flowering. Flowering initiates the reproductive process, so maybe some plants are as Puritan as some people.

But there aren't many of these shy types. Most houseplants are not affected much one way or the other because light from ceiling fluorescent fixtures is not nearly as important as the window light. So why not turn the lights off when you go home? It sounds as if you have good northern light, nice and even but without direct sun—perfect for painters or low-light foliage plants. 🌱

Let There Be Light

Q **I'd like to grow indoor plants, but I have no windowsill sun. What do I need to grow them under artificial light? Is this very expensive?**

A It is so easy to set up a small light garden that it's amazing more people don't do it. All you need are two fluorescent tubes and the reflector unit that holds them. Although special bulbs have been touted as the last word in light-garden technology, they are relatively costly. Instead, many gardeners have found that the light spectrum that most plants need can be produced inexpensively by using a cool light or daylight fluorescent tube, together with a warm light tube, either 20 or 40 watts each.

Economical two-tube reflector units and bulbs can be found at hardware stores, but be sure to measure your window space so you know what size to buy.

It's easy to set up a small light garden.

Position the light unit so that the plants are no closer to the tube than about 2 inches, and no farther away than about 10 inches. A typical "day" for plants growing under lights is 14 to 16 hours, and many growers use a timer to automate sunrise and sunset. 🍂

A LIGHT IN THE BASEMENT

Grow-light arrangements are usually recommended for one of two uses: starting vegetable and flower seedlings that will be planted out in the garden, in which case the whole setup is usually hidden; or growing light-loving indoor bloomers such as African violets, in which case the setup is somewhere prominent and the unlovely look of the grow lights is simply accepted as the price one pays.

But there is a third way. Be your own florist. Keep your grow lights out of sight but use them, in quantity, to grow flowering plants for display in the rooms where you live. Nurture the plants under the lights until they are ready to bloom, enjoy the flowers, and then return them to the grow room when the show is over.

This is the only way to get flowers if you don't have strong natural light, but even if you have bright windows, going the grow-light route can be worthwhile. Not only does it conceal plants that are undistinguished when out of bloom, it also enables you to grow a good assortment of flowering plants without sacrificing your own sunshine. (Though winter greenery does lift one's mood, a jungle that blocks out most of the daylight is not all that cheering in January.)

Having a secret garden room gives you a bit more temperature control, too. Many indeed are the flowering plants that find our living rooms too warm in the day or too cold at night .

Here are a few plant possibilities that can thrive under grow lights:

For cool places (north-facing rooms, basements; 50° to 55°F during the day, 40° to 50° at night): azalea, Canary Island broom, cineraria, cyclamen, freesia, geranium (*Pelargonium* spp.), gerbera, hyacinth, fragrant violets (*Viola odorata*), plumbago, primrose, tulip.

For hot spots (turn up the thermostat in the back bedroom—70° to 75°F or more during the day, 65° to 70° at night): anthurium, Arabian jasmine (*Jasminum sambac*), Cape primrose (*Streptocarpus*), gloxinia, hibiscus, night jessamine (*Cestrum nocturnum*), many orchids.

Clean Soil

Q I'd like to use soil from my garden for my houseplants, but I've heard it's not a good idea. How can I make outdoor soil safe for indoor use?

A It is true that garden soil is rarely practical for house-plants or seedlings because it contains insects and the pathogens that afflict plants. If you don't want to buy a commercial potting mix, which is already free of these problems, you can try pasteurizing your garden soil.

To do so, sift the garden soil through your fingers to remove pebbles and twigs. Then pour it into a deep baking pan and add enough water to wet it completely. Stir thoroughly so the water is uniformly distributed. Preheat an oven to 180°F and heat the soil mixture for about 45 minutes. The procedure will kill soil-borne insects and diseases.

After the soil cools, it can be prepared for houseplants: combine equal parts of soil, sand, or perlite, and composted leaf mold or peat moss. 🌰

Fertilizing Houseplants

Q Can you address the question of fertilizing houseplants? Should I fertilize year-round? If so, how often? Should I use an all-purpose chemical fertilizer, or the liquid fish kind?

A Your phrasing implies there is a single answer to this question, instead of several million. But fertilizing houseplants is like watering houseplants: there is no general rule, except that the average houseplant is more in danger of getting too much than of getting too little.

The best course is to watch each plant for changes that will signal its needs. Is it trying to put out new leaves? Do you see a suggestion of flower buds? Or is it just sitting there looking green? Plants are hungrier when they are in active growth or preparing to bloom than they are when resting, and unlike people, they won't automatically get bigger just because you feed them more. Most foliage houseplants do keep slowly making leaves and getting larger as long as they stay alive, but very little

Different plants have different appetites.

fertilizer is required to maintain this status quo. Feeding time comes when the plant is engaged in the sort of vigorous new growth that is usually set in motion by brighter light and lengthening days.

In spite of all this, many indoor gardeners do successfully simplify life by using a very small amount of fertilizer each time they water. If you want to try it, use the fish emulsion diluted to one-eighth the recommended strength. Fish emulsion isn't as strong as the chemical formulations, so it's less likely to burn roots or lead to a damaging buildup of mineral salts in the soil. And at this dilution, it won't be unpleasantly strong smelling once feeding time is past. 🌶

Fertilizer Leftovers

Q **The tops of my houseplant pots are coated with a crust. Is it harmful?**

A What you're seeing is a buildup of salts from chemical fertilizers. Although this is not harmful in itself, leaves touching the salt-coated portions will rot and fall off. The easiest way to dissolve salts from clay containers is to soak the pots for about 15 minutes in warm water. To prevent damage from future buildup, coat the rims with melted wax. And regularly water plants generously enough so that excessive salts are flushed out the drainage hole. 🌶

Strange Plant Food

Q **I've heard that gelatin is helpful to plants. Is it really, or is this just a myth?**

A At first blush it may seem like a lot of hooey, but gelatin contains nitrogen, an essential element for plant growth and particularly for lush, rich foliage. (A nitrogen deficiency is indicated by yellowish or pale leaf tones.) Because of the quantity and cost involved, though, gelatin is probably more useful for houseplants or window boxes than for large garden areas.

There are no official guidelines, but a safe dosage for foliage plants is one small envelope of gelatin (unflavored and unsweetened, please) dissolved in a quart of water.

Use the mixture to water the plants once every three weeks during the season of active growth. 🌰

Plants In, Bugs Out

Q My houseplants have spent the summer on my porch. I'll move them back inside soon, but I've noticed earwigs in my spider plants. Should I wait until the temperature drops enough to harm the bugs (but not, I hope, the plants)?

A Most houseplants are tropical or subtropical in origin while the bugs are local, so don't bet on giving the bugs the cold shoulder before the plants begin to suffer. Fortunately, earwigs and other insects in the soil can be forced to the surface by soaking the pot up to its rim in a sink full of water. What you do with the bugs as they surface is up to you. 🌰

Putting the Water on Automatic

Q I will be away for almost two months this winter. What is the best automatic watering system for houseplants?

A There are several automatic watering systems available for houseplants, though none is as good as a friend or neighbor who will stick a finger in the soil to see if water is needed.

Vacation watering systems mostly depend on the laws of physics to move water from reservoirs to dry pots. Some use wicks or tubes with sensors that go right down into the soil. Capillary mats bring the water in contact with the drainage holes on the bottom of the pot, where it can be absorbed and transferred to the soil. Either way, as the soil dries, water is drawn into the pot.

Another system, sold under various names, is a battery-operated pump that regularly delivers a set amount of water into the pot whether or not the soil is dry. Before you buy one, think about Mickey Mouse's broom running amok in the "Sorcerer's Apprentice" segment of *Fantasia*.

No matter which system you choose, expect some indignation from the plants. You'd better bring them back something better than a T-shirt. 🌰

HOME ALONE

Only a plant-savvy human being can give an assortment of houseplants the different amounts of water they're likely to need while they are home alone. But it isn't always easy to find a willing plant sitter, and it's even harder to find one who not only means well but has houseplant skills (returning to find that two-thirds of one's little green children have drowned is no better than finding them dried to a crisp). So if you must leave them untended, the following steps should keep them alive—if not happy—for up to a month.

1. One at a time, bring the plants into very bright light and check them over top to bottom for pests and diseases. Don't forget to look under the leaves and against the stems where they enter the soil. Problems that are very small now can balloon in your absence, and since the plants will be grouped together, those problems are likely to spread. Any afflicted plants should be treated and, for good measure, kept quarantined in a room of their own while you're gone.

2. Decide on a water-delivery system, ideally one that is triggered by the plant itself. Like the overzealous friend, timer-driven waterers usually deliver more than the plants need. Garden-supply stores and catalogs sell an assortment of capillary mats and water wicks that are less likely to drown plants, or you can go the low-tech route and opt for just supplying humidity (put the plants in plastic dish tubs lined with deep layers of pebbles or styrofoam peanuts and shallow layers of water.)

3. Set up the system where the plants will stay cool and get only a small amount of light. The bathroom is probably the best place since it is usually both cool and dark, and is the room best protected against water damage. If the plants will all fit in the tub, plan to put them there. Don't draw the shower curtain unless the room is very bright.

4. Water everything thoroughly. Soak clay pots until saturated; bottom-water plants in plastic pots until soil at the surface is wet. Let excess water drain, then group plants closely but not tightly—there must be a bit of air circulation or they'll all get fungus diseases.

5. Speak to them lovingly and close the door. They'll be fine.

Chlorine on Tap

Q **Is the chlorine in tap water harmful to my houseplants, and what are the signs of trouble? I read that water should be left for several days so that the chlorine evaporates. Does this work?**

A If chlorine does harm the plants, the injury will be to the root tips, said Len Morino, propagation manager for the New York Botanical Garden. "Although it's not a bad idea to leave the water you use for plants sitting around for about 24 hours if you can, we've found that the chlorine in the water hasn't proven to be a problem at all. In the New York Botanical Garden greenhouses, we use straight tap water for everything, and that includes seedlings."

Very likely, the reason chlorine rarely causes trouble in the tap water used for plants, he said, is that in the course of moving through the municipal system, most of it volatilizes, that is, it escapes into the air in the form of gas. "Chlorine just doesn't remain long," he added, "which is why it has to be added repeatedly to swimming pools."

That said, it must be added that some municipalities add heavier doses of chlorine, or add them closer to the end user, than happens in New York, so let your senses be your guide. If you can taste—or smell—chlorine, there's probably enough of it coming out of the tap to make aging it a good idea for the plants. Draw the water into wide-mouth jugs and let them sit uncovered for at least a day before you pour it on. 🌰

Softened Water

Q I have been told not to use softened water for my houseplants. Why not? If it is better for my own use, why isn't it good for my plants?

A The things that make water hard are minerals like calcium and magnesium. Water softeners remove these minerals (which plants like) by exchanging them for the sodium part of the salt (sodium chloride) that is found in the softener. Not enough sodium goes into the water to affect its taste, but there is much more than would be there naturally.

Sodium is a very active chemical. It also exchanges places with the potassium in plant cells, which is necessary for dozens of cell enzyme functions. When potassium is replaced by sodium, these functions can't happen and the plant could die. Different species have different tolerances, but eventually the sodium buildup will get to all but those that grow naturally at the seashore. 🌰

Recycling Water

Q **Is it O.K. to use water removed from the air by a dehumidifier to water my plants?**

A This sounds like a great idea. In fact, some indoor gardeners have written in to suggest it should be broadcast. But the General Electric Company, one of several manufacturers of dehumidifiers, does not advise re-using the water from these machines for anything. At the same time, though, no one at G.E. could say exactly why the company came to this conclusion.

If you don't use one of the solvents sold for cleaning dehumidifiers—these may contain chemicals harmful to plants—you might do a bit of experimenting yourself: use the water collected by your dehumidifier on one inexpensive plant for several weeks and see what happens.

And just to be on the safe side, don't use the water on anything you plan to eat. 🌱

Inspecting New Plants

Q **Every spring and summer, I buy petunias, jasmine, and assorted annuals for my apartment windows. I look them over carefully before buying. But last summer, one plant turned out to have tiny flying bugs (I don't think they were whiteflies). Do you have any tips for what to look for when buying so as not to infest a whole apartment?**

A There are two strategies: one to employ when shopping, the other to protect your older plants after the purchase. Start by checking the prospective adoptee for general health as well as for insects themselves.

Are there signs that a lot of leaves were removed? That may be because they were damaged by bugs. Are the leaves that are there unusually curly? Curled leaves can signal that there were aphids or red spider mites around while the seedlings were growing. Though the grower may have gotten rid of adult insects by spraying the plants with a pesticide or a blast of water, just one escaped aphid is enough to start a whole new infestation.

Thus, Strategy 2: the quarantine. Before letting a new plant join your old friends, keep it by itself for 10 to 12 days so you can monitor developments. Your apartment's best growing locations probably already have plants in them, but the newcomer will be all right cooling its heels in a less-favored place as long as its sojourn there is comparatively short. 🌶

Give Soap a Chance

Q **With the onset of spring, it seems that every bug in the book is attacking my houseplants. I've tried soapy water to no avail, and I don't like chemicals. Now what?**

A You're on the right track with the soapy water, but not all soaps are created equal in the bug-killing department. Though all of them are formed by the interaction of fat with an alkaline substance, the number and nature of the fatty acids they contain varies quite a bit. That doesn't matter when you're washing the dishes, but it can mean a lot when you are trying to cope with an aphid invasion.

So before you give up on soap, try a product specially formulated for houseplant care. Not only is it more likely to do the job for which it is intended, it is also less likely to burn the leaves of sensitive plants. 🌶

Be sure to spray underneath the leaves.

Washing Away Scale

Q **Is there any way to rid my houseplants of scale? I spray twice yearly with an insecticidal soap to no avail. What am I doing wrong?**

A You're not doing anything wrong. You're just not doing enough of what's right. Mature scale insects can be extremely frustrating because they're protected by a shell-like cover. But when this is removed, the insect dies. So one effective method to get rid of them is to use your fingernail and flick them off the plant (or use a brush if you're squeamish). Young scale insects, called crawlers, are less easily seen but are more easily wiped away.

In any case, a soapy spray is not as effective as a soapy bath. The real secret to eventual success is to bathe plants repeatedly, at least once a week. This is because the insects reproduce parthenogenically: even if only one survives, it can reproduce all by itself.

To make an effective bath, fill a sink or bucket with a gallon or two of warm water. Add the insecticidal soap, following the package directions if it is concentrated. If it is the prediluted mix, remove the spray top and pour in about a third of a cup for each gallon of water. Turn small plants upside down and hold the stems under the water for several seconds. (Keep the soil in place by covering it with tin foil or with a wet paper towel, and hold your hand over it when you turn the plant over.) Large plants can be laid on their sides and their limbs gently dipped into the sink.

A soapy bath

Strategies for Brown Scale

Q **I have had a hanging ivy plant indoors, in a window that gets quite a bit of light, for a couple of years. It hasn't really thrived, but it hasn't died either. For the last year or so, I've noticed a sticky substance on the leaves and the surrounding floor. What is it and what can I do?**

A That sticky mess, called honeydew, is—how to be delicate here?—sap from the ivy that has not been entirely digested. The culprits are soft brown scale insects, common on many houseplants. They are quite small, and as adults they form a flattish, oval, scalelike yellow-brown covering. Look for them on the undersides of the leaves, along the midrib, and on the stems. They are good at hiding (very nondescript, mostly just sitting there quietly), so you'll have to look carefully, using a small magnifying lens.

Juveniles, or crawlers, are even smaller than adults. They move about, looking for a place to settle down, and are more vulnerable.

What to do? If the ivy is that encrusted, it's probably best to throw it out and buy another plant. If you prefer, crawlers and adults can be killed with insecticidal soap. Or you can remove them one at a time, on an otherwise boring evening, with a cotton swab dipped in rubbing alcohol.

Whiteflies Indoors

Q **I have many houseplants, some on windowsills and others under fluorescent lights, but all have been invaded by whiteflies. I tried spraying but nothing has worked. Where did the whiteflies come from, and how do I get rid of them?**

A You are hardly alone in your fight with whiteflies. These pests are the bane of every indoor gardener, and they always seem to find a way to sneak inside. Sometimes it's via eggs hidden on new plant purchases; at other times, it's through open windows.

Your best defense is zealous adherence to sanitation: a weekly cleaning for every plant. Either dip the plants, upside down, in a soapy water solution or spray them with an insecticidal soap (first, read the label for application directions and the list of plants that cannot tolerate the soap). Some gardeners also find that after lightly shaking the plants, they can catch flying insects with a vacuum cleaner. Others gain some control by hanging strips of flypaper near the plants.

In any case, it is wise to isolate all new plants for several weeks, or until you are sure they are squeaky clean. And don't be afraid to be ruthless about eliminating plants that have passed the point of no return. Some may simply not be worth the time and effort needed to save them. 🍂

Ladybug Invasion

Q **For the past two autumns we have had a colony of ladybugs infesting the house. They cluster on the 30-foot-high ceiling of the family room. How can we prevent their entering, and how can they be removed? Vacuuming has been suggested, but is not possible because of the height.**

A Of all the ladybugs (also called lady beetles or lady bird beetles), the Asian ladybug, *Harmonia axyridis,* seems to be the one most likely to come indoors for the winter. It occurs in a variety of fashionable designs, with an orange or red body and anywhere from no black spots to 20.

Asian ladybugs were brought to this country and released in the late 1970s to attack agricultural pests but did not thrive. In the mid 1980s, though, they came in as stowaways through the port of New Orleans and did better on their own. Spreading by winds, they gradually adapted to new conditions. By 1990 they had reached Georgia, and only four years later, they were in upstate New York. Asian ladybugs are now found as far north as Maine.

Most ladybugs—and there are hundreds of species in North America—hibernate burrowed in leaf litter. But Asian ladybugs find buildings appealing. Just a few would suggest that they're probably coming in unnoticed through an open door. A gathering of ladybugs means that a window, chimney, or attic isn't completely sealed. That's worth finding and correcting: if ladybugs are getting in, heat is getting out.

In a cool spot—an unheated room, attic, or barn for example—their metabolism slows enough for them to survive the winter and emerge with a stretch and a healthy appetite in spring. Living areas, however, are too warm for them to hibernate in, and the ladybugs will die of dehydration, falling to the floor in a week or so. Now you can use the vacuum.

There are hundreds of ladybug species in North America.

Don't try swatting or sweeping them from the walls. When disturbed, ladybugs exude a blood-like orange liquid as a protective mechanism. It tastes bad to predators, but it also stains and stinks. It's the only unfriendly thing ladybugs do. ✿

New Office Problems

Q When my office moved to a location with an open layout, my plants and those of others became infested with tiny black flying insects. They seem to particularly like my amaryllis, which I'm reluctant to throw out because it is a small-flowered variety and hard to find. I've repotted the plants and tried insect spray, but the problem has only been reduced. Can you tell me what these insects might be and how to control them?

A Apparently, having an office door to close not only provides status and a quieter environment in which to work (or nap), but also a barrier for all sorts of pests, including flying ones. Someone either brought their fungus gnats along from the old office, or on a new plant.

The weak flying adults you observe are the final stage of a three-week life cycle. In the larval stage, they eat decaying organic material in the soil, and occasionally small root hairs.

You can verify that these are fungus gnats by slightly pushing a potato half, cut side down, into the soil. If larvae are present, in three to four days some will rise to the potato and tunnel up inside it.

Fungus gnats are more bother than trouble, but letting the soil dry out between waterings will help discourage them. Or you can buy one of the commercial controls for fungus gnats that uses Bt (*Bacillus thuringiensis*), a bacterium that is toxic to larvae when eaten, but this will have to be an office-wide treatment. 🍂

Frost Through the Window

Q **Maybe the snow outside has brought it to my attention, but lately I've noticed blackened areas on the leaves of several of my windowsill houseplants, including begonias, philodendron, and African violets. Other than that, they seem all right. So what is happening?**

A The culprit is probably the winter night. Very likely, you have no storm windows or other window insulation, and the leaves of these tropical houseplants are touching the glass and then being injured by frost.

Move the plants back from the windowpane to the innermost portion of the sill, and make sure that no foliage touches the glass. Then either remove the damaged leaves or cut the damaged portions back to about half an inch below the blackened part. The dead leaf area will not regenerate, but if the damaged sections are removed, no rot diseases will develop and move into healthy leaf tissue. 🍂

Plants for Dark Sills

Q **In my new apartment, the sunlight on the windows ranges from none to only a little. Can you suggest some easily grown plants to decorate my sills?**

Y ou're on the path to indoor success because you've already taken stock of the light you have and are seeking plants to match.

A windowsill that faces north, or is completely obstructed so that it has no direct sun but only bright light, is most challenging. Here you may try the rabbit's-foot fern (*Davallia fejeensis*), with its delicate, finely cut leaves. It demands only that its soil be kept evenly moist.

Or try the Swiss-cheese plant (*Monstera deliciosa*), whose large, heart-shaped foliage is deeply cut and perforated. The old-fashioned cast-iron plant (*Aspidistra elatior*), with its leathery-looking elongated leaves, is also . ideal for a north sill, as is the ox tongue or wart gasteria (*Gasteria verrucosa*), which has 6-inch-long, tongue-shaped leaves that are dotted with small white bumps.

Also challenging is a sill with only two hours or so a day of direct rays. But this exposure should suffice for the creeping fig (*Ficus pumila*), which has trailing, fingerlike branches lined with tiny, thin, heart-shaped leaves, or the staghorn fern (*Platycerium bifurcatum*), with its elegant, antlerlike silvery green leaves.

The graceful strawberry begonia, also known as mother-of-thousands (*Saxifraga stolonifera*), has rounded, deep olive-green leaves with ragged edges and silvery veins. It tolerates a scant two hours of sun, as does the slipper orchid (*Paphiopedilum* spp.), whose leathery oval leaves are often mottled with hints of red or silver. 🍂

Summer Greening Indoors

Q I'm an apartment dweller, but with summer coming I want to have greenery, too—indoors. What do you suggest?

A Imaginative planning can turn any windowsill into a Lilliputian tropical retreat. But be sure to match the plant with the available light.

Species that do well without sun but with bright reflected light include cast-iron plant (*Aspidistra elatior*), prayer plant (*Maranta leuconeura*), spathiphyllum, and many ferns. Plants for sills with three hours' sun include fuchsia, ponytail plant (*Beaucarnea recurvata*), kaffir lily (*Clivia miniata*), and jewel orchid (*Ludisia discolor*). On sills with at least five hours' sun, try pincushion cactuses (*Mammilaria* spp.), elephant bush (*Portulacaria afra variegata*), Madagascar palm (*Pachypodium lamerei*), or scented-leaf geraniums. 🍂

KEEP THE ASPIDISTRA FLYING:
10 BEST BETS FOR BLACK THUMBS

Because they are so widely used, the plants on this list have an image problem. But though they will never win prizes for originality, they are all both good looking and nearly unkillable—which is no small pair of virtues. Of course, there is a difference between "thriving" and "not dead"; like all plants, even these almost-indestructibles will be happier if you give them appropriate care.

Aloe (*Aloe* spp.). The true aloe, *A. vera,* with long, pale green, succulent leaves, is the best known and the one to choose if you want it for healing burns. But there are several other, more decorative types, such as the handsomely striped tiger aloe (*A. variegata*). Aloes are very easy to grow. They prefer bright, indirect light and comparatively cool temperatures, but will put up with almost anything as long as you pot them in soil that drains well, and don't overwater.

Boston fern (*Nephrolepis exultata bostoniensis*). If you imagine a fern on a pedestal in a Victorian parlor, this is the fern in your mind's eye. The fronds of the species make sweeping arcs and can be as long as 3 feet. Dwarf cultivars are smaller, and some of them are upright. These plants need some light but don't want bright sun, and they do best in soil that is constantly moist. That's moist, not wet, but this is still a good plant to choose if you tend to overwater things.

Cast-iron plant (*Aspidistra elatior*). Dark, strap-shaped leaves, streaked with cream in the cultivar 'Variegata.' Leaves grow from 12 to 18 (or more) inches long, on short stems that start at ground level. Because there is no upwardly mobile central stem, the cast-iron plant never gets very tall. It never gets very anything, but it doesn't mind the scant light and dry warmth that tend to be a houseplant's portion, and it is amazingly tolerant of erratic watering.

Zonal geranium (*Pelargonium* × *hortorum*). Most geraniums are easy keepers, but the zonal ones are the survivors *par excellence*. They have round leaves, usually with concentric stripes of colors around the edges. And if they are given a combination of cool temperatures and strong sunlight, they will repeatedly produce large flower clusters. The most important tool for nurturing them is a pair of shears; geraniums tend to become gangly even when conditions are perfect, and they can get extremely gangly if light is scarce. Frequent cutting back will keep them bushy and healthy.

Ivy (*Hedera helix*). Ivy is tough stuff, willing to spread in almost any light, willing to put up with almost any soil, as long as it neither dries out nor drowns. It's responsive to fertilizer but also able to grow for long periods without being fed at all. And while ivy's unhappy at temperatures above 75°F, it doesn't care how cold it gets, as long as it doesn't freeze. There are a gazillion cultivars, in a wide range of shapes, shades of green, and patterns of variegation, so if you shop at a well-stocked greenhouse, you can get a truly gorgeous assortment.

Parlor maple (*Abutilon* spp.). The name comes from the beautiful leaves, which, like true maple leaves, have figured out a lot of ways to vary their basic shape. Leaf colors are various as well, from a clear true green to one that is extravagantly mottled with gold. But the thing that makes these plants so popular is their ability to bloom year-round. As long as they get plenty of bright sunlight, consistent moisture, and monthly doses of fertilizer, they will keep right on pumping out their wide bells of white, yellow, orange, or red.

Philodendron (*Philodendron* spp.). The plant that built the houseplant industry. There are literally thousands to choose from: bushy or climbing, petite or enormous, shiny-leaved or velvety, as familiar as those in your local bank or as exotic as orchids (well, almost). Philodendrons ask only for consistently moist soil and a fair amount of indirect light; strong sun will burn the leaves. They aren't fussy about temperature, but warmer is better; days of 80° to 85°F don't faze them a bit.

Strawberry begonia (*Saxifraga stolonifera*). No relation to either namesake, except a visual one. The rounded leaves with scalloped edges look like begonia leaves. The gracefully trailing runners, each with a tiny plant at the end, look like those of strawberry

plants. The mother plant makes a tidy mound, the runners drape around the sides, and from the center (in the summer) rises a cloud of tiny white flowers on long, wiry stems. Strawberry begonias are moderates: not too much light, not too much heat, not too much to eat or drink. (Fertilize very sparingly and let the soil dry out an inch down between waterings.)

Swedish ivy (*Plectranthus* spp.). Natives of Africa and Australia, actually, but it was the Swedes who first realized that these handsome, fast-growing plants were ideally suited to indoor culture. We're talking about a bushy trailer (it's not a true vine) that will keep right on growing even in the depths of a Northern winter. All it needs is bright, indirect light and constantly moist soil. This is a plant that will not only root but grow in nothing more than a glass of water; so as long as you don't let it dry out, it's pretty hard to kill.

Tradescantia and zebrina (*Tradescantia* spp.; *Zebrina* spp.). These closely related groups of plants (known in less ethnically sensitive days as wandering Jews) all make fountains of long, drooping stems clothed in simple 1- to 3-inch leaves. They come in many colorations, most of them involving green and most of them involving stripes, as in *Z. pendula tricolor*, which is shades of light and dark green, white, and pink. All do best in bright, indirect light, but tradescantias like it a bit cooler than zebrinas do, and zebrinas like moist soil, while their cousins prefer to dry out a bit between waterings.

Indoor Tropics

Q We have an empty shelf near our bathtub. Although this area is bright, it does not receive direct sun. Assuming we add a lattice for support, what climbing plants could we grow?

A If you think of your bathroom as a quasi-tropical forest—with low light and regular periods of high humidity—it should help you determine which plants are most likely to succeed.

Among the trailing or climbing plants that should be content with your conditions are many cultivars of the arrowhead vine (*Syngonium podophyllum*), grape ivy (*Cissus rhombifolia*), Mexican breadfruit (*Monstera deliciosa*), the mosaic plant (*Fittonia verschaffeltii*), many hybrids of such philodendron species as *Philodendron lacerum, P. oxycardium,* and *P. sodiaroi,* and quite a few kinds of English ivy (*Hedera helix*). 🍎

Good Plants for Great Pots

Q I have two gorgeous urns that I want to put in front of the windows in our formal dining room. What can I put in them that will be out of the ordinary, spectacular, and long lasting, and that will survive in indirect light?

A How about loose bundles of long twigs, painted the color of the walls and tied with matching raffia? Goldfish could be impressive, assuming that the urns are large enough to accept the requisite bowls.

If you want to put plants in them, though, there are reasons to stick with tradition rather than lusting for novelty.

To start with, the urns are supposed to star: their contents should not compete for attention. And plants that merely survive won't do. They have to look very nearly perfect. They have to do it all the time. And they have to do it under less than optimal conditions.

Finally, life being imperfect, they have to be easy and inexpensive to replace. Unusual plants usually take unusual care, and if one of them starts declining, there goes the symmetry of your arrangement and your gorgeousness as well.

Rex begonia suits a wide, low urn.

One of the many versions of Boston fern will work well with simple urns, which are enhanced by a veil of green drapery. An upright grower like parlor palm (*Chamaedorea elegans*) might be a better choice if your urns are elaborately glazed or carved. If they are shallow, wide, and bold, consider coleus or rex begonia. Both are bushy and mound-shaped, with broad leaves in showy colors and patterns.

Size and splendor are pretty much synonymous in this case, but don't forget that any plant in front of the windows will be between you and the light. Something that is spectacular at night could give you deeply gloomy days if your windows are on the small side. 🌿

Houseplants That Bloom

Q **With the end of summer approaching, I want to add to my houseplant collection and would like species that flower. I have windowsill sun for about half the day. What plants do you suggest?**

Flowering plants need lots of light.

A Although half a day of sun is a good beginning, to keep houseplants in bloom you will also have to match each species with the humidity and temperature it prefers. So some experimenting is in order.

Among the plants that are relatively reliable indoor bloomers, given your light conditions, are browallia, gloxinia (*Sinningia speciosa*), shrimp plant (*Beloperone guttata*), chirita, cigar plant (*Cuphea ignea*), cyclamen, Cape primrose (*Streptocarpus* hybrids), and many kinds of begonias and African violets (*Saintpaulia* hybrids). Many orchids, too, are superb as houseplants. 🌿

Tall, Green, and Dramatic

Q **I just moved to a new apartment, and I would like to decorate with tall, dramatic houseplants. There is only bright reflected light, no direct sun. But I may add plant spotlights later. What species do you suggest?**

A The plants that should serve you best are the tropical species whose foliage has design potential on a grand scale. Although spotlights will definitely broaden your possibilities, plants that survive with low light include the fiddle-leaf fig (*Ficus lyrata*), gold dust tree (*Aucuba japonica*), schefflera (*Brassaia actinophylla*), dumb cane plant (*Dieffenbachia amoena*), and snakeplant (*Sansevieria trifasciata*).

You might also consider a number of palms, including the lady palm (*Rhapis humilis*), parlor palm (*Chamaedorea elegans*), Kentia palm (*Howea forsteriana*), curly sentry palm (*Howea belmoreana*), and petticoat palm (*Washingtonia filifera*). Also notable is the Sago palm (*Cycas circinalis*)— although it's a cycad, not really a palm. ❧

Greenery vs. Toxins

Q **I have read that certain houseplants are particularly effective at removing toxic substances from the air. (Those mentioned include the spider plant, English ivy, and dracaena.) Is there any truth to this?**

A The most impressive tests of this hypothesis were conducted in the 1980s by scientists of the National Aeronautics and Space Administration. They put plants and pollutants together in sealed containers and measured marked reductions in gases, including formaldehyde, benzene, and carbon dioxide.

Unfortunately, the sealed environment is central to the effect. Open a window, and the impressive results fly out of it. As skeptics have pointed out, it would probably take hundreds of plants to refresh the air as well as proper ventilation does.

Indoor air pollution is in large part caused by "outgassing," the release of toxic substances by a host of common products. From plywood to permanent-press fabrics, the synthetic rug to the ceiling tiles, many furnishings of daily life constantly exude unhealthy chemicals such as formaldehyde, xylene, toluene, ammonia, and benzene. Plants can remove small quantities of these from the air, but they cannot stop the outgassing itself; so control at the source should not be ignored. Score another point for natural fibers. ❧

TIPS ON PUTTING POTS IN POTS

- The outer pot is called a cachepot, from the French for "hide pot," and it can be made of any material, in any shape. As long as you can put a potted plant in it, it qualifies. Ironically, the one thing it is unwise to use is a valuable antique cachepot—or actually, a valuable antique anything. The minerals and algae that tend to collect on the inside of cachepots can discolor porcelain, bond to metal, or otherwise cause irreversible damage. Plastic liners are not reliable damage preventatives, though if you are determined to use an antique, a liner may help protect it.
- If the outer container is china or glass, use a plastic pot inside to minimize the chance of breakage if the interior pot hits it. If the outer container is metal, wood, or straw, line it with plastic for protection against rot, and use clay for the inner pot to give the plant roots a slightly better chance to breathe.
- Prop up the inside pot. Water is going to run out of it and collect in the cachepot, and if the plant sits in water constantly, the roots are likely to rot. Any water-resistant elevator will work: a piece of brick, an overturned saucer, or a short stack of plastic deli tubs (open end down). You can also just use a thick layer of pebbles, perlite, or styrofoam beads, though loose materials like these make routine maintenance more difficult.
- Remember to lift out the plant and empty the cachepot frequently; that water can get *nasty*. And if the assemblage is outside, mosquitoes can breed in it. Outdoor cachepots should contain small chunks of Mosquito Dunk (a biological control organism, widely available at garden stores).

Making Houseplants Feel at Home

Q **What triggers bloom in houseplants? I'd like to provide the conditions that will make my collection flower.**

A Plants bloom if they get good care—the right light, temperature, water, food, and growing medium—but the details depend on the particular species. If you can get one African violet to bloom, you'll be successful with any of them. But if you treat your kalanchoe the same way, it will probably never flower.

The goal is to provide an environment that's as close as possible to conditions in the plant's native home. Some plants, for instance, have learned to face adversity—periods of cold or dry—by going dormant for a while. For many, going through this dormant period is required to trigger blooming. In the wild, plants recognize when to go dormant by being sensitive to shorter days, lower temperatures, or reduced rainfall.

In a house, dormancy is induced naturally by shorter days, or by your withholding water or putting the plant in a cooler spot. Growth slows, and the plant needs less fertilizer and water. When days lengthen and become warmer or you resume more generous watering, you complete the cycle, and flowering begins.

Other plants come from environments where light, temperature, and rainfall are about the same all year. Those plants can grow and flower anytime, so they rarely need a dormant period to induce flowering. Since they are always growing, the amounts of light, fertilizer, and water you give them throughout the year remain constant. The amounts depend on the species.

There are many more refinements—almost as many as there are environments for plants to grow in. No one source covers every houseplant, but specialized books and university Internet sites are good sources of information about what particular plants need, as are the societies that seem to exist for nearly every plant except refrigerator mold. So think of every potential houseplant as a stranger you need to know more about before you bring it home. 🍂

Humidity Problems

Q **The warm winter seems to be inspiring high humidity in my greenhouse, causing some problems. What can I do?**

A Most plants love moist air. And high humidity is essential where seeds are germinating and cuttings are rooting. But when mold starts taking over the soil and diseases rage, there may be too much of a good thing.

Standard humidity control includes watering only in the morning, watering sparingly (just as needed), and using fans to circulate the air even when the greenhouse is sealed tight in winter. Ventilating moist air to the outside might be necessary in extreme cases, and you can also install an air-to-air heat exchanger. This device converts warm, moist air to cool, dry air and is available from greenhouse-supply stores. 🌶

Stop That Sun

Q **I have a greenhouse/sunroom with plants. I like to sit there, but the summer sun is unbearable. How can I stop it without losing good light?**

A All you have to do is choose from among the various shading materials designed for use in greenhouses and sold by specialty companies that advertise in garden magazines (look in the back) and on the Internet.

One option is shade paint applied to the exterior glass. It has a whitish hue on sunny days, but when it's wet, it becomes transparent, allowing light to penetrate on dark, rainy days.

An assortment of screens and panels is also available. Fabric sunscreens, for example, which come in charcoal, brown, or gray, are made of vinyl-coated fiberglass or polyester. Shade panels of polypropylene with an ultraviolet block come in a large assortment of widths, lengths, and prices depending on size and density.

Many suppliers will put together a customized package for you, or you might go for the gauzy tent look and just swathe the place with thin muslin. 🌶

Ultraviolet-Blocking Glass

Q **My company moved into a building that has ultraviolet blocking glass in the windows. I have heard that plants need ultraviolet light and I wonder whether I should bring some houseplants to work.**

A It depends. To block ultraviolet light (which causes colors to fade) and infrared (which heats the air), a special film is laminated to clear glass. There are several brands, but this type of glass is generally called "low-e" glass ("e" for "emissivity," the relative ability to reflect heat). Its function is to turn buildings into thermos bottles, preventing heat from moving inside in summer and outside in winter.

Plants use the blue part of the light spectrum, and a tiny bit of the neighboring ultraviolet to regulate their enzyme and respiratory processes and encourage compact growth with dark green leaves. They skip the green portion of the spectrum, simply reflecting it from the leaf surface. Red light stimulates stem and leaf growth.

Untinted low-e glass blocks light outside the range of wavelengths that plants use, so plants can get along quite well behind it. In fact, the Missouri Botanical Garden's spectacular Climatron is made of low-e glass. As long as there is enough light (brightness and duration) and the temperature is right, growth rates are not noticeably affected.

Plants may suffer, however, when low-e glass is tinted. If gray is added, all light is reduced. Too much gray and plants suffer as if they were in the shade. Bronze and green tinting are more serious. Bronze blocks blue light and green blocks both blue and red. Under these conditions, you may want to raise silk flowers instead of spider plants. 🍂

Houseplants in Particular

Pampering African Violets

Q **Where can I find healthy African violets? I often find them at a florist, take them home, and take good care of them, but once they have blossomed they refuse to blossom again. How can I keep them flowering?**

African violets need a light soil.

A More light, please, and a light, soilless potting mix. African violets insist on having bright indirect light, even preferring to be moved into full sunlight from November through March, and they never say no to additional artificial light (two fluorescent bulbs a foot above them, for 13 hours a day). Repot every year, using a light, free-draining soilless mix, such as Pro-Mix BX, with extra perlite and vermiculite added. Avoid those heavy, dark, soil-based African violet mixes. They may look like rich, fertile soil, but to violets they feel like muck that stays wet and prevents oxygen from reaching the roots.

Those are the most important requirements, but food and water cannot be neglected either. Add water (lukewarm, to keep from spotting the leaves in case you accidentally splash them) only after the surface of the soil is dry to the touch, but don't let the pot dry out completely. Using a balanced fertilizer, half strength to quarter strength, every time you water, will result in both flowers and deep, dark green leaves. 🍎

POTSHERDS OR PEBBLES?

I n the old days, garden experts were divided between those who told you to supply drainage for potted plants by putting in a layer of potsherds, and those who advocated pebbles for the same purpose.

These days, the word is one single shard, please, and put the pebbles back in the driveway. Even the one-shard recommendation is just to make traditionalists feel better about hiding the evidence when they break a clay pot (the only drainage help that the shard provides is to help keep the soil from leaking all over the windowsill before it has a chance to settle in).

Drainage is controlled by the structure of the potting soil or growing medium itself. The small particles of soil attract and hold on to water. When more water is added than the soil can hold on to, the excess drains.

It is reasonable to think that the larger pebbles or shards will help the pot drain faster, because there is so much more space between them than there is between particles of soil. But no matter how large those spaces are, they can only provide passage for the excess water that the soil gives up. They cannot reach up and suck water away from the soil particles.

About the only thing that the shards or pebbles do accomplish is negative: they reduce the amount of growing room for the roots. If the potting medium doesn't drain well on its own, don't depend on pebbles to bail you out.

Taming Tall Violets

Q **I have a house full of African violets that flower nicely. They are very tall, however, and toppling over. What is the solution?**

A As African violets grow, their stems—or necks—can elongate. They should be repotted, burying the neck. But with the pot in one hand and the plant in the other, it will be obvious that it is impossible to bury the neck with the roots attached. Drastic action is called for.

Cut all the roots off, leaving just a short neck, and remove all but four to six young leaves. Gently scraping the neck encourages roots to form, but don't go overboard and peel it like a carrot. Put the plant back into its old pot, now filled with a thoroughly moistened, light, fluffy soilless medium— one with a lot of vermiculite and perlite. Good contact between the plant and the potting medium is critical. Place the pot in a plastic bag, close it, and put the plant in bright light but not direct sun. The bag preserves the humidity, helping the plant get moisture until new roots grow. Leave it alone for a month. While you're waiting, look around and see if any others need your attention. 🍐

Dusty African Violets

Q **My African violets accumulate dust on their "hairy" leaves. I know that these plants do not like to have moisture sit on their leaves. Is there a way to remove the dust? A blow dryer set on cool and low produced no results.**

A African violet leaves get a bad rap for water spotting. Water won't cause spots, as long as it is lukewarm and you let the plant dry away from the sun. However, there is a better way. Rinsing with lukewarm water may not do the job because wet dust can be trapped by the hairs on the leaf surface and simply turn to mud. Violet fanciers who show their plants in competitions usually use a soft artist's paint brush, one leaf at a time. It is time-consuming but effective and gives you a chance to spend quality time with your plants. 🍐

Rotting African Violets

Q **As long as I can remember, I have raised African violets successfully. But this year the growing centers of my plants rotted and died. Why did this happen?**

A "The answer very likely is mites—either spider mites or cyclamen mites—which are virtually impossible to see," said Michael Riley, assistant director of the Horticultural Society of New York and an African violet fan for years.

"Mites are probably the most devastating thing that can happen to African violets because they destroy the plant's crown, which will not come back."

The safest course is to destroy all infected plants and begin again with sterilized soil. But you can salvage some of your favorites if you can find a healthy leaf to use as a cutting. Treat it with a pesticide such as insecticidal soap before propagating it in sterile soil.

In the future, at the first sign of mite infestation (typically, curled or distorted young leaves), dip the plants in a solution of insecticidal soap or other pesticide. Increasing the humidity also helps, since mites thrive in a hot and dry atmosphere.

And be sure to isolate new plants for a few weeks after you bring them home. They might be bringing unwanted guests with them, and when it comes to mites, prevention is far easier than the cure. ☙

First-Aid Plant

Q I burned my hand on a pot in a friend's kitchen, and she immediately covered the area with a soothing stem from what she called a "burn plant." I'd like one, too—what is it?

A Undoubtedly, your friend's plant is *Aloe vera*. It is also known as Barbados aloe because it is widely grown on that island, even though it is believed to be native to the Mediterranean and South Africa.

This plant's fleshy, somewhat spiny leaves contain rows of enlarged cells that are filled with a translucent yellow mucus. As early as the first century A.D., the Greek physician Dioscorides wrote of the benefit of using this substance as a healing herb for burns. The practice, which continues to this day, entails snapping off one of the spiky-looking leaves, slicing it down the middle with a fingernail, and spreading its gelatinous interior over the burned skin.

This sculptural-looking, easily grown plant prefers full sun but also tolerates as much as a half day of shade. Since the plant is a succulent, designed to withstand

Aloe vera,
the "burn plant"

dry conditions, watering should be on the spare side, particularly through winter, and well-drained soil is essential. Small aloe plants are frequently available at garden shops as well as dime stores, florists, and some supermarkets. 🌿

Willful Amaryllis

Q **I have been given many amaryllis bulbs as presents. When they finish flowering, I put them away to rest in a dark place. Then when they show green again, I repot them with rich soil, water them, and place them in a sunny window. The plants stay green a long time but make only leaves, no flowers.**

A For the next easy step, you can slack off on repotting; amaryllis (*Hippeastrum,* officially) flowers as well in tight quarters as it does when it has lots of room. It's good to scrape away a bit of the old soil each year and replace it with fresh, but repotting can wait until the roots start running out of soil and/or the bulbs threaten to start bulging out at odd angles.

When that time comes, the new pots should provide no more than an inch and a half between the bulb and the pot's edge. Don't forget to leave about one-third of the bulb exposed; burying it completely encourages leaves at the expense of flowers.

As for yearly care, start as soon as the flowers have finished blooming, cutting them right below the pod so they do not waste energy making seeds. The stems help nourish the bulb; leave them uncut until they turn yellow.

Encourage leaf growth by giving the plants as much light as possible. Fertilize monthly with a balanced liquid fertilizer. If you set the plants outside during the summer, choose a spot that gets some afternoon shade.

In late August or thereabouts, let the soil dry completely, then store the pots where it is dark and cool (but not below 50°F). In two or three months, retrieve the plants and cut off any lingering foliage. Remove and pot the offsets if desired.

Amaryllis mother bulb and youngsters in the same pot

Return the plants to a sunny window and resume watering, but be sparing. Do not let the pots sit in standing water. Flower stalks should appear anytime from three to eight weeks later, depending on variety and other circumstances. 🌰

Baby Amaryllis

Q **I split off the baby amaryllis bulbs from the mother plant and potted them up. The babies are taking an enormous time (years!) to get big enough to flower. What am I doing wrong?**

A The babies, or offsets, are behaving normally. It takes three to five years for them to reach blooming size. While you're waiting, treat them as you do their parents, letting them grow through winter, spring, and early summer, then giving them a dry rest period in late summer and fall. 🌰

Avocado Sprouting

Q **Can you tell me how to start an avocado plant from the pit?**

A Avocado pits are willing sprouters, sometimes sending out roots while still inside the fruit. If you have one of those, just plant it in potting soil, leaving about a third of the pit exposed.

If the root is small or not yet evident, hold the pit wide end down and stick three or four toothpicks in it around its equator. Fill a glass almost to the top with water, and set the pit on it—the toothpicks should hold it so the bottom third is submerged. Put the glass on a warm windowsill where it will get bright light but not direct sun; wait for roots and a shoot, and then pot it up.

Avocados make handsome, long-lived foliage houseplants and can grow to considerable size. They will not bear fruit indoors, but the leaves can be used as a seasoning in recipes for Mexican dishes. If you do intend to use the leaves, obviously the plant should not be sprayed. 🌰

Potted Azaleas

Q **I was given a large potted azalea at Christmas. It bloomed through January. Can I plant it outdoors in the spring? Or should I put it out in summer and then bring it indoors?**

A The azaleas sold for winter bloom indoors are usually from a group called Indica hybrids, plants that flourish in the Deep South but are not hardy in the North. Dr. Robert Hobbs, editor of *The Azalean,* the quarterly journal of the Azalea Society of America, said: "My idea would be to put it outside for the summer in a lightly shaded spot. The azalea should stay in its pot, with the pot buried in soil up to the rim. The plant has to stay moist but not wet, so if it's in plastic, repot it in terra cotta." (Unlike plastic, terra cotta is porous. Soil in terra-cotta pots dries out faster when they are exposed to air, but stays moist longer when they are buried.)

Leave it out for a month to six weeks around the first light frost. "In order to bloom," he continued, "the plant needs a chilling period at near-freezing temperatures (32° to 40°F would be ideal). Once temperatures go below freezing, bring it inside. Put it in a sunny spot, give it a little bloom-enhancing fertilizer, and water well. It should bloom around Christmastime."

Dr. Hobbs didn't mention aphids, whiteflies, and red spider mites, all indoor pests that are likely to find your azalea attractive, but he did point out that this branch of the rhododendron family was huge. There are hundreds of other azaleas, including scores of beauties far hardier than your houseplant. 🌿

Indica hybrid azalea

Secrets of Bay

Q **A few years ago, I bought some sweet bay plants. They are growing, but not very quickly. Are they slow by nature or is there a secret to success?**

A Actually, there's no great mystery to growing sweet bay (*Laurus nobilis*), which is really among the most undemanding of houseplants. Household bays can eventually reach about 6 feet tall, but in their native habitat of

Asia Minor and the Mediterranean, they may stretch to 40 feet or more.

The ideal conditions for good growth are a cool spot indoors in winter, a warm spot outdoors in summer, and a generous dose of sun all year. But since this is a most adaptable plant, it will also survive—but not prosper— with a lot less than the ideal.

Sweet bay
(*Laurus nobilis*)

Bay does best in rich, peaty soil that is evenly moist and has sufficient perlite or sand to insure good drainage. You can get away with twice-yearly doses of a balanced fertilizer (such as 20-20-20), but if it's real growth you're after, feed every other week from spring through late summer with a weak solution of fish emulsion. (Although generous feedings will inspire good growth, too rich a diet can reduce the flavor and aroma the leaves impart to soups, roasts, and stews, which after all is a main reason for growing this plant.) 🌿

What's Ailing My Begonia?

Q **I recently picked up a beautiful, big begonia plant at a tag sale. It has shiny leaves with saw-toothed edges. They are about 3 inches long, dark green with red splotches, and appear to be growing straight up from thick, horizontal brown stems. The plant completely fills the pot and is spilling over the sides. I have been watering it faithfully, but it just keeps wilting more and more. The leaves droop and sag and are starting to fall off. What's wrong? Does it need a bigger pot?**

A From your description, it sounds like your begonia is one of the rhizomatous tribe, and what it needs more than anything else is to be left alone. It isn't dying of thirst: it's drowning.

Rhizomatous begonias come in a wide variety of leaf shapes and sizes—leaves can be from about an inch across to about a foot—and most can live a long time, becoming quite large. The rhizomes (those stems) spread outward rather than up, so largeness is more a matter of width than height. Though grown for their foliage, they also offer delicate sprays of small white or pink flowers in late winter and early spring.

As a rule, these begonias are very easy to grow, thriving in east or west light, preferring the same temperatures agreeable to humans: 65°F at night, warmer during the day. They will endure considerable neglect and are seldom plagued by insects. Crowded pots are no problem—they can live wedged in for years, looking fuller and fuller.

But they hate soggy soil, so allow yours to dry out before you water again. They recover from drought more easily than from overwatering.

Just as insurance, you might want to take some cuttings to make a new plant in case your kindness has done in the original. Three- or 4-inch lengths of stem with most of the leaves removed will usually root if you simply stick them in a glass of water and put it in a dim spot.

When roots appear, plant several stems in a low, wide pot, using commercial potting soil labeled for African violets. Fertilize only during the growing season, March to October. 🌶

Getting Begonias to Bloom

Q How do I get my *Begonia* × *argenteo-guttata* to bloom? I have seen plants blooming in February at the New York Flower Show.

A *Begonia* × *argenteo-guttata* is often called trout-leaf begonia because of the silver spots that give it its Latin name. It belongs in the shrublike begonia group, and it blooms from spring to fall.

Trout-leaf has been around since the 1880s, and although it is still popular, it has to some extent been eclipsed by many new varieties that look a lot like your plant but bloom more generously.

So it is quite possible that the begonias you saw were cousins or half-siblings of good old trout-leaf. Or they may have been manipulated into early bloom. In any case, there is no reason to worry. Yours should start flowering before long.

To encourage it, water only when the surface of the soil is dry. Pinch it frequently to encourage branching. Give it bright but not scorching light and keep it relatively cozy, with temperatures in the 60s at night and low 70s during the day.

Around the middle of February, start fertilizing. Give the begonia a half-strength drink of bloom-boosting plant food (available at garden centers) with every other watering.

Trout-leaf begonia (*Begonia* × *argenteo-guttata*)

Continue this throughout the bloom season, alternating with a balanced fertilizer in the summer when the plant is in active growth.

In the fall, cut back on the fertilizer and enjoy the beautiful foliage until bloomtime comes round again. 🌿

Bird of Paradise

Q I've had a bird of paradise for four years. While it does produce leaves, it has never produced flowers. Is there anything wrong with this plant, and how can I make it bloom?

A This unusual South African native, whose botanical name is *Strelitzia reginae,* grows outdoors all year in southern Florida, California, and Hawaii. In colder climates it is strictly a houseplant, but only mature plants are capable of setting the striking orange-and-blue flower spikes. This may take as long as six years.

The bird of paradise must have its cool period of rest in autumn and winter, when nighttime temperatures should hover around 55°F.

Also, to encourage flowering, it needs sun all day and a rich, well-drained soil that is kept evenly moist all through the spring and summer, its period of active growth. During this time, fertilize regularly with any all-purpose fertilizer recommended for flowering plants, following package directions. 🌿

Bird of paradise
(*Strelitzia reginae*)

The Way of Bonsai

Q I just got a bonsai plant for Christmas. How do I care for it?

A You don't have a bonsai plant. You have a plant that has begun its training as a bonsai. While the words are Chinese (the characters *bon* and *sai* mean a "container" and "to plant"), it is the Japanese who have become most famous for creating miniature landscapes of windblown, ancient-looking trees in small pots. Not quite everything can be made into a bonsai, but tropical, semitropical, and temperate trees and shrubs, both evergreen and deciduous, are used, so there is no one way to care for them.

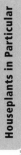

Bonsai enthusiasts have their plant preferences, but they all agree that to succeed you first have to know what you have. Luckily, the plants are mostly small enough to carry from garden center to bookstore to library until you find a book or person to help you identify it.

Caring for a bonsai has two aspects: first, keeping it alive and healthy, and second, continuing its training. Learning those things means getting involved.

A good place to start is to look at the fine examples at the National Arboretum in Washington or at the Brooklyn Botanic Garden, which has one of the largest collections outside Japan. Information on bonsai organizations can be found at the Web sites of Bonsai Clubs International (*www.bonsai-bci.com*) and the American Bonsai Society (*www.absbonsai.org*). If it all seems too much, just be glad you didn't receive one of those cute miniature pigs. 🖛

Bonsai requires a commitment.

WINDOWSILL BONSAI

Traditional bonsai plants are hardy outdoor species such as pines and junipers, which cannot live indoors year-round. If your bonsai must dwell where you do, here are some suggestions:

For full sun: Chinese elm (*Ulmus parvifolia*), dwarf pomegranate (*Punica granatum* 'Nana'), gardenia, snow rose (*Serissa foetida*)

For part sun: Australian myrtle (*Leptospermum scoparium*), camellia, citrus (many kinds, including orange, lemon, and grapefruit), coffee (*Coffea arabica*), jade plant (*Crassula argentea*), myrtle

For bright indirect light: creeping fig (*Ficus pumila* 'Minima'), false heather (*Cuphea hyssopifolia*), Norfolk Island pine (*Araucaria heterophylla*), star jasmine (*Trachelospermum jasminoides*).

Just One Bloom for Bromeliads

Q I have a bromeliad (*Aechmea fasciata*), which I keep indoors. For 10 months, it had a center spike with beautiful pink-and-blue flowers. Then it suddenly wilted and died. I don't believe I changed anything, so what went wrong?

A Sounds just about right. Many bromeliads, including your *A. fasciata,* are usually sold when they are in bloom or just about to open because they flower once and then die. They linger on a year or more after the bloom fades, like the heroine of a nineteenth-century novel, but they're just playing on your emotions.

All is not lost, however, assuming you haven't tossed it out. While you were admiring the flower, the plant was busy producing offsets, called daughter plants, around its base. Once flowering is over, you should remove the spent flower stalk and continue caring for the plant until the offsets are about half the size of the mother plant. They can then be carefully cut off (make sure you don't lose any roots) and placed in individual pots.

If the mother plant is looking too shabby, carefully cut it out, leaving the daughter plants until they are large enough to cut and pot on their own. In two or three years, the daughter plants will become mother plants, and flower.

Vacation for Cactuses

Q I know houseplants can go outside during the summer, but would it also be beneficial for my cactus plants?

A Most cactus plants will thrive outdoors, especially in early summer, when hot days and cooler nights mimic the temperature differences of the desert. Just remember that although they love the sun, they won't love it right away after a winter indoors. Set them out for a few morning hours each day for a week or so, then gradually lengthen their exposure time over the next fortnight, by the end of which they should be fully acclimated.

Also remember that desert rains are few and far between. Cactuses don't mind the odd summer shower, but their roots will rot if the soil stays wet. Be sure the pots have ample drainage holes, and if rain goes on for more than a day, move the plants to shelter.

Take them back inside around Labor Day, so they have time to adjust to indoor conditions (lower light and drier, warmer air) before these conditions are as extreme as they will be in winter.

Calamondin Calamity

Q I have a 4-foot calamondin orange tree that has thrived for years. This fall, leaves began shriveling and dropping off. I apparently had over-watered it, and I fear that it might have developed root rot. I trimmed the roots, repotted it, cut it back, watered it very sparingly, and have not fed it. I do continue to mist it. The plant keeps producing blossoms and fruit but not much new foliage. Can you offer any suggestions for encouraging growth?

A Time, sunlight, and a well-drained potting mix. Keeping a plant indoors is generally more of a mainte-nance situation than one designed for optimum growth, and this is particularly true of trees. The loss or damage of some roots has left your × *Citrofortunella microcarpa* (aka × *C. mitis*) unable to take up water and nutrients in enough quantity to grow additional leaves. Give the plant the most sunlight you can provide and return to watering. Always water it thoroughly after it dries out, giving it a soluble fer-tilizer with every third watering. Once the days lengthen and the roots fully recover, it will push out new leaves.

Stressed plants put their energy into seed produc-tion as a species survival strategy. But making fruit takes a lot of energy, delaying leaf production. Leave some flowers for their wonderful fragrance, but remove them before they start becoming fruit. Pick any ripe fruit you have now and, if you're fond of their bitter, sharp flavor, make some marmalade to remember them by. 🍎

Calamondin oranges
(× *Citrofortunella microcarpa*)

Creatures of the Night

Q Years ago I was given a small night-blooming cereus. It has grown and produces spectacular blooms that sadly last only the night. It appears to be thriving, but I have no idea what I'm doing right. I'd love to know its ori-gin, light requirements, and feeding needs.

A As a name, night-blooming cereus is the plant world equivalent of Smith. *Epiphyllum oxypetalum,* with its broad, flattened stems, is the most popular of about two dozen plants that share that common name. *Hylocereus undatus,* with triangular stems, and various species of

Nyctocereus and *Selenicereus* are also known as nig
blooming cereus.

All of these subtropical plants have similar requir
ments. They are cactuses but not desert dwellers. The
in moist, somewhat shaded areas, so they need a rich,
tile, well-drained potting medium that never dries out
pletely, and high light but not direct sun. They love
spend summers outside in light shade. Give them a
light dose of general houseplant fertilizer once a
month, starting when they finish flowering. A rest
period is necessary to set flower buds, so in winter, reduce watering (but not so much that the
plant begins to shrivel) and stop feeding.

For most of the year, there doesn't
seem to be a good reason to grow *E.
oxypetalum,* a large, rather gangly plant. But
during its short summer bloom period, owners frequently gather their friends to sit up all night and watch,
transfixed, as the white, 8- to 10-inch-wide flowers unfurl,
only to become limp dishrags by morning. Most species are
scented to attract the moths that pollinate them. The moths
must have wide-ranging tastes, because some plants smell
more like landfill than perfume. 🌿

Night-blooming cereus
(*Epiphyllum
oxypetalum*)

Unfruitful at Home

Q **While in Chile three years ago, we bought cherimoya fruit and successfully germinated seeds and grew houseplants. Now the leaves hang
limp and there are no flowers or fruit. What's wrong?**

A A northern Andes native, the cherimoya (*Annona
cherimola*) is sold in the metropolitan area at gourmet markets in winter. It vaguely resembles an artichoke.
Its botanical name means "corn" or "food," and the genus
includes such edibles as the custard apple, soursop, and
sweetsop. This tropical plant is also among the oldest of
cultivated New World fruits, said Debbie Peterson, editor of
The Pits, the newsletter of the Rare Pit and Plant Council.
"Pottery urns in the shape of cherimoyas have been found
in ancient Peruvian burial grounds."

In its native Andes, the cherimoya is primarily an understory tree reaching 15 feet in height; in Spain, it grows in sheltered valleys. Thus, full summer sun is definitely not to its liking. Grown as a potted houseplant, it should have rich, quick-draining soil and somewhat cool temperatures in winter, when it should also be watered sparingly. "It's possible your problem now is that your plant is ready for re-potting—remember, this is really a small tree—or your summer watering is insufficient for either the root system or the size of your plant," Ms. Peterson said. In any case, "flowers and fruiting are unlikely events for cherimoyas grown as houseplants. It's an easy plant to germinate but nearly impossible to fruit."

Christmas Cactus Woes

Q **My Christmas cactus has a very frustrating problem. Flower buds form, but they fall off before opening. Why?**

A The dangling, tubular flowers of the Christmas or crab cactus (*Schlumbergera truncata*) begin as buds that are set in autumn for a blooming period around Christmas. Unfortunately, the name "cactus" may be misleading. This plant is not from the hot desert sands. It is an epiphyte, or tree-perching plant, and a native of the humid jungle coastal areas of Brazil. It is also a plant that is at its best in soil that drains quickly, but must be kept barely moist during the summer growing season.

The flower buds start to form as autumn progresses with longer, cooler nights. The problem is that as the cool weather advances, the heating system in most homes is activated. The resulting hot, dry air can ultimately destroy the buds and shorten the life of any flowers that have managed to emerge. The only way to prevent this is to find a cool spot to keep your plant at night during the budding and flowering period. The optimum nighttime temperatures are around 60°F, although daytime temperatures can rise 15° higher.

Christmas cactus
(*Schlumbergera truncata*)

Passing On a Family Treasure

Q My aunt and uncle are relocating to a retirement community. They may not have room for the large Christmas cactus that my aunt inherited 30 years ago. Is there a way to subdivide this cactus and pass it on?

A Divide or subdivide, no; pass it on, yes. In spring, as the growing season begins, you can propagate any number of new holiday cactuses using cuttings. (There are many *Schlumbergera* hybrids, some of which start blooming around Thanksgiving, others not flowering until New Year's Day or thereabouts.)

To take cuttings, simply twist off (don't cut) pieces two or three segments long. Plant them deep enough to keep them standing straight in a freely draining potting medium. Keep the medium on the dry side.

They'll root after four to six weeks in filtered light. Increase watering once the roots grow, and transplant after six months. With luck, they could bloom at their usual time.

No matter how many cuttings you take, you'll still have a sizeable plant left over. A nursing home or library might be delighted to receive it. Everyone there can take cuttings, too. 🌿

What Kind of Cactus?

Q I recently saw an illustration of a Christmas cactus that had jagged leaf segments, but a plant that was sold to me as a Thanksgiving cactus resembles the drawing exactly. I have been told that the Christmas cactus has smooth-edged segments. Which is correct?

A There used to be a real difference, but then again, Thanksgiving and Christmas used to be two distinct holidays, not merely the bookends to a shopping season.

Schlumbergera truncata, which blooms around Thanksgiving, does have strongly toothed edges. In the 1800s it was crossed with *S. russelliana,* resulting in a hybrid, *S.* × *buckleyi,* with more scalloped edges and a later bloom period, closer to Christmas.

Further hybridizing has further blurred the distinction, and now there are more than 200 named cultivars, with bloom times that slide around from Halloween to Super Bowl Sunday, depending on who their parents were.

You will, of course, find people who insist on a neat fit into one category or the other, but those with less aggressive tendencies simply refer to any and all as holiday cactuses. 🌶

The Rare Yellow Clivia

Q **I have been longing to own a yellow flowering clivia for years, but they have been far too expensive for me. I wonder if the price has gone down at all, and if you can enlighten me as to the availability of these plants?**

A Depending on when you looked last, the price has gone down, but blooming-size clivias with yellow flowers still cost from three to almost 15 times more than the common orange cultivars. How one responds to prices like that illustrates the difference between a longing and a true obsession.

Why so pricey? When you cross-pollinate two naturally occurring yellow forms of clivia, you don't know what the flowers will look like for four or five years. If cross-pollination is successful, you propagate by division, and it's another few years before the divisions are ready to be divided again. When you have a few extras to sell, the demand from collectors is high, and so are prices because of rarity. By the time you have enough to sell inexpensively, you may have forgotten why you went into horticulture in the first place.

Japanese breeders are working on tissue-culture propagation, which will bring down prices by greatly increasing supply. In the meantime, seeds for yellow-flowering clivia are (relatively) inexpensive. But there is a small chance that the seeds won't come true to their parents, and that when they finally bloom, they won't have yellow flowers. 🌶

Helping Clivias Bloom

Q **I have had a clivia for about seven years. The plant bloomed four years ago for the first time and then again the next year. That was the end of that. I give it the best care, but why don't I get any flowers in return?**

A When winter is at its worst, a cluster of striking, trumpet-shaped flowers above the straplike, very dark green leaves of *Clivia miniata* can take the place of a Florida weekend, although the rarer clivias can cost nearly as much.

While it is possible to kill a clivia (pronounced CLY-vee-uh), it isn't easy. Clivias live in a variety of temperatures, tolerate shady windowsills, like to be potbound, and are immune to most insect pests.

What they do not do is bloom on command. Like many other plants, clivias don't recognize winter by looking out the window or watching the Weather Channel—they need to experience it for themselves.

A rest period of 8 to 10 weeks in a cool room (where temperatures are 40° to 50°F at night and only 10° warmer in the daytime), with a reduced water supply and no fertilizer, is necessary to produce flowering. Experts disagree about whether to allow them to stay completely dry or just nearly dry during the rest period. But they all agree that the cold period is necessary. 🍂

Clivias need a cool rest period in order to bloom.

Clivia Care

Q I have grown *Clivia miniata* for many years. Recently the flower appeared, as always, but it never grew up and out of the plant base. Why?

A To bloom, a clivia needs to be on an annual cycle of warm and cool temperatures, which you must have been providing. But it sounds as though there has been a change in your routine. Flower stalks that never fully elongate are a sign that the cooling period was not long enough, not cool enough, or both. 🍂

Clivia from Seed

Q I have a healthy clivia that produces many flowers and seedpods. How should I treat the seeds in order to grow new clivias?

A Once the berries, or seedpods, have turned shiny red, remove their seeds. Just barely cover the seeds with a well-draining potting medium, kept moist but not wet. Then grab a thick book and wait. The seeds can take months to germinate. When they do, place the seedlings in bright light (but out of direct sun), and go back to the book. If you're careful and do a good job, it shouldn't take more than three or four years before your new clivia is ready to bloom. ✿

Fragrant Flowers on a Corn Plant

Q **We received a corn plant (three trunks and 7 feet tall) nine years ago. A couple of weeks ago, for the first time ever, it sprouted a half dozen 18-inch shoots, and each shoot had four to six ball-like clusters of very fragrant flowers. What happened? I almost moved into the garage at night because of the overwhelming fragrance.**

A A blooming corn plant, *Dracaena fragrans* 'Massangeana,' is a mixed blessing. On the one hand, the long flowering stalks are an interesting surprise on a plant normally grown for its foliage. On the other hand, the night-opening flowers use scent to attract moths. In the tropics, these moths must either be quite a distance away or else have a pretty poor sense of smell, because when confined indoors, the fragrance is very much in-your-nose.

Why hasn't it flowered until now? Most likely, flowering resulted from a combination of two factors. First, and most important, the plant underwent recent stress that reminded it of its mortality and encouraged it to bloom and ultimately set seed. For a tropical plant like dracaena, a period of cold is often just the trigger needed. Dr. Dennis McConnell, professor of environmental horticulture at the University of Florida at Gainesville, has seen corn plants bloom following a few days of temperatures dipping to 50°F.

The scent of a flowering corn plant is overwhelming.

The second factor is that the plant has to have stored enough carbohydrates to produce the energy necessary to create a flower. Since it is sold as a low-light plant, it can take years of sitting in a dim location to pack enough away.

But no matter what the circumstances, if it lived long enough and grew large enough, its biological clock would have started ticking and one morning you would have awoken to the dubious pleasure of that distinctive aroma. ✿

The Touchy Croton

Q My croton is a small tree, about 4 feet tall. Last winter it lost all its leaves except three or four. In the spring I took it outdoors, and it came back to life. New healthy leaves grew all over. In October I brought it back in, and I think it went into shock because of the change. It started losing the smaller leaves. How can I help my croton so it will not lose all its leaves again?

A Moving to the edge of a tropical forest would be good. These handsome shrubs from Malaysia grow naturally where they get plenty of bright but indirect light, temperatures between warm and hot, high humidity, and frequent rain.

Most indoor environments offer only the heat—if that—and crotons respond to darkness and dry air by dropping their leaves. Drafts have the same effect.

Crotons hate change, as you have observed, and often drop their leaves when moved. They also lose lower leaves as they age, no matter how happy they are.

On the other hand, they are fast growers and will, as you have also observed, recover quickly once conditions are more to their liking.

To keep yours mollified over the winter, place it where it will get as much light as possible. Mist often. Fertilize monthly with a half-strength dilution of all-purpose houseplant fertilizer.

Allow the surface of the soil to dry out a half inch down between waterings, but make sure the soil below that is evenly moist. Dry soil and overwatering both promote (surprise!) leaf drop.

There are close to a hundred types of croton in cultivation, and some seem readier to disrobe than others. If you have room, you might try a couple of new varieties, just to see if one might be more tenacious than the one you have.

If you buy a new one in winter, be sure you have a way to keep it warm on the way home. Even a brief exposure to cold will make the leaves fall off. ✿

Crotons often drop their leaves, but they will recover.

Crowning Glory

Q I have a two-year-old crown of thorns, nearly 18 inches tall, with lots of leaves and flowers. The catch is they are all on the top 3 inches. How do I make it branch out?

A Crown of thorns (*Euphorbia milii*) is a spiny succulent that blooms almost constantly. There are many different colors, from brilliant red or pinkish to salmon, yellow, or white. It is perfect for the person who always wants a bit of cheer around the house. Since yours is flowering and healthy, it is getting enough bright light and warmth, but when the leaves are concentrated in a tuft at the top, it is telling you that you are keeping the soil too dry. Change your watering routine to keep it evenly moist, and you will stimulate it to produce leaves lower down the stem, lessening that feather-duster look.

Let it know you want it to branch by cutting a quarter inch off the top. Once it knows you don't want a telephone pole, it will branch just below the cut and also along the lower part of the stem. And later on, cut those new branches a quarter inch, too, to form a nice, bushy plant. The scars from cutting will be minimal because the tissue at the growing ends is soft, and the thick white sap will coagulate quickly. The sap can irritate skin, so be sure to make those cuts with scissors instead of a fingernail. 🖉

Saving Cyclamen

Q I adore the hardy cyclamens sold at my local greenhouse, but they always shrivel and die by Easter. Am I just observing their life cycle or is there a way I can keep them alive to flower again next winter?

A They may shrivel, but they don't die until you give up and toss them. After flowering, *Cyclamen persicum*, also known as florist's cyclamen, begins to go dormant. If you really want to save it, you can, although the plant will probably have fewer flowers, fewer leaves, and that "Look, Mom, I made it myself" appearance. If that doesn't bother you, give it a try.

Dr. William Miller, a professor of flower bulb and greenhouse physiology at Cornell University, said that you can extend the bloom period by keeping the plant cool (low 60s at night) and not overwatering—let the top inch of soil dry out between waterings. If the pot has a foil wrap, punch a few holes in it on the bottom to let the water drain, and never let it sit in water. Too wet encourages soil-borne fungus diseases.

As the leaves dry out, Dr. Miller contnued, start reducing the water, and once all of them are shriveled, let the soil go bone dry. Put the pot out of the way for two months since the cyclamen doesn't need light or any help from you. After it has rested, bring it out into bright light, start watering, and hope for the best.

This cyclamen may be hardy (in the sense of being vigorous) in the florist's shop, but it is not hardy (in the sense of overwintering outdoors) unless you live in a Mediterranean climate. Its relative, *Cyclamen hederifolium,* is a hardy cyclamen in zones 5 to 7. It looks like a petite version of *C. persicum,* blooms in the fall, and will come back as good as new every year—outdoors. 🌿

Cyclamens go dormant after flowering.

Desert Roses Need the Sun

Q **Last year in Barbados, I saw a lovely bush called desert rose. Once home, I actually found it in a local nursery and bought it. But now it's faltering and I don't know what it needs.**

A The handsome flowering shrubs known as desert rose, or impala lily, are succulents with thick, often bottle-shaped stem bases and rather fleshy leaves. They are natives of tropical and subtropical Africa and Arabia. You probably have the most common (some authorities say only) species, *Adenium obesum,* which has smooth bark and gray-green stems.

This plant wants as much sun as possible, and should be grown in coarsely porous, well-drained soil. Through winter, it should be watered only when the soil is almost dry. When summer comes, put it outside in your sunniest spot and it should rally.

In its natural desert home, the leaves of desert rose may be deciduous during the dry season. But if moisture is available, the plant remains evergreen. Although the shrub ultimately reaches about 6 feet in height, a potted house-plant can be kept as small as a bonsai and still produce its bright rose-pink, long-lasting flowers. But a word of warning: when cut, the adeniums exude a milky sap that is irritating to the skin and said to be poisonous when ingested. ✿

Dracaena Rises Again

Q **My faithful dracaena has survived three moves and is almost 5 feet tall. It seems healthy, but so many of the lower leaves are gone that it's no longer very attractive. Can it be pruned back?**

A It sounds as if you have one of the many varieties of *Dracaena fragrans,* all of which have long, straplike leaves and a tendency to shoot upward. In their native tropics, they are 20-foot trees with fragrant flowers, but most North American gardeners know them only as foliage house-plants. Yours has demonstrated the durability that endears them to so many (they're popularly known as the plant that will not die). Nevertheless, the best course of action is to have a nice goodbye party, throw it out, and start over.

If you do want to rejuvenate old faithful, you have two options: air layering and radical pruning. Air layering, which forces the plant to make roots in mid stem, is the more conservative option because you wind up with two plants. On the other hand, it is both slow and unattractive, so it's only worth it if the plant you're layering is very hard to replace.

Radical pruning also takes months to produce results, but it's pretty much effortless, and it's less visually offensive. Just cut off most of the plant, leaving a few inches of stem. In time, a new shoot or shoots will start from dormant buds near the base. You do have to leave the pot where those buds will get light, but you can park it behind other plants—or the couch—until it looks presentable again.

If your plant has multiple stems, cut off a couple of them, wait for regrowth, then cut off a few more of the old ones. Keep it up until the whole plant is rejuvenated. ✿

CREATING A NEW PLANT IN MID AIR

Layering is a propagation method that creates a new plant from a stem of the old one, while that stem is still attached to its parent. To layer a plant, you bend the stem to the ground and bury it. But with stiff-stalked plants such as dracaenas and rubber trees, bending is out. You must bring the ground to the stem in a process called air layering.

You can air layer the trunk of the plant—a good choice when it's time to lower something that has grown gawky—or you can use a good-size branch. Just don't try it on tender new growth; the layered area must be mature enough to root, and firm enough to support some added weight.

Choose a spot for the base of the new plant. Whether it is on the trunk or a branch, it should be within the upper third of the parent plant. Snip off any leaves that grow right above or below the spot.

Using a very sharp knife, make a slanting cut roughly 1½ inches long, about one-third of the way through the stem. Prop the cut slightly open with a bit of wooden matchstick, and dust the whole area with rooting hormone (available at garden centers).

Surround the wounded section of stem with a baseball-size wad of damp sphagnum moss, pressing it against the cut. Bind the moss tightly in place and enclose it with plastic wrap, so that no moisture is lost. In a month or two, roots will be visible through the plastic. Cut off the rooted plant, remove the plastic, and pot it up, moss and all.

The original plant will usually branch where the cut was made, but you often get more pleasing results by cutting the old-timer back even farther and letting it regrow from the base.

Wrapping the layered sections

In Need of Moisture

Q **Since I moved my elephant's ear (*Alocasia*) back into the living-room corner after having it outside all summer, it has "sweated" nonstop. Water droplets form on the tip and along the edges of each leaf, dripping to the floor. Why does this occur?**

A Your alocasia is a tropical plant, used to constant moisture and high humidity. It is having a tough readjustment period after being outside, but will eventually calm down. Dr. Dennis McConnell, a tropical foliage plant specialist at the University of Florida in Gainesville, said the most likely reason is the lower humidity indoors. Under that kind of stress, he said, the plant "turns on its water pumps and can't turn them off in time." More water is drawn up by the roots than is needed by the plant's tissues, and the excess escapes through the leaves.

Put the pot on a wide saucer filled with small pebbles, kept wet but not covered with water. If the water level is below the top of the pebbles, the bottom of the pot stays out of the water and the large surface area of the exposed pebbles evaporates a lot of water right around the plant. You might think you could just reach for your mister. Unfortunately, hand-misting raises the humidity for only a minute or so because it evaporates quickly unless you have one of those systems found in grocery-store produce aisles. 🌢

Elephant's ear needs a humid environment.

Trophy Fern

Q **I purchased a staghorn fern in a small pot. I've heard that such ferns are best planted or mounted on a wooden plaque. I can't seem to find any specific directions about how to do this, nor have I had success in locating the plaques at plant stores in my area. Can you help me?**

A Staghorn ferns (*Platycerium* spp.) are epiphytes, plants that hold on to trunks or branches. They have two kinds of fronds: flat, roundish sterile ones that turn brown and papery as they age; and the large, antlerlike green fertile ones that give the plant its common name. In the wild, the sterile fronds hold the fern to the bark and trap decaying organic material for nutrients. The ferns grow slowly but can reach 3 feet across. The whitish material covering the fertile fronds is protective and shouldn't be rubbed off.

You can mount yours now, or wait until it gets larger. Use a slab of cork bark or tree fern bark at least twice the width of the fern so it can get a good grip and have room to grow. Pound small nails in an outline an inch or two larger than the fern. Take a clump of damp osmunda fiber or sphagnum peat moss large enough to fill the hollow of the sterile frond, and lay it inside the outline. Place the fern on top, and lace the sterile frond to the nails by passing clear fishing line or plastic-coated wire over and through it. Slabs are available from orchid-supply companies. 🌢

Lace the sterile frond to the nails.

A Balding Ficus

Q **I recently purchased a hybrid *Ficus* 'Monique' tree that supposedly resists dropping its leaves. But since I bought it in June, it has lost about half of its leaves. I have it in a window that faces south. It is not in direct sunlight. I've watered it once a week.**

A Some of the leaf loss is probably a reaction to the drop in humidity and light from that of its former home in a commercial greenhouse, but improper watering may also be involved. Watering requires a finger, not a timetable. Dig in. When the top third of the soil is dryish, flood the plant. Use enough water so that a deep saucer placed underneath it fills, then let it sit 15 minutes before emptying the saucer.

Does 'Monique' really resist leaf drop? Hybrids often have more desirable characteristics than the straight species, but all ficuses are living things that respond to stress in the only way they can. 🍃

Homesick Ficus

Q **Last fall, I bought two 7-foot-tall ficus trees for my home in upstate New York. They began dropping leaves almost immediately, and now—three months later—one is nearly dead. Why?**

A Ficus plants are notoriously temperamental about any change, and the older they are, the more crotchety they are about readjustment. Unfortunately, your experience is a perfect example of what happens when a mature specimen undergoes a whole set of difficult transitions.

Growing conditions for the ficus are perfect at the wholesale grower's, probably somewhere in Florida. Then the tree gets put on a truck and sent to a Northern retail greenhouse. Conditions there are less than ideal, but it is still ficus territory: warm, full of bright but indirect light, and extremely humid. Then the poor thing has to move yet again, this time to the dim desert that is a Northern home in winter.

But don't be discouraged. As the widespread presence of healthy specimens makes clear, ficus *can* adapt to conditions like yours and (eventually) become quite large and treelike. Start with young plants, which are more adaptable than mature ones. Make the purchase in late spring or early summer, when the humidity is higher and the environmental change is less severe. And pay careful attention to growing instructions. 🌿

What's Eating Ficus?

Q I was washing the leaves of my ficus tree when I discovered that underneath every leaf, right at the base, there are small, pinhead-size bumps, whitish and waxy, always in the same place. I know ficus is susceptible to scale, so how do I deal with an infestation this large?

A Anything on a plant that is so uniformly spread, so consistent, is probably not an insect. Insects are free-thinkers, and are rarely much good at organizing (ants and bees excepted, of course).

In this case, the waxy spots on your *Ficus benjamina* are glandular spots, characteristic of ficus. Different species have different sites and numbers of spots. There is a theory that the glandular spots exude a substance that attracts tiny fig wasps, which are the plant's pollinators, but no one knows for sure. One thing is certain—they serve some purpose. Nature almost never does anything just for fun. 🌿

Glandular spots on
Ficus benjamina

Fragrant Frangipani

Q I brought back plumeria cuttings from Hawaii; one cutting rotted, and the other has grown only two tiny leaves and no roots in nine months. Last month I put it under fluorescent lights, and now it has two new leaves. Any suggestions about how I can grow this stubborn stub into something that approximates the lush shrubs we see and smell in tropical climes?

A It sounds as if the artificial longer days have awakened it. Dr. Richard Criley, a professor of horticulture at the University of Hawaii in Manoa, said that *Plumeria rubra*, or frangipani, the classic flower of the Hawaiian lei, needs at least 14 to 15 hours of light each day and temperatures above 50°F or it will go dormant. He said that tip cuttings, commonly available in tourist shops in Hawaii, should have the cut end dipped in rooting hormone before being planted in a well-aerated medium such as peat and perlite, and kept moist but not wet in a warm, brightly lit spot. It's not too late to apply the hormone to yours, but don't make a new cut.

Under the best conditions it takes four to six weeks for roots to grow, maybe longer. But the wait has just begun. Assuming the cutting is large enough, at least ¾ inch in diameter, and gets all those hours of light, it will set flower buds this summer and bloom next spring.

As a houseplant, plumeria tends to be tall and gawky, with few branches, and the leaves mainly at the top, so its attraction is strictly in the flowers. The waxy, simple pinwheel flowers range from white to dark red, rose-pink, yellow, orange, and multicolored, while the fragrance is unique but reminiscent of jasmine. One smell and it's clear why people love them, even though when shorter days lead to dormancy, and all the leaves fall off, they look exactly like an old walking stick jammed in a pot. 🌿

Pampering Gardenias

Q **I have a small gardenia bush in a clay pot on my apartment windowsill. It was flowering when I bought it but has not done well since. The leaves yellow, wither, and fall off. I have tried everything, including an iron-rich fertilizer. Any suggestions?**

Gardenia jasminoides 'Veitchii'

A You can treat gardenias like cut flowers from the florist, enjoying the glossy, deep green leaves, snow-white flowers, and drop-dead aroma as long as you can, knowing they are destined to die; or you can work hard to give them everything they want and still have them die for no apparent reason.

Gardenia paradise is easier to describe than to attain. Flood them with lots of very bright light, even full sun, all year long. Pamper them with cool nights (60° to 65°F) and warm days (70° to 80°) filled with fresh air, but no drafts. Indulge them with a constantly moist (never waterlogged), highly acidic (pH 4.5 to 5.5), well-drained potting medium, which is at least half peat moss and a quarter perlite, and regular feedings of acidic plant food. Above all, keep the humidity as high as you can. Trays of wet pebbles, hand-held misters, and humidifiers are in order. If your walls are not turning green, it is probably too dry.

Yellowing leaves can be caused by an iron deficiency, overwatering or underwatering, or having the pH too high. Gardenias are subject to scale, red spider mites, mealybugs, nematodes, and a canker disease. And even under the best of circumstances, some gardenias appear to be suicidal. 🍎

Flavor but No Flowers

Q **I've been growing ginger, a root I bought at an airport in Hawaii, for three years, but there have been no flowers. Can I expect them soon?**

A Probably not. Although there are several flowering plants that Hawaiians call ginger, all of them are tropical. It isn't easy to duplicate the conditions needed to bring them into flower on a windowsill in a cold climate.

But if the idea of ginger plants appeals, by all means try the easily grown *Zingiber officinale,* a native of tropical Asia and a favorite for flavoring Asian dishes. The lumpy-looking aromatic roots (actually underground stems or rhizomes) that are sold at produce markets will root with astonishing ease.

Simply place the root in a wide, shallow pot filled with any houseplant potting mix, cover with a scant half-inch of soil, and keep it evenly moist. Part shade is best. Graceful reedlike stems, 2 to 4 feet tall, often appear within a few weeks of planting.

Don't expect to stop buying ginger to cook with; a potted plant won't produce what you could call serious crops. And it's unlikely you will see this plant flower in your home. But in warm, humid climates with lots of sunshine, it produces fragrant yellow-green flowers in conelike clusters. 🍎

Seeking Glory Bower

Q **Can you tell me about clerodendrum (glory bower)? I saw this beautiful climber and want to give it a try.**

A The showy flowers of the clerodendrums are what make them compelling. This genus includes about 400 evergreen and deciduous vines, shrubs, and trees, most of them natives of tropical and subtropical Asia and Africa.

Clerodendrums do best in bright light with evenly moist soil. Good choices for indoor growing include *Clerodendrum splendens,* a twiner with long-lasting, tubular scarlet flowers, and *Clerodendrum thomsoniae variegatum,* whose white-and-red blooms are reminiscent of the flowers of bleeding heart. It's showy even when not in bloom, since the lime-touched leaves have cream-colored margins.

Regardless of the type you choose, a late-summer application of African violet fertilizer will encourage winter blooms. ✿

Some clerodendrums do well indoors.

Jade Plants Indoors

Q **My jade plant thrives outside all summer, but when I bring it in for the winter, it barely makes it to the following year. I heard that you should stop watering it when you bring it indoors. Is this true?**

A The tough, slow-growing houseplant called jade plant, a native of South Africa, is a member of the genus *Crassula* in the stonecrop family. The most popular is *Crassula argentea,* which has glossy, fleshy leaves that sprout from short stems along a treelike trunk.

It has been grown as a houseplant at least since the nineteenth century, and it can reach about 4 feet in height under ideal conditions. With a bit of luck, tiny pink or white star-shaped flowers will appear in winter.

In summer, the jade plant is happiest with hot days, filtered sun, shelter at high noon, regular watering (as much as two times a week, depending on its size), and twice-monthly diluted feeding. But these needs begin to change in autumn, when fertilizing should be stopped and the watering reduced severely—*but not completely,* as is too often mistakenly believed.

As winter progresses, a thorough watering should be administered once every two or three weeks or so, just before the leaves start showing signs of shriveling (as you pay attention to the plant and the soil, you'll develop a feel for this). In winter, too, the plant needs bright light, with a bit of sun if possible, but most important is a spot that's cool. Avoid a windowsill on top of a heater at all costs. 🌿

Jasmine Care

Q **I was recently given an Arabian jasmine as a gift. What does this plant do and how do I care for it?**

A The Arabian jasmine (*Jasminum sambac*) is an evergreen shrub from Southeast Asia with graceful, cascading stems that is treasured for its fragrant blooms. Unopened flower buds are used by the Chinese to perfume tea. And in Hawaii, the dainty white flowers are used for leis. Very likely you have one of two popular varieties, 'Maid of Orleans' or 'Grand Duke of Tuscany,' either of which is easily cared for.

These jasmines do best where they will stay warm and get at least four hours of bright light daily. An east or west window is better than a south-facing one. Keep the soil moist but not wet. To encourage blooms and good growth throughout the major flowering season (spring to late fall), feed the plants every two weeks, alternating a high-nitrogen organic fertilizer such as fish emulsion with any all-purpose water-soluble blend that is recommended for flowering plants. In late fall, cut back on the feeding schedule. While the plant is having its winter rest, a half-strength dose of all-purpose plant food every six weeks is all it needs—or wants. To keep the plant shapely and free-flowering, prune back by about a third in early spring, before the start of the new growing season.

Although very few insects are interested in jasmine, should spider mites or mealybugs take notice, control is quick and easy: dunk the plant upside down in a soapy water mix. 🌿

SUMMERING HOUSEPLANTS OUTSIDE

Almost all houseplants will enjoy spending the summer in the fresh air—just don't rush them out too fast. Many are of tropical or subtropical origin, and they're very sensitive to cold: "not freezing" is not warm enough for them to be comfortable.

Though there are a few—including ardisia, bay laurel, camellia, citrus, clivia, ivies, Norfolk Island pine, scented geraniums, oleander, and Christmas and Thanksgiving cactuses—that can go outside once night temperatures are consistently above 40°F, most should wait until the night lows will not drop below 50°.

And cold is not the only thing to be cautious about. The plants may look as if a good jolt of sun would cheer them up, but after they have acclimated to an indoor winter's much lower light levels, they could suffer from scalded leaves when suddenly thrust into full sunlight. Indoors, the light-gathering material in the leaf cells turns to offer the maximum surface area to the limited light. Outside, this material takes some time to reorient. Full sun before the change takes place will overwhelm the cells, bleach the chlorophyll, and generally wreak havoc.

Start by putting the plants out in the shade for a short period, then lengthen the time each day for about two weeks. Besides the obvious spot under a tree, consider the shady north side of a wall or fence, or beneath a patio umbrella. In fact, you may want to leave them there for the duration. Even after they are acclimated, most houseplants do best in dappled shade, not full sun.

Mountain Flower

Q Three years ago, for Valentine's Day, I was given a small jasmine covered with clusters of fragrant white flowers. It has grown into a big, beautiful, healthy vine, but it has never bloomed again. I fertilize it every six weeks and keep the soil evenly moist. It goes outside with the other houseplants for the summer, but I am careful to bring it in before frost. Last year it set buds, but they didn't open. This year there weren't even buds. How do I get it to flower again?

A It sounds as though you have a winter jasmine, *Jasminum polyanthum,* and if you do, the key to success is to keep your house as cold as your heart is warm. This jasmine is a native of the mountains of China. It needs a period of long nights and cool temperatures to set buds, then continuing cool growing conditions—think double sweaters—for the buds to open and bloom. Other than that, you're doing everything right (though you should cut back a bit on the fertilizer between late November and early April).

Leave the plant outdoors as long as possible. Ideally, it should get at least six weeks of night temperatures around 40°F. Bring it in to a place where it will get at least four or five hours a day of bright but not hot light—east and west, rather than south. Turn down the thermostat so that night temperatures stay around 50°F and days don't warm up much past 65°, and you should get flowers sometime between December and February. *J. polyanthum* blooms on new growth, so if it starts getting out of hand, feel free to prune it anytime between March and July. ꙮ

BRINGING THEM ALL BACK HOME

To avoid the shock of a drastic difference in temperature and humidity, all houseplants that have summered outside should be brought inside before the heat goes on.

Most need to be back indoors before the night temperature drops to 50°F, and though some hardy ones could stay out until it regularly approaches 40°, most of *them* will also do better if they can start readjusting before the difference between indoors and out starts getting extreme.

In most cases it's better to err on the side of safety, but it pays to know your plants. Several, including winter jasmine, cymbidium orchids, and Christmas and Thanksgiving cactuses, actually depend on cooler temperatures to start their flower-bud formation.

Before bringing in the plants, get the house ready by washing your windows (clean windows let in a lot more light). If possible, while the plants are still outdoors, move them into shade one to two weeks ahead to prepare them for the drop in light in the house. As you bring the plants indoors, soak the pots up to their rims in a sink full of water to force insects, especially sowbugs, slugs, and millipedes, to the surface, where you can make them pay the price of their audacious freeloading.

It's best to leave repotting until just before the new growing season begins in early spring. Moving to larger pots means more growing medium, which holds more water. With lower light levels and shorter days, overwatering is more dangerous than being a little potbound for the winter.

And quit fertilizing. They worked hard at growing all summer, so give them a rest until they start actively growing again in late winter.

Coaxing Kalanchoe to Bloom

Q **I always buy a kalanchoe for a little color in the winter, and then I always have to throw it out because I can't get it to bloom again. It seems such a waste. Can I get it to flower again?**

A There is nothing quite like coming in from a bitter winter's day and seeing the mass of bright red flowers of a kalanchoe (pronounced kal-an-KO-ee). Even the variations on red that are available—the softer apricot, deeper magenta, or singular yellow—brighten both the room and your soul. Compact, bushy, and about a foot tall, kalanchoe is common in winter, but once the flowers disappear, many people abandon them. That's a shame, because with a little effort, they can be forced to bloom whenever you want.

Kalanchoe is what is known as a short-day plant, but it is really the length of the night that matters. For kalanchoe to set flower buds, it needs six to eight weeks of days with 14 to 16 hours of uninterrupted darkness. And uninterrupted means exactly that, so you'll have to put it in the closet every afternoon—over in the corner where your poinsettia spends the fall, as it needs the same treatment. Pick the right closet because anything in it you might need won't be available until morning. About a month after the dark period ends, color should be showing as the buds begin to break.

Other than that, kalanchoe is a cinch to grow when given lots of sun (except when it's in the closet). It thrives in warmth, 65°F or more, although it tolerates temperatures just above freezing. It should have the chance to go a bit dry between waterings, and it likes a general fertilizer every two or three weeks when new leaves are growing.

When it gets too big, it can be cut back pretty hard, leaving only three leaves on each branch. If you do cut it back, wait until it has at least three pairs of new leaves on each branch (about two to three months) before tossing it back in the closet to initiate flowering. 🍎

Growing Fond Memories

Q **I am originally from the South, and have fond memories of night-blooming jessamine. I know I can't grow it outdoors in Michigan, but will it do okay in the house? Other jasmines are grown as houseplants, so I'm hopeful this one will work, too.**

A The common name night-blooming jessamine does suggest that the plant you remember is a kind of jasmine, which, just to confuse the situation, is sometimes called jessamine, especially in the South and Midwest.

But the two are not related. Jasmines are in the genus *Jasminum,* part of the family Oleaceae, along with lilacs, olives, and ash trees. Your jessamine is actually a *Cestrum* (*C. nocturnum*), and it's a member of the nightshade family, Solanaceae, along with peppers, tomatoes, petunias, and nicotiana.

But one thing the jas-jesses have in common, in addition to strong fragrance, is a willingness to live and bloom indoors where they are not hardy. If you want to try growing *C. nocturnum,* give it lots of bright light and plenty of water. Keep it on the cool side; high heat without outdoor-strength sun causes the kind of stress that leads to insect problems.

Feed only when it is in active growth and preparing to bloom (once a month with all-purpose plant food, from April to September). Prune it heavily in late winter so it stays bushy and compact.

And don't forget that this perfume machine is otherwise undistinguished. The long, narrow leaves are simple and plain, and the small greenish white flowers are closed during the day. It isn't ugly; it's just kind of blah, which doesn't matter in a large yard but is something to consider when you're giving out those precious sunny spaces indoors. 🌢

Night-blooming jessamine
(*Cestrum nocturnum*)

Rare Lepismium

Q **At a nursery, I saw what looked like a skinny Christmas cactus, but the label said *Lepismium*. What is this plant?**

A You're not far off in your observation, since this tropical houseplant is a cactus family member, an unusual cousin of the Christmas cactus. Like the Christmas cactus, the lepismium has elongated, flat or cylindrical jointed leaves that sometimes sport tiny tufts of hair. The white or pink flowers, which close up at night, eventually develop into small purple berries.

The lepismiums are a group of nearly two dozen epiphytic (aerial-rooted) plants from the jungles of Brazil, Bolivia, and Argentina. One of the more commonly grown is *Lepismium cruciforme*, also known as *Rhipsalis cruciformis*.

Some botanists consider all of these plants to be in the genus *Rhipsalis*, a group they certainly resemble. Apparently, there's a subtle difference in the pattern of their pendulous limbs, but one would be hard-pressed to tell them apart. 🌰

Exuberant Mandevilla

Q Last fall I brought a large mandevilla inside, where it is in a sunny south window. Should I have cut it back? It seems to be flourishing, and since it is so large, I hate the idea of touching it. Although I read it should be kept dry in winter, it seems to want a lot of water.

A There are a number of different mandevillas, but from your description, it sounds as if you have the old standby *Mandevilla × amabilis* 'Alice du Pont,' the one with the fuzzy foliage, bright pink flowers—and rampant growth habit. It doesn't need to be cut back to bloom, but since it does need to put on several feet of new growth to initiate flower formation, you can end up with quite the tangle if you don't take steps.

Mandevillas are tough plants and will come back after severe pruning, after a drought that makes them drop all of their leaves, or after a winter in the cellar. By continuing to water (and perhaps feed?) yours, you have prevented the semidormancy that helps ward off total takeover. According to John Enterline, the indoor display specialist at Longwood Gardens in Kennett Square, Pennsylvania, it will become unmanageable when it starts active growth again (in late winter or early spring). "It's going to put on at least 3 or

4 feet of new tendrils," he explained, "6 or 8 if it was a good-size plant to begin with."

The flower buds form on the old wood, so you don't want to cut it back by more than about half. An open structure that lets in light and air is best, Mr. Enterline said, in part because that makes it easy to fight off the mealybugs that often prey on indoor mandevillas. Ideal pruning time is January to February for bloom that starts in May. ❧

Maples for the Parlor

Q I'm planning to buy my wife a flowering houseplant for Christmas, either a miniature rose or a flowering maple. I realize aesthetics are personal, but is there a big difference otherwise?

A Go for the flowering maple, which is also known as parlor maple. Miniature roses do not make stellar houseplants.

Parlor maples are not related to maple trees. They are abutilons, members of the malva family, distant cousins of hollyhocks and hibiscus. The "maple" is from the shape of the leaves; the "parlor" from the Victorians, who grew vast numbers of these plants in the precursor of the living room.

Parlor maples, mostly *Abutilon × hybridum,* come in a broad range of colors, from pale pinks and creams through orange and brick. Plants may be upright or drooping. Foliage varies from narrow to broad, and leaves are often variegated.

Most of these plants will bloom indoors year-round, as long as they get plenty of sunlight and bloom-boosting fertilizer. Use it full strength once a month or dilute to quarter strength and use it each time you water. Keep the soil moist but not wet.

Abutilons prefer cool temperatures and tend to sicken in stuffy rooms. But they won't mind hot days as long as they have chilly nights (50° to 55°F). Turn down the thermostat at bedtime, and add a nice flannel nightie to the holiday gift list. ❧

Parlor maple
(*Abutilon × hybridum*)

More Sun for More Maple Flowers

Q I have a flowering maple that doesn't flower. It is large and bushy
and appears healthy. I feed it once a month with all-purpose fertilizer.
I know it can get sunburned, so it spends the summer outdoors in the shade,
the winter in a northeast window. How do I get it to bloom?

A Start by giving it a little more sun in the summer and
a lot more during the cold months. Flowering maples
do well in filtered light outdoors, especially where the sun is
very hot, but that doesn't mean they'll thrive in deep shade.
Indoors, they need at least a half day of sun, and will enjoy
having even more, as long as they don't suffer huge temperature swings. Try putting the plant near a southeast window,
or set it just a little back from a south-facing one.

Flowers form on the newer growth, so prune back by
about half when you bring your plant inside in fall. Then
prune again, lightly (only as needed to keep it shapely),
early in the spring.

Depending on the species, flowering can occur anytime,
though heaviest bloom is usually in late spring through
late summer. You can encourage flower-bud formation by
switching to a fertilizer that is high in phosphorus and low
in nitrogen, such as a 10-30-15. 🌿

In-Law Trouble

Q I have a mother-in-law plant in an area with no natural light, only
illumination from electricity. Shoots continue to sprout, but they are
extremely skinny, rather than the typical broad, fat shoots. What's wrong?

A There are several plants called mother-in-law. Yours
is most likely a *Dieffenbachia,* unless, of course,
it's a *Sansevieria,* which is also known as snakeplant and
mother-in-law's tongue because of its long, narrow, sharply
pointed leaves.

According to David Bulkeley, the manager of the greenhouse complex at the Institute of Ecosystem Studies in
Millbrook, New York, there are a lot of mother-in-laws. But
no matter which it was, he said, the likeliest cure for narrow

shoots is to give the plant more light. Spindly growth is generally a sign of light deprivation.

"Most sansevierias are high-light, low-moisture plants," he explained. "That's why they have those thick leaves." Though they will get by on almost nothing, they will thrive best in full sun and should at least be in an east- or west-facing window.

Dieffenbachias, on the other hand, are classed as low-light plants; they don't need or want strong sunshine. But that doesn't mean they will grow in the dark. If your mother-in-law is a dieffenbachia, try moving her to a spot where she will get bright but indirect light, like a north windowsill. 🍂

Frozen Oleander

Q **I had a beautiful oleander, grown from a little cutting 20 years ago, that got exposed to the bitter cold while wintering in my garage. Normally, the garage is above freezing, but someone left the garage door open overnight. It looks dead, but I am still watering it in the hope that it may revive. Is a freezing cold night always fatal?**

A Not necessarily. When a plant freezes, death comes as a result of cells bursting. If enough cells die, so does the plant.

The tricky part is figuring out how far below freezing the temperature has to go, and for how long, before damage is fatal. Leaves are out there in the cold air, so they freeze first. A plant can stand losing its leaves and a few branches as long as its roots survive. Since they are insulated by soil, it takes colder temperatures or a longer time for them to freeze.

How much soil was in the pot and how wet it was are important factors. Moist soil is a better insulator for the roots than dry soil is because the water has to freeze first.

Some or all of your oleander has obviously been damaged, but you may want to keep caring for it until it is very clear that reports of its death have not been exaggerated. 🍂

Oleander
(*Nerium oleander*)

Orange Blossoms for Perfume

Q I've moved from Florida to New Hampshire and miss the fragrance of orange blossoms. My new gardening friends all say you can't grow oranges indoors here, but I'm wondering if it would be worth a try if I'm willing to settle for just the flowers and don't try to have fruit.

A Most citrus trees like lots of light and quite a bit of humidity in addition to steady warmth, so even getting as far as "just the flowers" can be quite a challenge. But if you have a very bright spot in which to put your hopes of orange blossoms, the ones to try for are calamondins (× *Citrofortunella microcarpa*), kumquats (*Fortunella japonica*), ornamental mandarins (*Citrus reticulata*), and Otaheite oranges (*Citrus × limonia otaitensis*). All of these bear small, sour fruit, but they are more tolerant of indoor conditions than sweet oranges are.

Give your citrus plant bright light but protection from burning sun. Keep the soil moist. Consider getting a humidifier if you don't already have one. Feed every three to four weeks with an all-purpose plant food, diluted to half strength. And watch out for bugs; indoor citrus tends to attract every houseplant pest you ever heard of, as well as several that will probably be new to you. 🌣

Orchid Development

Q My orchid-loving friends talk about monopodial and sympodial plants. Can you explain these terms?

A They refer to how orchids grow and develop their bloom, and in general, there are two ways this happens. The sympodial orchid develops new flowers and leaves from the most recently formed rhizome, a horizontal-growing ground stem. In most species, once this area has matured and sent up its blooms, it does not do so again. If you look at an orchid with sympodial growth, it's often possible to trace the development of the rhizome from its oldest to its newest part. The cattleya and paphiopedilum are sympodial orchids.

The other orchid type is the monopodial. Instead of developing a separate new horizontal growth each season, it develops along a single vertical stem that continues to increase in height over the years. This orchid type develops its new leaves at the top, from its growing tip. The flowers develop from the area at the base of the upper leaves. The vanda and phalaenopsis are monopodial orchids. 🌿

Orchid Roots

Q **Although most of the aerial roots on my orchid plant are white, some are turning brown. Should I cut these off?**

A Definitely cut the brown ones off, because they are dead. Healthy roots of epiphytic orchids (orchids that grow above the ground, typically in trees) are covered with a whitish, spongy coat called velamen, which has a greenish tip.

This spongy coat is a covering that protects the inner conductive channel of the root. But its spongy surface also has the ability to absorb minerals and rain or moisture from the surrounding atmosphere. And it can fasten itself to any surface it touches. 🌿

Waiting for an Orchid to Bloom

Q **Last year I purchased two cattleya orchids that were in bloom. The orchids lasted a short time, but the plants have had no new blooms since. One is in the bathroom, where it gets light and air; the other is in a sunny room. I water only when dry. What should I be doing differently?**

A Maybe nothing. Cattleyas and their many hybrids bloom only from new growth and most flower only once a year. There are many cattleya hybrids on the market and each one always blooms at about the same time, generally sometime between late winter and early summer.

Two conditions are paramount for cattleyas to flower: enough light and a change in temperature between day and night. Cattleyas need more light than other common orchids: direct sun from November through March, bright light but not direct sun for the rest of the year. Leaves that turn pale yellow are a sign of too much light. Leggy, thin growth means too little light. Temperatures need to drop 10° or 12°F at night or the orchid won't set flowers. Low 60s at night is ideal, but it's the change that really matters.

If you picked the bathroom for humidity rather than light, move the plant. Humidity in a bathroom is too variable for these plants. It is better to put the pot on a wide tray of damp pebbles to increase the humidity consistently right around the plant.

The pseudobulbs, those large swellings at the plant's base, store water. Don't put orchids on a schedule; let them dry between waterings. When you do water, water thoroughly, and avoid getting water in the sheath, which can prevent flowering. Feed with quarter-strength balanced fertilizer every other watering. Flowering sheaths grow from the pseudobulbs and protect the flowers until they are nearly ready. There's swelling and lengthening, and then one day, there they are. ☙

Cattleya orchid

Mealybugs in the Orchids

Q **Please help! I grow orchids. I noticed that the phalaenopsis was being destroyed by mealybugs, so I cleaned the roots and repotted the plant. After four months, I still find the critters nesting in the folds of the plant. I am afraid that the bugs will make their way to other orchids and jade plants in my home. Where do these pests come from? Can they jump from plant to plant? How can I rid my home of them for good?**

A Mealybug is a common name for a family of scale insects. They came in hiding on one of your plants, and they are difficult to eradicate—truly the bug that came to dinner. There are at least five different species of mealybug that enjoy phalaenopsis, and most of them are indiscriminate when it comes to other orchids and houseplants.

The white fluff that you first notice is a female with an attached egg case, surrounded by a protective material. The crawlers that eventually hatch are smaller, darker, and pretty quick to move around and find their own lunch spot on that or another plant. Killing all of them will take time. A series of baths at three-week intervals, in a solution of insecticidal soap, should eventually solve the problem; or you can try the same routine with sprays of horticultural oil. But some orchids are sensitive to oil, so test it on a single leaf first and wait a week to see if the leaf turns yellow. 🌶

Repotting Orchids

Q **I have orchids that have bloomed profusely in past years, but this year they look very sad. I lightly feed them weekly with orchid food and blossom booster, as I have done for years. What can I do to get them going again? When I water them, I let the water drain out, and they have great light and not too much sun. Most are phalaenopsis, though this year an old cattleya rebloomed most unexpectedly.**

A Since you have not made any changes to a successful regimen, they probably need to be repotted. It's likely that the bark they're planted in, between being compressed by growing roots and broken down by micro-organisms living in it, is simply retaining too much water and not enough air.

A basic orchid bark mix contains coarse-grade perlite and fir bark. Chunky sphagnum peat moss is usually added to mixes for phalaenopsis because they don't like to go completely dry. Some growers add charcoal to their mixes. Others don't. It is a matter of what works for you.

But regardless of the composition, the mix needs to be replaced every other year. After flowering is finished and the tips of the visible roots begin to show some new growth, replace the bark. Soak the new orchid bark medium in water overnight before repotting. Otherwise, water will run right through without being absorbed. Mist the plant daily for a week, then resume regular watering.

Phalaenopsis orchids need coarse bark, but cattleyas prefer medium; small young orchids should have fine bark. A typical garden center, if it has orchid mix at all, won't offer the range of varieties, but they are readily available from specialty suppliers. 🌶

THE GREAT DEBATE: CLAY OR PLASTIC, AND A FEW OTHER OPTIONS

CLAY (UNGLAZED TERRA COTTA)

Advantages: Weight of the clay adds stability; pots in the classic tapered shape are less likely to tip over than are tapered plastic pots. Porosity enables water to evaporate, which has two benefits: roots are less likely to drown if the plant is overwatered; and evaporation cools the pot, helping to prevent over-heated soil.

Drawbacks: Clay is heavy, even before you fill it with soil. Evaporation means plants must be watered more frequently. Fertilizer salts build up on the outsides and rims of clay pots. And they are breakable. Another fault, though not of the clay itself, is that many good-looking clay pots are designed more for beauty than use: a pot that is narrower on top than it is at its widest point will probably have to be broken if the plant in it needs potting up.

PLASTIC

Advantages: Lightweight. Inexpensive. Easy to clean and compact to store. Plants in plastic need less-frequent watering. Fertilizer salts do not build up. Plastic is not unbreakable (in fact, many plastic pots become brittle after a few years), but it's not as fragile as clay.

Drawbacks: Tippy, especially if the plant is attractively large in proportion to the pot. Holds water so well it increases the danger of waterlogging. Can over-heat in a sunny spot, especially if the plastic is a dark color. There are now pseudo terra-cotta ones, complete with fake fertilizer salts, that look pretty convincing from a distance. But the beauty bottom line is still, well—they're plastic.

OTHER MATERIALS

Glazed clay pots don't transpire water as fast as unglazed ones, but they still provide more evaporation than plastic. Salts are less of a problem on glazed clay. These pots can be gorgeous, but that's not always a plus. Pots are there to support the plants; beware of using one that's so pretty it upstages its contents.

Glass is uncommon for good reason, as it combines the faults of clay and plastic without offering the benefits of either (unless you count weight). **Galvanized metal tubs** will rust where the seams are, no matter what the literature says, and **wood** will rot. Containers made of these materials should be lined with heavy plastic and used as cachepots (see page 597).

Windowsill Jewel

Q **A friend suggested I try growing a jewel orchid on my windowsill. Are they difficult?**

A Your friend has made quite a wonderful suggestion. Although there are several kinds of patterned-leaf plants known as jewel orchids, one of the easiest is *Ludisia discolor,* sometimes called *Haemaria.*

The ludisia is a terrestrial orchid, as opposed to the kind that perches on the branches of trees. It is exceptionally striking even when not in bloom because its narrow foliage varies in color from a velvety dark red to maroon, and has subtle silvery-gold veins. The leaves grow along graceful, somewhat brittle, succulent stems that cascade over the side of the pot. White flowers, which vaguely resemble large snapdragons, line foot-high spikes that can appear anytime from late winter to mid spring.

The ludisia is a native of Southeast Asia and does best with afternoon shade, cool nighttime temperatures, and soil that stays barely moist. 🌰

Mysterious Inheritance

Q **I inherited a plant I do not recognize or find in any of my houseplant books. It does, however, have a tab in the pot that says: "M3643 Den. New Horizon × *(canaliculatum × bigibbum)* MR7." To save the plant and my frustration, please advise on light, watering, etc.**

A Your understanding of frustration is just beginning. Eventually, you may even want to re-evaluate your relationship to the person from whom you inherited your dendrobium orchid.

Your plant is a complex hybrid, a cross between an older hybrid, *Dendrobium* 'New Horizon,' and another hybrid that is a cross between *D. canaliculatum* and *D. bigibbum,* two Australian species. (The tag numbers are just the breeder's records.) If you can get it to bloom, it will probably have two or more spikes holding small lavender flowers.

Dendrobium canaliculatum

But it won't bloom unless it is entirely satisfied with its living conditions. And living indoors isn't its idea of heaven. Dendrobiums need plenty of light and humidity. Keep yours in whatever window is getting the most light, and provide additional artificial light, since these orchids like 14 to 16 hours a day.

Watering depends on the state of the orchid-growing medium, which should be changed every couple of years as it breaks down. (Do any repotting in the spring, using the smallest pot that the roots will fit into.) Every watering situation is different, but keeping the medium a little too dry is better than too wet. Start by watering and feeding with 20-20-20 fertilizer once a week during the active growing season, early spring through fall. Quit feeding and reduce watering to every 10 days or so in the fall when the base, or pseudobulb, begins to swell.

Dendrobium bigibbum

If everything is right, it should flower in late fall. If it doesn't, you'll understand why you didn't find it in your houseplant books. 🌰

The Oxalis Tribe

Q **We recently purchased two small potted oxalis plants. I know that there are varieties too numerous to mention, but in general, what is the recommended care, indoor and outdoor; soil content; temperature; drainage preference; and watering and sun requirements? Do they winter over? If so, how does one treat them?**

A You're right about the size of the oxalis tribe. Unfortunately, a genus with species too numerous to mention is also one about which it is difficult to generalize. Though all oxalis are more or less rounded plants with cloverlike leaves, and all of them have delicate, five-petaled flowers, that's about it for family resemblance.

Pink-flowered *O. acetosella,* for instance, is a rhizome-forming woodland dweller that spreads readily into wide mats. It blooms in spring, stays green all summer, and comes through Canadian winters unscathed.

O. lobata, on the other hand, is a bright-light lover that can't stand frost. A tuberous-rooted native of Chile, it makes leaves in spring, goes dormant for summer, and then puts out new leaves and brilliant yellow flowers in the fall.

Many of the showiest oxalis have a dormant period, but since your plants didn't carry a warning label about one, they're probably from a species that doesn't mind skipping this step. If they have bands of purple at the top of grass-green leaves, they could be 'Iron Cross,' usually classed as *O. tetraphylla.* If they have large purple leaves and bright pink flowers, suspect *O. regnellii.*

Both are perennials that should be treated as house-plants north of the Carolinas. They do well in bright light but not hot sun, and can take some shade. A loose soil that drains well is best, since they like a lot of water but not soggy feet. Add some perlite if you have them in regular potting soil. Though they droop if they dry out, they have amazing powers of recovery once watered.

Feed monthly with a bloom-encouraging fertilizer as long as they're flowering, then let them rest. Avoid high-nitrogen plant food, which will encourage leaves at the expense of flowers and encourage rot at the expense of the plants. ❧

Low-Light Lady Palm

Q **I recently saw a plant called the lady palm, which supposedly does well with little sunlight. Is this true?**

A The graceful lady palms (*Rhapis excelsa* and *R. humilis*), with their deeply divided, fan-shaped leaves, arrived in England from South China in the eighteenth century and have been popular ever since. They're easily grown in extremely low light. If grown in full sun, the leaves may yellow and burn. Although the thin stems, which vaguely resemble bamboo, typically remain short for years, with ideal growing conditions they can eventually top 15 feet and expand to clumps several feet across.

The lady palm does best with its soil kept barely moist at all times, except through the winter, when it should be allowed to dry briefly. And since it is such a slow grower, fertilizing is minimal: a diluted liquid fertilizer should be added once every few weeks through the summer only.

There are some 150 named varieties of lady palms, including several variegated forms. One of these is 'Zuikonishiki,' which is easy to grow. 🍎

Vines to Fill the Indoors

Q Are there any vines that will grow indoors? I would love to grow some in pots in my living room, which has plenty of windows and a southern exposure. Are there any that would flourish, or even just live, in such an environment?

A *Philodendron scandens,* possibly the world's most common houseplant, is a vine, but perhaps you were hoping for something more unusual. What about a passion-flower (*Passiflora*)? There are several species from which to choose. Many will flower in the winter, and almost all are guaranteed to please since this is a plant that is almost as beautiful out of flower as it is when blooming.

Leaves are usually three-lobed and deeply cut, though those in the species *P. vitifolia* are nearly as broad as the grape leaves for which they are named. The flowers of most species have a flat ring of petals with crowns of filaments in the center and are usually purple, violet, lavender, or one of those three plus white.

P. vitifolia, however, has red flowers, as does the knock-your-socks-off *P. coccinea,* which is further distinguished by black filaments.

Some passionflowers, including 'Incense,' *P. caerulea,* and 'St. Rule,' also offer strong fragrance. Several even produce passion fruit, though don't expect big crops from anything in the living room. In short, it is hard to go wrong as long as you remember, when reading catalogs, that "everblooming" means "blooms in all seasons," not "blooms all the time."

Passion vines, as they are often called, do best indoors where they get lots of light and temperatures that stay between 70° and 80°F, though they will tolerate cool nights if they have to. Most are fairly well-behaved, but a robust specimen with sufficient root room and ample fertilizer may act like a sort of indoor kudzu, crawling around the window frames, infiltrating drapery rods, light fixtures, and anything else it can get its tendrils into or around. If you want to move yours outdoors in the summer, be sure to train it onto a free-standing frame of some sort. ✿

Passionflowers: What Now?

Q **I have three passionflower plants, growing in pots, that became 15-foot vines while they were outside over the summer. Now that they are in for the winter, what should I do next? Do I cut the vines back? Should I fertilize them?**

A As long as you got them untangled from their outdoor supports without damaging the main stems, there's no need to cut them back. Just provide an indoor trellis (preferably a portable one—the plants will be huge by spring), and let them keep on going. A passionflower's need for food depends on two things: its natural blooming habits and the brightness of its indoor home.

Some varieties, including the large-flowered purple-and-white *Passiflora caerulea,* the little yellow *P. citrina,* and the big, bright red *P. coccinea,* are year-round bloomers that will be glad for monthly feedings throughout the winter. Others, including the old-fashioned purple maypop (*P. incarnata*) and the little pink *P. sanguinolenta,* are spring and summer bloomers that rest from mid fall to early spring. Feed these, too, but half as often and at half strength.

Before you get out the fertilizer, bear in mind that all passionflowers need bright light. If yours are in a dim location, it won't matter what type they are. They will just hold on over the winter, growing slowly and greenly, and should be fed only sparingly—quarter rations—until stimulated by the brighter light of spring. ✿

Peace Lily

Q **The leaves of my peace lily get brown at the tips and gradually rot, and then I have to cut them off. What am I doing wrong? I always keep the plant moist.**

A Given a regular supply of water, peace lily (*Spathiphyllum* ssp.) can adjust to almost any indoor conditions. Consequently, large and small, the lilies are found everywhere: hotel lobbies, mall atriums, airport waiting rooms. And there they sit, quietly green, occasionally producing a slender stalk with a single white bract—a simple sail. With indoor plants, the harder they are to kill, the more popular they are.

The browning tips are probably a sign of excessive buildup of salts in the potting medium, a result of too much fertilizer. What we call low-light plants may tolerate low-light levels, but they don't necessarily thrive, and don't need as much fertilizer as they would in higher light. Spathiphyllum is not a heavy feeder to begin with, and needs even less in low-light conditions. Flushing the pot with at least a half gallon of water, two or three times, should remove the mineral salts. Wait an hour between flushings. In the future, fertilize at about half the rate recommended on the label, or less.

Frequently, peace lilies are bought bearing the only bloom their owners will ever see. To rebloom, they usually need about two weeks during the winter when the night temperatures are about 50°F. In addition, they need enough light. While they will survive just fine in light that is bright enough for you to read by, they should have about twice as much if they are to flower. 🌿

Growing Pineapple

Q **My daughter decided she wanted to grow a pineapple. Luckily, we all love pineapple because we have now eaten three in order to get the tops for her to start, all without success. Each time we have been careful to keep a thin layer of fruit attached to the leaves. I don't mind eating another one, but she is becoming disenchanted and I would like this one to actually grow.**

A Then eat all of the fruit so it doesn't have a chance to ferment and eventually rot, killing the top. Once you have a fresh top minus the fruit, leave the larger, spiky leaves alone but pull a quarter of the small lower leaves down and off, exposing the stem, where you'll see small brown bumps called root initials—the structures that will become the new roots.

Let the top dry overnight; then bury it up to the remaining leaves, in a well-drained medium in a 4- to 6-inch pot, and place it in a humid, sunny spot where the daytime temperature is around 75°F. Keep it moist but not wet, and new leaves should start growing in about a month. Once the plant is established, give it fertilizer diluted to half strength twice a month during the growing season, spring to fall. If it reminds you of a bromeliad at the florist, that's because it is a bromeliad, and the fruit will form in the top center of the leaves, just like a bromeliad's flower spike.

But not right away. It will take several years, as many as five, before it is ready to flower and fruit. In the meantime it will grow, and your daughter can practice the art of repotting and lugging it outdoors for the summer. By the time it is ready to produce fruit, it will be in a 2- or 3-gallon pot, she will be an expert at bromeliad care, and with luck, everyone will still love eating pineapple. 🌿

Poinsettia Rebloom

Q **Last year I was given my first Christmas poinsettia. I kept it alive, although with only two small leaves remaining, I thought it was a goner, but it revived over the summer and put out a number of new green leaves. Now that it's almost December, what should I do to ensure that it will color up for the holidays?**

Cut back to shape in spring and summer.

Deprive of all light on autumn nights.

A Either grab the spray paint or put off your holiday. Poinsettias don't just turn the color on with a switch; they need to be pampered, then convinced, with a process that takes many weeks.

Start with the pampering part: the indoor regimen should include bright light with a few hours of direct sun. Never let it dry out or stay saturated, and never let it get too cool (55° to 60°F at night is fine). In late spring after the weather is settled, cut the plant back to shape it, and put it outside. Cut it back again in early July to keep it shapely, and bring it inside around Labor Day.

Assuming whiteflies and spider mites don't kill it, it will be ready for convincing, the final step to make the bracts color up: eight to ten weeks of dark, 60° to 70° nights at least 13 hours long, with absolutely no stray light, and about six hours of very bright light each day. That means lugging it to and from a closet or covering it with a box every day—on its schedule, not yours. Start today and your poinsettia will be ready for Valentine's Day, but not Christmas.

Poinsettia sap may irritate your skin, but contrary to lore, poinsettias are not poisonous to people or animals. ☙

Beheading a Ponytail

Q **My ponytail plant is about 12 inches tall now. Is there any way I can induce the side shoots that I've seen in larger plants?**

A A corky, swollen stem topped by tufts of slender leaves assures a bizarre and sculptural look for the houseplant known as the ponytail plant (formerly *Beaucarnea recurvata,* now *Nolina recurvata*).

The best way to get the plant to branch is to chop off the top, and the best time to do it is in early spring. Use a sharp pruner and cut off about an inch. A day or two later, seal the open wound with hot candle wax. This prevents the stem from desiccating.

Maintain the plant as before, watering sparingly in winter, but more generously through summer when there's active growth. Eventually, the additional branches will appear. ☙

Prayer Plant Problem

Q **I recently bought a healthy-looking prayer plant but now its leaves are brown. What am I doing wrong?**

A Prayer plant (*Maranta leuconeura*) got its name because each night, its broad, strikingly colored foliage folds upward in a prayerlike position, and there it stays until daybreak.

The leaves of this curious plant from Brazil fall into three categories: those with brown blotches called rabbit tracks, which turn dark green with age; those with a herringbone pattern of prominent red veins; and those with black-green leaves and silvery veins.

Although easily grown, the prayer plant has rather specific needs. Among these are protection from direct sunlight and cold winter drafts, soil that is evenly moist but not sodden, and constant humidity.

Your plant may be suffering from air that is too dry. If you don't want it in your bathroom, keep it on top of pebbles in a shallow, water-filled tray. Spider mites may also cause brown leaves. If you find their webs (use a hand lens and examine the leaves' undersides), gently wash the leaves with mild, soapy water. 🌰

Rubber Plants

Q **I have a rubber plant, an old friend with nine lives, that has new growth starting about halfway up the stem. From the base there is a 1½-foot shoot growing out. Should I cut it off?**

A One of the nice things about the rubber plant, *Ficus elastica,* is that there are very few "shoulds" involved. The only two that really matter are "water sparingly" and "don't overfertilize."

Outdoors, rubber plants can become 60-foot trees, with multiple trunks that make them look like miniature forests. Indoors, size is limited mostly by the size of the container, the light available, and the determination of the owner.

If you remove the new shoot, you will maintain the columnar form you have become used to. If you leave it, and any more that follow, the plant will start bushing out.

To make more branches on the stem, shoot, or both, prune right above any leaf node, or above the scar where a leaf used to be. The plant will branch at the cut but may not do so evenly (rubber plants are famous for lopsided extensions). You might have to prune several times over the course of a year or so before you get a balanced plant.

Use a very sharp knife. Wear gloves. Protect the work surface. And have some powdered rooting hormone or some wood ashes handy; either of them will help seal the cut quickly, which is well worth doing. The white sap of the rubber plant doesn't make the best-quality tires—for that you'd want the true rubber tree, *Hevea brasiliensis*—but it is still copious, very sticky, and hard to remove. 🌰

Rubber plant
(*Ficus elastica*)

Sweet Flag Indoors

Q **Does sweet flag make a good houseplant? I love the swordlike foliage.**

A The sweet flag (*Acorus calamus*), a member of the arum family (Araceae), is native to North America from Florida to Nova Scotia, and must have bog or shallow-water conditions. It is also a deciduous garden plant that dies to the ground for its dormant period, beginning in autumn. There won't be much to look at if you take it indoors for the winter.

Members of the evergreen species *A. gramineus* might be better candidates for indoor growing. Of note is *A. gramineus variegatus,* which has striped leaves, and *A.gramineus pucillus,* which is only about 3 inches tall. If you decide to grow one of these sweet flags indoors, keep the pot in a shallow, water-filled saucer so that this bog plant never dries out. 🍂

Urban Lichens

Q **While walking in the woods behind my parents' home in Maine, I became fascinated by the profusion of lichen forms along the trail. They looked like structures one might find in the sea—sea fans, corals, and algae. They varied in color from light green to brown, and were stiff, yet not brittle. I gathered up a small example of each and brought them home to my New York apartment. I have done a little research and find that they are the symbiotic association of a fungus and algae, which grows very, very slowly. What I can't find is any information about how to keep them alive. When I spray them with water, they become soft and pliable, but I am not sure if my samples are still alive. If they are alive, is there any chance of keeping them alive in my vastly different environment, or should I send them home?**

A Send them home: they miss the woods. The relationship between the algae, which provide the fungus with carbohydrates through their own photosynthesis, and the fungus, which provides the algae with water, protection, and a place to live, is based on a very delicate balance of light and moisture. If the balance is upset, one or the other may die, or one may grow faster than the other. Either way,

Houseplants in Particular

the lichen—the combination of the two—won't be able to survive. A lot of interesting things grow in New York apartments, but lichens aren't among them. 🌿

Windowsill Yams

Q I'm intrigued by the idea of a windowsill yam or sweet-potato vine. I have heard they're easy to grow. What do you think?

A Windowsill sweet potatoes are indeed easy to grow, but they shouldn't be called yams (even though this misnomer is common). Whether they are red, yellow, orange, or white—whether they are labeled "yams" or not—the vegetables sold in the supermarket are all sweet potatoes, *Ipomoea batatas,* part of a genus that includes the morning glory, and is believed to be native to Central America.

True yams belong to the genus *Dioscorea*, and are very seldom sold in the United States.

Now that we have their name straight, here's how to grow the vines: sweet potatoes are easy to grow in their natural state, but they are sometimes treated with sprout inhibitors, so you'll have the best luck if you start with organic ones, which are not subjected to this method of preservation.

Choose firm, torpedo-shaped tubers with no signs of mold or soft spots. Place them pointed-end down in jars partially filled with water. The jar rims should support the tubers so the water covers only an inch or two of the potato. Put the jars where it is warm and light, but not right on the windowsill. Shoots should appear in two weeks or less.

Roots will appear somewhat later. That's when you decide whether you want to keep your plants in the water (which should be changed regularly) or transplant them to a deep pot filled with a light, fast-draining potting mixture.

If you do transplant, be sure to bury the whole tuber, even if it means covering some of the green shoots. The shoots will find their way to the light, so there's no need to worry about them. Once part of it has been buried, the exposed potato will rot, and may attract pests while it is doing so. 🌿

CHAPTER FOURTEEN

Container Gardening

Container Gardening in General

Getting Started

Q **I've decided I'd like to add window boxes to the rather plain front of our house, but now that I've made the decision I'm not sure what to do next. Can you get me started?**

A Window boxes bring color and spirit to barren streets, as well as considerable pleasure to those who tend them. Measure the width and length of your sill, then check garden shops or hardware stores for boxes in the appropriate size. (If you shop at a store with helpful clerks, you can get plenty of free advice about window-box attachment.)

Depending on your house style and budget, you can choose from wood, cast cement, molded terra cotta, plastic, or fiberglass. Avoid metal boxes, because they will very likely rust in a few seasons, and if placed on sunny sills will transmit heat, which burns roots.

Make sure the box is securely attached with wire or bolts. Don't count on just gravity, no matter how wide the support is. Prepare for planting by covering the bottom with a layer of landscape fabric or plastic screen. This will hold the soil in place while allowing water to drain.

Fill the box about three-quarters full with any all-purpose potting mix, then stir in several trowels each of perlite and organic matter such as leaf mold, aged manure, or compost.

There are no design rules to planting, but contrasting leaf sizes should be a goal, as should contrasting plant outlines. Use bushy plants for bulk, tall plants for a vertical accent, and pendulous species for a graceful cascade over the side. 🌶

THE RAPUNZEL EFFECT

Window boxes almost always look better if there is something draping over the edge, and for sheer drama, you can't beat drapery that hangs in long streamers well below the box.

Unfortunately, although there are many summer stalwarts that will swag down nicely for 12 to 18 inches or so, not many plants are willing to dangle unsupported for much more than that. Plants that will include ivy (*Hedera helix*), ivy geraniums (*Pelargonium peltatum*), nasturtiums (*Tropaeolum majus*), ornamental sweet potato (*Ipomoea batatas*), trailing lantana (*Lantana montevidensis*), and vinca (*Vinca* spp.)

The common houseplants pothos, tradescantia, and zebrina can also be used, though you have to start with good-size plants to get much of a show before autumn.

The list of likely trailers is short because most lax-stemmed plants are vines, and most vines would rather hang on than hang down. If they can't climb straight up, they'll climb any which way—on themselves, on the other plants in the box, on the brackets that hold the box up. The end result is a tangled mass instead of graceful tresses.

That said, if you have a situation where vines can't get a grip on anything, these are also worth a try: canary bird vine (*Tropaeolum peregrinum*), climbing snapdragon (*Asarina* spp.), grape ivy (*Cissus incisa*), and passionflower (*Passiflora* spp.).

Making a Window Box

Q **I plan to make my own wooden window boxes. Can you suggest a wood that's not budget breaking? What kind of paint can I use that's plant friendly? And if I decorate the front of a window box, can I seal it with polyurethane?**

A The first question to ask yourself is, How do I plan to attach this thing to the building? As a general rule, the problem with wood isn't what it costs; it's what it weighs.

Assuming you have a way to attach the box securely, you can use any wood you want, provided you don't plant edibles; treated wood should not be used anywhere around food.

Don't forget to consider looks and life span, as well as purchase price. Half-inch plywood, for instance, is inexpensive, strong, and less likely to warp than half-inch boards. But it must be painted. And constant dampness just about guarantees that it will start coming apart within three or four years, no matter how carefully you seal the joints.

Plain pine boards should last at least a little longer than plywood; rot-resistant cedar or hemlock, a few years longer than pine. No matter what wood you use, the box will be more durable if you use sheet aluminum or the fake wood made from recycled plastic for the bottom.

Wooden window boxes are easy to build, but heavy. Be sure they are attached securely.

After painting, line the inside with thick plastic sheeting so you have two layers of protection. (Remember to make drainage holes in the liner as well as in the box.) Paint and seal the outside with anything you like; as long as the stuff has cured completely and doesn't touch the soil inside, it will not harm the plants. 🐾

Looking for New Suspects

Q **Do you have a few winning suggestions for street containers? The local garden club plants 20 to 30 whiskey barrels with annuals each spring. They are the same from year to year; the center is planted with a dracaena, followed by petunias and geraniums, finishing up with vinca. The care of these barrels is hit or miss. Some are in full sun and some in partial shade. I would love to plan for some changes next year.**

A The list of inexpensive plants that will perform under the conditions you describe is not long, but there are a few directions in which you could branch out: marigolds, for instance. The little signet types, including 'Lemon Gem' and 'Tangerine Gem,' are just as foolproof as their larger, more familiar cousins, but they have prettier foliage and a more attractive fragrance—especially 'Lemon Gem,' which deserves its name. Alyssum and lobelia are also stalwart, carefree bloomers that put out a lot of color over a long season. All of these flowers are small—tiny, in the case of alyssum—but there are so many that the overall effect is bright.

If you need something with bigger flowers, don't forget nasturtiums, which are famous for thriving on neglect. Mixed-color assortments can be hard to blend with other plants, but single colors like the delicate primrose-yellow called 'Moonlight' are easy to work with. And what about dahlias? Though they take a bit longer to bloom, they look good even when all green, and the flowers are striking for a long time once they get going.

If you used ivy geraniums instead of the vinca, you would have trailing leaves and flowers to boot. Or if small leaves are important, the vinca might be replaced by *Helichrysum petiolatum,* sometimes called the licorice plant. The silvery-gray variety is more reliable than the chartreuse one called 'Limelight,' but 'Limelight' is a very handsome plant that will look great with deep blue lobelia or the equally blue, very low-growing *Anagalis monellii* (blue pimpernel). Your center height might come from a small canna like 'Tropical Rose,' or you could be daring and plant a clump of the multicolored Swiss chard 'Bright Lights.'

If you are willing to plant two kinds of barrels, consider fuchsias and trailing begonias for the ones that get some shade. 🌰

Container Cottage Garden

Q **I have a pair of large containers that sit on either side of my front walk, where they get sun for most of the day. I'd like to plant them with a cheerful mixture that has a cottage garden look. Any suggestions?**

A You can grow almost any sun-loving annual except space hogs like sunflowers. To get the cottage garden effect, be sure that the heights are varied, that some of the flowers are lacy, and that the colors are mostly pale ones, with bright reds, oranges, and pinks acting as accents rather than the main event.

Suitable plants include "patio" types of cherry tomato, dwarf dahlias, heliotrope, lantana, love-in-a-mist, blue lace flower, white dill, fennel, ageratum, miniature roses, verbena, zinnia, marigolds, petunias, cockscomb, and geranium.

The containers will look best if they are on the crowded side, but don't forget that crowding will put even more stress on the plants than simply being in containers (which is already stress enough). They will need more watering than you ever thought possible, especially in hot, windy weather, and it is a good idea to keep them constantly fed, as well. Either mix a timed-release fertilizer such as Osmocote into the planting mix, or add a quarter-strength dose of soluable fertilizer to every third or fourth watering. ⚘

A Partly Shady Sill

Q I am determined to have a window box garden—could you suggest plants for part shade?

A Plants for partly sunny sills include ageratum, basil, bay, bee balm (*Monarda didyma*), begonia, browallia, caladium, cigar plant (*Cuphea ignea*), dwarf Chinese astilbe (*Astilbe chinensis pumila*), ferns, four o'clocks, fringed bleeding heart (*Dicentra eximia*), lady's mantle, lantana, lobelia, and wishbone flower (*Torenia*); and English ivy, mint, or vinca to trail over the side. ⚘

No Sunlight at All

Q I would love to have a window box, but my ground-level sill receives no sunlight. Isn't there something I can grow there? The box is on the large side, but too small for trees or shrubs.

A No sun is no excuse for not planting a window box. Assuming you get at least bright reflected light, there are quite a few plants that will endure. Many of the best are perennials with comparatively short blooming periods, but if you choose plants with handsome foliage, the box will be attractive even when there are no flowers.

Container Gardening in General

The delicate, ferny foliage of Jacob's ladder, for example, contrasts nicely with the scalloped, round leaves of coral bells, and both remain fresh looking all summer. The Jacob's ladder will give you blue flowers for a few weeks in late spring. The coral bells will bloom (at least briefly) a short time later, in red, white, or pink.

Other possibilities with handsome foliage and at least a few weeks of bloom include dead nettle (*Lamium*), which has yellow, white, or pink flowers; variegated liriope, which has clusters of purple or white late-summer flowers; and the countless cultivars of small hostas.

During warm weather, continue the foliage theme with tropical houseplants such as asparagus fern, grape ivy, bird's nest fern, Chinese evergreen, and the purple passion plant.

If you are determined to have flowers all summer long, you can try shade-tolerant annuals, but keep in mind that even tolerance has limits. You'll probably have to experiment a bit to find which will perform under your conditions. Choices include wishbone flower (*Torenia*), with its small purple, snapdragon-like flowers; browallia, which has blue, lilac, or white trumpet-shaped blooms; begonia, both tuberous and wax, available in white and every shade of red and yellow from pale pink to screaming orange; and the ever-faithful impatiens, in a spectrum much like begonia's.

Don't forget to plant a trailer. Vinca and English ivy will both do fine. 🌿

Wind, Sun, and Privacy

Q **Overlooking my apartment terrace is a large building à la *Rear Window*, and I need privacy. What inexpensive trees can I grow in this space, which gets good afternoon sun but is very windy in winter?**

A Privet is by far the least expensive plant that will tolerate winter wind and afternoon sun and still add privacy a good part of the year, but the barrier will be more effective and will also look better if you use a combination of evergreen and deciduous trees or tall shrubs.

It's also best to plant them in multiple rows if there's enough room. Space and budget permitting, try mixing the privet with a few of the following wind-resistant trees and shrubs: 'Skyrocket' juniper, Japanese black pine, forsythia, pussy willow, crab apple, birch, lilac, arrowwood viburnum, Tatarian maple, mock orange, and tamarisk. 🌰

THE COMPANY THEY KEEP

When you're choosing the plants for a mixed container, it's easy to remember that those destined for a shady terrace must all be shade lovers, and that hot, bright situations call for a collection of sun worshippers. But while you're considering light requirements, don't forget that plants also differ in their need for water and food.

Both coleus and Boston fern thrive in semi-shade, for instance, but soil moist enough to suit the fern may make the coleus rot. Plant 'Wave' or other modern petunias in front of a screen of morning glories, and the heavy feeding those petunias need will drive the vine all to leaf. Hibiscus thrives when there's lots of food, moisture, and bright sun; nasturtiums are equally keen on bright light, but hate wet and will stubbornly refuse to flower if too well fed.

The easiest way to cope with this is to choose compatible plants, but you can also get around it by planting containers in the container. For instance, if you'd like a sedum (very well drained, lean soil) in the center of a pot, with lobelia (moist, well fed) trailing over the sides, put the sedum in its own plastic pot.

Place the potted sedum in the center of the container, on an inverted saucer or rock if necessary, to bring the rim of the sedum pot level with the rim of the outer container. Fill all around with fertile, moisture-retentive potting soil, stopping about 1½ inches below the rims of the containers. Plant the lobelia, which will rapidly hide the exposed lip of the sedum pot. Water and fertilize carefully.

Wind, Shade, and Green

Q **I have a windy rooftop terrace that gets very little sun. But I want to look out and see green, especially in winter. This year I lost my ivy. What other evergreens do you suggest?**

A Tough evergreens that shrug off wind and shade include rockspray cotoneaster, Japanese holly, wintercreeper, and the many yews. Evergreen perennials also worth considering include the variegated lilyturf, wild ginger, and wintergreen.

Even these will perish if they don't get enough moisture, so be sure to use generously proportioned containers.
And if there is little winter rain or snow during a period of
four to six weeks, get outside and add some water. Plan
on doing this early in the day when the temperature is
expected to remain well above freezing. ✿

For a Windy Aerie

Q **I wish to start a garden on my large sixteenth-floor terrace, where the winds are quite strong. Can you recommend a wind-protective mesh or any other way to deal with this problem?**

A Heavy Lucite panels are sometimes used to temper the winds, but they are not especially attractive and mesh is even worse. A better solution is a hedge of tolerant plants, ideally a combination of evergreen and deciduous species planted fairly close together and (if there's enough room) in a double row. A dense leafy barrier will decrease the velocity of the wind without cutting off air circulation altogether, and it will be a part of the garden rather than just a fence around it.

Evergreens for this mix might include 'Torulosa' and 'Skyrocket' junipers, arborvitae, false cypress, black pine, and Japanese holly. Deciduous choices include privets, bay-berry, and hornbeam.

Whatever you choose, plant your windbreak plants in the largest containers you have room for—the better to keep them well anchored. Keep them well watered all year if rain (or snow) is sparse. And brush up on your pruning skills; if the hedge gets more than 6 or 8 feet tall, it will cast too much shade on the terrace, unless by "large," you mean "huge." ✿

Drought-Resistant Annuals

Q **We have a weekend house and a number of whiskey barrels that have remained empty because we're not around to water during the week. What annuals can I plant that need very little water?**

A The standard rule on water needs is "1 inch of rain or its equivalent every week," but that assumes unconfined roots and widely spaced plants. The smaller and more tightly planted the container, the more frequently it must be watered.

So you're on the right track already just by having the barrels, which can hold quite a lot of soil and therefore store some moisture. As long as you don't overplant them, there are quite a few annuals that should thrive. Widely available choices include morning glories (give them bamboo poles to climb or plant bush varieties), nasturtiums, poppies, bachelor's buttons, California poppies (*Eschscholzia californica*), moss rose (*Portulaca*), calliopsis, and the haageana zinnias, of which 'Persian Carpet' is the best known.

There are also plants that can be described as hangers-in. They won't thrive, exactly, but they will survive a waterless week and revive when you come home. This group includes alyssum, geraniums, and nicotiana. 🍃

LIVING DIVIDERS FOR OUTDOOR ROOMS

Tall plants in pots make lovely screens, defining sitting areas, providing privacy, blocking the view of the trash cans. And they don't have to be the expensive evergreens so often seen in magazines. You can make a very effective "hedge" out of annuals like tithonia, old-fashioned tall cosmos, or cleome, or out of rampant vines such as passionflower, grown on individual trellises.

Since the plants will be tall, bushy, and prone to catch the wind, it is important to provide both root room and anchorage, i.e., large containers with wide bases. Plastic pots are usually O.K.; the soil should weigh enough to keep them steady, but if the location is very windy, it's wise to go for the extra heft that terra cotta provides.

Balcony plantings are a special case, since they need to be both lightweight and secure. Use plastic pots, lots of perlite in the soil mix, and if they are in a place where they might fall (or blow) over the edge, bungee cords or other strong ties to be sure they stay in place.

No matter how beautiful the pots are, a tidy line of large containers with large plants coming out of their tops will look stiff unless it is broken up a bit. Be sure to include some trailing plants at the pot edges, and place a few smaller pots at the feet of the big ones to add rhythm and variety (this is a great place to put vacationing houseplants).

When It's Hot and Dry

Q My rooftop deck is hot and dry most of the summer. I hate the idea of spending all my time watering, but would like to establish a perennial garden. Is this possible?

Sedums do well where it's hot and dry.

A Drought-tolerant plants, or those with minimal water needs, have become increasingly appealing, not just because they save gardeners work and time, but because in many parts of the country, water conservation has become essential.

Herbaceous perennials that manage with minimal water include artemisia, spurge (*Euphorbia* spp.), coreopsis, sedum, moss mullein (*Verbascum blattaria*), potentilla, yarrow, and yucca.

Woody plants that tolerate dry soil if they're situated in large containers include barberry (*Berberis* spp.), beach plum (*Prunus maritima*), cotoneaster, brooms (*Cytisus* spp.), shrub honey locust (*Gleditsia triacanthos* 'Elegantissima'), tamarisk, rugosa rose, juniper, and yew. 🍐

Terrace Space Savers

Q A friend suggested I use espaliered plants as space savers on my small terrace. What are they, and what plants do you suggest for containers that will be outdoors all year where temperatures sometimes go as low as 10°F?

A Espaliers are woody plants trained to grow flat against a trellis or other support. The plant grows all in one plane, typically a symmetrical shape (candelabrum, U, or fan), although a free-form design is possible, too. Espaliered plants have long been used in European orchards to achieve maximum yield of fruiting species such as grapes and apples in minimum space. The technique is believed to date from ancient Egypt.

Espaliered plants are the most artful way to soften a dreary wall. Any slow-growing shrub or tree that is hardy in the area can be espaliered in a container, as long as the container is large enough to allow for root development and to protect the roots in winter. Figure on a minimum size of 24 inches high, wide, and deep, although bigger is definitely better. Training espaliers is not difficult, but it usually takes several years to get results that look like something other than a bunch of leafy sticks. Fortunately, you can buy plants already trained. Look for cotoneaster, crab apple, euonymus, firethorn, forsythia, holly, Japanese dogwood, juniper, mock orange, quince, and yew. 🍐

Beautiful Weepers

Q **My terrace needs a focal point. A friend suggested a weeping tree in a tub. Do you agree?**

A There is no more striking plant sculpture than a weeping tree, but avoid weeping willows, rapid growers that grab too much space. Instead, choose such handsome plants as the weeping blue Atlas cedar (*Cedrus atlantica* 'Glauca Pendula'), the weeping Nootka false cyprus (*Chamaecyparis nootkatensis pendula*), the weeping willowleaf pear (*Pyrus salicifolia pendula*), the weeping Siberian pea (*Caragana arborescens pendula*), or any weeping flowering crab apples or cherries.

These weepers may be controlled with pruning and will grow in a terrace tub, which should be at least 18 inches in each dimension. 🍐

Container Shrubs in the Shade

Q **I live in a town house in Washington, D.C. It has a narrow terrace that gets little sun. Is there anything—other than dwarf conifers—that I could grow that will stay green all year? My planters are 2 by 4 feet, and I would like to have just one or two shrubs in each.**

A Easily grown broadleaf evergreen shrubs for shade in your area include holly, *Pieris japonica,* azalea, hardy camellia, and mahonia. Though the planters are large and won't get strong sun, the soil will still dry out quickly, especially after the shrubs become large. Don't forget to water regularly, summer and winter. 🍐

Potpourri on the Balcony

Q I would like to grow plants for my own potpourri but have only a small balcony. What do you suggest?

A For a fragrant summer and bountiful harvest of leaves with potpourri potential, grow plants with scented foliage. Quite a few are fine in minimal space, so all you'll need are several window boxes, or as many generous-size containers as you can comfortably fit on your balcony floor.

Scented geranium leaves

Among the outstanding plants for potpourri are the many species of scented geraniums, including peppermint, lemon, nutmeg, apple, and rose. Invaluable, too, are the leaves of lavender, lemon verbena, lemon balm, bay, thyme, and mint. Because your space is limited, you should start harvesting a few leaves from each plant as soon as it's established and continue cutting leaves all summer. Dry them thoroughly on a cookie sheet in an airy corner out of the sun, and store them in large labeled jars until you have enough to use.

Don't be shy about gently brushing the leaves and smelling plants before you buy; the perception of fragrance varies with each individual. As long as you don't harm the plants, no reputable nursery operator will mind. 🌱

A Sunny Terrace

Q I have a tiny terrace with an unobstructed southern exposure. What small perennials and annuals would you suggest?

A Your conditions are enviable and you should do well with many kinds of plants. But do keep in mind that with full sun, plants in small pots will need to be watered at least daily. Plant in the largest containers you can accommodate.

Some sun-loving annuals you might enjoy are African daisy (*Arctotis*), California poppy, portulaca, verbena, globe amaranth, strawflower, thrift or sea pink (*Armeria* spp.), love-in-a-mist, calendula, gazania, and nasturtium. Perennials to consider include some of the smaller artemisias, lavender, coreopsis, and sedum. 🌱

Old Potting Soil

Q **I've been rotating tomatoes among three beds, but this year I grew them in big pots. I assume I shouldn't grow tomatoes in the same pots again, but is it O.K. to grow other things in them? Does potting soil become unusable after a couple of years? Should I replace the soil each year? If so, is it O.K. to incorporate old potting soil into my organic garden beds?**

A Pests that overwinter in garden soil are likely to overwinter in potting medium, so continue to rotate. Potting medium doesn't just hold the plant upright and provide a spot to put those tiny trolls. The size and porosity of the particles control the supply and distribution of air, water, and the nutrients and minerals that are dissolved in the water. As organic material breaks down and compacts, the spaces between particles disappear. Air and water can't penetrate and circulate among the roots. Water either quickly slides between the medium and the pot's edge, or it puddles on top for what seems like a long time. The potting medium needs replacement if it shrinks down in volume or is no longer fluffy, or if a thorough watering takes too long.

Potting mediums are generally good for at least a year, but the actual length of their useful life depends on many factors, including their composition and what has been planted in them. Decide when to replace by looking at the medium, not the calendar.

When potting medium has given its all, just dig it into the garden soil, including any perlite and vermiculite. They're natural minerals, so your garden won't lose its organic status. 🍎

Homemade Potting Soil

Q **We grow many annuals outdoors in window boxes and in large pots. Do you have a recipe for potting soil that would be less expensive than the stuff that comes in little bags?**

A There are many recipes that will work in your situation. An easy, inexpensive one calls for the following:

1 part perlite

1 part moisture-retentive filler such as shredded coconut fiber or peat moss

1 part all-purpose potting soil

1 part compost or composted cow manure

This mixture will provide good drainage while being water-retentive enough to help counteract the tendency of containers to dry out. But even with the compost, it will not be fertile enough to support blooming annuals over the course of a whole season, so don't forget to feed the plants frequently. You can do this with soluable fertilizer, or by adding ¼ cup timed-release fertilizer pellets for each two gallons of soil mix before you fill the containers. 🌶

Mixing homemade potting soil.

Perlite and Vermiculite

Q Most soil mix recipes call for perlite, vermiculite, or both. What are they, and what's the difference between them?

A Perlite and vermiculite are both minerals that are processed at high temperature to make them explode into small, lightweight, puffy pieces.

They share many traits that make them valuable components in a growing medium. Their size and shape make channels for the flow of air and water, helping to aerate the soil and providing drainage. They also prevent the growing medium from drying out too quickly because they hold on to water. But they do it differently, and that difference is important. Perlite holds water only on its surface; vermiculite absorbs water, as much as 16 times its weight, making a much wetter growing medium.

Perlite is white and nearly round, and comes in several sizes from a grain of sand to about ¼ inch in diameter. No matter where it is mined, all perlite is the same chemically. It is inert, its pH is neutral, and it does not break down.

Vermiculite, on the other hand, has a shiny brownish metallic color, and comes in squared-off pieces. Depending on where it is mined, its pH may range from neutral to strongly alkaline. It is chemically active, binding or releasing various minerals, and eventually needs to be replaced. 🌾

Small-Space Composting

Q **I have a rooftop terrace that is not large enough for the three-bin compost system recommended by most garden periodicals. But I would like to make compost. Can I? And if so, how?**

A You can make compost in even the tiniest space using a pair of large plastic garbage pails.

First, line the bottom of one pail with several thicknesses of newspaper. Then start adding the fallen leaves from plants that are free of diseases, along with small pieces of soft kitchen vegetable matter, if you wish.

Every few inches, add a thin layer of packaged cow manure. (Fresh horse manure is actually better, but most gardeners are too embarrassed to roam bridle paths or follow mounted police with a plastic bag.) Top the manure with a few inches of straw, shredded dry leaves, or newspaper cut in strips, then start adding plant debris and kitchen waste again.

Keep the materials moist but not wet, watering if the weather is dry, covering the pail in rainy weather. Continue layering in materials until the pail is full, then let it sit for two weeks.

Line the second pail with newspapers. Empty in the contents of the full pail, stirring a bit as you go. Let the compost sit for two weeks, then repeat the pail-switching routine. Repeat again two weeks later. Etc. As long as the materials were small to begin with (no grapefruit halves!), the compost should be ready to use in about two months from the time you first filled the pail.

Alternatively, consider buying a polyethylene composting unit that keeps the ingredients together in a neat, unobtrusive container. You can find this easily through mail-order garden-supply companies. 🌾

Those Gelatinous Blobs

Q **While walking by some outdoor flower boxes that are maintained by our local garden club, I noticed transparent, gelatinous blobs nearly covering the soil. A friend told me it was a water-saving gel added to the soil, and that the recent heavy rains must have caused the problem. Since it looks so peculiar, I am wondering if there is a way to prevent this from happening, and whether the gels are worth the effort?**

A Follow the directions and don't expect miracles. Hydrogels, sold at most garden centers under several brand names, are small granules of polyacrylamide or other similar materials that can absorb up to 400 times their own weight in water. As the soil around them dries out, these water-savers gradually release the water, thus keeping the soil moist. Using them in a well-drained potting mixture can extend the period you don't need to water by two or three days at most.

Intuitively, you would think using more than the recommended amount (about a teaspoon for an 8-inch pot) would let you water once and take off for a trip around the world, but it doesn't work that way. Using too much can leave the soil soggy and the roots gasping for air. Sorry, the art of watering is still important.

The other instruction the package will give is not to use the gels in the upper 2 inches of soil. The manufacturers say the reason is that you want to have the gels down where the roots are, but since the water they release will disperse throughout the pot, the real reason may be to avoid having the water-saturated granules rising to the top like bloated bodies emerging from a lake in a bad mystery. ✿

Winter Window Boxes

Q **Will hydrangeas, statice, and other dried flowers hold up in a window box through the cold?**

A There is nothing quite so forlorn as an empty window box in winter, which is why you so often see them filled with arrangements of evergreens. But if you prefer dried material, there are quite a few choices that should last until early spring as long as they are protected from high winds and heavy snow.

You can experiment with any plant that has an interesting outline or decorative parts. Among those with long-lasting seedpods or berries are clematis, Queen-Anne's lace, bittersweet (*Celastrus scandens*), roses, gas plant (*Dictamnus albus*), love-in-a-mist, and honesty.

Possible flowers include cockscomb, globe thistle, sea holly, globe amaranth, goldenrod, strawflower, yarrow, and many plumed grasses.

For a contrast, use silver-leaved species like dusty miller: 'Silver King' or 'Silver Queen' artemisia, or lamb's ears. 🌱

Wintering on the Terrace

Q I recently moved from one side of Philadelphia to the other, relocating my potted trees and shrubs from a terrace open to the elements to a covered terrace with wind, some sun, and no rain. Should the plants be watered over the winter? Is it necessary to wrap the pots with burlap?

A Wind can be very hard on plants, but unless the former location was unusually well protected, yours should be used to it. Same story with the sun; it doesn't sound as though too much is going to be a problem.

The only thing to watch out for is a narrowly southern exposure. Trunks and branches that get strong heat on one side while the other side stays cold can develop cracks.

You'll be on watering duty big time during the summer, but during the winter be careful not to overdo. Your plants should be dormant (or close to it) when the weather is freezing, and although they still need some water, too much will lead to rot. All that's necessary is enough to keep the roots moist.

The only thing you would wrap with burlap would be the plants, not the pots. Burlap is an overcoat that shields trees from drying wind, scorching sun, and branch-breaking ice and snow. But don't use it unless you absolutely have to. Burlap's sunblock aspect means plants can bleach or starve if you don't take it off soon enough. The dank environment it creates can lead to fungus problems. And you have to look at it.

As long as your new terrace isn't absolutely arctic, you can just group the plants away from the wind near an inside wall, and let them wait out the winter relatively undisturbed. 🍎

THE ELEPHANT IN THE BACK BEDROOM

Several of the finest summer container plants are problem children in winter: unable to withstand frost, yet also ill-suited to life indoors. They don't die if you bring them into the living room, but they look so bad you almost wish they would. Lantanas drop all their leaves. Hibiscus drop many leaves and pick up bugs. Brugmansias and fuchsias keep most of their leaves and even make pale, weak new ones, the better to support even *more* bugs.

Off to the basement! Except that you can't. Unlike, for instance, fig trees, these tropical and sub-tropical plants don't go truly dormant. Short-term dark storage is possible, but only for six to eight weeks. They may not be actively growing, but they still need light.

What to do? The ideal off-season environment for such fussbudgets is about 50°F, with moderate humidity and low but consistent light. If you have an unheated room with north-facing windows, group the plants there. A sunporch (with a space heater for supercold nights) will also work, if you keep the plants well away from the windows and don't mind opening them on bright days when the room warms up.

You can even try the basement if you're willing to invest in grow lights, though it may take a bit of experimenting to determine the right number of lights, and a bit of ingenuity to rig them up at the proper distance from the plants.

No matter where you put your plants, don't let out of sight be out of mind. It takes only a few hours for temperatures to rise or fall significantly enough to require adjustment. The plants will need minimal care, but they will need water from time to time, and may develop insect problems. Keep the soil just moist enough so the roots don't dry out. Watch for bugs, and spray with insecticidal soap as soon as they show up.

In other words, as a general rule, the best way to keep these plants over the winter is as memories: allow them to die—or give them away—at the end of the season, and start over with fresh ones next year. The only exceptions that make sense are for rare plants that cannot be replaced, huge plants (same problem), and of course, homemade standards, the training of which is a multi-year proposition.

Protected Winter Pots

Q **I would like to grow hostas in some large clay pots, but if they are left outdoors through winter, the pots will crack. Will the plants survive in the pots in a toolshed if the soil dries?**

A No. If the soil dries out completely enough to protect the pots, the hostas will dry completely enough to die. If you are determined to keep the plants in the clay pots, you might follow the method used by the greenhouse manager at Klehm Nurseries in South Barrington, Illinois.

She suggested that you move the plants to a cold but frost-free space in late autumn. Water them thoroughly and then mulch the pots heavily with straw, wood chips, or burlap to help retain moisture. Sometime in early winter, certainly by mid January, check the soil, and if it's no longer moist, water the plants again.

"It's very important to make sure that water penetrates the complete pot and not just the top," she said. A few weeks later, check to see if more water is needed. "Plants must not stay bone dry for any length of time."

As late winter melts into early spring, remove the mulch, and with an eye on the temperature, move the plants outside. They can remain there permanently after nighttime frost is no longer a danger. 🌰

Container Gardening in Particular

Agapanthus

Q **I have an agapanthus plant that did not bloom the first year but bloomed the second year. I was told it had to be potbound to bloom, and it is quite potbound now. My problem is that the roots are coming out of the drainage holes, and the pot will not stand straight because of it. I have just brought it in for the Connecticut winter. Should I repot, or will I sacrifice next year's bloom if I do?**

A You're going to have to figure out a balancing act for the winter, because agapanthus have permanent, fleshy roots that are touchy, and the plants will do best if divided in the spring, just before the new growth starts.

The rest of the bad news is that waiting until spring will still delay the bloom for a year while the plant settles in and grows into its preferred state of being slightly potbound. When agapanthus are too potbound, the situation that yours seem to be in, they also refuse to flower, so avoiding dividing them isn't the answer.

How you overwinter your agapanthus depends on whether you have a deciduous or an evergreen species. Evergreen species will slow down for the winter but do not completely stop growing. They should be kept in bright light, with just enough water to keep the soil from going completely dry. Deciduous species go dormant, and can be kept dry and in the dark. Both kinds need storage temperatures between 40° and 50°F degrees well into the spring.

Luckily, the tall blue agapanthus flowers with their strappy leaves are worth the fuss.

A Durable Bouquet

Q We recently received a small, potted balsam fir tree as a holiday gift. We live in the middle of the city, with only a small patio for gardening. Will the tree survive there in a large pot or half barrel?

A Not for long. In fact, it has probably perished already (balsams make great Christmas trees in part because they hold their green needles for months after they die).

The balsam fir, *Abies balsamea*, is a tree of the far north and the high mountains, where both air and soil are constantly cool and moist. It pines away when it gets warm, so it seldom does well south of zone 5 even when planted in the damp, acid, shady ground that should remind it of home.

And there is also size to consider. Although dwarf forms are available, the average height of a standard balsam is about 60 feet. The sensible course is to think of your gift as an unusually durable bouquet. Enjoy it as long as it lasts, and then throw it out.

PROTECTING POTTED PERENNIALS

Tough, mid-size perennials such as day lilies, hostas, sedums, and coreopsis are all good candidates for long-term pot culture, but before you plant them, think ahead to the rigors of winter.

These plants don't mind frozen ground. But they suffer when subjected to repeated freeze-thaw cycles, and most pots hold so little soil that they make such cycles likely. Repeated freezing and thawing is also hard on the pots themselves: plastic becomes increasingly brittle, terra cotta chips and cracks, and even cement may break if tiny fissures get filled with water that swells into ice over and over.

You can store potted perennials in an unheated garage or shed where temperatures stay between 32° and 40°F. Check the soil from time to time to be sure it doesn't dry out completely; roots should be moist but not wet.

Alternatively, you can protect both plants and pots by burying pots right up over the rim. Make sure the soil around clay pots is free of rocks that might shift and cause damage. Mulch after the ground freezes to help it stay frozen.

Truly huge "estate-size" planters (think the bottom third of a telephone booth) may be left in place; there's safety in volume. But if there is no frost-free place to store them, pots that fall in the middle—too big to bury, too small to trust—should be emptied. Same goes for planters made of wood, which is vulnerable to rot. Transfer the plants to plastic pots, and store or bury them as above; then turn the planters upside down so water doesn't collect in them.

If you don't mind taking a gamble, just water thoroughly in late fall, group the pots together in a place where you won't have to look at them, and insulate the whole assemblage with fiberglass batting or a huge pile of leaves or straw. Cover the mound with plastic sheeting and anchor it securely. As long as temperatures stay above zero, there's a good chance they'll come through fine.

Bundling Up Bamboo

 Please tell me how I can best protect tall bamboo trees, planted in containers on a windy Manhattan terrace, against winter's cold.

A Presumably, these are hardy *Phyllostachys* species, something like yellow-groove (*P. aureosulcata*) or fish-pole (*P. aurea*). "If it's a bambusa, it's tropical, and it's probably going to die no matter what you do," said Michael Bartholomew, a horticulturist at Cornell Cooperative Extension in Albany, who is on the board of the American Bamboo Society.

Mr. Bartholomew, who takes his own bamboos inside for the winter, said that there are two threats to your plants' survival. One is cold sufficient to freeze the rootball; the other is wind, which can freeze-dry the canes.

A large container, 2 feet or more in diameter, is essential. Smaller ones will not provide enough insulating earth. Even a large container should be further insulated, if possible, and though the heap of mulch you'd use in the country is probably not an option, fiberglass batting or a triple layer of bubble wrap should work just as well. To improve the look of the thing, cover the wrapping with burlap.

Get lots of insulating material—you'll also need it to wrap the canes. Even when bundled up, many of the leaves will die, but the canes themselves should survive and put out new leaves next year. Asked about the aesthetic implications of Christo-on-the-terrace, Mr. Bartholomew said that there wasn't much to be done about it, but that the period of need was short: "January and February have the worst winds, so that's the danger point."

If you're willing to put up with all this, you might like to join the American Bamboo Society: 750 Krumhill Road, Albany, NY 12203; *www.bamboo.org/abs/.*

Begonia Power

Q **Until last year, my north-facing window boxes held beautiful tuberous begonia displays. But powdery mildew became a problem, and it looks as though it is about to strike again. Must I switch to something else? (I'd rather have begonias.)**

Tuberous begonias need breathing room.

A Pests and diseases tend to flock in when you put the same plant in the same place over and over, and powdery mildews are diseases that need no extra encouragement. They are always around, like the common cold, waiting for an opportunity.

The mildew that attacks begonias is hard to get rid of. Infected plants can seldom be cured, and removing them won't remove the spores left behind—in the soil, on plant debris, and on surfaces nearby.

To make your window boxes safe for begonias, empty them, and, wearing protective gloves, wash them with a solution of two tablespoons of bleach in a gallon of water (do *not* use bleach on treated wood). Fill the boxes with fresh potting material, choosing a light, quick-draining mixture formulated for begonias, then bring in a new mildew-free team. Begonias look prettiest when they are crowded, but mildew sees a closed space as an open door. It's better to leave plenty of room between plants for air to circulate. It also helps to let the top inch of soil dry out between waterings. Mildew thrives in the humid conditions created by damp surface soil.

Cleaning the boxes yearly will probably let you keep planting begonias, but it wouldn't hurt to think good thoughts about ferns, just in case. 🌺

Bougainvillea Blues

Q How do I take care of my tree bougainvillea indoors during the winter in Connecticut? How much water and fertilizer does it need? It's starting to look slightly unwell, and I'd like to keep it healthy and blooming.

A There are bougainvilleas that bloom all year, but none that will do it indoors in the Northeast under ordinary household conditions. They need a great deal of warmth and bright light to put out those big, colorful bracts. (Though the bracts are often called the flowers, they aren't; they're the flower wrappers. The true flowers, which grow inside the bracts, are tiny.)

It's easy to provide as much warmth as would come from summer sun, but you'll do the plant no favors by keeping it toasty when it can't get the summer sun's light. It will continue to grow, especially if you feed it, but the new growth will be lanky, pale, and tender, highly susceptible to invasions of whiteflies and spider mites.

The solution? Don't try to keep it growing and blooming; just; try to keep it alive. That's easy if you think of winter as a rest period.

Put the plant where it stays cool, 50° to 60°F. A bright eastern or northern exposure is best; hot midday sun can

Bougainvillea blooms mostly at the ends of new growth.

create unhealthy temperature swings. Let the soil start to dry out between waterings. Bougainvillea can take quite a bit of drought, and it's better to let it start to wilt than risk drowning the roots. Don't fertilize at all while the plant is resting, and don't worry if it drops lots of leaves.

Bougainvillea is by nature a fast-growing vine, and it blooms mostly at the tips of new growth. The tree form needs your help to stay in shape, so around mid March, when spring is in sight, get out the pruning shears.

Remove any stems or leaves growing from the straight trunk section. Above the trunk, shorten the main branches slightly and cut the secondary limbs back by about one-third. Begin to water more frequently, and start fertilizing every other week with a bloom-boosting fertilizer diluted to half-strength.

Before long, the cut limbs should put out new branches. When the new branches have three leaves, pinch off the tips so they branch again.

Most bougainvilleas bloom from spring to fall. Assuming yours is one of them, flowers should start about a month after the second pruning. 🍎

Wintering Brugmansia

Q **I have been growing brugmansia cultivars in containers on my porch and would like to overwinter them. Given their size, it would be easiest to store them in a dormant state in an unheated garage. Is this feasible?**

A In theory, yes. In practice, it's a bit tricky because brugmansias are fast-growing tropical shrubs that do not have the slightest natural inclination to go truly dormant. You have to force them into it, and they are reluctant to stay there.

The first thing to do is bring them inside—all but the lightest brush with freezing temperatures will kill them. Once they are safe from the weather, begin preparing them for winter by letting the soil dry out until they start to wilt. Then cut them back severely, removing roughly half of the top growth, and cut at ground level any stalks that are spindly.

Ideal storage conditions are cold, about 40°F, and dark. The garage will do as long as it doesn't freeze. Just set the brugmansia pots out of the way (some gardeners lay them on their sides, which may help keep them dormant and may not). From time to time, water very sparingly, just enough to keep the soil from drying to dust. Don't worry when all the leaves fall off.

The brugmansias will probably behave themselves until February or March. Then they're likely to start growing even though you haven't done anything to encourage them. There will be flushes of pale chartreuse, hungry-looking leaves, and then, almost surely, aphids. At this point, dormancy is over. Bring the plants into a room that gets as much light as possible. Water and fertilize sparingly, so they don't take over the whole house, and keep the aphids to a low roar with insecticidal soap.

As soon as the danger of frost is past, put the brugmansias outside. Resume normal watering and fertilization, and they'll be back, even bigger and more beautiful, in just a couple of weeks. ✿

City Camellia

Q I have a *Camellia japonica* that grows outside on a terrace until frost. It grows very well and sets many buds. But when I bring it in, very few of the buds open, some dry up, and the ones that do open are not always in full flower. It is in a cool room, fed and watered about every other day.

A Dried flower buds are the camellia's response to the stress of low humidity and high temperatures indoors. Not exactly a nervous breakdown, but close enough. You may think the room is cool, but to a camellia, a cool room ranges roughly between 50° (nights) and 65°F (days). At temperatures warm enough that people are comfortable, the camellia needs nearly enough humidity to grow mold on the walls.

Getting camellias to bloom indoors is difficult—unless you have a cool greenhouse, which is where they grow the potted camellias you see for sale at the florist's. So you can congratulate yourself that you're getting any flowers at all, especially since you're watering and fertilizing too often.

Water only when the potting medium's surface dries, and fertilize once or twice in spring.

If you have a spot where it could be planted in the ground, you might consider starting over with a hardy camellia that wouldn't need to be moved back and forth. There are camellia hybrids introduced by the National Arboretum and the University of North Carolina that are hardy even in zone 6.☙

Container Clematis

Q I would like to plant something—preferably with flowers—that will climb a trellis and grow in a container. I'd love to have clematis but have been told that they won't survive our cold winters in a pot outdoors. Please advise.

Clematis can survive in a pot if the pot is big enough.

A Clematis is quite likely to survive winter in a container, and the same is true for several other hardy climbers, as long as the container holds enough soil for insulation from repeated freezing and thawing. Where temperatures dip as low as 0°F, a tub should be at least 24 inches high, wide, and deep to insure winter survival.

Moisture is crucial for winter endurance, so add a deep mulch of straw or shredded leaves after the first frost, and water sparingly during thaws if there has been little snow or rain. Remove the mulch in early spring. (You can leave a thin layer to help keep roots cool, but be sure it doesn't touch the stems).

Other hardy flowering climbers for trellis growing include wisteria, variegated kiwi, hops, and climbing roses, but all of these make larger root systems than most clematis. If you want to grow them in containers, you'll have to add root pruning to your list of occasional gardening tasks. ☙

Dangers in the Night

Q I use my city terrace garden mostly in the evenings, so I prefer night-blooming flowers with scents strong enough to stand up to wafting car fumes. Daturas are favorites, but one time I got some sap in my eye, and the pupil was dilated for days. Just how poisonous are these plants, anyway?

A The short answer is "very," though whether datura will simply dilate your eye or also deaden your senses, roil your guts, produce wild hallucinations, induce convulsions, or all of the above (and more) before it kills you depends on many factors.

These include how much you absorb, the species involved, how the plant was grown, and even when the poisoning occurs. Living plants tend to put out more toxins at night.

The most common ornamental species are *Datura meteloides, D. suaveolens,* and *D. metel.* They are closely related to jimsonweed (*D. stramonium*) and to the shrublike brugmansias, with which they are sometimes confused.

All daturas and brugmansias produce similar toxins, primarily atropine, hyocyamine, and scopolamine. Yet all (except the jimson-weed) are also good choices for summer container gardens.

Pretty and poisonous. Plant datura with care.

The plants are handsome and easy to care for, with wide green leaves and a steady output of the huge white, purple, pink, or yellow flowers that give them the shared common name of angel's trumpets.

As long as you don't eat daturas and don't let the sap enter your system—through cuts or your eyes, for example—there is little reason to worry. But it is probably unwise to grow daturas where small children or plant-eating pets might play. 🌿

Freesias Are Hard to Fool

Q I bought a potted clump of blooming freesia. Will they rebloom in the pot next year? I know they were grown in California, and I live in New Jersey.

A The freesias think they are in South Africa, their original home. They will not bloom again unless they remain under this impression, and they are very hard to fool.

Freesias are tender members of the iris family, Iridaceae, which grow in winter and flower in early spring. While the plant is growing, the underground corm that gave birth to it is withering away, and a new corm is forming.

681

A month to six weeks after the plant flowers, every-thing aboveground dies, and the plant goes dormant to wait out three or four months of hot, rainless summer. When cool rains and winter weather arrive, the new corm springs into action, sending up green shoots and then, if (and only if) the green plant has gathered enough nourishment, bright flowers.

You could probably duplicate most of this cycle, but it is hard to provide a South African winter without a greenhouse. You need at least three months of bright light, with temperatures between 45° and 60°F, in order for the growing plants to build sufficient strength to bloom. 🌰

Freesias are very particular about growing conditions.

Caring for Fuchsia

Q **I just purchased my first fuchsia, an expensive, beautiful all-red one. How do I care for it through the summer? Is there any chance it could overwinter outdoors in Rhode Island?**

A Most fuchsias aren't hardy north of zone 8, and some are strictly zone 10 types. There are only a few that might—with a lot of protection—survive outdoors in Rhode Island. If the people who sold you yours didn't make a point of extolling its toughness, you can safely assume it will need to winter inside.

During the summer, keep it in a warm, semishaded place, out of the wind. While it's blooming, feed it every other week with a half-strength solution of balanced fertil-izer. Water just enough so that the soil stays evenly moist.

Most fuchsias bloom from spring to fall, but always on new growth. As each branch stops flowering, cut it back to a strong node (where you see incipient branches forming at the base of both leaves). The plant will put out fresh branches and, in a month, another round of flowers.

If your fuchsia was in a greenhouse and is now out-side for the first time, don't be surprised if it needs cut-ting back quite soon. The rude shock of fresh air often makes these coddled beauties drop some of their flowers.

It's disappointing but not a disaster; the plant will recover as soon as it adjusts. Repotting often has the same effect, so don't repot unless the roots are so crowded that no soil is left. 🌰

Fuchsia Cuttings

Q **My neighbor has a large, beautiful fuchsia that has been growing on her porch all summer. When I admired it the other day, she said I was welcome to take a cutting and start my own plant. Can I do it now, with fall approaching, or must I wait until spring?**

A Fuchsia cuttings root most easily in spring, but they will also do fairly well in fall. Since that's also the time to cut plants back for storage indoors, your neighbor will probably be willing to let you take three or four pieces, tripling or quadrupling your chances of success.

Choose strong growing tips about 4 inches long that have three or four pairs of leaves.

Clip off the set of leaves nearest the cut, and remove any flower buds. Dip the cut ends in commercial rooting hormone (available at garden centers), and insert them in a bed of moist sand or vermiculite. Make sure the nodes where you removed the leaves are buried.

Keep the cuttings out of the sun. Water from the bottom so they aren't jostled. Don't overwater; rot is the most common cause of failure. The cuttings should make roots in six weeks to two months. 🌰

Fuchsia cuttings root best in spring, but fall is O.K., too.

Impressive Ivy Geraniums

Q **On a visit to Germany last year, I noticed many terraces from which blankets of pelargoniums draped down. Some of them were several feet long and almost as wide. I tried to do this here by planting ivy pelargoniums on the rim of my terrace in two 3-foot by 6-inch wooden boxes. A fair number of nice blossoms sprouted, but nothing like the big spreads I saw in Europe. In fact, the plants hardly draped at all. What do I have to do to achieve a lush spread?**

A Fine food and displays of ivy geraniums (*Pelargonium peltatum*) are the strongest memories for many visitors to northern Europe. Many people fail in their attempts to reproduce either once home, because both require attention, a bit of skill, and the right ingredients.

For the ingredients: 'Balcon Royale' (red), 'Princess Balcon' (light orchid), and 'King of Balcon' (light coral) are commonly used cultivars, said Gary Barnum, the director of horticulture for the Clark Foundation in Cooperstown, New York, whose mid-summer displays could bring tears to a German eye. He advises using a soilless mixture to promote good drainage, and packing the container with enough plants to be pot-tight right away.

Since these cultivars of ivy geranium tend to be rangy, pinch them back at the second node (second set of leaves from the base) to encourage lateral growth. Then pinch at the second node of each lateral, continuing until the number of laterals has you completely confused and unable to keep track of which have or haven't been pinched. When to stop? Since it takes six to eight weeks for flowers to appear after you stop pinching, it's a trade-off between early flowers and big spreads.

Pelargoniums are sensitive to both drought and inconsistent moisture. With a container full of roots in a relatively small volume of growing medium, they will need watering and feeding daily, using an all-purpose fertilizer diluted much further than the label advises.

Ivy geranium
(*Pelargonium peltatum*)

Start the food and water when you plant, and continue the daily regime until you are fed up and ready to rip the whole thing out. And if you really want to match the European displays, don't forget to come home at lunchtime to water. ✿

Overwintering Geraniums

Q **Can you recommend a method for overwintering window-box geraniums? An old-timer suggested hanging them, dry, upside down in a cellar.**

A To do that, you need just the right cellar, so even though it's possible, many geranium pros advise against it. "We get this question all the time," said Joe Heidgen, whose family's nursery, Shady Hill Gardens in Batavia, Illinois, has specialized in geraniums since 1974.

"We have any number of people who swear by any number of methods for winter," he continued. "And that includes hanging plants upside down in a brown paper bag. Some insist they must be cold, others say warm; some say dry, and others swear they must be kept damp. But we don't recommend any of these methods because geraniums really don't have a dormant season—they are good on windowsills all year."

Mr. Heidgen's suggestions for winter maintenance begin with digging the plants up from outside well in advance of the cold weather and repotting them in any all-purpose mix with good drainage. Trim them back by a third to half.

"Just be sure to retain a number of large, healthy leaves, not the yellow, sickly ones," he said. "And place them on a reasonably sunny sill. From late autumn through late winter, water sparingly and don't fertilize at all. Keep in mind that with the short days, the plants are not growing; they're just marking time."

As winter nears an end, water more frequently and start fertilizing with a diluted solution of any flowering-houseplant food. By summer, your geraniums should be ready for another season of window-box bloom. 🌶

Container Trees in Winter

Q My neighbor and I have several hazelnut trees in containers on our patios. Will they survive the winter outdoors in southern Connecticut, or should they be brought inside?

A If you move these plants indoors, they will die. Hazelnuts (*Corylus avellana*) are deciduous trees that must have a period of winter rest. Any plant that is winter hardy in the ground in your locale—and hazelnuts are—will also survive the winter in a container, provided the tub is generously proportioned, at least 24 inches high, wide, and deep. 🌶

Repotting Hibiscus

Q **I am getting conflicting advice about why my hibiscus's leaves are turning yellow and dropping after spending the summer outside. Some friends tell me that I am watering too much, others that I am watering too little. Is this the result of too much or too little water?**

A It is probably a case of too little water, but increasing your watering schedule is not going to help. A hibiscus grows quickly during the summer, and the increased root mass displaces the soil in the container. The water—as well as the fertilizer you probably applied religiously every two weeks—is traveling straight through rather than soaking in. You pour water in, see it come out through the drain holes, and naturally assume that the hibiscus has been watered and fed. Unfortunately, the soil around the roots remains dry, and the plant remains thirsty.

Knock the hibiscus out of its pot and take a look. Overcrowded roots signal that moving to a larger container is necessary. When repotting, score the root ball with a knife or pull through the roots with a hand cultivator and tease some away so that they will grow into the fresh medium. If you don't, the roots will remain wound tightly, occupying the center of the container, and you'll have the same starved, thirsty plant—just in a larger pot.

Of course, no matter what you do, a hibiscus will probably sulk in the winter. It is a full-sun tropical plant, and the low light, short days, and low humidity that come with spending a Northern winter indoors are even more depressing for it than for us.

One further note that may fall under the horticultural truth-in-packaging principle: small potted hibiscus, frequently sold in the spring, appear to be dwarf plants covered with large flowers. Most, however, are treated with a growth retardant to keep them small. When the retardant wears off after a month or two, the 2-foot plant is on its way to becoming a 6-footer. This can be disconcerting to anyone who has not seen the same phenomenon occur in a teenage boy. ❧

Bringing Hibiscus Indoors

Q I have two beautiful Chinese hibiscus plants in pots outdoors. How do I prepare them for the long Northeast winters, when I know they must be brought indoors? I heard they should be placed in a basement with little light and watered only occasionally.

A Wintering over large, flowering tropical plants like *Hibiscus rosa-sinensis* is always a challenge. They never thrive in the living room the way they do outdoors. Leaves turn yellow and drop, flowers seldom appear. Assorted pests do appear—in droves. No wonder gardeners dream of exiling these shrubs to the basement, where they can be out of sight and out of mind until spring.

This kind of hibiscus never sleeps, however, and trying to store yours as though it were dormant may give you a rude awakening. If you want to try it anyway, keep the plants cool, 45° to 50°F. Expect them to drop all their leaves. They will likely get bugs. And they will still need to be brought into light well before summer planting time.

A better choice is a room that gets lots of light and is cool enough to slow growth, 60° to 65°. If you must put hibiscus plants in the living room, keep them in the sunniest place, away from direct heat and far enough from the window so they don't suffer big temperature swings from night to day. There is no point in misting, but if you don't have a humidifier this would be a good excuse to get one. Keep the soil barely but consistently moist, and don't feed unless flowers appear. Watch out for aphids, whiteflies, and red spider mites. If you see them, treat promptly with insecticidal soap.

Hibiscus is tough. The plants will not be glorious inside, but they will survive. Cut them back in late April, removing leggy branches and working to create a pleasing shape. New growth should start almost at once. It is tempting to set the plants out as soon as the danger of frost is past, but hibiscus is a heat lover that will be happier inside until it is warm out day and night—late May or early June.

Alternatively, treat hibiscus as an annual indulgence. While they are still beautiful, give your plants to somebody with big

Chinese hibiscus
(*Hibiscus rosa-sinensis*)

windows and no qualms about getting rid of ailing ornamentals. Enjoy a carefree winter, and get new ones next year. 🍎

Hardy Hibiscus in a Tub

Q **I have been given a large *Hibiscus syriacus* 'Diana' in a tub. What kind of plant is this? I live near Chicago. For the winter, should I leave it in the container or transplant it to the garden?**

A You have been given an old-fashioned flowering shrub called rose of Sharon, or althaea, which can grow 12 feet tall and wide. A native of China and northern India, it has been grown in the United States since the eighteenth century. 'Diana' is a cultivar that was developed in 1963 by Dr. Donald Egolf of the National Arboretum. It bears large, shallow, bell-shaped white flowers from mid to late summer through early fall, in both sunlight and light shade.

Altheas are hardy to zone 5 when grown in the ground. Yours can stay in the container as long as the container is at least 24 inches high, wide, and deep, and you give it some extra help. Late in the fall, surround the tub with an insulating mulch of shredded bark or pine boughs. Roots should not be allowed to dry out, so water sparingly through winter if there is little rain or snow. They won't need a lot and can easily drown, so be careful not to overdo.

By the end of next year (if not sooner) 'Diana' will be a strapping specimen bursting the bounds of her container. Store over winter as before, then the following spring, before new growth starts, root-prune, repot with new soil, and trim back the upper growth. 🍎

Honeysuckle in a Bucket

Q **I remember honeysuckle growing around the house at the shore where I spent my childhood summers. Now I live in an apartment with a balcony on the south. Is it possible to grow honeysuckle in a container there?**

A It is if you are the patient type. Honeysuckles usually don't flower much until they are established, which may take a couple of years. And the container should be at least 16 inches wide and deep, though bigger is better. It has to hold enough soil to insulate roots in winter.

Because most honeysuckles want lots of room, be sure to choose a comparatively small variety like *Lonicera periclymenum* 'Serotina.' Its fragrant red-purple flowers open to cream centers, bloom from mid summer into fall, and are followed by bright red berries. You could also try the fragrant scarlet and yellow *L.* × *heckrottii* 'Gold Flame.' It has stronger color than 'Serotina' and blooms longer, but is somewhat less likely to be happy in confinement.

Both plants are vigorous vines that will require trellises to climb and regular pruning to keep them in bounds. If you want something smaller and bushier, consider the new yellow-flowered hybrid called 'Honey Baby,' developed for pot culture.

'Honey Baby' is a cross between *L. periclymenum,* which is well-behaved, and *L. japonica,* one of the most invasive species ever to hit these shores. So to be safe, keep it deadheaded. If it can't make berries, birds can't eat them and spread the seeds all over the countryside. ❧

Straggly Impatiens

Q I brought my New Guinea impatiens inside last fall and they flowered for a long time. But now they have dropped leaves and gotten leggy. I cut some back, but the stems died. How can I have healthy, attractive plants?

A The New Guinea impatiens, known for their elongated bronze, green, and red leaves, are tender perennials believed to be descendants of *Impatiens schlechteri,* a native of New Guinea. Like most impatiens, they are sold as annuals, with the expectation that they will be allowed to die at frost.

Unlike their shade-loving cousins, these impatiens must have sun, and they must have it all year, so it's likely that your light in winter was not bright enough for their needs. They must also have warm temperatures, around 70°F.

If your plants survive through spring, a return outside in summer should bring renewed growth, although it's probably best to start over with fresh young plants. If you bring them in again next fall, try adding grow lights to supplement the limited sun of short winter days, and closely monitoring the room temperature. 🌿

Creating Tropical Trees for Containers

Q This fall I saw a collection of beautiful lantana trees at Planting Fields Arboretum in Oyster Bay, New York. I thought lantana was an annual flower plant and was stunned to see the trees. Where can I purchase one? Do they have any special requirements? Are they hardy?

When the stem is long enough, pinch out the tip.

Pinch the branch tips.

A The common lantana, *Lantana camara,* is a woody shrub in warm climates, an annual anywhere it encounters freezing temperatures. Though lantanas are not difficult to grow (in the tropics, they're weeds), considerable training is required to turn them into the 7-foot trees you saw at Planting Fields, which are known in the trade as standards.

The technique can also be used on abutilon, heliotrope, geranium, fuchsia, and hibiscus, to name five other common tropicals that take well to standardization, and if you use one of the first three, you can enjoy it all year long. (Fuchsia, hibiscus, and lantana must be stored frost-free over winter but don't do well in the living room.)

To create a standard, start with a small plant (about a foot tall) that has a long central stem, and transplant it into an 8- or 10-inch pot. Supply it with a plastic stake that can act as a guide and anchor until the standard can stand up straight on its own (somewhere between three years and never). The stake can be anywhere from 3 to 6 feet long, depending on your ambitions, but don't use anything longer. Place it as close as possible to the long stem and be sure to sink it all the way to the bottom of the pot.

Take off the side branches, and as the plant grows, pinch out all of the side shoots. Using soft florist's tape (available at craft stores), tie the stem to the stake frequently so it doesn't sag. Keep it up until the stem is about three-fourths of the height you want. Be sure there are at least eight or ten growth nodes below the top, then

Time to
pot up.

pinch off the tip to encourage branching. Pinch the tips of the branches once they get going to make them branch again.

You will have something presentable in two or three years. But even before then, as the standard starts filling out on top, the pot will start getting tippy and the plant will start wanting more root room. Be sure pot up to a bigger container before disaster strikes.

Making standards isn't really a lot of work, but it does require patience. If you prefer instant gratification, you can buy one ready-made. They are widely offered in spring by large garden centers. Look for a straight, undamaged trunk, and main branches that are evenly distributed around the top. 🍎

Aliens in the Garden

Q Last summer I gave a Mexican heather plant to friends who are gardeners. They told me they took it indoors in the fall, and it seemed to be thriving in a sunny window. Is it an annual, as I thought?

A Mexican heather, *Cuphea hyssopifolia,* is native to Mexico but is no more an annual than a true heather. It is a small woody shrub that won't survive frosty winters, so in the North it is grown as an annual or overwintered indoors.

Plants that we are used to thinking of as houseplants have been doing summer duty in the garden. Some gardeners don't want to be limited to traditional flower gardens or join the nothing-but-natives movement. Instead, they use "houseplants" and other exotics to create the illusion of anything from a Costa Rican rainforest to their own private Eden.

Old favorites that never left your grandmother's piano, such as oxalis, begonia, *Hypoestes* (polka-dot plant), and tropical ferns, are going outside to join *Abutilon* (flowering maple), *Strobilanthes* (Persian shield), *Justicia* (shrimp plant), *Bouvardia,* and cigarflower.

In window boxes, groups of pots, or in the ground, tropicals (and temperate plants that look like tropicals) mix in and provide contrasting spiky, broad, glossy, tiny, or variegated foliage, irrationally exuberant flowers, and an otherworldly look. 🌰

Trouble with Poppies

Q I live in Houston. For four years, I have been trying to grow annual lettuce-leaf poppies, using seeds from plants that grow on abandoned lots here and elsewhere around the state. I plant them in March or April, in wooden containers that provide good drainage. The soil is rich but light. Each year, the plants sprout rapidly, grow to about 4 or 5 inches, then develop spots on the leaves, turn pale, and die. I have never thinned them out, preferring to let the process happen naturally. Am I doing something wrong, or is Houston's hellish humidity to blame?

A Since the wild ones are doing all right in Hades, it's likely your problem is a combination of rich soil and late planting. Most poppies, including the *Papaver somniferum* you've been collecting, are adversity fans: they like it lean and cold. They also like a bit of breathing room. Think of your urge to thin them as a natural one and indulge it.

It's also possible that the soil has become infected with fungus spores. To be on the safe side, empty the containers and, wearing rubber gloves, wash them with a bleach solution (1 tablespoon of household bleach to each gallon of water). Replace the soil with a new batch, cutting its richness by adding one part sand to every three parts soil.

Scratch the soil surface and scatter the seed in November or December. Press it in firmly, but don't cover with extra soil. Baby plants will be one of your first signs of spring, with flowers following about 14 weeks later. 🌰

Strawberry Jar Blues

Q I've failed abysmally at growing anything in a strawberry jar. Watering floods the top, while the bottom stays bone dry. What can I do?

A These pots with pocketlike openings around the sides make wonderful decorative subjects no matter which little plants you choose—they're especially nice for collections of drought-tolerant things like thymes and sedums.

But even drought-tolerant plants need water (and strawberries need a lot of it). The trick to success in this regard is a watering tube down the middle of the pot.

Cover the jar's bottom drainage hole with a wire screen. Buy a length of polyvinyl tube, 2 or 3 inches in diameter, that's 2 or 3 inches shorter than the jar's height. (You may have to buy a standard length and cut it.) Drill half-inch holes in the tube to correspond roughly with the holes in the jar. Fill the tube with pebbles, tie a screen over the top with wire, and place the tube in the center of the jar.

Add several inches of soil to the jar, to a level just below its lowest holes, then use a chopstick to coax the root balls of small plants into the lower holes of the jar. After adding soil around the roots, repeat the procedure up the length of the jar for each planting pocket, tier by tier.

At watering time, fill the tube first, then water each pocket as well. When the weather is very hot and dry, it's a good idea to soak the pot itself while you're at it. The large expanse of terra cotta wicks a lot of moisture out of the soil, and the watering tube means there's less soil in there to start with. Just set the jar in a container filled with 6 inches or so of water and let it soak until it's dark right to the top.

A watering tube is essential in a strawberry jar.

Overwintering Strawberries

Q My large terra-cotta strawberry jar is flourishing, with plants producing both berries and runners. I live in Providence, Rhode Island, and would like to winter it over instead of starting fresh next spring. Do I take the jar indoors, leave it outside, mulch it, or what?

A Freezing won't bother the strawberries, but it could crack the jar, and mulch won't help unless you use a pile the size of a haystack. The best storage place is an unheated basement or garage where it's dark, slightly damp, and cold (35° to 45°F). The goal is to let the plants go dormant and then keep them that way.

Cut off all the runners before storing the jar. Over the winter, water sparingly if at all; the soil should be just moist enough to prevent total desiccation.

Feed with soluble fertilizer when you set the jar out next spring, and feed again when blossoms appear. Expect to start over after the next cycle. By then, the soil will be tired and so will the plants, which bear most heavily when they are young. ✿

Store planted strawberry jars where they won't freeze.

Container Vegetables

Q I would like to grow some vegetables in containers. How deep and wide should the pots be, and what kind of soil should I use?

A Basically, the bigger the plant, the bigger the container. Shallow-rooted choices like radishes and lettuce can be grown in window boxes; tomatoes need big tubs, at least 16 inches high, wide, and deep.

Vegetables need rich soil that drains well. You can make a fertile mix by blending equal amounts of loam, compost, or dehydrated cow manure; peat moss or coconut fiber; and perlite. Stir ¼ cup of balanced slow-release fertilizer into each 16-inch pot of the mixture. ✿

PART FIVE

Garden Keeping

CHAPTER FIFTEEN

Soil

Enriching the Soil

Controlled Release

Q I've heard the term "controlled release" applied to fertilizers, and I wonder if you might explain what this means.

A Controlled-release fertilizers, also known as slow-release, are fertilizers that dissolve over a period of time, releasing their nutrients slowly. It is true that the slow-release action can occur naturally, as in the case of granite dust, cow or horse manure, and other organic materials that need time, moisture, and/or bacterial action to make them available to plants. But when you see "controlled release" or "slow release" on a label, it usually means the contents are chemical fertilizers that have been formulated in coated pellets. The pellets dissolve over the course of three to six months, depending on the soil's temperature and moisture, and the nutrients pass by osmosis into the root area.

When using controlled-release fertilizers on shrubs and trees, don't forget these plants need to harden off any new growth before the onset of cold weather. Be sure to time the fertilizer so it's all used up at least six weeks before the first frost. ✿

WHAT IS SOIL, ANYWAY?

All soils are composed of roughly equal quantities of weathered rock particles and the spaces between them, along with a small but absolutely crucial amount of organic matter. The different types of soil are defined by the particle size of the rocks—sand, clay, or silt—and how much of each you have.

Sand particles are large enough to be clearly visible, and you can feel them as grit when you rub the soil between your fingers. The spaces between them are big, so they keep soil open, providing good drainage, and there is lots of room for oxygen. When there is too much sand in the mix, soil cannot hold water, and nutrients wash away.

Clay particles are tiny. You can't see them, but you can feel them as sort of slippery when the soil is wet. The spaces between them are very small, so they hold water and nutrients for a long time. But that very smallness can make it hard for plant roots to get at the goodies. Soils that contain too much clay waterlog when wet, and tend to turn rock hard when dry.

Silt falls between sand and clay. Particles are still quite small, but the spaces between them aren't as tight as in clay, so drainage is much better.

Loam is the garden ideal, the rock part composed of roughly

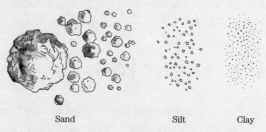

Sand   Silt   Clay

40 percent each silt and sand, with 20 percent clay, which is just enough to hold water and nutrients without causing problems. Most gardens fall short of this Shangri-La, tending more toward clay or sand, based largely on the geological history of the area where they are located.

Deciphering Fertilizer Labels

Q **I often see three numbers on fertilizer labels, and I know they refer to the nutrients the fertilizer contains. But exactly what are these nutrients, and what do they do?**

A The three hyphenated numbers that appear on fertilizer labels—for example, 5-10-5 or 14-14-14—indicate the percentage of nitrogen, phosphorus, and potash that the product contains. Often these nutrients are represented by their chemical symbols: N for nitrogen, P for phosphorus, and K for potassium (also known as potash). These three primary plant nutrients are listed in that order on fertilizer labels. The listing is required by law and is found on packages of organic fertilizers as well as synthetic or chemical ones.

Nitrogen stimulates foliage formation and gives leaves their healthy green glow. Symptoms of insufficient nitrogen include stunted growth and pale leaves.

Phosphorus encourages strong root formation and maturity, which means good flowering and fruit set. Signs of insufficient phosphorus include leaves with a reddish or purple hue, and reduced or nonexistent blossoms.

Potassium promotes hardiness and disease resistance. Deficiency symptoms include reduced vigor, leaf-tip scorch, and small, thin-skinned fruit.

In addition to nitrogen, phosphorus, and potassium—the Big Three—more than 20 other nutrients are also needed for healthy plants. When any of these additional nutrients are present, they too are noted on the fertilizer label, often flagged by the marketing phrase "plus minors." Although they are required in smaller quantities, this equally essential group includes iron, calcium, magnesium, zinc, and molybdenum. 🍎

Balanced Fertilizers

Q **Can you tell me what is meant by the term "balanced fertilizer"?**

A A balanced fertilizer is one that provides equal parts of the three major nutrients: nitrogen (N), phosphorous (P), and potassium (K). The percentage of these nutrients, listed in the order N-P-K, is indicated on the fertilizer label by three numbers. In the case of a balanced fertilizer, the numbers might be 10-10-10 or 5-5-5. 🍎

POTASSIUM SOURCES

Sulfate of potash (potassium sulfate) and greensand marl are two good sources of potassium that are available at most nurseries. Granite dust and seaweed, if you can find them, are equally useful. Wood ashes, which are often recommended as a way to raise soil pH, are an excellent source of potassium for soil that is on the acid side. Any of these sources is preferable to the more commonly found muriate of potash (potassium chloride) and potassium nitrate, which are very strong and may injure your plants.

Wet vs. Dry Fertilizer

Q **Is it better to feed my plants with wet or dry fertilizer? I've tried both, but I'm not sure I see any significant difference.**

A Dry fertilizers are easier (and quicker) to apply, especially when large areas are involved, and though they are slower to take effect, they last longer. In most gardens, wet fertilizers are used for foliar feeding, sprayed directly on plant leaves for immediate uptake. They produce rapid results, but their action is short-lived.

Dry fertilizers are usually mixed with the soil before planting. Later in the season they are used as side dressing, spread in a narrow band about a foot away from growing plants and then scratched in.

Ideally, dry fertilizers break down slowly, providing a steady stream of nutrients with minimal danger of root burn, weak hypergrowth, and other problems caused by too much, too soon. In practice, however, this doesn't always work out. Dry chemical formulations are highly soluble, and while they are more durable than liquids, they disperse rapidly in warm, wet weather. They can work well, but it is important to use minimum amounts, mix them well with the soil, and keep them away from plant roots.

Most organic amendments, on the other hand, are minimally processed. They must be broken down by weather and soil microbes before the nutrients they contain are available to plants. While there are exceptions, as a general rule these natural products pose none of the dangers of rapid breakdown, and unlike chemical fertilizers, they offer long-term soil-building benefits. But there's no denying they're slow to download; you have to plan well ahead. 🍎

Safe Leaves for Compost

Q **Can leaves pick up herbicides from lying on treated grass? I'd like to glean some of the bagged leaves that are left at curbside in my town, but don't want to contaminate my compost.**

A The leaves would not carry damaging amounts of herbicides unless they were down when the lawn was treated, but there could be contaminated soil in the bags with them. Vigorous raking scratches up some dirt, and if the weather has been dry, leaf blowing can blow along substantial amounts of topsoil.

To be on the safe side, shake the bags up and down several times so the dirt falls to the bottom, and then lift the leaves out. 🍂

Beyond Compost and Manure

Q **I am determined to have an organic garden. What, if anything, should I add to my soil beyond compost and manure?**

A Organic or not, the key to good garden soil is humus, organic matter at various stages of decomposition. Where humus is plentiful, water is easily absorbed, beneficial bacteria and earthworms thrive, and pH is more likely to be balanced, assuring that the nutrients present are available to plants.

The best way to build humus is to do just what you're doing, adding large quantities of organic matter—compost, composted animal manures, chopped leaves, seaweed, and green manures (plants, especially leguminous plants, grown specifically for tilling back into the soil). In the long run, if you are faithful about these additions you probably won't need anything else.

When you are just getting started, however, it's impossible to know just what nutrients your garden might be lacking until you test the soil. There are numerous home-testing kits on the market, but more accurate results usually come from the tests performed (for a very small fee) by your county agricultural extension service.

A soil test will determine the pH and, if requested, look for major nutrients such as nitrogen, phosphorus, potash, magnesium, and calcium. If there is an imbalance or deficiency, the test report will tell you, and in most cases it will also tell you what's needed for correction. Make sure you ask for organic recommendations when you submit the sample; otherwise you may be advised to use products that have no place in an organic garden. The best time to test is in early fall; most organic amendments should be applied before winter and allowed to weather in. 🍎

Never Too Much Compost

Q Can you ever add too much compost? It's the only thing I use in the garden besides manure. I add it at the beginning of the season before I till the soil; use it to mulch around the plants throughout the season; and then again at the end of the season, I spread a nice generous layer. It is not all from my own compost pile. I get a small truckload at the beginning of the season.

A Compost, compost, and more compost can only do good—assuming there's nothing deleterious in it. You know the homemade sort is fine, but don't make hasty assumptions about the stuff you buy.

In its backyard incarnation, compost is the glorious refutation of "garbage in, garbage out." You put in banana peels, egg shells, and dead flowers; out comes the basic building block of healthy soil. But not everything nasty is capable of transformation. Some commercial compost is made from sewage sludge, which often contains heavy metals that composting does not remove. Other large-scale producers might use paper bleached with dioxin. And some sellers may offer "compost" that is actually nothing more than partially composted bark or sawdust.

These products are almost all carbon, though they can look very much like compost made from a proper mixture of carbon and nitrogen. They take nitrogen from the soil in order to finish decomposing, and when they're done they don't give much back except improvements in texture.

On the other hand, many commercial compost makers are environmental heroes, entrepreneurs who saw the diamonds hidden in rough stuff like fish waste. When in doubt, just ask—and don't buy from anybody who won't give you an ingredient list. 🍎

Manure or Chemical Fertilizers

Q I know farmers have always used manure as a fertilizer, but I wonder if it is really that useful in the garden, compared to standard products like 5-10-5. Also, is it safe to use manure as-is, or must it be composted first?

A Anywhere from 75 to 90 percent of the plant nutrients fed to animals are excreted in their manure, so it should be no surprise that the stuff is an excellent fertilizer. Don't be misled by the NPK numbers that suggest manure is less powerful than chemicals. It is actually far better because it contains large amounts of organic matter, so it feeds and builds the soil while it is feeding the plants.

If manure is applied at least two months before planting, and nothing is harvested for two months after that, there is no need to compost it before working it into the soil, where it will break down quite quickly. If you can't get it tilled in that soon, or want to harvest earlier, manure should be thoroughly aged or composted before it is used. Completely apart from any human health considerations, there is also a danger to plants. Many of them, including potatoes and peonies, will be damaged by fresh manure.

There are a few manures that should not be used, primarily those of meat eaters. Cat, dog, and human droppings all contain pathogens that may not be killed by time, exposure, or even careful composting. Otherwise, the sky's the limit, as those zoos that are now marketing giraffe and elephant manure have discovered.

Most gardeners have a far more limited menagerie to choose from—if they have one at all. The small farms that can afford to retail fresh manure are as endangered as condors. Nevertheless, in some areas it is still possible to buy a truckload or two, and if you do, your garden will thank you for it.

No matter what sort of manure you use, use it as a soil amendment, not a mulch. Even after it has been composted, it should not touch plants or be spread where rain might splash it onto plants. Wear gloves when you are working with it, wash up afterwards—and don't forget to rinse the vegetables well before you eat them (always a wise idea whether you use manure or not). 🍂

THE VALUE OF MANURE

Nutrient values of manures vary greatly, depending on the diet and age of the animals, and the nature and quantity of bedding in the mix. There's also freshness to consider: the older the manure, the fewer nutrients it will contain. On the other hand, the older it is, the sooner it will be safe to use and the less fragrant it will be.

These variables make precise nutrient listings impossible, but there are significant differences between manure types that are useful to know.

Poultry: Hen dressing, as it's known in the country, is higher in nitrogen than other common manures. It also contains a significant amount of phosphorus, and some potash. Chicken manure from a farm where birds run around in straw will be considerably less potent (and probably less full of antibiotics) than manure from an egg factory where birds live crowded together in wire cages. Chicken manure is famous for burning plants if it is used when too fresh.

Sheep: Comparatively high in nitrogen, an excellent source of potash, with moderate phosphorus. Manure from sheep fed hay and grain will be more potent—and more likely to be available—than manure from animals that live on pasture.

Horse: About half as rich in nitrogen as chicken, with a good amount of potash but only a modest dose of phosphorus. Amounts of bedding vary greatly, which means potency does, too. Horse manure can be a powerful carrier of weed seeds.

Cow: Cow manure has the lowest nutrient numbers, in part because there is so much bedding mixed with it. But that low nutrient concentration makes it safe to use in unlimited quantities. Try to find manure that's mixed with straw or shredded newspaper, rather than the more common sawdust. If you get the sawdust kind, expect it to take a year before it starts to deliver results.

Specialty: Rabbit manure is very high in nutrients and less likely to cause nitrogen burn than chicken manure. Most rabbit owners know this and do not give it away. Bat guano is like supercharged chicken, but it's hard to gather, getting rare, and priced accordingly. Zoos need the money more than you need hippopotamus droppings, but if you have enough land to pile weird manure until it's composted, the charity you spread will improve your soil.

Going Green

Q I know "green manure" is made from plants and is supposed to be a
good thing, but I don't understand how it works. Aren't animal manures
much better?

A Most commonly used animal manures are simply
plants that have been partially digested and concentrated. Green manures actually go them one better by providing far more organic matter, much of it supplied in situ
by their decaying roots. And green manures do not require
transport, storage, or spreading.

In other words, the key to the magic of green manures
is that their full name is "green manure cover crops." Unlike
animal manures, they start and finish in the same ground
they are designed to nourish. You plant the seed, you cut
down the top growth, you till that in, and then you plant.
None of the nutrients are lost to age, leaching, or the other
problems that are common with animal manures.

Most green manures are legumes, which add lots of nitrogen (legumes have nodules on their roots that fix nitrogen from
the air). Many have very deep taproots that help loosen compacted soils, and these same roots bring deeply buried trace
minerals up to the surface where plants can make use of them.

You can sow some green manures in fall and till them
under in spring, but maximum benefits come when they are
used as part of a rotational system that gives them a full
growing season to do their work.

If you plant cowpeas, soybeans, or buckwheat, which is
not a legume but is an excellent soil builder, the land that's
being improved by the cover crop will also yield an edible
harvest, although, of course, the portion of nutrients you
harvest as beans or grain will not go back into the soil. 🍒

Looking for Greensand

Q What exactly is greensand?

A Greensand, which is also called greensand marl or
glauconite greensand, is an undersea mineral deposit

with many important elements naturally found in sea water. It is valued as a fertilizer primarily for its potassium or potash content, although it may also contain some 30 other elements important to plants, including silica, magnesium, and phosphorus.

Greensand releases its nutrients slowly—a single application lasts several years. It is applied at rates of anywhere from 2½ to 10 pounds per hundred square feet of soil, depending on the severity of the need. A handful sprinkled in occasionally will help stimulate bacterial action in compost heaps. 🍎

Wood Ashes

Q **Every winter, my mother empties the ashes from her wood-burning stove and puts them in our vegetable garden. Is this beneficial to the soil?**

A It is, with two big *ifs*. The first is *if* you have acid soil, which is most common in the East. Wood ashes are alkaline, roughly half as alkaline as lime, so they are good for balancing acid soils, but they make matters worse where soils are alkaline, as they are in much of the West.

The second is that wood ashes are beneficial *if* they are from natural unpainted wood or ordinary (nonshiny) newsprint, which uses nontoxic inks. Paint, especially old paint, and the inks used with shiny paper can contain heavy metals and other contaminants that fire will not destroy. Plywood, treated lumber, and those "logs" made of pressed wood chips and/or sawdust are similarly suspect.

In addition to their effect on pH, dry wood ashes also contribute useful nutrients. Composition varies with the species of tree, but you can expect them to contain a small amount of phosphorus and a significant amount of potash. Phosphorus is important in fruit development and hastens plant maturity, while potash improves stem strength and contributes to winter hardiness. 🍎

No Magic Potions

Q We will soon move into a new house, and at 65, I don't want to wait
20 years for small plants to mature, nor do I want to pay for large
plants. Gibberellic acid, the plant growth hormone, is available from a mail-
order nursery that also sells small, inexpensive trees and shrubs. Would that
hormone be the answer to my problem?

A Sounds logical, but you probably won't be the first
person to be disappointed that it isn't a magic potion.

Gibberellins are plant hormones that occur naturally and
help control growth. Gibberellic (pronounced jib-er-EL-ic) acid
makes some plants grow taller, but it does so by an unnatural
elongation of the cells, not the production of healthy new tissue. And there has been no research into its effect on trees.

Gibberellins do have uses in horticulture, including in
the testing of dormant seeds to see if they are still viable, but
instant landscaping isn't one of them. Buy medium-size, well-
grown plants you can enjoy watching grow, and let the future
take care of itself. 🍅

For Peat's Sake

Q Every gardening resource I read suggests using peat moss about every
other page, but I have also read that peat bogs are endangered. Are
they, and if so, what's a gardener to do?

A Technically, it's moss peat, created when sphagnum moss
decays under very acid water. But whatever you call it,
it's great stuff: sterile, absorbent, and lightweight, moderately
acid in pH. Although it is almost nutrient-free, it has long been
considered a vital ingredient in potting mixtures, an invaluable
aid to improving soil texture, useful for pH adjustment, and the
ideal winter packing material for summer bulbs and tubers.

Unfortunately, there is some danger of ecological damage
if everybody keeps on blithely using tons of it. The primary
problem is in Europe, where the bogs are comparatively small
and have been mined for a very long time. In Canada, the
source of most of the U.S. supply, the bog acreage is far larger
and only a small percentage of it is being mined.

Canadians are well aware of the issues involved. Increasingly, bogs are being "restored" rather than simply left to regenerate in their own time, and peat moss processors claim these restorations are adequate replacements.

Whether this is true is a matter of some contention. All parties agree that virgin bogs destroyed by mining will take several hundred years to return to their original condition. The processors' argument is that "not original, but quite similar," a matter of decades rather than centuries, is good enough. And they may have a point. Although less rich in diversity and stripped of the geopaleontological history they once held, the restored bogs do act like bogs, growing new moss, holding and filtering water, while sheltering wildlife.

Extensive debate and reams of data are available on the World Wide Web, but those who want to behave responsibly without becoming peat moss mavens can do so simply by thinking of it as—distantly—analogous to petroleum.

Just as there will be times when you have to drive, and situations in which plastic is the best material for the job, there will be places where peat moss performs better than anything else; but it can only do good to use more sustainable substitutes whenever they are available and appropriate. 🌿

BEFORE YOU REACH FOR THE PEAT MOSS

Peat moss is frequently recommended as a soil additive or storage medium, but before you use it, consider the following options:

To improve the water-holding capacity of soil: compost, shredded leaves, green manures, all of which will go peat moss one better by adding nutrients as well as textural improvement (Peat moss is very nearly nutrient-free.)

To lower soil pH: pine needles, sulfur, oak sawdust (Compost the sawdust before use so it doesn't tie up nitrogen while decaying.)

To provide lightweight, sterile bulk in potting mixes: coconut fiber (an industrial by-product); aged, finely shredded pine bark

As a component of seed-starting mixes: This is a place where there is no equally suitable substitute; go ahead and use peat moss. Be sure to dampen it thoroughly before mixing it with the other materials.

As a winter-storage medium for summer bulbs: vermiculite, shredded newspaper, coconut fiber, styrofoam peanuts

Keep the Earthworms

Q **How do I get rid of earthworms? In early spring I use lime, but by late summer they are back.**

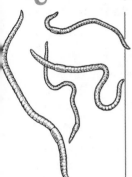

Earthworms are a gardener's best friends.

A You don't know how you're blessed. Earthworms are a gardener's best friends, and the good they do truly outweighs their occasionally messy habits. You would do better to take pride in their presence and encourage their work. It's not for nothing that they are called nature's plows; they have the ability to burrow to depths of several feet. Their churning loosens the soil and improves its structure so that air and water can penetrate to roots. The organic matter they feed on passes through their bodies and is excreted as castings, a rich source of nutrients readily available to plants. 🌿

Mantra for a Worm

Q **I'm considering putting a small worm composting bin in my garage, and plan to fill it with moist newspaper and vegetable scraps. The temperature in the garage is above 35°F, even on very cold days. Will the worms perish at this temperature? My wife says no worms in the basement, so the garage is my only choice.**

A How about giving her a large bunch of homegrown flowers and promising always to take care of the wiggly little dears yourself? Point out that a properly constructed and maintained worm box will not smell unpleasant. Assure her that fruit flies will be few—as long as you are careful to bury everything you put in—and that nothing nastier than fruit flies will show up as long as you compost only paper, fruit, and vegetable scraps.

Perhaps it would be better to go on at length about how fluffy, rich, and great for the garden the finished worm compost will be.

However you do it, mollifying your wife is Step 1, because the red worms (aka wrigglers, *Lumbricus rubellus,* and *Eisenia foetida*) you should be using for this project do their best work when it's warm, 55° to 85°F. They won't perish of cold at 35° or 40°, but they won't eat your garbage, either. 🌿

An Abundance of Worms

Q **Are worms a sign that the garden is okay? My soil seems fertile. It's loaded with worms and the plants seem to be happy, but I have never tested it. Under these circumstances is there really any need to?**

A If it ain't broke, as the saying goes . . .Worms may not have yellow feathers or melodious voices, but they still function like the canaries in the coal mine. Worms thrive in the same conditions that favor the health of plants, and when the soil has been abused they will be driven away, or killed, long before the plants appear to be failing.

Worms are scarce in soils that have been damaged by the overuse of chemical fertilizers, pesticides, and herbicides. And they can't live at all in soils devoid of the organic matter that also gives life to plants.

On the other hand, they don't seem to be especially fussy about things like lead, so if your garden is near old buildings or by a busy roadway, you might want to have the soil tested for heavy metals, just to be on the safe side.

It sounds as though you have been gardening in the same place for some time, and since things are going so well you must have been adding lots of organic matter (compost, manure, chopped leaves, etc.) each year. Keep it up.

Sandy Seaside Soil

Q **I have very sandy soil near my seaside cottage. I don't have a lot of time there, so I wonder if I should just throw in the towel and plant things that naturally grow in this kind of environment. If I take the time to amend it dramatically this season, will I have to do it every year?**

A Paying attention to your environment isn't throwing in the towel; it's the key to all good gardening. Working with nature instead of against it makes all the sense in the world, ergonomically and aesthetically.

That said, it must be admitted Mother Nature doesn't care if you don't have any home-grown vegetables. If buying them at the farmer's market just won't do, or if you must have lilacs, you will have to amend the soil and you will indeed have to keep putting in organic matter, year after year after year.

That's true no matter where you garden, actually. It's just that the seaside sand will suck the goodies down with daunting speed. To get the most benefit from your labors, confine them to raised beds or small, well-defined plots, and go for the natural look on the rest of the property. 🍎

Amending Soil

Q **My sister and I both moved to the country at about the same time. Since we are both first-time gardeners, we had our soil tested. I have been told I have too much clay. She has too much sand. But we have both been told the key to improvement is more organic matter. How can the same product cure both conditions?**

A Organic matter improves all soil structures by helping the soil particles—too small in your case, too large in your sister's—bind together into clumps called aggregates. The spaces between these clumps form a network of open pores through which water, oxygen, and plant roots can move freely.

In the case of sand, having the particles aggregated means there are fewer large pore spaces; water and nutrients can't drain away as fast as they do from plain sand.

In the case of clay, the clumps mean there are *more* large spaces. Water has multiple places to go, so it's not all bound up in the clay, and plant roots have an easier time moving through the soil in search of the things they need.

No matter what their rock composition, soils rich in organic matter will be crumbly and easy to work, a highly desirable condition known as "friable." 🍎

A Useful Time-Out

Q **The recent birth of our third child in three and a half years has led to a gardening moratorium for this season. Could you suggest some sort of cover crop that would leave my four 4- by 6-foot raised beds in excellent shape for next year?**

Planting a cover crop isn't a moratorium: it's an advance. When you give your beds a season filled with crops such as buckwheat, clover, and alfalfa, you're using a very low-tech (and low-cost) but highly effective natural system to give them a major boost. Legumes like alfalfa, which can gather nitrogen from the air, are best for increasing fertility. But all cover crops will improve soil structure, prevent erosion, and forestall the invasion of weeds.

As a bonus, many of these crops are as beautiful as they are useful. Choose crimson clover and you will have carpets of rich red flowers. With alfalfa in the mix you get endless subtle shadings of blue-green that shift with every wind. Grasses offer deep greens that turn to gold at season's end.

The hardest decision will probably be between hardy plants and those that die over the winter. Buckwheat, for example, will be knocked down by frost and rot to almost nothing by spring. Winter rye, on the other hand, will persist long into the fall and sprout again early in the season. Tender plants mean less work next year when it's time to till them into the soil, but perennials tend to give you more soil-building power and look better, longer, while they do it.

Warning: Many cover crops flower heavily, attracting large numbers of assorted bees. Most bees are not aggressive, but if you're planning to turn the toddlers loose nearby, it might be wise to stick to grasses.

Soil pH

The Mysteries of pH

Q I often see the term pH in reference to soil but don't really understand what it means. Please explain.

A The degree to which soils are either acid or alkaline is indicated on the pH scale, which runs from 0.0 (the most acid) to 14 (the most alkaline). The explanation of what this means has two levels, one technical and one practical.

If we are being *technical,* the thing being measured is the concentration of hydrogen ions. (The "H" in pH is the chemical symbol for hydrogen.) The more hydrogen ions there are, the more acid the thing measured is. That's easy to understand.

What gives non-mathematicians pause is that the pH scale is not a linear one, with equal intervals between numbers. Instead, it is logarithmic, in base 10. And it's negative logarithmic to boot (the "p" in pH is the mathematical symbol for negative logarithm).

Translation: every number on the pH scale shows ten times *less* H concentration than the number below. Soil with a pH of 5 is ten times more acidic than soil with a pH of 6, and a hundred times more acidic than soil with a pH of 7. Seven is neutral, right in the middle of the scale, but it still has ten times more hydrogen ions than soil with a pH of 8. (Above 7, there are more hydroxyl ions than there are hydrogen ions, which is what makes those soils alkaline.)

Got it? Doesn't matter. From the *practical* gardening standpoint, all you really need to know are two things: The number 7 is neutral, below 7 is acid, above 7 is alkaline; and although there are exceptions at each end (rhododendrons for soils of 5.5 or so, yucca for those around 7.6), most plants do best in soils that are slightly on the acid side of neutral, while those that prefer alkalinity don't want too much of it. This is because the organisms that make nutrients available to plants function best in the 6 to 7 range. There may be nutrients present in highly acid or alkaline soils, but it won't matter because the plants won't be able to get at them.

Soil pH is important, in a general way: lilacs will never thrive where it is too acid, and potatoes will be discouraged if it's at all alkaline, but you don't need to fall into a cookbook funk about measuring pH exactly. As long as other growing conditions are salutary, you should be able to grow nearly anything in soil that falls between 6 and 7.5. If you get a thorough, professional testing when you start out with new ground, then keep an eye on things by using a home soil-test kit every other year or so, that should be enough. ❧

TESTING, TESTING, 1, 2, 3

Whether you send your soil away to be tested or use a home kit, results cannot be accurate unless the sample has been gathered correctly.

1. **Collect** a couple of tablespoons of soil from each of 7 to 10 different parts of the area to be tested. Scrape aside the top 2 or 3 inches and get the stuff that's right underneath.
2. **Thoroughly mix it all up,** then spread it out on a glass, ceramic, or stainless steel surface to dry (paper or reactive metals could contaminate the sample).
3. **When the sample is dry,** rub it through a coarse sieve to remove pebbles and lumps.

Bear in mind that even comparatively small gardens can vary quite a bit from place to place, especially if there are complicating conditions such as sloping ground, both shade and sun, or a layout that's part newly turned sod and part previous garden. If you average it all into a mixed sample, the test will give you an equally averaged result. Where differences are minor, this won't matter, but if part of the garden is severely acid and part of it is almost neutral, an averaged test will be misleading to the point of uselessness. For the most accurate results, have each distinct part of the garden tested separately.

Alkaline Soil

Q I recently bought a house in Rhode Island with a large yard, where I intended to plant vegetables, herbs, fruit trees, and flowers. But when I had the soil tested, it was way too alkaline. How can I remedy this?

A Most soils in the Northeast are naturally on the acidic side, so the first thing to do is figure out why the test came out the way it did. Perhaps it's an accident of nature. Your house might sit squarely over a vein of limestone, in which case the remedy is a combination of acidifying soil amendments (sulfur is the most common) and learning to love the many plants, including pears, asparagus, peonies, and pansies, that prefer slightly alkaline conditions.

But over-alkalinity might also be a gift from the previous gardener. If he or she found acid soil and added too much lime in an attempt to compensate, all you have to do is spread lots of compost, then wait a year or two for the rain to right things.

The happiest possibility of all is that the problem is simply a bad sample. If a large part of the soil you had tested came from a spot where old bricks (and their alkaline mortar) had been piled, or from a place where wood ashes, another famous antacid, had been dumped for years, it could have been alkaline enough to throw off the reading completely.

How can you tell what's really going on? Consult the trees and plants that are thriving now in your yard and the yards of your neighbors. Walnuts, wisteria, lilacs, columbine, and white clover do best in slightly alkaline soils. Spruces, white birch, rhododendrons, and wild strawberries all require acid conditions. ☞

CHALKY SOIL

In British garden books, it is not uncommon to come across the word "chalk" or "chalky" in reference to soil. Chalk is a form of limestone made of calcium carbonate. For gardeners, this reference is important because it means that the soil in question is alkaline, or has a high pH.

Sweet Soil

Q **I have an old garden book that says of several plants: "does best in sweet soil." What is that?**

A Sweet soil is alkaline, with a pH of at least 7.5; sour soil is acid, 6.5 or lower. It's not just a figure of speech. Though the sweetness of sweet soil is hard to taste unless conditions are extreme, sour soil really does taste sour. A soil test is more accurate than your tastebuds, however. ☞

Gypsum for Winter Woes

Q **The de-icing products I used are now apparently affecting my shrubs— several branches appear dead and much of the new growth is scanty and looks burned. Short of replacing the soil, is there anything I can do?**

A The toll exacted by de-icing compounds used on sidewalks, driveways, and roadsides becomes apparent in spring, when perennials, shrubs, and trees that should be rejoicing in new growth appear to be dead or dying.

What you can do will depend partly on the magnitude of what you did and partly on the nature of your soil. If you really loaded on the de-icer and your soil is on the heavy side, replacement is probably your only option.

If, on the other hand, you didn't use *too* much, and/or the soil is well drained, the best way to counter the toxicity is to add gypsum, the common name of hydrated calcium sulfate, available at garden centers.

Work it into the soil at the rate of about 10 pounds for each 250 square feet of soil. Gypsum is part sulfur and will increase acidity, so it is best used around plants that prefer an acid soil. 🍎

INSTEAD OF SALT

When winter comes, it's important to keep walkways safe, but the chemical compounds sold for de-icing all contain some form of salt, which you don't want leaching into your soil. Although calcium nitrate or high-nitrogen fertilizer is often recommended as a more benign alternative, an overdose of nitrates isn't really any better than a buildup of salt itself. In either case, soil organisms are damaged, plant roots can be burned, and leached-out excess winds up in the groundwater.

So what to do? Start with prevention. There will be very little ice to worry about if you are careful to keep the walkway well shoveled in the first place. Remove snow right down to the path surface as soon as it falls (walking on snow compacts it and makes it stick). Pile the snow on the downhill side, so it doesn't flow over the walkway when it melts.

Next, cover any ice you do get with something that will provide traction. Clay cat litter and coarse sand both work well and won't be much of an indoor problem if you keep a bootbrush by the door.

Alternatively, you can add traction to the walkway by covering it with temporary "paving" that has a nonslip surface. There are specially designed flexible metal grids sold for this purpose at hardware stores and through specialty catalogs. Or you can use panels of asphalt roofing shingle. They cost less and work just as well, although they are less than lovely (sprinkle sand under the shingles so they don't slip around).

Digging & Bed Making

Working the Soil

Q **Many of the seeds I want to plant have instructions that say to plant them as soon as the soil can be worked. Is there a date for that as there is for the last frost? What would be the danger in working soil too early?**

A Getting out there too early and stomping around the garden, turning beds over, and trying to force the return of spring should be avoided. Walking on wet soil or working it with garden tools will compact it, making it difficult for air and water to reach plant roots.

Once the soil is damaged, it can take years for microbial action to re-establish the structure of small clumps that gardeners refer to as good tilth.

There is no easy date to give because soils and microclimates differ so much. Just try picking up a handful of soil and squeezing it. If it stays together, it is still too wet. When it begins to crumble into smaller pieces, gardening season has begun. 🌱

Serious Digging

Q **I keep coming across the term "double-digging," as if I should know what it means. I don't. Kindly explain.**

A Double-digging is most commonly used when preparing new garden beds. It loosens and improves the soil more deeply than ordinary cultivation. Double-digging does indeed give plant roots a very encouraging environment, but unless the soil below your topsoil is badly compacted or severely deficient in organic matter, it is a refinement rather than a necessity.

Start double-digging at a top corner.

If you want to try double-digging, here's an easy way (lefties, just reverse direction):

1. Divide the planting area into horizontal strips that measure about a foot from top to bottom. You'll be working on one strip at a time.

Finish off the strip with the first top spit.

Double-dug ground will be raised, but not for long.

2. Starting at the top left corner of the area, dig into the soil and remove one spadeful of the top strip—that's called a top spit—and set it aside on a piece of burlap.

3. The exposed area beneath is called a second spit. Stir a half-spadeful of compost or manure into it.

4. Move to the right along the strip and remove the top spit of the adjacent area. Place it upside down on the second spit to the left, the one you just finished working on, and top the whole thing with a thin layer of compost or manure. Return to the area now exposed, and add compost or manure as you did in Step 3.

5. Continue moving along the bed to the right, repeating this procedure until you reach the end of the strip. Finish off the last section by topping it with that first top spit you had set aside on the burlap.

6. Move down to the next strip and do it all again. (As the project continues, remember to always stand on the unworked ground; you don't want to compact the soil you just worked so hard to loosen.)

After all of this digging and amending, the area will be slightly raised above the surrounding ground, but it will soon subside to its previous level. 🌿

Dealing with Hardpan

Q Do I have hardpan? My soil is certainly rock-hard, but I'm not sure that fits the definition. I do know it's very difficult to get anything to grow in it.

A Rock-hard soil is usually soil with a high clay content. When it dries out, it becomes a solid mass from the surface right down to the subsoil. A hardpan, on the other hand, is a very thin but continuous layer of compacted soil. It's even more rocklike than clay, and though most common where conditions are alkaline, it may be buried in almost any kind of soil.

A hardpan can be located anywhere from a few inches below the surface to a couple of feet down, but wherever it lies, it forms an impenetrable barrier; neither water nor

MAKING YOUR BED

One of the best ways to get good soil—and keep it—is to use raised beds for the plants, with paths between them for walking.

When you use raised beds, resources such as water and compost are conserved—you only put them where they're needed—and soil is spared the compacting pressure of the gardener's weight. The concentration of good things enables you to plant more closely, and that in turn means fewer weeds. Over time, as rocks and weeds are removed while compost and other amendments are added, the beds become filled with super-soil: loose, fertile, and moisture retentive.

Raised beds are usually no more than 4 feet wide (you have to be able to reach in from the sides to plant, weed, and harvest) but they can be as long as you want. Height doesn't matter as long as the walls are easy to build and to reach over; in practice that means somewhere between 8 and 14 inches. (The waist-high boxes of soil that border decks and make gardening easier for wheelchair users are planters, not raised beds.)

You can build a raised bed with butted boards, or by sinking 4 × 4 corners and nailing boards to them. Or you can buy a kit. Many catalogs offer packages that make bed-construction as simple as spending money. But the easiest raised beds of all are the ones you make by just piling up the soil.

Piled beds are space hogs compared with those that are enclosed; earth sides must slope where lumber stands straight up. But you can't beat the price, construction is swift, and piled beds are easy to move, which is handy in the vegetable garden where plant rotation is important for disease prevention and nutrient balance.

Raised beds made with butted boards

Raised beds warm up more quickly and drain more rapidly than flat soil, even when the paths between them are mulched. In many circumstances this is an advantage, but if you have sandy soil and/or problems with drought, reverse the shape and plant in pits, so you can catch rainwater and use the insulating powers of the soil to keep bed contents cool.

plant roots can go down through it and subsoil minerals can't move up.

Since water can't percolate down for storage, and plant roots must spread sideways rather than go deep, anything growing above a hardpan is highly vulnerable to drought. It is also vulnerable to rot if there is a rainy spell; water that can't move down just sits there.

That's how hardpans near the surface usually reveal themselves—you get enduring puddles in every low spot, every time it rains. Hardpans that are more deeply buried are harder to confirm. Dig a few test holes and check the side walls for a layer of rocklike material ⅛ to ½ inch thick.

Hardpan is so tough most hand-tillers can't break it up, but you can still rent a heavy-duty tiller (or a special tool called a soil ripper or sub-soiler) and do the job yourself if the garden is a small one. Otherwise, you're better off hiring a professional.

Alternatively, if you can afford to wait, plant the whole area with buckwheat in year one and alfalfa in year two. Both of these green manure crops have roots so determined to go deep they can even break up hardpan. 🌾

Crops of Rocks

Q I know New England is famous for giving crops of rocks, but how does it work? I've been removing rocks for years but there are new ones every spring.

A Each winter, the water in the ground freezes and thaws, usually several times. Water expands as it freezes, so everything around it has to move, and since there's a lot more room to move up than there is to move down, each freeze lifts the things that are closest to the surface.

Once lifted, the solids don't subside much, but the water sinks back down as soon as it thaws, finding tiny channels through the subsoil, underneath the rocks. It can take decades, sometimes centuries, for a basketball-size rock to "float" to the surface as water trickles underneath and freezes, over and over and over again. But sooner or later it will appear. 🌾

Unwanted Sod

Q In the spring, I plan to remove a large amount of sod to expand a garden. I know I can throw it in the composter, but I will have much more than my composter can hold. And it is too heavy to put in much at a time. Any suggestions beyond just piling it up and letting it decompose on its own?

A What's wrong with just piling it up? There are few enough garden chores that have "just" in the description; why make work where none is needed? As long as the sod is from average lawn, with only the usual assortment of weeds, it will break down on its own.

On the other hand, if the sod is well peppered with (or largely composed of) tough perennial weeds such as quack grass, it will resist breaking down. You can use it to fill low places where weeds won't matter (by the roadside, for instance), or you can lay it out in a single layer, upside down, until the weed roots are dry and dead. Put the layer at the edge of the driveway or somewhere else that's paved, so it can't take root and won't kill what's underneath it.

Whatever you do, don't make super-weedy sod into a pile unless you want an interesting new landscape feature. 🌶

Mulch

Mulching Time

Q Is September too late to put down shredded cedar as a mulch on my perennial garden in the Adirondacks?

A It's never too late to put down 3 or 4 inches of organic mulch, but if you have also put off other chores, it may be a bit too soon. Before you add an earth-covereing blanket that will still be in place next spring, make sure the bed itself is ready for summer.

Divide plants that are in need of it. Weed thoroughly, paying special attention to deep-rooted invaders like dandelion and burdock. Put on a 2-inch layer of compost.

And if there are evergreens in the garden, make sure the cedar is not freshly shredded, exuding lots of strong-smelling volatile oils. Although these oils seldom cause damage, some plants are sensitive to them, and drought-stressed plants are likely to be more sensitive than usual.

To be on the safe side, let fresh cedar mulch age for a couple of weeks, turning it frequently, until the smell becomes faint (it won't completely vanish).

When both the bed and the mulch are ready, go for it. But don't go whole hog. Keep the mulch at least 8 inches away from woody stems, and don't pile it on too thickly. Plant-eating rodents are lurking in the weeds, watching to see if the mulch will be deep enough to thread with cozy nests. ✿

Save the Salt Hay

Q **Something called "salt hay" is often suggested as a winter mulch. Is this just a fancier name for hay?**

A No, it's a different plant altogether. Salt hay, which is sometimes called salt-marsh hay, comes from the grasses that are found only in salt marshes. But it is cut and dried the same way that ordinary hay is.

Salt hay has several advantages. It provides a better covering because the stems don't mat down or rot as quickly as ordinary hay. And because salt-hay seeds germinate only in damp, saline soil, it doesn't produce the weed crop that frequently appears with other hay.

Unfortunately, using this marvelous mulch could damage native wetlands; all the salt hay sold in nurseries has been gathered from the wild. And as with any wild plants, overharvesting can have serious environmental consequences.

In winter, salt-marsh grasses shelter both animals and waterfowl. Marshes themselves are spawning areas for fish. Rather than further deplete fragile and rapidly disappearing marshes for mulch, gardeners should use ordinary straw or leaves from deciduous trees. If you use leaves, it's best to chop them first so they don't mat down and cause rot. ✿

Waste Paper as Mulch

Q I would like to recycle shredded computer paper as mulch in my garden. Should I be concerned about the ink from a laser printer? Can shredded newspaper (or even flat sheets) be used as mulch? What about junk mail? Are the inks O.K.?

A The good news is that a lot of studies have tested the safety and usefulness of shredded paper in the garden. The bad news is that they came up with slightly different answers. Black and colored newsprint get the O.K. from almost everybody, because the inks are almost always soy-based. But the bright inks on slick paper inserts and magazines can have dangerous components, and paper bleached with dioxin may be of more concern than the inks used on it.

The main problem with paper mulches is that even when they're safe, they're inert. They are barriers against weeds and evaporation (and havens for slugs), but not much good as soil improvers. Unless finely shredded, they don't decompose, and if they *do* decompose, they take nitrogen from the soil while they're doing it. Other things being equal, it's better to put your paper in the recycling bin and use straw, grass clippings, or shredded leaves in the garden. ◈

Leaf Sweep

Q Each year I have major leaf-raking chores. Is it O.K. to allow the leaves in the foundation planting areas to remain until spring, or must I remove them now?

A It's not just O.K., it's absolutely the thing to do. Leaves are a free mulch that helps conserve moisture. Leaves also stabilize the soil temperature, reducing the fluctuations of freeze and thaw that tear plant roots and heave them from the ground.

A 2- or 3-inch mulch of autumn leaves will at least partially decay over the winter, releasing vital nutrients and improving soil structure, but be sure to rake away any leftovers in very early spring, before the perennials and bulbs start peeking up. Large piles of whole leaves will provide great insulation, but they often fail to decompose completely, leaving you with soggy mats that smother emerging plants. 🍂

Seaweed Mulch

Q I have a home near the ocean and am just putting my first garden in. I notice that a few of my neighbors use seaweed as a mulch, although my next-door neighbor doesn't—she says it adds too much salt to the soil. Who is right? Frankly, I'd love to use it, because there's an endless free supply on a nearby beach.

A Seaweed is seldom salty enough to cause problems, especially if you stick to the stuff above the high-tide mark and gather it after a rain. It makes a good mulch in an orchard or other places where you don't spend lots of time, but it smells pretty funky while it's decaying, and it's very slippery. You'll get most of the benefits (lots of great micronutrients) and fewest drawbacks (far less odor, no banana-peel effect) if you put it in the compost instead of spreading it around raw. 🍂

Beware the Chips

Q Our neighbors have taken down some old trees and offered us as much of their huge pile of wood chips as we would like. Can I use them to mulch my flowerbeds?

A It would be better to use them on the paths, where they will suppress the weeds without competing with your plants for nutrients.

Fresh wood chips that touch the soil use nitrogen to break down—nitrogen that should be nourishing your flowers. They don't steal as much as was formerly thought, but they are not innocent either.

And the "huge" pile does prompt a further warning: chips from large piles are sometimes sour, tainted through anaerobic decay with plant-damaging, volatile acids. If you smell vinegar, say no thanks, unless you can air them thoroughly before they enter the garden. 🍂

Licorice Mulch

Q A friend told me about a very natural-looking mulch called licorice root. Do you have any idea what it is?

A Unlike typical bark mulches, licorice-root mulch is fibrous, knits together, and is very dark when wet. It is a by-product, made from what's left over after the licorice flavor is extracted from the rhizomes of *Glycyrrhiza glabra*, which is grown commercially from the Middle East to western China.

Only one company makes it in the United States, and it is primarily sold (under the brand-name Right Dress) in the Northeast, although in the age of the Internet, everything seems to be available everywhere. It costs about twice as much as standard bark mulches, but it must have its fans because the company says it sells all it can make. There is even a competing product called I Can't Believe It's Not Licorice Root. 🌱

Mulch, Rain, and Rot

Q Our vegetable garden suffered badly in a drought last year, so this year we mulched the lettuce and peas with straw as soon as they came up. We also put a thick layer of it around the peppers and tomatoes. But we've had a lot of rain and now we are afraid this will lead to problems with rot. Should we take the mulch off again and allow the garden to dry out a bit?

A Straw mulch timing depends on the crop, as well as on the weather. Cool-weather crops like lettuce and peas should be mulched early, not only because mulch holds in moisture but also because it moderates temperature. An insulating layer of straw will keep the soil around their roots nicely chilly. Hot-weather crops like tomatoes and peppers, on the other hand, don't like cold feet. They should not be mulched (or ideally, even planted) until the soil is thoroughly warmed. If you have to set them in cool soil, mulch with a thin, dark, porous weed barrier rather than thick pale straw.

Arrange straw around tomatoes, peppers, eggplants, and okra after the soil is well warmed but before it's hot.

(continued on page 728)

MULCH MADNESS

Though anything that covers the ground under plants is a mulch, there are vast differences between the many available choices.

BLACK PLASTIC

Advantages: Very effective weed control. Inexpensive. Warms soil. Retains moisture.

Drawbacks: Short useful life. Repels water. Creates anaerobic conditions, smothering soil and killing worms. Environmentally destructive (made from petroleum, winds up in the landfill). Provides no soil nourishment. Ugly.

POROUS LANDSCAPE FABRIC

Advantages: Very effective weed control. Inexpensive. Warms soil. Holds in moisture without excluding air or water. Provides a useful barrier between soil and coarse, decorative mulches such as wood chips or stones.

Drawbacks: Environmentally destructive (made from petroleum, winds up in the landfill). Provides no soil nourishment.

HAY

Advantages: Controls weeds. Inexpensive. Keeps soil temperature even and cool (don't apply to warm-season crops until after soil warms up). Holds in moisture. Prevents splashup of soil-borne disease spores. Improves soil texture when tilled in.

Drawbacks: Contributes weed seeds as fast as it smothers the ones that are there. Nutrient poor.

STRAW

Advantages: Controls weeds. Keeps soil temperature even and cool (don't apply to warm-season crops until after soil warms up). Holds in moisture. Prevents splashup of soil-borne disease spores. Improves soil texture when tilled in. Informally handsome and pleasant to walk on barefoot.

Drawbacks: Nutrient poor. May contribute "weed seeds" in the form of stray grain in the straw.

COMPOST

Advantages: Some weed control and moisture retention, but principal benefit as mulch is in disease prevention. Organisms in the compost out-compete or actively destroy deleterious bacteria and fungi. Safely feeds plants throughout the season and does not require tilling to become part of the soil.

Drawbacks: Not great at weed-prevention compared to other mulches (in fact, weeds will thrive in it unless you keep piling on more). Expensive if purchased.

GRASS CLIPPINGS

Advantages: Some weed control—let dry a day, then use while still pliable. Warms soil. Holds in moisture. Feeds plants and improves soil when tilled in.

Drawbacks: In the South, can cause too much heat if used in high summer. Can cause rot if placed too close to plant stems. May contain weed seeds. Frequently contaminated with herbicides; be sure any clippings you use are from lawns that have not been treated.

NEWSPAPER

Advantages: Whole or shredded, provides excellent weed control. Free. Retains moisture. Keeps soil temperature even and cool (don't apply to warm-season crops until after soil warms up). Very long lasting if used in stacks; cover with a thin layer of straw or bark to improve appearance and keep top layers from blowing away.

Drawbacks: Can create anaerobic conditions when used in stacks. Does not improve soil texture unless tilled in, but then ties up nitrogen in order to decompose. Nutrient poor.

SHREDDED BARK

Advantages: Very long lasting. Attractive. Retains moisture. Keeps soil temperature even and cool (don't apply to warm-season crops until after soil warms up).

Drawbacks: Comparatively expensive. Can exude chemicals that harm tomato plants. Does not improve soil texture unless tilled in, but then ties up nitrogen in order to decompose. Nutrient poor.

WOOD CHIPS

Advantages: Stays put through high winds and heavy rains. Retains moisture. Controls weeds.

Drawbacks: Does not improve soil texture unless tilled in, but then ties up nitrogen in order to decompose. Nutrient poor. Will harm plants if used when sour (acetic acid builds up in chips that spend time in large piles; spread out to air and do not use until the smell is gone).

SHREDDED LEAVES

Advantages: Free, and you get recycling points. Retains moisture. Keeps soil temperature even and cool (don't apply to warm-season crops until after soil warms up). Improves soil texture without needing to be tilled in. Very earthworm-friendly.

Drawbacks: Weed control only moderate. Labor intensive, as leaves must be shredded. Slug heaven.

Mulch

(continued from page 725)

If you used a barrier at planting time, just pile the mulch on top. Once the mulch is in place, close to but not touching the plants, don't mess with it unless you see rotting stems, moldy leaves, or an invasion of slugs. 🍂

Mulch Invaders

Q **What are those little sprouts that are growing all over my new mulch? My husband thinks something has infested it. I think the problem is related to a massive maple-pollen surge we had around here recently, and that the sprouts are maple seedlings. Any ideas?**

A Armies of Norway maples are indeed invading many areas, but even these aggressive spreaders have to start with seeds; pollen alone doesn't generate anything but allergies. And baby maples develop maple leaves right after the initial pair of seed leaves has fully opened. They are a plague, but they aren't confusing. You know them when you see them.

If the mulch is straw, your sprouts are probably oats. Stir the straw around to uproot them, and let them perish in place.

Otherwise, there is no telling what the sprouts might be. Whatever they are, it is unlikely that pulling them up one by one will solve the problem. It would be better to remove the mulch and start over with fresh. 🍂

The Artillery Fungus

Q **Along my driveway is a shrub bed with wood mulch. Vehicles parked nearby get small black specks that are nearly impossible to remove. I'm told that these are spores shot out by a fungus in the mulch. Is there any way to prevent this fungus from growing?**

A It's easier if it isn't your problem, of course, but you do have to admire the ingenious solution that a simple fungus came up with for the age-old question of how to give its offspring a good start in life. For the artillery fungus, the answer is a small, rigid, spherical structure. Inside is a spore mass mixed with a sticky substance that expands as it absorbs water during cool, wet weather in spring and fall. The structure tilts toward the light, and when the expansion pressure is high enough, the gluey spore mass blasts out.

It is aiming for a place in the sun, but it can be fooled by light reflected from a house or a car. Small consolation. The spots, which are dark brown, slightly raised, and about ⅛ inch in diameter, contain an adhesive that is so good that it is an expensive problem for insurance companies. Many policies explicitly exclude artillery fungus damage.

The fungus earns its living by taking the nutrients released as it rots wood. Mulches that contain wood are big favorites. The fungus population rises and then falls as the wood breaks down, so a really bad year for spots is often followed by a better one.

Dr. Donald Davis, a professor of plant pathology at Pennsylvania State University in State College, has researched artillery fungus and recommends mulches made from large pine-bark nuggets or cocoa hulls, the bark of Atlantic white cedar or cypress, or licorice root. While not immune, these are less likely to encourage large populations.

Discretion being the better part of valor, surrender the parking spot during howitzer season. 🌂

Compost

Pruning and Burning

Q **I have been reading a book on pruning. Several times the author mentions removing dead, diseased, or damaged branches and burning them. He gives no explanation why burning is necessary. In these days of recycling and compost making, is there a particular reason he says this?**

A Even a well-made home compost pile may not heat up enough to kill the disease spores on sick plants, so anything of this sort that you remove should leave the garden permanently. In addition, wood takes much longer than other compost ingredients to decompose, even when shredded.

Where the law still permits, the easiest way to get rid of this stuff is to burn it. Fire is a great purifier—no fungi or bacteria can survive the heat—and it quickly reduces huge piles of prunings to small piles of ash.

If open burning is out of the question, bury any sick material at least a foot deep, burn it in the fireplace, or send it to the landfill. Anything that isn't sick can go through a chipper (rentable if you don't have one) and then be used as mulch. Or your town may have a "wood dump" where it can be taken. 🍎

Composting Deer Contributions

Q Deer often visit our backyard to eat fallen apples, leaving behind quite a mess. Recently, as my assistant gardener was helping me mix some of the droppings into the compost, she asked, "Grandpa, is it O.K. to put deer droppings into compost that will wind up in the tomato patch next year?" I was stumped. Is it?

A Your young helper is right to be wary, but not because the deer dropping will end up in the garden, said Dr. Eric Sideman, who is the technical services director for the Maine Organic Farmers and Gardeners Association and helped draft the United States Department of Agriculture rules covering manure use by organic farmers. (The agency does not regulate manure use on conventional farms.)

It's the fresh material that causes problems, he explained. "If you look at all the contaminations of produce by lethal *E. coli* bacteria, you see that they were due to failures in sanitation, not agronomic practices. The vectors of transmission are things like dirty hands, dirty water, food harvested from a garden where fresh manure has just been spread."

The federal rules say manure must be hot composted, to 131°F, in order to kill pathogens. Otherwise, harvesting must be delayed: until 90 days after application for produce that doesn't touch the ground, like tomatoes; 120 days for crops that have soil contact, like lettuces and carrots.

As long as you observe the waiting periods—spread that compost early in the spring—you should have no problems. But do think of the waste in your yard as potentially hazardous. Wear gloves. Remember that your work clothes will have manure on them. Wash up carefully when you're done, and remind your garden helper to do the same. 🍎

Dangerous Compost?

Q The London plane trees in my neighborhood are all afflicted with what a Parks Department employee told me was anthracnose disease. The city offers free compost in the fall and spring. Do the leaves from these and other diseased plants end up in the compost? Am I better off buying sterilized, bagged stuff to avoid infecting my garden plants?

A Sycamore anthracnose, a fungus disease, affects American sycamore and London plane trees. A badly infected mature tree may completely defoliate by the end of June, giving its owner a bad attack of jitters until it begins leafing out again a few weeks later. Trees rarely die, even if infected year after year.

Some of the fungus is present on the leaves that end up in community compost piles, along with other pathogens. But don't put the Parks Department in the same category as Typhoid Mary. The microbial activity in a compost pile, along with the warmth generated, renders practically all of these particular pathogens harmless.

So use the city's compost, and don't blame it for next year's outbreak—the fungus overwinters mainly in cankers it produces on twigs and branches throughout the tree. 🍎

Turning the Pile

Q I've got a bad back and turning my compost pile is murder. Any suggestions other than to leave it be?

A There are numerous commercial products that turn the compost for you. At one end of the spectrum, for use with a free-standing pile, are mechanical stirrers, called aerators, some hand-powered, others that use gas or electricity. At the other end are plastic compost drums, mounted on frames and equipped with turning handles.

If possible, test the aerator you choose before you buy—or at least make sure you can return it. They are far less costly than compost drums, but they can be difficult to use, putting as much strain on your back as turning would have done.

Most of the drums are easy to use (check for solid construction and a well-weighted frame), but they don't hold much, so it's important to follow instructions and make them do their work as efficiently as possible.

You can also improve on leaving it be by adding a few air vents when you start building the pile. Use the perforated 4- or 6-inch PVC pipe sold for use in leach fields, cut into lengths about a foot taller than you expect the finished pile to be. Stand them straight up like chimneys, spaced about 2 feet apart in all directions. (You'll have to prop them up with bricks or stones until the pile is a couple of feet tall.)

Yes, the holes do get clogged, but a fair amount of air finds its way in as long as the tops remain open. ✿

Hot and Cold Compost

Q **Although my compost pile eventually turns to compost, I am certain it never gets to the temperatures I read about. Does this matter? I don't add any meat products, just garden and vegetable refuse.**

A As you have observed, garden wastes will decompose into a useful soil amendment no matter how warm the pile gets—or doesn't. Hot piles decompose faster, and even those that are merely warm will produce useful compost in a few weeks, instead of the many months it takes for cold piles to perform.

In theory, a carefully constructed and maintained heap, with just the right proportions of ingredients, moisture, and oxygen, can reach and hold temperatures high enough to kill most bacteria, fungi, and weed seeds. But in practice, "just right" is seldom achieved, so it's better to assume that there will be at least some cool spots.

That means it is crucial to keep diseased material out of the compost and wise to avoid adding weeds that have gone to seed. Not adding meat is also important, and the same goes for cheese or any other animal-derived product. Even if they don't contain pathogens, these things attract skunks, raccoons, and rats; and fats (of any sort) discourage the beneficial bacteria that break down plant material. ✐

Woody Refuse

Q **Should I add my rose canes and other woody garden refuse to my compost pile? It seems to take forever to break down.**

A few twigs here and there can be beneficial, precisely because they *don't* break down. By keeping their shapes, they help keep the mix aerated and make it easier to turn. Larger amounts, though, make turning difficult. They also add work, since you have to sift them out before you can use the compost.

What to do depends on how much woody refuse you have. If there's a lot, year after year, it might be worth investing in a chipper/shredder. Once shredded, the soft "wood" of roses and the thin branches of shrubs decompose fairly quickly as long as they are mixed with other compost ingredients, and they can also be useful as a path covering.

Of course, you could pile the woody bits in an out-of-the-way place, then rent a chipper every few months and grind it all up at once. This method is a bit more of a bother and takes up more space, but it is far less expensive.

If you have only a small amount of genuinely woody material but lots and lots of breakdown-resistant things like thick cosmos stems and dead pepper plants, gather it all into a foot-high pile and carefully, slowly, lower the lawnmower on it. The shredded material will shoot out the discharge hole; be sure it's facing in a suitable direction. ✐

Coffee in the Garden

Q **Can coffee grounds go directly in the garden or do they have to be composted?**

A Coffee grounds do not need to be composted before being used in the garden. In fact, some growers recommend using them as a mulch in order to repel rabbits, squirrels, and other four-footed pests. Before you try this, be warned that they may repel you, too. Few elements of vegetable garbage are as garbagy-smelling as week-old wet coffee grounds.

For best results outside of the compost, work the coffee grounds into the soil. They are quite high in nitrogen and will be especially welcome around onions, lettuce, corn, and other nitrogen lovers.

Coffee grounds are also quite acid. In the old days, nobody had enough of them for this to be a problem, but now that the known world is spangled with hip coffee shops eager to recycle their garbage, truckloads of grounds are sometimes available just for the asking. Don't use more than about six pounds per 100 square feet of soil unless you want to change the pH. 🍎

Compost Thief

Q **Any suggestions for keeping animals out of the compost? Raccoons are always going to mine, even though I do my best to bury any food under a layer of garden clippings.**

A No matter how conscientious you are about burying things that say "food" to you, it's likely you'll miss at least a few that say "food" to raccoons. Even if you don't, they'll dig around just in case. All else failing, there are likely to be some tasty worms near the bottom of the pile (if the skunks haven't already eaten them).

In fact, raccoons and skunks do such a good job of stirring the compost you could think of them as helpers. They aren't even all that messy; it's crows that fling everything around like children having a food fight.

That said, it must be admitted the compost area can look unpleasantly untidy if there are too many visitors. To keep them out, build a sturdy compost bin that has a heavy, latchable lid, and remember to keep it closed. The lid should let a bit of water in and allow plenty of air circulation, so make it from something fairly porous like heavy-duty chicken wire stapled to a wide wood frame. 🍂

Sheet Composting

Q **Our garden is small and it's right in front of the house, so we can't have a compost heap, yet it seems crazy to throw away the organic garbage and then go out and buy compost. Is there any way around this problem?**

A Sure. It's called sheet or trench composting, though decent burial might be a better description. (Once the compost is in place, you don't move it again.) The system works best in gardens laid out in rows, but you should be able to adapt it to any situation where there is a bit of mulch-covered space between the plants.

Work well away from the plants, so you don't damage major roots. Scrape aside the mulch and dig a hole about a foot deep. (Don't cheat on the depth or it's likely that a skunk, opossum, or other interested party will smell the buried goodies and dig them up.) Put in roughly 5 inches of kitchen scraps, dead flowers, or other organic garbage, tamping it down as you go. Refill the hole and replace the mulch. You may have a bit of a hump for a week or so, but the earth will subside to its former level as soon as the garbage starts to break down.

In large vegetable gardens, it's easy to dig trenches between rows and you don't have to be fussy about breaking up the stuff you bury; time will take care of everything. Where space is limited, it pays to chop or shred the material. The finer the grind, the less space it will take up, and the faster it will break down. (Some gardeners have an extra processor or blender dedicated solely to this purpose. It works if you have either a very small garden or very little garbage.) 🍂

Compost

Watering the Compost Heap

Q All the instructions say to be sure the compost heap stays moist, but mine is far from the house (and the hose). How moist is moist, and does it really matter?

A Think moist as in a wrung-out towel that's been hanging on the line for about 10 minutes on a sunny spring day. It's still definitely not dry, but it isn't soggy either.

The bacteria that break down organic matter must have moisture in order to do their work. If the heap is allowed to dry out completely, decay will come to a standstill. On the other hand, the desired bacteria are aerobic, which means they must also have oxygen. When the heap is soaking wet, there's no room for oxygen; anaerobic bacteria take over and you get rotten slime instead of fluffy "black gold." Excessive water will also leach nutrients from the mix.

A wire lid for the compost bin should be a big help. With the addition of a plastic cover, it can hold moisture in when rain is infrequent, and it can keep moisture out when there is an excess. A rain barrel near the heap will also cut down on hose-dragging. Don't forget to use a screen cover for the barrel so mosquitoes can't use the rainwater as a breeding puddle.

Shady Compost

Q The only out-of-sight site for my compost heap is in the shade of the house next door. Is it okay to put a compost heap where it doesn't get any sun?

A Although sunlight is often recommended, that's largely because the process goes faster when the pile is warm. The desired organic activity is taking place deep in the pile where it's dark, so—other things being equal—the heap won't care where you've put it.

How the people next door will feel is another matter, especially if you are the neglectful type. A frequently turned compost pile is very nearly odorless; compost that's left to sit and ferment soon conjures memories of the city dump. Both will eventually yield valuable soil amendments, but only the former is what might be called neighborly. 🌶

Winter Compost

Q I have a small compost heap to which I've added leaves, vegetable matter, and cow manure. Should I continue adding kitchen vegetable scraps through winter and then try to turn it? Will it continue to "cook," or should I hold these scraps till spring?

A Absolutely continue adding chopped vegetable scraps to your compost through winter as long as you have room, and don't worry about trying to turn a frozen pile. Add a covering layer of cow manure periodically. This will increase the beneficial microbes in your small heap, and when the weather warms, the decaying process will continue.

Whatever the season, there is no great mystery to composting. Any loose pile of vegetable matter eventually decays, even if the gardener stands around and does nothing. Making and turning a formal compost pile is simply a way of organizing and speeding nature's own process of decomposition. 🌶

CHAPTER SIXTEEN

Troubleshooting

Allelopathy

Q Can you explain allelopathy? I don't understand how one plant can prevent another from growing.

A Although the reasons for it are not fully understood, allelopathy (pronounced al-lull-LOP-path-ee) is a kind of antagonism between two plant species. It is believed to be a protective device that enables one plant to prevent certain other plants from intruding into its territory, said Doris Stone, a botanist and former head of education at the Brooklyn Botanic Garden.

The black walnut may be the best-known example. Its roots, leaves, and branches produce a substance that is toxic to some other plants grown in the same soil. Tomatoes and alfalfa are among the susceptible species.

Allelopathic effects have also been found on the balsam poplar (*Populus balsamifera*), whose roots inhibit the growth of the green alder (*Alnus crispa mollis*). The toxins produced by the roots of the desert sagebrush (*Salvia leucophylla*) and the California artemisia (*Artemisia californica*) result in their being surrounded by 3 to 6 feet of bare space. It's likely that this is a survival strategy, insuring the allelopathic plants have more of the available water and nutrients.

The allelopathic property of the annual sunflower (*Helianthus annuus*) is frequently mentioned, but it is not as strong as many fear. It spreads only a foot or two, and can be mitigated by regularly raking up the seed hulls and discarding them. 🌰

Allergies of Autumn

Q **I know that goldenrod is not the same as ragweed, which seems worse than ever this year. Can you explain the difference?**

A It's a shame that goldenrod is blamed for the sneezes and wheezes of autumn allergies. The reason is probably because goldenrod produces its brilliant yellow flowers just when ragweed also blooms, but no one notices the culprit's small homely pale green blooms. Goldenrod's pollen is heavy and is moved about only by bees, whereas ragweed pollen is tiny and light and meant to be spread by the wind.

There are some 15 species of common ragweed, whose botanical name is *Ambrosia* (a misnomer if ever there was one). Ragweeds grow naturally from coast to coast, adapting to both country meadows and gritty city environments.

The plant has fernlike leaves similar to those of wormwood (*Artemisia*), and is actually a tasty treat for pigs and cattle.

Ragweed is also an excellent soil preserver and conditioner, one of the group, sometimes called pioneer plants, that spring up rapidly after floods, fires, or bulldozers have ravaged the earth. 🌰

Meadow goldenrod
(*Solidago
canadensis*)

Ragweed
(*Ambrosia
artemisiifolia*)

Controlling Aphids

Q Would you please tell me what to do about the black bugs that are making a home and multiplying on my nasturtiums? I don't know what to spray them with because I would love to use nasturtiums in my salads.

And another reader wrote: My rose has been attacked by aphids since last month, and I've been spraying it with a hot chili pepper spray. It worked for a while, but now there are more. I tried garlic water, and mild soap, too. Is there something else I can use without resorting to harsh chemicals?

A Although the second questioner might try planting a diversionary "trap crop" of nasturtiums, which, as the first questioner has observed, aphids adore, nasturtium growers will obviously have to consider something else.

Aphids come in so many varieties it sometimes seems like there's a special one for every plant that grows. But all of them have the same basic habits, and the first line of defense is always the same: attend to the health of the plants. Aphids concentrate their attacks on the weak and sick.

Start by being sure the victim has plenty of water; drought-stress is notorious for inviting hordes of aphids. Then try a spray of immune-system-boosting liquid seaweed. Avoid fertilizers that contain a lot of nitrogen; the soft, lush growth it promotes is another favorite aphid target.

First aid for the plants, along with a strong spray of water to wash off the more persistent stragglers, will usually bring aphid populations down to tolerable levels within a week or two (total elimination is not an organic concept). If the infestation is still severe and you have no plans to eat whatever is being infested, insecticidal soap or, in extreme cases, a pyrethrum-based insecticide will help. Spray carefully in the evening, when beneficial aphid-eating insects like ladybugs are least active.

Unfortunately, insecticidal soap doesn't taste very good, pyrethrum is really nasty, and neither one can be completely washed off, so when it comes to edible leaves and flowers, they can't be used. All you can do is be very careful in the kitchen. And if one *does* get into the salad, just smile brightly and mention "more protein." Ours is not an insect-eating culture, but the truth is, a couple of aphids never hurt anybody. 🌣

THE SOAP STORY

Insecticidal soaps kill insects by destroying interior cells, so their first job is to penetrate as much as possible of the target's outer covering. This is no problem with soft, slow movers like aphids, juvenile (crawler-stage) scales, and beetle larvae, but adult beetles, wasps, grasshoppers, flies, and bees are both swift and well defended; they seldom succumb to soap sprays.

The good things about insecticidal soaps—their extremely low general toxicity and their rapid dissipation—are also their limitations. Even when your pest population is a relatively small one, you will have to apply the soap regularly in order to get it under control.

Insecticidal soaps are most useful for controlling aphids, juvenile scales and sawflies, spider mites, and thrips. They also work well against greenhouse whiteflies and fungus gnats, especially if you spray at night when these airborne pests are less likely to fly out of reach.

Whatever bug(s) you plan to attack, remember the soap is also hitting the plants, some of which can be burned by it. Read the label on the soap, and then, as the cleaning products *meant* for cleaning always advise: "Be sure to test on an inconspicuous spot before using." Spray one or two tender leaves and wait two days to be sure they're O.K. before blasting away.

Aphids on Nicotiana

Q **Last year I grew nicotiana in containers on my balcony. They bloomed profusely but were infested with aphids. I tried a pyrethrum spray and also insecticidal soap, but both destroyed the blossoms. Is there any other way I can control such pests?**

A If you have no pets or young children, and don't mind using toxic chemicals, you can try a systemic insecticide, which works from within the plant to kill feeding insects. Systemics are added to the root area, where they are absorbed directly into the plant's system. (This is why systemics must never be used on or near edibles.) Wear gloves and take care to read all label directions carefully.

Bats Beyond the Belfry

Q **I've seen bats flying around my garden at night and have to admit I wish they weren't there—too scary. I know they are supposed to be good guys, but are they really? Or are the tree-huggers exaggerating?**

A Bats are definitely good guys; in fact, "great" may not be too strong a word when you consider that one bat can eat up to 4,000 mosquitoes in a single night. There are about 40 bat species in the United States, and they are important garden helpers in many ways.

Bats help gardeners by dining on pests like cutworms, corn borer moths, potato beetles, and cucumber beetles. They also eat scorpions. And they are major plant pollinators and seed spreaders, especially in the tropics.

Admittedly they do get rabies, but as long as you don't pick up a sick one, you're more likely to win the lottery than you are to get bitten. And all you have to do to protect your pets is be sure their vaccinations are up to date. 🐾

Beetle Mania

Q There are little yellow beetles eating the petunias and cosmos in my roof garden. They are the size of ladybugs and have similar black dots, but they're pointier in front. What are they, and is there an organic way to get rid of them?

A It sounds as though you may have 12-spotted cucumber beetles, which in spite of their name are equal-opportunity eaters, damaging a wide range of crops; they are particularly fond of late-summer flowers.

If the bodies are narrow, the heads black, and the spots correct in number, you know the name of the enemy. But the truth is, that doesn't matter too much. Almost all the possible culprits will be killed on contact if you spray them with a pyrethrum-based pesticide. Pyrethrum comes from a plant, *Chrysanthemum cinerariaefolium,* and is approved for organic gardening.

Apply it in the evening, after the bees have gone home and the beetles have settled in. Pyrethrum dissipates quickly; most of the toxicity will be gone by morning. But while it is working, it is lethal to beneficials as well as pests, so target only those areas where the problem is severe.

There are several pyrethrum-based products available. Those labeled as containing *pyrethrum* are made using parts of the plant itself; they are the least toxic, which means they are also the least potent. If you want something a little stronger, look for a product that contains *pyrethrins*, the toxic chemicals themselves, extracted from the plant.

But if you are eager to stay organic, beware of products that contain *pyrethroids*. Pyrethroids are synthetic compounds that operate in similar ways but are a great deal stronger than either of the natural versions, and they are frequently compounded with other, even stronger toxins. 🍎

Bt (*BACILLUS TOTALLYWONDERFULLUS*)

Bacillus thuringiensis, known as Bt, was named after Thuringia, Germany, where this useful pathogen was discovered in 1911. It was occasionally used as an insecticide in the '40s and '50s, but really took off in the '60s, when very strong strains were developed for use against specific types of insects.

One strain does in the larvae of *Lepidoptera* (such as cabbage worms), others are more useful against *Coleoptera* (potato beetles, to give one example). There are also Bt strains that work against mosquitoes and other pests, and more are being developed all the time.

The beauty part is that all of the strains of Bt are very specific. When you apply them to your plants—or water garden—they do not harm anything but the insects they are designed to kill. (In fact, what you are applying is usually not the bacteria themselves but a mixture of the toxins they produce and spores that will, in time, give rise to more bacteria.)

When used in appropriate amounts to combat specific outbreaks of pests, Bt is both very effective and very safe, a near-perfect pesticide. But unfortunately, that very perfection may end up causing problems. It attracted the notice of biotechnologists, who figured out how to move some of the toxins into crop plants like cotton, corn, and potatoes. Instead of being sprayed with Bt only when protection is needed, the bioengineered versions of these crops are now, effectively, all Bt all the time.

In the short term, crops bioengineered to contain Bt radically reduce the amounts of other, more toxic pesticides farmers must use, which sounds like a good thing. And it is—in the short term. In the long term, however, it's likely that Bt will be rendered ineffective through overuse, and the toxic treadmill will start up again.

Why? Because *almost* all of the pests are killed when Bt toxin is part of all the food they eat, but a few manage to resist. Those few pass on their resistance to their children, who do the same in their turn. Insects make a lot of babies, and one generation follows the next very quickly. Before you know it, the few are many, and there's a whole new breed of bugs that can eat Bt for breakfast and your crops for lunch.

Replanting a Rose Bed

Q Deer and black spot have caused me to give up on one small rose bed. When replanting with some deer-proof plant, do I need to do something to get rid of the black spot fungus?

A The only good thing about *Diplocarpon rosae* is that it's specific to roses. If you don't plant them, black spot won't come. The deer, however, will, and you might as well know now that there is no such thing as a deer-proof plant. The best you can hope for is things they won't eat unless they are extremely hungry (see pages 749–50).

No matter what rose replacement you choose, for best results let the bed lie fallow for a year before you plant it. Deer often operate on automatic, returning to a favorite restaurant and chowing down (or at least having an appetizer) before deciding that they don't like the new menu. If you close the place for a while, there's a better chance they'll forget it's there. ✿

Cabbage Worm Culprits

Q I'm having problems with cabbage worms. Is there a natural control, other than frequent sprays of Bt?

A The adult and larval stages of several species of ground beetle (members of the family Carabidae) are fond of eating cabbage worms. Many in this large, widely distributed family of beneficial insects are dark and shiny, with prominent eyes, threadlike antennae, and segmented silhouettes. Typically, they are found under stones and debris. Ground beetles active during the day tend to be brightly colored or metallic looking; the species active at night are black.

So be careful not to kill these beetles if you see them. Unfortunately, you either have them or you don't; ground beetles are not commonly offered by companies that sell beneficial insects, and there is no practical way to collect them from someplace else and bring them home with you. ✿

Alerting Birds

Q **Birds keep flying into my penthouse picture window and committing suicide. What can I do to stop their unfortunate actions?**

A It is not uncommon for some species of birds to become confused by the reflection of the sky in window glass. They are trying to fly through what they believe is an open space. Interestingly enough, the "city-wise" species like finches, sparrows, and pigeons rarely make this mistake. It is only the less widely seen birds, as well as migrating passers-by, who do, making the self-destruction all the more poignant.

One solution to this problem, devised some years ago by savvy nature centers, is to place a silhouette of a diving sparrow hawk in the window. The image of this natural predator apparently repels many of these birds, and it also breaks up the window reflection.

Unfortunately, the repellent aspect is limited—effective for only a small portion of a large window—and for a comparatively short time. Before long, birds regard the silhouette as part of the home's surroundings and are no longer chased away by it.

Other ways of breaking up the reflection work better in the long term. You can use fluttering strips of ribbon outside the window, or drape netting over it, or you can try installing drapes. Check carefully if you go for the drapes; they don't always halt the mirror effect. 🍂

Keeping Cats Away

Q **I've read that a plant called rue prevents animals—particularly cats—from digging up gardens. Is this true, and can you tell me about the plant and where it's available?**

A Animals may be even more unpredictable than humans, so while the acrid scent of rue (*Ruta graveolens*) will discourage some cats, it will not necessarily deter them all. Rue's lengthy history of herbal uses dates to ancient Greece, when it was valued for its ability to repel fleas. In the Middle Ages, it was also considered a fine defense against witches, and useful for restoring hair. The strong odor was considered prophylactic, so small bouquets were placed on judges' benches to keep them from being infected by the "gaol fever" of prisoners.

In the garden, rue is a handsome, hardy perennial that grows to about 2 feet tall. It is evergreen and somewhat shrubby where winters are mild, but in the North it usually dies to the ground and reappears in spring.

The small, rounded leaves are a beautiful blue-green, topped in early summer by bright yellow flowers. Rue grows easily in any well-drained soil and tolerates a bit of shade. It grows readily from seed, but you can find small plants at many garden shops (usually tucked in among culinary herbs) or by mail.

Scat, Cat

Q **How can I dissuade roaming cats from using my flower garden as their personal litter box?**

A Start by removing all the droppings—cats go where their noses tell them cats have gone before. Follow up with a commercial cat repellent, to cover any smells left behind. (Don't expect the repellent to perform like Hercules; you really do have to start by cleaning up).

Once the odor problem is solved, make it hard for cats to dig by covering any open soil with landscape cloth or a very loose mulch such as pebbles or bark nuggets. This leaves newly planted soil as the only vulnerable area. Cover it with chicken wire until the new plants have achieved fair size and can be further protected with mulch, and you should have the little dears thoroughly thwarted.

Caterpillar Controls

Q **I use *Bacillus thuringiensis* to control destructive caterpillars, but I'm concerned about harming the caterpillars of butterflies I want, like the monarchs. Can this happen?**

A Between them, the various commercially available strains of *Bacillus thuringiensis* (Bt) can kill all leaf-eating caterpillars; and this means that the Bt you count on to destroy tomato hornworms, cabbage loopers, cabbage worms, leafrollers, and tent caterpillars will have the same effect on baby butterflies.

But only if they eat it, which means the danger is minimal. Monarch caterpillars eat milkweeds, swallowtails are partial to the Umbelliferae family (Queen-Anne's lace, parsley, carrot, celery, and parsnips). As long as you don't spray these plants, the caterpillars that eat them will be fine. If the plants that need Bt protection are very close to known butterfly plants, either cover the butterfly plants or paint on the Bt solution instead of using a spray or dust, either of which can drift, even when the air is still. 🌶

Uglynest Caterpillar

Q **There are hideous-looking webs at the ends of my hawthorn trees. What should I do?**

A Those silk webs at the branch endings of woody plants like hawthorn, cherry, and rose are the home of the uglynest caterpillar. The caterpillar feeds from late spring through summer. As autumn approaches, the adult moths begin to emerge to lay eggs and start the cycle anew. These webs can be distinguished from those of the tent caterpillar or fall webworm, which are located at the crotche of a branch, not at the ends.

Since the nests are usually out of reach, the easiest way to get rid of these pests is to use a pole pruner to cut off the webbed limb tips (destroy them after they fall down). Where the webs are low enough, you can also try turning a hose on the area and knocking the webbed structure and the caterpillars out of the plant. 🌶

Preserving Garden Sculptures

Q **How does one best protect statues in the garden from snow and ice damage? Ours are cast cement with steel reinforcing rods and will be left out all winter. Is it appropriate to wrap them in burlap, lay them flat on the ground, leave them standing, or what?**

A Ice has always been a problem because water expands as it freezes, forcing tiny cracks apart, and creating cracks where there had been only small depressions.

Snow, on the other hand, is a comparatively new hazard. It wouldn't bother anything if it were pure, but these days, like rain, it tends to be acid, and if it doesn't melt off quickly, it's melting whatever it's sitting on.

Though the damage is different, the key to prevention is the same: keep your sculpture dry. Burlap is unwise as it will retain moisture. And there's no point in laying the sculpture down unless you fear high winds.

At Kykuit, the Rockefeller estate in Pocantico Hills, New York, where the gardens are complemented by an extensive collection of sculptures, caretakers take different approaches for different materials.

Bronzes are simply waxed to repel the elements, but Cynthia Altman, the curator, said, "We cover the marble with Gore-Tex covers. It breathes and sheds moisture so nothing can freeze and thaw." She added that with a metal armature, it's even more important to prevent condensation."

When Kykuit's garden was built in 1908, its designer, William Welles Bosworth, created a wooden pyramid to protect the huge reproduction of Giambologna's "Oceanus and the Three Rivers" that anchors Kykuit's forecourt, and he put decorative lattice on the wooden boxes that covered smaller sculptural elements. Now, Oceanus and his pals have to make do with a vented plastic wrapper (the granite basin is left uncovered because it is less vulnerable than the marble to ice damage), so it may be a good thing that Kykuit is closed in the winter.

Which brings us to the heart of the dilemma: the best protection is so unlovely that unless you've got museum pieces, you may conclude that the cure is worse than the disease. If your sculptures are in good condition, without places where water can collect, you may prefer to chance the ice and rush out with a broom when snow falls. ❧

"DEER-PROOF" FLOWERS

I t seems that every week, letters arrive lamenting the feeding habits of deer and complaining that some of the plants recommended as deerproof are in reality expensive deer food. In an effort to determine what deer find tasty and what they do not, David H. Chinery, the Cornell cooperative extension agent in Westchester County, New York, polled a local group of master gardeners and compiled a list based on their observations.

Although many factors determine what a deer will eat (the time of year and the size of a herd, for example), Mr. Chinery said he was surprised to discover that there are quite a few flowers they rarely consume. The survey indicates these include cleome, four-o'clock, verbena, heliotrope, globe thistle, goatsbeard, coreopsis, verbascum, Jacob's ladder, bee balm, ajuga, lily of the valley, and wisteria.

Admittedly, all the deer in the survey were in or near Westchester County, but that is one of the most deer-pressured areas in the United States.

To Make Deer Frown

Q This year we have more damage by deer than ever. How can we prevent damage next year?

A An adult doe needs about eight pounds of food daily during the winter. With herd sizes increasing, territorial battles between deer and suburbanites are also increasing.

The deer eat a swath from ground level to a height of several feet; branches appear torn, not cut neatly, because deer do not have upper front teeth.

Controls fall into three categories: repellents, fences, and plants. Repellents are popular, but their effectiveness depends on how hungry the deer are. Since they work by training the deer away from plants, they should be applied before browsing starts in October or early November, and many of them need to be reapplied frequently. Don't skimp: treating part of a plant, or just some of a group of plants, will not keep deer away from the untreated ones.

Some gardeners have had more success with repellents based on thiram, a fungicide, than with products based on soap or putrescent eggs. Be sure to read the label for suitability and application instructions with all repellents.

Eight-foot fences are the most effective barrier, but control through plant choice has the most appeal for most people. Woody plants that are often cited as distasteful to deer include common boxwood, *Potentilla fruticosa*, Japanese pieris, drooping leucothoe, paper birch, barberry, bumald spirea, and Colorado blue spruce. But this is all relative. As with people, the hungrier deer are, the more things on the menu look good to them. 🍎

Oil on Troubled Gardens

Q **What does a dormant oil do and when does it do it?**

A Dormant oils, which are usually petroleum based, kill insects (aphids, mealybugs, scales, mites, and psyllids, among others) by smothering them. They kill insect eggs both by smothering and by penetrating the casing and interfering with development. And they prevent the spread of some fungus diseases by blocking their contact with the target.

Traditionally, these oils were heavy and strong. They killed a lot of bugs, but they also damaged leaves and the needles of evergreens. You could only use them on deciduous trees and shrubs, and then only when those trees and shrubs were leafless—hence the "dormant" in the name.

The name persists, but old-fashioned dormant oils have been replaced by lighter formulations, called horticultural oils or superior oils, that are (usually) safe to use throughout the growing season. There are also formulations based on vegetable oils, but no matter what type you use, it's crucial to follow the label directions precisely for the correct dilution for different plants, and for different times of the year.

Petroleum-based oils break down quickly and the residue is not toxic to birds or mammals. They are toxic to aquatic life, though, and should not be used near ponds or rivers. 🍎

WHEN TO ADD OIL

For every tender new leaf heralding spring's arrival, there's a pest lurking. Many overwintering insect populations boom following a mild winter, so gardeners should be especially vigilant in early spring, when many pests are out and in a stage of their life cycle that is vulnerable to the smothering effects of refined horticultural oil.

Scale insects, for example, have a crawler stage, when horticultural oil can easily kill them. But once inside their protective shells, many scales simply laugh off any attempt to deal with them.

From the end of April into early May, a number of common pests are vulnerable, and scouting will show you if populations are large enough to warrant treatment. Follow directions carefully. Different dilutions of horticultural oil are used depending on whether leaf buds have broken.

Scale insects are common on hemlock, privet, juniper, euonymus, and *Prunus* species. Mealybugs, mites, and adelgids are also susceptible to spraying with horticultural oil. Watch for mealybugs on yew, and occasionally on dogwoods and crab apples. Look for adelgids of one sort and another on Douglas fir, Norway and white spruce, pine, and especially hemlock. Mites can be found on spruce, pine, hemlock, arborvitae, hawthorn, apple, *Prunus* species, holly, azalea, and other broadleaf evergreens.

Bye-Bye, Earwigs

Q **Do you have an organic suggestion for ridding a garden of earwigs? They seem to be more plentiful than usual this year.**

Adult earwigs

A Earwigs are night feeders that seek dark hiding places near target plants during the day. Bear in mind that they do eat aphids and young slugs, as well as your prize dahlias. The easiest way to control them is with tubular traps. Use lengths of hose, fat sticks of bamboo, toilet paper cores with an end blocked—any dark hiding place that you can easily empty into a can half full of water with a slick of detergent on top to prevent their crawling out.

Earwigs also flock in large numbers to slug traps that have been baited with vegetable-oil-soaked breadcrumbs instead of beer. Unless the traps have one-way entrances, these, too, must be emptied, preferably early in the morning before the earwigs have staggered off to bed. 🐛

Fire Blight

Q The new leaves on my weeping crab apple look burned and deformed. What is this, and how can I treat it without toxic chemicals?

A It is likely that you are seeing symptoms of the bacterial disease fire blight, which affects various members of the rose family, including apple, hawthorn, pear, pyracantha, and cotoneaster. The disease was first recorded in the United States in the late eighteenth century and has had some devastating effects in orchards. The name fire blight is an apt description of the blackened flowers, leaves, and twigs, which look as though they were burned.

The bacterium, *Erwinia amylovora,* spends winters on sunken lesions called cankers, and oozes in spring when it is spread by wind, rain, and insects to new shoots and blossoms. By mid summer, there may be extreme branch and twig dieback. Fire blight is especially persistent during warm, wet weather. The best thing to do is to prune away and destroy all the infected twigs and branches, cutting at least a foot below the injured area. Between cuts, sterilize the pruners by dipping them into a disinfectant— either rubbing alcohol or a solution of water and household bleach. When you are finished, rinse the pruners and dry them well.

Avoid fertilizers high in nitrogen, which lead to a rapid growth of vulnerable shoots and suckers. Early next spring, before leaves or flowers emerge, consider trying a preventive spray of copper sulfate. If the plant succumbs, plant elsewhere with a variety that is resistant to fire blight. 🍂

Taming Driveway Fungus

Q For the last several years, I've had some white fungus growing through the asphalt of my driveway in late summer, breaking it with an astonishing strength. On occasion, a few of these growths, which are about 3 inches big, pop on the lawn. I dig them out, but the next year they come back. This year two big ones have pushed through already. Do you have an explanation or a cure?

A Ain't nature grand! All that force from a little fungus. Actually, the fungus producing those growths is not little at all; it's a netlike webbing of living tissue that has, from the sound of it, spread through a good portion of the soil beneath your lawn and driveway.

The webbing is called a mycelium, and it can live for many years, feeding on buried organic matter. When conditions are right, it sends up mushrooms, which are the spore-carrying "fruiting bodies" of the fungus. (They aren't fruits, because fungi aren't plants, but it's the same idea.)

The only way to get rid of them is to get rid of the parent fungus. Yours is probably *Coprinus comatus*, commonly known as the shaggy mane. These mushrooms have a bullet shape, almost a point, so they are very well suited to pushing through things, including asphalt. They come up through blacktop so frequently that it's almost as though they had an affinity for the stuff.

No matter what it is, the fungus under the driveway will eventually run out of food and stop producing mushrooms. If you can't wait, you'll have to rip up the asphalt and remove at least a foot of the soil underneath. Replace the soil with a bed of sand or gravel and pour new asphalt. The mycelium grows quite close to the surface and needs organic matter to feed on, so this treatment should discourage it. 🍂

Grub Problem? Maybe

Q I have a lovely *Malva* in the garden, but unfortunately it attracts Japanese beetles. Can Japanese beetles cause a grub problem in the lawn?

A The adult Japanese beetle's well-known appetite for leaves of *Malva*, rose, grape, hollyhock, pussy willow, and others is easily matched by its larvae's appetite for grass roots. Controlling grubs successfully means planning your attack. Knowing when your enemy is weakest is the key.

First, scout out the situation to see if you have a grub problem worth treating.

Dr. Frank Rossi, assistant professor of turf grass science at Cornell University in Ithaca, New York, said that Japanese beetle grubs are commonly found in well-irrigated, shady sections of the lawn. In early September, when the grubs are actively feeding on grass roots, peel back some of the turf and look for ½- to 1-inch-long, milky white grubs with brown heads. The problem is not bad enough to treat if the population is less than 10 per square foot.

More serious infestations should be treated when the larvae are small and most vulnerable. In the Northeast, this period is from early August, when the eggs hatch, into September, when the grubs begin migrating down into the soil to avoid the colder weather. They overwinter below the frost line and return to the surface in the spring.

Effective biological controls for grubs are a Holy Grail of horticulture. Milky spore disease, which infects young larvae and is passed on like an epidemic, can be used, but it takes several years to spread through a population and is rarely more than 15 to 25 percent effective.

There are also products that attack the grubs when they molt. These are less toxic to everything else than conventional grub-killers, and they are just as effective, but they have to be applied in mid May in order for them to be there at the right time.

Later in the year, you can—if you must—use a traditional lawn product labeled for grubs. But take a peek under the lawn first. There may not really be a problem worth worrying about. 🍎

Adult Japanese beetle on a rose

Grub underground

Heat and Poison Don't Mix

Q The heat seems to have brought out an unusual number of bugs, so I bought some all-purpose pesticide at my local nursery. The clerk warned me not to use it until the weather cools down some, but by then everything will be eaten! Why must I wait?

A Extraordinarily high temperatures stress plants, making them more vulnerable to any damage that comes their way. And some pesticides—or the "inert ingredients" used to bulk them out and help them adhere—are phototoxic; when sunlight hits plant leaves that have been coated with them, it burns.

This combination makes it risky to apply pesticides when the sun is bright. Even after temperatures moderate, it's best to put the pesticide on in late afternoon or early evening. As an added advantage, that will be after many beneficials, including bees, have gone to bed, so you will be doing a better job of targeting your wrath. 🍎

Mystery Tomato Eaters

Q **My tomato plants were quite healthy until recently, when I suddenly noticed that most of the leaves had been chewed and the flowers had disappeared. What happened, and what can I do about this?**

A Your plant was probably under attack by tomato hornworms (which can also do a job on your petunias, peppers, and nicotianas if they're so inclined). It is amazingly easy to miss seeing these plump, leaf-green caterpillars, which average 3 to 4 inches long. Check the leaves and the area around the base of your plants for the caterpillar's dark green droppings.

The best control for these pests, which have white stripes and distinctive reddish "horns," is hand-picking. (Kill them by drowning unless you have a strong stomach— they're too big to squish easily.) But before you kill a hornworm, check to see if there are small white oval bumps protruding from its back. If so, leave it alone. These are the eggs of its natural enemy, the braconid wasp, which may already be destroying the pest at hand. The wasp's young will emerge to attack yet another generation of hornworms. 🍎

Death to Bugs. All Bugs?

Q **This is my first year to have a garden. I have corn, tomatoes, onions, bell peppers, and cucumbers. I have encountered some minor insect problems and was wondering what insecticide I might be able to use on everything, as well as around my house.**

A Surely not everything! Not the beneficial ladybugs that eat pests like aphids. Not the harmless little wasps that keep whiteflies at bay. Not the . . . well, you get the idea. It's natural to want to get rid of damaging insects, and it certainly would be convenient if one product fixed every problem, but gardens—even the simplest ones—are fantastically complex ecosystems where one size never fits all.

It sounds as if you are in an ideal place to start out right. Your insect problems are still minor, and you haven't yet started poisoning everything in sight and wiping out all your helpers. Natural predators need a wide variety of habitats. Encourage them by planting lots of different flowers, vegetables, and herbs. Keep your plants healthy; sick ones are much more likely to suffer from insect attacks. And start learning to recognize the many beneficial insects that help keep the garden free of pests. Being able to tell friend from foe will do a lot more good than any pesticide you could buy. 🍎

Fighting Weedy Vines

Q **I am desperate. How do I cope with a yard that's overgrown with all kinds of vines? If the roots run among ground covers and barberries, how can I hope to extricate them? The vines are pulling down the lilacs. And there's some poison ivy. Must I resort to scorched earth, starting over from scratch? Please keep in mind that I'm only there on weekends and would prefer not to use chemical herbicides.**

A In this case, it might be wise to emulate General Sherman. Do you really want all those barberries? Are the ground covers wonderful and rare?

But though starting over is the best idea, there's no need to really scorch the earth. You can easily restore order without resorting to huge applications of herbicide. All you need is a lawnmower. (If you want to save the ground cover, dig out a few dozen clumps and transfer them to a holding bed.)

Begin by cutting unwanted barberries and the thickest vine stems at ground level—start with the ones that are killing the lilacs. Cut by hand if possible, to minimize flying debris that might contain poison ivy. Wear gloves at all times, of course, along with long sleeves, and long pants tucked into boots. If you must use a mechanical cutter, protect your face with one of the clear masks sold at well-stocked hardware stores.

After clipping or sawing the thick-based things, pick up all the cut material and pile it in an out-of-the-way corner. Cover it with a dark tarp and let it decompose—it should not be burned because the poison ivy smoke can cause reactions.

Then start mowing, setting the mower at about 2 inches from the ground. A year or so of consistent close mowing (don't let up until hard frost, and start again first thing in the spring) will destroy the established vines, including the poison ivy, which should not cause problems as long as you wear protective clothing while mowing.

A chopped sprig or two of young poison ivy among the grass bits can be left to decompose in place, as long as no one goes barefoot in the area, but if there is more than a handful, protect yourself as described above, rake up the clippings, and pile them on the heap to decompose along with everything else.

During your year of mowing instead of planting, think about what you really want in the landscape department. When the yard is ready, you will be, too. 🍎

The Lovely Lacewing

Q **I've read that lacewings are good insects to have in the garden. Just what do they do and how can I recognize them?**

A Of the more than 700,000 kinds of insects that scurry, jump, flit, or slither about our planet, quite a few are good guys. The green lacewing is one of the best; its larvae eat more pest species than even the highly regarded ladybug. Like ladybugs, they are fond of aphids, and they also eat mites, whiteflies, and the eggs of several kinds of destructive beetles.

The green lacewings vary in length from about ½ to ¾ inch. Some have prominent golden or copper-colored eyes. But most easily recognized are their pale-green, oval-shaped wings that they fold tilted above their bodies. Lacewings are often seen flitting about plants

Adult lacewings

in relatively open areas. If touched, they give off an unpleasant odor.

It's important to distinguish between the beneficial lacewing and the destructive lacebug, which also has gossamer green wings. The lacebug, which feeds on plants, holds its squarish-shaped wings horizontally and flat against its body. 🍂

Milkweed Takeover

Q **I've always had milkweed around the fringes of the garden for butterflies. Lately, it has become rampant, even invading the vegetable plot. Has the lack of a deep freeze the last few winters caused this? The roots are too deep to dig out. Help!**

A Fringe is not a meaningful concept to the common milkweed, *Asclepias syriaca.* Once a stand is well established, its deep, eagerly spreading roots and multitudinous seeds make it a takeover specialist, and since milkweed is hardy to about 50 below, don't count on help from a freeze.

Instead, mow the perimeter of the garden so the nearest milkweed is at least 10 feet away. In the garden itself, pull all shoots as soon as they appear. Wind-sown seedlings won't have a chance to put down strong roots, and although the roots that are already there will keep sending up new plants, depriving them of top growth will eventually starve out the network. 🍂

Moldy Steps

Q **We have railroad ties as steps between the levels in our shady garden. These steps have become greasy with mold. Since we are reluctant to cut down trees to expose the steps to more sunshine, is there any treatment for the wood that will inhibit this problem?**

A Your problem is almost surely not mold, but moss or algae. There are several products designed to get rid of it, including some made from (relatively) benign ingredients that will not will not hurt the surrounding trees.

The products are sold at garden-supply stores, often shelved with the pesticides. Read labels carefully before buying; some products stop a lot more than algae. 🍂

Coping with Moles

Q I seem to have a lot of mole holes and tunnels in my garden, and I worry that some of the root vegetables will be attacked. One suggestion has been to use nematodes to kill the grubs the moles eat and thus drive them away. What should I do?

A Fear not. Or rather, no need to fear yet, since moles don't eat vegetables. As long as they stay in the food garden, they're doing mostly helpful things, like aerating the soil and removing grubs. They'd be assets if they didn't also eat your valuable earthworms, and (unwittingly) lend their tunnels to vegetable-hungry mice and voles.

And they do breed. So sooner or later you're going to have more moles than you need, at which point you'll discover that, along with gophers, they are the hardest of all animal pests to get rid of. You can't fence them out; and folk repellents, including human hair, seldom work.

You can try spraying the earth near the tunnels with castor oil solution (6 ounces of castor oil and 2 tablespoons of dishwashing liquid in 1 gallon of water). That sometimes drives moles away. But they might just go to the lawn, and then you'd *really* have problems.

Mole-plagued lawn owners, whose sorrows range from dead grass to broken ankles, have no recourse except trapping or using poison gas. These methods work only until the next group of moles moves in. But if employed in early spring, before breeding season starts, they will help somewhat. Farm-supply stores sell the equipment and provide instruction on how to use it. 🍎

Buzz Busters

Q Are the battery-operated mosquito-repellent gadgets effective? The ads say they work by emitting sounds made by mosquitoes' enemies, but I don't know if I believe it.

A Numerous scientific studies have failed to find any use for these devices, and once you hear them, you're

(continued on page 762)

759

MASTERING THE MILDEW PROBLEM

Unless your life is charmed indeed, sooner or later your garden will be visited by the mildew brothers, Downy and Powdery. Leaves will be disfigured, plant health will decline, flowers will be few and faltering. Powdery mildew is far more common, and though hideous, less destructive. It shows white on top of the leaves, darker on the bottom. Downy mildew is less widespread but more devastating. Leaves get brownish purple to black spots on top and gray fuzz underneath.

Grapes
(prone to downy mildew)

Mildews are fungus diseases, spread by microscopic spores that can live for years on dead leaves or in the soil. Once established, they are very hard to control; preventive action is far more effective than any amount of cure.

PREVENTION

Look for mildew-resistant varieties, which will be labeled as such. Make sure all plants get good air circulation. If weather is damp but not rainy for several days in a row, spray vulnerable plants with one of the fungus fighters listed below. If you have had fungus problems in a given place and want to grow susceptible plants there in succeeding years, spray them once every 10 days to two weeks no matter what the weather is doing.

Remove afflicted annuals as soon as you see damage, and clean up any dead material under or around perennials. Bring a plastic sack with you to receive the debris, so you don't spread spores as you carry it through the garden. Composting frequently fails to kill fungi, so burn the bodies or send them to a landfill.

CURE (SORT OF)

Most of these work by changing the pH on leaf surfaces from acid, which the fungi love, to base, which they don't care for. If possible, spray on overcast days; bright sunlight through the fungicide can damage plant tissue. Be sure to cover all parts of the plant, paying special attention to the undersides of the leaves. The potions below are comparatively nontoxic to everything except fungi, but it is important to observe all precautions on the labels.

* Starred products are preventive only; once the mildew has taken hold, they don't help much.

- **Sulfur/fungicidal soaps.** Sulfur is a natural fungicide. It comes as a powder for dusting, a wettable powder to make into spray, and as a component of commercial fungicidal soaps. It can damage plants if used when temperatures are above 80°F. More effective against powdery mildew than downy.

- **Fixed copper compounds.** These are stronger than sulfur, and more effective against more kinds of fungus. Unfortunately, copper is likely to damage plants when used in the sort of cool, damp weather most likely to cause mildew problems. This means copper is less useful against mildews than it is against rusts and blights, but it's still worth trying in emergencies. Look for products that contain basic copper sulfate, copper oxychloride, or cuprous oxide, and follow label instructions scrupulously.

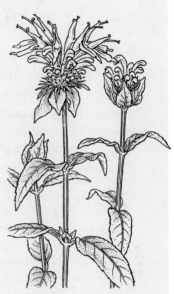

Bee balm
(prone to powdery mildew)

- **Baking soda*.** The following mixture is easy and inexpensive to make, and very effective at preventing mildew when consistently applied. (Test on a few inconspicuous leaves before using in quantity; sometimes sun on the oil damages plant tissues.)

  Mix 1 tablespoon each of baking soda (sodium bicarbonate) and summer-weight (or lightweight) horticultural oil with 1 gallon of water. Spray weekly, making up a fresh batch each time.

- **Water*.** The lowest-tech approach of all, and quite effective against powdery mildew, which spreads most aggressively on dry leaves. The spores must dig in to grow, and they can't do it if the leaves are wet. Just spray leaves with a strong shower of water every morning, early enough so the sun can dry them quickly. The only difficult part is the "every morning." It won't work if you slack off, and damp (as opposed to wet) leaves give the spores a chance to slide from place to place.

Forget-me-nots
(prone to downy mildew)

(continued from page 759)

likely to conclude that the only thing they repel are human beings driven mad by their high-pitched whine.

There are several low-toxicity mosquito-repellents available that will provide some relief, but none of them, unfortunately, works as well as DEET (N,N-diethyl-3-methylbenzamide), the active ingredient in most chemical-based repellents. It is comparatively safe if used sparingly, but it is by no means benign. It can cause serious side effects, especially in children, and particularly if overused.

DEET is absorbed through the skin, so one way to avoid problems is to put it on your clothes instead. Choose an outfit for gardening: shirt, pants, socks, hat or kerchief, and gloves. Spray lightly with a product that contains a high concentration of DEET, and let dry before dressing. Take a shower when you take your DEET duds off, and store them in a plastic bag between wearings. ✿

Death to Mosquitoes

Q I am using self-watering pots and window boxes this summer. They have a water reservoir with an access hole for filling with a hose. Since there will be standing water, will I be guilty of encouraging the breeding of mosquitoes?

A They may be encouraged, but you won't be guilty as long as you use a biological control called Bti, which kills the larvae when they eat it. (It is not a contact insecticide and will not harm mammals, birds, or fish.)

Bti stands for *Bacillus thuringiensis israelensis.* It comes in various forms. The easiest to use is a pelleted product that does not need any mixing or special applicators.

Many hardware stores and garden centers sell pelleted Bti, occasionally as granules, more commonly in the form of handy little doughnuts called Mosquito Dunks. Wherever you see a likely breeding ground, throw in a doughnut—or a small chunk—suiting the quantity to the situation.

Mosquito Dunks come packaged with application rates. Their simplicity should not lure you into overuse, which could speed the development of Bti-resistant mosquitoes. ✿

EXTENDING A HELPING HAND

When the land-grant college system was set up, back in 1862, one of the things it was set up to do was to make sure farmers had access to the latest research. In 1887 the colleges were awarded funds for agricultural experiment stations, to broaden the knowledge base. And in 1914, Congress authorized the creation of the Cooperative Extension Service, an educational outreach effort jointly run by the land-grant colleges, the experiment stations, and the U.S. Department of Agriculture. Almost immediately, state and local governments also got into the act.

Now, nearly a century later, this publicly funded information machine has offices in every county of every state. And every office has an expert available to answer—at no charge—any question about growing things that you might care to ask. (The extension service offers information on many other subjects as well—including food and water safety, nutrition, and natural resources—but we're talking about gardening.)

The service is unexcelled at pinpoint diagnosis: testing your soil, putting a name on the disease that's doing in your apple tree, suggesting the varieties of turf grass that will do well in your particular yard. The only fly in this all-purpose ointment is that there are still some extension agents who rely on agricultural chemicals to solve every problem. Be sure to ask for low-impact remedies if that's the kind you want.

Using the phone book to find your local extension office is not always easy. If "Cooperative" and "Extension" both fail, and it isn't listed with the county offices in the government pages, try the closest branch of the state university. Alternatively, go directly to the Web for a national list: *www.reeusda.gov/1700/statepartners/usa.htm.*

Mosquito Plant

Q **Last year I heard about a plant that would repel mosquitoes. What is it and does it work?**

A In recent years, a weedy-looking geranium with a citronella-like odor has been touted as a mosquito repellent and called citronella, citrosa, or mosquito-repellent plant.

But it is only "the latest gimmick to prey on people's fear of insects," said Dr. Dave Shetlar of the Ohio State University extension service, and there is no scientific basis for claims of any repellent qualities for this plant.

Said to be a cross between an African geranium and something called grass of China, the plant does contain some citronella oil. But the amount is so small, Dr. Shetlar said it would take a great number of plants to drive any self-respecting mosquito away. 🌢

Moss Rash

Q **I've heard of rashes developing from handling moss. Can you explain this?**

A A fungal infection called sporotrichosis, which causes a red or purple rash, may develop a few weeks after handling sphagnum moss. But it's important to differentiate between sphagnum moss, which can cause the rash, and sphagnum peat moss (or more accurately, sphagnum moss peat), which does not.

Sphagnum moss is the live plant that grows on the top of peat bogs in Canada, Minnesota, and elsewhere. Harvested as flat green sheets, it is perhaps most often used to line hanging baskets. It is in this live plant that the fungus may live.

Sphagnum peat moss, on the other hand, is found below the bog's surface, dead and partly decomposed. It is the material that comes in bales and is used to make seed starting mixes. (It is often recommended as a soil improver, as well, though there are several better choices for that purpose.)

Wearing gloves is the simplest way to avoid any possibility of a rash when using the allergenic moss, and if you think you might be sensitive, it's a good idea to wear a mask so you don't inhale the dust. 🌢

Get Out the Neem

Q **Recently, my yard and garden have been plagued with small, flying light brown beetles. They eat peonies, irises, and roses, though seedless ash leaves are chomped on, too. Picking them off the plants has been a losing battle, but I don't want to use pesticides that might harm birds, fish, or beneficial insects like bees. Is there anything I can use?**

A For everything except the ash tree, you might try a mild, noncontact formulation of neem, an organic pesticide derived from the tropical neem tree (*Azadirachta indica*).

Neem does not harm birds. It will kill fish, but only when it is fresh out of the bottle, so keeping it out of the water is largely a matter of not pouring it in.

Neem is effective against a wide assortment of insects, including several chewing beetles that shrug off most low-impact poisons. But it is important to shop carefully when you go out to buy some. There are several formulations available, and they differ markedly: in the ways they attack the insects, in their general toxicity, and in the damage they may cause plants. The details will be on the labels.

To have neem fit your criteria, be sure to choose a formula that does not kill on contact, one that requires the insects to ingest the neem before it can destroy them. As long as you don't spray a lot of it directly on flowers' pollen-bearing parts, it won't bother bees. And beneficial insects that eat other insects will be largely unaffected. (The amount they consume when they eat their prey is relatively small.) 🐌

Pill Bugs

Q **Every time I pick up a pot on my patio, I find a pill bug. What mischief are these creatures up to?**

A Probably not much, since their favorite food is decaying matter. Pill bugs, like their cousins the sow bugs, have hard, dark gray or brownish segmented bodies about half an inch long, and if disturbed, they roll into protective balls. They are crustaceans, related to shrimp.

Pill bugs do their feeding at night, and if their numbers are minimal, they do no harm. Problems arise if their numbers grow so large that they increase their menu to include the fine rootlets of young plants. If that happens, the best control is to eliminate the moist, dark areas under flower pots, boards, or rocks, where they like to hide during the day. 🐌

Pill bug

PLANT-DERIVED PESTICIDES

The organic arsenal does include a number of pesticides, but organic gardeners, knowing that "natural" is not the same thing as "harmless," use the ones on this list only as helpers of last resort. Although they are comparatively benign, all can hurt non-target organisms like birds, fish, and beneficial insects. Some, including ryania, are very strong poisons to mammals as well; while if rotenone gets into your system, it may help trigger the development of Parkinson's disease.

Always wear protective clothing when applying pesticides. Read the label carefully to be sure the pesticide you're using is approved for the pest (and plant) you want to use it on. Follow dosage directions; this is definitely one place where more is not better.

Neem, from the neem tree, *Azadirachta indica.* Multiple actions: repels pests, destroys their appetites, kills them by disrupting their growth. Also has some fungicidal properties. Useful against a wide range of pests including flea beetles, whiteflies, corn earworms, cabbage loopers, and root-knot nematodes.

Pyrethrum, from flowers of *Chrysanthemum cinerariifolium* and *C. coccineum.* Instant knockdown, which is very gratifying. But it doesn't always last; if the dosage is improper or the insect has resistance, the victim gets up and staggers away as soon as you turn your back. If you use the proper amount, however, and manage to get it to land on the target, pyrethrum is useful against almost any invertebrate that may be plaguing you. (Be very careful about using pyrethrum or its derivatives on cats; small amounts rid them of fleas, but if you overdo it, you will also be rid of Puffy.)

Rotenone, from several species of legumes in the genus *Lonchocarpus.* Use it and watch the beetles die. Mexican bean beetles, potato beetles, cucumber beetles—even the adults of these hard-to-kill scourges are not immune. Neither, unfortunately, are fish, birds, small mammals, or much of anything else. Rotenone degrades rapidly, but it's very strong stuff while it lasts.

Ryania, from a shrub called *Ryania speciosa,* and like rotenone, short lived but no joke. Use on the caterpillars of codling moths and cabbageworms, and the larvae of Japanese beetles, bean beetles, and potato bugs.

Sabadilla, from the South American plant *Schoenocaulon officinale.* Use only when all else fails, on things like thrips, squash bugs, and tarnished plant bugs. Sabadilla is extremely toxic to bees; be sure to apply it only after they have gone home for the night.

Peperonyl butoxide (PBO) may or may not be plant derived; it can come from sesame oil but is also chemically synthesized. It is an insecticide in its own right, but it is most commonly used as a synergist, combined with other pesticides (especially pyrethrum). It destroys an insect's ability to fight off the pesticide, making the product more effective, and at lower doses, than it would otherwise be. But PBO is not on everyone's organic-acceptable list, and may cause health problems, so you may prefer to avoid it.

Poison Ivy in Winter

Q **Is it possible to get a poison-ivy rash in winter, even though the plant is dormant?**

A Unfortunately, it is. Poison ivy (*Toxicodendron radicans*) is a native North American trailing or climbing vine, and occasionally a shrub. Every portion, including roots and stems, contains an oil called urushiol, which is capable of producing a nasty dermatitis even in winter.

Although in winter the plant is without its distinctive three leaflets, the bare vine can be recognized by the hairy appearance of its brown, leafless stem, which can scale trees to great heights. The numerous dark rootlets and fibers make it look fuzzy.

Urushiol from the stem and rootlets can remain on tree bark even after the vine has been removed, so if you get the rash and can't remember seeing any likely cause, the problem may be your firewood.

Poison ivy's garb at other times includes a handsome crimson leaf in fall (often tempting unwary flower-arrangers), tiny green flowers in spring, and white grapelike berries in late summer that may linger through winter. This fruit is a valuable food for birds, which, unaffected by its oil, help spread the plants when the seeds pass through their system.

Poisonous Plants

Q **I have young children, so I want to be sure not to plant anything that would poison them if they ate it. Can you help?**

A There are so many potentially toxic plants that if you are determined to eliminate every edible hazard, you won't have much of a garden. In addition to plants like nicotiana and oleander, which are poisonous in every part, there are some plants that have both edible and toxic components, such as tomato and rhubarb. The tomato fruit is safe, as are the red rhubarb stems. But eating the leaves of these plants can cause nausea, convulsions, comas, and in extreme cases, death. Similarly, apricots, peaches, and plums are fine, but

Monkshood
(*Aconitum* spp.)

their seeds are not, and the bark and leaves of the trees that bear them can be dangerous, too.

Potentially dangerous parts of ornamentals include daffodil bulbs; clematis leaves; the leaves and flowers of mountain laurel, rhododendron, and azalea; leaves and stems of wild black cherry (*Prunus serotina*), chokecherry (*P. virginiana*), and pin or wild red cherry (*P. pennsylvanica*).

Also on the list are English ivy berries; the corms and seeds of autumn crocus (*Colchicum autumnale*); the stems, flowers, and leaves of monkshood (*Aconitum* spp.), cardinal flower (*Lobelia cardinalis*), and Jerusalem cherry (*Solanum pseudocapsicum*); the leaves and flowers of tansy (*Tanacetum vulgare*), and truth to tell, several hundred more.

Instead of trying to keep poisons out, focus on teaching young children not to put random pickings from the garden—or anywhere else—into their mouths. 🌿

Is Proximity Poisonous?

Q **If I plant edible plants like herbs and vegetables next to plants that are listed as poisonous, will the edible ones still be safe to eat?**

A As a general rule, toxins being formed by growing plants don't migrate through the soil, and wouldn't be taken up by the neighbors even if they did. So the short answer is sure, no problem.

But there are a couple of things to watch out for: cross-contamination, in which toxic plant parts fall on the innocents next door, and skin rashes, known to doctors as contact dermatitis.

Cross-contamination is seldom a problem, since you must eat a measurable amount of most poisonous plants before they can hurt you. But a few, including angel's trumpet (*Datura*), foxglove, oleander, and some lobelias, are potentially so virulent, you could be sickened just by nectar or sap that fell on a nearby edible and wasn't washed off.

Contact dermatitis is a lot more common. It's easy to brush against adjacent plants as you reach for the food. Allergic reactions to plants vary widely, but many people get rashes from such garden stalwarts as comfrey, spurge, and feverfew, and the beautiful blue-flowered *Phacelia parryi* is devastating to those who are sensitive.

Of course, all bets are off if small children will be visiting the garden. They might easily come to the wrong conclusions if they saw pretty poison in the vegetable patch, and they're a lot more likely to be seriously hurt if they make a mistake. 🍎

Useful Purslane

Q **The weed purslane has appeared in my garden, and I was trying to get rid of it when a friend told me it's edible. Is it?**

A Yes, indeed. Purslane (*Portulaca oleracea*) is a smooth, succulent-looking annual with creeping, 5- to 10-inch reddish green stems; small, somewhat oval leaves; and in late summer, tiny pale yellow flowers. It grows in sunny fields and gardens, thriving best in sandy soil and dry conditions.

The leaves and stems have an agreeable sweet-sour flavor, and when raw, a crisp texture that is welcome in salads. Cooked purslane is popular in the Middle East, but before you try it, bear in mind the texture becomes mucilaginous, rather like that of okra.

Adding a bit to the mixed greens is well worth it, though; purslane is a nutritional powerhouse that contains heart-protective omega-3 oils, in addition to iron, beta carotene, vitamin C, and several minerals. 🍎

Creating a Rabbit-Free Zone

Q **Every year, I have to replant my flowers at least three times because the rabbits eat them. I have tried moth balls, dried blood, repellents, and even fences. They just hop over the fence and have a buffet. I have seen them standing on their hind legs to reach up into my bushes. Help!**

A Remain calm. All you have to do is amend your fences. Rabbits excel at the long jump, not the high hurdles. They can't climb. And although they are burrowing animals, the burrows are comparatively shallow; their hearts aren't really in it when it comes to digging straight down. They can, however, squeeze through tiny gaps, and they love to do the limbo.

Help is available at the lumberyard: farmers' rabbit fencing, a wire grid 4 feet tall, with very close mesh at the bottom. Bury it 8 inches deep, and be sure the gate hugs the ground so the rabbits can't slither underneath. If you are also conscientious about keeping the gate tightly closed, the fenced area should be rabbit-free.

Unfortunately, the unfenced areas will remain vulnerable until you get a dog. 🍂

Scale Invasion

Q **I am having trouble with scale on my Harry Lauder's walking stick. What can I do?**

A Scale insects are immobile round or oval creatures that come in assorted colors and blend nicely with plants. Several kinds, in particular the lecanium scale and the oyster-shell scale, damage this shrub, which is also known as the contorted European hazel (*Corylus avellana* 'Contorta').

Scales infest many different shrubs and are often hard to see until they have done considerable damage, at which point it is way too late to just scrub them off. Yet an uncontrolled infestation can kill a plant within two or three years, so you are wise to realize you do have to do something.

Eggs are laid on the leaves or bark and from spring through mid summer; the young, called crawlers, migrate to other areas. This is when they are most vulnerable, and if you catch them at this stage, repeated sprays of insecticidal soap or lightweight (summerweight) horticultural oil should bring them under control.

Since the brief crawler stage is variable, depending on both the scale and the weather, you may find it easier to spray with dormant oil each winter. Dormant oil will smother the eggs, so you won't have to worry as much about being on the spot when the crawlers appear. 🍂

Skunks in the Suburbs

Q I live in a lovely suburb 15 minutes outside Boston, and we have a large skunk community. How can I keep them out of my yard? Is there some kind of plant or shrub or other organic matter they will avoid? It wouldn't be a problem, except that my dog cannot stay away from them. Is there a way to get rid of them?

A Getting rid of them is not to be. Skunks have adapted very well to the suburbs, where there are lots of good things to eat—lawn grubs, earthworms, mice, and rats—and plenty of sheltered places to build dens. When you remove a skunk from such habitat, all you do is open territory for the next one.

The best way to keep them out of your yard is with a low, tight wire-mesh fence. Skunks don't do much climbing, so a height of 2 feet should be adequate. They do dig, though, so you'll want to bury the fencing 6 to 8 inches deep.

Nothing repels them, but they are easily attracted, especially by grub-infested lawns and anything fishy, meaty, or sweet. (Although they are carnivores, they love moldy cake and stale cookies almost as much as raccoons do.)

Some authorities suggest drenching the lawn with pesticides to get rid of the grubs, but even doing that is unlikely to solve the skunk problem completely.

It's important to keep the garbage covered, and to be aware that fertilizers of animal origin such as blood meal and bone meal are powerful lures. Keep unused supplies in tightly lidded containers, and be sure to work these materials well into the soil as soon as you use them.

Since, as you note, the problem is not so much with the skunks as with your dog, the easiest solution is probably to control the pooch rather than the polecats. 🍎

SLUG AND SNAIL PATROL

The first thing to realize is that snails and slugs cannot be vanquished. Pressure from these slimy scourges may abate for a while in a drought, but with the rains they will be back, as inevitable as death, taxes, and telemarketers at dinner-time. But although they will be with you always, populations can be kept to tolerable levels through a variety of controls.

Not counting predators, of which there are mercifully many (wild birds, ducks, geese, chickens, toads, turtles, and snakes, among others), control methods include poisons, traps, hand-picking, and barriers.

The **poisons** are metaldehyde, a chemical that is also toxic to mammals and birds, and iron phosphate, a natural mineral that its marketers claim harms nothing except slugs. The **traps**—fancy plastic "snail hotels" or unfancy empty tuna fish cans—are filled with an attractant, most commonly beer, and are buried just below ground level. Slugs and snails come to drink, fall in, and drown. Traps can often be effective, but they sometimes attract more pests than they kill, thus compounding rather than solving the problem.

Hand-picking is self-descriptive: you wander around at night, when slugs and snails are most active, finding them with a flashlight and plucking them off the plants. Then, to kill them, you either sprinkle them with salt or drop them in a can of soapy water. Hand-picking is time consuming, messy, and in the case of the salt, somewhat grisly.

There are two main **barriers.** The most commonly recommended one is diatomaceous earth, the powdery remains of prehistoric shellfish. It feels smooth to the touch but is unbearably gritty to slugs and snails, which must exude so much slime to crawl over it, they dehydrate themselves and die. Unfortunately, once it becomes thoroughly wet, they can slide over it on the water layer, so it's least effective when most needed.

Diatomacious earth is environmentally benign, no danger to fish or friendly insects, and harmless to birds and mammals—assuming they don't inhale it. Remember to wear a mask if you're sprinkling out large amounts.

If you have raised beds or other confined garden areas around which to use it, the longest-lasting and most effective barrier is copper, which reacts electrochemically with the beasts' slime so they will not cross it. Strips of copper at least 2 inches wide around a raised bed will keep lettuce safe in a rainstorm, which is really saying something. Be sure to install the strips in dry weather and to keep checking from time to time for stragglers and newly hatched babies. The pests can't get in, but they can't get out, either.

Slug Love

Q **You've written about controlling slugs, which I know do a lot of damage. But don't they provide a balance in a garden? Or put another way, what good are they?**

A It is hard for a gardener to think positively about slugs, but many of the gardener's most valuable pest-controllers, including snakes and toads, find them delicious. They also provide food for fireflies, a particularly comforting thought when you're contemplating the ravaged delphiniums. 🍃

Slugs, Worms, and Dust

Q **I've heard that diatomaceous earth controls slugs. But does it harm the beneficial earthworms if mixed into their soil?**

A No. Many pests are repelled by diatomaceous earth and it can kill slugs and snails, but it appears to be completely digestible by earthworms. 🍃

A Foamy Garden

Q **I'm noticing white, frothy blobs along the stems of my yarrow and on lots of different plants in the garden. The blobs don't seem to be causing a lot of damage, but I am wondering what they are and whether I should try to get rid of them.**

A The froth is a big disguise for a little larva. As an adult spittlebug, the insect will be nondescript, but its protective coating as a youngster gives it its name. From late May until early August, that white mass will usually show up along the stem or, on many plants, where the leaves join thee stem. Somewhere inside, the larva is happily sucking sap, secure in the knowledge that the coating (made by mixing air with a drop of fluid from undigested plant sap and a binding material produced by certain glands) renders it impervious to assault from pesticides, and invisible to predators.

You can root around in the froth and crush the larvae, or you can wash them off with a strong spray from a garden hose. Or you can ignore them. The spittlebugs that attack pines and other conifers can cause serious damage, but the ones that show up in the garden like so many splashes of beer foam cause little real damage. 🍎

Pepper vs. Squirrels

Q **I have read that cayenne pepper can be used to ward off squirrels. How does it work? Are the peppers hung like tree ornaments? Sprinkled on the ground? I tried using camphor balls around the plants, but the neighbors complained about the smell and when I last looked the squirrels were thriving.**

A The active ingredient is capsaicin (pronounced cap-SAY-ih-sin), the chemical that makes hot peppers hot. It burns anything it touches and is particularly excruciating on the sensitive membranes of the eyes, nose, and mouth of mammals. Birds appear to be unaffected; in fact, capsaicin is used as a coating for birdseed to discourage squirrel raids.

To defend against rabbits, squirrels, deer, and muggers, you can buy commercial repellents that contain pure capsaicin, or you can make a kitchen-cupboard version. One formula calls for mixing ½ cup finely chopped jalapeños or the much hotter habañeros with ½ gallon of water. Boil for 20 minutes, strain, and use as a spray. Be sure to use gloves while working with the peppers. Keep the pot covered, let it cool covered, and don't inhale the vapors; hot or cold, capsaicin is highly volatile and those vapors can burn.

You can also just buy large quantities of ground cayenne and, observing the same cautions, sprinkle it on the cherished items. Either way, the pepper will have to be reapplied at least once a week and after every heavy dew or rain.

It is not as foolproof as it sounds. You have to assure contact; vapors dissipate rapidly, and the smell alone won't do it. Many animals rapidly become used to, if not fond of, spicy food. And it's easy to forget and get burned yourself, especially if you touch the protected plant and then rub your eyes.

That's primarily how it works against squirrels, by the way. They rub their faces with their peppery paws and wind up in agony. But squirrels are not stellar learners; some of them make the connection and some don't. 🍎

Keeping Thistles at Bay

Q **I rent a small plot in a community garden. The problem: thistle, every-where. I've tried pulling those vicious plants and came out the loser. What's worse is that all the neighboring plot holders just let theirs flower. Short of dropping a bomb, what can I do? I'd prefer to go organic, as I am growing vegetables, but I'm desperate.**

A Warlike thoughts are perfectly understandable, but why not look on the bright side? At least your laissez-faire compatriots are not attacking the weeds—and your vegetables—with chemical herbicides. As soon as you feel better, you can begin a two-pronged program of cut and mulch.

Biennial weeds like thistles are famously difficult to pull up, but you can get rid of established plants by cutting them off at the base each time they put out new growth. As long as you don't let any root-nourishing leaves develop, they will exhaust themselves and eventually die.

To foil new invaders, mulch all the exposed soil with thick planter's paper or water-permeable fabric. If the seeds can't get through, they can't take root. 🍎

Mystery Irritant

Q **Recently, while clearing overgrown honeysuckle, I pulled up 30 or 40 young thistles. Shortly afterward, I developed itchy, localized blebs on my hands and face. Could the thistle juices on my leather gloves have caused an allergic reaction? In the past, I've pulled up thistles barehanded without any problem.**

A The highly invasive Canada thistle (*Cirsium arvense*) has occasionally been described as "a vicious weed," and you could probably raise a rash by rubbing your skin with its prickly leaves. But neither this nor any other thistle shows up on standard lists of common allergens.

You might have an unusual allergy; almost everything disagrees with somebody. But before you go to the doctor, consider the likelihood of plain old poison ivy. It often lurks unsuspected in overgrown places and is frequently seen (or, alas, not seen) in conjunction with honeysuckle. 🍃

Benefits of Toads

Q **There are toads living in my garden. I know they're harmless, and I don't want to kill them, but I would like to improve conditions so that they go away and don't come back.**

A It would be much better if you'd improve your attitude toward your warty little friends. Toads are far better than harmless; they are a major asset, capable of scarfing three times their weight in insects and slugs every day. Some of the bugs are beneficials, but about 80 percent are pests: earwigs, cutworms, Japanese beetles, grasshoppers, even cucumber beetles, which most other predators won't touch.

You must have a nicely organic garden; toads can't coexist with pesticides (the poison goes through their skin). If you don't have any water around, they will eventually fade out; they need shallow ponds to reproduce. Toads also need dark, damp spots for shelter. Garden-supply stores sell cute little artificial caves, but a flowerpot turned on its side and partly buried does just as well. 🍃

Rainfall: It's the Timing, Not the Total

Q **A hurricane season is predicted, and I'm wondering if the additional rain will make up for the drought that has devastated our landscape all summer.**

A The rain will refill the reservoirs, but as far as trees and shrubs are concerned, the damage is already done. Leaf scorch, browning of the edges, is already apparent, and some trees, especially maples, are showing early fall color as they prepare to give up and wait for next year.

But many signs won't show up until next spring or even the next couple of years. Drought-stressed trees and shrubs may become more susceptible to disease and insects. Twigs and even entire branches may die. Some maples' crowns may not seem as full as they were before the drought. And more years of summer drought will do more damage.

Watering trees slowly and deeply during dry summers can be boring, and where there are watering restrictions, it may not even be possible, so think carefully before you plant if a drought is predicted. During a hot summer, newly planted trees should get thoroughly watered every four to five days (allow 20 gallons for a 6- to 8-foot tree), and you may need to devote all the water available to the trees you already have. 🍎

Counting the Drops

Q **After several weeks of drought, we had two quite heavy rainstorms just five days apart. But when I went out to work in my vegetable garden, the soil was dry just a couple of inches down. I know it didn't run off, so what happened to all that water?**

A The rainstorms may have been quite heavy, but if they weren't also quite long, they probably didn't deliver as much water as you thought they did.

The soil has already told you all you really need to know: however much it was, it wasn't enough. But if these disappointments are frequent, it might not be a bad idea to start measuring. That way you'll know if you are just over-hopeful or if—just perhaps—your soil is so sandy it needs major infusions of organic matter to help it hold water.

You can buy an inexpensive rain gauge, but these are no more than simple clear cylinders with measurement marks. You can get the same information from a straight sided glass and a ruler. The only advantage of the gauges is that they come with mounting devices, so you're more likely to have one in place when the heavens open.

Of course, it won't tell you the straight story unless it is well away from trees, roofs, powerlines, or any other rain-aggregators. You don't want extra dripping or blowing in. 🍎

Watering Myth

Q Can you please clarify the issue of keeping water off foliage in full sun? I've been told that it is best to water from the base of plants in full sun because water can act like a magnifying lens and burn leaves. I can understand that base watering is the most effective way to get the roots saturated, but why keep leaves dry when they get wet naturally?

A Along with those gift plants that suck the oxygen out of hospital rooms, possibly suffocating their recipients, magnifying water droplets are a most persistent horticultural myth. Water droplets do magnify a bit, but not enough even to warm the leaves, let alone burn them. 🌰

Wasteful Evaporation

Q I keep reading that using a sprinkler is a great waste of water, but I don't understand why this should be so. Doesn't it all get absorbed by the leaves or else fall to the ground?

A No, it doesn't. Water that lands on leaves is not absorbed. It evaporates before it reaches the ground, as does some of the water thrown into the air by a sprinkler. Watering the soil at the base of plants really is more efficient. Even if there are no summer droughts to cause watering restrictions, it makes sense to conserve by watering effectively.

It is best not to water in the evening because leaves stay damp much longer, and damp leaves are a terrific breeding ground for many fungus diseases. The smartest gardeners water at dawn or in the early morning. With the whole day ahead, any water that does land on leaves has a chance to evaporate long before sunset. 🌰

Dealing with Deadly Drought

Q This summer's drought is hurting my annuals and vegetables. Perennials look O.K. but not great. The water supply is limited, so I can't water everything. I have put on lots of mulch. Is there anything else I can do?

A Keep your eye on the long term and give that rationed water to the most important plants. Annual flowers and vegetables will be history by winter, no matter what, while expensive and slow-growing items like Japanese maples should be once-in-a-lifetime purchases.

It's tempting to try to rescue the neediest; yellow-leaved plants with hanging heads are heart-wrenching, but plants already stunted by drought are the least likely to thrive later, even if they do survive. It's better to water things that are O.K. but just a little peaked. And don't forget that spring-flowering shrubs like lilacs start building next year's blossoms as soon as they finish this year's show. They need water to do it, so don't let appearances deceive you into shortchanging them.

If possible, water whole areas rather than single plants. Dry soil wicks moisture away, so spots watered in isolation are surrounded by the enemy. Select the few healthiest tomatoes and peppers, give those all the water they need, and let the other vegetables go. Your crop will be smaller but better tasting (it takes a lot of water to make good fruit). If you're determined to save annual flowers, shear them back. If rain comes, they will rapidly put on new growth and a burst of bloom. 🍂

New and Improved Rain Barrel

Q I recently saw an "improved" plastic rain barrel advertised in the newspaper. The ad didn't describe the improvement and I'm wondering what it could be. A rain barrel is a rain barrel, isn't it?

A Well, yes. You put a large, leakproof vessel under the drainpipe and boom—rain barrel. The "improved" ones have fitted lids that keep out debris and breeding mosquitoes, where old-fashioned types just put screen on top.

Some fancy models have a faucet near the base, so you can draw water without lifting the lid. Check this feature carefully before buying; there should be a way to remove the faucet and cap the hole if you don't want to use it. And be sure it is high enough to be useful—some are so close to the barrel's base that you can't get any kind of pail underneath if the barrel is on the ground. 🍂

Gray Water

Q **With reservoir levels dropping, I'm concerned about my plants. Can you advise about safely recycling our household gray water?**

A Most households do generate a lot of gray water (technically, everything that got used once except what got used in the toilet), but unless you start talking about complicated purification systems, the only safe source of "recycled water" is the kitchen.

Once in the habit, you will find that it is not inconvenient to keep a large pot or a gallon watering can near your sink, ready to catch leftover water. This includes water run from the tap before it gets hot, water used to rinse off fresh vegetables or fruit, water used for steam-cooking, water used to boil eggs (which is also a good source of minerals), and water used to boil frozen-food packets. Just remember to let hot water cool before tossing it on plants.

Gray water from the dishwasher, clothes washer, and shower should not be used; it's usually contaminated with soap, bleach, fat, or bacteria (and may be illegal to use, depending on where you live).

Webworms

Q **My apple tree, which was fine in the spring and for most of the summer, now has several gauzy nests. All of the leaves inside the nests have been eaten. I don't want to spray them with pesticides, but how do I take action? Should I cut them off, burn them, or what?**

A Put away the ax, blow out the torch. Apple, maple, oak, and about a 100 other deciduous trees host fall webworm without suffering serious consequences. By the time webworms emerge from the eggs laid by tiger moths in mid summer, build their protective nests, and begin eating, the leaves have done their job and are just marking time until fall.

When the webworms finish, they'll lower themselves on thin silken ropes, like miniature Alpine climbers, and over-winter at the base of the tree or underground. Next year they might be back, but they're just as likely to find another tree or be eaten by predators.

There's not much point in trying to prevent them from overwintering; tiger moths are very common and since they move around so freely, thwarting the group that caused you problems this year will not protect your trees in the future. 🍎

Safe Weedproofing

Q **What can I do to stop the weeds from growing through the gravel paths in my herb garden? I've been using chemical weed killers but I don't want to continue.**

A The easiest way to keep weeds out of gravel paths is to line them with heavy-duty, porous landscape fabric before the gravel is spread. In your case, the gravel will have to be removed first, but the task won't be too onerous if you do it a little at a time, and the results will be worth whatever hassle you have to go through.

That is, they will if you don't cheap out on the fabric. It comes in various grades, from inexpensive, lightweight stuff meant for use in vegetable gardens, to serious material, meant for sale to landscapers, which should keep your path weed-free for up to a decade.

Don't be tempted to use black plastic instead. It blocks weeds, but it also blocks water and the movement of air. Put it under your gravel and you'll get puddles underfoot, along with sour soil and fungus growth underneath the plastic. 🍎

Death Between the Flagstones

Q **We have a flagstone terrace, laid in a bed of cinders, with unsightly weeds growing in the cracks. What is the best way to get rid of them? Hand-weeding is time-consuming. Could I use a flame gun? I've also thought of using coarse salt in the cracks, but I'm pretty sure it poisons the soil. How about herbicides?**

A You're right about the salt. It can poison the soil it's poured on. How far the poisoning extends depends on many factors, including the amount you use, how sandy your soil is, and how much rainfall you get.

Other than that, much depends on whether you really want the hard, sterile look of an expanse of stone where absolutely nothing grows. Even very formal gardens usually include the softening effect of a bit of green, and if you decide to go that route, hand-weeding is less of a chore. Just use a dandelion digger on coarse invaders and leave attractive low-growers like ground ivy, chickweed, and small grasses in place.

A flame gun works best on broad-leaved annual weeds and on broad-leaved perennials that have just gotten started. Use a light touch; the idea is to heat the sap until it bursts cells, killing the plant. Well-established weeds are likely to require several treatments before they succumb, but they will be vanquished in time as long as you keep at it.

Herbicides vary. Those mild enough to be (comparatively) benign environmentally won't work on all of the weeds and will have to be reapplied frequently. Those that are powerful enough to eliminate all greenery are likely to do just that, eventually giving you—and your neighbors—more sterility than you bargained for. 🌰

A Weed Raw or Sautéed

Q **Can you really eat garlic mustard? A colleague insists it's delicious, but I'm not sure I believe him. This weed is the bane of my existence, so it would be great to learn of a use for it.**

Garlic mustard in flower

A Though the toothed, heart-shaped leaves of *Alliaria petiolata* have been cooked and eaten in Europe for centuries, they tend to be tough and sharp flavored, so you are right to be suspicious of "delicious."

The nicest use may be in salads, where the small white flowers and tender top leaves add a welcome bite. But that doesn't use up much compared with cooking, which shrinks a large pile of leaves to a small serving and also helps tame the mustard flavor.

For the tastiest results, use leaves from plants that have not yet flowered. (Discard the stems.) Sauté in olive

HEAT VS. WEEDS

While the world is waiting for something that kills every mortal plant but grass, yet doesn't harm any other living thing, there is a powerful ally against weeds that is environmentally safe, easier and faster than hand-digging, and (depending on how you harness it) inexpensive, too.

That ally, of course, is heat. Whether it is conveyed by boiling water or a living flame, heat kills weeds by destroying their protective outer coatings and expanding internal cells so they rupture and die. This means a light touch is all that's needed. You're not trying to melt or incinerate them, and since heat is non-selective, you want to use as little as you can to do the job.

Death is very nearly instantaneous for the plant tops. But deep roots are another story; even when you target them directly, the roots of well-established perennial weeds are unlikely to be killed. Before long, they'll put out new growth. Expect to treat them two or three times before they give up.

And most of the lurking weed seeds won't be affected; they'll sprout soon as the removal of the dead weed gives them an opening. If the weed you're removing is in the lawn, keep a little grass seed handy to drop in the hole. If the offender was between paving cracks, plug the hole with sand or a paste of corn gluten and water. (Corn gluten is a natural product that will prevent many weed seeds from growing; it won't kill any living plants that are already in place.)

Boiling water works very well, but it kills more beneficial soil organisms than flame weeders do. And there are limits to how much time you can spend trotting around the yard with a kettle. (There are machines that spray boiling water or live steam, but they are truck-size industrial models meant for commercial or municipal use.) Boiling water works best when you have only a small area, such as a paved path or terrace, that needs attention.

Flame weeders. There are dozens on the market, from inexpensive light-weight handhelds with small fuel tanks to jumbo drag-alongs meant for use in orchards and other commercial settings. All of them will (of course) scorch surrounding grass or any other proximate plants, and all of them can set fires. Don't use flame weeders when things have been droughty or in areas where there is a lot of dry debris. It's a good idea to have a hose handy, too, just in case.

oil until wilted, add a sprinkle of water, cover, and steam until tender, about 10 minutes. Stir in a few raisins or toasted pine nuts. Add salt and lemon juice to taste.

And hope you don't enjoy it so much that you want to eat all you can get. Overindulgence can have a laxative effect. 🌶

Young garlic mustard

Witches'-Broom

Q I've heard gardeners discuss witches'-brooms. What are these things?

A Branches of trees and shrubs sometimes develop a peculiar looking cluster of small twigs that, with a bit of imagination, do indeed resemble a rather messy-looking broom. Foliage in the area becomes sparse, shrunken, and sickly looking. The cause may be an attack, either by an insect, a plant disease, or more seriously, mistletoes, which are parasitic or semiparasitic plants.

Alternatively, witches'-broom can be genetic mutations, and these can be a source of interesting and desirable new plants. One example, the popular dwarf Alberta spruce, is now available in many variations.

Among the scientists who have devoted themselves to the development of plants derived from witches'-broom is Dr. Sidney Waxman, formerly of the University of Connecticut. He has propagated more than two dozen new dwarf conifers from seedlings taken from various witches'-brooms, including white pines named 'Old Softy' and 'Soft Touch,' and a larch named 'Varied Directions.'

And since he's especially partial to his relatives' names, there is also a white pine 'Paul Waxman,' a larch 'Deborah Waxman,' and hemlocks 'Florence Waxman' and 'Howard Waxman.'

If you suspect your witches'-broom has been caused by a problem, not a mutation, prune it off right away. If the cause is an insect or disease, the problem may be sufficiently localized so that eliminating the damaged area will suffice. But if the witches'-broom is a result of one of the mistletoes, a professional arborist should be called in. 🍏

Woodchuck Woes

Q Woodchucks have destroyed our garden, and no repellants will work. Local trappers cost a fortune, with no guarantees. And we definitely don't want to kill them. Any suggestions?

A If you are determined not to kill them, the only way you can get rid of woodchucks is to trap them without harming them, then transport them far enough away so that they cannot possibly find their way back. Of course, this means you are passing the problem along to someone else. And you may not be doing the woodchuck much of a favor, either—they have their territories, and will defend them.

The only way to trap woodchucks (aka groundhogs) unharmed is with a box trap such as a Havaheart. The traps, made of reinforced galvanized wire, are available in various sizes at well-stocked hardware stores. For woodchucks, you'll need one that is at least 10 inches high and wide, and 30 to 36 inches long.

Woodchucks aren't smart, but they are wary and tend to avoid anything unusual. Live trapping is most successful very early in the season, when there isn't much for a woodchuck to eat except that delicious-looking lettuce with the wire around it. If lettuce doesn't work, try apple slices; they may fall for the sweet treat without noticing it's not apple season yet. ✿

Xeriscaping Defined

Q **Now that we are having drought warnings, I keep hearing the word "xeriscaping." Just what does this mean?**

A Xeriscaping is water-sensible gardening, or using plants that survive on the water that nature provides, with minimal supplementation. The word is derived from the Greek *xeros,* which means "dry." Though water-wise gardening has been around for millennia, the modern xeriscaping movement began in the 1980s, in Denver, where landscapers worked with the water department to develop more conservation-oriented plantings.

Plants with minimal water needs are becoming increasingly important in communities where water shortages are a concern. But these plants are also superb for containers on sunny rooftops, terraces, patios, and decks. Xeriscape plants include Bar Harbor junipers and honey locust trees, as well as dusty miller, goldenrod, lavender, mullein, portulaca, Queen-Anne's lace, Russian sage, sedum, thyme, yarrow, and yucca.

Mulching is also stressed by xeriscape gardeners, as is good soil preparation with the addition of organic matter and the use of the most efficient irrigation system, like a soaker hose or low-volume dripper. 🌸

Yellow Jackets at Home

Q This summer I noticed a proliferation of yellow jackets in my garden. I tracked them to a nest in my front porch roof, which they reach through a small hole behind the gutter. Spraying into the hole at dusk proved futile. Since fall is here, can I just ignore them? Or will they hibernate over the winter and be back in larger numbers next spring?

A Though yellow jackets usually build nests in the ground, they are also willing to exploit cozy cavities in houses and barns. And they don't mind long front halls when they undertake construction. The nest may be 30 or more feet away from the entrance hole, far too distant for your spray to have had any effect.

As long as they are no longer active, you can ignore them. The colonies do not overwinter and old nests are not reused. Colonies propagate by making a new queen, who leaves the nest in the fall, hibernates in a stump or under some bark, and then goes house-hunting in spring.

When she finds a likely spot, she starts a nest and soon brings many, many little yellow jackets into the world. With any luck, she'll do it a good distance from your house. 🌸

USDA Plant Hardiness Zone Map

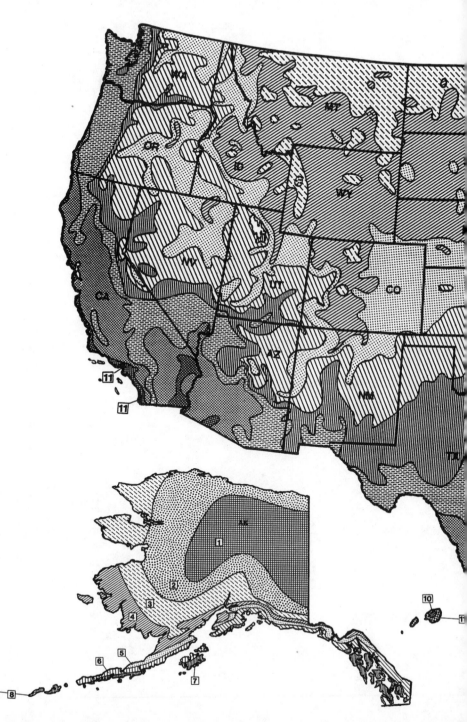

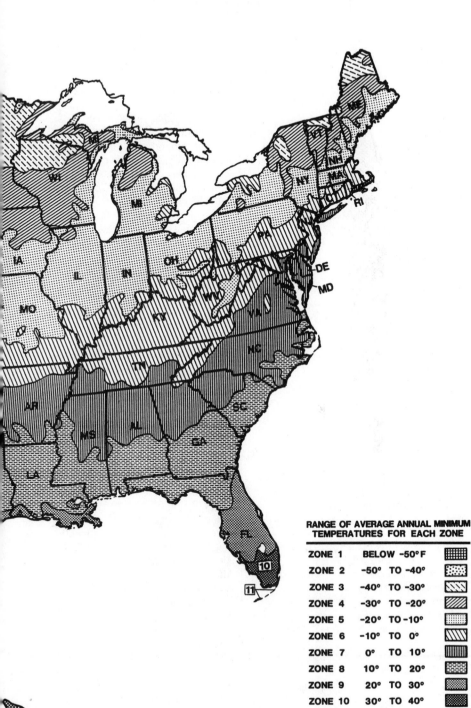

RANGE OF AVERAGE ANNUAL MINIMUM
TEMPERATURES FOR EACH ZONE

ZONE 1	BELOW −50° F
ZONE 2	−50° TO −40°
ZONE 3	−40° TO −30°
ZONE 4	−30° TO −20°
ZONE 5	−20° TO −10°
ZONE 6	−10° TO 0°
ZONE 7	0° TO 10°
ZONE 8	10° TO 20°
ZONE 9	20° TO 30°
ZONE 10	30° TO 40°
ZONE 11	ABOVE 40°

Courtesy of USDA Agricultural Research Service

Index

B

Index

Index

Index

H

Index

S

Index

Smiley, Ruth H., 412
Smith, Betty, 362
Smokebush (*Cotinus coggyria*), 293, 298, 300
Snails. *See* Slugs and snails
Snail vine (*Vigna caracalla*), 251–53
Snakeplant, or mother-in-law's tongue (*Sansevieria* spp.), 596, 637–38
Snakeroot (*Cimicifuga* spp.), 142
  black (*C. racemosa*), 73, 77, *77*, 80
Snakeroot, white (*Eupatorium rugosum*, or *Ageratina altissima*), 78
Snakes, 446, 772, 773
Snapdragon (*Antirrhinum majus*), 5, 9, 17, 27, 48, 143
  dwarf, 15
  growing from seed, 55
  pelleted seeds for, 24–25
  predicting color of, 16
Snapdragon, climbing, or asarina (*Asarina* spp.), 228, 252, 656
Snout beetles, or plum curculios, 561–62, 564
Snow:
  de-icing products and, 715–16
  protecting garden sculptures from damage in, 747–48
  around trees, melting of, 360
Snowdrop (*Galanthus* spp.), 178, 186, *186*, 217–18, 364
Snow-in-summer, 412
Snow-on-the-mountain, or ghost weed (*Euphorbia marginata*), 56
Snow rose (*Serissa foetida*), 610
Snow-seeding, 279
Soaker-hose systems, 444
Soaps, insecticidal. *See* Insecticidal soaps
Soapwort, bouncing Bet, or wild sweet William (*Saponaria officinalis*), 143–44, *144*, 412
Socrates, hemlock and, 377
Sod, 278
  decomposition of, after removal, 721
  removing for vegetable garden, 436
Sodium, in softened water, 584
Softened water, for houseplants, 584
Soil, 697–737, 786
  building up bed with, 82
  clay. *See* Clay particles and soils
  compaction of, 353
  crop rotation and, 429–30

digging and bed making and, 717–21, *717*, *718*, *719*;
  see also Digging and bed making
enriching, 262–63, 697–712; *see also* Soil amendments
"in good tilth," 435
for ground covers, 262–63
hardpan and, 718–20
for houseplants, 580
humus in, 701
piling around tree trunks, 352
potting medium, 667–68
preparing for lawns, 272, 273, 274, 279
rocks brought to surface of, by freezes and thaws, 720
sandy. *See* Sand particles and soil
for self-sown seeds, 4, 21–22
structure of, 711, 712
temperature of, for seed germination, 25–26
testing, 701, 710, 713, 714, 715
tilling for vegetable garden, 431
types of, 698
water-holding capacity of, 708
working, earliest date for, 717
working with nature and, 710–11
worms and, 709–10
Soil amendments, 701–8
  compost, 407, 701, 702, 708, 715
  determining need for, 701
  double-digging and, 718
  green manure (cover crops), 444–45, 701, 705, 708, 711–12, 720
  manures, 407, 697, 701, 703–4
  organic matter, 433–34, 700, 701–2, 703, 711, 786
  peat moss, 707–8
  pH and, 714–15, 716
  for sandy soils, 407
  wood ashes, 699, 706
  see also Fertilizers
Soil pH, 308, 701, 712–16
  acid rain and, 330
  coffee grounds and, 330, 734
  de-icing products and, 715–16
  hydrangea color and, 315
  lowering, 708
  moss and, 399, 401
  pH scale and, 712–13
  raising, 699, 706
  testing and, 701, 713, 714, 715
  tomatoes and, 505
  for vegetables, 435

X

Y